FREEDOM, THE INDIVIDUAL AND THE LAW

Geoffrey Robertson QC

SEVENTH EDITION

PENGUIN BOOKS

PENGUIN BOOKS

Published by the Penguin Group
Penguin Books Ltd, 27 Wrights Lane, London w8 5TZ, England
Penguin Books USA Inc., 375 Hudson Street, New York, New York 10014, USA
Penguin Books Australia Ltd, Ringwood, Victoria, Australia
Penguin Books Canada Ltd, 10 Alcorn Avenue, Toronto, Ontario, Canada M4V 3B2
Penguin Books (NZ) Ltd, 182–190 Wairau Road, Auckland 10, New Zealand

Penguin Books Ltd, Registered Offices: Harmondsworth, Middlesex, England

First published in Pelican Books 1963
Second edition 1967
Third edition 1972
Reprinted with revisions 1975
Fourth edition 1977
Fifth edition 1982
Sixth edition 1989
Reprinted in Penguin Books 1991
Seventh edition 1993
1 3 5 7 9 10 8 6 4 2

Copyright © H. Street, 1963, 1967, 1972, 1977, 1982, and
Geoffrey Robertson, 1989, 1993
All rights reserved

Set in 10/12pt Monotype Bembo
Typeset by Datix International Limited, Bungay, Suffolk
Printed in England by Clays Ltd, St Ives plc

Geoffrey Robertson QC has appeared as counsel in landmark cases involving civil liberties in British and Commonwealth courts, in the Privy Council and in the European Court of Human Rights. He has conducted missions for Amnesty International to South Africa and Vietnam, served as counsel to the Royal Commission investigating gun-running to the Columbian drug cartels, headed the defence in the Matrix Churchill trial and led the 1992 human rights mission to Malawi on behalf of the Bar and Law Society.

A Rhodes Scholar, he has been a visiting fellow at Warwick University and the University of New South Wales, and is the author of *Reluctant Judas* (1976), *Obscenity* (1979), *People against the Press* (1983), *Does Dracula have AIDS?* (1987), *Geoffrey Robertson's Hypotheticals* (1986 and 1991) and *Media Law* (with A. Nicol, 3rd edition, Penguin, 1992). His play *The Trials of Oz* won a BAFTA 'Best Single Drama' nomination in 1992 and he received a 1993 Freedom of Information award for his writing and broadcasting.

Geoffrey Robertson lives in London where he is head of Doughty Street Chambers. He is an Assistant Recorder, and a member of the executive councils of Charter 88, Justice and the Institute of Contemporary Arts.

Contents

CHAPTER 1: Personal Liberty and Police Powers   1

A POLICEMAN'S LOT (*police accountability*)

ARREST (*'reasonable grounds to suspect'; the duty to give reasons; 'reasonable force'; the summons alternative*)

DETENTION (*length of custody; terrorist suspects; the right to a lawyer; other physical restraints*)

POLICE INTERROGATION (*the right to silence; recording interviews; confessions*)

RELEASE FROM CUSTODY

REMEDIES FOR POLICE MISCONDUCT (*damages for civil wrongs; complaints; prosecution; inquests; tricks and traps*)

CHAPTER 2: Public Protest   65

LACK OF POSITIVE RIGHTS

PROCESSIONS

PUBLIC MEETINGS

POWERS TO PREVENT DISORDER (*arrest for breach of the peace; bind-overs; bail conditions*)

PUBLIC-ORDER OFFENCES

THE LIMITS OF PROTEST

THE LIMITS OF POLICING PROTESTS

INCITEMENT TO RACIAL HATRED

OFFENSIVE WORDS

BROADCASTING BANS

ELECTIONEERING

CONTENTS

Preface to the Seventh Edition

Freedom, the Individual and the Law made its first appearance in the summer of 1963. Stephen Ward was standing trial at the Old Bailey and two reporters had just been gaoled for refusing to disclose their sources to the Vassall spy tribunal, while in Beirut MI5 was furtively offering an immunity from all prosecution to Mr Kim Philby, OBE. Sheffield police had been caught beating suspects with rhino whips, Detective-Inspector Challoner had been framing political protesters, while throughout Britain consenting adults were facing criminal charges relating to abortion and homosexuality. The Lord Chamberlain had stopped the Royal Shakespeare Company from performing a play because it was 'anti-American, beastly and left-wing'. Penguin Books had good reason to commission a work on civil liberties: it had recently been accused at the Old Bailey of corrupting wives and servants by publishing *Lady Chatterley's Lover*.

Thirty years on, Penguin Books have survived bombs and blasphemy charges for publishing *The Satanic Verses*. Judith Ward, the Birmingham Six, the Guildford Four and the Maguire Seven have been released after serving collectively 288 years of wrongful imprisonment. Sado-masochists whose sexual rituals hurt no one but themselves had just been gaoled at the Old Bailey, a fate narrowly avoided by the businessmen who sold arms to Iraq, once the Government's secret complicity in their enterprise was publicly exposed. Journalists had recently been threatened with custody (and Channel 4 with liquidation) for refusing to disclose their sources. Policemen no longer wielded rhino whips, but had used unlawful force in mounted baton charges against demonstrators. Small children had been snatched by social workers in Orkney hell-bent on saving them from imaginary satanic abuse, and teenagers placed in care were cared for by unlawful and cruel 'pin-down' techniques.

British libel law was declared 'anti-American' and unenforceable in the US courts, while the villainy of our leading litigant, Robert Maxwell, was finally revealed once he was no longer in a position to issue writs for defamation. The Prime Minister was collecting substantial damages for a *New Statesman* article which suggested that he was not being unfaithful to his wife. Meanwhile, his Government was girding its loins for battle against the thirty thousand British citizens who had paid to decode the satellite signals of Red Hot Dutch. The seventh edition of *Freedom, the Individual and the Law* is, regrettably, the longest: threats to civil liberties may have changed, and become more sophisticated, but they show no signs of diminishing.

The original edition of this work, by Professor Harry Street, was the first modern account of the legal basis for executive interference with the liberties of British citizens. His last edition – the fifth – was completed in 1981, before the avalanche of legislation passed by Thatcher Governments. Some of these laws enhanced liberty, usually because Britain was obliged by its European treaty obligations and by decisions of the European Court of Human Rights to make better provision for the fundamental freedoms of its citizens. The Contempt of Court Act (1981) and the Data Protection Act (1984) were examples of positive legislation enlarging the right to comment on *sub judice* issues and providing some protection for privacy, which came about only because of our European commitments. But the Video Recordings Act (1984), Interception of Communications Act (1985), Public Order Act (1986), Security Service Act (1989) and Official Secrets Act (1989) were examples of new laws which directly embodied Thatcherite preoccupations: secrecy, censorship and unfettered executive discretion. Together with the 1984 Police and Criminal Evidence Act (which extended police powers while providing some new methods for controlling them) and the numerous court decisions which surveyed, with increasing scepticism, government claims to confidentiality and infallibility (such as the *Spycatcher* saga and the acquittal of Clive Ponting), these developments required a complete rewriting of the text for the sixth edition, published in 1989.

Since 1989 we have had DNA sampling, the Asylum Act, acid house parties, the Broadcasting Act, PNC 2, Camillagate, Iraqgate, and the creation of the Press Complaints Commission; there has been a host of leading cases, and important rulings from the European Court of Justice and the European Court of Human Rights. But the most dramatic development since the sixth edition has been the public perception of that 'appalling vista' (described as unimaginable by Lord Denning in 1979) of police perjury, prosecutorial unfairness and forensic systems failure, which have combined to produce so many notorious miscarriages of justice. Inquests into these wrongful convictions demonstrated that civil liberties are not satisfactorily protected by neat laws and strict procedures for police paperwork, as the framers of the 1984 Police and Criminal Evidence Act imagined. Much more attention must be paid to the 'Ways and Means Act' operated by the police, the Home Office, customs officials, lawyers, and others who exercise power over citizens because their decisions reflect the etiquette and assumptions (often hostile to civil liberties) of their social and occupational milieu. It is remarkable that none of the present 'casebooks' on civil liberties have any section devoted to the right to a fair trial. This key chapter has been expanded for the seventh edition, to emphasize the importance of introducing further safeguards against wrongful convictions. The Royal Commission on Criminal Procedure (the Runciman Commission) which reported in July 1993 has set a controversial agenda for reform: some of its recommendations would produce more miscarriages of justice, while others would make them more readily detectable after they have occurred. I have tried in this book to focus on changes required by commitment to fundamental principles of justice, while recognizing that reforms must be able to work not only at street level but also in the hard-bitten cultures of police canteens and barristers' robing rooms.

The scope of this book is confined to the law in force in England and Wales: there are differences, especially in regard to minor offences, in Scottish law, while civil liberties in Northern Ireland is a subject which deserves a separate book. I have not sought to deal with second-generation rights – to housing and health and education and social security and other such concerns of the European Charter of Fundamental Social Rights, nor with 'third-generation' rights to a protected environment. Although termed 'collective rights', they are as important for the development of the individual as the first generation of civil and political freedoms discussed in this book. To some extent they involve policy decisions about the allocation of resources which are not appropriate for determination by the courts, and in any event their acceptance as social goals is in this country rather more secure (government cuts and thrusts notwithstanding) than the civil freedoms which this book is concerned to explain and to enhance.

The views expressed herein have been formed over many years of advising and representing individual clients and to them I owe my first debt of thanks. My colleagues Andrew Nicol, Jill Peay, Camilla Palmer and Quincy Whittaker provided valuable comments on individual chapters, while Helen Bramford, Jonathan Riley and Domenica Matassa wrestled the manuscript into shape. The right to family life is sorely tested by new editions: Kathy Lette, who suffered my husbandry, and Georgina, our newest addition, helped me to labour with love.

Geoffrey Robertson   1 September 1993
Doughty Street Chambers

Introduction

If liberty means anything at all, it means the right to tell people what they do not want to hear.

George Orwell (from his unpublished introduction to *Animal Farm*)

Liberty in Britain is a state of mind rather than a set of legal rules. Unlike most Western democracies, the United Kingdom does not have a constitution embodying written guarantees of personal freedoms. Instead, it relies upon formal procedures and established institutions to protect the individual from oppressive behaviour by those Orwell termed 'the striped-trousered ones who rule'. Since the institutions are manned, and the procedures operated, by the self-same 'striped-trousered ones', the rights which are allowed to citizens in practice are no more than officialdom, at any particular time, will tolerate. That the extent of that toleration has been considerable is a tribute to a civilization whose history, literature and cultural values have conjoined to produce a presumption in favour of the liberty of the subject to speak freely, protest openly and be judged fairly. Members of Parliament do not hesitate to raise constituent grievances and to pressure ministers; the civil service is untainted by corruption; the judiciary is philosophically committed to fair play. Why change such an agreeable system? As the British Government explained to the Human Rights Committee of the United Nations in 1991:

The country has not felt the need for a written constitution or a comprehensive Bill of Rights: the principle has been that the rights and freedoms recognized in other countries' constitutions are inherent in the British legal system and are protected by it and by Parliament unless they are removed or restricted by statutes.

But fundamental rights and freedoms *are* consistently restricted by statute. They are not in any meaningful sense 'inherent in the British legal system': on the contrary, the courts cannot give them the force of law *unless* they are enshrined in statutes. In other words, rights and freedoms are in Britain at the mercy of Parliament, which passes the statutes which give them and take them away. And Parliament is controlled, with rare exceptions, by the executive government, as unwilling to have its power curbed by principles applied by the courts as it is to share power with its political opponents or its own back-benchers. A democracy that subordinates fundamental rights to the exigencies of executive government leaves them dilapidated, outdated and legally insecure. For example, in 1993:

There is no right to *privacy*. The use of electronic eavesdropping devices and lie detectors is not subject to regulation, and nor is the burgeoning private security industry which operates them for espionage purposes. There is no legal limit to police use of surreptitious surveillance devices, nor to the collection of information by the state about individuals. There is no law against obtaining, by deception, information about bank and building-society accounts. Security-service bugging, burglary and letter-opening is done at the Home Secretary's discretion, and cannot be approved or disapproved by the courts. Perverts and nosey-parkers enjoy intercepting private conversations, which they occasionally record and sell to newspapers, which regularly seek out and publish details of private lives, feeling free to ignore the rulings of the Press Complaints Commission because the newspaper industry controls it. There are few rights of access to files kept by private organizations on individuals, let alone to those built up within Government departments. The Data Protection Act of 1984 provides belated and limited rights of access to certain computerized files, but fails to impose satisfactory measures to protect against leakage and linkage of information and does not cover the new Police National Computer (PNC 2) which lists citizens who are HIV positive or who have had the temerity to complain about the police. All the other Western democracies now protect their citizens' privacy more effectively than Britain.

There is no right to *public protest*. Demonstrations are held by police permission, or not at all. Processions may be 'blanket banned' by the authorities for periods of up to three months. Except at election time, there is no right to hold meetings in public halls or parks. Demonstrators who commit no criminal offence may none the less be sent to prison if they refuse to submit to 'bind-over' orders, or may have their freedom circumscribed by bail conditions. The Government has blithely announced plans to make human-rights demonstrations unlawful outside the embassies of countries which infringe human rights, and has already passed 'criminal trespass' laws aimed at gypsies and 'new-age travellers'. Paramilitary police squads have been trained to deal with demonstrations by using unreasonable force – baton charges and truncheon assaults – as well as CS gas and rubber bullets. Public servants who wish to speak out against waste, mismanagement or dangers to public health risk prosecution under secrecy laws, or discipline through internal Whitehall procedures. Foreigners who demonstrate risk deportation if they commit minor public-order offences, or if their presence is deemed 'undesirable' on inscrutable 'national security' grounds.

The right to *personal liberty* is subject to the discretion of police forces that are not answerable to Parliament or to local authorities. Suspects are not properly informed of their rights, and thousands are unnecessarily taken into police custody (occasionally in 'dawn raids' staged for the benefit of the media) instead of being proceeded against by summons. The rules governing arrest, detention and interrogation are not backed up by a satisfactory system for handling complaints against police misconduct. The right to silence has been abolished in Northern Ireland and is in jeopardy on the mainland. There is no legal inhibition against the use of *agents provocateurs*: citizens may be convicted of crimes they would not have committed but for the instigation of a police agent, and the courts are approving 'sting' operations that create crimes in order to solve them. The British Government admits that detention under the Prevention of Terrorism Act breaches international human-rights law, but remains unrepentant. Britain was the only Gulf War ally to imprison and deport alleged Iraqi sympathizers, without allowing them *habeas corpus* or any proper right of appeal.

The right to a *fair trial* is effectively denied to several hundred persons each year who are wrongfully convicted and imprisoned, sometimes for life. The Government has for many years resisted demands to establish an independent body to investigate and rectify miscarriages of justice, or to change rules and practice which have been shown to conduce to injustice. It uses 'Public-interest Immunity Certificates' in an attempt to avoid disclosing relevant evidence to the defence. Trial by jury is denied in some cases of importance, and there is no law against jury vetting. The magistracy and the judiciary are not independently selected, and are not sufficiently representative of the community. The Asylum Act removes effective rights of access to the courts from some refugees who may be sent back to persecution, and even to death.

Freedom of speech is subject to numerous restraints: libel, contempt, breach of confidence and copyright, obscenity, blasphemy, official-secrecy legislation and the like. Some of these restrictions are justified, to some extent, but they can have the result of curbing and suppressing stories of public importance. In general, they impose more restrictions on the press than are found in comparable legal regimes in North America and Europe, and our libel law has been declared so 'antipathetic to the free-speech protections of the first amendment' that US courts refuse to enforce it. The European Court of Human Rights in *Spycatcher* has condemned the unnecessary prior restraint imposed by the English law of breach of confidence, but this law remains unreformed and threatens journalists with imprisonment for refusal to disclose their sources. Films and videos and television programmes are heavily censored for sex, violence and political incorrectness. Representatives of Sinn Fein (a lawful political entity with one MP and many local councillors) cannot be heard to speak on radio or television. The Official Secrets Act of 1989 obliges tens of thousands of citizens employed on security-related work to maintain silence about it unto the grave. The most noticeable difference between the British and other Western governments is its persistent refusal to enact freedom-of-information legislation, which would give the public access to the facts and arguments behind major policy decisions. Official secrecy is bolstered by rules which unjustifiably require public records to be kept secret for thirty years and, in some cases, allow civil servants to suppress information for all time.

*

The picture which emerges, when British liberty is measured against standards that have won international acceptance, is not reassuring. The absence of any constitutional guarantees of freedom means that courts often lack the legal power to protect individuals against abuses by agents of the state. The inventory of the current condition of civil liberties in England – our national intangible assets, so to speak – shows a poor growth rate, a lag in production compared with other Western democracies, and a failure to adapt to the challenges of modern technology. But the Government remains complacent. In 1992 it issued a glossy propaganda booklet entitled *Human Rights* to convince itself and the rest of the world that liberty in Britain was thriving as never before. It begins:

The British legal systems provide a number of remedies to deal with human rights abuses . . . the remedy of *habeas corpus* secures the individual's right to freedom from any unlawful and arbitrary detention. These rights are guaranteed by the judicial system which is strictly independent of the executive.[1]

This is seriously misleading. The courts are powerless to grant any remedy against arbitrary detention – by *habeas corpus* or otherwise – if that loss of liberty is pursuant to a power enjoyed by the Government. All detentions for interrogation beyond four days are contrary to the European Convention of Human Rights, yet the Government has decided to derogate from that Convention to enable persons to be detained and interrogated for seven days under the Prevention of Terrorism Act. The writ of *habeas corpus* would not run to assist dozens of people who were wrongfully imprisoned to await deportation during the Gulf War, by order of the Home Secretary under his power to remove those whose presence he thinks unconducive to the public good. At the very time *Human Rights* was published, an army captain had been held in solitary confinement for seventy-five days under suspicion of leaking information to what was left of Boris Yeltsin's secret service: the courts declined, after secret hearings, to grant her *habeas corpus*. Judges are not, in fact, 'strictly independent' of the executive – they are appointed by the Government and not by an independent appointments commission, and John Major's government in particular has compromised their independence by using them for political tasks, and by involving them in behind-the-scenes work 'monitoring' the security services. In any event, judges cannot 'guarantee' rights that they have no authority to enforce. The power of the High Court to review government decisions which directly affect individuals is limited to ensuring that they are made rationally – which means that if the minister who made them has a reason, however lame or unmeritorious, his decision will be upheld.

The Government's propaganda booklet continues:

In addition to legal remedies, the citizen can obtain impartial scrutiny of action by public bodies if he or she feels that there is cause for complaint.

No sensible society would expect all or even most infringements of human rights to be rectified by courts. Public bodies are necessary to investigate complaints, award compensation and condemnation, and to monitor compliance with rulings aimed at protecting the right in question. But for these tasks the public body must have independent direction, and legal powers to obtain evidence and enforce its rulings. The Police Complaints Authority inspires little confidence: it has no investigators at all, it manages to substantiate an insignificant fraction of complaints, it fails to protect complainants against police reprisals and it is powerless to discipline policemen whom it believes to be guilty of misconduct if it cannot prove the case against them beyond all doubt. Other complaints bodies open to the citizen are enfeebled by lack of adequate legal powers or by irresolute direction from weak government appointees. The two vital anti-discrimination bodies, the Equal Opportunities Commission and the Commission for Racial Equality, are hamstrung by limited powers; the tribunals which receive complaints about security-service misbehaviour and unlawful telephone tapping are wholly ineffective (and have never upheld a single complaint), while the Press Complaints Commission, funded and dominated by the press, is no more than a public-relations exercise for the newspaper industry.

Unfazed, the Government *Human Rights* hand-out continues:

There are also some non-legal safeguards against the abuse of Government power, including unwritten parliamentary conventions, the vigilance of Parliamentary Opposition parties, the influence of a free press and public opinion, and the right to change the Government through free elections by secret ballot.

These 'safeguards' protect the majority against oppression: they offer little or no comfort to individuals or groups which suffer abuses of power. 'Unwritten parliamentary conventions' do little more than require ministers to answer MPs' questions, but permit answers which are 'economic with the *actualité*' and relieve a minister from dealing with any issue of 'national security' (as the minister chooses to define it) or any matter which is *sub judice*. Parliamentary opposition parties rarely espouse unpopular causes, and are in any event by definition powerless to reverse Government actions. The press is far from free; much of it supports the government, and many newspapers are more interested in invading civil liberties (by infringing privacy or prejudicing fair trials) than they are in highlighting abuses of power. The right to change the Government comes once every five years, and is generally decided by popular judgements on economic management and taxation policy rather than on promises about civil liberties. In any event, such promises are widely and rightly distrusted: some of the worst abuses of power discussed in this book were committed by the last Labour Government, and its deathbed conversion to a Bill of Rights just before the 1992 elections lacked credibility.

The very fact that the Central Office of Information engages in human-rights propaganda exercises does show a new Government sensitivity about Britain's domestic human-rights record. The Thatcher Government treated such concern with disdain: human rights were something that other countries needed to observe, but were irrelevant to the management of Britain. John Major's Government has accepted the importance of citizens' rights, but has attempted to divert attention from its refusal to provide them with legal force (the only way 'rights' have meaningful existence) by a public-relations initiative called 'The Citizen's Charter'. This is an exercise in promoting 'courtesy and helpfulness' in public services by encouraging the wearing of name badges, speeding up the time taken to answer telephones and awarding prizes (a 'Charter Mark' to emboss on promotional material) to public organizations which have achieved 'good Charter practice'.[2] This is all very commendable, but it has nothing to do with empowering citizens to protect themselves against violations of their fundamental rights.

What is really required is a political resolve to make better provision for civil liberty, and that resolve is notably lacking at a time of low budgets and rising crime. Liberty is, after all, an expensive and inconvenient idea, far removed in its common application from the romantic associations evoked in its rhetoric. The plain fact is that most accused persons are guilty of crime. 'Free speech' can be a euphemism for foul obscenities. Demonstrations drain public resources and clog the traffic. Anti-discrimination laws are bad for businesses which aim to give the public what it is thought to want. A data-bank society has the advantage of isolating those unworthy of credit or credibility. The lie-detector test may catch out the odd spy, just as the random 'stop and search' may pull up an incautious drug trafficker. Another day in the cells and the unconfessed criminal may crack – a prospect which might be jeopardized by a solicitor's visit or the presence of a video recording camera. There is a pragmatic case to be made against any civil liberty, on grounds of cost and of convenience.

The cost of liberty is already being used to justify its diminution, in unscientific and ill-judged ways. Massive cut-backs in legal aid were announced in 1993. Whitehall opposes a Freedom of Information Act on the basis of the cost of photocopying and collating, conveniently ignoring the value of allowing public opinion to play on policy debates. The judiciary, too, have allowed cost-consciousness to motivate their decisions to curtail traditional rights: recent cases have limited the right to make bail applications, to have the full prosecution case presented at committal proceedings and to cross-examine. The Home Office long resisted demands for an independent tribunal to review dubious convictions by claiming that this reform would be too expensive at a time of financial stringency. It is a poor society indeed which finds justice too expensive, although it has taken an accountant, not a lawyer, to point out the omission in the costing:

The costs resulting from the wrongful conviction of an innocent party are likely to depend upon two factors, namely the costs of the punishment imposed and in addition any general loss of confidence in the effectiveness of the system ... In addition to the resource costs entailed by mistakenly imprisoning an innocent party are the more general costs which may result in the event that the mistake comes to light ... If it becomes known that mistakes are frequent, public confidence in the criminal justice system will decline and some of the deterrent impact of punishment may be lost. Any increase in the sense of insecurity experienced by citizens as a result of their coming to fear that they run an increased risk of being imprisoned for crimes they have not committed will represent a loss of aggregate happiness or social welfare.[3]

We should apply the same accounting principles which so generously value the 'goodwill' of a business to the value of fairness in the business of justice. Not only in the cases where rights protect the innocent, but where they protect the guilty as well. For example, how do we begin to value the right of suspects to be fairly treated? If police break the rules in order to extract a confession, the trial judge will none the less be asked to admit that confession into evidence. The discretion is his, and by admitting the confession he will make it more likely that a public nuisance will be put behind bars. But the value he will sacrifice is the value of due process, the value of living in a society in which the agencies of Government – in this case the police – work according to rules. If the case is thrown out because the police have broken the rules, it might mean that a lot of expensive police time had been wasted. But to convict on the basis of an unfairly obtained confession would also mean that a principle had been sacrificed: the principle that all suspects must be fairly treated. Is there not a value to be placed on a system which acquits a person, not because he or she is necessarily innocent, but because the rules of fair play were breached in the course of drumming up the evidence of guilt? Every time that evidence is rejected because of breach of a rule, it means that the police will be less likely to break that rule again. They will get their evidence properly, or not at all. A system which allows defendants to walk free when police break the rules is, more significantly, a system which is genuinely concerned to ensure that police do *not* break the rules.

Rights can be understood, and even appreciated, through such arguments without necessarily becoming popular. There will always be more votes for the party which promises to bring back the death penalty than for the party which promises to guarantee to suspects the right to silence. When Home Secretary Merlyn Rees was confronted over the last Labour Government's failure to deliver its manifesto promise on freedom-of-information legislation, his cynical reply expressed the political wisdom which still prevails: 'Only two or three of your constituents would be interested.'

That is why much of the impetus for liberalizing British law comes from the European Court of Human Rights in Strasbourg. In 1930 the Lord Chief Justice of England could slightingly refer to 'continental despotism': ironically, it has been only as a result of commercial and political arrangements with other European states that many advances in the protection of human rights in Britain have been secured. They have forced the United Kingdom Government to legislate for data protection, to reform the law of contempt, to make changes to the prison and immigration rules, to abandon 'in depth' interrogation in Northern Ireland, to control telephone tapping, to end birching in the Isle of Man, to provide additional rights for mental patients – and much else besides.

The British people have never entered into a written pact with their rulers defining the thresholds of power. Magna Carta was a compromise between the King and his barons which set the seal on aristocratic privileges rather than citizens' rights. The Bill of Rights in 1688 was a political settlement designed to protect the position of what was, by modern standards, an undemocratic Parliament. The reform movements of subsequent centuries secured the fundamental rights to vote and to combine, but these advances decided *who* should exercise power rather than *how* it should be exercised. British history has bequeathed no statute of liberty, no comprehensive Bill of Rights forged on the anvil of revolution, to serve either as a check on overweening authority or as a checklist against which to measure the standards of justice achieved by legislation and legal decisions. Remarkably, a language rich in the rhetoric of liberty has never been deployed to enumerate, in an authoritative and binding code, the content of the 'rights' which those who speak it shall possess.

Instead of a set of basic principles, which can be taught and understood and valued by all citizens, we have a vast array of disparate statutes and decided cases from which, as often as not, no satisfactory principle can be derived. The litigation over the Government's attempt to ban reports of *Spycatcher* provides a good example: nobody knew, from one day to the next, what 'law' the courts would declare to exist or to what extent, if at all, the public interest would be permitted to counter the claims for secrecy which sounded so convincing at the outset but which were proved bogus by the end. Much of our policing is done not according to law, but by reference to 'Home Office guidelines', which make unenforceable suggestions about matters as basic as the criteria for secret surveillance and use of informers. Vast discretion is reposed in the 'Home Secretary' – not so much a person as a cipher for the decisions taken behind closed doors by Whitehall mandarins. Many of these decisions – ranging from the issue of warrants for telephone-tapping to the length of time which prisoners sentenced to 'life imprisonment' will actually serve – should be made by the courts, by application of known legal principles, rather than by ministers or public servants acting subjectively and secretly.

The following chapters examine the state of English law as it relates to the liberties that are recognized as most fundamental to the fulfilment of human aspirations. Law has a limited but crucial role in securing individual freedoms: criminal law must not, in terms or in operation, infringe basic rights; administrative law must offer a remedy against the unfair actions of officialdom; statute law may additionally establish avenues and institutions to combat discrimination and to discipline over-zealous or corrupt agents of the state. In each of these three areas, British law remains defective, notwithstanding the reforms which have been made in recent years. That most progress in the protection of civil liberties over the past decade has been directly inspired by the EEC or by the European Court of Human Rights in Strasbourg stands as a reproach to our own institutions, where slothfulness and secrecy, rather than any desire to oppress, have been the major obstacles to necessary reforms. Our preference for pragmatism rather than principle has been convenient in the short term; its cost may be measured in the gaps which still remain in the rights of British citizens to obtain speedy, effective or indeed any remedy against abuses of private and public power.

There are other victims of Britain's failure to make proper provision for the protection of citizens' rights who are not citizens of Britain at all. They live in its former colonies, now Commonwealth nations, which have inherited British law and whose rulers exploit its weaknesses to commit the most serious human-rights abuses. Opposition politicians and newspaper editors are regularly prosecuted and jailed for offences of *sedition* and *criminal libel* and *contempt of court*; English Court of Appeal decisions denying *habeas corpus* to Gulf War detainees and aliens deported by the Home

Secretary are used to deny liberty to political dissidents detained without trial; powerful politicians use civil libel laws to drive their accusers into bankruptcy with the help of the pliant judges they have personally appointed. In 1993 Malawi's unpopular despot, Dr Hastings Banda, hired English lawyers to use his country's English sedition laws to gaol for two years the recipient of the John F. Kennedy Peace Prize, merely for demanding a change to multiparty democracy. British laws (and some British lawyers) have done much to diminish human rights throughout the Commonwealth. Better provision for civil liberties in the United Kingdom will be of value not only to its own citizens, but to all peoples who suffer at the hands of governments which defend their abuses of power by reference to the law of England.

CHAPTER I

Personal Liberty and Police Powers

There are 140,000 police in England and Wales, and each year they arrest over one and a half million citizens. Every arrest involves some deprivation of personal liberty, as the suspect is detained in the police station for hours – sometimes for days – before being set free or released on bail or brought before a court which may order further detention in police custody. The act of arrest is a dramatic moment, pregnant with legal consequence, and what goes on in the police station in the period before the suspect is charged with an offence is often fateful. What goes on is interrogation, and what comes out, very often, is a claim that the suspect has confessed to a crime. Hence the decision to arrest and the treatment of suspects in police detention prior to charge are of central importance to civil liberties: the rules which govern police conduct at this point are our basic protections for personal freedom, and our most important safeguards against forced or fabricated confessions. We look to the law to ensure that no person is arrested without substantial cause, and that those suspects detained in police custody are treated fairly. Otherwise, there is a danger that justice will miscarry – either because the innocent are convicted on the strength of false confessions, or because the guilty are acquitted by juries who refuse to believe in the truth of confessions tainted by police misbehaviour.

English law attempts to strike a balance between the public interest in ensuring that criminals are caught and the interest of members of the public in going about their business without interference. For the most part, this involves a common-sense political compromise: the detection of crime ceases to be the prime consideration at the point where detective methods upset law-abiding citizens or put so much pressure on suspects that the results are questionable. The present law governing arrest and detention was hammered out in detail during the parliamentary passage of the Police and Criminal Evidence Act (PACE) in 1984, and it was influenced by the Government's basic trust in the police and willingness to tolerate increased police powers in the interests of combating crime. None the less, the Act was inspired by the Report of a Royal Commission which was sensitive to the dangers of justice miscarrying, having itself been set up in response to the Confait Report on three youths wrongfully convicted of murder on the strength of false confessions.[1] The Act was additionally influenced by Lord Scarman's report on the Brixton riots of 1981, a wise and robust warning against heavy-handed policing of the impoverished inner city.[2] PACE provided police with additional powers, but sought to control their exercise by more rigorous procedural requirements for fairness in the arrest and detention of suspects.

The PACE reforms had barely come on stream before a series of shocking revelations about miscarriages of justice in criminal trials in the 1970s undermined the Royal Commission's complacent assumption that procedural changes would be sufficient. The trials of the Birmingham Six, the Guildford Four, the Maguire Seven and Judith Ward had miscarried for more fundamental reasons: police brutality and perjury, Government scientists who economized with the truth, non-disclosure of key evidence by prosecutors and emotive trial atmospheres which swept judges and juries towards wrongful convictions. Serious miscarriages of justice were not confined to 'terrorist' cases: the behaviour of particular police squads in London and the West Midlands was exposed as so rotten that many convictions of 'professional' criminals had to be quashed. And some detective work had been so slipshod or overbearing that innocent suspects had been gaoled for long periods even without police perjury or fabrication. These scandals were brought to light by developments in forensic science (notably the ESDA test which can X-ray police notebooks and tell a different story from that told by officers in the witness-box) and by retrospective discovery of documents withheld from the defence. Although many of these revelations were made by conscientious teams from other police forces, ordered to investigate many years later, these orders were only issued because of long and bitter political campaigns to reopen these cases, sometimes with the assistance of *Rough Justice* and other media spotlights. The Government's response to these scandals was to establish another Royal Commission under Lord Runciman, which reported in 1993 to the effect that many more changes in police practice were required before evidence obtained from suspects under arrest and detention could be relied upon as a basis for conviction.

This chapter focuses upon the police and their powers over the person up to the point at which they make a formal charge. It is convenient to consider, at the outset, the office of the constable and the merits of the controversial tradition which frees the police from political control. Police discretion, be it noted, is severely limited by the law: the citizen has inalienable rights of non-cooperation and even forcible resistance to the over-zealous bobby. There is an analysis of the power of arrest and the rights of the suspect in detention and under interrogation. A 'right' is empty rhetoric unless it can be enforced, and the remainder of the chapter examines in some detail how abuses of police power may or may not be brought to book by civil actions, official complaints and rules about exclusion of evidence. Police powers to stop and to search, to mount covert surveillance and to break up protest meetings are dealt with in later chapters, while the problems of avoiding miscarriages of justice at the trial stage are the subject of Chapter 8.

A POLICEMAN'S LOT

The modern police officer has evolved from the ancient office of the constable, a man hired by local magistrates to help keep the peace. As every citizen has a right to maintain order and arrest criminals, there is a romantic notion that the policeman remains a 'citizen in uniform' – 'a person paid to perform, as a matter of duty, acts which if he were so minded he might have done voluntarily'.[3] Today, this principle has little basis in reality: Parliament has armed police officers with a battery of powers unavailable to ordinary citizens, who would risk heavy damages if they dared to exercise them. The principle does serve one useful purpose, however, in reminding us that any and every power exercised by the police must be based on a law: however sensible or meritorious a police action may be, if it is not justified by some specific law it is an abuse of power which the citizen is entitled to resist, by force if necessary, or by suing the police for compensation.

3

The principle is illustrated by the case of *Rice* v. *Connolly*. Police officers were patrolling at night in a burglary-prone area and noticed Rice loitering in the shadows. Sensibly enough, they asked him to account for his movements. He gave some doubtful information, so again quite reasonably they asked him to come down to the police station where it could be checked. Rice refused, and was arrested for obstructing the police in the execution of their duties. The Lord Chief Justice ruled that police had no power to insist upon answers to their questions or to detain Rice while they checked up on him.

It seems to me quite clear that though every citizen has a moral duty or, if you like, a social duty to assist the police, there is no legal duty to that effect, and indeed the whole basis of the common law is the right of the individual to refuse to answer questions put to him by persons in authority, and to refuse to accompany those in authority to any particular place; short, of course, of arrest.[4]

It follows that the police have no power to compel citizens to assist them with inquiries into crime – either by detaining them or merely questioning them in situations where they are not suspected of any offence. There is no offence of 'refusing to help police with their inquiries' – a euphemism invented by the media to avoid libel actions from those arrested by police but not subsequently charged. 'Police officers either arrest for an offence or they do not arrest at all.'[5] If any citizen is detained against his or her will, in a situation falling short of an actual arrest, this is the wrong of false imprisonment, for which the victim can recover damages. Still less, of course, do police have power to insist that a witness visit the station to make a statement or answer questions, or indeed answer police questions at any time or place. Citizens can be served with subpoenas ordering them to attend as witnesses when a case comes to court for hearing, but that is all. They are entitled to ask an inquisitive policeman, 'Are you arresting me or not?' and, if not, to go their way unhindered.

The Police and Criminal Evidence Act gives some statutory force to the common-law position by providing that people who voluntarily go to a police station to assist inquiries 'shall be entitled to leave at will' unless specifically told that they are under arrest.[6] Regrettably, it imposes no duty on the police to inform those they invite to *inhibiting personal freedom?*

assist inquiries that they are free to decline, or that, having arrived at the police station they are free to cut short their assistance and to leave at any point. This is a good example of the British reluctance to admit or to advertise 'rights' which may prove inconvenient to authority – it is better to keep citizens in ignorance than to encourage them to assert their rights at awkward moments. When this section of PACE was being debated in Parliament, a formidable case was made for an amendment which would have required police to be honest with citizens whom they invited to 'assist inquiries', but the Government claimed that this would impose 'an enormous administrative burden on the police'. In consequence, many suspects against whom there is insufficient evidence for arrest are inveigled to police stations in the hope that the atmosphere of confinement and interview will elicit an admission sufficient to justify an arrest.

In practice, of course, most citizens recognize a public duty to aid the detection of crime by giving the police all possible assistance. Innocent suspects will welcome the opportunity to clear themselves, witnesses will want to do their public duty, and most of them will probably not realize that the police have no compulsive power. The device of voluntary attendance is used by some police officers to postpone the operation of legal safeguards which apply after caution and arrest. Most suspects asked with a meaningful stare to 'come down to the station for a chat' will interpret this as a demand declined at their peril rather than as an invitation they are at perfect liberty to refuse. Once inside the oppressive environment of the police station their 'chat', unrecorded and unregulated, can be fashioned into a confession which the suspect can be pressured to repeat on the record after a formal caution. The US Supreme Court, in *Miranda* v. *Arizona*,[7] has recognized the reality that 'all custodial detention is inherently coercive' and requires safeguards that operate from the outset. There would be no 'enormous administrative burden' in requiring police to advise voluntary attenders that they are free to leave at any time, or (if they choose to stay) that they can do so in the presence of a friend or a solicitor.

Police accountability

The Runciman Royal Commission reported that between 80 and 90 per cent of offences are brought to the notice of police by victims, bystanders or other members of the public, and that 'the proportion of crimes solved by the police without help of any kind from members of the public is negligible'. A community which has little trust in the police or is angered by policing policies will be reluctant to provide voluntary assistance. People will only give information which may incriminate neighbours if they are confident that police will use it fairly: they will not allow their homes to be used as surveillance posts if they believe that police hold unjust suspicions or routinely discriminate against certain classes of citizen. Regrettably, the independence of chief constables from any meaningful political or community accountability has, at least in some parts of Britain, hampered the partnership between the police and the public which is necessary for effective control of crime.

It is obviously desirable to keep the police politically independent, in the sense that their operations and the exercise of their discretions should not be dictated by or made in the interests of a particular political party. In Britain, however, this has been taken to an extreme, by endowing forty-one chief constables, together with the Commissioners of the Metropolitan Police and the City of London Police, with a freedom of action on questions of policy which cannot be called to account by central or local Government. As Lord Denning put it, in flourishing phraseology:

I hold it to be the duty of the Commissioner of Police, as it is of every chief constable, to enforce the law of the land. He must post his men that crimes may be detected; and that honest citizens may go about their affairs in peace. He must decide whether or not suspected persons are to be prosecuted; and, if need be, bring a prosecution or see that it is brought; but in all these things he is not the servant of anyone, save of the law itself. No minister of the Crown can tell him that he must, or must not, keep observation on this place or that; or that he must, or must not, prosecute this man or that one. Nor can any police authority tell him so. The responsibility for law enforcement lies on him. He is answerable to the law and the law alone.[8]

The law − or at least the judges who enforce it − will not call upon police chiefs to answer for very much. They will only interfere if satisfied that there has been an abdication of responsibility; in effect, a determined refusal to enforce the law. They will order a chief constable to think again about a policy, based on a misinterpretation of the law, of not enforcing gaming regulations,[9] and they will find a police officer guilty of misconduct for turning his back while a man was being beaten to death in a brawl.[10] But they will not pass judgement on the exercise of police discretion, for example by ordering a police chief to enforce more vigorously the law against pornography[11] or heeding a pacifist's complaint about political discrimination in the decision to arrest her for obstruction of the highway at a place where speakers with more acceptable messages had long been unmolested.[12] To say that police are 'answerable to the law alone' means that they are not answerable to anyone in the way they choose to enforce the law. They are free to take decisions and exercise discretions which may have dramatic consequences on the community (the clumsy 'Swamp 81' stop-and-search operation led to the Brixton riots) or on individuals, whose prospects of being prosecuted rather than cautioned for minor offences often depend upon the particular patch where they are arrested.

Some uniformity in deciding which cases to bring before the courts is achieved by the Crown Prosecution Service (CPS), but the all-important decisions about which cases to send to the CPS as appropriate for prosecution are still made by the police. By 1992, seven years after the CPS was established with the purpose of supervising police discretion, the evidence was that police remained very much in control of the crucial decisions which determine whether a prosecution is brought to court. Lawyers in the service have lacked the authority to intervene at early stages or to drop charges which senior police are determined to pursue. Instead of acting, as the 1981 Royal Commission expected, to filter out weak prosecutions and thereby reduce the number which have to be dropped at a late stage or thrown out of court by the judge at the close of the Crown case, the proportion of those 'directed acquittals' has actually increased (from 44 per cent of all acquittals in 1980 to 59 per cent in 1991) in the years since the CPS was created. This is an abject record for a service which lacks the confidence and the power to curb over-zealous policemen, and amounts to a scandalous waste of public resources as well as an unconscionable infliction of misery on defendants who have, at the end of the day, no case to answer. The Runciman Commission made concerned noises and wishes that the 'friction' it detected between police and the CPS would diminish, but declined on principle to give prosecution lawyers any muscle over police behaviour at the investigatory stage. It is precisely that 'principle' of police inviolability and unaccountability which must be abandoned before real improvements can be made in eliminating unjustifiable prosecutions.[13]

There is a deeply entrenched distaste for anything approaching a 'national police force', although some uniformity has been achieved through the device of the 'Home Office circular', advising all chief constables as to how particular policing tasks (e.g. the use of informers and surveillance devices) should be approached. These circulars do not have the force of law, and are merely 'guidance': there is no sanction for disobedience. The 'Codes of Conduct' which accompany PACE have provided a better basis for achieving uniform treatment of suspects throughout the country but they impose no constraint on police chiefs who adopt controversial policies, in relation, for example, to equipping their forces with rubber bullets and riot shields or mounting heavy-handed operations against pubs or clubs popular amongst ethnic communities.

Each police district has a 'Police Authority' comprising local councillors and magistrates: they appoint the chief constable and have a duty to maintain an 'adequate and efficient' force for their area.[14] But their powers are extremely limited and attempts by some police authorities to direct chief constables on matters of operational policy have been implacably rebuffed: Merseyside's chief constable laughed off his Police Authority's attempt to remove him with the comment: 'I have every Christian virtue except resignation.' ACPO, the Association of Chief Police Officers, has become the most powerful club in the country, promoting policies agreed amongst its members, resisting attempts to introduce measures for accountability and actively entering the political arena by lobbying against legislation which impinges upon policing methods. It operates the National Reporting Centre (NRC), a clearing-house for information about policing problems which spill over several geographical areas (such as the 1985 miners' strike). It reports direct to the Home Secretary, and with the advent of PNC 2 is slowly and secretly becoming a centralized intelligence agency, without any charter to limit its operations.

Local communities have no say over what form of policing they would prefer: the chief constable is the expert on 'operational policy' who must not be trammelled in deciding whether to put bobbies on the beat with truncheons, or with sub-machine-guns.

Few Western countries permit police forces such organizational independence. Most police chiefs in the USA must submit themselves for election and may be called for cross-examination by public representatives. In Europe, police are generally servants of Ministries of State which are themselves politically accountable. In his report into the Brixton riots, Lord Scarman recommended the establishment of formal procedures for police consultation with representatives of the community, and Section 106 of PACE implements his proposal to the extent of requiring all local authorities to 'make arrangements' for obtaining 'the views of people in that area about matters concerning policing of that area' as well as 'securing their cooperation with the police in preventing crime'. The Section does not condescend to suggest what arrangements might be made, and Home Office guidelines emphasize that consultative groups cannot intervene in police operations, although they must work to enable 'decisions which are properly for the police [to] be more closely informed by the discussion of local needs'. But most police/community liaison meetings have been found to have little significant impact on local policing, precisely because the law bestows no significance on them at all.

The lack of organizational accountability of the forty-three police authorities in Britain is an anachronism which was recognized by the Home Secretary in 1993. He promised some reduction in their number and a greater degree of Home Office supervision. The Home Office would set 'national objectives', and appoint the chairman of each police authority as well as five 'business people' in addition to the existing mix of local councillors and magistrates. But this proposal is almost as objectionable as the present arrangements. Magistrates should have no part in organizing the police: their job is to be independent of them. A few 'local councillors and business people' are acceptable, but not to the exclusion of representatives of lawyers, voluntary organizations and ethnic groups in the areas, who will be at the sharp end of police behaviour. In addition, police authorities must be entitled to demand more access to information and have more influence over policing policy, while the Home Office's secret circulars giving 'guidance' to chief constables must all be published. The tradition which protects the police from overtly political control is not put at risk by requiring informed community consent to policies which otherwise risk alienating the community from the police.

ARREST

Personal freedom ends at the point of arrest. This is a formal act by which the power to detain someone reasonably suspected of crime is exercised by a police officer or a citizen. If an arrest is made on insufficient or unreasonable suspicion, or if certain procedures are neglected, it will amount to an excess of power and the arrestor will be liable to damages for falsely imprisoning the victim. 'Citizen's arrest', a relic of the pre-police days when every available member of the community was expected to join in the 'hue and cry' after a felon, is expressly retained by PACE in relation to murder, offences which may carry more than five years' imprisonment (such as theft) and a rag-bag of other 'arrestable offences' ranging from indecent assault and taking bribes to offences under the Official Secrets Act.[15]

In practice, the ancient right to perform a 'citizen's arrest' mainly serves as a protection for those who break up fights or answer the denuded shopkeeper's cry of 'Stop thief!' In the latter case, however, we act at our peril, as W. H. Smith discovered when one of its employees arrested a Mr Walters, believed to be stealing books from its King's Cross shop.[16] Walters was acquitted on the grounds that he intended to pay for them, whereupon he sued W. H. Smith for false imprisonment. He recovered damages, because of the rule that a citizen who arrests must not merely have reason to suspect his victim of committing an 'arrestable' crime, but that such a crime must in fact have been committed, at least by somebody. Police powers of arrest are not limited in this way – an officer may arrest on reasonable suspicion, even if it turns out that no crime has in the event taken place.

This distinction between police and citizen powers is preserved in PACE, and may be hard on a citizen who responds to the cry of 'Stop thief!' by tackling an innocent who flees after a false alarm. The alarm may even be real at the time: a man who took a chocolate bar from Woolworths without paying for it was pursued by a store detective and assaulted a citizen who tried to arrest him in the street. The jury acquitted him of theft (because he had honestly forgotten to pay) but convicted him of assaulting the citizen – a conviction which had to be quashed by the Court of Appeal in 1992 because the citizen had no power of arrest (there having been no offence of theft) and the defendant had in consequence been entitled to use reasonable force to escape the citizen's well-intentioned but retrospectively unlawful assault.[17] The rule has a certain Gilbertian quality when applied in such situations, but at least it has the merit of obliging department stores to report suspects to the police if they wish to avoid the risk of damages for false imprisonment. Store detectives generally ask suspects to accompany them to the nearest police station, and supply their evidence to the police who make the arrest if they believe the evidence is sufficient to justify the charge. There is no obligation to assist a store detective with inquiries, much less to accompany him to a police station: the innocent suspect should insist on being made the victim of a 'citizen's arrest' to preserve a claim for damages against the store.

The police have the power to arrest without a warrant (i.e. an arrest authorization from a magistrates' court) in a wide variety of circumstances. They may arrest if they have reasonable grounds for suspecting guilt of crimes carrying maximum sentences of five years or more or for the special 'arrestable offences' listed in Section 24 of PACE. In addition, they may arrest someone reasonably suspected of having committed an offence, however minor, if they have reasonable grounds for *believing* (rather than *suspecting*) that detention is necessary to prevent the suspect causing harm to himself or to anyone else, or damaging property or obstructing the highway (Section 25). They may arrest rather than proceed by the more civilized method of summonsing the suspect to appear in court wherever this latter course would be impracticable – i.e. in cases where the suspect refuses to give a name and address, or provides a name or address reasonably believed to be false. Police may even use the power of arrest in order to stop a suspect committing an offence against public decency, in cases 'where members of the public going about their normal business cannot reasonably be expected to avoid the person to be arrested'.[18] (Those who wear T-shirts with rude messages can expect to be thrown into the cells for a few hours while relatives or duty solicitors bring a change of clothing.) Before 1984, the police managed quite satisfactorily with a law which allowed them to deprive of liberty only citizens suspected of moderately serious crime: Parliament, by providing various statutory excuses for taking people off to the cells in the most minor cases, has unnecessarily diminished the liberty of the subject. Section 25, with its ominous title 'General Arrest Conditions', signals the change from a society where police powers were limited by reference to specific offences to a state where these powers may be exercised in most circumstances where the police find them convenient.

None the less, PACE does not displace the three great safeguards for every arrest: it must be (1) based on reasonable suspicion, (2) effected by no greater force than is necessary, and (3) the suspect must be informed of the grounds for the arrest at the time it is made. Failure to comply with these fundamental requirements can give rise to civil liability in damages, and can provide a defence for any person charged with resisting arrest or assaulting or obstructing police in the execution of their duty. It is no part of an officer's duty to engage in an unlawful arrest: when police get it wrong, they have no remedy against physical violence inflicted on them by a suspect who attempts to escape. Others may come to the suspect's rescue, with all the force necessary to free him from the unlawful arrest. The force must, however, be directed to securing release from police clutches, and not to chastising the officers for abusing their powers. It is a curious liberty which entitles a citizen to punch a police officer who makes a mistaken arrest: it is, perhaps, the most dramatic reminder of the common law's insistence that every act of detention must be legally justified.

'Reasonable grounds to suspect'

The meaning of this phrase is crucial to the liberty of the subject. It is the formula which permits police officers to set their coercive powers in motion. It means that the officer must act on more than a hunch, but not much more: 'suspicion' is conjecture without hard proof, and a reasonable possibility, rather than the probability, of guilt is sufficient. The best definition has been given by Lord Devlin: 'The circumstances of the case should be such that a reasonable man acting without passion or prejudice would fairly have suspected the person of having committed the offence.'[19] This test allows the constable to take into account material which could never stand up as evidence in court – hearsay, gossip, tip-offs from informants and the like – and to apprehend the suspect at a point where the odds in favour of conviction would be much less than 50 per cent. But it does require a fair appraisal of existing evidence, subject to the circumstances (which may demand a hasty decision) and the application of common sense and logic. Common sense is not the same as common prejudice: judges these days are prepared to hold that it is not reasonable to arrest a man on suspicion of dealing in drugs simply because he is black, drives a BMW and frequents cafés in Notting Hill Gate. As the PACE code for stops and searches emphasizes, personal factors such as colour, age, hairstyle, dress and 'stereotyped images' of likely offenders (of the sort promulgated by the tabloid press) can never alone amount to 'reasonable suspicion'.

In deciding whether an arrest is lawful, the court must be satisfied[20]

(1) that the constable did *in fact* suspect his victim of an arrestable offence. Suspicion of a non-arrestable offence is insufficient,[21] because he will then be unable to give proper reasons for the arrest (see below). Arrest for ulterior purposes (e.g. to facilitate inquiries or to neutralize potential trouble-makers) is unconstitutional.

(2) that there was reasonable cause for the officer's suspicions. This will be decided objectively, by the court determining whether, on the facts known to the constable, his suspicion was rational. Where a policy decision has already been taken not to prosecute persons guilty of the offence, there can be no rational justification for an arrest of anyone reasonably suspected of it.[22]

Courts will decide whether an arrest is based on reasonable suspicion after hearing evidence of the objective facts and the constable's thought processes as applied to them at the time. In one recent case, a court held that a man wearing long hair and blue jeans, carrying a large canvas bag and loitering with a woman and a dog could not be 'reasonably suspected' of going equipped for theft, women and dogs being unlikely burglarious companions.[23] A jemmy protruding from the canvas bag would have been sufficient to make the suspicion 'reasonable', although had the bag been marked 'swag' it might have been unreasonable to suspect the man of going equipped for more than a fancy-dress party.

The duty to give reasons

Suspects must be told that they are under arrest, and have the reasons for the arrest explained to them, either at the time or 'as soon as practicable' afterwards should they resist or attempt to run away. This rule, now contained in Section 28 of PACE, was established by the House of Lords in the leading case of *Christie* v. *Leachinsky*.[24] Leachinsky had attracted the sort of suspicion which frequently attaches to totters and rag-and-bone merchants – that of being in unlawful possession of stolen property. The police, who in fact had reasonable grounds for suspecting him of theft, arrested him under a municipal by-law which only applied when a suspect's name and address were unknown. Christie, the police officer, admitted that he knew Leachinsky and his address, but had found it 'more convenient' to arrest for the wrong reason. In 1947, before police convenience had become a factor to be reckoned with in the development of the criminal law, the House of Lords laid down a strict rule:

If a policeman arrests without warrant upon reasonable suspicion of felony, or of other crime of a sort which does not require a warrant, he must in ordinary circumstances inform the person arrested of the true ground of arrest. He is not entitled to keep the reason to himself or to give a reason which is not the true reason. In other words a citizen is entitled to know on what charge or suspicion of what crime he is seized.

Leachinsky was entitled to damages against the police for false imprisonment. Although the police are not required to give technically precise or detailed reasons for arrest, 'in this country a person is, *prima facie*, entitled to his freedom and is only required to submit to constraints on his freedom if he knows in substance the reason why it is claimed that this restraint should be imposed'. The rule in *Christie* v. *Leachinsky* has the merit of requiring police to crystallize their suspicions prior to arrest sufficiently to give a reasoned statement, and permits the suspect to know the nature of the allegation which he can, if so minded, try to refute then and there. The arrest will be unlawful if no reasons for it are given, or if those reasons are irrelevant or insufficient or the power has been exercised for the wrong reason or in bad faith.

'Reasonable force'

In effecting an arrest, a police officer or citizen may use 'such force as is reasonable in the circumstances'. Unreasonable force will make the arrest unlawful, and the victim will be entitled to damages for assault. For example, damages have been awarded against police for restraining a recalcitrant prisoner in a body belt for twenty-four hours, and for arresting a middle-aged woman for a minor traffic offence by twisting (and fracturing) her wrist. It will be for the police to justify their need to use headlocks or handcuffs or the threat of unleashing of trained dogs (fondly known to their handlers as 'furry Exocets', and much favoured for rounding up football hooligans). Handcuffing is only justifiable when there is a reasonable apprehension that the prisoner would otherwise escape or turn violent, and if used unnecessarily will constitute a trespass to the person, even if the arrest itself has been lawful.[25] Public handcuffing is a degrading and humiliating action which should never be taken without good reason. The Metropolitan Police rarely use handcuffs, but this B-movie tradition lingers in other police districts. The riot in St Paul's in Bristol in 1980 began with a police raid on a popular black café. The crowd which gathered was in good humour as the police carried away endless cases of Red Stripe beer from its unlicensed cellar, but the mood turned ugly at the sight of the proprietor, a popular and entirely peaceable figure in the local community, being led away in handcuffs. It was the spark which ignited a riot that caused £2 million damage. Parliament omitted to restrict the practice of handcuffing when extending police powers in 1984.

Any show or use of force should be the minimum consistent with protection of the arresting officers in the circumstances, and police who shoot to kill without very good reason will often face murder charges if they can be identified. They will almost always be acquitted, however, because juries are understandably reluctant to bring back a verdict which will result in life imprisonment for a policeman or soldier who has acted in honest error as to the 'reasonableness' of discharging his weapon. The law, by applying too strict a test, allows those who respond excessively and unnecessarily to escape all punishment. There is need for an 'in between' verdict of manslaughter in these situations, to bring British law into line with Article 2(2) of the European Convention which requires that no more force should be used in these situations than is *absolutely* (rather than 'reasonably') necessary.[26]

The police have internal regulations about the use of firearms. With true British passion for secrecy, these regulations are contained in a confidential ACPO manual. In 1982, after a public outcry over the gunning down of Stephen Waldorf in mistake for a dangerous criminal, the inevitable 'Home Office circular' directed that firearms should only be used as a last resort, and should be issued only when a senior officer has reason to suppose that officers will have to face armed or very dangerous criminals. But this circular is no substitute for careful criteria governing the supervision and use of lethal weapons, as subsequent police shootings have demonstrated. There is an urgent need to draw up detailed and restrictive legal guidelines for lethal weapons based on the 'absolute necessity' principle of the European Convention. Allegations that the army and the RUC have operated a 'shoot to kill' policy, exemplified by the SAS killing of three IRA members in Gibraltar, make it internationally unacceptable for British law to permit assassination in circumstances which are 'reasonable' rather than imperative.

The British bobby, with truncheon and faintly ridiculous helmet, is a reassuring figure compared with the pistol-packing cops who patrol the streets in almost every other country. But the pretence that the police on the mainland go about their business unarmed is belied by the increasing number of officers in every force who have undergone firearms training and are 'licensed to kill' when circumstances reasonably require. Accurate statistics are deliberately withheld by the Home Office in order to promote the myth of the 'unarmed force', but as long ago as 1986 there were fifty-six full-time training officers teaching firearms use in the Metropolitan Police alone: the annual budget for their courses (occupying seven thousand man hours) was £2 million. Many police officers in fact carry firearms, under both plain clothes and uniforms, or in special 'armed-response vehicles' which now cruise city centres in wait for calls to arms. These developments may be inevitable: what is objectionable is the secrecy which has accompanied them. Secrecy has misled the public; it has lost any deterrent benefit from the overt wearing of firearms, and it has required officers to wear their guns in places from which it is difficult to draw them (PC Trevor Lock might have held the Iranian Embassy against terrorist attack had his gun been in a holster by his hand rather than hidden under his uniform).[27] It is ironic, if unsurprising, that Britain is more concerned to maintain the fiction that its police do not carry any lethal weapons than to regulate the way in which they do in fact increasingly carry and use them.

The summons alternative

Police have alternatives to arresting without a warrant. They can obtain an arrest warrant from a magistrate, or can simply summons the suspect to appear in court at a particular date to answer the charge. The extension of police power to arrest without a warrant (Sections 24 and 25 of PACE) has reduced the demand for magistrates' warrants: the detective's traditional doorstep greeting – 'I have a warrant for your arrest' – is now heard a little less frequently. (Search warrants, as we shall see in Chapter 3, are still keenly sought.) But why arrest at all, when there is no objection to bail and a summons sent by registered post will secure a court attendance by the defendant? Many suspects who are arrested and detained for a day or so could be quizzed at their home or at a solicitor's office and be subsequently served with a summons if the evidence warranted prosecution. That was the view of the 1981 Royal Commission on Criminal Procedure, which pointed out that 'arrest represents a major disruption in the suspect's life', and recommended that the option of arrest should be strictly limited to cases where detention was genuinely necessary (e.g. where police intended to oppose bail) and not be used routinely or for police convenience.[28] PACE, however, extended police powers of arrest generally, and hence provides no incentive to use the summons procedure.

Whether citizens will be summonsed rather than arrested may depend on who they are and where they are. Police are more inclined to summons well-to-do persons than to arrest them, unless there is valuable (i.e., prejudicial to the suspect) publicity to be obtained. There was no question of arresting Mr Jeremy Thorpe – he was interviewed, by appointment, in his solicitor's office and summonsed to attend court to face charges of conspiracy to murder without suffering the ritual indignities of searching and fingerprinting and a night in the cells. Unnecessary humiliation, however, was visited upon the Maxwell brothers, who were arrested at their homes at dawn, and upon Asil Nadir, who was arrested at Heathrow on his return to Britain, in both cases after press and television had been 'tipped off' so as to ensure maximum publicity. These suspects could easily have been summonsed, and had in any event volunteered to attend at police stations with their solicitors. The behaviour of the Serious Fraud Office, in choosing to parade them at a media circus, was a disgraceful abuse of the power of arrest.

The Royal Commission discovered that some police forces hardly ever use a summons (the Met and Greater Manchester in only 1 per cent of cases), while Derbyshire summonsed 72 per cent of its suspects and North Wales 53 per cent. The picture which emerges is that a summons can be used effectively, even in large cities, in about 50 per cent of cases: the enormous variations from police district to police district are unacceptable. Some police chiefs are hostile to the summons procedure because they prefer to play against their suspects on home ground – the police station. Arrested persons can be disoriented and frightened by the sights and sounds of police custody, and by the bare interview room and the long waits in cells reeking of tobacco, urine and cabbage. These atmospheric influences may be powerful inducements to confess, but not necessarily to make a true confession.

DETENTION

The period between arrest and charge is the time between the ending of personal freedom and the commencement of court-supervised custody. Persons reasonably suspected of crime are cautioned, interrogated, searched, often fingerprinted and photographed: in due course they will either be set free (if the accumulated evidence is insufficient to prosecute) or else charged and brought before a court, which will consider whether to grant bail or to remand them in prison pending subsequent stages in the prosecution process. It is a crucial time, in which their treatment is determined by a compromise between different public interests – the desirability of getting at the truth about an offence, the importance of the individual's 'right to silence', the need to maintain certain minimum standards of fairness and humanity, and the necessity of guarding against false confessions produced by fear or force or a simple desire to obtain bail. Occasionally police officers extract confessions by physical violence, although more often the inducement comes from offers of bail or threats to charge friends or relatives. The rules governing interrogation are designed to prevent such blandishments, which obviously render confessions unreliable. But a more subtle form of pressure is atmospheric. The very experience of being confined in a police cell, the fear – of police or of other prisoners – the disorientation, the smell, can all work to sap the will. So can lack of sleep – a common handicap for prisoners in police cells where lights burn all night. The psychologist who studied the mental impact of arrest and detention for the 1981 Royal Commission has described the 'softening-up' process that inevitably occurs:

Say you are brought in for questioning and you are, in effect, a suspect. You're brought into the police-station yard, a door with a special locking device opens, you get out of the car, into the cell blocks, through another large iron door with a grille again with special locking devices, and you pass through into the charge room, where your property is taken from you. You will then be put in a cell which is a bare room, with bars that obviously are a guarded window, wooden bench, nothing much on it, or a lavatory next door, and the door is locked on you. There is a very small grating in the door, and you are obviously locked in, and very much alone, in a totally alien environment. You've got no shoes on by this time, and your belt has been taken away, and so have all your possessions – you no longer feel in control of yourself, you are under somebody else's control and authority. That sets the scene for effective use of interrogation techniques of all kinds.[29]

This psychological softening-up, deriving from the very fact of police detention, makes many people an easy target for relatively simple interrogation techniques – the 'Mutt and Jeff' routines set out in police textbooks:

The suspect may be placed in a chair with no arm-rests, probably fixed to the floor. The interrogator, behind a desk, endeavours to establish friendly relations and to draw the suspect out. If this fails he may change tactics, pretend that the case is sewn up by the discovery of an eye-witness or the confession of an accomplice, and suggest that the suspect's only course is to make a statement. Another routine is for the first, friendly interrogator to be alternated by a verbal bully; or the interrogator may try to unnerve the suspect by addressing questions to him from behind.[30]

As the strongest pressure to confess undoubtedly derives from consciousness of guilt, is there any need for concern about oppressive atmospheres and techniques which fall short of torture or inhumane treatment? The problem for a society which rightly regards the conviction of the innocent as a greater evil than acquittal of the guilty is that oppressive circumstances can produce the very sort of false confession which juries find credible. Take the case of Albert Hudson, planning officer for Kensington and Chelsea Council. At 6.30 a.m. on a Sunday morning he was arrested at his home and taken to Chelsea police station, where he spent the next five days, much of the time taken up by answering seven hundred questions from police officers. At the end of that period, he broke down and confessed to many things which simply could not have happened. 'Why should a man make an incriminating statement when the evidence was to the contrary?' asked the Court of Appeal, when it later quashed his conviction.

The feeling of captivity starting with the police officers arriving at 6.30 a.m. at his house and arresting him; the fact that he was taken from his home in Farnham to Chelsea police station; the experience of being a prisoner in a police cell; the twenty-five hours of questioning; and the fact that he was always accompanied by a police officer except when he was in his cell and was in custody out of his cell for fifty hours. All of that with a man of fifty-nine who had never been in trouble before would inevitably provide a strong inference of oppression.[31]

In 1992 the Court of Appeal quashed the unreliable murder convictions of the Cardiff Three, which were based on confessions extracted by 'verbal bullying' as police bellowed at and browbeat suspects over several hours of intensive interrogation. The PACE Codes of Practice do not address this form of pressure, and although the interview was tape-recorded the lawyers concerned in the case had been content to put before the jury only a typed transcript which failed to evoke the oppressive atmosphere apparent to the appeal judges after they listened to the recordings. This case provides a warning of how false confessions may be extracted notwithstanding compliance with all the procedural safeguards in PACE, through psychological techniques which exploit the fear and disorientation caused by captivity. Many confessions forthcoming in such circumstances will, of course, be true; but the danger of miscarriages of justice can only be acceptably reduced by a rule which requires their credibility to be bolstered by some item of independent evidence which connects the confessor to the crime to which he has confessed.

Length of custody

How long are police entitled to keep a suspect in their custody? The danger of the oppressiveness which bore down on Albert Hudson and others who have falsely confessed must be balanced against the need to give investigating officers a reasonable time-frame within which to conduct their inquiries. The Royal Commission on Criminal Procedure recommended that the law should provide a specific limit, which could be subject to a court-approved extension in complicated cases. That limit was set, by PACE, at twenty-four hours in the case of ordinary offences, and at thirty-six hours when 'serious arrestable offences' are being investigated and a senior police officer is satisfied that the additional time is necessary to secure evidence or to complete questioning. After thirty-six hours, the police must apply to a magistrates' court for a warrant authorizing continued detention, which may be extended for up to another thirty-six hours if the justices are satisfied that the investigation is being conducted diligently and further detention is *necessary* to preserve or obtain evidence. The magistrates may extend the warrant for yet another period, so long as the total time spent in police detention by the suspect prior to charge or release does not exceed ninety-six hours.

The 'serious arrestable offences' which may cause a suspect to spend up to four days in police custody include murder, rape, incest, causing explosions, using firearms, kidnapping, and terrorism. Regrettably, Section 116 of PACE adds to their number *any offence at all* which has serious consequences for public order, national security or the administration of justice, or involves substantial financial gain or 'serious financial loss to the person who suffers it' (you can thus be held for four days on suspicion of picking a vagrant's pocket, but only for twenty-four hours on suspicion of stealing money from a millionaire who would not really miss it). This lack of clarity over what constitutes a 'serious arrestable offence' is a major defect in PACE, and one which leads to some innocent suspects being kept in custody for almost four days before being released.

PACE is at its weakest when purporting to provide 'safeguards' against unjustified detention. The first of such 'safeguards' is the custody officer on duty at the police station, who is obliged by Section 37 to refuse an arresting officer's request to detain a suspect unless it is 'necessary' to do so. 'Necessary' is a strong word in theory, but one which commands no respect in practice – studies published in 1991 reveal that custody officers refuse to detain in less than 1 per cent of cases brought to them. The independence of the custody officer from the investigation – a central assumption of the detention safeguards of PACE – is a fiction. The Runciman Commission reported that custody officers are 'trained' for only two days, that the job is unpopular and that it may be 'unrealistic' to expect them to take an independent view of a case investigated by colleagues. In view of persistent complaints about police behaviour at the stage of receiving a suspect into custody, the Commission recommended that a continuous video recording should be made of every police station's custody reception area ('custody suite' is the new official euphemism). This is a valuable suggestion which would resolve many disputes at trial and would encourage custody officers to display more concern about the rights of those whom they are depriving of liberty.[32]

For the suspect who has been detained, the arrival of a police inspector (who must approve continuation of any detention beyond twenty-four hours) provides no independent safeguard. This only comes in the form of review by magistrates after thirty-six hours have elapsed, although this time may be extended by the device of making the arrest on Friday night or Saturday morning (as the time for seeking court approval does not run on Sundays).[33] Local justices, as we shall see, are more renowned for rubber-stamping police requests than for championing the liberty of the subject. In issuing a warrant for further detention they will at least have the suspect before them, with the right to have a lawyer to contradict and cross-examine the police case. The writ of *habeas corpus* remains available to secure the release of any suspects held in breach of the time limits, although it is likely to take at least twenty-four hours to prepare the High Court application and have it listed for hearing. Anomalously, PACE does not apply to protect persons held in military custody. When Captain Carole Maychell, an officer in the Territorial Army, was arrested on suspicion of breaking the Official Secrets Act, she was held in solitary confinement for seventy-five days while the investigation continued. In 1993 the Divisional Court decided that 'excessive delay had not been demonstrated' and refused to release her on bail.[34] The charges against her were later dropped.

Detention of terrorist suspects

A severe incursion into civil liberties is specially authorized in the case of suspects detained on suspicion of involvement in terrorism. They may be held incommunicado for two days, and the Home Secretary may grant a warrant to hold them for a further five days, in the course of which they may see a solicitor but only on condition that the interview is 'within sight and hearing' of a uniformed officer. These powers were extended in the angry aftermath of the Birmingham pub bombings in 1974, when twenty-one people were killed. The Prevention of Terrorism Act was then described as a temporary and emergency measure, but successive Governments have reimposed it. The Act proscribes membership of the IRA and INLA and permits the exclusion of suspects from the country, but it is doubtful whether its extended detention provisions have assisted the apprehension and conviction of persons who could not have been dealt with under existing police powers. Only a small percentage of the thousands of suspects detained under the legislation have been charged with any criminal offence, and there is some evidence that the seven-day detention period is used mainly for low-level intelligence gathering on Irish activists.[35] The Home Secretary's warrant procedure is objectionable: the decision to detain for up to five days after the initial forty-eight hours should be decided by a court, and not by the prerogative of a party politician who in practice will rarely have the time or the ability to consider the police request with any degree of scepticism.

This was the view of the European Court, which decided in 1988 in the case of *Brogan* v. *UK* that holding persons under the Prevention of Terrorism Act for longer than four days without the approval of a judicial authority was a violation of Article 5(3) of the European Convention of Human Rights, which requires that all persons detained after their arrest 'shall be brought promptly' before a court. The Court made full allowance for the need for flexibility in response to terrorism, but refused to countenance this as an excuse for denying a fundamental right to have loss of liberty considered 'promptly' by a judicial authority independent of the state. The UK Government angrily reacted by derogating on this point from the European Convention and from the International Covenant on Civil and Political Rights, on the basis that a 'public emergency' existed in Northern Ireland, where Brogan had been detained. This reason does not, of course, justify the detention of suspects for seven days without having to convince a court, rather than a Government minister, of the necessity for doing so. The excuse for flouting basic human-rights standards is thin in any event, as Northern Ireland studies demonstrate that terrorist suspects tend either to confess within a few hours of arrest, or not at all. If there is any reason to believe that reliable information will be obtained after four days of detention, this could be presented to a court in support of a request to approve detention for three extra days – but the UK Government declined to amend the Act in this simple way so as to comply with human-rights standards.

Official reports into the operation of the Prevention of Terrorism Act have drawn attention to the danger of police abusing the extra detention powers to fish for intelligence or obtain evidence of non-terrorist offences, and have recommended that the Act should only be used where no other police power is appropriate.[36] This recommendation has not been heeded, and police invariably arrest terrorist suspects under its extended powers. The official explanation is that hardened terrorists are trained in anti-interrogation techniques, so seven days' detention may be necessary to break down their defences. This is not only an ugly admission that the end justifies the means, but an argument supported by neither logic nor evidence. Well-trained terrorists will easily withstand questioning for seven days, while innocent suspects may unreliably confess as late as day six or seven. Persons detained and then released without charge are, quite unjustly, not entitled to have their fingerprints or photographs destroyed, and police will retain photocopies of any interesting documents found in their possession for possible use against them later on. It is difficult to see how communication with a solicitor can be of any advantage when it takes place in the presence and hearing of a police officer. The case for a special power, unique in English law, to detain on suspicion (which need not be reasonable) for a period in breach of maximum human-rights standards, must rest on evidence that some guilty terrorists have been convicted by use of the special power in circumstances where they would have been acquitted, or not even charged, if processed under the 'serious arrestable offence' provisions of PACE. No such evidence has ever been produced.

The right to a lawyer

In the USA, the 'right to counsel' is absolute: *Miranda* v. *Arizona* requires suspects to be told immediately on arrest that they are entitled to have private access to a lawyer and that either their own will be contacted or one will be provided at state expense.[37] Section 58 of PACE begins with a similar flourish: 'A person who is in police detention shall be entitled, if he so requests, to consult a solicitor privately at any time.' However, the entitlement is far from absolute. Broadly speaking, access to a lawyer must be provided at the very latest after thirty-six hours of arrest for 'a serious arrestable offence'. Access may be delayed if police fear interference with evidence, hindrance to recovery of property or the alerting of other suspects as a result of notifying a solicitor or permitting him to consult with the arrested client. The same considerations also permit delay in giving effect to the right, established by Section 56 of PACE, of having one friend or relative notified of the arrest. In other words – which are certainly not the words with which the section commences – a suspect may be held completely incommunicado in a police station for thirty-six hours. Parliament was swayed by the image of gang members disposing of drugs and gold bullion on hearing from helpful solicitors that one of their number had been arrested. Although the Law Society, on behalf of practising solicitors, undertook that its members would accept a solemn obligation in such exceptional cases to pass no communication from the suspect to others, the risk of 'coded messages' was deemed too great.

The real reason, of course, why police are generally reluctant to contact a solicitor is their belief that a lawyer will advise the suspect to exercise the right of silence and refuse to answer their questions. This police belief is in many cases a misapprehension: solicitors frequently advise clients to put forward their explanation at the first available opportunity, and even if they counsel silence, that is merely reminding suspects of a right which they are fully entitled to use. The Code of Practice for police questioning[38] specifically states that access to a solicitor must not be denied on the ground that the lawyer might advise the suspect not to answer questions – which means in practice that police who do deny access must be able to justify their decision by reference to one of the three exceptions in Section 58. The so-called 'right' under Section 58 may be avoided by police who conduct their interviews while driving the suspect to the police station ('we're taking you on the scenic route'), or who, once there, promise that if they cooperate by agreeing to an immediate interview they can go home rather than face a long wait in the cells before the solicitor arrives.

Although the Code of Practice issued pursuant to PACE requires a notice about the availability of legal advice to be prominently displayed in the charging area, and the custody officer has a duty to inform the suspect shortly after arrival at the station of his entitlement to free legal assistance, there are commonly used ploys for deterring requests for solicitors.[39] One device is for custody officers to read rights quickly and incomprehensibly, while obtaining the suspect's signature on that section of the custody form which requires his confirmation that no solicitor is needed. A very effective ploy is to state (dishonestly, given legal aid, but credibly) that a 'lawyer would cost you a lot of money'. Even more effective is the line 'Of course you can have a solicitor, but we'll have to bang you up in the cells until he gets here.' Although a majority of detainees still decline – many as a result of such ploys – to contact solicitors or to take advantage of 'duty solicitors' on call to most police stations, the Code provisions have produced a significant increase in requests for legal assistance. Moreover, the Court of Appeal has been more than usually prepared to exclude from evidence confessions obtained after police disregard for Section 58, on the grounds that it would be unfair to convict a person who has been improperly denied access to legal advice prior to interrogation. In the *Winston Silcott* appeal, where three young men were found to have been wrongly convicted of killing a policeman during the Broadwater Farm disturbances in Tottenham, the Court was particularly sceptical of police claims that the presence of a solicitor during their interviews would have resulted in interference with evidence or the alerting of other suspects. Although much will depend on the circumstances of each case, the Court of Appeal's many decisions on this point indicate that trial judges should seriously consider rejecting confessions obtained after denying or delaying requested access to a solicitor, unless the chosen solicitor (or solicitor's clerk) was reasonably believed to be untrustworthy or the defendant was well aware of his right to silence, and remained confident and self-controlled during the interview session.[40]

Ironically, the commendable work done by appellate judges to strengthen the right to a solicitor has been undermined not by police so much as by solicitors themselves. Research projects instigated by the Runciman Commission reported in 1992 that except in 'high profile' cases, experienced solicitors opted out of advising suspects during interviews, and for the most part dispatched untrained and unqualified staff (sometimes 'retired' police officers or 'resting' actors) to police stations for hand-holding exercises designed only to sign up the suspect as a client.[41] The research establishes that suspects are unlikely to receive any competent advice (or anything which could be fairly described as 'advice') from supine young solicitors or their clerks, who sit silently while their client is subjected to bullying and unfair interrogation. This extraordinary passivity may be explained by inexperience or (more cynically) by the desire of solicitors to maintain good relations with police officers who help to drum up their business. But it demonstrates that the solicitors' profession (and the law faculties) must begin to comprehend the crucial significance of interviews in police detention, give attendance higher priority and status, and start to teach those who do attend how and when to object to police questioning when it assumes guilt or asks leading questions or is designed to demoralize or trick or bully a suspect into confessing guilt.

The Runciman Commission emphasized the need to improve the quality of legal advice available to suspects by urging the Legal Aid

Board to scrutinize the competence of a solicitor's services in this respect before paying public money for them. Surprised that only 32 per cent of suspects actually tick the box on the custody form to indicate their wish for a lawyer, and suspicious of the ploys described above, the Commission recommended that a suspect's refusal should be recorded on tape and that he should be invited to state his reasons for waiving this right. He should then be invited to speak on the telephone to a deputy solicitor before finally deciding to undergo an interview unrepresented. These would be valuable safeguards, if only solicitors would live up to the trust reposed in them to protect their clients from oppression.

Other physical restraints

What other powers do police have over suspects once they are in custody? Fingerprinting and photographing can sometimes be necessary to assist identification or to eliminate the suspect from the inquiry: before PACE was passed, however, these had become routine at many police stations even for the most minor offences. In 1981, the Divisional Court was shocked to find that police in Kingston upon Thames had insisted on fingerprinting 'a middle-aged lady of good character' after a trifling motoring offence, and issued a stern warning that such humiliating infringements of personal liberty should not be undertaken without good reason.[42] PACE now purports to confine the compulsory taking of fingerprints to cases where a senior police officer has reason to believe that the prints would 'tend to confirm or disprove' the suspect's involvement in a crime. The code of conduct for identification procedures permits photographs to be taken for criminal-record purposes, but in cases where the suspect is released without charge or subsequently acquitted, any photographs or fingerprints must be destroyed, and the ex-suspect has a right to witness their destruction, although once again there is no duty to inform suspects of this right. In fact, routine fingerprinting and photographing of suspects continues at most police stations because PACE 'safeguards' are hopelessly inadequate. These invasions of privacy are permitted in relation to *any* offence, no matter how minor. Because there is no effective sanction against the senior police officer who gives approval, they are often deployed without any intention to use them to 'confirm or disprove' the victim's involvement in crime. They are, rather, used to humiliate and 'soften up', and for record-keeping purposes. Political protestors are often forcibly fingerprinted and photographed on their arrest for minor obstruction offences: their dabs and mug-shots will end up in Special Branch files, and will stay on them after conviction, even though they should never have been taken in the first place.

People are often misled by US films and television into thinking that police can put a suspect on a 'line-up' whenever they choose. In Britain, attendance at an identity parade is purely voluntary. It is a method devised, with careful safeguards, to test the most unreliable kind of evidence. Wrongful identification is a potent source of miscarriage of justice, and a parade offers a better means of checking it than such alternatives as inviting a witness (who may have had but a fleeting glimpse of the criminal) to associate the memory-image with a 'mug shot', or to identify a suspect who is sitting in a cell or a court dock. Where police believe that an identification check would be useful, they may ask the suspect to stand on parade, pointing out the less satisfactory alternatives. They are obliged to hold a parade if the suspect insists. Obviously the evidential value of any identification which takes place at a parade is destroyed if the witness has been shown a photograph of the suspect beforehand, or if the suspect's appearance is significantly different from that of all the other persons paraded. Police often have difficulty finding 'matching' members of the public to stand on the line, and although a defence solicitor is normally present there are often subsequent disputes in court over the manner in which the witness made the identification. The Runciman Commission recommended that all identity parades should be video-recorded, to enable juries to make better assessments of their reliability.

Some police practices relating to the search of suspects prior to the enactment of PACE and its codes of conduct were unnecessarily degrading. The courts were unimpressed by police claims that they were entitled forcibly to remove brassières from female suspects lest they do themselves an injury, and saw no need for custody officers to seize jewellery or watches.[43] PACE directs custody officers to record all items possessed by a suspect on entering the station: they can only be confiscated if there is reason to believe that they might be used for self-injury or to assist escape, or are otherwise relevant to the offence being investigated. An 'intimate search' of 'bodily orifices' may be conducted by a 'suitably qualified person' if there are reasonable grounds for believing that the orifice conceals a 'Class A' drug or something which could cause physical injury. This provision was made the subject of much agonizing debate in Parliament: while customs officers have similar powers to deal with suspected drug smugglers, there is no evidence that drug-dealers walk the streets with cocaine or heroin secreted in anus or vagina. This provision was inserted against original Government intentions as a result of back-bench hysteria about 'Class A' drugs, and affords an opportunity for police to invade personal integrity which is out of all proportion to the harm sought to be averted. The Act does not explain what classes of person are 'suitably qualified' to examine body orifices for non-medical purposes: the power is both degrading and unnecessary.

A more sensible and civilized approach is taken in relation to 'intimate bodily samples' such as blood, semen, urine or clips of pubic hair, which are sometimes required for forensic examination that may confirm or disprove the suspect's involvement with a crime. The suspect must consent before these can be taken, and a refusal will not be met by forcible extraction but by permitting the jury at the trial to hear of the refusal and to regard it, where appropriate, as an indication confirming other evidence of guilt. This provision has been of increasing importance with the recent development of 'genetic fingerprinting' techniques that enable semen taken from rape victims, or blood shed at a murder scene, to identify positively a suspect with the same unique configuration of DNA. It is a mistake to suggest that these provisions breach the rule against self-incrimination: refusal to allow a physical examination that could provide conclusive evidence of linkage to a crime can fairly be held against a suspect, while a refusal to answer police questions proves nothing. As Justice Holmes once remarked, 'the prohibition of compelling a man in a criminal court to be witness against himself is a prohibition of the use of physical and moral compulsion to extort communications from him, not an exclusion of his body as evidence when it may be material'.[44]

The results of DNA testing are not infallible and should be excluded from evidence unless the prosecution can negative any real prospect of contamination, leakage, confusion or statistical error in the testing laboratory. At this stage of its development, it would be preferable that convictions should not be based solely on DNA profiles, and that this class of evidence should not be admitted unless the defence has had the resources to test the validity of the findings. Given the probable consequences of consent to DNA sampling (as well as refusal to undergo it, which can give rise to an inference of guilt) suspects should be required to take legal advice prior to consenting, and should ideally be given the opportunity to have the samples tested at a different laboratory to that used by the prosecution. The Government has admitted to planning a 'national DNA database' of convicted offenders, an enterprise enthusiastically supported by the Runciman Commission, which recommended that all persons arrested for serious offences should be profiled from DNA compulsorily extracted from their saliva or their plucked hair. Once convicted, their DNA would be entered in the database in the hope of clearing up their past or future crimes. Runciman's boundless faith in DNA evidence may yet prove premature and become, ironically, a source of more wrongful convictions.

POLICE INTERROGATION

The right to silence

Statements made to the police constitute important evidence in criminal detection, and the conduct by police of their interviews with arrested persons is a focal point in most criminal trials. Each and every interview must begin with the traditional caution: 'You do not have to say anything unless you wish to do so, but what you say may be given in evidence.' If they do indicate a wish to stay silent, however, there is nothing to prevent the interrogator from attempting to goad or sting or prompt them into a response. There are certain well-established limits to efforts to coax a silent suspect: threats must not be made, nor promises of bail or favourable treatment held out as an inducement to 'spill the beans'. There must be no 'oppression' of the suspect, and no trick or other unfair practice employed, otherwise the resulting confession may not be allowed in evidence at the trial.

The caution embodies the 'right to silence' – the rule against self-incrimination which is one of the most notable features of British criminal law. Its origins go back to the heresy trial of John Lilburn, the Leveller, who in 1637 accused his judicial interrogators of 'trying to ensnare me, foreseeing the things for which I am imprisoned cannot be proved against me'. The Star Chamber had him set in the pillory for refusing to take an oath to answer their questions, but the House of Lords later condemned his treatment, holding it to be 'contrary to the laws of nature and the kingdom for any man to be his own accuser'. While the rule can assist the guilty, it has also protected innocent suspects from making ill-considered explanations while disoriented after an arrest or in panicked responses to aggressive questioning. It places a premium on police *investigation*, emphasizing the need to gather objective evidence rather than relying upon suspects to trip themselves up. The value of applying the rule to police questioning is underlined by research which shows how the atmosphere of custody may exert a degree of oppression and confusion that can render unreliable confessions obtained after intensive questioning. There may be reasons for abrogating the rule in special circumstances, or in relation to special people. The Companies Act, for example, requires persons responsible for public companies which crash to answer questions about their stewardship put by Department of Trade Inspectors, and their answers may be used against them in subsequent criminal proceedings. They will, however, have had ample access to documents and legal advice before being called upon to respond. The Serious Fraud Office is also entitled, under Section 2 of the Criminal Justice Act 1988, to require suspects to answer questions on pain of six months' imprisonment if they refuse, although their answers may only be used in evidence if they give a different story in the witness-box at their trial. Once again, most persons suspected of serious fraud will have had ample time to prepare for their interview. For inexperienced or vulnerable suspects, interviewed within a few hours of a sudden and traumatic arrest, the right to silence can be a valuable safeguard.

The 'right to silence' has stood out as one of the proudest boasts of Britain's commitment to civil liberties, contrasting most starkly with the forced interrogations and explanations required of suspects under inquisitorial systems. It has been adopted by Commonwealth countries, and in the United States the protection is entrenched in the Fifth Amendment to the Constitution. In Britain, however, the right was summarily abolished by the Government in 1988 in relation to Northern Ireland, where suspects are required to answer specific questions put by police officers: their failure to do so permits the judge or jury to draw adverse inferences at any subsequent trial. Silence may, in addition, be used to corroborate evidence which would otherwise be insufficient to secure a conviction. Worse still, the jury is entitled to draw an inference of guilt from the refusal of an accused to testify at his trial. The result of these changes has been to make a severe inroad on the presumption of innocence, by establishing a virtual 'presumption of guilt' concerning any defendant who chooses to put the police or the prosecution to proof by refusing to answer questions or to give evidence.

The debate over the 'right to silence' tends to be exaggerated on both sides. Police claims that it regularly protects the guilty have been demolished by research conducted for the Runciman Commission, demonstrating that it is actually exercised by less than 5 per cent of suspects who undergo police interrogation, half of whom are eventually convicted. Rarely are 'ambush defences' (where surprise evidence is sprung on the prosecution at trial) advanced.[45] It follows that abolition of the right would not lead to a significant increase in convictions of the guilty. On the other hand, it would make false confessions more likely in those cases where it remains the suspect's only protection against bullying and oppressive questioning: to deprive of any legal force the only rational and dignified response to such tactics would serve to encourage their use. The rule against self-incrimination is not, however, a fundamental human right: like jury trial, and the burden of proof on the prosecution 'beyond reasonable doubt', it is a basic feature of an adversarial system of criminal justice which lacks the safeguards of inquisitional systems in Europe (where interviews are conducted by magistrates and not by police, and the answers are assessed by judicial panels). When similar safeguards exist – as they do for businessmen called upon to explain to liquidators where their missing millions have ended up – the prospect that their answer may subsequently be used against them can hardly be regarded as unfair or oppressive. The fact that the Maxwell brothers were facing criminal charges did not entitle them to silence when asked to help the liquidator of the *Mirror* pension fund to trace money which had disappeared,[46] although it fully justified their refusal to cooperate with a publicity-seeking parliamentary committee which tried to usurp the role of the courts by questioning them before their trial.

A sensible and principled compromise would be to retain the right for all suspects in police detention, and for all persons placed on trial, but to require those who have enjoyed special positions of public trust to account for their conduct when there is evidence that it has been abused. Directors of collapsed public companies fall within this category, as would police officers reasonably suspected of corruption or brutality. (Police organizations are, ironically, the loudest in demanding abolition of the right to silence, but the most implacable in insisting that it should be claimed by their own members, even when the claim is made in order to cover-up serious crime.) The majority of the Runciman Committee sensibly concluded that abolition of the right to silence in relation to police questioning would produce more wrongful convictions, either by inducing unreliable confessions or by encouraging juries (in some cases, illogically) to infer guilt from silence. Less sensible was the Commission's proposal to require pre-trial disclosure of the defence – a subject which is discussed in Chapter 8.

Recording interviews

The vast majority of suspects do speak, and it is crucial that their police interviews are accurately recorded. The greatest single reproach to English criminal procedure used to be the vaudeville routine of the 'police verbal', in which officers present at an interview would, hours later, put their heads together and produce an allegedly verbatim account of what was said, only to be cross-examined endlessly in court at a later date about their presumed gift of total recall.

Relief had long been at hand, in the simple form of the tape recorder, but irrational fears blocked experimentation until 1984. Police were afraid that suspects would be less likely to talk, or would record statements of the 'please stop beating me up' variety, or that defence lawyers would successfully allege that tapes had been tampered with. These fears have proved groundless, and in 1992 tape recordings were required to be made of police interviews relating to all indictable offences save those concerning terrorism on official secrets. Suspects have shown no disinclination to talk into a microphone – on the contrary, this symbol of the *vox pop* society seems to be a positive encouragement to answer questions. Those who confess on tape generally plead guilty rather than seek acquittal by deriding 'police verbals', and recordings have led to substantially increased conviction rates and cut back the length of some trials.

Some problems remain. It is absurd not to tape-record interviews of suspects held under the Prevention of Terrorism Act or the Official Secrets Act – these are the very cases where accurate recording is vital, and where interview notes have been fabricated by police in the past (e.g. the Birmingham Six and the Guildford Four). The Government's excuse – that recordings may fall into the hands of terrorist organizations – is threadbare, because so too may the present written notes of interviews. In other cases, gaps remain as the result of uncertainty as to what constitutes an 'interview' for the purposes of the recording requirement. Too often do police claim that suspects blurt out their guilt on arrest, or while watching their homes being searched, or during exchanges of pleasantries in the police car on the 'scenic route' to the station, or during what are euphemistically called 'social visits' by the police to their suspect in the cells before the interview begins. The PACE code of practice gives far too much latitude in this respect, and the Court of Appeal, while aware of the danger, has permitted police to give evidence of 'discussions' at the scene of the crime and 'chit-chat' in the police car.[47] On the other hand it is hardly reasonable to require police to behave like Trappist monks until they enter the interview room, and questions asked at the scene may exculpate the suspect. One simple solution in many cases would be to issue police with portable tape recorders, and to install recorders in police vehicles (like the aeroplane 'black box'). 'Social visits' to the cells should be discouraged when the object is to elicit information about the crime.

Logically, the next step is to require that all interviews should be video-recorded. There would be obvious advantages in observing the demeanour of the participants, and in understanding the atmosphere. There is, however, the danger that innocent suspects will appear suspicious when seen under interrogation shortly after the trauma of arrest, and that their physical symptoms of nervousness and anxiety may be mistaken for consciousness of guilt. This problem caused the Runciman Commission sufficient concern to suspend judgement on the wisdom of video interviews, although a reasonable compromise would be to record them on video but only to admit the tape in evidence with the consent of the defence. It must never be thought that video-recording is a panacea for the problem of the false or forced confession. As any student of Stalin's show-trials will know, the most imaginative and self-abasing *mea culpas* are conditioned by what happens off-camera. Offers of bail, or to drop charges against lovers or friends, or other routine behind-the-scenes inducements, if made conditional on a good performance on videotape, will produce convincing confessions.[48]

Confessions

There are three classes of confession which cannot be used in evidence against the maker:

(1) *Confessions obtained by police oppression* – a concept which includes torture, inhuman and degrading treatment, and threats of violence (Section 76, PACE). The list is not exhaustive – overbearing behaviour designed to pressure a suspect to the point at which his will to claim the right to silence crumbles will amount to oppression. Bright lights and heavy-handed interrogation routines, and even the protracted interviewing periods to which Albert Hudson was subjected, may make any consequent confession unusable. 'Inhuman and degrading treatment' is a phrase taken from the European Convention on Human Rights. The European Court held that it covered the 'in-depth interrogation' to which the Royal Ulster Constabulary (RUC) subjected Irish internees in 1971. They were forced to stand for many hours spread-eagled against a wall, barefoot and hooded while listening to a high-pitched monotonous noise. They were deprived of sleep and kept on a diet of bread and water. These techniques were 'inhuman and degrading' because they caused physical and mental suffering and acute psychiatric disturbances, making use of fear and humiliation as a means of breaking down physical and moral resistance. They did not amount to 'torture' – a label reserved for very serious and cruel suffering.[49] Interviews which are excluded on the ground of oppression will inevitably require some proof of improper behaviour by the police: rudeness or emotional blackmail will not suffice.[50]

(2) *Confessions which are likely to be unreliable as a result of anything said or done to the suspect* (Section 76, PACE). This overlapping test additionally catches more subtle inducements to confess, which may be offered without any impropriety on the part of the police. A confession obtained by persistent questioning of a mentally defective youth, for example, might be ruled out as unreliable without any suggestion of police malpractice. As an innocent suspect will want nothing more badly than to get out of the police station, an offer of bail in return for a confession is a potent incentive to tell the police what they want to hear, irrespective of the consequences. For the criminally experienced suspect, offers not to pursue more serious charges or inducement to turn 'Queen's Evidence' can have a similar effect. Where there is evidence which also implicates close family members, such as wives and girlfriends who have already been arrested, offers to 'drop them out of it' frequently crack the most defiant of suspects. Whether a confession elicited by such ploys is 'unreliable' will be for the trial judge to decide by considering whether what was said or done by police at the time of the interview was likely to induce statements made for reasons other than a wish to tell the truth.

(3) *A confession which 'would have such an adverse effect on the fairness of the proceedings that the court ought not to admit it'* (Section 78, PACE). This is the general discretion to exclude unfairly obtained evidence, and it can be applied to confessions obtained by police through deceit or misrepresentations. An example of such malpractice is provided by *R. v. Mason*, a case remarkable not only for the dishonesty used to secure the confession but for the honesty of the police officer who admitted to it in the witness box.[51] He suspected Mason of fire-bombing a car but had little evidence against him. So he arrested Mason and told both him and his solicitor that his fingerprints had been found on glass shards from the petrol bomb. 'This was play-acting – a trick,' he confessed proudly in the witness box. 'The fragments of the bottle had not even been sent for fingerprint testing at that stage. We set about "conning" the defendant. We had only a suspicion against him and we realized we needed more proof – I felt the only way to get the truth from him was to do this.' The trick worked – Mason's solicitor, conscious no doubt of the virtual impossibility of challenging fingerprint evidence, advised his client to give an explanation of any involvement

in the incident, whereupon Mason confessed in reliable detail to having constructed the petrol bomb. His trial judge allowed the confession to go before the jury, which duly convicted and the defendant was imprisoned for two years. The Court of Appeal said that the trial judge was wrong to have allowed the confession into evidence. To hoodwink a suspect in this way was reprehensible, and it was even more reprehensible to hoodwink his solicitor. Although the confession was obviously true, it had been elicited by such serious misbehaviour on the part of the police that its admission into evidence adversely affected the fairness of the proceedings. The case is a valuable reminder that the end of convicting the guilty cannot justify means which are patently dishonest. Police officers tempted to lie to suspects about the state of the evidence against them, in order to give the impression that 'the game is up', must be made to realize that their misconduct is likely to lose the case when it comes to court.

This approach can be justified on grounds of social morality: it is better that the guilty should walk free than that agents of the state should be permitted to play an ignoble part. Section 78 of PACE defines the court's discretion to protect a defendant against unfairness in terms of the moral imperative: was the evidence obtained so unfairly that the court *ought* not to admit it? Even when the accuracy of a confession obtained by oppression and therefore inadmissible under Section 76 is confirmed by, for example, finding stolen property or a 'smoking gun' as the result of what the defendant has said, the fact that it was found as a result of what the defendant said should be withheld from the jury unless he goes into the witness-box and gives an explanation at variance with the truth. This may not be much comfort if the defendant's fingerprints are found on the smoking gun, but even this devastating evidence might conceivably be kept from a jury if the court decides, under Section 78, that the police misbehaviour was so gross that no advantage whatsoever should be taken of it. If a policeman points a revolver at a suspected terrorist and threatens to shoot him unless he confesses the whereabouts of an unexploded time-bomb, the court should on principle exclude not only the ensuing confession and the fact that the bomb was found as a result of it, but also (under Section 78) any forensic evidence connecting the bomb with the defendant.

The exclusion of a confession on grounds of unfairness is a decision calling for a value-judgement by the trial judge, and no hard and fast rules can fetter his discretion. A confession made after improper denial of the right to see a solicitor may, as we have seen, lead to its exclusion from evidence – or not, if the court takes the view that the defendant was already well aware of his legal rights. The Court of Appeal has indicated that records of interviews conducted in breach of the rules of PACE and its codes will not normally lead to exclusion unless the breaches are both 'significant and substantial'.[52] Decisions by trial judges have not been consistent, and exclusion rulings have been variously motivated by fears about reliability, upholding the rule against self-incrimination, and the need to condemn police impropriety and rule-bending. Many more confessions are now thrown out of court than before PACE was enacted, although this is less to do with Section 76 and Section 78 than with an increased judicial resolve to avoid the shameful miscarriages of justice which were exposed in the 1990s and largely attributed to false and fabricated confessions. The Runciman Commission failed to recommend the ultimate solution to the 'false-confession' problem, namely to disallow any prosecution based solely upon confession evidence. It did, however, recommend that judges should warn juries about the dangers of convicting on uncorroborated confessions, and that they should have additional powers to stop a trial if they assessed the prosecution evidence as weak or unreliable. Once again, this is the spirit of pragmatism rather than principle: a strict rule against conviction on the strength of an uncorroborated confession would require police to find the independent evidence (which will always exist if a confession is true) rather than to stop investigating once a suspect has told them what they want to hear.

A special danger is encountered when the suspect is young or mentally handicapped – factors which were both present when three youths falsely confessed, in remarkably convincing detail, to participation in the killing of a man named Confait. They were convicted of murder as the result of a series of prosecution errors and oversights which began with police interviews held in the absence of any parent or solicitor. An inquiry by Sir Henry Fisher exonerated one youth and a subsequent confession to the murder by a man in prison for other offences made it clear that the other youths were innocent as well. Even after the publicity surrounding the Confait report, and the advent of PACE, the same mistakes were made in the case of Braithwaite and Raghip, two mentally handicapped and 'abnormally suggestible' youths wrongly jailed for life on the strength of their confessions to murder of a policeman during the Broadwater Farm disturbances.[53]

Where such confessions are the only evidence against a 'person at risk' it would be better for the trial judge to exclude it as unreliable under Section 76, or to stop proceedings at the close of the prosecution case on the grounds that there is insufficient evidence upon which a jury could properly convict. This latter course was recommended by the Court of Appeal in R. v. Mackenzie, the case of the serial killer who turned out to be a serial confessor.[54] As there was no independent evidence to corroborate his confessions to the two murders of which he had been convicted, and he had confessed to several other murders which he could not have committed, the trial judge should have withdrawn the case from the jury. His confessions had not been obtained unfairly or oppressively, and their unreliability did not result from anything 'said or done' by police, but because there was no other evidence to support them, and they contained no factual details which only the true killer could know, no rational jury should have been satisfied of Mackenzie's guilt 'beyond all reasonable doubt'.

The Court of Appeal's common-law approach to confessions volunteered by unstable and vulnerable people in police detention, developed in the cases of Mackenzie and Raghip, is much to be preferred to the less extensive protection offered to such persons by Section 77 of PACE and its codes of practice. 'Persons at risk' (juveniles or the mentally handicapped) must be interviewed in the presence of a person who has some duty of care towards them, failing which Section 77 merely requires judges to warn juries of a special need for caution in convicting on the strength of their confessions. The dangers here have proved so great that it would be far better to have a strict rule preventing prosecution at all unless some external evidence connects the confessor to the crime, or the confession itself contains such verifiable detail that it could not have been volunteered by an innocent person. This is the approach that should be applied to confessions made by persons under other disabilities which are not catered for by PACE, such as temporarily incapacitating mental states (e.g. produced by drink or drugs, or hysteria or traumatic shock).[55]

RELEASE FROM CUSTODY

Suspects must, by the end of twenty-four hours or any specially extended period, be either released or charged with an offence. Once charged, they must be brought before a court 'as soon as is practicable', at which stage they may make an application for bail. The magistrate may at this point remand the defendant in police custody for up to three further days, but only if and for so long as this is strictly necessary to allow inquiries to be made into other offences. The defendant has a right to bail, and the Bail Act of 1976 entrenches a statutory presumption in favour of liberty unless the court is satisfied that there is an unacceptable risk of failure to surrender to custody or the commission of further offences while on bail or interference with witnesses.

There are occasional retrospective press outcries when a person is convicted of an offence committed while on bail for a similar crime: the magistrates or the judge who granted bail are blamed in strident editorials for freeing a public menace. The benefit of hindsight is uniquely vouchsafed to the editors of popular newspapers: the court will on examination usually be found to have applied the law, and if blame is sometimes to be attached it generally rests on the prosecution for failing to apprehend the danger of the accused committing further offences.

There remains an unfortunate tendency for persons entitled to bail to be remanded in custody for a week or so after their first appearance in court. The Bail Act allows a court to refuse bail if it has not been practicable to obtain sufficient information to decide the issue, and this is an easy way out for magistrates when police object on the irrelevant ground that they have yet to complete their inquiries. The Divisional Court has held that a bail application, once made and rejected, cannot be renewed until the defence can show some change in the circumstances[56] – a ruling that obliges solicitors who have just met their client to wait a week and to gather the evidence for a considered application. The reluctance of courts to concede that circumstances have changed frequently means that a bail application, once fully made, cannot be renewed until committal, many months later.

The court may grant bail unconditionally, or on any conditions designed to secure the accused's presence at later hearings of the case. In dealing with demonstrators, local justices sometimes abuse their power to impose conditions by requiring that bailed defendants do not return to the scene of the protest (see later, page 79). It is unacceptable to make the right to liberty, after what is usually an arrest for a minor offence, contingent upon abandonment of the rights to free speech and assembly. In appropriate cases, sureties may be required in considerable sums, passports may be confiscated and the accused can be required to report regularly to the local police station. These conditions are frequently 'offered' by the defence and 'accepted' by the prosecution – they must be designed reasonably to secure attendance or protect witnesses, and not as a pre-trial punishment. The 1688 Bill of Rights, which is still in force, provides 'that excessive bail ought not to be required', noting in its preamble addressed to William of Orange that his predecessor's 'evil judges' had 'required excessive bail of persons committed in criminal cases to elude the benefit of the laws made for the liberty of subjects'. This at least prohibits the absurd and distasteful device used by US judges to keep an accused person in custody by setting bail at astronomical levels.

The last resort to obtain release from custody is to apply for a writ of *habeas corpus*. This is a direction by a judge to anybody who has a person in custody to bring that person before the court so that the legality of the detention can be investigated. Traditionally, 'the great writ' has been regarded as being of the highest constitutional importance: the means whereby release from illegal detention is assured. The slave brought by ship into British territorial waters,[57] the demobilized Army officer pulled from his civilian bed for alleged military crimes over which the army no longer has jurisdiction,[58] the Polish seamen who feared punishment for their political opinions if they were not freed from their ship in the Thames before it sailed back to Poland,[59] the inmate of a mental hospital who was illegally detained there by the hospital authorities,[60] the woman imprisoned by the Vice-Chancellor of Cambridge University for 'walking with a member of the University'[61] all secured their release upon a writ of *habeas corpus*. Even the validity of detention by order of either House of Parliament may be challenged in this way. An application for *habeas corpus* takes precedence over all other business before the court. A recent and dramatic example of *habeas corpus* effecting freedom from wrongful detention is provided by the release of 112 Muslim insurgents, charged with treason and murder after they had invaded the Trinidad Parliament and held the members of the Government as hostages. The President offered them an amnesty if they surrendered without further loss of life: when they did so they were immediately arrested and detained to await trial on charges which carried the death penalty. The Privy Council decided that *habeas corpus* should secure their immediate release once the amnesty was proved to be valid.[62]

Valuable though *habeas corpus* can be, its limits must be noted. It operates only where there is no legal authority to detain. Prior to PACE, *habeas corpus* occasionally secured the release of suspects detained for unlawfully long periods in police stations. Now that strict time limits apply to detention, with provision for magistrates' court warrants to extend detention periods, there is very little scope for *habeas corpus* applications in relation to suspects in police custody. However, if a suspect were held for longer than thirty-six hours without a warrant, or a warrant were granted in respect of an offence which was not a 'serious arrestable offence', an action for *habeas corpus* would, if made speedily, secure release. Some protection for persons denied bail on serious offences was provided by the custody time-limits imposed in 1987, requiring bail to be granted if committal for trial is delayed more than seventy days from their first court appearance, or if arraignment (the formal start of a jury trial) is delayed more than a further 112 days from the date of committal. The value of these safeguards is undermined by permitting police to start the time running all over again by the simple ploy of bringing an additional charge shortly before the time-limit expires or (if this device is too bare-faced) to apply for a further extension of time on the grounds of 'good or sufficient cause' (e.g. the defendant is regarded as dangerous) and the prosecution has acted 'with all due expedition'. 'Due' means 'reasonable' or 'appropriate', and although the High Court has granted bail on *habeas corpus* applications where the only reason for delay has been lack of court facilities to have the case tried, it has declined to do so when police and prosecuting authorities have been slow in bringing the case to trial.[63] If custody time-limits are to have real effect, the only 'good and sufficient cause' for disobeying them should be a justifiable request by the defence for extra time to prepare.

REMEDIES FOR POLICE MISCONDUCT

Rights only exist to the extent that they can be enforced when authorities abuse their power. In Britain, the citizen can sue for serious violations of personal liberty, and obtain damages as compensation for humiliation and indignity and even, in bad cases, as a measure of punishment for outrageous official misconduct. There is also a system for making complaints about police behaviour, which can in turn lead to disciplinary action within the police force against officers who have contravened codes of practice or behaved bloody-mindedly or from racist motives. Where there is evidence that officers have committed crimes, the Director of Public Prosecutions can bring them to trial. The rules which permit a court to exclude evidence of confessions extracted by oppression or unfairness are part of a general judicial discretion which can occasionally protect even guilty defendants from suffering punishment for an offence which police have themselves instigated or investigated in flagrant violation of suspects' rights. The families of those who have died in police custody or as a result of police action are entitled to be represented at the inquest, and police actions which have had serious social repercussions may be made the subject of a public inquiry. There is no remedy at all for the consequences of police incompetence or stupidity. The mother of the 'Yorkshire Ripper's' last victim was not permitted to sue the West Yorkshire Chief Constable for his force's negligent failure to detect the deranged killer before he struck yet again.[64] If there is outrageous dereliction of duty – as in the case of the policeman who calmly stood back to watch a man being kicked to death – there may be a prosecution for the offence of 'misconduct of an officer of justice'.[65]

At first blush, an impressive panoply of remedies seems available to the citizen: closer scrutiny demonstrates that some are in practice hedged about with unsatisfactory qualifications and restrictions. The police complaints machinery, for example, has many defects and does not enjoy public confidence, despite improvements made to it by PACE, and the role of the courts in excluding improperly obtained evidence is in some respects undefined and discretionary. The constable, unaccountable to public representatives for the exercise of police duty, is still but imperfectly accountable to the law for doing constabulary duty wrongly.

Damages for civil wrongs

Actions for damages may be brought against chief constables when police under their command commit civil wrongs (torts). An arrest without reasonable suspicion or a lawful arrest followed by an unjustifiably long period of detention involves the tort of false imprisonment, and where force is used to make an unlawful arrest this will amount to the tort of assault as well. A prosecution brought against a person whom the police know to be innocent amounts to the tort of malicious prosecution; unlawful entry on to private premises will constitute trespass to land and (if property is wrongfully seized) to goods; police may additionally be sued for any negligence which has resulted in the death of someone in their custody. The advantages for the citizen of taking civil action rather than making a complaint to the Police Complaints Authority are overwhelming: the case need be proved only on the balance of probabilities (rather than beyond a reasonable doubt), these actions can in many cases be heard by a jury, and there is the prospect of being awarded exemplary damages as a mark of public disapproval of intolerable behaviour.

One of the worst cases is *White* v. *Metropolitan Police Commissioner*, where a husband and wife received £40,000 exemplary damages for what Mr Justice Mars-Jones described as 'monstrously wicked' police behaviour, on top of £13,000 compensation for false imprisonment and malicious prosecution. The couple had been dragged out of bed in the early hours and beaten up 'in a brutal and inhuman way', then unlawfully arrested and detained for some hours at the police station. In order to cover up their own crimes, the police then fabricated charges of assault against the couple.[66] In cases where police conduct has not been outrageous or the plaintiff has suffered no serious harm, damages will be limited to a few thousand pounds. In one 1989 case, however, a plaintiff who had been 'planted' with cannabis, wrongly detained and maliciously prosecuted was awarded £10,000 for false imprisonment, £20,000 for malicious prosecution and exemplary damages of £70,000.[67] Exemplary damages are awarded to punish police for conduct which is oppressive, arbitrary or unconstitutional, generally in circumstances where insult is added to injury. Thus a West Indian who had been unlawfully detained was entitled to punitive damages for a racist policeman's action in throwing peanuts into his cell with the words, 'Here you are, monkey.'[68] Even when circumstances justify an arrest, excessive force can provide the basis for a civil claim for assault. A middle-aged woman lawfully arrested for a minor traffic offence recovered damages for being subjected to a ju-jitsu 'hammer-lock and bar' in which her wrist was held behind her back and twisted by the arresting officer until it fractured.[69]

Cases of this kind present such an unedifying picture of police conduct that considerable effort is expended in keeping them out of court and out of the public eye through a negotiated settlement. In 1992 the Metropolitan Police alone paid out £401,000 to settle civil actions, and a further £193,000 in damages awarded in contested cases. Twelve of the cases settled for more than £10,000 were for false imprisonment, and in 1990 one negligence action resulted in agreed damages of £130,000. The Government declined to tell Parliament how many policemen had been prosecuted or disciplined as a result of these actions. It should be important for the public to learn the details of such cases, and to be able to confirm that officers whose high-handed behaviour has led to the payment of public money in damages have been appropriately disciplined. Where secret settlements are made, however, such reassurance is not provided. The officers at fault do not pay the damages out of their own pocket, and while individual plaintiffs are doubtless happy to be compensated without the stress of a court action, the adverse publicity which serves to deter repetition of such conduct is lost. The £75,000 paid by police to the family of Blair Peach in order to avoid a trial had the consequence of suppressing details of the internal police investigation into reponsibility for the death, which was a matter of the gravest public concern.

Complaints against police

Civil actions will not lie against many kinds of police misconduct, including breach of most of the rules in the 'Codes of Practice'.

Such matters fall to be dealt with, if at all, by internal disciplinary proceedings supervised in the case of serious public complaints by the Police Complaints Authority (PCA). This body was established in 1984 after widespread public criticism of the lack of any independent element in the investigation of complaints against the police. Lord Scarman, for example, was concerned by the evidence at his Brixton inquiry that 'there is a widespread and dangerous lack of public confidence in the existing system'. Public confidence has not been much enhanced by the PCA: it has no autonomous powers of investigation, which falls to be carried out by the police themselves, subject to the PCA's duty to oversee inquiries into serious complaints and to ensure they are conducted expeditiously, thoroughly and impartially. The statistical evidence of its failure is stark: in 1990, 34,894 complaints against police were dealt with: only 847 (2.4 per cent) were substantiated and only 106 police officers were disciplined as a result, the majority being merely fined or reprimanded. A suspiciously large number of these complaints – 42 per cent – were withdrawn, although independent research has suggested that one third of these could have been substantiated, and that many were withdrawn because of police discouragement and intimidation.[70]

The stumbling block in the campaign for an independent police complaints system has been the Home Office's implacable belief that you must set a policeman to catch a policeman: the notion of an outside investigative body, comprising lawyers, administrators, retired senior police officers and customs officials, has been repeatedly resisted on the unconvincing argument that detective skills are 'unique' to the police service. While there have been impressive examples – notably under Sir Robert Mark – of vigorous searches for 'rotten apples' in the police barrel, there have been more notable failures – such as the inability of the PCA-supervised investigation into the West Midland Serious Crimes Squad to produce evidence sufficient to justify a single prosecution, notwithstanding the large number of wrongful convictions attributed to that squad. The efficiency of inquiry teams in other public and professional areas refutes the notion that detective prowess is vouchsafed only to serving policemen. The clarity of PCA 'oversight' of police investigations may be doubted after its extraordinary failure to act on evidence produced by an inquest into the death of Cynthia Jarrett, who had collapsed from a heart attack during a police raid on her home in Tottenham, a factor which incited a serious riot on the Broadwater Farm Estate. The subsequent PCA report not only misunderstood the jury verdict, but took no action on matters which emerged at the inquest. A subsequent unofficial inquiry into the incident, chaired by Lord Gifford, QC, concluded that, 'Given these failures in one of the PCA's first major investigations, it is not surprising if confidence in the new machinery is low.'[71]

The present procedure has at least the merit of simplicity: complainants set out their grievance and the investigation is conducted without further effort or obligation on their part. They may complain about a broad range of misconduct, from rudeness and indifference to breach of a Code of Practice or serious crime. Conduct which is disorderly or likely to bring discredit on the reputation of the police force is a disciplinary offence, as is any abuse of authority or behaviour which is racially discriminatory. Minor public complaints are made the subject of informal conciliation proceedings which can lead to explanations and apologies, while complaints substantiated after investigation are dealt with at disciplinary hearings before the chief constable or, in London, a disciplinary board. The complainant may attend, and can cross-examine accused officers if they elect to give evidence. Punishments range from reprimands to dismissal from the force. Although the procedure is internal, in the sense that all investigation and decision-making is done by police officers, the PCA has a duty to supervise the investigation of complaints which are serious (e.g. where death or injury has resulted from police action) or where the public interest requires some independent oversight. It has certain powers to direct reluctant chief constables to hold disciplinary proceedings or to send reports to the DPP for consideration of criminal charges.

One serious deficiency in the system is that it makes no provision for any compensation to successful complainants, even when they have suffered quantifiable loss. Another unhappy feature is that police officers complained against may sue the complainants for libel – their initial complaints are not covered by the absolute privilege from defamation action which protects statements made in court. The position is made intolerably unfair by the lack of any legal aid for libel defendants and by the willingness of the Police Federation to finance libel actions brought by its members. Although the complainant has a 'qualified privilege', the qualification (that the complaint was made without malice) can be expensive to establish in court, and there is no doubt that the possibility of being sued for libel has a powerful deterrent effect on potential complainants. The House of Lords failed to appreciate how the prospect of expensive and intricate libel actions deters complainants when in 1993 it ruled that qualified privilege was lost because a letter of complaint contained one untrue allegation against an arresting officer accused of racism.[72] The fact that victims of police misconduct may exaggerate their tribulations does not prevent their story from being basically true, and they are unlikely to have a libel lawyer at their elbow to help them tell it with care and precision. Where an investigation proves that a complainant has fabricated allegations out of malice, the appropriate remedy is to prosecute him or her for the offence of wasting police time.

One particular concern of potential complainants is that they may suffer reprisals from the police. The PCA has no power to investigate if victimization does occur, and the only remedy is by civil action. In 1985 a jury awarded £4,000 damages against Merseyside police for harassing a man without reasonable cause, allegedly because he had previously lodged a complaint against them.[73] One deplorable feature which follows from the internal aspect of the complaints system is that the PCA has no control over the use to which police may put evidence which they gather about a complainant in the course of investigating his or her complaint. After Cynthia Jarrett died of a heart attack while police were searching her home, her daughter cooperated with the investigation which was supervised by the PCA. Information she supplied was duly reported back to the Metropolitan Police Commissioner, and was used by the police at the inquest into Mrs Jarrett's death in an unsuccessful attempt to discredit the daughter's evidence. This incident is a glaring example of how the present complaints system can be perceived as partisan and of how the PCA is powerless to protect complainants from whatever use chief constables decide to make of their complaint. In 1990 the Government admitted that the police national computer contains a special entry for those who have made 'false allegations against the police'.[74] If 'false' means no more than 'not proven beyond reasonable doubt', then 97 per cent of complainants end up with a computer entry to this effect, calculated

to provoke any constable who calls PNC 2 to check their car registration.

The insignificant number of public complaints which are actually
upheld demonstrates that the system does not work, rather than that
police behaviour is almost always exemplary. In 1989, after 300
complaints of racial harassment had led to only three officers being
disciplined, the Metropolitan Police Commissioner accepted that 99
per cent of complainants could not be lying: 'we are failing because
officers are committing offences, and we are not getting them'. One
reason why the present system does not get them is because it is
loaded in their favour, as a result of government capitulation to
pressure applied by the Police Federation. It insisted that disciplinary
offences must be proved 'beyond reasonable doubt', which puts the
police in a privileged position compared with other employees,
whose reason for dismissal need only be proved at an industrial
tribunal on the balance of probabilities. For an occupation which
should be above suspicion, and in relation to disciplinary charges
which have no criminal consequence, this is a privilege which is not
justifiable on public-interest grounds. This explains why lawyers
advise complainants wherever possible to bring a civil action for
damages which can be proved on the balance of probabilities, and
why police officers whose misconduct can be proved to this standard
may nevertheless remain in the force. In its recent reports the PCA
has confessed that the unnecessarily high standard of proof is causing
the police disciplinary process to fall into disrepute: in the absence
of independent evidence, it can rarely decide a complaint 'beyond
reasonable doubt' when police deny it. Complainants are not dis-
believed, but they will not be sufficiently believed for their complaint to be upheld if it comes down to their word against that of a
police officer.

Another aspect of the complaints system which runs counter to
the public interest, at least in cases which have aroused community
concern, is the secrecy which attends all stages of the investigation.
Inquiries supervised by the PCA cannot be published, even when
chief constables wish to reassure the public by issuing the final
report. Secrecy may be desirable in many inquiries in order to
encourage witnesses to come forward, especially officers who 'break
ranks' to give evidence against their fellows or their commander,
but in cases where serious and apparently substantial allegations are

publicly made against the police the community is entitled to demand satisfactory evidence of thorough investigation. Far too many important complaints are inadequately and inexpeditiously investigated, and the PCA is too remote from the investigation to exercise any meaningful supervision. One unhappy example is provided by the collapse of all the prosecutions against police officers alleged to have been involved in the brutal beatings cases (as seen on television news) of demonstrators at Wapping in 1989: so dilatory and lackadaisical was the investigation that the High Court had to abort the trials.[75]

In some of the most controversial cases, there can be no disciplinary action at all because criminal proceedings have been brought unsuccessfully. This is another privilege unique to the police. It is based, inaccurately, on the rule against 'double jeopardy' – the principle that a person cannot be tried twice for the same offence. So where policemen kill a suspect and are acquitted of murder because they acted in self-defence or without intending to pull the trigger, they cannot be disciplined for careless handling of firearms. This rule overlooks the obvious fact that disciplinary procedures do not amount to a 'trial' – they may result in loss of seniority or even job, but not in a criminal record. Many police officers properly acquitted of criminal offences have nevertheless acted discreditably in the course of the incident and deserve to be disciplined. Other disciplinary bodies are not constrained by acquittals from probing discreditable conduct, and employees may suffer dismissal for behaviour which a jury finds to fall short of an actual crime. Frequently evidence which is inadmissible at a criminal trial may help to prove a disciplinary offence. While it would be wrong to subject police officers to special disabilities when confronted with accusations of misconduct, the present complaints and disciplinary system provides them with privileges other employees do not enjoy, which sit uneasily with their possession of unique legal powers.

There can be no public confidence at all in a police disciplinary system which fails to discipline officers where corruption and brutality has been proven to the satisfaction of a civil court and has resulted in large payments of public money to compensate their victims. In 1993 three Wapping demonstrators proved that they had been beaten up by six policemen who then made false statements so that they could be prosecuted. The three plaintiffs were awarded

£87,000 compensation, but the six police officers were permitted to remain on active duty with the Metropolitan Police. They had originally been charged with conspiracy to pervert the course of justice, but this prosecution failed on technical grounds because of a delay in bringing it to trial.[76] Although the Metropolitan Police Commissioner apologized in court for the violence and dishonesty of these six officers, they were not even subjected to disciplinary proceedings, let alone to the dismissals they deserved. The Runciman Commission rightly condemned the present disciplinary system as ineffective, and demanded that police officers should be disciplined or dismissed, like other employees, once misconduct had been proved against them on a civil rather than criminal standard, and that they should be expelled from the force, notwithstanding the failure of any prosecution, if their conduct had demonstrated their unsuitability for service. These recommendations must be implemented urgently to avoid further affronts to justice and common sense of the kind illustrated by the Wapping case.

Prosecution

Where there is clear evidence of a criminal offence, police officers may face prosecution. There is a division of opinion, however, on the test to be applied in putting a policeman on trial. The DPP adopts the '51 per cent solution' – only if conviction is a better than even bet will action be taken, and prosecutors are all too aware of a low conviction rate from juries which tend to prefer a policeman's word to that of his often unprepossessing accusers. Others maintain that the public interest of ensuring that those who enjoy authority do not abuse it demands prosecution whenever there is a clear *prima facie* case. In principle, they are correct: police officers should be brought to trial, just like other citizens, when there is evidence upon which a properly directed jury would be entitled to convict. By applying a more favourable test to police officers, the DPP is putting them if not above the law, at least some distance beyond its reach. This debate masks the real question of how to go about producing a convincing case against those who abuse power within an institution whose members have a strong sense of solidarity and a professional awareness of their rights. During the investigation into the killing of Blair Peach, the right to silence became a right to *omertà*, as police officers who must have known the truth about which of their comrades killed him simply refused to tell it. The myth of the over-merciful jury makes the trial process a scapegoat for inadequate investigation and inability to prise open ranks which masonically close. In 1992 there was criticism of the DPP's decision that no members of the West Midland Serious Crimes Squad would face prosecution, although the behaviour of that squad had produced so many wrongful convictions that the chief constable had been forced to disband it. In the United States, the special difficulties of unravelling police corruption are handed over to 'special prosecutors', who are senior lawyers with investigative powers. Company collapses, as we have seen, attract the special investigation powers of Department of Trade inspectors, whose reports usually lead to successful prosecutions. Some day, we may come to recognize that an unsolved police murder of a political demonstrator is as worthy of special investigative procedures as the death of a public company.

Inquests

Death, the ultimate loss of liberty, is made the subject of a special inquiry when it occurs in police or prison cells or as a result of police operations. The agency which seeks to satisfy the public conscience in such cases is the coroner, who must summon a jury whenever death results from an injury caused by a police officer.[77] In the Middle Ages, the coroner was given the task of inspecting dead bodies to discover the cause of death – a matter of great interest in those days to the King, who benefited from the estates of the slain. To assist him, in an age long before police forces and medical science, the coroner summoned a jury from the neighbourhood. The medieval coroner and his jury would squat around the body – often by a roadside or in a ditch – and look for tell-tale signs of disease or violence or suicide. Pooling their local knowledge, they would try to come up with the name of a likely suspect whom they would present for trial. Although these important functions were in due course taken over by professionals – policemen and doctors and lawyers – the coroner survived, as a public official appointed by local councils to investigate unnatural deaths. In this century, coroners lost most of their powers of criminal inquiry: in cases of suspicious death, they in effect unveil to the public the evidence upon which the police have failed to reach any conclusion.

Inquests are unlike any other judicial proceedings. Coroners need not be lawyers: they may be doctors of at least five years' standing. Unlike lay justices, they do not have the assistance of a legally trained clerk. The closest equivalent at an inquest is a policeman who acts as the 'coroner's officer'. This does not help to create an appearance of impartiality where the death is alleged to have been caused by the police. In addition, an inquest does not follow the usual adversarial pattern of most legal proceedings, where the truth is expected to emerge from the clash of opposing evidence and submissions. Instead, the coroner takes the initiative and leads the investigation. The police collect the evidence and discuss it privately with the coroner, who is not obliged to show it to representatives of the deceased's family.[78] This means that lawyers are sometimes unprepared for the evidence which the coroner decides to call. It means, too, that at inquests where police misconduct is alleged, the police lawyers will have exclusive access to statements taken by police officers, and so have an unfair advantage over the deceased's family, who are further handicapped by the fact that legal aid is not available to pay for legal representation.

At inquests, no advocate may address the coroner or the jury on the facts. There are no final speeches. So the jury never hears the contentions of the parties about the cause of death; the only coherent account is provided by the coroner in the summing-up. This may be an unsatisfactory account, or even, as in the Helen Smith case, a preposterous account.[79] It is to the credit of juries that they occasionally refuse the coroner's dictation, and bring back verdicts highly inconvenient to the authorities. In 1992, for example, the 'friendly fire' jury found that nine British soldiers had been victims of aerial manslaughter committed by reckless USAF pilots in the closing stages of the Gulf War, and in another inquest the jury decided that Oliver Pryce, a black man who died from asphyxiation in the back of a police van in Cleveland, had been unlawfully killed. No attempt was made to identify (let alone to extradite) the American pilots, nor to discipline (let alone to prosecute) any Cleveland police officer.

In cases where coroners sit with juries, public esteem for the jury system in criminal courts invests the 'verdict' with a degree of acceptability. But all the coroner's jury can do is to announce one simple fact – how the deceased met with death.[80] The law requires a narrow answer to a narrow question, but in cases where police are responsible for death, the public rightly expects much fuller answers to a whole range of questions. Until 1980, a coroner's jury could add a rider to its verdict and make recommendations to prevent the recurrence of similar deaths, and the Blair Peach jury used this power to make several critical comments about the Special Patrol Group. (It recommended that the SPG should be better controlled by its officers, that its relations with local forces should be improved, that no unauthorized weapons should be available at police stations and that regular inspections should be carried out.) But an amendment to the Coroners' Rules has now taken away the jury's right to add a rider to its verdict.[81]

All these procedural handicaps work collectively to prevent a coroner's inquest from fulfilling public expectations as a mechanism for getting the truth out and for drawing lessons from it. There are cases – fortunately only a handful each year – which involve serious factual disputes about deaths in custody and in the presence of police officers, and which raise wider public-interest questions. Liddle Towers, Jimmy Kelly, Blair Peach, Colin Roach, Oliver Pryce and Cynthia Jarrett are examples of deaths which should have been investigated by High Court judges at public inquiries at which the families were legally aided and proper rules were followed. Such an inquiry could then have ended with a reasoned judicial conclusion as to the cause of death, setting out in detail any grounds for public disquiet, after all the evidence had been properly presented and put coherently into place first by advocates and then by the judge in his report. In 1988 the refusal of the British Government to hold a judicial inquiry into the killing by the Special Air Service (SAS) of three IRA members in Gibraltar, and the defects of the inquest which subsequently took place, received international condemnation. Any society which values civil liberties must take exceptional measures to examine why a life was lost through the actions of agents of the state: coroners' inquests, which serve useful purposes in uncontroversial cases, are inadequate for this task.

Tricks and traps

Should criminal courts play a part in punishing police misbehaviour by excluding improperly obtained evidence from the trial? This is a fundamental and very polarized debate. The US Supreme Court has long adopted the principle that it is better for the guilty to go free than for the state to play an unworthy part, a principle supported by the common-sense consideration that the only realistic way to stop police obtaining evidence illegally is to remove the incentive by forbidding them to use it. Thus when a suspected drug dealer seen swallowing capsules was illegally stomach-pumped to force him to regurgitate the evidence, the capsules found in the vomit were 'fruit of the poisoned tree', and excluded from evidence at his trial. Orson Welles makes the argument in the film *Touch of Evil* through his portrayal of a corrupt police chief who frames only the guilty: his dying fall down a slippery river slope in the final scene symbolizes the reason for the rule. Once the courts start endorsing the principle that the end justifies the means, unfairness and illegality may become routine.

British courts have over the past decade become much more alive to the dangers of false or fabricated confessions producing miscarriages of justice, so confessions obtained in breach of PACE rules are often now excluded from evidence. There are other kinds of evidence that are equally questionable, yet against the reception of which few safeguards exist. For example, although complicated rules govern the taking of statements from defendants, there are no rules at all to ensure the accurate recording of statements by witnesses. Police usually insist on writing these themselves, and often exaggerate, or put words in the mouths of unsure or unwilling civilian witnesses. The danger is greater when police are themselves called to testify to what they have seen, for example after surveillance operations (the logs of which can easily be doctored) or after demonstrations, when memories and imaginations may be refreshed in the police canteen. Much detective work involves the cultivation of contacts with informants, who may provide information (and later give evidence) out of malice or for money or in order to obtain a lesser sentence for their own crimes. Some may actually create crime, by acting as *agents provocateurs*. Police at high level are now approving 'sting' operations and other tricks and deceptions which are of dubious propriety, using bugging and surveillance techniques that are not subject to any legal control. In these areas of police discretion, the only way of deterring abuse and setting standards, in the absence of proper legislation requiring prior authorization by court warrant, is for judges to use their powers of exclusion rather than to swallow the fruit of the poisoned tree. Thus far, however, the courts have preferred to digest the infected crop rather than to destroy it.

British law dodges the issue of principle by leaving the decision in the discretionary lap of the trial judge. There are special rules, as we have seen, for excluding improperly obtained confessions, but the admissibility of other sorts of evidence – obtained by tricks or entrapment – is decided by reference to Section 78 of PACE. Having regard to all the circumstances, including the circumstances in which the evidence was obtained, 'Would its admission have such an adverse effect on the fairness of the proceedings that the court ought not to admit it?' It follows that 'the circumstances in which the evidence was obtained', if attended by police misbehaviour, can provide a basis for exercising the discretion. Thus when police officers pursued a motorist into his own back yard and demanded that he take a breath test, knowing that they had no right to make this demand on private property, they were acting oppressively and in bad faith: the evidence that the breath test was positive was excluded under Section 78.[82]

When courts exclude reliable evidence like this because of police misconduct, it is difficult to accept that they are not in effect seeking to deter police misbehaviour by depriving them of its fruits. In *Mason* (where a true confession was obtained by pretending to the defendant and his solicitor that his fingerprint had been found on a petrol bomb) the Court of Appeal ended its judgement as follows: 'We hope never again to hear of a deceit such as the present being practised on an accused person and still less on a solicitor bound to advise.' Where misbehaviour is serious, exclusion of evidence in this way is a mark of authoritative disapproval. The problem, however, is that while this police trickery received Court of Appeal condemnation, other deceptions have been accorded Court of Appeal acclaim.

The decision in *Mason*, for example, should be compared to that in the 1993 case of *R.* v. *Bailey and Smith*, where a specially bugged cell was prepared for a couple of robbery suspects.[83] Police then prevailed on magistrates to deny them bail, on the grounds that they wanted to put them on identity parades (they did not, of course, say that they really wanted to put them in a bugged cell).

They then acted out a charade in which a bad-tempered custody officer insisted, over the 'protests' of the detectives, that both men be put in the same cell. Thus hoodwinked, the suspects were tape-recorded discussing their robberies. The Court of Appeal had no doubt that this police conduct was fair, although it involved dissembling to the magistrates, exploiting the 'independence' of the custody officer and lying to the robbers. The Court did concede that such stratagems 'should only be used in very grave cases' – in other words, so long as the end justified the means. But Mason's crime of petrol-bombing was no less grave than robbery, and it can hardly be more morally objectionable to mislead a solicitor than a bench of justices. Mason was creatively deceived about the strength of the evidence against him, which was a stronger inducement for a guilty person to confess than a deception about the soundproof nature of a shared cell, but this is hardly a satisfactory basis for distinguishing between good and bad police tricks. Indeed, there are more far-reaching civil-liberty concerns about *Bailey and Smith*, if that case presages the routine bugging of police and prison cells, and the use of courtroom submissions as smokescreens. English law is unsatisfactory in leaving trial judges to decide, subjectively, whether (with hindsight) the end justifies the means. If a secret bugging operation is to be mounted, police should be required to obtain a judicial warrant to carry it out, on the same basis as they must obtain a warrant to seize confidential documents (see later, page 131). At present, their power to engage in trickery is unfettered and it is difficult to predict whether the evidence thus obtained will be ruled admissible when the case is brought to court.

Apart from its statutory right to exclude tainted evidence, every court has an inherent power to stop a trial for 'abuse of process' – behaviour by the police or the prosecution which has had the consequence of eroding any real prospect that the trial can be fair. This valuable jurisdiction to stop a trial in its tracks should be invoked where the court is presented with a situation where a defining characteristic of a trial – namely fairness – cannot be achieved, because no court of justice can allow its proceedings to be used so as to produce injustice.[84] Most exercises of this exceptional power have been as a result of unconscionable delays in investigating a case or bringing it to trial, where the defendant has suffered real prejudice through the mounting stress or the fading memory of witnesses. In 1993 the High Court invoked it to stop proceedings against a youth who had been an accessory to murder, but who had been solemnly promised by police that he would not be charged if he assisted them to solve the crime and gave evidence against the killer. The CPS thought it could go back on the deal, and charged the youth despite his assistance given to police in reliance on their promise. Although neither police nor prosecutors had acted improperly or with any intention to deceive, the continuation of proceedings in these circumstances was considered morally wrong.[85]

Deals are routinely made with informants, and the relationship between coppers and their narks has long been the murkiest area of policing, unregulated by statute or court rulings and subject only to elastic and widely ignored Home Office 'guidelines'. Detectives under pressure to get results, and subject to promotion by reference to their record as thief-takers, will cultivate informants from the criminal community, offering them small sums of money (which may turn into very large amounts if they recommend them for insurance awards) and the opportunity to settle old scores or to be 'dropped out' of their own criminal offences in return for helping to catch other criminals. Some detectives have exploited their criminal contacts for criminal purposes – demanding shares in insurance money, for example, or some of the proceeds of crimes to which a blind eye has been turned. Police/villain relationships involve dirty and intricate games, without rules or referees. The problem is exemplified by the case of Inspector Lundy, Scotland Yard's most successful detective, forced into early retirement after revelations about his contacts with major criminals. 'Is he brilliant or bent?' asked the press. Neither his police superiors nor the courts could decide.[86]

The most dramatic example of the dangers of unsupervised informers is the story of Kenneth Lennon, a Special Branch agent who infiltrated an IRA team in Luton.[87] To maintain his cover, he was prosecuted on one occasion, with the evidence doctored to assist his acquittal without revealing his true role. The cover-up did not fool the IRA – Lennon was apprehended and executed, but not before he had made a 'confession' to the National Council for Civil Liberties alleging that he had been instructed by the Special Branch to act as an *agent provocateur*, setting up men for crimes which carried long prison sentences. The ensuing official inquiry published the secret 'Home Office circular' which purports to govern police relations with informants.[88]

Although it instructs police not to encourage informants to 'create offences', the circular is not part of the law and in any event police may be in no position to judge whether their informant has exceeded instructions. The practice of not disclosing the identity is apt to mislead the court and often to permit the trial to proceed on a false basis. Yet research for the Runciman Royal Commission discovered that police, particularly in drugs cases, were refusing to disclose the existence of 'participating informants' to the CPS.[89] This means that prosecutors, as well as defendants and their lawyers, will in some cases remain unaware of the prospect that the criminal activity has been set up by the police. The courts will protect the identity of informants unless the accused can demonstrate that the revelation is important to establish his innocence; a failure to disclose the existence of an informer to prosecuting counsel can result in misleading the court and in depriving the accused of the opportunity even to argue that further disclosure is essential in the interests of fairness.[90]

There are many dangers inherent in accepting informer evidence as the basis for a criminal charge against a defendant who is not permitted at his trial to test it by way of cross-examination, or even, in many cases, to learn of its existence. Informer evidence may be obtained by fear, by guilt, by greed, by self-interest or by spite. The spy, secure in the knowledge that his version of events will normally go unchallenged, tends to supply his controllers with the information he feels they want to have, or at least will pay to obtain. He may feed them with stories that support his role, stress his own importance or perception and justify his continued employment. If, like Lennon, he is being paid on 'results achieved', he will have an incentive to achieve those results by using methods that he hopes will go undetected both by his masters and by his victims. The incentive to distort and exaggerate will be all the greater if he has become financially dependent on his controller, or if he needs a favour – immunity from prosecution or suppression of some dark corner of his past.

The unfairest evidence of all relates to crimes which have been incited or encouraged by police officers, often with the help of informants who have become or been used as 'agents provocateurs'.

Failures in orthodox detection work have encouraged some senior officers to approve 'sting' operations in order more easily to tempt and trap offenders. Such trickery is acceptable if it works to collect solid evidence of previous crime, or of ongoing criminal conspiracies, but should not be countenanced if it serves to incite crimes which would otherwise never have been committed. This crucial distinction is overlooked by British law, which affords no defence of entrapment to persons who would not have engaged in crime but for temptations offered by agents of the state.

The absence of any 'entrapment' defence is a serious gap in constitutional protection, and serves to encourage a particularly dangerous form of police trickery. In the United States, it has long been accepted that a positive defence of entrapment may be advanced 'when the criminal design originates, not with the accused, but is conceived in the minds of the government officers'.[91] Thus where a police informer befriended an ex-addict, and persuaded him to revert to heroin-taking in order to inform on him and so earn police favours, the Supreme Court quashed the conviction. The entrapment defence helps to ensure proper standards in the exercise of Government power, but it has, regrettably, never been adopted in Britain. Although Lord Goddard once complained that 'it is wholly wrong for a police officer or any other person to be sent to commit an offence in order that an offence by another person may be detected', the only rules against permitting undercover policemen and informers to overstep the mark are contained in Home Office circulars. There have been several serious miscarriages of justice involving the imprisonment of men for robberies which were 'set up' and even led by police agents who were not charged, and much of the corruption which crippled Scotland Yard in the late sixties and early seventies stemmed from unhealthily close relationships between police officers and their criminal informants, who were permitted to act as *agents provocateurs* so as to boost arrest rates.

The House of Lords decided in *R.* v. *Sang* that there was no defence of entrapment in English common law, although the judge had a general power to exclude evidence in order to achieve a fair trial. Section 78 of PACE, as we have seen, now requires exclusion of evidence if in all the circumstances ('including the circumstances in which the evidence was obtained') it would have such an adverse effect on the fairness of the trial that 'the court ought not to admit it'. This would permit an argument that evidence obtained by entrapment techniques which had encouraged the commission of the crime in the first place 'ought' (as a moral imperative) not to be used to convict persons who succumbed to police temptation. An example is provided by the case of *R. v. Ameer*.[92] The defendant claimed he had been 'set up' by a man named Buckley, all trace of whom had disappeared from the prosecution evidence, along with much of the cannabis he had been possessed of when arrested. Buckley was subpoenaed by the defence to give evidence and described himself as 'licensed' to deal in drugs on behalf of certain police officers. He claimed to be employed by these officers to 'set up' cannabis deals, and subsequently to sell part of the seizure. He told how he had befriended Ameer, given him cannabis on social occasions and originated the idea of a drugs deal, using 'every trick in the book' to obtain Ameer's participation. The judge was satisfied that Buckley had acted as an *agent provocateur*, playing a major role in drawing the defendant into a criminal enterprise which he would otherwise never have contemplated. The judge excluded all evidence relating to the cannabis and ordered the defendant's acquittal; subsequently, twenty-six other persons awaiting trial for drugs offences involving the same informer had all charges against them dropped.

Those who argue that criminal trials are not the place for inquiry into police malpractice ignore the fact that many of the worst cases of police corruption have only come to light as the result of barristers cross-examining police officers in the course of seeking to convince the judge to exercise a discretion to exclude unfairly obtained evidence. Section 78, by permitting a forensic examination of the circumstances in which police obtain evidence, at least permits the exposure of methods which are underhand. Whether such methods will be deterred, however, depends on whether the evidence is allowed to secure a conviction. It was permitted to do so in the case of Stardust Jewellers, a shop established in Tottenham and run for three months by undercover policemen posing as fences willing to pay large cash sums for stolen goods.[93] Thieves flocked to the shop, to exchange their ill-gotten jewellery and credit cards for public money in transactions recorded by secret video cameras, and thirty of them were 'stung' at the end of the operation. The

Court of Appeal declined to rule that the entrapment evidence made their trials unfair: 'The trick was not applied to the appellants: they voluntarily applied themselves to the trick.' This approach is too glib. What the Court should have considered was the extent to which the existence of Stardust Jewellers, by brazenly offering large cash sums for stolen goods, had actually encouraged the stealing of the goods concerned. There can be no objection to undercover operations which entice criminals to provide evidence of completed or ongoing offences, but the public interest is hardly served by a police force which drums up its own criminal business.

The 'Stardust Jewllers' decision has been used to endorse and encourage more blatant forms of police entrapment. In *Williams* v. *DPP* in 1993, the High Court approved a 'crime initiative' whereby a transit van was left unattended in a busy shopping centre, with apparently valuable cartons of cigarettes plainly visible and easily removable through the half-opened roller shutter at its rear. After an hour and a half observing honest bypassers passing it by, the police arrested two eight-year-old boys who helped themselves to a carton (and were reprimanded) and then the two defendants, who had toyed with temptation for ten minutes and then succumbed. Although they obviously would not have committed the theft had the police set-up not provided them with the opportunity, the court found no basis in the wording of Section 78 of PACE to exclude the evidence against them, since they had not been pressured or persuaded by police agents to commit the offence. This decision appears to allow Section 78 to operate in cases where the incitement to crime comes from the mouth of an *agent provocateur*, but not where the temptation, however hard to resist, results from a carefully laid trap which contains its own lure. The distinction is artificial, but it has permitted police to take 'crime initiatives' which initiate crime (and even initiate small children into crime), yet which are described by the courts as 'entirely legitimate enterprise'.[94]

The question of whether a person guilty of crime should be acquitted if he can prove that he would never have participated without pressure and persuasion from an undercover policeman or a paid police agent goes to the crux of the balance between civil liberty and police power. We do not have quite the commitment to liberty to say, with the Americans, that entrapment should be a defence, but we are now inclined, by Section 78 of PACE, to let it in through the back door of judicial discretion. The Law Commission, reporting on a possible 'entrapment' defence shortly after the Lennon affair, said that the arguments were finely balanced, and the decision should be made at a political rather than a legal level. On one side is the view that informers ought to be protected at all costs even if there is a suspicion that they may have broken the rules and that people who succumb to temptation to participate in serious crime deserve to be punished anyway. The better view is that courts should not be lied to and misled, that rules against creating crimes where none would otherwise have been committed ought to be observed, and that it is a contradiction in terms for officials charged with maintaining the law to arrange for it to be broken.

CHAPTER 2

Public Protest

Demonstrations helped to win the democracy we enjoy today. The right to stand for Parliament, the right to vote and the right to join trade unions were all hastened by meetings and marches and protest movements – as, more recently, has been the right not to be subjected to poll tax. The right to assemble, to stand up and be counted among the believers in a cause or crusade, still marks the most obvious difference between liberal democracies and totalitarian states, where protest is banned and protesters are taken off to have their heads examined – and not only for bruises. Although public protest is still a powerful means of bringing the reality of grievance home to politicians and bureaucrats, it can also be high-pitched, brainless and brutal, spreading fear in minority communities, intimidating workers and clogging up traffic. More than any other freedom it comes at a price, and a price moreover which Governments are increasingly reluctant to pay. Despite much sentimental rhetoric, the right to protest has never been entrenched in English law: the police have always had power to stop speeches and demonstrations whenever a breach of the peace might occur. Inner-city riots, violent clashes between police and striking miners, provocative racist marches by the National Front and the persistent defiance by the women of Greenham served as a backdrop to the Public Order Act of 1986, which enlarged police powers to control meetings and processions and to arrest those who cause alarm or distress to bystanders. These changes in the law have brought an increase in the numbers of prosecutions for minor offences and new opportunities to harass those whose lifestyles police find offensive, but have done little either to protect genuine protests or to define the acceptable limits of paramilitary force in coping with unruly demonstrations or outbreaks of violent discontent during long hot urban summers.

LACK OF POSITIVE RIGHTS

Although the virtues of peaceful protest are frequently extolled, there is in England no legal right of peaceful assembly or procession or (except at election time) even to hold meetings in public places. Cars and horses have more legal rights on the highway than people, as a small group of Islington social workers discovered when they were stopped by court order from spending their Saturday mornings distributing protest leaflets outside the offices of a local estate agent. They were complaining about the agent's tactics of 'winkling' working-class Islingtonians out of houses which were then profitably sold to the upwardly mobile. The demonstration was held with police approval and caused no obstruction, yet the Court of Appeal (over Lord Denning's vigorous dissent) put paid to any notion that there was a 'right to demonstrate' in English law.[1] The estate agents claimed the leaflets were libellous, and that the demonstrators were causing a 'nuisance' outside business premises: the court ruled that the 'balance of convenience' (i.e. the balance of business convenience) required that the protest should stop until these claims could be tried, a year or so hence. This case, *Hubbard* v. *Pitt*, is a classic example of how property rights can prevail in law over basic principles of free speech and assembly. The court asserted that the only right members of the public have on the highway is to move along it in a reasonable manner, otherwise the owner of the highway can sue in trespass.

Local authorities usually own the surface of main roads, so that they could sue in trespass anyone who used those roads for purposes other than that of passage. Other roads are often owned by the possessor of the adjacent land, who can sue for trespass if members of the public go beyond their right of way. Thus the racehorse trainer who objected to press racing correspondents timing from the highway his horses' practice gallops on his adjoining land[2] and the landed duke whose pheasant shoot was interfered with by somebody deliberately opening and shutting his umbrella on the highway[3] had their remedy in trespass. A landowner can also eject a trespasser with reasonable force after first requesting him to desist from the trespass. The courts have had no hesitation in granting injunctions to extirpate demonstrators and picketers from highways running past places of controversial employment; this was the device used to clear colliery entrances during the miners strike in 1985[4] and to make way for the Murdoch newspapers after News Ltd moved to Wapping.[5] It is a criminal offence wilfully to obstruct free passage along a highway without lawful excuse, and policemen may arrest offenders without a warrant; the courts have decided that the offence may be committed although only part of the highway is obstructed, and even though no nuisance results. The scope of the crime is illustrated by what happened to Pat Arrowsmith: her conviction for obstruction was upheld although the area was frequently used for meetings, the police had been notified and she believed her meeting was lawful.[6] It follows that meetings and demonstrations on highways are always potentially unlawful: the owners of the appropriate part of the highway can always have the public removed, the targets of the protest can have the demonstrators injuncted and any 'obstruction' will constitute a criminal offence.

Restrictions on the right to demonstrate might be tolerable if there were a right to hold protest meetings in public places, like parks and open spaces. In the United States, for example, there is a constitutional *right* to use the streets and parks for purposes of public assembly. The Supreme Court has held:

Wherever the title of streets and parks may rest, they have immemorially been held in trust for the use of the public, and time out of mind, they have been used for purposes of assembly, communicating thought between citizens, and discussing public questions.[7]

Compare that imaginative approach with the mean-spirited words of a former Lord Chief Justice in a leading British case on the right to demonstrate. It arose when a member of the National Council for Civil Liberties was arrested trying to address a group of people outside a Jobcentre. She was causing no obstruction, but the police thought that her speech might excite the unemployed and so lead to dissatisfaction inside the centre. The Chief Justice held this was ample ground to justify a police order to descend from her soapbox, and approved her conviction for obstructing them when she refused:

There have been moments during the argument in this case when it appeared to be suggested that the court had to do with a grave case involving what is called the right of public meeting. I say 'called' because English law does not recognize any special right of public meeting for political or other purposes. The right of assembly is nothing more than a view, taken by the court, of the individual liberty of the subject.[8]

The views taken by the courts, in a series of cases around the turn of the century, have been uniformly hostile to the liberty of the subject to hold public meetings in public places, at least without the prior written consent of officialdom. Although it is possible to acquire rights by 'prescription' as a result of custom and usage, the judges in these early cases were simply unable to conceive how a 'right' to assemble or to protest could ever exist in law. They dismissed evidence that public meetings had been held 'from time immemorial' in places like Hyde Park and on Brighton Beach: these were merely 'enjoyments the public have had by the gracious concession of the Crown', or by local authorities in whom parks and foreshores are vested.[9] These petty and authoritarian decisions are now so entrenched in law that they could only be reversed by legislation, or by a Bill of Rights which guaranteed freedom of assembly.

Most Western European countries permit meetings in public parks, and have laws requiring local authorities to hire halls to citizens for political meetings.[10] There is no equivalent in Britain, except for certain rights given to candidates at election times. Try to make a speech in the street, and you will be moved along, or, if you persist, arrested for obstruction of a police officer. In a park, your speech will probably be contrary to local by-laws forbidding meetings and distribution of literature in the interests of civic cleanliness. In most parks, dogs have more rights than demonstrators. You cannot even stand on a soap-box at Speakers' Corner or in Trafalgar Square – those world-famous symbols of freedom of British speech – without prior permission from the Department of the Environment (DoE). Organizations which have been refused permission to speak in Trafalgar Square – for no better reason than that their message was not acceptable to the Department of the Environment – include the Campaign for Nuclear Disarmament (CND), Save Greece from Fascism, the Northern Ireland Civil Rights Movement – and indeed, since 1972, *any* organization of *any* kind which has anything to say about Northern Ireland. The DoE is obsessed with the desire to live a quiet life. In 1992, amongst proposals for new laws to silence late-night car alarms and stereos, it recommended a legal ban on all political demonstrations outside diplomatic missions. It is extraordinary that the department in charge of permitting protests should be so concerned to suppress them, in the very places where it is most vital to have them heard. Embassy premises must remain inviolable under the Vienna Convention, but the streets outside are the appropriate places for demonstrating against the brutalities and inhumanities of their Governments. When Bill Clinton, as a student at Oxford in 1968, participated in the mass demonstrations outside the US Embassy at Grosvenor Square, he joined vast numbers of British students in sending home the message that his Government's Vietnam policies were intolerable. Visual messages of this sort, if the DoE has its way, will not be allowed to discomfort foreign Governments again.

If a political group wants to hire a hall, the fate of its protest is in the hands of the local authority. Some local authorities will not allow the National Front to hire their halls – others have refused bookings from the Anti-apartheid Movement. Indeed, Scarborough Council has preferred to pay large damages to the National Front by breaking a contract to hire its hall for a conference, rather than to permit the expression within its precincts of offensive political views.[11] These restrictions on protest are increasing. Until 1978, Oxford Street was a popular venue for processions. So was the route from Tower Hill to Westminster through the City. Quietly, without any fuss at all, the police have used their powers to close these areas off to marchers. The centre of consumerism and the citadel of capitalism may not be deaf to the voice of protest – they are just not permitted to hear it.

If a particular organization believed that it was being discriminated against by refusal of permission to hold a meeting, it is not clear what legal remedies, as distinct from the obvious political steps of having the matter raised in council and the local press, would be available. It is a defect in the law that there is no clear-cut legal process for preventing political discrimination on the part of the local authority in controlling public meetings in its parks and open spaces. The citizen has no right to use premises belonging to local authorities for meetings, except a statutory right to use school or other premises controlled by the local authority upon payment of a reasonable fee for meetings organized by a candidate in connection with a parliamentary or local-government election. Of course, many local authorities habitually let meeting-halls to local associations and societies, but as the law stands this is purely a private business arrangement completely at council discretion. Ratepayers could secure the court's intervention if the local authority charged lower fees to one political body than to another, yet it is very doubtful whether they could have any legal remedy if the local authority systematically refused to allow particular associations the use of its premises on payment of the ordinary fee.

The citizen's rights are inadequate here: the rights given in respect of elections should be made of general application. There is much to be said for the proposal that English law should be brought into line with that of North America and most European countries, by the introduction of a statutory right to hold a public meeting, backed by a corresponding duty placed upon local authorities to set aside public land, or public halls, for such occasions. This recommendation was made by Lord Scarman in his report on the Red Lion Square disorders, but has been ignored. Ironically, the only places where freedom of assembly is protected by law are at universities, polytechnics and colleges, whose governors are bound by Section 43 of the 1986 Education Act to 'take such steps as are reasonably practical' to ensure freedom of speech within their cloisters for students, teachers and visiting speakers. This curious clause was inserted by the Government after several of its own members had been stopped from speaking at universities by demonstrations (or the fear of demonstrations) against their policies.

Liverpool University was first to breach Section 43, by prohibiting a visit from the South African ambassador, after hearing of police concern about demonstrations which might be called in the city to protest against the visit.[12] The Divisional Court ruled that the Vice-Chancellor and the governors had no business to take into account what might happen outside their precincts: their duty was to do their best to secure a free market-place in ideas, however offensive, on their own campus. This is all very well, but on what principle can public freedom of speech and assembly be legally protected only within the private precincts of universities, where they should least need that protection? Section 43 is objectionable because it gives as a privilege to students and their campus visitors something which should be available by right to all who wish to hear or deliver political messages in public.

Article 11 of the European Convention of Human Rights guarantees 'the right to freedom of peaceful assembly and to freedom of association'. It is subject, of course, to considerations of public order and the rights of others, but these exceptions must be 'necessary in a democratic society'. When Parliament debated the 1986 Public Order Act, the Government was pressed to include a right of peaceful assembly to balance the extremely broad powers it was providing to the police. The Government refused, but solemnly undertook to issue a 'Home Office circular' requesting the police to bear this 'right' in mind when exercising their new powers to control meetings and processions. Whether that undertaking was given out of cynicism or naïvety, it exemplifies Whitehall's ingrained fear of providing citizens with statutory rights, and illustrates the extent to which 'rights' are represented in England by polite letters to police chiefs rather than by rules of law.

PROCESSIONS

A political procession is a perfectly proper use of the highway, at least so long as it processes. The basic right to pass and re-pass along the highway exists for all reasonable users, and the Divisional Court had no hesitation in acquitting a CND official of incitement to obstruct the highway by directing a crowd to march down a particular route.[13] No obstruction or public nuisance is caused by a procession, whatever its size, unless, in all the circumstances, including the tradition of tolerating public protest, its use of the highway is unreasonable. Nevertheless, the Public Order Act 1986 gives police extensive powers to ban or reroute processions before they begin, however reasonable and peaceful their organizers' intentions, if public-order problems are expected.

Organizers of all 'political' processions – whether protests or campaigns or merely marches to commemorate historical events – must give notice to the police in writing of the time and route at least six days before the date, or as soon as reasonably practicable,[14] unless the decision to take to the streets is of the spontaneous, 'Let's march on the town hall' kind. The notice must designate at least one person as organizer, and a variety of footling offences are committed by organizers whose procession deviates from the route given in the notice or who fail to give notice at all or as soon as practicable. The notice requirement, imposed nationally for the first time by the 1986 Act, is of little value to public-order law. Over 80 per cent of marches were already being notified, and any demonstration large enough to pose a major public-order problem will obviously be known about well beforehand. The notice requirements merely discourage sensible people from volunteering to 'organize' a procession which would lay them open to a criminal charge if it took an unnotified turning or started an hour late because the band failed to arrive. The new offences may be committed in numerous petty ways, and there is ample scope for harassment of organizers of marches in support of controversial causes. The notice provision might have served some purpose had it provided that police approval of (or failure to request changes in) the notified route would be a defence to any marcher charged with obstructing the highway. This would have overcome the unfair decision in Pat Arrowsmith's case, when a brief and entirely unforeseeable obstruction caused by a meeting approved beforehand by police none the less resulted in her conviction for obstructing the highway.[15]

The 1986 Act gives senior police officers new powers to impose conditions as to the time or route of proposed processions if they reasonably believe that serious public disorder, serious damage to property or 'serious disruption to the life of the community' would otherwise result, or that the real purpose of the organizers is to intimidate others.[16] This power tilts the balance against civil liberties, in favour of the quiet life. Serious damage and disorder might be predictable as the result of a particular route, or a time which makes the march clash with a rival event, but 'disruption to community life' is an altogether too vague yardstick for ordering a protest march to keep to the back streets or the local playing fields, or to comprise no more than twenty demonstrators. Senior police officers are not required to consult representatives of the community whose life they allege will be seriously disrupted, and police decisions on this ground inevitably involve political value-judgements. So too does the new power to impose conditions to avoid the intimidation of others 'with a view to compelling them to do or refrain from doing lawful acts'. If strikers decide to march to the place where 'scabs' are still working, the police power to route them elsewhere will depend on whether the strikers intend to use persuasion or compulsion – a distinction which is often difficult to make, even after the event. The first prosecution brought under the Act was against a demonstrator who shouted 'Apartheid murderers!' at visitors to a reception being held at South Africa House, and who refused to obey a police direction to move out of their earshot. The charge was dismissed after police admitted that the direction had been given merely to avoid discomfiture to the visitors rather than to intimidate them.

Where a chief constable considers that his powers to impose conditions on a procession are insufficient to protect the area from serious public disorder, he may apply to the district council for an order banning all processions in the district for a period of up to three months.[17] The order must be approved by the Home Secretary (who approves it directly, without the interposition of any council, when requested by the Metropolitan Police Commissioner in London). At first sight, this seems reasonable enough: the Home Secretary is entitled, at the request of police and local councillors, to deny a particular organization the opportunity to march, at a particular time, if that would stir up serious public disorder. But if the Home Secretary does that, the law insists that a most remarkable and illogical consequence should follow: *all* marches in the area must be stopped, for a period which could be as long as three months. In other words, he is required to impose a *blanket ban* on all street marches, however harmless, in order to stop one particularly dangerous protest. These 'blanket bans' originated in the Public Order Act of 1936, which was rushed through Parliament when Mosley's Brownshirts were fighting pitched battles with Communists in the East End of London. Why, if only one march is going to cause a problem on one day, ban *all* marches on *all* days in the immediate future? That tactic may have made sense in terms of pacifying the East End battleground in 1936; it has no relevance to conditions today, when problems have mainly been caused by brief National Front sorties to different areas with high immigrant populations. The theory behind the law no longer makes sense – but the power unleashed *by* the law is formidable. In 1936, that power was justified on the basis that its very formidability would make Home Secretaries think twice before using it. And, sure enough, between

1936 and April 1980, there were only eleven bans imposed in Great Britain – an average of one ban every four years. But between April 1980 and June 1982 there were fifty-one total bans – prohibiting *all* marches in an area, sometimes for only a fortnight, sometimes for the full three months.

Most of these recent blanket bans have been imposed to stop just one march with a racist message. But a banning order is a scatter-gun which hits and hurts all sorts of innocent targets. For example, Friends of the Earth lost 5 per cent of their annual income when an entirely unobjectionable march against nuclear power, planned months in advance, had to be cancelled at the last moment because it fell within a banning period imposed to stop a National Front march. On another occasion, it lost a 'Save the Whale' rally for the same reason. Traditional events, like Trade Union May Day proces-sions, have suffered the same fate. But even if the reasons for imposing a blanket ban are tenuous, the courts will not intervene to uphold the right to protest. That was discovered by the Campaign for Nuclear Disarmament, which became fed up with having its marches stopped because of other people's disturbances. After losing its seventh demonstration in five months, it marched into the Court of Appeal and sought to quash an order banning all demonstrations in London during the month of May 1981.[18] This particular blanket ban meant that there could be no wedding processions, no fairs on the common, no carnivals and no CND marches for four whole weeks in any part of the 786 square miles of Greater London. Although the court said that the police reasons for the ban were meagre, it could only overturn the order if there were no reasons for it at all. It is virtually inconceivable that judges would ever say that the Metropolitan Commissioner of Police and the Home Secretary had reached a decision which no reasonable person could make, so judicial review of banning orders offers only illusory protection to the right to protest.

Blanket bans have become an easy way out of difficult policing problems. But the consequence has been to give hooligans a new importance – a power, in effect, to dictate the terms upon which others may exercise their freedom to assemble. It is difficult to understand why the Government did not change this 1936 law when transferring it to the 1986 Act, so as to enable the Home Secretary to ban individual marches. The minister of state claimed that chief constables were worried that a power to ban a single march would lay them open to charges of political bias – an illogical argument, since on every occasion a blanket ban has been imposed it has been well known which particular organization has triggered it.

Special criminal trespass provisions were hastily framed to increase police powers over the 'peace convoy' which was passing unpeacefully through the West Country as the Public Order Bill was passing through Parliament. It subsequently transpired that much of this violence was inflicted on, rather than instigated by, these 'new-age travellers', whose colourful caravanserai had provoked the local constabulary to paroxysms of unreasoning brutality: a court held that thirty convoy members had been assaulted and falsely imprisoned during 'the Battle of Bean Field', and awarded them damages against the chief constable of Wiltshire. The marks which were left on public-order law are found in Section 39 of the 1986 Act, which makes it an offence for trespassers who have insulted the landowner or his family, or who are travelling with more than twelve vehicles, to disobey a police order to leave the land upon which they are camped. These special criminal provisions were unnecessary, given existing police powers and the availability of speedy civil remedies to extirpate trespassers, but they have been used in combination with banning orders (routinely imposed in the Stonehenge area during the summer solstice) to criminalize followers of a lifestyle which may appear more old-age than New Age, but should not for that reason be legally objectionable. These powers for interrupting spiritual journeys have proved convenient for clearing squatters from unused urban land, although courts have insisted that police directions should be clear and should preferably allow sufficient time for vehicles to be repaired and removed as well.

In 1992 the Government signalled its intention further to harass the travelling community by proposing to abolish the duty on local councils to provide caravan sites, and to create a new criminal offence of 'stationing a caravan for the purpose of residing for any period within England and Wales on any land within the boundaries of a highway or any other unoccupied or common land'. At present, Section 6 of the Caravan Sites Act 1968 requires local authorities to provide a minimum number of campsites, but this duty is widely ignored and has never been enforced. The answer to what the DoE describes as 'the problem' of gypsies is not to abolish this duty but to enforce it, especially at a time when gypsies in Germany are once again suffering vicious outbreaks of public hostility. The right to choose, or to persist in leading, a nomadic lifestyle should be protected, rather than criminalized as another form of vagrancy.

PUBLIC MEETINGS

The most controversial new provision in the 1986 Public Order Act is Section 14, which extends to police officers the power to give directions to organizers or participants at public meetings of more than twenty persons. The power operates at two stages: before the demonstration, the chief constable may impose written conditions on the organizers; at the scene of the demonstration, the senior policer officer present may impose them in any way he thinks fit. The power can only be exercised on the same grounds as the power to impose conditions on processions, namely on the reasonable belief that his direction will help to prevent serious public disorder or damage to property, or serious disruption to the life of the community, or deliberate intimidation. The conditions imposed can relate to the place of the demonstration, its length and the number of persons permitted to attend. Failure to comply with a police direction is an offence, punishable by up to three months' imprisonment, unless the failure arises from circumstances beyond the defendant's control. It is hard to see how an organizer could be held responsible for failing to comply with shouted directions lost in the tumult of an angry crowd, or with conditions which are broken by others who insist on swelling ranks beyond the allowed numbers or who refuse to disperse at the ordered time.

None the less, Section 14 is a recipe for conflict and confusion at demonstrations, as police officers shout directions, then wade in to arrest for non-compliance. It can permit chief constables to destroy the purpose of a protest in advance, by imposing conditions which make it futile. A vigil outside the South African Embassy could be ordered to move across Trafalgar Square to the New Zealand High Commission, a 'mass picket' might be directed to reduce itself to twenty-one persons, and so on. The direction itself does not have to be reasonable or fair, so long as it subjectively appears to the particular police officer to be necessary at the time to thwart disorder or disruption or intimidation. The prospect of a gaol sentence makes it a more serious charge than obstruction of the highway, which carries only a financial penalty, and it is a regular police tactic to order demonstrators to move and then to arrest them under Section 14 for failure to comply with a direction. In effect, it provides the police with power to bring mass demonstrations to an end, by imposing a time limit by which the number of protesters must be reduced to below twenty, thereby limiting severely the scope and impact of demonstrations held in public places.

Section 14 was designed primarily to curb mass picketing. In some cases it will be possible for police to entertain a reasonable apprehension of serious public disorder or disruption to community life, but for the most part they will rely upon the ground that the purpose of the assembly is 'the intimidation of others with a view to compelling them not to do an act they have a right to do, or to do an act they have a right not to do'. Striking workers mustered at factory gates to deter others from working may have the object of persuading rather than compelling by intimidation: in *News Group* v. *SOGAT* it was held that 'abuse, swearing and shouting' did not amount to a threat of violence for the purpose of intimidation.[19] However, violent incidents accompanied by efforts to block entry will be sufficient to enable police to invoke their Section 14 powers to give directions.

The most unsatisfactory aspect of the Section 14 power, as of the power to ban or restrict processions, is the difficulty of appealing against restrictions. There is, in fact, no appeal from police decisions to impose conditions – only the possibility of having them reviewed for procedural errors or 'unreasonableness' in the High Court. To quash an order on the basis of 'unreasonableness' the court must be satisfied that it has been made by a police officer who has, in effect, taken leave of his senses. A preposterous condition, which would destroy the whole point of the protest, might be struck down, as might a condition irrationally imposed on a traditional meeting which had never shown any signs of turning violent. But the High Court is reluctant to 'second-guess' police apprehensions about public disorder, or apply a presumption in favour of freedom of speech and assembly: if there is some evidence, no matter how meagre, of potential dislocation, the belief will probably be upheld as one which a reasonable chief constable could entertain.[20] The potential of Section 14 conditions for diminishing the impact of legitimate political protest is yet another example of the advantage of incorporating the European Convention in domestic law: this would provide a presumption in favour of freedom of speech and assembly which the High Court could invoke to abolish or minimize conditions imposed by lazy or over-cautious police officers.

POWERS TO PREVENT DISORDER

Arrest for breach of the peace

The police and the magistrates have certain preventive powers at common law to restrain persons who are likely to create public disorder. The proper exercise of these powers turns upon whether there is a reasonable apprehension of a 'breach of the peace', in other words, behaviour which is likely to lead to harm to people or property or to put others in fear of suffering harm.[21] Mere annoyance or disturbance or insult is not sufficient: the peace is not broken by bad language or disobedience. The better view is that passive resistance will not amount to a breach of the peace, so long as protesters allow themselves to be removed without struggling, although one judge has noted that 'Even Mahatma Gandhi discovered to his sorrow that in the conduct of ordinary mortals passive resistance only remains passive so long as the resistance is successful.'[22] Those who sit down on highways can, of course, be arrested for obstruction, but police have no such power where the 'sit-in' takes place on private property. They are entitled to intervene only if there is forcible resistance to the owner's efforts to remove them. Police do have power to enter private property when they apprehend a breach of the peace, so they may attend public meetings (or even 'closed' meetings) on private premises, against the wishes of the organizers, if they believe that violence is likely to occur unless they are present. There is one case, *Thomas* v. *Sawkins* (1935), where police conduct in entering private premises without a warrant on the off chance that seditious speeches would be made and remaining after being ordered to leave was approved; like *Duncan* v. *Jones* this was a decision of the century's most illiberal and least able Chief Justice (Lord Hewart).[23] The better view is that police need an invitation or a warrant before entering meetings on private premises, unless a breach of the peace is reasonably apprehended. In this situation, the police do as a duty what any citizen is entitled to do by right, namely take reasonable steps to prevent breaches of the peace, if necessary by forcibly detaining the person whose conduct threatens public order.[24] That conduct must be 'likely', not 'liable', to breach the peace: the duty does not justify restraints on those who may possibly cause trouble.[25]

The police power to restrain breaches of the peace was used to controversial effect during the 1984 miners' strike, when police intercepted car-loads of picketers some miles from the collieries and forced them to turn back. The Divisional Court accepted that police were entitled to act because of recent violence from pickets at the colliery, and the likelihood of a breach of the peace by reinforcements was 'a real possibility'.[26] This test dilutes the requirement that the likelihood of violence must be imminent and immediate before prophylactic action is justified, to such an extent that the courts in applying it were able to approve police behaviour in stopping car-loads of southern NUM supporters at the Dartford Tunnel, several hundred miles and many hours away from the place of the intended demonstration. This is a clear infringement of liberty, but courts are unlikely to object when its victims are supporters either of soccer teams or of Arthur Scargill.

Another device used by the courts during the miners' strike for limiting the right of individuals to join flying pickets was to impose a condition of bail on those arrested for a public-order offence that they should not henceforth engage in picketing other than at their own place of work. Such conditions involved a presumption of guilt prior to trial, and were particularly objectionable when imposed by magistrates as a routine policy rather than by reference to the facts of individual cases. A person who commits another public-order offence while on bail risks a much higher sentence at the second trial, and this fact should itself serve as a deterrent to misconduct, without the need to impose bail conditions which prevent the exercise of the right to assemble and express opinion. The Divisional Court, which approved the application of these bail conditions on men of good character upon their first arrest for a minor public-order offence, made no reference in its judgement to any such right: it accepted police evidence that all the mass pickets involved violence and intimidation, and that justices were therefore entitled to decide there was a 'real risk' that defendants would commit offences by returning to the picket line.[27]

These generalized preventative powers to avoid breaches of the peace have been taken to extremes by police in their efforts to thwart the first discomforting lifestyle phenomenon of the nineties, the 'Acid House' countryside party. A middle-aged generation of peace-keepers brought up to believe that 'Acid House' connotes an Aladdin's cave of LSD rather than a style of music, have treated these 'raves' as illegal breaches of the peace, advising landlords to annul contracts for hire of farms on the grounds of illegality, setting up roadblocks to turn away party-goers, and attending themselves in full riot dress to declare the party over. The power to prevent breaches of the peace entitles closure of noisy parties, but not all-night events in remote parts of the countryside. There are ample powers to arrest drug-dealers on the spot, without making a collective assumption of the guilt of thousands of young party-goers. One common police strategy, which has no legal basis, has been to alter road signs and to point them in the wrong direction. This tactic was last deployed by Dad's Army to confuse any Nazi invasion force: Dad's Constabulary appears to feel similarly threatened by an invasion of young people having fun, to endlessly repetitive patterns of instrumental music.

Bind-overs

Magistrates may make an order binding over any person in their court to keep the peace in future. This power was given to lay justices in 1361 as a means of containing the depredations of drunken soldiers roaming the country after the French wars, and it still has valuable uses to calm neighbourhood disputes and to prevent domestic violence. It does not count as a conviction, and may be imposed without any trial at all, so long as the magistrates foresee future misbehaviour. Refusal to accept a bind-over may be punished by up to six months in prison – a fate some protesters are prepared to suffer rather than fetter their future conduct. In 1961,

Bertrand Russell and some of his distinguished CND colleagues were sent to prison for refusing to be bound over, and in 1969 Pat Arrowsmith became Britain's first 'prisoner of conscience' when she was gaoled for six months for refusing to provide sureties for future good conduct after participating in an anti-Vietnam demonstration. They had not been convicted of any offence: they simply refused to put themselves in a position which would make it more difficult for them to organize or participate in future demonstrations.

There have been several unedifying cases of the bind-over power being inflicted by country justices on anti-hunting demonstrators appearing as prosecution witnesses against huntsmen who have beaten them up. The latter were given discharges or small fines for assault, and the witnesses were sent to prison for refusing the magistrates' demands to be bound over. Not even Kafka envisaged a judicial proceeding where the victim is gaoled and the assailants go free, yet that is exactly what has happened in recent years in courts in Rye and Market Bosworth.[28] Anti-hunt campaigns may be provocative, but it is wrong to seek to deter further protest by demanding that participants who have not themselves been proved to have breached the law should submit to a bind-over. It is especially unjust that protesters should be gaoled, not merely in circumstances where they have committed no offence, but where the offence that the court fears they might otherwise commit is minor and would only result in a small fine.[29]

Bail conditions

The preventive powers to arrest for potential breach of the peace, to bind over on suspicion of future misconduct and to impose bail conditions pending appeal permit police and magistrates to restrict the rights of persistent but peaceful protesters. One favourite police tactic which was developed against anti-hunt demonstrators in the 1990s is to arrest them before the hunt begins on grounds of suspected breach of the peace, and then to 'de-arrest' them as soon as the hunt is over. This is a calculated and unconstitutional form of preventative detention. Those who refuse to be bound over will often receive short prison sentences with release on bail subject to conditions that they do not return to demonstrations until their appeal has been heard. By such devices the rights of those who wish to protest regularly against perceived environmental hazards are severely circumscribed, without any finding that they have committed an offence. The High Court has been reluctant to intervene in the misuse of preventive powers, beyond insisting that justices should have some evidence (and not instinct or police assertion) for predicting further misbehaviour, and must set a time limit to their orders.[30] The continued existence of these powers is always justified by reference to their utility in defusing domestic squabbles and public displays of loutishness and aggression; in the absence of any legal recognition of a right to demonstrate, they will continue to be used to treat political protesters as if they were mindlessly motivated drunks and hooligans.

PUBLIC-ORDER OFFENCES

The two offences most commonly charged against demonstrators are obstructing the highway and obstructing police in the execution of their duty. Section 137 of the Highways Act makes it an offence wilfully to obstruct the free passage along a highway without lawful authority or excuse. The test is invariably one of reasonableness, and the court must consider the length of time the obstruction lasted, whether any passers-by were forced to detour, whether any request was made by police to clear the area, and so on.[31] It is not unreasonable to stand on a street corner holding a placard or making a political speech, and it is entirely reasonable to demonstrate, even in large numbers, until police seek to clear the road to make way for vehicles or pedestrians. The Divisional Court quashed convictions of animal rights protesters who had been handing out leaflets condemning the fur trade in a shopping precinct: the prosecution had failed to prove either that pedestrians had actually been obstructed in going about their business or that the protest had been conducted in such an unreasonable manner that there was no 'lawful excuse' for it.[32] Decided a decade after *Hubbard* v. *Pitt* (above, page 66) where an injunction was granted against demonstrators in almost identical circumstances, the court in this case was willing, at least as a matter of criminal law, to accept that protest about issues of public concern would provide a defence of 'lawful excuse'.

The offence of obstructing the highway cannot be committed on private property or on a road to which some members of the public have been denied access: a 'highway', in law, entails 'the right of all Her Majesty's subjects at all seasons of the year freely and at their will to pass and repass without let or hindrance'. This caused difficulties for the police when they made use of statutory powers to divert vehicular traffic from the roads leading to Rupert Murdoch's plant at Wapping, and then sought to arrest demonstrators for obstructing those roads – which had ceased to be 'highways' in law as a result of the restricted access.[33] A test case involving Tony Dubbins, Secretary of the NGA, ended when he was acquitted of obstruction on the basis that he had not heard the police order to clear the road and had sat down for his own safety when police charged and attacked those who ran away. Whether or not the road was a 'highway' at the time, he had acted reasonably in the circumstances.

The offence of obstructing police in the execution of their duty is committed by any action which makes it more difficult for them to do their job – by resisting arrest, for example, or trying to hinder the arrest of someone else. Contested cases generally turn on whether the police were in fact acting in the execution of their duty, as a citizen is entitled to use reasonable force to resist an unlawful arrest. Thus it will be a good defence to charges of obstruction or assault if the police action which provoked them cannot be justified on grounds either of reasonable suspicion of an 'arrestable offence' or of reasonable apprehension of a breach of the peace. At industrial disputes, many arrests for obstruction of both the highway and the police arise from attempts by pickets to 'persuade' drivers and workers to turn back. There is nothing to stop pickets from communicating their case; equally, there is nothing to oblige drivers to stop and listen to it.[34] When reason prevails, police will allow pickets to stop and converse briefly with drivers, and then move them back when the driver indicates that he wishes to proceed. Unless some such system is agreed between police and picket organizers, ugly confrontations are likely, in which pickets can be charged with obstructing the highway by blocking the passage of vehicles, and obstructing the police by refusing to budge or by resisting arrest. Obstruction offences are difficult to prosecute, at least in courts which apply the proper standards of proof, because the evidence will inevitably reflect the confusion of the mêlée, and it may be difficult to determine which side has acted the more reasonably. Obstruction is not an offence triable by jury, however, and lay justices tend to be biased against protestors (especially 'outside agitators') who disrupt their local peace and quiet.

A more effective weapon against pickets has been found, in recent industrial disputes, in civil actions for injunctions against the unions to which they belong. Especially where there is evidence of workers being intimidated or assaulted, or commercial contracts being interfered with by the turning away of lorries, the High Court is generally prepared to grant injunctions which oblige the union to restrain its members from such actions, on pain of heavy financial punishment for contempt of court and further damages payable to the employers. It is now customary for the courts, in recognition of traditional 'rights', to exclude from the ambit of the injunction 'peaceful, disciplined and orderly marches' and 'pickets, provided they do not exceed six in number, at the entrance to the main gate for the purpose of peacefully obtaining or communicating information'.[35] These exceptions define the 'right to protest' in industrial disputes. The number of six is taken from the Employment Code of Practice (1980) and is inevitably arbitrary. Unfortunately, it is becoming a magic number for police-approved picketing on non-industrial matters.

There is an important difference, which some civil libertarians are reluctant to recognize, between mass pickets organized and financed by trade unions as part of a battle to obtain better conditions for members, and political demonstrations which touch the conscience rather than the hip pocket of those who attend. This is not to deny that trade unionists fighting to keep their jobs are entitled to the same rights of protest as disinterested demonstrators against human-rights violations, but it is wrong for police to apply an arbitrary rule designed to keep factories open for business during strikes to a candlelight vigil outside a foreign embassy. While six pickets may be the maximum number permitted to communicate with strike-breaking workers or drivers, there is no law or code which limits the number entitled to attend non-industrial demonstrations, so long as those numbers pose no imminent danger to public order.

A new rod for the backs of violent pickets was fashioned by the offence of 'violent disorder' in Section 2 of the 1986 Public Order

Act. This makes it unlawful for three or more persons to use or threaten violence in a way which would cause 'a person of reasonable firmness present at the scene to fear for his personal safety'. No 'person of reasonable firmness' need be present at the time, although police officers, as persons of unreasonable firmness, will generally give observation evidence of strike-breaking workers being spat upon and threatened with violence. Threats uttered when there is a strong police presence would be unlikely to cause reasonable fears for personal safety, and 'abuse, swearing and shouting' will not be sufficient of itself to constitute the 'use or threat of violence' necessary to obtain convictions.[36] A single demonstrator who makes a physical (as distinct from simply a verbal) threat of violence which would intimidate a reasonable person present at the scene can be prosecuted for the new offence of 'affray' contained in Section 3 of the Act.

Both violent disorder and affray are triable in magistrates' courts (where the maximum penalty is six months' imprisonment) but the defendant may elect trial by jury – the greater chance of acquittal being counterbalanced by the prospect of a heavier sentence (five years maximum for 'violent disorder' and three years for 'affray'). As the two offences will often overlap with the less serious crimes of obstruction, assault on police and 'insulting and threatening behaviour', which do not carry a right to jury trial, Crown prosecutors will generally prefer to charge the latter offences so as to have the charges dealt with more speedily by magistrates. This is the preferred approach where picketing is likely to continue for some time. Where serious violence has occurred, however, the prosecution may decide that the case is grave enough to warrant Section 2 or Section 3 charges, and to request a crown court trial.

The most serious public-order offence is riot, which carries a maximum penalty of ten years' imprisonment. It is committed by any person who uses unlawful violence for a common purpose shared by at least twelve persons, whose collective conduct would make the hypothetical 'person of reasonable firmness' fear for his personal safety. The offence was retained in Section 1 of the Public Order Act, although Parliament's sentimental attachment to the word and the concept over-looked the historic tendency of juries to acquit alleged rioters with political motivations, from trade unionists at the turn of the century to Fascists in the 1930s to miners in the

1980s. Over six hundred miners were charged with riot or 'unlawful assembly' (now abolished) as a result of the 1984 strike: overwhelmingly they were found 'not guilty' or had the charges dropped. A prosecution of nineteen persons for riot after the disturbances in St Pauls, Bristol, in 1980 hindered efforts to 'let bygones be bygones' in that community, and the long trial cost half as much as the damage done by the disturbances before the defendants were acquitted. Riot is a blunderbuss of a charge, posing great difficulties for prosecutors in associating particular defendants with a 'common purpose' or in proving that they used unlawful violence in pursuit of it or at all. It invites 'political' defences: the miners charged with riot put the police tactics on trial, and the Bristol riot trial jury heard about the history of racial oppression in the area from the days of the slave trade. It was noticeable that the DPP declined to bring riot charges against participants in the 1990 'Battle of Trafalgar Square' and other violent anti-poll-tax rallies, and generally tried to avoid jury trials on the (unstated) ground that most jurors would be over-sympathetic to the defendants' cause.

THE LIMITS OF PROTEST

There is a fundamental conceptual question which is raised throughout the law relating to public order. To what extent are police entitled to restrict lawful protest because of disorder apprehended from lawless reactions by others? In the USA, the right to protest is absolute: those who exercise it cannot be stopped merely because they are provocative. In Britain, the approach has been much more pragmatic. In the last century the courts protected obstreperous Christians who provoked attacks, but the same tolerance was not vouchsafed in the 1930s to left-wingers and pacifists whose speeches provoked Fascist wrath. These latter decisions were meanly argued and much criticized, but they provided a basis, in the 1970s, for police actions which turned the historic tables and stopped the National Front from flaunting its racist doctrines in the face of ethnic communities and provoking angry attacks from left-wing organizations. The European Court of Human Rights has now held that states must take positive action to protect demonstrators from fear of physical violence from counter-demonstrators, and to enable lawful demonstrations to proceed peacefully. However, it ruled that Austrian police had fulfilled this duty by separating opposing groups only when tempers had risen to the point at which physical violence became likely: they were not obliged to intervene to protect the original demonstrators from lesser forms of disruption.[37]

The leading British case of *Beatty* v. *Gillbanks* arose from Salvation Army processions in Weston-super-Mare in 1882.[38] Their object, 'lawful and laudable', was to 'reclaim and draw away from vicious and irreligious habits' those hitherto dead to religion. They regularly clashed with 'The Skeleton Army', a jeering mob egged on by the brewery trade, and on several occasions 'free fights, blows, tumult, stone-throwing and disorder' erupted. The burghers of Weston-super-Mare objected to the disruption of the customary quiet of the town, and the justices bound the Salvation Army captains to find sureties to keep the peace – in effect, putting an end to their participation in processions which would be sure to disturb it. The Divisional Court quashed the order, on the principle that persons acting lawfully could not be held responsible merely because others were thereby induced to act unlawfully and create a disturbance. Had the Salvationists been more directly responsible for the disturbances – by abusing and insulting their opponents – the bind-over might have been upheld.[39]

A less principled result was reached in *Duncan* v. *Jones* (1936) where a speaker was arrested for obstructing a police officer who ordered her down from her soap-box outside a training centre for the unemployed.[40] A year previously there had been a restlessness amongst the unemployed after the same speaker had addressed them, and the police claimed they feared repetition – the topic, ironically enough, was the threat to free speech posed by the Incitement to Disaffection Bill. The Divisional Court had no hesitation in holding that the police had reasonable grounds for apprehending a breach of the peace, and that the speaker wilfully obstructed them by refusing to desist from what was otherwise lawful conduct. *Duncan* v. *Jones* is a miserable decision for civil liberties, all the more so because the judges purported to find no difficulty of principle in it. Australian courts have recently refused to follow it in a case involving women who protested on Anzac Day (a hallowed remembrance of war dead) against the propensity of soldiers to rape in wartime.[41] Although they refused a police order to desist from a demonstration which would probably have provoked old soldiers to breach the peace, they could not be convicted of obstructing police because they were committing no offence themselves. The remedy – as the court had pointed out in *Beatty* v. *Gillbanks* – was for the police to arrest those who allow themselves to be provoked into violence by lawful demonstrations.

Protesters may none the less break the law if their actions are calculated to goad bystanders beyond endurance. Even in the USA, the right falsely to shout 'fire' in a crowded theatre is overridden by considerations of public order and safety. The British Parliament redefined the permissible limits of non-violent protest in Sections 4 and 5 of the Public Order Act 1986 and showed a distinct preference for curbing speech and behaviour which could end in violence or tears. Section 4 makes it an offence punishable by up to six months in prison to use threatening, abusive or insulting words or behaviour towards another person, or to distribute threatening, abusive or insulting pamphlets, either with the intent that others should fear or be provoked to violence or in circumstances where it is likely that such fear or provocation will result. The key adjectives – 'threatening', 'abusive', 'insulting' – are 'all very strong words'[42] which must be given a common-sense interpretation: vigorous, distasteful, unmannerly, offensive and annoying words and behaviour are permissible. When anti-apartheid protester Dennis Brutus disrupted a tennis match at Wimbledon featuring a South African player, the audience was provoked to fury – fists were shaken and attempts were made to hit him. But the House of Lords held that he had been wrongly convicted under the predecessor of Section 4, because his conduct had not in any ordinary sense been 'insulting', let alone abusive or threatening.[43] But if this test is satisfied, speakers take their audiences as they find them, and British Fascists have been convicted for proclaiming that 'Hitler was right' in speeches at Trafalgar Square which insulted and were likely to provoke to violence Jews and Communists who happened to be in the audience.

This is a dangerous precedent, because it would mean that a person who seized the microphone at a Fascist rally to proclaim 'Hitler was wrong' would also be liable to conviction. The core problem is the weasel word 'insult'. Insults are a common feature of heckling and political speech and should not be deemed in law to be capable of provoking violence, unless coupled with threats. The notion of 'insult' has been allowed to develop quite illogically in public-order contexts: the Divisional Court has upheld the absurd conviction of two homosexuals for 'insulting behaviour' likely to cause heterosexuals to breach the peace by kissing and cuddling at a bus stop in Oxford Street at 1.55 a.m.[44] It has also described as 'insulting behaviour' the act of masturbating at a urinal in the hope of attracting some fellow-feeling from the only other occupant (an undercover policeman) on the grounds that the average heterosexual would find it 'insulting' to be assumed to have homosexual tendencies.[45] These cases prove nothing more than that the sooner the word 'insult' is removed as a test of guilt from public-order legislation, the better.

This conclusion is strengthened by the attempted private prosecution of Salman Rushdie and his publishers under Section 4(1)(b) for distributing to bookshops *The Satanic Verses*, which was alleged to be insulting to Muslims and likely to provoke unlawful violence. The Divisional Court dismissed the attempt on the grounds that the 'unlawful violence' required by Section 4 had to be 'immediate' – not necessarily instantaneous, but short in time and close in causation.[46] This is a welcome ruling, which should protect speakers and writers from prosecution based on the actual or likely behaviour of those who have brooded on their words, but it does not restrict the meaning of the word 'insult'. At least the Act requires that defendants must intend their words to be insulting, or must be aware that they may be insulting, before being convicted of a Section 4 offence, so that those who preach that 'Hitler was right' cannot be convicted if they think they are addressing a Nuremberg rally.

Section 4 requires the insulting words to be used 'towards another person', so there can be no conviction unless the speaker directs his diatribe towards people likely to take offence, or be put in fear of violence. It is not enough, of course, merely to prove that the speaker is abusive or insulting: the prosecution must prove that, in the circumstances in which the words were uttered, people addressed would either be provoked to unlawful violence or would be likely to believe that unlawful violence would be used against them. The standard abuse hurled at those who walk to work through picket lines will not be sufficient, although belief in an imminent attack would be justified if similar abuse had been followed, on previous occasions, by attacks on workers. It is not clear how the Australian women protesting against wartime rape would fare under Section 4 with their placards 'Patriots Kill' and 'Heroes Rape': it would be for the court to decide whether these words were insulting and liable to provoke violence from those present at the time. By 'court' is meant the local magistrates: Section 4, like most public-order offences, carries no right to jury trial. For all our rhetoric about the jury as guardian of liberty, successive Governments have been careful to avoid having to submit fundamental free-speech issues to juries. Magistrates are assumed, with some reason, to be more likely to convict. Yet the question of whether we should tolerate a protest which causes deep offence and anger to those remembering the war would be more acceptably decided by a jury rather than a lawyer-magistrate or a group of lay justices.

Section 5 of the 1986 Public Order Act contains a catch-all offence of using threatening, abusive, insulting words or behaviour, 'within the hearing or sight of a person likely to be caused harassment, alarm or distress by the above conduct'. This minor offence of 'disorderly behaviour' carries a maximum fine of £1,000, and police can only arrest after having first given a warning to desist which has not been heeded. If there are no civilians present, a police officer may consult his own feelings in the matter: if he reasonably suspects himself of being harassed or alarmed or distressed, then he has the power to arrest his tormentor. He must consider himself carefully; the Divisional Court accepts that 'very frequently, words and behaviour with which police officers will be wearily familiar will have little emotional impact on them save that of boredom'.[47] This new offence was introduced in 1986 ostensibly to give the police power to deal with hooliganism and rowdy late-night behaviour, but the notion of 'disorderly behaviour' is so elastic that police could use it to victimize people in the community who cause alarm and distress by acting differently rather than dangerously. The wide words of the statute make it applicable to many peaceful protests, especially those with banners and placards which abuse Governments and politicians and employers, and cause distress to bystanders with different political perspectives. 'Distress' is a weak and weasel word: a lot of art and literature, and speeches at political meetings, are designed to distress those responsible for or indifferent to injustice or poverty or oppression. The Crown Prosecution Service covered itself with ridicule during the 1987 general election by its unsuccessful attempt to use Section 5 against students displaying a satirical poster depicting Mrs Thatcher as a sadistic sexual dominatrix.

It is a defence under Section 5 'for the accused to prove that his conduct was reasonable' – which can lead to some interesting, if long-winded, political exercises in magistrates' courts. Could Greenham women argue that the horror of nuclear Armageddon makes a disorderly or abusive protest against cruise missiles entirely reasonable? Once again it will be magistrates rather than juries who decide, applying an objective test (i.e. what *they* think is reasonable). When anti-Vietnam demonstrators set a match to an American flag in Grosvenor Square in 1969, they were convicted of the crime of 'insulting behaviour' – on the basis, according to the Marlborough Street magistrate, that it would distress American tourists. Yet that very same action for the very same reason, if it were committed outside the White House in Washington, would under American law be a form of symbolic speech, protected by the First Amendment. In the words of the Supreme Court in a flag-burning case, 'We are unable to sustain a conviction that may have rested on a form of expression, however distasteful, which the constitution tolerates and protects.'

Section 5 has recently been tested in relation to the picketing of licensed abortion clinics by protestors displaying photographs of aborted foetuses to the obvious and intended distress of women attending the clinics. The prosecution failed to convince the court either that the placards were 'insulting' or that the defendants, blinded by their religious zealotry, knew or were aware that the placards might be 'insulting'.[48] A further charge under Section 7 of the Conspiracy and Protection of Property Act was also dismissed: the pickets were 'watching and besetting' the clinic, but with a view to dissuading, rather than compelling, its doctors and nurses to desist from lawfully terminating pregnancies. The callousness of anti-abortionists who redeploy the tactics of anti-Vietnam demonstrators may make liberal blood boil, but the right to protest claimed by a political cause cannot be denied to others who are acting from conscientious motives. The only difference in principle which may emerge is that anti-abortionists who confront patients (rather than doctors or nurses) with curses and condemnations are infringing their right to privacy, at a time when that right is most deserving of respect. Because that 'right' has no legal substance in the UK and there is no likelihood that the victims will be provoked to breach the peace, police have no powers to protect them, provided their passage is not physically obstructed. One useful reform would be to provide that the 1875 Act offence of 'watching and besetting' is committed if the intention is to invade unreasonably the privacy of any person. This would give citizens some relief in their homes and hospital rooms against harassment, whether by protestors or by journalists.

THE LIMITS OF POLICING PROTESTS

All large demonstrations have a potential for violent disorder; much will depend upon police strategies and capacities for avoiding provocation and defusing anger at any necessary arrests. When riots ensue, right-wing newspapers and politicians tend to blame anarchist infiltration of the crowd, while their left-wing counterparts argue that social deprivation and legitimate grievances have erupted spontaneously in response to police aggression. There is a mass of sociological literature seeking common themes in British mob behaviour, from the seditionists of George III's time to the football hooligans two centuries later. The most satisfactory accounts, however, are judicial inquiries into the causes of specific riots, notably Lord Scarman's analysis of Red Lion Square (1974) and Brixton (1981), and Lord Taylor's report on the Hillsborough disaster. These have been moderately critical of police behaviour, and have led to changes in tactics which have reasonably reduced public-order problems in the context of counter-demonstrations, inner-city racial tensions and soccer crowds. The Taylor reforms gave police some special powers exercisable at football matches, but otherwise these reports urged greater restraints and discretion in the use of existing crowd-control mechanisms. The British public has not had the benefit of a judicial inquiry into disorders exacerbated by officially sanctioned police aggression, such as Orgreave, Wapping and 'The Battle of Trafalgar Square', so that recent developments in crowd-dispersal techniques and weapons have not – perhaps deliberately – been subject to independent public scrutiny. The ghost of Blair Peach, the schoolteacher killed in 1979 by a policeman in the course of a rampaging baton charge against demonstrators, haunts because the crime was covered up at every level: the Government refused a judicial inquiry, the courts refused to order the police to produce evidence at the inquest, the policemen who knew the culprit refused to give evidence against him and the Metropolitan Police Commissioner paid a large sum in damages to the murdered man's family to stop their civil action coming to an embarrassing public trial. The operational principles upon which police believe themselves justified in using potentially lethal force are kept as secret as possible.

The overriding legal principle is stated in Section 3 of the Criminal Law Act 1967:

A person may use such force as is reasonable in the circumstances for the prevention of crime, in effecting or assisting in the arrest of offenders or persons unlawfully at large.

The preconditions for the use of lawful violence are the apprehension of crime and the application of no more force than is reasonable in the circumstances to combat it. The first condition is hardly satisfied by the existence of a demonstration – the force which is justified to clear a passage through it would, in peaceful circumstances, be no more than pushes and shoves – and intelligence reports about lurking anarchists do not justify aggressive dispersal operations unless and until there are attacks from the crowd. This condition was frequently breached at Wapping, where baton charges and mounted police advances were inflicted on angry but non-violent protest groups. The second condition is breached where riot police pursue fleeing demonstrators to belabour them with shields and truncheons – as seen on television during the miners' strike and some of the anti-poll-tax rallies, and as found by the Police Complaints Commission when it accused some officers of 'indiscriminate violence' at Wapping. These excesses are not capable of correction by the prosecution of individual officers, who are usually acquitted on technical grounds, or by civil actions which are 'bought off' by settlement (see earlier page 46). Individual miscreants will be interpreting orders or carrying out strategies which encourage the use of 'unreasonable force', and responsibility lies to some extent with the senior officers who have ordered offensive operations. Two common crowd-dispersal tactics are of doubtful legality: baton charges and orders to mounted police to advance into the crowd at a canter.

The police instructions for baton charges were exposed and condemned at the Orgreave riot trial. A secret Association of Police Chief Officers' 'Tactical Options Manual' revealed that teams of riot police armed with short shields and long truncheons would, on the command 'charge', run thirty yards into the crowd 'and *incapacitate* missile throwers and ringleaders by *striking in a controlled manner* with batons about the arms and legs and torsos so as not to cause serious injury'. This amounts to an unlawful incitement to assault, given that the adrenalin set running on the charge makes the notion of 'controlled striking' a contradiction in terms, the prospect of accurately identifying 'missile throwers' and 'ringleaders' a hopeless hope, and the risk of causing serious injury while 'incapacitating' very substantial indeed (as in the case of Blair Peach). A charge by mounted police, instructed to ride towards the crowd 'in a way indicating they do not intend to stop' may trample people underfoot or cause panic and hysteria. These tactics are indiscriminate and inevitably inflict unbridled violence on many protestors who have committed no criminal offence other than possible obstruction of the highway. Psychological studies suggest that during those manoeuvres police are, literally, 'out of control' – the pent-up frustration of stationary duty is followed by a release of inhibition and an actual pleasure in the adrenalin rush of 'sanctioned violence'.[49]

When crowds do riot, there are safer ways to disperse them. Ironically, the least dangerous method, by using water cannon which drenches and dyes without injury, has been rejected by the Home Office on grounds of expense. It is cheaper to use the more noxious CS gas (which causes coughing and nausea) and cheaper still to use plastic bullets (which incapacitate, occasionally by killing). These are weapons of last resort, which Lord Scarman recommended should only be used in 'grave emergencies', where lives may otherwise be lost, and only by personal order of the chief constable. He was critical of public use of CS gas during the Brixton disturbances, but the Home Secretary would only promise to confine future use to 'situations of serious public disorder'. In 1986 the Home Office offered to supply chief constables direct from the central store if their local police authorities withheld approval for purchasing CS gas and plastic bullets. The Court of Appeal rejected an application by a Labour-controlled police authority to stop the Home Office from going behind its back.[50] It ruled that the Government is entitled to supply police forces with any weapons appropriate for dealing with breaches of the peace, and the decision to use those weapons is entirely one for the chief constable, uncontrolled by court or local council. On these matters, local police authorities have no authority whatsoever. The question remains, who does? And by what rules are these weapons to be issued and authorized for use? The answers will no doubt be provided by a judicial inquiry into some future débâcle caused by paramilitary policing, which might not have occurred had the secret instructions now governing that style of policing been publicly revealed, debated and revised.

INCITEMENT TO RACIAL HATRED

There are few issues in the field of human rights that are more difficult to resolve than the head-on collision between the right to express unattractive ideas and the right to live free from racist vilification. In 1974 the US Civil Liberties Union lost a substantial proportion of its funds and many of its members by supporting the right of the American Nazi Party to march through the predominantly Jewish town of Skokie; ten years later the National Council of Civil Liberties in Britain was condemned by many of its most distinguished members when it took the opposite position by refusing to support the civil rights of a racist political party, the National Front. There is no easy answer to the dilemmas posed for a tolerant society by racial intolerance and the questions have become much harder for those European countries where race hatreds, previously contained by Communist regimes, have recently and violently erupted.

Freedom of expression entails the right to entertain ideas of any kind, and to express them publicly. The mode or the manner of the expression, however, may properly be regulated in the interests of the freedom of others to go about their business in public without being gratuitously assaulted or defamed, and may properly be curtailed in order to avoid public disorder which may follow provocative dissemination of racist ideas. This was the basis of the first anti-incitement laws, passed in Britain in 1965 after several years of racial violence of the most serious kind, by a Labour

Government whose commitment to freedom of speech was weakened after the infamous Smethwick by-election in which a Labour majority evaporated in the face of the slogan, 'If you want a nigger for a neighbour, vote Labour.'

This law has been amended on several occasions – the 1986 Public Order Act being the last – in an effort to make convictions easier to obtain. Nevertheless prosecutions, which can only be brought with the Attorney-General's consent, are rare, because of the counter-productive consequences of acquittals. There was only one prosecution in 1989 and another in 1990. In 1991 a Cheltenham Tory who described the black candidate foisted on the local constituency by Central Office as a 'nigger' was charged, but died before his trial. This prosecution was misconceived: the speaker had not been 'stirring up' racial hatred, he had been appealing to the racism of fellow party members in order to provoke them to resist the *diktat* of Central Office. (His racist views were dramatically, if more discreetly, endorsed by Cheltenham Tories who defected *en masse* at the 1992 General Election to deliver their safe Conservative seat to the white Liberal candidate.) The only prosecution to succeed in 1991 was of the Dowager Lady Birdwood, an obsessive anti-Semitic nuisance who sent her racist pamphlets to relatives of concentration camp victims. The judge sensibly declined to make her a martyr, and discharged her with an order to pay the costs of her prosecution. (The Government of Kenya, mildly criticized by Britain for use of torture and terror to silence its critics, issued a statement condemning the UK for thus denying 'an elderly political opponent' her right of free speech.) It will be more in keeping with free-speech standards to deal with the Dowager's ilk in future by way of the 1988 Malicious Communications Act, which creates the summary offence of sending grossly offensive or malicious threats or messages with the purpose of causing distress and anxiety to their particular recipient.

Section 18 of the Public Order Act makes it an offence to use threatening, abusive or insulting words or behaviour with the intent of stirring up racial hatred or in circumstances where racial hatred is likely to be stirred up. 'Racial hatred' means hatred against a group defined by colour, race or national origin, thereby including Jews, Sikhs and Romany gypsies, but excluding Zionists, Muslims and gypsies (and 'travellers' in general). The offence can now be committed by television companies (including the BBC) and programme producers, as well as by the person recorded making the incitement. This is a recent and undesirable change in the law, which means that television and radio programmes about racism must take care to ensure that the racists they interview say nothing to stir up racial hatred. The result will be to censor their more rabid and disgusting utterances and thereby to make them more attractive figures than if they were allowed to speak for themselves. Even if the producer's intention is to condemn racism, the objective prospect that the programme would excite some extremists would be sufficient for a conviction.

The offence can also be committed by the public performance of a play, although a drama's propensity to stir up racial hatred is to be judged with regard to all the circumstances and 'taking the performance as a whole'. Racist abuse heaped on Shylock and Othello by Shakespearian characters is therefore defensible, and there have been no prosecutions of stage plays. However, the Royal Court Theatre's cancellation of the play *Perdition* in 1987 after pressure from Jewish interests shows that the question may not be of entirely academic interest in the future.

Further potential for inhibiting free speech is contained in the offence of possessing racially inflammatory material with a view to its publication in circumstances where racial hatred is likely to be stirred up. Authors and journalists who collect such material in order to condemn it will not be at risk, but it might be argued that uncritical displays of Nazi memorabilia or unvarnished publications of *Hitler Diaries* and the like could revive old hatreds. The protection for books of genuine historic interest is provided, not by the words of the Act, but by the need to obtain the Attorney-General's consent to prosecution. It is unfortunate that Parliament did not make these sections of the Act subject to a defence that the play or the publication or collection was in the interests of drama, literature, history or other subjects of general concern.

When the offence of inciting racial hatred was first introduced it was severely criticized as a counter-productive attack on the right to free speech. Since then, it has been enlarged and stretched to what may be hoped will be its limit, although some want it further amended to catch racist ideas expressed without threat or insult or abuse. Has the advent of the crime helped or hindered race relations?

Few would assert that it has measurably diminished racism in British society, although it has provided a standard for condemning racist utterances. It has helped to stigmatize racists as persons involved in antisocial behaviour, and has been used to justify deployment of police resources in monitoring their organizations and plans. Although prosecutions have been few, the majority have been successful, because successive Attorney-Generals have adopted the policy of only prosecuting when there is a very strong case. Some of the most crude and hurtful racist utterances have been removed from the public domain, and the editor of a National Front comic for schoolchildren has been sent to prison. (Whatever view may be taken of the right of racists to put their doctrines on display in a free market-place of ideas, attempts to indoctrinate schoolchildren with specially tailored propaganda are less defensible on free-speech grounds.)

However, the incitement to racial hatred law in Britain has had a number of counter-productive consequences. It has changed the *style* of racist propaganda: by making it less blatantly bigoted, it has made it more respectable. As a Home Office review of the law pointed out:

Whilst this shift away from crudely racialist propaganda and abuse is welcome, it is not an unmixed benefit. The more apparently rational and moderate is the message, the greater is its probable impact on public opinion.[51]

There is no doubt that the law has a potential for punishing the expression of genuine political statements, albeit couched in crude or insulting terminology. This can apply particularly to activists from oppressed minorities, whose rhetoric is designed to jolt what they perceive as white complacency. In Britain the law was used, at least in its first decade of operation, more effectively against Black Power leaders than against white racists. The first person to be gaoled for a race-hatred offence was Michael X, convicted by a white jury in 1967 for some fairly routine black-consciousness rhetoric of the period.[52] Although prosecuting authorities have taken care to avoid creating martyrs, the publicity attendant upon acquittals has been counter-productive. When members of the Racial Preservation Society were acquitted for publishing a newspaper claimed to be 'innocently informative' rather than 'intentionally inflammatory', they derived benefit from the publicity surrounding the trial and reissued the edition, overprinted 'Souvenir Edition – the paper the Government tried to suppress'. There was an increase in this type of quasi-educational racist literature after the acquittal. Similarly, racists were encouraged by the acquittal of one National Front speaker who 'joked' in reference to the murder of an Asian immigrant, 'One down, one million to go.'

Laws against inciting racial hatred create more expectations than can be fulfilled by prosecution authorities anxious to avoid giving racist utterances the publicity of a trial and the endorsement of an acquittal. There is no objection in principle to prosecuting racist speeches or writings which either occasion a real threat of public disorder, or which are maliciously forced on citizens in public places or in their homes against their wishes in terms so gross as to cause serious affront or deliberate distress. In such cases, freedom of speech is not at stake: what is being prosecuted is not the idea behind the utterance, but the occasion chosen for making it. Suggestions that the law should go further, by punishing opinions which favour discrimination, would make too great an inroad on the principle of freedom of expression. Once protection is denied to one socially unacceptable belief it can be denied to others: sexism, communism, anarchism or whatever. Any abuse is hurtful, whether on grounds of race, sex, religion or physical or mental handicap: racism is a special case because of its particular propensity to cause public disorder, but a law which does not confine its operation to that particular mischief offers a cure which may well serve only to promote the disease.

OFFENSIVE WORDS

Protests are usually collective expressions of anger and outrage, and individual protesters may give vent to their feelings in unrestrained language and offensive slogans. They can fall foul of various laws against public indecency, which courts in Britain will judge according to the circumstances of the utterance rather than by the high-flown jurisprudential principles deployed in the USA to decide, for example, that a 'Fuck the Draft' badge enjoyed constitutional protection. The leading case on bad political language is *Wiggins* v.

Field, which arose from a public reading of Allen Ginsberg's poem *America*, including the line 'Go fuck yourself with your atom bomb'. The reader was charged with using 'indecent language' in contravention of a local by-law, but the Divisional Court said that the case ought never to have been brought.

Whether a word or phrase was capable of being treated as indecent language depended on all the circumstances of the case, the occasion, when, how and in the course of what it was spoken and perhaps to a certain extent what the intention was.[53]

It decided that in the work of a recognized poet, read without any intention of causing offence, the word 'fuck' could not be character-ized as 'indecent'. The same robust attitude was expressed by the court in quashing a doctor's conviction for using indecent language when he described workmen as 'a pair of stupid bastards' for making a noise outside his surgery. 'It is quite impossible to say that the word in this context was indecent.'[54]

A message will be 'indecent' if it outrages the sensibilities of reasonable people – a quality which it is not always easy for prosecutors to prove beyond reasonable doubt. Slogans on T-shirts have come in for some attention: the arguably political (or at least defiantly apolitical) message 'Fuck Art, Let's Dance' has been acquit-ted, but the more commercial message, on a T-shirt issued by Stiff Records, 'If it ain't stiff it ain't worth a fuck', resulted in a conviction. In 1977, Virgin Records, promoters of an album entitled 'Never Mind the Bollocks, here's the Sex Pistols' were acquitted of indecent advertising, after the court heard evidence from a professor of English who traced the etymology of the word 'bollocks' from its original meaning of 'testicles' to its modern connotation of 'rubbish'. The turning-point apparently came with the King James edition of the Bible, which had replaced 'bollocks', used in the original sense in earlier editions, with the word 'stones'. The acquit-tal relieved the promoters from retitling their album 'Never Mind the Stones, here's the Sex Pistols'.

The place of the protest can make all the difference. In 1966 a group of anti-Vietnam protesters interrupted a church lesson being read by the Foreign Secretary, Mr George Brown, with cries of 'Oh you hypocrite. How can you use the word of God to justify your policies?' The Divisional Court upheld their conviction for indecent behaviour, on the grounds that 'an act done in a church during divine service might be highly indecent and improper, which would not be so at another time'.[55] This principle is unexceptionable, although it may be doubted whether the court applied it correctly in the actual case, which arose from a church service at a Labour Party conference where Government ministers were ostentatiously displaying their piety for the benefit of television cameras. Lord Soper, a defence witness, testified to 'the tradition of vigorous disputation in Methodist churches', and it would be unfortunate if politicians or partisan clerics could be protected from reasonable interjections by delivering their messages in a church. Normally, of course, religious feelings do deserve special protection when they are being solemnly celebrated in places of public worship, and public-order laws have been used, for example, to punish racists who intruded a pig into a Muslim mosque. A range of arcane laws punish disturbers of 'decent and quiet devotions' and those guilty of 'riotous or indecent behaviour in church precincts', 'molesting vexing or misusing preachers' and 'unauthorized addresses at the graveside' (Hamlet and Laertes would face two years' imprisonment under the Burial Laws Amendment Act 1880).[56] These laws are all justifiable when used to punish the deliberate disturbance of religious devotions, although the rise of political evangelism in the USA underlines the need for some protection for peaceful protest on occasions that are more political than religious.

BROADCASTING BANS

In October 1988 the Government used its powers over radio and television broadcasting to order that no interviews should be transmitted with representatives of Sinn Fein and other Irish organizations which have supported the political use of violence, nor should statements which incite support for such organizations. This is the first peacetime prohibition on public statements by or about lawful organizations, and it serves as a clear example of how the IRA has succeeded in diminishing liberties traditionally enjoyed in Britain. The ban applies to interviews with elected local councillors (of whom Sinn Fein has sixty) and with Sinn Fein MPs as well as with persons who manifest support for Sinn Fein or the Ulster Defence Association. It does not apply to candidates at election times, or to parliamentary broadcasts, but it operates to prevent any representative of these organizations from being heard on the electronic media discussing local political issues far removed from terrorism, such as voting intentions on rate increases or measures to prevent dogs from fouling the pavements. It prevents the broadcast media from using direct quotations as part of an analysis (even a historical analysis) of such organizations, and it prevents the public from hearing representatives cross-examined about any aspect of their policies. It is a measure of direct political censorship, denying the air waves to specific organizations whose policies, however unattractive, none the less command some support in Northern Ireland.

The Home Secretary's reasons for imposing the ban were that such interviews caused outrage to many viewers, and gave 'a spurious authority and respectability' to interviewees. These reasons are, of course, self-contradictory: viewers who are offended are unlikely to respect the person causing them offence. The philosophy of a free market-place of ideas which underpins the 'freedom of expression' guarantee in the European Convention is based on the principle that citizens should be entitled to judge for themselves the odiousness of politicians and their platforms, and the great value of television interviews is that it enables this judgement to be made by seeing and hearing representatives under a form of cross-examination. (A *World in Action* programme prior to the ban severely dented the credibility of Gerry Adams precisely because it was able to put him under interrogation.) The very fact that up to 100,000 people in Northern Ireland vote for Sinn Fein at local elections makes its representatives and their policies a matter of public interest in the United Kingdom, however 'offensive' such interviews may be to the Government (the evidence suggests that viewers, on the whole, are not offended by the fact that such interviews have been screened in the past). The ban operates a political censorship which is unnecessary and unjustifiable in a democratic society. Citizens are entitled to form and promote organizations which are not conspiracies to break the law, and it makes no sense for Governments to deny them one outlet for expressing their opinions merely because the power to shut off that outlet exists fortuitously in the law which regulates broadcasting. One of the first casualties of the ban was a song recorded by an Irish pop group The Pogues, with lyrics claiming that the Guildford Four were innocent. The Independent Broadcasting Authority refused to allow the record to be played on radio or television, even after the Court of Appeal had declared that the Guildford Four *were* innocent.

ELECTIONEERING

In a democracy, elections should be the time at which protest is most valued. Ironically, it is at this very time that public confrontation of candidates is most tightly constrained. Under section 75 of the Representation of the People Act 1983, it is a criminal offence for persons not authorized by election agents (who are appointed by political parties) to incur any expense exceeding £5 by holding meetings or distributing leaflets 'with a view to promoting or procuring the election of a candidate'. The courts have given this law the widest possible interpretation, making it an offence for CND, the Society for the Protection of Unborn Children, anti-hunting groups and the like to supply electors with information about candidates' voting records or intentions on these moral issues.

Section 75 is an anachronism. In origin, it was an important measure for establishing a 'level playing-field' in local elections, setting limits on expenses by candidates and their supporters and preventing corrupt vote-buying practices in days before the advent of radio and television and mass-media political campaigning. Now that general elections are largely fought at a national level, with funds totalling many millions supplied without limit to the major parties by companies and trade unions and corporate criminals, it seems absurd to stop pressure groups from trying to make their concerns a matter of constituency interest, especially where they seek to raise moral issues on which candidates, if elected, will have a conscience vote. The current position is both undemocratic and an infringement of the right to freedom of expression.

CHAPTER 3

Privacy

The right to privacy has many applications: it can mean freedom from snoopers, gossips and busybodies; or being treated by state officials with a measure of decency and dignity; or being entitled to indulge in harmless activities without observation or interference. At base, it is a right to be left alone, to be able to live some part of life behind a door marked 'do not disturb'. The guarantee in Article 8 of the European Convention of Human Rights, that 'Everyone has the right to respect for his private and family life, his home and his correspondence' reflects both the individual's psychological need to preserve an intrusion-free zone of personality and family, and the anguish and stress which can be suffered when that zone is violated. We shall see that the fond boast that 'an Englishman's home is his castle' needs revision in an age when the battlements are defenceless against electronic surveillance devices, journalists have no difficulty getting their foot in the drawbridge, and several hundred different kinds of officials are endowed by law with power to walk on the water of the moat.

The most glaring deficiency in English law is its systemic failure to protect the privacy of its citizens. That failure reflects the nature of a society both prurient and prudish, where the newspapers which are most despised for invading private lives are at the same time the most popular. No other nation in the world could experience a year – 1992 – in which the matters of consuming public interest were:

- the leader of a political party 'exposed' for a short affair with his secretary, five years before, with evidence stolen from his solicitor's office and handled by a national newspaper;
- a Government minister forced to resign after evidence of his affair with an actress, consisting of telephone conversations

secretly taped by a newspaper after payment of £45,000 to the actress's landlord, was published in excruciating detail;

- the Princess of Wales's intimate car-phone conversation, intercepted by an amateur snooper and sold to a newspaper, both published and (for a short time) played on a British Telecom 'entertainment line';
- photographs of the Duchess of York bathing topless on a French beach, surreptitiously taken from a distance through telephoto lenses, featuring on the front pages of every tabloid newspaper.

By 1993, attention had turned to 'Camillagate' – another intercepted telephone conversation, although whether it had been intercepted by MI5 or MI6 or GCHQ or the CIA or any of the thousands of nosey parkers whose hobby is to scan and record private conversations was anyone's guess. Some may regard royalty and politicians as fair game, but many 'ordinary' victims suffered in comparative silence. The Duchess sued her telephoto tormentor under French law and received £75,000 in damages – her own country offered her no redress. It is ironic that the editors of British newspapers who devote so much space to condemning human-rights violations in other countries are incapable of recognizing that privacy is also a fundamental human right. By their obsessive opposition to enactment of any law to protect privacy, they join the ranks of those who violate human rights in Britain.

The deficiency in English law was well illustrated in 1991 by the behaviour of a journalist and photographer from the *Sunday Sport* who sneaked into the intensive-care hospital room of *'Allo, 'Allo* star Gordon Kaye, as he was coming round after brain surgery.[1] They photographed him and recorded his ramblings for publication as a 'world exclusive' scoop. The actor's family failed to stop the publication: they had no remedy in libel, or even in trespass (the entry was not unlawful) and the best that sympathetic judges could do was to grant a limited injunction preventing the newspaper from pretending that the actor had consented. The judges all lamented their inability to give a satisfactory remedy for this 'monstrous invasion of privacy'. In America, judges have fashioned such remedies from the plasticine of the common law, and it might still be possible to build on 'breach of confidence' precedents here to erect a protected zone of privacy around bedrooms – in private houses as well as hospitals. However, since our judges have resisted such creative lawyering, reform must be left in the unsafe hands of Parliament. A Government elected with the support of the tabloid press is unlikely to act so as to damage its circulation. By 1993 back-bench MPs from all parties were convinced that 'something must be done' about invasions of privacy, although there was little consensus on what it should be. The Lord Chancellor's Department produced a splendid 'consultation paper' outlining a new civil wrong whereby a victim could sue over the infliction of substantial distress by harassment or invasion of rights to keep health, family and personal relationships private, subject to a broad public-interest defence. Reform of this kind is advocated later in this chapter, and in earlier editions of this book: indeed, legislation to secure it has been introduced regularly, by way of Private Member's Bills, over the past thirty years. There must come a time when 'consultation' has to stop, and British citizens are given the same rights to privacy protection enjoyed in other European countries, and throughout most of the civilized world.

EAVESDROPPING

The first recorded protection for personal privacy is a 1360 statute, still in force today, which provides that

> such as listen under walls or windows, or the eaves of a house, to hearken unto discourse, and thereupon to frame slanderous and mischievous tales, are a common nuisance, and are punishable by finding sureties for their good behaviour.

It is occasionally invoked to deal with those who install bugging devices in their neighbours' bedrooms, although a bind-over to keep the peace is hardly a satisfactory punishment for perverts whose activities have caused their neighbours to suffer nervous breakdowns. The absence of any modern statute incriminating prurient or malicious invasion of privacy makes Britain something of a haven for the peeping or listening Tom with access to infinity bugs (which pick up any conversation in a room), metallic contact bugs which can tap any telephone, stethoscope microphones which listen through walls, directional microphones which pick up conversations at fifty paces, infra-red cameras which see in the dark, microwave antennae which pick up and translate vibrations on window panes, and so on. These devices have been on open sale for many years, through specialist shops or mail-order advertisements in *Exchange & Mart*. In 1993 DIY bugging kits, which can pick up conversations a quarter of a mile away, were selling for £4.99, while at the other end of the market scanners which could track and record any mobile phone in the country were on offer for £7,000. The cash-strapped Russian Government was exporting night-vision goggles previously issued to its fighter pilots for sale at £345 to customers in Britain eager to study the nocturnal activities of their neighbours.

There is no law against the use of surreptitious surveillance devices, whether for fun or for profit, unless the device uses wires to intercept messages or to transmit electronically in a way that might interfere with a radio channel, in which case a minor offence will be committed against the Wireless Telegraphy Act 1949. In 1985 it was made an offence to intercept a telephone conversation without a Home Secretary's warrant, although the Interception of Communications Act does not cover bugging and other forms of surveillance which are used far more frequently than intercepts to monitor electronic communications. Thus Mr David Mellor's conversations with his actress girlfriend were lawfully intercepted by a sophisticated bugging device attached to the telephone in the flat where she had been generously allowed to live by a landlord who gave the *People* permission to install the device for a much larger sum than he could have obtained in rent. Princess Diana's conversation was taped by a retired bank manager, Cyril Reenan, whose hobby was eavesdropping on other people's conversations with the assistance of a £1,000 radio scanner linked to a twenty-foot aerial in his garden. (He insisted he did not want to hurt the royal family, so he delivered the tapes to the *Sun* for safekeeping.)

The general legal principle is that everything is permitted which is not expressly prohibited, as Lord Bernstein discovered when he failed to stop aerial photography of his home.[2] The court did say that harassment by constant aerial surveillance and photographing of the plaintiff's every movement would be 'such a monstrous invasion of his privacy' that it might award damages for the tort of nuisance, but there is no law which deters surveillance by telephoto cameras and wireless listening devices which do not involve any trespass on private land. Most civilized countries have such laws, and a series of official reports from the Younger Committee on Privacy in 1972[3] to the Law Commission in 1981[4] and the Calcutt Reports of 1990 and 1993[5] have recommended criminal prohibitions against obtaining information and photographs by improper use of secret surveillance devices. But we still have no real deterrent against those who spy for prurience, profit or politics. The shadowy hypothetical presence of the electronic eavesdropper has made 'de-bugging' a growth industry – many company boardrooms are now swept not only by cleaners, but by counter-espionage experts.

The professional privacy-invader, the private detective, operates lucratively in an area where law is either non-existent or inadequate to deter abuse. Individuals cannot complain if they are profiled from public sources or observed going about their business, but many private investigators – of whom there are 10,000 employed in the UK – have no difficulty tapping into the Police National Computer, the DVLC, and repositories of confidential information in DHSS and other Government departments. If money is paid for the information then offences of corruption are committed, but many private detectives offer the service to clients none the less. Some private detectives have criminal convictions, and others are ex-police officers who resigned under a cloud, but there is no agency empowered to license, regulate or discipline them. While the Government is understandably reluctant to issue 'licences' which could easily be misrepresented to gullible members of the public as official sanction for requests to snoop, most Western countries have found ways to contain the behaviour of private detectives by regulatory authorities which can discipline or expel those whose conduct or methods involve unacceptable invasions of privacy. Such an agency would not, of course, be able to stop practices which are permitted by law: the use of lie detectors and 'psychological stress evaluations' to screen candidates for employment, for example, or the circulation amongst employers of 'blacklists' of persons with records of trade-union activism. One private organization, the Economic League, supplied information on 'left-wingers' in trade unions to over 2,000 employers who subscribed for many years to its blacklist services. The failure of British law to develop any general right to privacy has allowed these practices to grow without any check.

In the United States, the courts have moulded the common law so as to award damages whenever a person's interest in seclusion, or in personal dignity and self-respect, or in being free from emotional upset, is interfered with by conduct which is regarded as intolerably antisocial. They have awarded damages in the following situations: installing tape recorders secretly in hospital wards in order to hear the account given by the victim of an accident to her relatives; publishing lurid photographs of the victim of a car accident; publishing X-ray photographs of the deformed pelvis of a woman celebrity; photographing the body of the plaintiff's dead husband; photographing a mother's Siamese twins and publishing the picture. As the Gordon Kaye case demonstrates, in none of these situations would the English courts be likely to afford any remedy to the victim.

Private information which is accurate may be circulated and published without any redress, unless it involves a breach of copyright (e.g. by the publication of family photographs without payment or permission) or a breach of confidence. The scope of this action is unclear: the few cases decided in relation to domestic confidences have mainly been brought by members of the royal family (who succeed) and pop stars (who fail). Thus the Duchess of Argyll was able to stop the Duke from publishing sordid details of their marriage,[6] and the Prince of Wales obtained an injunction against the publication of purported tape recordings of premarital and long-distance conversations with Lady Diana, but John Lennon,[7] Tom Jones,[8] and Soraya Kashoggi[9] all failed to ban stories of their marital and extramarital dalliances. No sensible distinction has emerged from those cases between public interest and public prurience, with the result that 'kiss and tell' stories are now staple fare of Sunday newspapers. The pop stars, politicians, churchmen, television personalities and sports stars, the details of whose sexual performances are sold by erstwhile partners (or by thieves or buggers) to the *News of the World*, must suffer in silence, victims of a new form of blackmail. Indeed, the crime of blackmail has largely become redundant with the rise of Rupert Murdoch: those possessed of sordid secrets about celebrities now offer them lawfully to newspapers for much larger sums of money.

This is just one of the disquieting developments as entrepreneurs take commercial advantage of the lack of any real remedy for breach of privacy. The courts are reluctant to act against them, on the principle that 'England is not a country where everything is forbidden except what is expressly permitted'.[10] There have been occasional and very weak legislative initiatives against a few abuses – the Rehabilitation of Offenders Act withdraws protection from libel actions in the case of malicious publication of truthful details about very old criminal offences, and the Unsolicited Goods and Services Act makes it a criminal offence to send brochures describing or illustrating human sexual techniques to unsuspecting households, but successive Governments have consigned recommendations for more fundamental law reform to the 'too hard' basket. The courts have granted injunctions to stop publication of confidential material (such as Myra Hindley's application for parole and jockey John Francome's tapped telephone conversations) when the information is of minimal public importance and has been obtained by illegal methods, but have refused to create a more general tort of invasion of privacy.[11] There is also the possibility of victims of invasion of privacy suing for wilful infliction of physical harm, if the nervous shock occasioned by the invasion was foreseeable and has caused long-term suffering.[12] It would take courage, however, for victims to relive the trauma by bringing test cases, and the results, as the law now stands, may not be worth the effort. When one plaintiff successfully sued his neighbour for trespassing in his house to install a bugging device (so that his bedroom conversation could be 'listened to and chuckled and chortled over'), the court awarded damages of only £52.[13]

The real problem is that English law is far more attuned to property rights than to human rights. Unless victims can demonstrate damage to physical property, e.g. by trespass or by theft of private papers, their prospects of recovery are slim. Press opposition to a privacy law is justified only to the extent that it may threaten revelations of real public interest: the fact that America has the most free press in the world, as well as privacy laws, is a simple refutation of this argument. The best way forward would be to reform the laws which shackle the British media in other respects (see Chapters 5 and 6) as the price for inhibiting their present freedom to invade privacy. That is not the solution which is likely to be adopted. The Calcutt Commission recommended criminal offences to punish journalists who enter private property uninvited or photograph individuals on private land, but this prosecutional approach is misconceived and would give police unparalleled powers to arrest reporters and camera crews as they go about their proper business investigating crooks and con-merchants. Law should not be used to jail those who seek the truth, nor should it be used proactively to suppress publication of the truth. It can, however, usefully work to deter publication of unimportant private truths if it provides an effective remedy for victims of invasion of privacy. An effective remedy – the right to bring a civil action, legally aided where appropriate, and to obtain compensation and damages – is precisely what English law does not, at present, offer. The Press Complaints Commission is a hollow pretence and its 'code of conduct' is no longer publicly acceptable as a privacy safeguard. If, however, that code were made the basis of a statutory tort, so that any breach of it that could not be justified on public-interest grounds would render the newspaper liable in damages, a significant advance would be made in the protection of human rights in the United Kingdom.

THE PRESS COMPLAINTS COMMISSION

The British newspaper industry not only deploys its editorial space to campaign against a privacy law, it has established a sophisticated public-relations exercise called the Press Complaints Commission (PCC), with an annual budget of £1 million, to convince Parliament that its ethics are susceptible to what it optimistically describes as 'self-regulation'. But the PCC is a confidence trick which has failed to inspire confidence, and forty years' experience of 'press self-regulation' demonstrates only that the very concept is an oxymoron. The worst feature of the failure of this voluntary tribunal is that it encourages the thought that it might succeed if turned into a statutory quango like the Broadcasting Complaints Commission (see p. 295) with Government appointees empowered to issue injunctions and to punish newspapers for misbehaviour. This was foreshadowed by the Calcutt Commission in 1990, and was the objective of a Bill which attracted wide cross-bench support in 1993. What the British press has so signally failed to understand is that its freedom to serve the public interest would be better secured if privacy were protected by law rather than by systems which depend either on self-restraint (which is unworkable) or on extra-legal and unappealable powers wielded by Government-appointed quangos.

The newspaper industry first decided that it needed to insure against the advent of privacy laws and statutory regulation in 1953, when it established the Press Council to set ethical standards and receive complaints from the public. The Council's performance was severely criticized by the Royal Commission on the press in 1977, which found 'flagrant breaches of acceptable standards' and 'inexcusable intrusions into privacy'. The Council responded by speaking out more loudly against the harassment and chequebook journalism which took place after the arrest of the 'Yorkshire Ripper',[14] but a study of its work published in 1983 revealed that even successful complainants were overwhelmingly critical of the services it offered.[15] Its principles were confused and inconsistently applied, rulings were not respected and it did not work to improve the ethical standards of the British press. This was also the conclusion of the Calcutt Committee in 1990 which recommended its replacement by a smaller and more expert body called a Press Complaints Commission which would adjudicate complaints speedily and more effectively. If the PCC did not succeed as a voluntary body, Calcutt recommended that it should be replaced by a tribunal chaired by a judge, with statutory powers to order publication of corrections and apologies and to award compensation to victims of press abuse. Newspaper proprietors took this threat seriously, and established the PCC in 1991. It comprises a number of editors (two of them from the tabloid press) and several distinguished lay persons. Its rulings to date have done nothing to improve press standards: if anything they became worse during the circulation wars of 1992, as hysteria mounted over the break-up of royal marriages and the sexual behaviour of leading politicians.

The PCC pretends to police a 'code' which proclaims that intrusions into private life without consent 'are not generally acceptable' unless justified on public-interest grounds. Such grounds are limited to detecting or exposing 'crime or serious misdemeanour or seriously antisocial conduct' or protecting the public health or safety or preventing the public from being misled by the target of the intrusion. It cannot be contended that adultery or homosexuality or run-of-the-mill heterosexual behaviour amounts to 'seriously antisocial conduct', although such revelations have remained the stock-in-trade of the tabloid press.

One of the PCC's first adjudications, designed especially to impress Members of Parliament, was to condemn *News of the World* editor Patsy Chapman (one of its own members and chair of the committee that drafted its code of conduct) for her vendetta against Clare Short, MP. The newspaper had decided to punish the MP for attacking its 'page 3' sexism by trying to dig for dirt on her private life, and found a suitable bedfellow in the police from the crooked West Midlands Serious Crimes Squad (also attacked by Short, for fitting up suspects), who supplied details of a man with whom the MP had a close friendship twenty years before. The newspaper also offered money to Ms Short's ex-husband (who had been in and out of psychiatric institutions since their marriage break-up twelve years previously) for any 'revealing' pictures of the MP. Neither the newspaper nor its editor bothered to apologize after the adjudication, publishing it in small print on page 8 ('despite it being the longest we've ever seen') alongside a picture and the original headline: 'Flashback: The *News of the World* story which led to the right to privacy case.'

Before long, the PCC was forced to condemn the conduct of another of its members, the homophobic editor of the *Daily Star*, for encouraging the persecution of homosexuals by a front-page story about the army under the heading 'Poofters on Parade' and attacking gay-rights groups as 'strident mincing preachers of filth'. The editor had continued the vilification (which was based on incorrect facts) in his own column.

In 1991, the PCC condemned the *People* for publishing a secretly taken picture of the Duke of York's baby daughter frolicking naked in the garden, whereupon the newspaper republished the picture together with a picture of the naked Duke of York, and invited its readers to participate in a telephone poll over whether the pictures were offensive. In other words, the PCC's privacy judgements were counterproductive because newpapers only seized the opportunity to repeat the offence. This was precisely the reason why the Press Council did more harm than good: when it condemned the *Sun* for taking telephoto pictures of a pregnant Princess Diana on a private beach, the *Sun* made a grandiose apology. To illustrate the apology it reprinted the pictures, under the banner headline: 'THIS IS WHAT THE ROW'S ALL ABOUT FOLKS!' Then it proceeded to illustrate the genuineness of its concern for royal privacy by selling the pictures to newspapers around the world.

Royalty is a bizarre institution, and there is not much to choose between contempt for a press which affords it no privacy and a press which, before the war, loyally refused for months to tell its readers about the constitutional crisis developing over King Edward's relationship with the divorced Mrs Simpson. Of much more concern is media behaviour towards ordinary citizens, especially when they are struck by exceptional grief or tragedy. When the daughter of a vicar at Ealing was brutally gang-raped, the *Sun* published her picture, taken as she was leaving church the next Sunday, over three full columns on its front page. The thin black line marking her eyes left no doubt as to her identity and the additional ordeal was deeply distressing. The *Sun*, however, showed no remorse. Its managing editor told the Press Council that the picture was published to highlight the victim's 'ordinary-girl-next-door qualities'.[16] (It was doubtless this managing editor's capacity for humbug which secured his appointment as the *Sun*'s ombudsman, dealing with complaints from its readers.)

The press may have little sympathy for victims of crime, but even more worrying are the occasions when it provides financial support for criminals and those who break confidences in order to obtain money rather than to expose a genuine scandal. The Press Council would occasionally (and to no avail) condemn 'chequebook journalism' and 'stories sold on the back of crime', but the PCC has no provision in its Code relating to payments to sleazy informants, jilted lovers and other familiar sources of kiss-and-tell stories. There is often no public-interest justification for such tales, and on occasion the tabloid press has paid large sums of money to drug addicts and prostitutes in order to tell them. It is ironic that the people who would be prosecuted for the serious crime of blackmail if they threatened their victim with public exposure unless they were paid a sum of money can now obtain that sum quite legally by taking their story direct to a newspaper. It has been suggested that newspapers that purchase sensational stories of this sort should be required to disclose the amount of the payment when publishing them: this would serve to alert their readers to the possibility that the sensation in the story may be related to the sensation of receiving a large amount of money for telling it.

Of course, the scope of private matters which do not bear on public performance is necessarily limited: the hypocrite who preaches a return to Victorian values whilst committing adultery, the left-wing politician who takes advantage of private medical treatment, the bankrupt financier who lives it up in casinos and the dowager who charters an airliner to fly her pet dogs to a tax haven are all fair game. Social butterflies can hardly complain if their activities provoke gossip – there is a difference between snooping and recording the obvious. What powerful people do with their money or their credit is always a matter for the public domain, although what they do to each other in the privacy of their own houses deserves some veil of secrecy.

The PCC will continue to operate unsatisfactorily to protect citizens from press intrusions into their private lives, simply because it has no legal power to deter competing newspapers from publishing circulation-boosting stories. The Advertising Standards Authority – also a voluntary body – works because its rulings are backed by the threat that an expensive advertising campaign will have to be abandoned if it flouts the ASA's code. The PCC might begin to function effectively if it were provided with contractual powers to oblige newspapers to publish its adjudications with front-page prominence and to award compensation to victims, but the newspaper industry has balked at giving this public-relations exercise any real teeth. In consequence, it will continue to face demands for criminal trespass laws and statutory tribunals – cures which could well prove to be worse than the disease. The only reasonable and feasible alternative is a legal right to privacy, enforceable in courts required to pay attention to the public interest but empowered to award damages to victims for the distress they have suffered in cases where that interest cannot justify the violation of their privacy.

The PCC has also failed to raise the tone or the profile of debate over media ethics. Its adjudications are short and usually oversimple, reflecting on editors who do not appear discomforted in the least by its statements that they have breached a code of practice. Perhaps its most fateful decision in its first year was to take the *Sunday Sport* seriously and to treat it as a newspaper. The distinguished members of the PCC embarked upon a solemn investigation into a front-page story entitled 'THIS NUN IS ABOUT TO BE EATEN'. ('She's soaked in sauce, barbecued, then carved up like a chicken . . . turn to pages 15, 16 and 17 if you dare.') The editor of the *Sport* entered into the PCC's game with relish, describing his article as 'pioneering investigative journalism at its best', which he was proud to have published, and dared the PCC to condemn him for exposing necrophilia in a Buddhist monastery in Thailand, 'a country regularly visited by British tourists'. The PCC rose to the bait, describing the story as 'an extreme breach of the spirit of the Code of Practice and the standards which the newspaper industry sets itself'. In fact, the story was not a breach of the Code of Practice at all, whatever its 'spirit' may be, and if the PCC regards a pornographic paper as part of the newspaper industry that it affects to regulate, then its doom is already sealed.

CONTROLLING THE DATA BANKS

There are over a million people in Britain employed in the business of collecting information on fellow citizens – not by spying or snooping, but simply by gathering facts and forms and feeding them into files and computerized data banks. The average adult has private information about himself or herself on over two hundred separate files, and by 1982 Government departments alone boasted 220 different computerized data banks. From birth certificate to death certificate, our lives are printed out on school and NHS records, tax and VAT returns, insurance, mortgage and credit ratings, social-security files, motor-vehicle licences, police records and the like.

By 1992 there were no less than 164,500 companies or organizations processing or using personal data which had registered under the Data Protection Act. Yet the problem of 'data matching' – the linkage of two or more sets of records, assembled for different purposes, to enhance the profile of each – had not yet been addressed in Britain, despite laws regulating the practice passed years ago in Canada, Australia and the US. As Lord Browne-Wilkinson observed in 1990 when contemplating police powers to collate records, 'if the information obtained by the police, the Inland Revenue, the social security services, and other agencies were to be gathered together in one file, the freedom of the individual would be gravely at risk. The dossier of private information is the badge of the totalitarian state.'

The gossip of neighbours has nothing like the potential for

damage of the chattering of computers, as they link and match scraps of information from different data banks to build up an incomplete jigsaw of the individual on record. As computer technology enters its fifth generation, processing psychological and motivational analysis to determine fitness for jobs or promotion, the implications for privacy become particularly serious. There may be data so sensitive that they should not be on file – details of sexual behaviour or past illnesses or voting habits. The data may be out of date, such as a psychiatric report on teenage depression or an old criminal conviction, raked up to tip the odds against being offered a job or a loan. The data may be inaccurate: it is common for individuals to be recorded as bad credit risks after they have simply refused to pay for defective goods, or have been confused with people of similar name who have criminal records. The more that hard facts rub shoulders with unchecked gossip and ill-considered opinions, the more the prospects for fair evaluation of an individual recede. We look to the law to provide adequate guarantees that confidential data will not be transmitted without permission, that there are safeguards against information being used for purposes for which it was not provided, and that data which have been collected are accurate and up to date.[17]

Information is not property which can be 'stolen' for the purposes of the law of theft, so no offence is committed by tricking banks and insurance companies and hospitals into giving information about their client accounts.[18] In 1982, a newspaper hired a private investigator for £500 to report on the private life of an MP: in a matter of days he was able to obtain access to criminal records, bank statements, credit agency reports and insurance files. Subterfuge thrives on the negligence of data handlers – one survey in the *Lancet* concluded that anyone wearing a white coat and stethoscope could obtain any record he cared to name from an NHS hospital. A social-work lecturer conducted an experiment by having students call up different agencies on various pretexts to obtain information about his clients, and only once was the request refused. The Law Commission has, since 1974, consistently pointed out this gap in the criminal law: to the relief of the private-investigation industry there has been no attempt to fill it by creating an offence of dishonestly obtaining sensitive private information.

The Data Protection Act

In 1984 major legislative action was at last taken to regulate data banks. The Data Protection Act owed more to EEC pressure than Orwellian fears: the Council of Europe's Data Protection Convention required signatories to withhold transmission of data to countries which had no laws to protect it, and British firms had started to lose overseas contracts which involved the swapping of information, because European businesses were not permitted to deal with firms in countries which could not guarantee the confidentiality of computerized information. The Act requires all companies which process or use computerized personal data to register their operations with the data protection registrar in sufficient detail to enable his office to be satisfied, if necessary after inspection, that use of computerized data is in accordance with principles laid down in the Act. Citizens may inspect the Register, and may apply, on payment of a small fee, to inspect any information which is being held about them and may apply to a court to order correction or removal of any factual errors.

The 'data-protection principles' which all companies should observe, on pain of being struck off the Register and hence unable to use or collect computerized personal data, are:

(1) The information to be contained in personal data shall be obtained, and personal data shall be processed, fairly and lawfully.

(2) Personal data shall be held only for one or more specified and lawful purposes.

(3) Personal data held for any purpose shall not be used or disclosed in any manner incompatible with that purpose.

(4) Personal data held for any purpose shall be adequate, relevant and not excessive in relation to that purpose.

(5) Personal data shall be accurate and, where necessary, kept up to date.

(6) Personal data held for any purpose shall not be kept for longer than is necessary for that purpose.

(7) An individual shall be entitled:
   (a) at intervals and without undue delay or expense:
      (i) to be informed by any data user whether he holds personal data of which that individual is the subject; and

.   (ii) to access to any such data held by a data user; and

.   (b) Where appropriate, to have such data corrected or erased.

(8) Appropriate security measures shall be taken against unauthorized access to, or alteration, disclosure or destruction of, personal data and against accidental loss or destruction of personal data.

The Act requires all data users who 'process personal data automatically' to register, giving details of the kind of information they collect, their purpose, sources, and the persons or organization to whom it may be disclosed. The registrar may (subject to an appeal to the Data Protection Tribunal) refuse to register where insufficient information is provided, or where he is satisfied that the data-protection principles are not being observed, and any business which processes personal data without being registered commits a criminal offence, punishable by an unlimited fine at crown court. The registrar has certain powers to inspect the premises of data users, to obtain search warrants for this purpose, and to serve an 'enforcement notice' as a warning before taking de-registration proceedings. The Act's provisions relating to rights of citizen access allow 'data subjects' (in the unlovely computerspeak terminology adopted by the statute) to make a request to see copies of information held about them which is not exempt, does not identify other individuals who have provided the information, and relates to facts and opinions but not to the 'future intentions' of the data use (e.g. prospects for promotion of the data subject). The business must respond within forty days: if the information turns out to be inaccurate, the applicant can obtain compensation for any harm suffered and a court order to correct factual errors and erase opinions and assessments made on the basis of facts which are false.

There are, needless to say, broad bans on citizen access to information held by police, prosecution authorities and tax departments, and the Home Secretary may exclude any review of 'information as to the physical or mental health of the data subject' held by Government departments or local authorities or voluntary agencies. 'National security' is a catch-all exemption from the Act, decided conclusively by a ministerial certificate. These exemptions are far too wide, and were decided before the formation of the National Criminal Intelligence Service in 1992 (which links information ranging from suspected drug users to over-enthusiastic football supporters) and the introduction in the same year of the new Police National Computer (PNC 2) with formidable powers of data matching. PNC 2 will even indicate whether individuals are HIV/ AIDS positive – a data practice the registrar has approved, although this questionable judgement at very least demands a right of subject access to correct the indication if it is in fact false. In 1992 the registrar discovered that the Metropolitan Police forensic labatory was retaining the DNA profile data resulting from samples given freely by citizens who were then eliminated from suspicion. The law (PACE) requires fingerprints to be destroyed in such circumstances, but has not kept pace with DNA developments. The danger is underlined by the fact that in 1990 Parliament's Home Affairs Committee found that Government departments and agencies had checked police records on over half a million job applicants, and it expressed alarm at the high level of inaccuracies in these records.[19] None the less, the UK has been the only Council of Europe nation to refuse to comply with EC directives requiring that individuals should ultimately be informed as to whether information recorded without their knowledge is being kept on file, and prohibiting collection of data on individuals 'solely on the basis that they have a particular racial origin, particular religious convictions, sexual behaviour or political opinions or belong to particular movements which are not proscribed by law'.[20]

The Data Protection Act came into full operation in 1987, and the registrar has been active in encouraging professionalism and caution in the handling of data and permitting rights of access and correction. Its overwhelming defect is that it applies only to computerized information: data users who wish to breach every principle in the Act can continue to do so with a manual filing system. There is ample scope for companies to make applications for access difficult, by delaying any response for the full forty days and insisting on extravagant requirements for applicants to prove their identity. The compensation provisions are grossly inadequate, as damages may only be awarded for inaccurate information compiled directly by the data user, and not for inaccurate material supplied to the user by malevolent or incompetent third parties. This kind of rumour and gossip is, of course, precisely the kind of information which is likely to prove most damaging. The Home Office justified this exemption by asserting that 'Where a data user records inaccurate information supplied by someone else, the data are accurate. They are an accurate record of what someone else said' – a distinction of which Pooh-Bah would have been proud. The result is that the victim of false information maliciously provided to a data user cannot either obtain compensation from the user for circulating it, or obtain the name of the malicious person who provided it in order to sue for defamation.

[margin handwritten note: result of Defect]

Some serious deficiencies have already become apparent in the Data Protection Act's 'protection'. The most dangerous data errors are in criminal records, motor-vehicle registration details, and 'wanted person' information transferred to the Police National Computer (PNC) to which subjects are allowed no access at all. Yet official access to the PNC is vouchsafed to Government departments and authorities and to numerous professional bodies and organizations ranging from the BBC to the National Gallery, and improper access is obtained by many private-detective agencies. Almost 120,000 calls are made to the PNC every day, but very few are monitored to ensure that the request is *bona fide*, despite the inevitable 'Home Office guidelines'. Moreover, local police computers store information provided by 'collators' at each station, which includes gossip and innuendo about persons who are not even suspected of crime. These compilations fall outside the provisions of the Act. The existence of the Act nobably failed to deter British Airways from hacking into the computer files of Virgin Atlantic in order to identify and poach its first-class clientele. This scandal, exposed in the wake of Richard Branson's libel action against BA in 1993, raises serious doubts about the effectiveness of a law which gives the Registrar no power to prosecute powerful companies which profit from breaching it. They do so because the risk of detection is slight and could only lead, at most, to a modest compensation order. If Board members and executives of companies like BA were made subject to criminal proceedings for authorizing blatant breaches of the Act, there would be a much greater level of compliance with it.

The Data Protection Act permits access only to personal information held on computer. There is, however, a legally enforceable right of access to information held on any personal file by credit agencies,[21] and the 1987 Access to Personal Files Act allows individuals to inspect and correct manual files held on them by local council social services and housing authorities. This Act covers all factual data and personal opinion recorded since it was passed (although not statements of future intentions) and it provides that the Home Secretary may make regulations to include other local-authority records within its ambit. In 1992 the Data Protection Registrar became concerned that the limited rights of subject access under this and other Acts was being abused by employers and licensing bodies which are requiring individuals to undertake these searches and reveal the results before their employment is confirmed or their licence (e.g. to drive a cab) is granted.[22] This ironical development demonstrates the need for continued vigilance: the appetite for personal information is such that even laws passed with the object of protecting privacy may be exploited so as to diminish it.

Security data

Special problems arise in relation to data which are collected by Special Branch and by MI5 on persons who are thought to harbour 'subversive' thoughts or intentions. In a glossy brochure published in 1993, MI5 officially admitted that it targeted 'the subversive element within' legitimate protest groups, and it is unofficially reported to have a central registry with dossiers on 500,000 citizens, while the Special Branch (with whom it works closely) has some 2,000 officers throughout the country collecting information, usually on individuals who have committed no criminal offence. Both services have computers, which are outside the provisions of the Data Protection Act, and access to the fruits of telephone-tapping, mail interception, electronic surveillance, infiltrators and the GCHQ monitoring of overseas communications. The secret directive establishing MI5 in 1953 invites its Director-General to 'arrange to have such access to the records of Government departments and agencies as you may deem necessary for the purposes of your work' and to 'arrange that all Government departments and agencies submit to you for inclusion in your records all information bearing on security which may come into their possession'. This directive would suggest that security service files on individuals will contain material from the Inland Revenue and DHSS, together of course with reports from informers, agents and 'assets' in different walks of life.

The collection and transfer of information about individuals by the Special Branch (and, for that matter, by GCHQ, military intelligence and MI6) falls outside the provisions of the Data Protection Act and is entirely unregulated by law. There are serious questions about the criteria upon which targets are chosen and the basis upon which information is divulged to third parties. In 1981 Madelaine Haigh, a teacher who had no political involvements, wrote to her local paper complaining about the lack of controls over American nuclear missiles on British soil. In consequence, she was clumsily investigated by her local Special Branch, who gained entry to her home under a subterfuge and lied about the reason for their interest in her. The chief constable criticized them for 'unprofessional' behaviour, but strenuously defended their right to investigate anyone with views which might lead them to participate in public protests. Another chief constable, John Alderson, has admitted to discovering that 40 per cent of the information on the files of his Special Branch related to persons who posed no security or criminal threat, but who were merely outspoken on public issues or members of pressure groups. In 1985 the Home Secretary disclosed the inevitable 'Home Office guidelines' which recommend against data collection on persons 'solely' because they espouse unpopular causes, but as Madelaine Haigh's case shows, the blanket label of 'potential subversive' may be attached simply by assuming that those who feel strongly enough to write to newspapers may one day be prepared to break the law in the same cause.

The collection and dissemination of secret information on individuals by MI5 is purportedly 'regulated' by the Security Service Act (see later, page 183) which the Government introduced in 1989. This measure came about as a direct response to applications to the European Court of Human Rights by Harriet Harman, MP, and Patricia Hewitt, who had been NCCL officials at a time when that organization, like CND and various trade unions, had been targeted by MI5 as 'subversive'. In 1984 an ex-MI5 officer named Cathy Massiter revealed this surveillance on a television programme, and the victims complained to Strasbourg that it breached their right to privacy guaranteed by the European Convention. It was apparent from recent European Court decisions that they would succeed: their right to privacy had been invaded by secret collection of information on them by an organization which had no legal powers or even at that time legal existence, and against whose behaviour they had no remedy. The Government introduced the Security Service Act in an effort to meet the minimum standards required by the Convention, and in the hope of allaying fears generated by publication of *Spycatcher*, in which Peter Wright confessed to 'burgling and bugging his way around London' in the service of MI5. Wright and his cronies had by this time been shown to have collected private (and often inaccurate) information about a large number of left-wing politicians, trade-union leaders and friends of Harold Wilson, and to have used this in attempts to destroy or damage their careers. It transpired that even in the late 1970s MI5 had been secretly and irresponsibly at work in the BBC, stopping the employment of the respected journalist Isabel Hilton because she had as a student been secretary of a China friendship association regarded as subversive, and trying to stop Anna Ford from reading the news on the BBC because an ex-boyfriend had been a Communist. It has now been revealed that the head of MI5's anti-subversion section who ordered the targeting of Harriet Harman and Patricia Hewitt and their NCCL colleagues, and who directed a special MI5 study on anti-establishment but influential journalists, left the service to publish a clandestine right-wing paper called *Background Briefing* which as late as 1989 was describing Shelter (the organization which helps the homeless) as having 'Communist affiliations' and muck-raking against Labour MPs and trade unionists.[23] It is highly unlikely that the Security Service Act will provide satisfactory safeguards against resurgence of such McCarthy-like behaviour, and it is doubtful whether it satisfies the minimum requirements of the European Convention.

Under the Act, MI5 is entitled to collect and to use information to the extent that is necessary for the protection of 'national security'. This term is not defined other than by examples (which are not exhaustive) including 'actions intended to overthrow or undermine parliamentary democracy by political, industrial or violent means'. The notion of undermining Parliament by political means seems a veiled invitation to maintain surveillance on political agitation outside the mainstream parties – even the campaign to introduce a Bill of Rights was described by Prime Minister Thatcher as 'undermining parliamentary democracy'. The definition of 'national security', of course, may be very much wider – the Government White Paper in 1985 which led to the Interception of Communications Act defined 'the interests of national security' to include steps taken 'in support of the Government's defence and foreign policies'. The only limitation on the security service is that it must not 'take any action to further the interests of a political party' – a clause inserted as a result of Wright's admission to participating in a plot to bring down the Wilson Government and Massiter's claim that information collected on CND found its way to Conservative politicians bent on discrediting Labour's defence policies. The Act recognizes that MI5 may need to trespass, burgle and steal to obtain information: such actions merely require the Home Secretary to sign a warrant. MI5 is free to use the private information it collects as it sees fit in the national interest, except to influence employment decisions, in which case it must follow procedures which the Home Secretary secretly authorizes. The minister will not be required, under this clause, to approve specific MI5 blackballs on individual careers, but only the procedures by which they are thrown (presumably, he insists that such decisions are made at a senior level within the service).

The Act, in effect, serves to legitimize every complaint hitherto made about the operation of MI5, other than its involvement in promoting party-political interests. There are new safeguards, modelled on the scheme established in 1985 for the supervision of telephone tapping (see later, page 137). A tribunal of senior lawyers has been appointed to receive and investigate complaints from members of the public who believe they have been burgled or blacklisted or have otherwise suffered as targets of MI5. The complaint will only be upheld, however, if the targeting was based on information that MI5 had no reason to believe was true, or (in the case of a Home Secretary's warrant) that it was granted for reasons that no minister in his right mind could conceive was really necessary in the interests of national security. The tribunal's function is so restricted that it offers no meaningful oversight – the Act specifically provides that it is 'reasonable' to target entirely innocuous complainants if they happen to be members of a group 'regarded by the service as requiring investigation'. (Madelaine Haigh would on this basis have no cause for complaint if she were monitored by MI5, so long as it regarded CND as 'requiring investigation'.) The tribunal has certain powers to refer targeting decisions to a senior judge, who has been appointed to review the working of the Act and to report to the Prime Minister, although any part of his report which might be prejudicial to the functioning of the service (including, presumably, revelation of any targeting decision) will not be made public. In short, the complaints procedure established by this Act offers no remedy for persons who are victims of mistaken judgements rather than mistaken facts. Even those who are targeted as a result of clerical errors and administrative confusion of names will rarely have cause to complain, for the simple reason that the Government's Official Secrets Act of 1989 (see later, page 167) makes it a crime to reveal any detail at all of MI5's operations even when such revelations (e.g. of mistakes in targeting) are in the public interest. There will be no more Cathy Massiters: the Government's 1989 legislative package was designed to outlaw the very class of revelation which forced it to bring MI5 within the law in the first place.

The reports by the Commissioner established under the Security Service Act have been brief, bland and uninformative. He has refused to disclose even the number of warrants for burglary issued under the Act, and has given no indication of the nature of the targets. Of the eighty-one complaints investigated by the tribunal in its first two years of operation, not one has been upheld – the Commissioner has suggested that many complainants are suffering from delusions. This cannot be accepted in the case of the redoubtable Mesdames Harman and Hewitt, who demanded that the Tribunal allow them to see the contents of their files, or at least assure them that these files had been destroyed. The tribunal found it impossible, in terms of its restrictive mandate, to accede to their request, so they have complained once again to Strasbourg that the Act which was passed as a result of their previous complaint still does not satisfy the requirements of the Convention. It is extraordinary, at a time when Britain's three traditional partners in intelligence gathering and sharing – Canada, Australia and the United States – have passed laws which make their secret services fully accountable to independent bodies or to Parliamentary Committees, that MI5 has no real accountability and MI6 has not even an unreal accountability (although in 1992 the Prime Minister admitted, for the first time, that it did actually exist). In 1993 Parliament's Home Affairs Committee demanded the right to scrutinize the activities of security services, noting that MI5's headquarters at Millbank were being refurbished with state-of-the-art computer equipment at a cost of £100 million, while MI6 was moving to a new office building overlooking the Thames at a cost of £240 million, on top of an annual budget for both services of £185 million. It rejected the assertion of the then Home Secretary, Kenneth Clarke, that MPs should not ask questions about security matters, and argued that their right to do so would 'meet an important public interest and help to protect against any possible abuse of power'. The Government declined to accept the report's conclusions, notwithstanding that its own backbenchers were in a majority on the Committee.

POLICE SEARCHES

The great boast that 'an Englishman's home is his castle' goes back to a court case in 1604,[24] and was much embellished by several splendid decisions in the 1760s when the courts awarded damages to John Wilkes and his radical supporters who had their homes ransacked by Government officers in search of evidence to connect them with seditious newspapers. These decisions were based, not on any considerations of personal privacy, but upon the pre-eminent respect that English law has always accorded rights of property ownership,[25] although they inspired William Pitt's famous declaration:

The poorest man may in his cottage bid defiance to the Crown. It may be frail – its roof may shake – the wind may enter – the rain may enter – but the King of England cannot enter – all his force dares not cross the threshold of the ruined tenement.

The modern council flat is a good deal less sacrosanct, however, since police need do no more than obtain the rubber stamp of a lay justice on warrants permitting them to enter, search and seize property related to a myriad of possible offences. The heady defiance of John Wilkes is no longer permitted to his journalistic successors like Duncan Campbell, whose personal library was entirely uplifted by a police pantechnicon in 1978 and whose films about *The Secret Society* were removed from the cutting rooms of the BBC in 1986.

The modern counterparts of the eighteenth-century printers and booksellers who could slam the door on 'the King's messengers' are powerless to withstand the warrants and 'writs of assistance' (see later, page 135) displayed by police and customs officials to remove dangerous books from their shelves: 'Operation Tiger' in 1985 denuded one Bloomsbury bookshop, Gay's the Word, of its stock of literature by Gore Vidal, Oscar Wilde, Jean Genet and Christopher Isherwood.

The Police and Criminal Evidence Act 1984 (PACE) now largely governs official search-and-seize operations, and confirms the police power to enter private premises whenever there is reason to believe there may be evidence of serious (and certain not-so-serious) offences within. Although it discourages 'dawn raids' and ensures that searches are carried out reasonably and without obvious provocation, it pins far too much faith on the ability of lay justices to control the extensive police power which a search-warrant represents. From the viewpoint of the citizen, the drawback of PACE is not so much that it awards greater powers to search and seize, but that it fails (except in its special provisions relating to confidential material) to provide a proper system of review.

The eighteenth-century cases of *Entick* v. *Carrington* and *John Wilkes* v. *Lord Halifax* at least established the permanent principle that no state official may enter a citizen's premises without the authority of law. Halifax, convinced by the informers he interviewed that Wilkes had written a seditious attack on the King and his Government, himself issued a warrant for Wilkes's arrest and for the search of his home to remove all his papers. Wilkes sued for trespass, and was awarded £1,000 in damages (the equivalent of £200,000 today) while crowds in the street roared their approval of 'Wilkes and Liberty'. The court ruled that Lord Halifax, as Secretary of State, was not a Justice of the Peace and had no legal power to issue a warrant. Moreover, the 'general warrant' to seize any evidence of any crime by anybody was itself illegal: search warrants had to specify the kind of material which was sought, and only material of that specific description could be seized.[26]

What is left of 'Wilkes and Liberty' more than two centuries later? It remains the case that police officers who enter without a warrant are liable for damages for trespassing on private property unless they either enter by invitation, or to make or follow up an arrest, or to put down a breach of the peace. Of course the police, like all members of the public, have an implied licence to go up the garden path to the front door of a house to make legitimate inquiries: they become trespassers if they refuse to leave within a reasonably short time of being ordered out by the occupier or owner.[27] The case of *McArdle* v. *Wallace* illustrates these restrictions: One night policemen found new car parts in a passage outside a factory. They proceeded along the passage to the yard of a café in order to pursue their inquiries about the parts, which they reasonably believed had been stolen. The café proprietor's son ordered them off the premises, but they did not leave and asked further questions about car parts, whereupon the son struck the policemen. The son was prosecuted for assaulting the policemen in the execution of their duty. The court pointed out that the policemen had no reasonable grounds for expecting to find and apprehend the thief on the premises, so that they had no right to remain once somebody acting with the authority of the occupier asked them to leave. Accordingly the son was not guilty – indeed, the café proprietor could successfully have sued the police for trespass.[28]

What constitutes a request to leave, or the withdrawal of an implied licence to walk up the garden path, is a question of fact: several courts have perversely declined to construe the statement 'fuck off' as a request to depart.[29]

A timely reminder that the spirit of 'Wilkes and Liberty' is not dead came in 1991 when the Divisional Court awarded £25,000 exemplary damages to the victim of an 'oppressive, arbitrary and unconstitutional search' conducted by a Government department under cover of a warrant issued to the police. The police had not satisfied themselves that the search was necessary, the warrant was general in its terms and the justices had permitted any number of Government officials to join the raiding party; irrelevant and confidential documents were taken from a company, which was then denied access to inspect them. The warrant was declared null and void by a High Court in judicial review proceedings, and it went on to award general damages to the company for disruption and inconvenience and exemplary damages to mark 'a deplorable abuse of power by Government officials'. This case should be required reading for all magistrates: it was clear to the court that insufficient inquiries had been made by the justices before they issued the warrant.[30]

In other respects, however, the chant of 'Wilkes and Liberty' has failed to echo down the corridors of legal time. In 1763, the Chief Justice declaimed

that to enter a man's house by virtue of a nameless warrant, in order to find evidence, is worse than the Spanish Inquisition . . . the Government sought to exercise arbitrary power, violating Magna Carta, and attempting to destroy the liberty of the kingdom with the general search warrant.

More recent court decisions, extended by PACE, have virtually turned every search warrant into a general warrant. Section 19 of the 1984 Act, ominously headed 'General Power of Seizure', is precisely that: once lawfully on private premises, police may seize anything they reasonably believe to be evidence of any offence, whether or not related to the offence under investigation and whether or not that offence was committed by the person under investigation. The only condition is that they must believe that seizure is necessary to prevent the evidence being 'concealed lost altered or destroyed' – a belief which will normally be entertained about any evidence of crime. Section 19 undermines the 'search warrants – safeguards' section of PACE, with its requirements that in applying for such warrants police shall 'identify so far as is practicable, the articles or persons sought', that entry should if possible be at 'a reasonable hour', and that the search 'may only be a search to the extent required for the purpose for which the warrant was issued'.

The fundamental weakness of the search-warrant procedure is that it relies on lay justices to safeguard citizen's rights. Lawyers have long known what academics are just beginning to discover from research, namely that lay justices almost invariably 'rubber stamp' police requests to sign search and arrest warrants. Indeed, many police stations select a few favoured local justices who can be relied upon to issue warrants at any time of the day or night without asking difficult questions, and direct all warrant requests to them. Justices of the Peace are not lawyers, but local worthies who do not critically examine police requests – often made on their doorstep late at night – to issue warrants on 'reliable information'. PACE requires that warrant applications shall be supported by 'an information in writing' – generally a formal document providing little actual information – and that constables must answer on oath any questions that JPs may ask. A study just before PACE came into operation revealed that only rarely were serious questions asked at warrant application hearings and in most areas it is virtually unheard of for a JP to refuse to sign a warrant.[31] (If one does, he or she is unlikely to be asked again.) A follow-up study, five years after PACE, concluded that 'magistrates are no more questioning now than they were before the Act'.

It is unfortunate that Parliament grasped at such a weak reed to support its 'safeguards' for searches of private homes. In 1968, there was a great fuss about a JP who acted as a 'mere formality' in granting a warrant to search Lady Diana Cooper's home for drugs, after police had received an anonymous telephone call that turned out to be a hoax. Although it is technically possible to quash a warrant that has been issued without adequate scrutiny, and to sue for trespass where a warrant has been wrongfully obtained, a successful legal action is made virtually impossible by the paucity of detail required on the 'written information', and the fact that justices are not required to give written reasons for signing the warrant. As the leading work on the law of search and seizure concludes,

The lack of any record of reasons undermines the protection for citizens which a judicial procedure for vetting applications for warrants is designed to provide: it becomes difficult to make the officer or the magistrate accountable for their behaviour ... the warrant is likely to be uninformative, and the provisions in the Act do not adequately protect an individual's civil law remedies.[32]

Seizure of confidential material

The protection of scrutiny by a crown court judge rather than a magistrate is required in cases where police wish to seize confidential papers – including medical and social-work records, journalistic material and personal records created in the name of any business or profession. Where such documents are sought for the purpose of a police investigation into a 'serious arrestable offence' (see earlier, page 21), a crown court judge must be satisfied that police have reasonable grounds to believe that they are likely to be of substantial evidential value and that their seizure under a warrant is likely to be for the public benefit. (Certain documents of a highly confidential nature are classed as 'excluded material', and can only be seized if the judge is satisfied that a warrant would have been granted under an enactment prior to PACE.) The importance of the protection awarded to 'special procedure' and 'excluded' material is not only that a crown court judge rather than a magistrate decides whether to issue a warrant, but that the owner or occupier is entitled to be represented at the hearing, which may be in open court, to argue that the warrant should not be granted. One outrageous anomaly, which the courts have declined to correct, is that there is no duty on the police to notify the owner of the property if it is sought from a third party, such as a bank, which may not wish to contest the application.[33] This can mean that confidential material is wrongly handed over by court order, because the owner has not been notified in time to challenge the application.

These are complicated provisions, but their very existence has been an encouragement to law-enforcement agencies to make use of them to obtain information in circumstances where, prior to PACE, no search power existed or where social scruples might have stayed the police hand. It was hardly surprising that newspapers were the first to experience the 'special procedure' provisions, as police in Bristol went on a fishing expedition to obtain all photographs, whether published or not, taken by press photographers who had covered a 'riot' in the St Paul's area of the city. Prior to PACE, media organizations had refused to hand over untransmitted film and photographs taken at public-order disturbances, fearing that cameramen could be put in danger if they were perceived by the mob as agents of the police. This argument cut no ice with the judge: there was reason to believe that pictures of a fast-moving series of incidents would help to identify persons committing serious crimes, and the public benefit from handing them over to the police outweighed any added danger to photographers or the possibility that sources in the area would no longer cooperate with the press.[34] ITN protested loudly when its untransmitted film was seized by South African security police investigating black protesters, but the Bristol decision shows that the same result would be reached in Britain.

In all cases involving contests between confidentiality and police applications for access, there will be a clash between the right of privacy and the demand to prosecute serious offences effectively. Crown court judges will have to weigh the testimony about 'public benefit' presented on each side. The only class of material which is exempt from seizure under any circumstances is that relating to communications between lawyer and client, or between lawyers and third parties (such as potential witnesses) in relation to legal proceedings. Documents covered by 'legal professional privilege' are sacrosanct: the law, understandably, regards it as the highest possible good that citizens should be entitled to take legal advice without fear that their confessions should be made public.

'Stop and search' powers

By far the most controversial police power to invade personal privacy has, at least in recent years, been the power to stop and search citizens in the street. 'Operation Swamp', which preceded the Brixton riots of 1981, involved 943 stops on suspicion of theft – over half of black people, more than two-thirds of whom were under twenty-one. The arrest score was one burglary charge, one attempted robbery and twenty minor thefts. When two young police officers noticed a black minicab driver put money in his sock, they suspected – with no more evidence – that it might be the proceeds of drug dealing. So they searched him, in full view of a gathering crowd, while he laughingly explained that he kept his money there for safe-keeping. Undeterred by finding him 'clean', they began to search his car, while the crowd started to mutter about 'police harassment'. This incident, against the background of hostility engendered by 'Operation Swamp', sparked off the worst rioting Britain has seen this century. The two young policemen, Lord Scarman observed, acted without judgement or discretion.[35]

Although the power to search for stolen goods is necessary to combat street crime, there must be safeguards against police officers acting on 'hunches' which are no more than prejudices. The power to stop and search for drugs has been especially open to abuse: in the sixties, long hair and beards or attendance at a pop festival was enough to provoke police suspicion, and ten years later it was being young and black and standing on a street corner (or driving a

BMW). Studies done shortly before PACE revealed that about one third of all police stops were random, in the sense that there was no cause to suspect the individual detained, other than that he was black or young or walking in a neighbourhood associated with drug deals. Fewer than 10 per cent of those stopped and searched were found to be in breach of any law, and generally the offences uncovered were trivial (such as possession of a small amount of cannabis).

PACE does not, unfortunately, confine the power to cases where possession of stolen property or 'Class A' drugs is suspected. However, the Act has introduced a number of safeguards by requiring constables to justify their decision to stop, both to the suspect at the time and subsequently in a written report. The Code of Practice stresses that 'reasonable suspicion' must be founded on fact, and have a concrete basis which can be evaluated objectively. Suspicion must relate to a fact about the individual, and not to the group or class to which he or she belongs.

A person's colour of itself can never be a reasonable ground for suspicion. The mere fact alone that a person is carrying a particular kind of property or is dressed in a certain way or has a certain hairstyle is likewise not of itself sufficient. Nor is the fact that a person is known to have a previous conviction for unlawful possession of an article.[36]

The extent to which this Code of Practice has been put into practice is doubtful: the temptation to 'show them who's boss' in city areas frequented by defiant young blacks is difficult for police to resist, especially where there are resident complaints of real street crime such as mugging and burglary. At least police stops in public must now be carried out with a minimum of decorum: the power only permits them to remove a suspect's outer coat, jacket and gloves.[37] Any more intimate search will require the exercise of a power of arrest, and consequent detention. Evidence since the adoption of PACE casts doubt upon whether its safeguards have been effective. The Home Office refuses to publish statistics in relation to police 'stops' (the vast majority of which are unproductive) and its figures still show that over 80 per cent of stops and searches are fruitless acts of harassment. It is difficult to believe that police suspicions are generally reasonable, given the extent to which they are unfounded.

OTHER SEARCH POWERS

Several hundred different officials have been given statutory powers to enter private homes, generally after court orders and usually for entirely acceptable purposes like reading the gas and electricity meters or checking up on the welfare of children. VAT inspectors have the most draconian powers of search and seizure, but only after obtaining a warrant from a High Court judge. The Court of Appeal was very critical of the zeal with which dawn raids were conducted on the homes of those suspected of revenue offences in the *Rossminster* case,[38] when the bedrooms of five-year-olds were turned over in search for cheque-books, although others may feel this is an occupational hazard for very young children who have active trading accounts.

One constitutional anomaly which invites abuse is the 'writ of assistance', an ancient prerogative granted to customs officers searching for contraband. This curious document, couched in what was doubtless common parlance when it originated three hundred years ago (it begins 'To all and singular our officers and ministers – Greeting') is issued by the 'Queen's Remembrancer' at the beginning of each reign, and contains a blanket power for every customs officer carrying a copy to search any premises at any time and to seize smuggled goods. It is a general warrant which is executed, without any judicial or magisterial scrutiny, on about five hundred occasions each year, often for no better reason than that customs officers (who have the alternative power to obtain a magistrate's warrant) have a sentimental attachment to this relic of despotic royal power. On over half the occasions on which the writ is run, no smuggled goods are discovered – which suggests that it is being abused to conduct raids on suspicions which a court, if asked, might not find reasonable. There are no 'codes of practice' to govern the execution of the writ, which was used as the basis for the Customs and Excise assault on books by, for or about homosexuals imported by Gay's the Word bookshop. The 'writ of assistance' has produced one great historic consequence, namely the American Revolution. Oppressive use of these writs by British customs officials to raid Boston merchants in efforts to extract revenue for George III was, according to the US Supreme Court, 'perhaps the most prominent event which inaugurated the resistance of the colonies to the oppression of the mother country'.[39]

In recent years the Chancery Division of the High Court has provided a means whereby private plaintiffs in civil actions can search the homes of defendants and seize disputed property. This exceptional remedy was developed to enable film and record companies to deal with 'pirates' who produce counterfeit articles or simply run off copies of tapes and cassettes in direct breach of copyright. Until 1983, film and video piracy was a minor offence and police were not much interested in it: the producers had to band together to take civil action against persons who were capable of selling or hiding the pirate copies long before the action came to trial. The courts, with good intentions but without the ability to control the consequences (a defect which commonly characterizes judicial law-making), sat in secret to issue *Anton Pillar* orders (which required suspected pirates to admit the plaintiff's solicitors to their premises to inspect their stock and carry off items relevant to their breach-of-copyright claim) and *Mareva* injunctions (which froze the bank accounts of the alleged pirates). Solicitors were generally accompanied by private detectives, and these raiding parties sometimes resulted in the closing down of High Street video shops and the ransacking of premises allegedly used for copying tapes.

In 1985 the High Court, in the first contested case resulting from an *Anton Pillar* raid, awarded £10,000 damages in trespass against solicitors who had over-zealously executed the order and Mr Justice Scott expressed serious misgivings about the manner in which such orders had been applied for and carried out.

What is to be said of the *Anton Pillar* procedure which, on a regular and institutionalized basis, is depriving citizens of their property and closing down their businesses by orders made *ex parte*, on applications of which they know nothing and at which they cannot be heard, by orders which they are bound, on pain of committal, to obey, even if wrongly made? . . . even villains ought not to be deprived of their property by proceedings at which they cannot be heard.[40]

The court emphasized the need for applicants to produce overwhelming evidence of piracy causing considerable damage and of imminent danger of destruction of evidence before *Anton Pillar* orders could be made. The remedy should be confined to highly exceptional cases, and should not be granted at all where there is an allegation of criminal conduct capable of proper police investigation. The need for widespread *Anton Pillar* action only arose because police forces did not perceive copyright theft as criminal behaviour: legislation in 1983 which massively increased the punishment for piracy has changed that perception, and there is now less scope for court-approved invasions of privacy by private litigants.

TELEPHONE TAPPING

Telephone tapping and mail interceptions are conducted by British Telecom and Post Office employees at the request of police and security-service officials who have obtained a warrant from the Home Secretary authorizing the intercept for a particular period of time. The Home Secretary is a party politician whose ministerial duties leave little time for proper discharge of the serious responsibility of authorizing state invasion of the privacy of many thousands of citizens each year. Although there were only 874 telecommunications warrants and 92 postal intercept warrants in force at the beginning of 1993, many of these related to organizations and it has been estimated that up to one million private communications are intercepted each year. There can be no doubt that the state requires powers of interception in order to gather information about serious crime and terrorism, but these powers are not limited by law to acceptable and definable targets. As a result, interception as practised in the UK has three disadvantages: it is not used in court to convict criminals; there is insufficient independent safeguard against abuse; and there is a good deal of unnecessary paranoia amongst those whose telephones malfunction. Telephone tapping is carried out by BT employees who record the conversations. Transcripts of those regarded as relevant to police, Customs or MI5 investigations are transcribed, and one copy is kept on file by a special unit of the Metropolitan Police, usually for at least a year. Senior officers involved in the particular investigation are permitted access to the master file, and may copy extracts into special-issue notebooks, which must never be taken near a courtroom (so that defence lawyers will never discover – as they did in *Malone*'s case (page 139) – that their client's telephone has been tapped).

By the 1990s, the great majority of the warrants being issued by the Home Secretary related to serious crime, especially to customs investigations of drug conspiracies. The end of the cold war had reduced the demand to listen to 'subversives': there were many warrants issued against them in 1985, but only two in 1990 and none in 1991 (although warrants justified for counter-terrorism purposes had increased).[41] There is no reason to doubt these reassuring statistics, other than to point out that they apply only to cases where the Home Secretary has been involved. He is not involved in surveillance by GCHQ or MI6, nor is his warrant required for use of bugging devices or remote interception of digital signals.[42]

Given the historic principle of *Entick* v. *Carrington* that an official has no power to interfere with a citizen unless that official can prove affirmatively that the law confers on him such a power, it is surprising that the first inquiry into telephone tapping, conducted by a group of Privy Councillors led by Lord Birkett in 1957, was not more concerned about a practice for which it could find no clear legal sanction.[43] In 1937 the Home Secretary had secretly begun to issue warrants for intercepting telephone calls to detect breaches of exchange-control and emergency food regulations and the posting of Irish sweepstake tickets in violation of the Lotteries Act. In 1951 a secret 'Home Office circular' was issued, stating that intercept warrants could only be issued where serious crime was suspected or the national interest was at stake. The Birkett Committee approved these principles, and recommended that transcripts should not be passed on to persons outside the public service. It criticized as 'mistaken' the Home Secretary's decision to pass to the Bar Council intercepts of communications between a barrister and a target criminal, although it did not criticize the Bar Council's decision to disbar the barrister for 'unprofessional behaviour' on the strength of the intercepts.

After the Birkett Committee's report, Post Office interception of mail and telephones continued under a Home Secretary's warrant (other forms of surveillance, such as bugging devices, required no authority at all). The warrant procedure still had no legal sanction, and the authorities were careful never again to reveal that any particular intercept had taken place. Even when telephone taps provided the clearest evidence of guilt, they were not revealed, as a matter of policy, to a court. But in 1979 a young police officer, giving evidence in a case against Mr James Malone involving theft of antiques, made a historic oversight. Under cross-examination he produced his police notebook, in which he had scribbled some extracts from an intercept authorized by the Home Secretary on Malone's telephone. This provided sufficient evidence for Malone to challenge the lawfulness of the Home Secretary's warrant procedure in the High Court. The judge, Sir Robert Megarry, reluctantly concluded that he had no power to intervene, but he was scathing about the lack of legal safeguards: 'This is not a subject on which it is possible to feel any pride in English law ... telephone tapping is a subject which cries out for legislation.'[44] Malone took his case to the European Court of Human Rights in Strasbourg, which held that the warrant procedure violated the Article 8 guarantee of privacy in the European Convention. The lack of adequate or effective safeguards and indeed the total absence of any rules governing tapping or any remedy against abuse, meant that interceptions were not carried out 'in accordance with the law' – a precondition required by the Convention before official invasion of privacy can be justified to combat crime or protect national security.[45] This ruling obliged the British Government to introduce legislation, which took the form of the 1985 Interception of Communications Act.

This Act gives statutory effect to the Home Secretary's warrant procedure, establishes a commissioner to keep it under review and a tribunal to consider complaints from persons who believe their telephone may have been tapped or their mail interfered with. The entire purpose and effect of the legislation, however, is to remove official interception from any independent examination, and to ensure that the embarassment caused by the violation of Malone's privacy can never happen again. Section 9 outlaws any evidence or questioning in court proceedings which might tend to suggest that any interception warrant has ever been issued. The object of Section 9 was to make the subject of state interception taboo in British courts: there can be no questioning of police as in the *Malone* case, no affidavits by persons like Cathy Massiter, an ex-employee of MI5 who has accused the Home Secretary of granting warrants for party political purposes. With a genius for turning defeat into victory, the British Government has sought to fulfil its obligation to protect privacy by the simple expedient of ensuring that violations of privacy are henceforth never to be exposed through court hearings.

The quid pro quo for demolishing any possible remedy in the courts against unauthorized or unjustified tapping is a tribunal of five senior lawyers empowered to investigate a complaint from any person who believes that he or she may have been the subject of an intercept. But their powers to 'investigate' are confined to considering whether a warrant has been issued, and if so whether, 'applying the principles applicable on an application for judicial review', it was properly issued. This formula means that they cannot critically examine the evidence available to the Home Secretary: so long as there was some information before him from which a reasonable person could conclude that a threat to national security or a serious crime needed investigation, the tribunal can take no action. They merely inspect the Home Secretary's paperwork, and make no examination of the reality or reliability of police or security-service assertions. An application to tap a telephone in relation to an utterly trivial crime, or an innocent activity which it would be wholly perverse to regard as a threat to national security, would enable the tribunal to quash the warrant and compensate the victim. But no senior policeman or security official would be so stupid as to make a written application on perverse grounds, and in 1984 it took a senior judge only a few days to satisfy himself that the 6,129 warrants issued since 1970 had been formally in order. Whether the evidence upon which a formally correct application is based is sufficient or reliable involves questions that the tribunal will be unable to consider. Nor, remarkably, does it have any power to investigate *unauthorized* interception. Not surprisingly, given its limited terms of reference, the tribunal has never upheld a complaint. The Act provides for a senior judge to be appointed as 'commissioner', a part-time officer with a roving brief to assist the tribunal and generally to monitor the warrant procedure. He has no obligation to examine the background to every application, but merely makes 'random checks', and on discovery of any contravention of the rules he is to notify the Prime Minister in secret and not the victim. His public reports have been uninformatively reassuring, disclosing little more than the rare occasions when clerical errors have led to taps being placed on the wrong phone.

The sum total of these arrangements is: to stop the courts from ever providing any redress to victims of unauthorized or wrongly authorized interceptions; to permit a number of senior lawyers to read transcripts of private conversations, without having the power to do anything about them unless the warrant application is perverse; and to pretend to the public that the system is working fairly because a senior judge is keeping an eye on the paperwork it generates. The complainant, of course, will hardly ever discover whether his telephone has in fact been tapped: the uninformative response from the tribunal will normally be to deny that it has discovered any contravention of the Act. (The only way to discover with any certainty whether your telephone is tapped is not to pay the bill: the state's appetite for information being greater than its appetite for money, disconnection will not automatically follow.)

Whether these 'safeguards' satisfy the requirements of Section 13 of the European Convention, which requires an effective remedy for every violation of a right, is open to doubt.[46] The Royal Commission on Criminal Procedure recommended in 1981 that no warrant should be issued until the Official Solicitor, on behalf of the unsuspecting suspect, has had an opportunity to consider and to question in court the grounds for the application.[47] While these proposals may not be appropriate to national-security intercepts, there would be obvious advantages in adopting them where warrants are sought to obtain information about crime. The faith reposed in the Home Secretary, who does not have the time and may not have the relevant experience to consider judicially whether an application fulfils the stated criteria, is wrong in principle and misplaced in practice. Moreover, it has led to the absurd consequence that evidence of serious criminal conspiracies contained in intercepted letters or on transcripts of telephone conversations is never produced in court. The obsession with secrecy is such that the state prefers criminals to walk free rather than have them convicted by revealing the secret transcripts which contain the evidence of their guilt. If intercept warrants were, like search warrants, issued by courts (preferably, by High Court or at least crown court judges) there could be no objection to introducing the transcripts as part of a prosecution case. Indeed, American experience suggests that this class of evidence can be crucial to the conviction of Mafia leaders like Jimmy Hoffa and 'inside dealers' like Ivan Boesky. The British obsession with secrecy, in this respect, is a positive handicap to effective law enforcement.

These secrecy obsessions about telephone tapping at first surprised the courts. In one 1992 case, *R. v. Effik*, police had listened through an FM radio device and taped the conversation from a cordless telephone, which is not part of a public telecommunications system and thus no warrant was required.[48] The Court of Appeal said that 'astonishing results' would follow if Section 9 was to be interpreted so as to prevent telephone intercepts being received in evidence if that were the only way to prove a serious crime, or equally was the only way by which a defendant could prove that he had been framed. A few months later, a differently constituted Court of Appeal in *R. v. Preston* gave fuller consideration to the interpretation of Section 9, and decided that it intended and achieved exactly these 'astonishing results'.[49] Telephone intercepts could be used only for investigation, and not for prosecution, other than in the highly exceptional situation where the intercept had taken place by consent. But suppose the intercept contains material of vital assistance to the defence? Section 9 creates the 'far from ideal situation' that its contents cannot be revealed to the judge or the defence counsel or the appeal court. The best the Court of Appeal could do was to urge that new 'guidelines' should be drawn up by the Attorney-General, which would impose a duty on prosecuting counsel to study the secret transcripts and ensure that public presentation of the Crown case did no injustice to the defendant. This is wholly unsatisfactory, because the only persons who can properly appreciate whether evidence assists the defence are defendants and their counsel.

In any event, the prosecution position when *Preston* reached the House of Lords was to argue that the Act prevented the police from making transcripts available to even the *prosecution* lawyers, so that the DPP and the Attorney-General would never be in a position to consider whether they contained material which could assist the defendant to prove his innocence. This was an extraordinary argument, since the Government had solemnly undertaken during Parliamentary debates on the Bill in 1985 that any prosecution would be dropped if the DPP or CPS lawyers found evidence consistent with innocence on telephone-tap transcripts.[50] The fact that they have never, since that undertaking was given, sought in any way to honour it, and that the Home Office now argued that it could not be honoured because of the terms of the 1985 statute, demonstrates just how devious the Government was at the time it promoted the measure. It has to be said, however, that the Government was not put under much pressure by an ill-informed Opposition. The senior judges appointed as Commissioners have had little experience of criminal law, and have not even noticed the potential for wrongful conviction inherent in the Home Office refusal to make the product of intercepts available to prosecution and defence lawyers.

The only solution consistent with a real commitment to avoid miscarriages of justice is to abolish Section 9, to allow telephone taps with the approval of a judge and to make all the evidence obtained thereby available for use by prosecution and defence alike. There can be no security concern about allowing defendants to re-hear their own telephone conversations, and the result (as with the recording of police interviews) would be to save legal time and money, to convict more of the guilty and to protect some of the innocent.

The Interception of Communications Act sets out three grounds on which a warrant may be issued:

(1) in the interests of national security;

(2) for the purpose of preventing or detecting serious crime; or

(3) for the purpose of safeguarding the economic well-being of the United Kingdom.

Ground (3), according to the Home Secretary when moving the bill, is not concerned with promoting British trade but rather with securing supplies of essential commodities and with obtaining information about significant threats to the national economy.[51] He was being economical with the truth, according to Robin Robison, a former member of the Joint Intelligence Committee, who told *World in Action* in 1991 that GCHQ (which is outside the Act) furtively intercepts communications to and from large foreign companies and passes the information to their British competitors. Ground (3) would also seem to permit a Home Secretary to order taps on the telephones of trade unionists who organize strikes in major industries. (The 'person' against whom a warrant may be granted 'includes any organization and any association or combination of persons'.)

A crime is 'serious' if it is likely to result in a sentence of more than three years' imprisonment, or in substantial financial gain, or if it involves the use of violence or conduct by 'a large number of persons in pursuit of a common interest'.[52] This formula too would permit the tapping of the telephones of those involved in large-scale political protests. The Government defines 'the interests of national security' to include combating 'terrorist, espionage or major subversive activity' and supporting 'the Government's defence and foreign policies'.[53] This affords a broad scope for intercepting communications between those concerned with peaceful protests against the politics of the Government of the day. Cathy Massiter, the MI5 'case officer' on CND, claimed that the real reason for the application she had been instructed to make for a warrant to tap the telephone of John Cox, a member of CND's executive, was to gather information which might help the Defence Minister, Mr Michael Heseltine, to discredit the peace movement for political purposes. In the application, she had alleged that Cox's membership of the Communist Party indicated a subversive intent: in reality, she claimed, he was chosen because he lived in Wales and frequently communicated by telephone with the executive members.

In 1986 CND brought a High Court action based on Massiter's evidence, arguing that the repeated Government statements and White Papers promising that tapping would be confined to subversives and would not be used for party political purposes had created a 'legitimate expectation' that the court could oblige it to honour. Mr Justice Taylor (now the Lord Chief Justice) agreed that the courts were entitled to review unfair actions by Government stemming from failures to live up to 'legitimate expectations' aroused by repeated publication of policy criteria, even in areas such as phone tapping where it had no obligation to hear representations on behalf of a proposed victim. (This principle marks a significant extension of administrative law's ability to protect the liberty of the subject, and may in due course enable the courts to review official actions taken in breach of Home Office 'guidelines' and 'circulars' which are so often used as substitutes for law.) He succinctly stated the principles which should govern security-service surveillance:

The function of the Security Service is the defence of the realm as a whole from, *inter alia*, the actions of persons who and organizations which may be judged subversive to the state. Subversive activities are those which threaten the safety or well-being of the state and which are intended to undermine or overthrow parliamentary democracy by political, industrial or violent means. A warrant to intercept should issue only where there is reasonable cause to believe that major subversive activity is already being carried on and is likely to injure the national interest. The material reasonably likely to be obtained by the interception must be of direct use to the Security Service in its functions which include keeping up to date its information about subversion. Normal methods of investigation must either have failed or be unlikely to succeed. Interception must be strictly limited to what is necessary to the Security Service's defined function and must not be used for party political purposes or for the purposes of any particular section of the community.

On the facts, CND's case was rejected, as Massiter's evidence did not exclude the possibility of other and more legitimate reasons, of which she was unaware, being given to the Home Secretary to justify the issue of the warrant. None the less, the decision stands as an important authority on the limits of state interception, especially as it is unlikely ever to be repeated. Section 9 of the Interception of Communications Act puts an end to any further applications to the court, and requires these to be considered only by the tribunal. Ironically, Mr Justice Taylor rejected the Government's argument that national-security considerations should have stopped the court from hearing the case at all:

I do not accept that the court should never inquire into a complaint against a minister if he says it is his policy to maintain silence in the interests of national security . . . Totally to oust the court's supervisory jurisdiction in a field where *ex hypothesis* the citizen can have no right to be consulted is a dangerous and draconian step indeed.[54]

It is precisely this 'dangerous and draconian step' which the Government has taken by enacting the Interception of Communications Act. That Act, of course, applies its 'safeguards' only to intercepts authorized by a Secretary of State. GCHQ operates a microwave system which scans overseas telephone calls and scoops up those containing 'key words', and reportedly has facilities which intercept telex and facsimile messages, at home or from abroad. In 1967, it was revealed that the security services were reading all foreign telegrams – a disclosure which the Government sought to prevent by a D notice. There is a vast array of electronic bugs and surveillance devices available to security agencies and police which require no authorization at all. Peter Wright went 'burglaring and bugging' his way round London for MI5 without the Home Secretary's approval, and in 1982 security officials were interrupted while installing a bug on a public telephone serving a council estate in Wales.

In 1979 a hidden video camera was discovered in the bar of a Hartlepool pub: the publican disclaimed any knowledge, so it was commandeered by a group of his customers. They were later arrested and held for a day before the police owned up to planting the camera in an attempt to obtain evidence of small-scale trafficking in cannabis.[55] This was a breach of the inevitable 'Home Office circular' recommending that the use of secret surveillance devices be confined to the investigation of serious crime, but as a senior officer commented in a similar case a few years later, they could not see any reason why they should respect 'an obscure piece of paper brought out five or six years ago'. Fresh guidelines were issued by the Home Office in 1984 to 'regulate' use of aural and visual surveillance devices, recommending (since 'guidelines' and 'circulars' are not legally binding on anyone) that use be confined to the investigation of serious crime (or obscene telephone calls) where more routine methods would be unlikely to succeed, and that attention must be paid to the risk of interfering with privacy, especially when devices are placed in homes or hotel bedrooms. The use should be approved at chief or assistant chief constable level, and bugging devices should not be used to pick up telephone calls in a way which would circumvent the Home Secretary's warrant procedure.

These 1984 guidelines are fundamentally defective, because they completely ignore the rights of the person whose privacy is being invaded. They envisage that a decision will be made by senior policemen to use sophisticated surveillance devices to record conversations in private residences and hotel bedrooms, but they provide no independent supervision over the use which is made of the product, nor do they give the target any right to learn subsequently of the surveillance and to ensure that the product is destroyed. Targets who are prosecuted may never learn that their privacy has been invaded, and have no access to recordings or records which may contain evidence which helps to prove their innocence. The whole process of police authorization of listening devices is unregulated by law, in blatant breach of Article 8 of the European Convention as interpreted in *Malone*, and is not even made subject to the rudimentary safeguards of the Home Secretary's warrant procedure and the 1985 Interception of Communications Act. Once again, the British obsession with secrecy has been permitted to override the standards basic to any civilized system of law, namely that state interception of private conversations in private homes and bedrooms should either be authorized by court orders made according to published and acceptable criteria, or should not be authorized at all.[56]

Surreptitious surveillance is now a regular incident of policing, and is largely beyond control by the courts. Telephone and mail intercepts cannot be mentioned, let alone challenged, in any court, and breaches of 'Home Office guidelines' on listening devices will rarely be discovered, because these forms of electronic surveillance are not even subject to the minimal 'safeguards' available in respect of telephone tapping and mail opening. This whole subject is a disaster area from all rational viewpoints: victims of state privacy invasions have little or no redress; the product of these invasions is not actually used to convict serious criminals; and innocent defendants who have been targets of surveillance cannot demand to see the evidence which might exculpate them. The time has surely come, in the interests of rational law enforcement, to end the counterproductive Home Office attachment to secrecy and ministerial discretion, and to oblige police to go to court to obtain a warrant from a judge before deploying surveillance devices of any sort in places not open to the public. The criteria set out in the Interception of Communications Act and in the Home Office guidelines are best applied by a judge: the Home Secretary lacks the time and the qualifications for the role of objective scrutineer of police suspicions. If intercept and surveillance warrants were applied for and granted by courts on the same basis as search warrants, there could be no objection to the fruits of that surveillance (subject to the 'fairness' provisions of Section 78 of P A C E) being used as relevant evidence of criminal conduct or conspiracy. The gathering of national-security information does present problems with which courts are less familiar, but the abuses alleged by Cathy Massiter and Peter Wright make it difficult to maintain confidence in a secret procedure authorized in certain cases by a Government minister and in others by anonymous senior civil servants in the security service. If 'national interest' surveillance were in every case to be undertaken upon a warrant issued by a senior judge, overseen by an all-party committee of Privy Councillors, there would be less cause for disquiet. The US Supreme Court has convincingly refuted the executive's claim to a unique ability to authorize secret surveillance on those suspected of domestic subversion:

We cannot accept the Government's argument that internal security matters are too subtle and complex for judicial evaluation. Courts regularly deal with the most difficult issues of our society. There is no reason to believe that federal judges will be insensitive to or uncomprehending of the issues involved in domestic security cases. Certainly courts can recognize that domestic security surveillance involves different considerations from the surveillance of 'ordinary crime'. If the threat is too subtle or complex for our senior law enforcement officers to convey its significance to a court, one may question whether there is probable cause for surveillance ... By no means of least importance will be the reassurance of the public generally that indiscriminate wiretapping and bugging of law-abiding citizens cannot occur.[57]

VETTING AND PURGING

To what extent is the state entitled to probe the private life and political views of its employees to eliminate security risks? In 1952, after the defection of Burgess and Maclean and the conviction of several scientists for supplying nuclear secrets to the Russians, a 'positive vetting' (PV) procedure was introduced to enable closer scrutiny of employees with access to security information. A measure of the extent to which the 'Secret State' has grown is provided by the increase in positively vetted employees, from 1,000 at the time the system was introduced to 68,000 in 1982, including civil servants, employees of the nuclear industry, British Telecom and defence contractors, and police officers.[58] 'Positive vettees' are at least told that they will be the subject of MI5 inquiries, unlike the 700,000 people who are secretly made the subject of 'negative vetting', to check whether MI5 has anything about them on file. (This is called the 'nothing known against' procedure.) The 'positive vetting' procedure is expensive and time-consuming, and the vast number of checks has undoubtedly contributed to reduce their comprehensiveness and has led to such spectacular failures as MI5's Michael Bettany (who flaunted Fascist beliefs at Oxford), GCHQ's Geoffrey Prime (who sexually molested small children) and Commander Trestrail, the Queen's bodyguard who openly consorted with male prostitutes. The PV procedure involves interviews of the employee, his referees and his previous employers, and checks into family background, associations and lifestyle. Security clearance is denied if there is an indication of 'unreliability', such as sympathy with a subversive organization, or 'character defects' which may expose the employee to blackmail or to temptation offered by foreign security services. The MoD regards as 'character defects' the following: 'Major indiscretion, drunkenness or drug-taking, dishonesty, conviction for serious crime, having substantial financial difficulties, being vulnerable as a result of irregular sexual behaviour and significant mental illness.'

Positive vetting is a necessary precaution for members of the security services and for police officers and others who deal with information of potential use to terrorists, and there can be no objection to it in principle. The definition of a 'character defect', however, is open to debate. What really matters is whether a civil servant who is subject to an adverse PV report has an effective means of challenging it – and this is far from the case. Where the civil servant is refused clearance on the basis of alleged character defects, his appeal is merely to the permanent head of department, who is hardly an independent judge, and the courts will not intervene even if the appeal is unreasonably turned down. One young data processor had worked at GCHQ for some years before he recognized his homosexuality. He immediately disclosed it, and in consequence lost his PV clearance on the grounds that he might be subject to blackmail.[59] This was an irrational decision, since his openness about his sexuality would preclude him being blackmailed on that ground alone. None the less, the High Court held that it was not entitled to interfere with 'positive vetting' procedures other than to check that they had been conducted with basic fairness. The

Government was entitled to hide behind 'national security', irrespective of whether the decision had been made unreasonably, irrationally or in bad faith. The Security Commission has recommended that homosexuality should not be an absolute bar to a security clearance, and the revelation in 1981 that Sir Maurice Oldfield, the most distinguished of spymasters, was that way inclined serves only to emphasize the belated wisdom of this approach.

When security clearance is denied on the basis of suspected Communist or Fascist links or suspected susceptibility to blackmail, the employee has the right to invoke what has become known as the 'purge procedure', and to state his case to 'three advisers'. Until 1962, an accused person was not allowed any formal representation: since then, he has been permitted to bring a 'friend', who could be a lawyer or trade-union official, but who has no right of audience. The civil servant is given no opportunity to confront or cross-examine his accusers, and no power to subpoena witnesses. 'Chapter and verse' of the allegations is very rarely provided, on the ground that to do so might compromise sources. The three advisers meet and report in secret, they do not see witnesses, and the minister is not bound to accept their recommendations. In 1982, the Government announced that they would have a judge as chairman.

This 'purge procedure' is a relic from the depths of the cold war. An inquiry by Privy Councillors into the Burgess/Maclean defections decided that the three advisers must 'tilt the balance in favour of offering greater protection to the security of the state rather than in the direction of safeguarding the rights of the individual'.[60] The sole question that the advisers should ask themselves was, 'Are there or are there not reasonable grounds for supposing that the individual has or has recently had Communist sympathies or associations of such a type as to raise legitimate doubts about his reliability?' The Privy Councillors indicated that marriage to a Communist or Communist sympathizer would be sufficient to raise such doubts, and ICI was forced by the Minister of Supply to dismiss its assistant solicitor, Mr J. Lang, or suffer cancellation of all Government contracts. Lang's wife had once belonged to the Communist Party, although she had disaffiliated before her marriage. The minister refused to tell Lang of the allegations against him, or to explain to Parliament why he should be debarred from drafting contracts relating to secret work. In 1962 the Radcliffe Committee extended the 'purge procedure' to independent contractors working for Government departments.[61]

It is the consistent policy of British Governments to avoid putting themselves under judicial controls whenever possible. If a person is not accorded the protection, such as it is, allowed by the arrangements already described, there is no court to which a complaint can be taken. This defect is particularly important in cases pivoting upon vague words like 'security'. 'Security' is an abstraction, and the citizen is at the mercy of administrators who will define it as they please. The justification is always the same: ministerial responsibility. In the words of Lord Kilmuir, then Lord Chancellor, the balance 'must be struck by a minister who is responsible to Parliament ... and who is there to be shot at'.[62] The value of this protection can be measured by looking at the proceedings of the House of Commons ten days previously. The Minister of Supply was asked on what grounds he had denied access on the part of Lang to secrets: he refused to answer. What is the point of stressing the right to ask a question on matters of security when the minister can be relied on never to answer? The political accountability of a minister does not extend to security matters, and is a completely inadequate substitute for the right to take one's case before the courts. The rules laid down by the Government in 1957, as revised by the cabinet office in 1985, do not envisage the employee being given details of the allegations or permit him to be represented at the hearing before the advisers, or to cross-examine the evidence against him.

It may well be that these manifestly unjust aspects of the purge procedure will be the subject of future challenge in the courts, which have in recent years developed broader powers to review administrative actions and to strike them down on grounds of unfairness. The 'three advisers' system is also available to aliens threatened with deportation on national-security grounds, and was challenged by American journalist Mark Hosenball when he was made the subject of a deportation order in 1977 and by Gulf War detainee Abbas Cheblak in 1991 (see later, page 401). The Court of Appeal accepted that the procedure was unfair, but upheld the order on the grounds that national-security considerations justified a shortfall in the rights which could be accorded to an alien suspect.[63] A British citizen whose job is at risk falls into a different category, and in 1984 the House of Lords was prepared to insist that there should at least be some evidence of a security threat before the Prime Minister was entitled to prohibit civil servants at GCHQ from joining trade unions.[64] The court is not prepared to evaluate evidence relating to national security, but will use its powers of judicial review to ensure that the basic rules of natural justice have been complied with. In the case brought by the homosexual data processor against GCHQ, the High Court confirmed that it would supervise the 'fairness' of dismissals on grounds of national security, ensuring that employees were given at least an indication of what was alleged against them and an opportunity to present arguments against their sacking. In the light of this case, it may be that courts would strike down a dismissal or refusal of security clearance where legal representation had not been afforded or no reasons at all had been forthcoming.

Individual litigants cannot expect British courts, as presently minded, to look very closely into Government claims that actions taken against them are based on national security. Unlike breach-of-confidence actions (where such claims must at least be weighed against a specific public-interest defence) judicial review is strictly limited to ensuring that proper procedures are followed and that there is *some* evidence – however slight and however dubious – that national-security interests were at stake. All assessment of that evidence will be left to the executive, no matter how much the decision strikes at civil liberties. The Government's ban on trade-union membership at GCHQ was a plain denial of the right of freedom to associate. It was struck down by a High Court judge on the basis that the Government had acted unfairly in imposing it without giving the unions the opportunity for consultation that they had a legitimate right to expect. On appeal, however, the Government succeeded by arguing that a national-security consideration had been present in its decision, because the monitoring centre had been adversely affected by union strike action several years previously. This was hardly an impressive argument: the Government had not thought to make it in the initial proceedings, and the unions were in any event offering a 'no strike' agreement which would have guaranteed no further disruption. The Government could not prove that its ban was necessary, or even justifiable, in the interests of national security, but the House of Lords required merely to be satisfied by some evidence (a passage in an affidavit by Sir Robert Armstrong, the Cabinet Secretary whose credibility was later to be severely shaken in *Spycatcher*) that the decision had been motivated by security concerns. Judges are often accused of being too deferential to the Government in this area, and there is no doubt that they could go a little further, within the constraints of judicial review, by requiring national-security decisions to be made rationally. But this test is easily satisfied, and it is unfair to expect the courts to protect civil liberties unless they have the power to judge whether a withdrawal of a fundamental right is *necessary* in the interest of national security. That is the test applied by the European Convention of Human Rights for abrogating rights to freedom of speech and assembly, and only by enactment of the Convention as part of British law would the courts of this country be properly empowered to safeguard citizens from losses of liberty by unjustifiable invocations of 'national security'.

CHAPTER 4

Official Secrecy

'Can you shed any light on the disappearance of Burgess and Maclean?'

'No I can't ... I am debarred by the Official Secrets Act from saying anything which might disclose to unauthorized persons information derived from my position as a former government official.'

> Mr Kim Philby at a press conference in 1956 after being
> cleared by the Prime Minister of any taint of disloyalty

Secrecy, said Richard Crossman, is the British disease, and it has reached epidemic proportions. No other Western democracy is so obsessed with keeping from the public information about its public servants, or so relentless in plumbing new legal depths to staunch leaks from its bureaucracy. The laws and practices which are examined in this chapter cast a blanket of secrecy over 'official information' irrespective of its triviality, or its importance for public health and safety, or its revelation of bungling and incompetence. There is no compelling legal reason why much of this information should not be revealed: successive Governments, advised by successive bureaucrats, have simply made political decisions to protect it from Parliament, press and public, other than by way of 'authorized' disclosures through departmental press releases and ministerial statements, or by dishonestly briefing journalists on non-attributable 'lobby' terms. This has obvious advantages for the party in power, because it can control the flow of information so as to reduce political embarrassment for senior civil servants, whose performance is not subject to sensible public scrutiny until they are long retired or deceased. One of the most remarkable sights Britain has to offer is the annual queue of journalists and historians waiting at Kew for the Public Record Office to open its doors and reveal the secret papers which will explain how and why the British

Government acted as it did thirty years before. The occasion deserves to be a tourist attraction: it symbolizes the governance of modern Britain a good deal more accurately than the Trooping of the Colour.

The cult of secrecy amongst our mandarins is not entirely explained by self-interest: there is a genuine belief that decisions are made better if made without publicity. (As Sir Humphrey Appleby of *Yes Minister* felicitously puts it, 'Open government is a contradiction in terms. You can be open, or you can have government.') The difficulty of squaring this belief with any acceptable view of democratic accountability leads them to shelter behind a political fiction called 'ministerial accountability' which holds that information emanating from Whitehall should only come from or with the approval of a responsible minister. But the truth is that ministers neither control nor are in practice answerable for thousands of decisions made by middle-ranking bureaucrats – decisions which may vitally affect individuals. Freedom of Information legislation, which allows inspection of information accumulated by and acted upon by officials, is fast becoming a defining characteristic of democracy in countries throughout Europe, North America and Australasia, underpinned by Madison's vision of representative government:

> Knowledge will for ever govern ignorance. And a people who mean to be their own governors must arm themselves with the power knowledge gives. A popular Government without popular information or means of acquiring it is but a prologue to a farce or a tragedy, or perhaps both.[1]

The evidence shows that public participation in government leads to better government. But when the Freedom of Information campaign was launched in 1984, it was condemned by Mrs Thatcher: a Freedom of Information Act, she proclaimed, is 'both inappropriate and unnecessary ... ministers' accountability to Parliament would be reduced, and Parliament itself diminished.' The notion that ministers would be less accountable if there was more information about department blunders for them to account for is curious, to say the least, and it is not clear how Parliament would be diminished, other perhaps than by a fuller public appreciation of how little influence it has on civil-service decision-making. None the less, constitutional fictions like 'ministerial accountability' and 'parliamentary sovereignty' are invariably paraded in opposition to proposals to increase citizens' legal freedoms: left-wing politicians, as we shall see, oppose a Bill of Rights by reference to a view of Parliament as protector of civil liberties which is just as absurd as Mrs Thatcher's.

Mr John Major has paid lip service to the need for more open government, and has even appointed a minister with this objective as one of his responsibilities. This commitment is meaningless, however, unless it is backed by a legal right of citizen access. Its hypocrisy was exposed in 1992 at the Matrix Churchill trial, when four ministers signed 'public-interest immunity certificates' in an effort to stop pre-Gulf War documents about secret shifts in British policy towards arming Iraq from becoming public knowledge.[2] They claimed that it was 'necessary for the proper functioning of the public service' for the documents to be withheld, because they would reveal 'the process of providing for ministers honest and candid advice on matters of high-level policy'. This claim was shown to be bogus when the documents were ordered to be released, revealing that the advice had been in favour of dishonesty and lack of candour. Senior civil servants had in 1988 approved exports to set up large munitions factories in Iraq, in breach of 'guidelines' publicly declared to Parliament: they had advised their ministers to 'keep as quiet as possible about this politically sensitive issue' in order to avoid 'presentational difficulties', i.e. political criticism. The documents exposed the culture of secrecy in Whitehall and the presumption in civil service minds that ministers should avoid if at all possible explaining contentious policy to an informed public. The advantage of FoI, of course, is that it would create a presumption in favour of informed debate: the prospect that advice will become public sooner rather than later will not mean that the advice will be *less* candid, it will mean that the advice will be *in favour of* candour.

The 'Iraqgate' documents also demonstrated the hollowness of the notion that 'ministerial accountability' is a safeguard for the democratic process in the absence of a Freedom of Information Act. They revealed that the stringent guidelines for sale of defence equipment to Iraq which had been announced in Parliament in 1985 had been secretly liberalized by ministers in 1989, although for the next three years they still publicly pretended that the 1985 guidelines remained in place. After the ministers had met to change the rules, they agreed that these changes should not be revealed to Parliament. As William Waldegrave (later to become minister for 'open government' in the Major administration) recorded at the time:

The form of words we agreed to use if we are now pressed in Parliament over the guidelines was the following: 'The guidelines on the export of defence equipment to Iraq and Iran are kept under constant review, and are applied in the light of the prevailing circumstances, including the ceasefire and the development in the peace negotiations.'

This formula was a masterpiece of equivocation. How, under this formula, could MPs divine that the guidelines for defence sales to Iraq had fundamentally altered, so as to allow a new range of defence equipment to go to Iraq but not to Iran? This is an example of how Mrs Thatcher's ministers regarded their obligation of 'ministerial accountability', which she had invoked to resist calls for a Freedom of Information Act.

The central issue – should we arm Saddam and, if so, to what extent – was appropriate for public debate in a democracy. The policy considerations were obvious: they were political, economic, social and moral. In favour were considerations of boosting British exports, of competing with European rivals (whose Governments displayed no moral scruples in attracting petrodollars) and of weaning a powerful country away from Soviet influence. Against were humanitarian considerations of refusing to help prolong the Iraq/Iran war and, after it had ended, of declining to contribute to the armoury of a megalomanic and brutal dictator, engaged both in reprisals against an ethnic minority and in seeking to obtain weapons of mass destruction.

These pros and cons of defence-related trade with Iraq should have been argued out in Parliament, in editorials, in pubs and clubs and common rooms. Had the Government declared its policy and publicly defended it, then everybody would have known where they, and HMG, stood on the issue. And that stand could have been altered, as the result of the play upon it of public opinion. Had ministers and civil servants known their policy shift would become public knowledge in a few years' time, rather than in thirty years' time, it is much more likely than they would have allowed that debate to take place.

The Government's policy of promoting some 'conventional' arms sales to Iraq, both during and after the Iran/Iraq war, is now criticized, with the benefit of hindsight, as an error. Had it been seen – and debated – at the time it was under way, it would have been a mistake made within the democratic process. Because it was undeclared, and justified privately by reference to the 'elasticity' of published rules and the 'flexibility' of the unpublished rules that replaced them, it became a mistake made by a Government which lacked the spur to democratic action provided, in other Western countries, by freedom-of-information legislation. Indeed, in the US, sufficient information became available about 'Iraqgate' by 1992 to undermine George Bush's claim to have been a wise formulator of foreign policy, and the scandal played an important part in his defeat in the presidential elections. Had the British Government's involvement with the same scandal been known to the public by the time of the UK elections in April 1992, it might well have affected the result. There can be no better evidence that freedom of information is crucial to the democratic process, and no other reason why the present British Government is so adamant that it must not be introduced.

SECRECY LAWS: THEN AND NOW

The first Official Secrets Act was passed in 1889, after a clerk in the Foreign Office had passed details to the *Globe* of a secret treaty between Britain and Russia. He had, sensibly, committed these details to memory, and much embarrassment was suffered by the authorities when he was duly acquitted of the only available offence, that of removing a state document. In an era where secret treaties were necessary to effect imperialist ambitions, some protection against the disclosure of such high policy matters did not seem unreasonable. A much more significant protection was afforded by the Prevention of Corruption Acts of 1889 and 1906, which make it a criminal offence for any employee to receive bribes or kickbacks as an inducement to use his position to favour an outsider. This covers the selling of information derived from an office or employment, and is a much more satisfactory method of prosecuting public servants who have tainted motives for disclosing official information. It only applies while the employee holds office, and so does not catch those who write reminiscences in retirement, nor those impelled to speak out, without payment, by reason of conscience or political belief. It was this that worried civil-service chiefs at the beginning of the century and they prepared legislation – secretly, of course – to gag any public servant who might feel morally impelled to talk to the press. The law which was to become Section 2 was recognized by its sponsors to be a draconian infringement of civil liberties: they bided their time, waiting for a suitable opportunity to slip it through Parliament.

That opportunity was provided in 1911, when German 'gunboat diplomacy' at Agadir caused national panic, and coincided with sensationalized newspaper stories about German spies posing as tourists and photographing the fortifications at Dover harbour. The Government, to the acclaim of the press and the opposition, instantly produced the Official Secrets Act as a measure to protect the nation from enemy agents. Astoundingly, the bill passed through all its parliamentary stages in one day, with no more than one hour's debate, in the course of which Section 2 – cunningly inserted between sections dealing with espionage – was not mentioned once. Until 1989 Section 2 forbade any of our one million public servants, or any of the further one million civilians employed under Government contracts, from revealing any information about their jobs, or any information obtained in the course of their jobs, if the disclosure had not been 'authorized' by a superior. In legal theory, it was a crime to reveal the number of cups of tea consumed each day in the MI5 canteen.

In 1989 the Government introduced a new Official Secrets Act to replace Section 2, which would make it the clearest possible criminal offence to reveal the number of cups of tea served in the MI5 canteen on any day in the eighty-year history of the security service.[3] The purpose of this legislation was to refurbish the criminal law as a weapon for punishing leaks from the intelligence community or which relate to defence and foreign policy, by removing or narrowing potential defences that may have been available under the old Section 2. In practice, as we shall see, the new law would make it easier to convict all persons who had in the past been controversially prosecuted under Section 2, and would enable the state to gaol people like Cathy Massiter whom it had not previously dared to prosecute because of the public importance of their revelations. The impact of the 1989 legislation can be appreciated in the context of what the state had previously thought it necessary to punish under Section 2.

Section 2 was for many years taken quite seriously. An early decision confirmed that, despite its title, it did not apply to information which was 'secret', and in 1932 the distinguished author Compton Mackenzie found himself in the dock of the Old Bailey for publishing a collection of reminiscences about his intelligence activities in the First World War. The Crown conceded that the book had not prejudiced the public interest, other than by revealing the names of long-retired intelligence officers who, it was argued, might be brought back from retirement in the event of another war. Mackenzie pleaded guilty in return for a promise of a small fine, and heard the Attorney-General explain to the judge that his worst crime had been to reveal the dangerous consonant – C – by which the Chief of the Security Service was known, and that the position had been occupied by Sir Mansfield Cumming. 'Surely this officer's name was perfectly well known during the war, Mr Attorney, in clubs both you and I belong to?' asked the astonished judge. The Attorney-General demurred, and was unable to explain what secret occupation Cumming was currently engaged on until the defendant, from the dock, reminded the court that C had died ten years previously.[4] Mackenzie was none the less fined £100, a sentence which did not deter *Daily Telegraph* journalists from publishing the Government's secret plans to arrest Mahatma Gandhi. They were held in custody and interrogated about their source, until their proprietor let it be known that the source for the story was the Home Secretary himself. (Under the 1989 Official Secrets Act, Mackenzie would have no defence at all to the charge of disclosing information learnt in the course of long-past intelligence activities.)

Needless to say, politicians have never been prosecuted. In 1934 no action was taken against Labour MP George Lansbury, who gave a Cabinet paper to his son (who published it and was fined), and two years later J. H. Thomas, a Cabinet Minister who should have been prosecuted for leaking Budget secrets, was allowed to resign in disgrace. Parliament protects its own: in 1938 the Attorney-General was criticized by the Privileges Committee for threatening Mr Duncan Sandys, MP (described in a secret War Office memo as 'a slippery young gentleman who is certainly backed up by Winston'), with an Official Secrets Act prosecution for obtaining and disclosing information about the lack of anti-aircraft defences in London.[5] (Under the 1989 Act, the MP's source would be guilty of the crime of revealing information about defence equipment.) Parliamentary privilege will protect any MP from prosecution for disclosing an official secret, even when it is alleged to affect national security: Kim Philby's treason and Colonel B's identity were disclosed by questions in the House, and a former Labour minister was said to have damaged the national interest by blurting out the fact that Britain had been intercepting Argentinian Government communications for many years before the Falklands War.

When in office, ministers are assumed to have the power to authorize themselves to disclose secrets, however deviously or improperly. This 'self-authorization' doctrine saved J. H. Thomas, and doubtless Home Secretary Sir Leon Brittan when he flagrantly violated convention by leaking to the press the Solicitor-General's opinion on an aspect of the takeover bid for Westland Helicopters, in order to damage the credibility of a fellow minister. There was a half-hearted police investigation when Ms Sarah Keays claimed that her lover, Mr Cecil Parkinson, had spilled intimate details of the War Cabinet proceedings during the Falklands conflict: Section 7 of the Official Secrets Act (which is not repealed by the 1989 law) makes it an offence to 'knowingly harbour' a person you have reason to believe is about to communicate an official secret, so Miss Keays may have taken a risk by allowing her loquacious Cabinet lover to stay the night. Such speculations are in practice idle: the Attorney-General's consent is required for any official secrets prosecution, so Cabinet Ministers and their mistresses are unlikely to be seen in the Old Bailey dock.

The decline of Section 2 dates from the prosecution in 1970 of Jonathan Aitken, a journalist and parliamentary candidate, who came by a secret army document about the state of the Biafran war which contained information at variance with Prime Ministerial statements to Parliament. He was given it by a general, who had received the report from a colonel attached to the British Embassy in Nigeria. Aitken, to the general's embarrassment, arranged for it to be published in the *Daily Telegraph*. The Attorney-General authorized a Section 2 prosecution of the colonel, Aitken and the editor of the *Daily Telegraph*, with the general cutting a sorry figure as chief prosecution witness. Various technical defences were canvassed, based on the prosecution's difficulty in proving that original disclosure by the colonel to the general, his former commanding officer, was 'unauthorized'. Both journalist and editor additionally claimed that they had a moral duty to make the information public in order to rectify false statements in Parliament. The defence claimed the case was a 'political prosecution', initiated by a petulant Labour Government, and the trial judge in a sympathetic summing-up told the jury that it was high time that Section 2 was 'pensioned off'. All defendants were acquitted. (Under the 1989 reforms, all defendants would have been guilty of making disclosures about army logistics and deployment which would be likely to jeopardize British defence interests abroad.)

The outcry provoked by the Aitken prosecution led to the establishment of a committee headed by Lord Franks to examine Section 2 of the Official Secrets Act. It condemned the width and uncertainty of the section, and urged its replacement by a law narrowly defining the categories of information which deserved protection. The Government, in a White Paper in 1976, accepted that mere receipt of secret information by the press should not amount to an offence.[6] But its White Paper promise was almost immediately betrayed by its prosecution the following year of investigative journalist Duncan Campbell, for interviewing an ex-soldier about his work many years before at the GCHQ base at Cyprus. The 'ABC case' as it came to be known (after the defendants Crispin Aubrey, John Berry and Duncan Campbell) marked the first public admission that the function of GCHQ, which had been established in 1920, was to intercept communications. Campbell, who was then working for *Time Out*, faced not only a Section 2 allegation but two 'spying' charges laid under Section 1 of the Act and carrying fourteen years' imprisonment apiece. The Government (a Labour Government, be it noted) was determined to put behind bars for a very long time a twenty-four-year-old journalist with a discomfiting ability to read between the lines of glossy Ministry of Defence handouts and to conjure official secrets out of telephone books. Although his entire library had been transferred by pantechnicon to Scotland Yard, the Section 1 charge accusing him of 'collecting information' collapsed as it became apparent that all the information was available from public sources (for example the microwave facilities alleged by the prosecution to be 'top secret' were all shown on a map issued to Aeroflot pilots by the Department of Civil Aviation). The judge threw out the second Section 1 charge as 'oppressive',[7] Campbell and his fellow journalist Aubrey were given conditional discharges for breaching Section 2, and John Berry received a suspended sentence: a counter-productive result of a case which had done little more than to put GCHQ on the public, as well as the Aeroflot, map.

Duncan Campbell has not been deterred by his prosecution from probing official secrecy. In 1984, when he fell off his bicycle, a policeman helped him to hospital while others helped themselves to the contents of his saddle-bags, confiscating his copy of *The Army Manual on Personal Protection* with its secret 'Instructions on Defecating in the Arctic'. The following year, Campbell was retained by the BBC to make a series of films entitled *The Secret Society*, with results which will shortly require examination. (Duncan Campbell's journalism could be made the subject of prosecution under the 1989 law, because it included the use of information of a class regarded as 'likely to damage' the intelligence services or the defence establishment.)

In the meantime, however, the cases of Sarah Tisdall and Clive Ponting re-emphasized the counter-productive consequences of using Section 2 to punish those who leak from motives of conscience or concern for democratic accountability. Tisdall, who pleaded guilty to sending to the *Guardian* documents revealing the date of cruise-missile arrivals at Greenham Common, was gaoled for six months, a sentence which many believed to be harsh for an impulsive act taken when she read in them that the Defence Minister planned to dodge questions in the House and that there was official concern that American military personnel might shoot at women who stormed the base in protest at the arrival of the missiles. Many journalists, mortified that the evidence against her had been provided by the *Guardian* itself, in obedience to a court order to hand back the documents, vowed henceforth to destroy such documents immediately after use.

Tisdall's fate did not deter Mr Clive Ponting, OBE, a senior MoD official, from priming Tam Dalyell, MP, with information which undermined the truth of ministerial answers to questions he had been asking in Parliament about the sinking of the *Belgrano*. (When confronted in court with these parliamentary fibs, the minister's private secretary riposted that 'one man's ambiguity is another man's truth' – a worthy precursor, in the Whitehall book of euphemisms for lying, to Sir Robert Armstrong's more notorious phrase about 'being economical with the truth' and Mr Alan Clark's sophisticated improvement, 'being economical with the *actualité*'.) Ponting was prosecuted under Section 2, and acquitted. It was very much a 'sympathy verdict' – in which sympathy for Ms Tisdall's fate may have played some part, together with a feeling that Ponting had a duty to expose ministerial evasiveness. A jury, of course, has a constitutional right to acquit a defendant irrespective of the evidence, and the only defence open to Ponting under Section 2 – that Dalyell was 'a person to whom it is his duty in the interests of the state to communicate [the information]' was in effect foreclosed by the judge's controversial ruling that 'the interests of the state' referred to the policies of the Government of the day. The jury presumably took the view that Ponting had a moral duty to let MPs know that answers provided by ministers, and drafted by their civil servants, had been positively parsimonious with the truth.[8] (The 1989 law forecloses any defence based on 'moral duty' or public interest.)

The message that juries could not be trusted to convict where apparent breaches of Section 2 had been motivated by conscience came through loud and clear, and no attempt was made to charge Cathy Massiter when she revealed details of MI5 operations against trade unionists, civil libertarians and the peace movement in a Channel 4 programme tauntingly entitled *MI5's Official Secrets*. The IBA loyally postponed the screening of the film for a month to give the Government an opportunity to prosecute its makers, an action which only served to have the transcript published widely in the press while video-cassettes of the film were marketed by Virgin Records under the label 'The Programme That Couldn't be Shown'. The purpose of the 1989 law is to ensure that any person like Cathy Massiter shall have no defence at all to charges of disclosing information about the work (however controversial or even unlawful) of the security services.

All civil servants and most experts who sit on Government committees go through the routine of 'signing the Official Secrets Act' (a legally pointless exercise, as they, like everyone else in Britain, are bound by it anyway). Although the likelihood of prosecution is negligible in the case of disclosures which are not made corruptly or are not damaging to national security, this ritual conduces to an atmosphere in which outspokenness and open debate are officially discouraged. To take but one example, a detailed and disturbing study of the eating habits of British schoolchildren, completed in 1983, was kept under wraps until it was leaked in 1986. The scientist who had conducted it, by then retired from Government service, was warned by DHSS lawyers that she could not publicly discuss it – her obligation of confidence continued even unto the grave. The need for open debate on food policy is obvious, given the 'behind the scenes' influence of the agriculture and food-processing industries, yet independent scientists seconded to DHSS committees are still required to 'sign the Official Secrets Act' and to hold their tongues. The media's absorption with the debate about national security leads it to overlook how the absence of a Freedom of Information Act prevents disclosure of information relating to pesticides and radiation and petrol and drugs and microwaves and housing and education and product testing and welfare benefits and so on – all areas of vital concern to individuals whether as consumers or voters or as human beings who simply want to go on living.[9]

The Official Secrets Act offers remarkably extensive powers of search and seizure which sidestep some of the safeguards in PACE. This came dramatically to public attention in 1987, when Special Branch officers raided the BBC offices in Glasgow and seized all master tapes of Duncan Campbell's *Secret Society* series, raided the homes of three *New Statesman* journalists and spent over four days examining files in the offices of that magazine.[10] Because the London warrants were issued under Section 2 of the Official Secrets Act, the normal requirement in PACE that 'special procedure' applications for journalistic material shall be preceded by a notice to the person in possession of it, so that the application can be contested in court, did not apply.[11] Because the information was alleged to be covered by a secrecy law, and was in the possession of persons who were journalists and therefore likely to disclose it, the search warrant could be granted at a secret court hearing without representations from the *New Statesman*. The same result would follow under the 1989 law, which made no change to search and seizure provisions. In addition, both Campbell and the BBC would have committed the new crime of conspiring to make a damaging disclosure relating to 'defence policy and strategy, and military planning and intelligence'.

The whole episode related to Duncan Campbell's exposure of 'Project Zircon', a £5-million spy satellite being planned by the MoD to put Britain in the business of eavesdropping from space. Campbell's argument, supported by BBC executives, was that public interest required debate over both the politics of the decision – which arguably distorted the defence budget in merely replicating US technology – and the fact that its cost had been hidden from the Parliamentary Accounts Committee. The Government's case for suppression was undermined both by the fact that the project seemed to be common knowledge amongst defence contractors and by the impossibility of keeping the satellite a secret from the Russians once it was launched. (This last consideration has never weighed with the defence establishment. The D Notice Committee once tried to expunge references in a book by Tom Driberg to the disastrous SIS (Secret Intelligence Service) attempt to overthrow the Albanian Government. When Driberg protested that Philby and Burgess had told the KGB all about it at the time, the committee's secretary replied, 'Good heavens, old boy! It isn't the Russians we worry about, it's the British public we don't want to know about it.')[12] With similar logic, the Treasury Solicitors tried to stop other newspapers from referring to the transcript of the Zircon project, which had been published by the *New Statesman*, and the Government stopped the BBC from transmitting it by the simple expedient of keeping the master tape. No charges were ever brought under Section 2, which had been used as a pretext for searches and seizures of journalistic material unparalleled in peacetime since the 'King's Messengers' went in search of John Wilkes and his seditious newspaper more than two centuries before.

It took eighteen years from the report of the Franks Committee before a Government was prepared to attempt such an overwhelmingly necessary law reform as the replacement of Section 2. Unfortunately, that reform came just before the collapse of Communism in Eastern Europe, and the end of cold-war justifications for high levels of military and intelligence secrecy. By 1993, the 1989 Act was an anachronism: the KGB was no longer an implacable enemy – on the contrary, its secret files had been sold to an American institution which was promising to translate and to publish them in annotated volumes over the next few years. But the thinking behind the 1989 Act assumes that Britain and the Western alliance have mighty enemies from whom any details of our defence or intelligence or diplomatic networks must be hidden, on pain of imprisonment. The Act postulates a world which has ceased to exist, and the law it lays down is in consequence both unreal and unnecessary. Although it still remains vital to keep intelligence secrets from terrorist groups and terrorist states, the 'new world order' of international cooperation in military peace-keeping ventures requires a public which is well informed on Britain's contribution to such initiatives. Ironically, it is precisely this area of informed comment on diplomatic and international relationships that the Act is designed to inhibit.

The 1989 Act

The British Government unveiled new plans for reforming Section 2 in a White Paper published whilst it was still smarting from its *Spycatcher* defeats. A High Court judge had pointed out that the absolute protection it was seeking in that case 'could not be achieved this side of the Iron Curtain', but the Official Secrets Act of 1989 certainly made the attempt. Its primary purpose is to deter all leakage of information about security and intelligence matters by making disclosure and publication of insider information an absolute criminal offence, without any scope for acquittal on grounds of public interest or even on the common-sense basis that the information had already been published, in Britain or abroad. In addition, a range of new criminal offences was created to punish the disclosure or publication of information about defence, foreign policy, police operations and relations with other countries and international organizations. To obtain a conviction in relation to disclosures in these categories, the prosecution must at least prove that they are likely to be damaging, but the statutory tests for determining damage are exceedingly broad and much easier to satisfy than the 'serious injury' test proposed by the Franks Committee[13] The new law threatens imprisonment for up to two years not only of civil servants who make such disclosures, but of journalists and editors who encourage them or publish their information with reason to believe that it has been divulged 'without lawful authority'.

The litigation associated with *Spycatcher* demonstrated that the judiciary, however supportive of the Government in granting injunctions, would at the end of the day apply a 'public interest' standard to permit important disclosures made in breach of confidence. So the Government could not rely on civil litigation to deter media organizations which could afford to fight for freedom of expression in the courts. A serious risk of imprisonment was necessary to frighten editors and television executives, yet juries could be expected, after the *Ponting* trial, to acquit them unless Section 2 was replaced with offences which made a defence difficult or indeed impossible. The 1989 legislation was designed to achieve this level of deterrence, by making convictions more likely (and in some familiar cases, unavoidable) while at the same time removing from entirely theoretical liability under Section 2 a host of disclosures which the Government would never have dreamed of prosecuting in the first place.

The Government launched its new legislation with extravagant and dishonest claims that it would usher in a new era of openness. But it did nothing for freedom of information – not a single document has been released as a result of its enactment. It narrows the absurd breadth of the discredited Section 2, but left the disclosure of everything that the section previously covered by penal sanctions to be dealt with by specific secrecy laws, disciplinary offences and civil actions for breach of confidence. In the armoury of criminal sanctions, it replaced a blunderbuss with an Armalite rifle, trained on those who disclose precisely the kind of information which has caused political controversy and embarrassment in the past. The most objectionable new offences are those which allow of no defence at all, namely revelations about any aspect of intelligence work by persons engaged, or formerly engaged, in it. Not only must all employees take their secrets – however trivial or however scandalous – with them to the grave, but so too must any person who is 'notified' by the Home Secretary that he is bound by this absolute duty. Anyone who comes into contact with the Security Services – by being approached to work as a spy, or by witnessing a bungled operation – may be silenced for ever by a Home Secretary's notice. The duty of absolute secrecy extends to the revelation of serious crime, or breaches of the Security Service Act, or to any information obtained by telephone taps or burglaries authorized by the Home Secretary's warrant. It will not only be an offence to blow the whistle, but even in some circumstances to hear it: journalists who conspire to obtain security-related information or 'aid abet counsel or procure' any divulging of it to them can be prosecuted as accomplices. If they publish such information with grounds for believing it has been disclosed to them without official approval, they will also be guilty. Under these arrangements, it will be difficult to learn anything of security and intelligence operations other than what the Government chooses to make public.

The disclosure of other categories of information is punishable only if 'damaging', but this test is readily satisfied by statutory assumptions that 'damage' is occasioned by any act which 'endangers the interests of the United Kingdom abroad' or 'damages the capability of any part of the armed forces' or 'impedes the prevention or detection of offences'. Once the prosecution proves this level of damage, the burden shifts to the defendant to prove that he or she had no reasonable cause to believe that the disclosure would have any such consequences. Reversal of the burden of proof in a criminal statute restricting freedom of expression is objectionable, but at least gives some scope for mounting a defence. In practice, however, the odds will be stacked in favour of the Government, which has access to senior military and police experts who will be permitted to make damage assessments in closed court-rooms. Prosecutions under the Official Secrets Act can only be brought with the consent of the Attorney-General, and nervous editors and television executives will prefer to submit material to his office for 'vetting' rather than to run the risk of criminal prosecution by publishing. This form of back-door Government pre-censorship may be the worst consequence of overbroad laws, which encourage 'winks and nods' from establishment quarters like the D Notice Committee and the Attorney-General's Department.

The scope of the 1989 legislation, while not the theoretical dragnet of the old Section 2, is none the less considerable. Revelations about defence which are potentially actionable include any disclosure about the 'size, shape, organization, logistics, order of battle, deployment, operations, state of readiness and training of the armed forces of the Crown', anything relating to the research or development or operation of weapons and equipment, 'defence policy and strategy' and plans for civil defence. Publishers will be guilty if their information comes from a civil servant or Government contractor and if it 'prejudices the capability of the armed forces' or 'endangers the interests of the UK abroad or seriously obstructs the promotion of those interests by the UK'. Stories about deficiencies in protecting the Falklands, or projected troop withdrawals from Hong Kong, or plans to send more ships to the Gulf, or the development of sinister weapons at Aldermaston, or plans to reintroduce internment in Northern Ireland, might all be held to satisfy the standard for guilt by juries instructed to ignore any public interest which might be served by the story. It is a crime to publish information from police sources which 'impedes the prevention or detention of offences' – even if such information additionally promotes the public interest of learning about police corruption or controversial operational policies or breaches of data protection principles by the Police National Computer.

The most confusing and potentially important category of information protected by the new criminal law is that described simply as 'relating to international relations'. Any unauthorized disclosure which 'endangers the interests of the UK abroad' or 'seriously obstructs the promotion or protection by the UK of those interests' is deemed to be 'damaging' and hence prosecutable. This includes disclosure of any information provided in confidence by the Government to any foreign country or international organization (which would include the United Nations). This new offence is designed to limit media coverage of foreign policy and diplomacy, much of which is informed by unauthorized leaks from embassies and from within the Foreign Office. It is here that the 'damage' defence looks most threadbare, in light of the White Paper's insistence that any leakage of information 'endangers the UK's interests abroad', because it will make foreign governments and organizations more reluctant to trust British diplomats. If 'damage' is ascertained by reference to diplomatic embarrassment, there will be few revelations that can be made about dangerous alliances and dubious deals with dictators. One of the great scandals of the 1970s – how British ministers and Foreign Office officials connived with oil companies in busting the Government's own sanctions policy against Rhodesia – would fall within the prohibition, and so would any prior insider revelation of the British 'Iraqgate' affair which emerged at the Matrix Churchill trial in 1992.

Section 5 of the new law makes it a specific offence for journalists and editors to publish information which they know is protected by the Act, although the prosecution must additionally prove that they had reason to believe that the publication would be damaging to the security services or to the interests of the United Kingdom. If charged under Section 1, editors can at least testify as to their state of mind in deciding to publish, and will be entitled to an acquittal if the jury accepts that there was no rational basis for thinking that the disclosure would damage British interests. This defence will not be available, however, if they publish information from former or serving members of the security services (or 'notified' persons), and are charged instead under Section 1 with aiding and abetting, or conspiring with, such persons to disclose information about their secret work. Any editors minded in the future to publish information derived from the likes of Cathy Massiter and Peter Wright – or even from defected agents like the late Kim Philby – run the risk of being charged as accomplices, with no defence.

In the course of Parliament's debates on the new law, most attention was focused on the need for a public-interest defence. The Government adamantly and successfully resisted amendments which would have provided a defence where the information revealed the existence of serious misconduct (defined as 'crime, fraud, abuse of authority or neglect in the performance of official duty') in circumstances where the benefit of revelation outweighed any damage which might be caused by it. (Civil servants, to make good the defence, would have had to show that they had taken all reasonable steps to bring the misconduct to the attention of the authorities, but to no avail.) The consequence of rejecting this amendment is that disclosure of a public scandal – such as corruption in naval procurement or lives negligently lost in the course of a secret army mission – will be a criminal offence if it is 'damaging' as defined by the Act (e.g. by revealing details of 'secret' military movements or equipment). The virtue of the disclosure and the social value of its consequences will be irrelevant: in official secrecy law, nothing can matter more than the needs of defence, intelligence and foreign policy.

It would have been possible to reform Section 2 by confining its operation to information of real security importance. In Canada, this was achieved quite simply when the courts ruled, in relation to an identical Act, that its very title required it to be confined to information which was truly 'secret' and which had not already been made public.[14] The criminal law need extend only to information the disclosure of which would be liable to cause serious injury to the national interest: any document classified 'secret' or 'top secret' would be presumed to fall into this prohibited category unless it could be proved that the classification was mistaken. Unauthorized disclosures of the kind made by Sarah Tisdall and Clive Ponting can be dealt with by disciplinary action within the public service, the 'trade secrets' and commercially sensitive material which government departments frequently receive is protected by the civil law of confidence, and leaking information for reward is punishable under the Prevention of Corruption Act. The 1989 legislation rejected this sensible reform in favour of a blanket ban on security disclosures and wide-ranging offences of 'damaging' rather than 'seriously injuring' defence, policing and foreign policy.

The 1989 Official Secrets Act deserves to be derided as the last hostile Act of the cold war. It evinces hostility towards publication of exactly the sort of information which is necessary for informed public debate about British involvement in international peace-keeping efforts, about the appropriate role of the security and intelligence services, and about questionable diplomatic relationships with foreign countries. The fact that it has not, four years after its enactment, been deployed in any significant prosecution is a measure of its irrelevance to legitimate security concerns, but it is by no means a 'dead letter'. That it operates effectively to deter 'leaks' from within Whitehall was demonstrated by the Matrix Churchill affair, which illustrated how no civil servant had dared to leak information about the British involvement in arming Iraq, even after the Gulf War had given this secret policy a considerable political importance. The Act (unlike American legislation) gives no comfort to 'whistle-blowers', and the puny civil service arrangements for bureaucrats with a 'conscience' to take their concerns to the Cabinet Secretary were never invoked by any of the many civil servants who knew of the secret policy. There is no encouragement for civil servants impelled by moral duty to reveal acts of dishonesty, double-dealing or malfeasance to any independent internal arbiter, or to the media. Secrecy will continue to be enforced, if not by prosecution, at least by disciplinary proceedings or by refusal to promote anyone minded to speak out. The Act makes no change to the individual statutes – over one hundred of them at the last count – which make it a specific crime to disclose information obtained by certain Government agencies, for the most part with duties relating to health and safety. Moreover, it includes within its ambit not merely government employees and persons 'notified' by the Home Secretary, but employees of a number of private concerns (such as British Nuclear Fuels) and supposedly 'independent' agencies, such as the National Audit Office, the Health Service Commissioner and the Parliamentary Commissioner for Administration (the Ombudsman).

[handwritten: To Mon the 1989 HG expires]

FREEDOM OF INFORMATION

The Government, in its 1993 White Paper, adamantly refused to countenance a legal right of access to information collected or generated by civil servants. This, in most Western democracies, is the function of a Freedom of Information Act, which generally works to require departments of state to publish annual lists of all their reports and surveys and advisory opinions and working files. These Acts establish a procedure for applying for copies of desired documents, and a time limit of a month or two within which a request must either be granted, on payment of a small fee, or else refused by reference to a category of exemptions set out in the legislation. Applicants whose requests are refused in whole or part may then appeal to a court or tribunal, which inspects the document and decides whether the refusal has been properly made. Exemptions are usually on grounds that disclosure would prejudice national security or foreign relations, impede law enforcement, invade the privacy of individuals, disclose trade secrets or commercial confidences, or reveal Cabinet discussions. FoI legislation assumes that citizen access to bureacracy records is a right rather than a privilege: the exceptions are narrowly defined, although public servants whose opinions are disclosed are immune from libel or other legal action as a result of any opinions they have expressed in the course of their duties. Applicants in Australia and Canada tend to be successful

[handwritten: How FOI legislation works in practice]

about 70 per cent of the time, and partly successful in most of the remaining cases. They include journalists and MPs, historians and authors, interest groups, consumer organizations, research scientists, businesses, parties to litigation and individuals seeking access to records about their own personal affairs or simply wanting to know how a decision affecting them has been made. FoI is not merely a minority interest: there are 25,000 applications a year in Australia and 250,000 in the United States. The costs are considerable, although overseas experience suggests they would be about half of the £27 million the British Government spends each year on its heavily controlled press and information services.

FoI is becoming almost a defining characteristic of accountable democratic government elsewhere in the world, at a time when it is implacably opposed by the British Government and its senior bureaucrats. Their objections on grounds of cost have been much exaggerated. Their objection of principle is based on the 'ministerial accountability' theory, which assumes that ministers give true answers to questions asked by informed MPs. Neither assumption is, in many cases, correct. In any event, ministerial involvement in departmental decisions occurs only at levels of high policy: ministers neither control nor are in practice answerable for thousands of decisions made by middle-ranking departmental officers, decisions which may vitally affect individuals and communities. It is often claimed that civil servants would be less candid in offering advice and writing reports if they knew their words would be publishable within a year or so rather than after thirty or fifty years' anonymity which the Public Records Act currently provides. This argument does little credit to the civil servants who advance it, and overlooks the fact that statutory privilege from libel action will give no cause for them to fear about frankness. As the Matrix Churchill affair demonstrated, the advice routinely given to ministers in relation to controversial policy is to be devious or deceptive in answering questions from MPs or members of the public. FoI would encourage them to choose the option of openness and public debate.

Overseas experience suggests that the prospect of early public scrutiny does concentrate the civil service mind: judgements are more careful and considered, and advice is not tendered lightly. FoI provides, in fact, an incentive to perform better, to produce analysis that will withstand contemporary public scrutiny and may often receive accolades a good deal more genuine than the honours routinely handed out to senior public servants in the Queen's Birthday list. There is, of course, a congenital fear of having to defend secrecy decisions in the courts, and no amount of logic will convince ministers and mandarins that a High Court judge might be in a better position to determine the public interest than they are. None the less, the skies have not fallen on Westminster-style democracies in Canada and Australia with the advent of FoI: on the contrary, most public servants there have not only come to terms with the legislation, but have even come to like it. Tax and social-security forms contain messages about FoI rights, telephone books contain basic instructions on how to make an application and media campaigns promote awareness of the Act. Not content with merely making memoranda available to the public, in 1978 the USA provided legal protection for civil servants who take the initiative in revealing misconduct. The Civil Service Reform Act of 1978 – known as 'the Whistle-blowers Act' – protects civil servants from any form of retaliation, legal action or demotion if they disclose wrongdoing or malpractice. Thanks to this legislation, US civil servants are protected if they disclose, to Congress or, through the press, to the people, any evidence of: violation of any law, rule or regulation; mismanagement; gross waste of funds; abuse of authority; or any substantial or specific danger to public health or safety.

What has Britain missed in not having had FoI? In the USA, the public have been able to measure rules of official thumb through access to: guidelines used by tax inspectors; the Parole Board's guidelines and decisions; military rulings on internal discipline; criteria used by law-enforcement agencies in deciding whether to prosecute; environmental impact statements and other submissions by corporations; internal policy directives on immigration control; contracts between government departments and private contractors; guidelines and manuals on drug analysis, highway management and supervision of social-security benefits; and reports by the Government analysts on food additives, pesticides and vitamin pills. Documents disclosed under the Act have revealed: radioactive contamination of state water supplies; an increasing incidence of cancer among workers in nuclear plants; risks inherent in the use of silicone in cosmetic surgery; and potentially corrupt connections between public servants and big business. The Freedom of Information Act has assisted spectacular press revelations of illegal and ignoble activities by Government agencies. It provided evidence of the perverted mind of J. Edgar Hoover, who bugged Martin Luther King's bedroom and gloatingly played the tapes to his cronies. It exposed the CIA programme of LSD experiments on unsuspecting citizens (one of whom died as a result) and CIA plots to assassinate Castro, Trujillo and other Third World political leaders. The army report on the My Lai massacre has been disclosed, and the public was informed for the first time of their Government's interpretation of the Vietnam peace agreements when a judge ordered the legal opinion to be released pursuant to the Act. The FBI's programme of illegal harassment and disruption of dissidents and left-wing groups came to public attention when courts ordered production of Bureau documents.

If reform of Section 2 had been accompanied by the enactment of FoI, we would have three classes of official information: a 'secret' category of facts and material the revelation of which would attract a criminal sanction; an intermediate category of sensitive information (e.g. trade secrets supplied under legal obligation by companies) which would not be disclosable under FoI and could be protected by breach-of-confidence actions or by prosecution under the Prevention of Corruption Act if leaked for reward; and the remaining, largest, category which would be discoverable pursuant to an FoI application. The effectiveness of such a system would depend on a sensible classification policy — and since it is unlikely that any policy concocted in Whitehall would be sensible, the system would need to be defined by law and be reviewable by the courts. Classification categories should correspond to realistically apprehended injury to the national interest — reviewable in the spirit of Justice Stewart's injunction to government in the *Pentagon Papers* case:

The very first principle [of a wise security system would be] an insistence upon avoiding secrecy for its own sake. For when everything is classified, then nothing is classified, and the system becomes one to be disregarded by the cynical or the careless, and to be manipulated by those intent on self-protection or self-promotion. I should suppose, in short, that the hallmark of a truly effective internal security system would be the maximum possible disclosure, recognizing that secrecy can best be preserved only when credibility is truly maintained.[15]

SPIES' STORIES

The United Kingdom has, at every level, an extraordinary obsession with spying, which makes it particularly difficult to draw acceptable distinctions in law between the interests of freedom of expression and the real interests of national security. The code-breakers of Bletchley helped to win the last war, and even today an increase in tank traffic on some benighted border, picked up by a GCHQ monitoring station strategically located in some former colony, may signal the commencement of new hostilities. Signals Intelligence (Sigint) is by far our most valuable intelligence asset, and is shared with the United States, Australia and Canada under the UK/USA agreement of 1946. Human Intelligence (Humint) is a distinctly more dubious commodity, and the list of traitors, ideological and mercenary, since the last war is long and embarrassing. It is, none the less, the stuff of which spy novels are made, and the popular imagination which has been gripped by Smiley's people and James Bond's women is easily and lucratively attracted to 'truths' about MI5 which seem stranger than the fiction. 'Insiders' who have been privy to secret work want to write autobiographies for all sorts of motives: money, boastfulness, the settling of old scores, a natural desire to put one's life in perspective for one's grandchildren, a burning sense of duty to alert the public to security lapses or Communist infiltration, and so on. There will be a variety of obvious public benefits from such revelations, but there may also be detriments: disclosure of information which may still be security sensitive, invasion of privacy and accusations against those who cannot answer back.

In the United States, which has intelligence secrets that are more vital to the West than Britain's, these conflicting interests are sensibly resolved contractually, by requiring ex-CIA officers to submit their manuscripts to a Publication Review Board, which requests deletion of disclosures that would damage national security. By the end of 1986 there had been 430 manuscripts submitted, and none had ever been rejected in whole or substantial part – any changes required were modest. The penalty for failure to submit a book is not an injunction preventing publication: the US Supreme Court has ruled in the *Pentagon Papers* case that the First Amendment prohibits such prior restraint, save in cases so serious that lives would be lost or wartime troop movements disclosed. In Britain, however, the Government claims that books by 'insiders' are by very definition damaging to the national interest, and it has invited the courts of this and other countries to develop the elastic doctrine of breach of confidence to prohibit all of them.

The principle of a total embargo has been slow to emerge, and did not really crystallize until the case against Peter Wright concentrated the minds of the Government's legal advisers. Until then, Section 2 of the Official Secrets Act had been fitfully invoked to intimidate publishers, although quite a few memoirs slipped through its net. The turning-point came in 1976, with the threatened publication of Richard Crossman's diaries, which detailed discussions in Cabinet. The Government, reluctant to take proceedings under the Official Secrets Act against the executors of its own former minister, chose instead to argue that Cabinet meetings were confidential. The Lord Chief Justice agreed that, in principle, the law against breaches of confidence could be invoked to restrain publication of confidential Government material, although he found Crossman's diaries such heavy going that he declined to suppress their 'stale' secrets.[16] None the less the principle was established, and the Treasury Solicitors who lost that particular battle were soon using it to claim that other 'insiders' were bound by contract or by moral obligation to keep their activities secret for ever.

The first casualty was a book by Jock Kane, a former security officer at GCHQ stations, who had resigned in order to campaign against the corruption and incompetence he had discovered hiding beneath the veil of Sigint secrecy. Kane was an archetypal 'whistle-blower' – a man of unquestioned loyalty who had (as the Prime Minister conceded in Parliament) done much to improve security at GCHQ. He had taken his evidence of petty corruption and lack of security consciousness to all available departmental channels, and tried to go public only when he believed his complaints had fallen on deaf ears. Interestingly, the Government put its case against his book on two separate grounds: it listed in its pleadings a number of revelations which it maintained would compromise national security, and it then made the general argument that Kane was debarred by his conditions of employment from ever publishing *anything* about his years of service. Clearly, a sensible compromise could have been reached by making the 'national security' deletions, but the Treasury Solicitor was determined to press the broader claim.

That claim was made and considered in the litigation about *Spycatcher*.[17] The background to the book and its author is of some importance. Wright entered MI5 as a 'boffin' – an electrical engineer initially seconded from Marconi because he was a dab hand at bugs and concealed microphones. Wright's scientific expertise was employed on bugging embassies and diplomatic residences and international conferences – an activity contrary to the Vienna Convention but engaged in as a matter of course by most Governments. In 1963 his pre-eminence as an eavesdropper, and a severe shortage of qualified staff, led to his rapid promotion to interrogator and then to chairman of an internal committee inquiring into Soviet infiltration of the security services. Wright and his cronies were convinced that MI5's record for incompetence and bungling in the fifties and sixties was only explicable on the basis that it was still infiltrated, at the top, by Soviet double-agents. This embarrassing thesis was at least convenient, as it avoided the alternative and more embarassing hypothesis that MI5 was indeed full of incompetents and bunglers.

Wright's suspicions settled on the head of MI5, Roger Hollis. He was formally interrogated, but no evidence of any substance was discovered. Meanwhile, with an obsession matching that of Senator Joe McCarthy, Wright proceeded to discover reds under the pre-war beds of Cambridge and Oxford colleges. He interrogated hundreds, hounded some out of Government jobs and caused at least one of his suspects to commit suicide. Consumed with the presumption of guilt, Wright and his colleagues managed to convince Harold Wilson that one of his best junior ministers was a security risk because his wife had once been a Communist: Wilson, to his discredit (and one hopes his subsequent mortification), arranged for the man to leave Parliament. Wright, by now a chief interrogator, amassed copious files and used them to damage individuals who disturbed his overly suspicious mind.

It was only a matter of time before the paranoia exemplified by Peter Wright took an insidious political turn. Accepting a view of the world in which things are the opposite of what they seem (Dubček was a KGB agent and the Sino-Soviet split a KGB disinformation plot), Wright came to believe that Harold Wilson himself had been installed by the KGB, which had poisoned Hugh

Gaitskell, and that victory by the Labour Party at the 1974 elections would not be in the national interest. He fomented a half-baked plot hatched at this time to feed anti-Labour gossip and tittle-tattle from MI5 files to pro-Conservative newspapers. He retired from 'the service' and left the country in 1976 because there were 'too many blacks' – which was not a problem in Tasmania, whose aborigines had all been massacred in the previous century by English settlers and convicts. His Tasmanian stud farm was on the brink of bankruptcy when Lord Rothschild summoned him back to Britain and introduced him to Chapman Pincher. Wright had brought with him a dossier of his case against Hollis, and went into partnership with Pincher to exploit the material. The security services were well aware of the contents of Pincher's book, *Their Trade is Treachery*, before it was published, but deliberately did nothing to stop it, doubtless preferring that the allegations against Hollis, if they had to surface, should do so through the perspective of a Chapman Pincher rather than a Duncan Campbell. Wright was not satisfied with the result – a Prime Ministerial statement in Parliament to the effect that Hollis had been 'cleared' – and he broke cover in 1984 in a television interview to voice his conviction that Hollis was guilty. This led to his own book, *Spycatcher*, in which he developed the case against Hollis and gave his version of the plot against Wilson.

The Government claim that a book by an 'insider' is more damaging than a book containing the same information which has been written by a journalist has at first blush a certain force: to a lawyer, first-hand eyewitness evidence is always preferable to hearsay. But the evidential rule against self-serving statements reflects the fact that autobiographies are notoriously unreliable – vitiated by memory lapses, self-interest, and skewed perspectives. The historian and the investigative journalist, sifting numerous sources, are better placed to produce approximations to the truth than individual participants in events. And autobiographies by patriotic ex-security officials pose a particular problem for the reader who really matters – the KGB analyst assumed to weigh every word in his office in the Kremlin. How much is truth, and how much is disinformation? (Applying Wright's own system of intelligence analysis – what might be termed the Little Buttercup approach to a world in which things are seldom what they seem – the whole furore over *Spycatcher* appears as a carefully laid disinformation plot, in which the British security services have planted Wright as a novel kind of double-agent, defecting not to the Soviets but to the press, and endowing his 'revelations' with a spurious credibility by deliberately bungled legal attempts to stop them.) Of course it must be conceded that an 'insider', however security-conscious, may expose a detail or an identity which could prejudice current security operations. This is why it is so much better to have a CIA-style Publications Review Board which can require the deletion of such material. Wright and Kane would have been perfectly happy to submit their manuscripts to a sensible vetting process, and indeed offered to do so. By imposing a blanket ban on publication of any kind by an 'insider', and refusing to negotiate deletions, the Government has adopted an 'all or nothing' policy which damages national security when unex-purgated books are published abroad.

A more weighty objection, underplayed by the Government in the *Spycatcher* case, is based on invasion of privacy. The information which Wright was marketing related to the private lives of individu-als he had, for the most part inconclusively, investigated for 'disloy-alty'. Using the special, above-the-law position of MI5, he had spent much of his life prying into the backgrounds of many people who were not under suspicion of any crime, but whose past associations might or might not have made it undesirable for them to hold security-related positions. Quite apart from the unattractive-ness of Wright's mercenary motives, there is a strong public interest in protecting, even after death, the reputations of those whose private peccadilloes may have found their way into secret police files. In the best of possible legal worlds, public curiosity would be no excuse for publishing details on inconclusive loyalty investiga-tions other than by way of access to files granted either to the subject of the investigations or in the fullness of a time sensibly fixed for releasing historical records.

The genuine public interest which overrides the claim to privacy lies precisely in the revelation of how individual privacy was invaded, for purposes which had little to do with the defence of the realm, by people like Wright whose appreciation of the 'national interest' was distinctly warped. In any proper study of whether the security service has worked effectively to combat genuine enemies, the paranoia of Peter Wright must be exhibit number one. How and why did this technical assistant come to don the mantle of grand inquisitor, to an extent that gave him an apparent hold over Lord Rothschild, and drove one of his targets to suicide? How many 'spies' did he really catch, and how many honourable careers did he ruin by passing on gossip and innuendo? If there was a genuine fear about high-level penetration, why was it not fully and properly investigated by a special commission, rather than allowed to drag on in a part-time committee staffed by conspiracy theorists? In this sense, the real public interest in Wright's book lay not in its accusations against Hollis (which even Wright's co-author rejected and which now appear to be wholly false) but in what it revealed about the mentality of its author, and the standards within MI5 which allowed people with that mentality to occupy positions of power outside any legal or democratic control.

The Wright case serves to show the absurdity of a blanket ban on security-service memoirs, in a world where British court writs do not run beyond the three-mile limit. Those who serve the state should not thereby lose their right of self-expression for all time: the interests of national security can be safeguarded by obliging them to submit manuscripts to a committee empowered to delete only those disclosures which would cause serious damage to current security operations, with a right of appeal to a High Court judge. The present policy of objecting to any publication by an 'insider' can have absurd results: in 1986 it successfully stopped publication in Britain of *One Girl's War*, a Mills & Boon-style account of how a débutante secretary working in MI5 during the war fell in love with her boss, only to find her romantic hopes dashed by the dawning realization that he was happier in the arms of men. The book was published in Ireland, where a British Government attempt to suppress it was laughed out of court.[18]

CONTROL OF THE SECURITY SERVICES

The Wright and Massiter revelations have served to emphasize the need for some oversight and accountability in the security services, to ensure that its practices and policies really do protect the country from external enemies and internal subversion, and do not go beyond what is strictly necessary for that purpose. There can be no doubt that the operational activities of MI5, MI6 and GCHQ require secrecy: the IRA is a permanent threat to British soldiers and civilians, and London has had more than its share of international terrorist outrages. There can be no objection to the gathering of information about individuals or organizations which espouse extreme or violent views, so long as there are clearly defined limits to the use to which such information is put. Citizens cannot demand to know what is going on, but should at least be able to live in confidence that it is going on effectively and fairly. This can only be achieved by setting independent guards to watch over the guardians, representing a public which has a right, if not to know, at least to be positively reassured.

The security service was established in 1909 by royal prerogative as part of the defence forces of the realm. Its purpose was carefully spelled out by Lord Denning in his Profumo report:

The cardinal principle is that their operations are to be used for one purpose, and one purpose only, the *Defence of the Realm*. They are not to be used so as to pry into any man's private conduct, or business affairs: or even into his political opinions, except in so far as they are subversive, that is, they would *contemplate the overthrow of the government by unlawful means*.[19]

These principles are clear enough, but are they complied with? The constitutional position of the security service could scarcely have been more carefully devised to remove its operations from democratic scrutiny. The Director-General has direct access to the Prime Minister if he wishes to discuss a particularly sensitive matter, but ministers are specifically enjoined not to inquire into its day-to-day operations. MI5 directs the operations of the Special Branch, which is part of the Metropolitan Police Force, whose Commissioner is responsible to the Home Secretary on matters of general policy. The courts have held that in operational matters, police discretion cannot be interfered with by ministers of state. In 1964 the Government set up a Security Commission – a panel of public figures from the judiciary, the armed forces and the civil service. It is chaired by an eminent judge, but activated by the Prime Minister only to examine particular scandals that have come to public notice. The Ombudsman is specifically excluded from examining any action taken for the purpose of protecting the security of the state.

In 1989 the Government introduced legislation to establish MI5 on a statutory basis, in an effort to forestall condemnation by the European Court of Human Rights (see earlier, page 123). This measure merely provides that MI5's function shall be to protect national security, 'in particular' to guard against espionage, terrorism and sabotage and actions 'intended to overthrow or undermine parliamentary democracy by political, industrial or violent means' and 'to safeguard the economic well-being of the United Kingdom' against actions by foreigners. This is a very much broader definition of 'subversion' than that provided by Lord Denning ('contemplating the overthrow of the government by unlawful means'), but his definition has demonstrably been ignored in the past by a service that was not properly accountable. Given that any functional definition in this area is bound to be elastic and to require the application of subjective judgement, what matters is accountability and oversight. In this respect the Security Service Act is notably deficient. It provides for a director-general to be appointed by the Home Secretary and enjoins him to ensure that no information is collected or passed on 'except so far as be necessary' for safeguarding national security or detecting serious crime. How far is 'necessary' is again a question of judgement. The courts regard the term as denoting something more than 'expedient' and less than 'indispensable'. So what is really needed in the interests of national security will remain a matter for the judgement of those within the service in deciding which targets to select as 'subversive' and which of those 'subversives' to subject to deceptive or illegal measures. That their judgement has not always been acceptable in a democratic society is demonstrated by their targeting of NCCL officials, trade-union leaders, 'left-wing' journalists and politicians, CND members and a host of other citizens whose careers, it now transpires, have been damaged or put in jeopardy by judgements made within MI5 to collect information about their private lives and to use it to block their employments or appointments. As one former Home Secretary, Roy Jenkins, said in 1988: 'I am convinced now that an organization of people who live in the fevered world of espionage and counter-espionage is entirely unfitted to judge between what is subversive and what is legitimate dissent.'

The Security Service Act, however, ensures that such judgements will not be subject to the kind of democratic scrutiny which operates in the United States, Canada, Australia and European countries other than the UK. The Government resisted all proposed amendments to have the service overseen by a Select Committee of Parliament or even by an appointed body of Privy Councillors. Nor was it prepared to allow independent oversight in the form of an inspector-general, who functions in Canada and Australia (in addition to parliamentary committees) as a watchdog empowered to monitor all aspects of security operations to ensure that they are within the law and respect civil liberties. Instead, the Security Service Act provides merely that a senior judge will serve as a part-time 'commissioner', with the limited task of 'reviewing' the Home Secretary's decisions to grant warrants allowing MI5 to trespass and burgle. He is not permitted to question the Home Secretary's judgement in signing the warrant, but merely to consider whether his action was procedurally proper – i.e. whether he had before him some material, however slight, that justified the exercise of judgement. It is difficult to believe that this will provide any real measure of control: in the unlikely event that the commissioner concludes that the Home Secretary has taken leave of his senses by signing a warrant, his only power is to report the fact to the Prime Minister, who may exclude any mention of it from the commissioner's annual report to Parliament. The commissioner's other function is to investigate in the event that the secret tribunal established to consider complaints from possible victims of MI5 operations stumbles across unreasonable behaviour within the service. The likelihood of such reference is minimal, given the severe restrictions on the scope of the tribunal itself. But even if a reference is made and the commissioner concludes that MI5 has acted unreasonably, he has no power to do anything about it. He can only report the matter to the Home Secretary, 'who may take such action in the light of the report as he thinks fit' – and the Home Secretary may, of course, think it fit to take no action at all. To describe the commissioner as a 'safeguard' is to argue in a circle: his remit is limited to a small area of MI5's operations and any malfeasance he uncovers can merely be reported to the Prime Minister or Home Secretary who need neither correct it nor bring it to public attention.

There is evidence that the Act has actually operated in a manner damaging to the liberty of the subject. In the first place it compromises the independence of the judiciary by involving a judge (as commissioner) and a number of 'trusted' Queens Counsel, who will soon be judges (as members of the Complaints Tribunal) in the work of the security service. This is objectionable both in principle and because it adds to the number of senior lawyers who are exposed to the cult of secrecy (others are the judge and QCs who monitor telephone taps, the judge who chairs the Security Commission, and the judges who chair 'purge procedure' and internment tribunals). Further, the existence of the Tribunal and the possibility of retrospective investigation has given MI5 an excuse to keep records that it would otherwise have shredded on persons wrongly classified as 'subversive' or who turn out to be not subversive enough to warrant a permanent file. As the commissioner points out in his 1991 Report, 'it seems somewhat ironical that the service now retains such records, which it does not require for its own purposes and which it would otherwise have destroyed'.[20] The Tribunal in its first two years considered eighty-one complaints, none of which was upheld. The commissioner publishes short and uninformative reports confirming that warrants had been issued to MI5 by the Home Secretary but it is 'not in the national interest' to say how many. These are warrants 'to interfere with property' (i.e. to burgle homes) and it is quite unacceptable that the number should be secret when the number of warrants for mail and telephone intercepts are published.

The Act stages a typical Whitehall farce: real victims of secret and unacceptable MI5 operations will never know they have been targeted, while persons psychologically suffering from delusions will occupy the expensive legal time of the Tribunal. The only statutory limit imposed on MI5 operations by the Security Service Act is that the Director-General is placed under a 'duty to ensure that the service does not take any action to further the interests of a political party'. Since the 1989 official secrets reform prohibits any revelations at all about MI5 actions, it is difficult to envisage a breach of this duty ever becoming public, unless an officer were to publish memoirs from abroad. The duty is in theory enforceable by the High Court at the behest of a disfavoured political party, although it would have to show that the Director-General was unreasonable in his belief that the objectionable action was not designed to promote party-political interests. When what is being furthered is the interests of the Government and its policies (especially in defence and foreign relations), the courts would be unlikely to intervene. Given the difficulties of obtaining credible evidence, the duty is for all practical purposes unenforceable in law, and if the commissioner stumbles upon a breach of it his only remedy is to report to the Prime Minister, who will almost certainly be the leader of the party which is being favoured. It is no secret that individual MI5 officers 'leak' private information on political figures to chosen journalists, or by way of anonymous contributions to *Private Eye*. The practice is longstanding (in 1924 no less than four different security officials leaked copies of the 'Zinoviev telegram' to discredit the Labour Party). Such practices will only cease by the encouragement of an ethos of professionalism and impartiality within the service – a task that would be assisted by independent oversight, but to which part-time commissioners and tribunals will make little contribution.

The iron curtain of secrecy surrounding the activities of MI5 and MI6 has been penetrated in two recent court cases. In 1990 the Divisional Court ordered Special Branch officers and a retired MI5 case officer to give evidence about the investigation of the prison escape by MI6 traitor George Blake.[21] It appeared that two of the culprits – CND activists Michael Randle and Pat Pottle – had been identified as long ago as 1970, but no effort was made to obtain evidence until they provided it themselves with a book in 1989 confessing to the crime. A jury subsequently acquitted them, doubtless taking the view that their offences were historical rather than requiring present punishment. The suspicion remains that MI5's inactivity in 1970 was designed to foster an illusion that Blake had in fact been sprung from prison by a KGB of awesome power and penetration, rather than by amiable amateurs upset by the length of his sentence. This illusion, of course, would have served to bolster MI5's claims for additional pay and resources to meet the KGB's 'threat'.

More damaging to public confidence in the security services was the revelation of their role in the prosecution of Paul Henderson, the managing director of Matrix Churchill, who had helped to implement the secret British policy of supplying arms-making equipment to Saddam Hussein in the years before his invasion of Kuwait. The case collapsed in November 1992, when former Thatcher minister Alan Clark admitted that he had encouraged Henderson to be 'economical with the *actualité*' in applying for export licenses for machine tools intended to equip Iraqi arms factories. (This was 'a matter of Whitehall cosmetics – to keep the records ambiguous'.) The public was amazed that Henderson had been prosecuted, after his MI6 case officer admitted in court that he was a very brave man who had risked his life by informing regularly on Iraq's procurement network. What appeared most questionable was the role that MI6 had played in supporting the customs prosecution of its loyal agent, and the fact that it had been involved in the preparation of that prosecution from its earliest stage. It was also unacceptable that the intelligence officers who gave evidence were provided with special protection against the possibility of perjury charges (they were allowed anonymity, and a special witness box was built to hide them from the press). If MI5 and MI6 officers are to give disputed evidence which might expose their own agents to conviction and imprisonment, they can hardly claim a special status for that evidence which is not given to any other witnesses' testimony.

In the wake of the Matrix Churchill trial, and the questions it raised about MI5 and MI6 handling of their volunteer agents and the confused internal procedures for passing analysis of their information to Government departments, the blanket-secrecy tradition became intolerable. MI5 finally broke cover in July 1993, by publishing a glossy public-relations brochure about itself and making its Director-General, Stella Rimington, available to pose for press photographers. It was officially admitted that MI5 had two thousand employees, half of them women and a quarter of them recruited from Oxbridge, and that since the end of the cold war 70 per cent of its resources were devoted to gathering intelligence about terrorism. The brochure concedes that MI5 assists Government departments and 'organizations' to vet employees who might have access to classified information, although the nature of non-Government organizations which receive its data were not specified. MI5 denied that it targeted any legitimate protest group 'as such, but the subversive element within it' – which must be read as an admission that it does target members of legitimate protest groups, upon a definition of 'subversion' which is neither vouchsafed to the public nor subject to any independent oversight. MI5's first photocall was an historic moment in the annals of the British secret service, but it falls abysmally short of the accountability now expected of such agencies in all other democracies. MI6 remains resolutely under wraps, notwithstanding the vast public expenditure on its new headquarters, although another historic watershed was breached in 1992 when the Prime Minister officially admitted, for the first time, that it did in fact exist.

Both bodies have large staffs and enjoy very large budgets, yet remain entirely beyond parliamentary control. The security services have had notable achievements in recent years against the IRA and terrorist groups, and have attracted several important KGB defectors. It is difficult to see how this legitimate work would be compromised by independent oversight which provides reassurance that the secret services are not targeting trade unionists and civil liberties groups as 'subversive', or leaking information obtained by invasions of privacy for party-political purposes, or conducting internecine feuds of the kind which have been alleged in recent controversies over the disciplinary proceedings against John Stalker or the whispering campaign against the late Sir Maurice Oldfield. In the USA, a satisfactory degree of control and accountability for the CIA has been achieved by the enactment of a legally binding charter, and by inquiries conducted by Congressional committees into activities which may be in breach of it. The Australian and Canadian intelligence communities have been placed on a firm democratic footing as the result of Royal Commissions which discovered numerous inadequacies and malpractices. There is no evidence that national security performance in these nations has been damaged by democratic controls over forces whose methods of operation and selection of targets can vitally affect the liberty of the subject.

D NOTICES

A curious institution known as the D Notice Committee was established in 1912 – the year after the Official Secrets Act was passed – for the purpose of applying behind-the-scenes pressure on newspaper editors in relation to national security issues. The Committee comprises a handful of representatives from the media together with civil servants and officers from the armed forces, and it worked for forty years before the press dared even to mention its existence. In 1963 Mr John Profumo tried unsuccessfully to have it issue a D Notice to stop the publication of Christine Keeler's memoirs, and in 1967 it fell into some disrepute when the *Daily Express* published the identities of the heads of MI5 and MI6 in contravention of a D Notice and revealed MI5's practice of monitoring all overseas cables. The Secretary of the Committee, Colonel Sammy Lohan, had taken journalist Chapman Pincher to lunch in an attempt to persuade him not to publish the cable-monitoring story: when it did emerge, Lohan resigned his job and became restaurant critic of the *Evening Standard*. There are now only eight permanent D Notices, made public for the first time in 1993, and they warn in general terms against publication of details of defence plans and equipment, nuclear weaponry, codes and communication interceptions, the security services, civil defence and the photography of defence installations.

It is important to appreciate that a D Notice has no legal force whatsoever, and 'guidance' from the Committee or its secretary is of no effect at all. In 1980 the *New Statesman* published a series of articles by Duncan Campbell about telephone tapping, despite a warning from the Committee's secretary that this contravened a D Notice, yet no prosecution followed. Conversely, an editor who assiduously follows the Committee's advice is not guaranteed immunity from prosecution under the Official Secrets Act. The editor of the *Sunday Telegraph* faced charges along with Jonathan Aitken for receiving the Biafran War report, although the secretary of the D Notice Committee had told him that its publication would create no danger to national security. In 1987 the secretary of the D Notice Committee assured the BBC (which cravenly sought his guidance) that *My Country Right or Wrong* was in no way a threat to national security: the Government then turned round and obtained injunctions against transmission of the programme on the grounds that its breaches of confidence *were* potentially damaging to national security.

The D Notice Committee is a confidence trick, which does some damage to freedom of speech through those media executives and editors who cooperate with it. It certainly cannot be trusted: in 1985 its secretary (who is always a retired military officer) politely requested a sight of the manuscript of Jock Kane's book on GCHQ in order to offer 'guidance' which would help its publication: when

Kane's naïve publishers complied, the D Notice secretary sent the work immediately to the Treasury Solicitors, who obtained an injunction against it ever being published. In 1988 the secretary of the Committee tried to put a D Notice on certain names mentioned in books about to be published by David Leigh and Rupert Allison, M P. Some were dead, while others had served with Philby, who had blown their cover forty years before. Both authors insisted that their books be published with the names intact. A few weeks before the 1991 Gulf War commenced, a lap-top computer containing details of force deployment was stolen from the car of a careless R A F officer. The Government issued a D Notice on any mention of the missing computer, and falsely claimed that all the 'lost' information had been recovered. All the British media complied with the D Notice for a week until the true story was published by an Irish newspaper, but the D Notice was only lifted when the *Sun* (of all newspapers) broke British ranks and decided to publish the truth.

In 1980 a House of Commons Committee reviewed the system and published a damning indictment. It reported that major newspapers had stopped consulting D Notices; that the foreign and fringe press had never received them; that the notices were so vaguely worded as to be meaningless; that the notices had not been amended in the previous ten years; and that some categories of sensitive information were not covered by the notices.[22] The Conservative majority of the Committee (which had finally split on party lines), thought the system could be reformed. It was supported by both the BBC and the IBA, on the grounds that they welcomed 'official' advice. Evidence to the contrary was given by the *Sunday Times*, *World in Action* and the Press Association, which argued that the freedom of the press is incompatible with the cosy cooperation which the D system envisages. They convinced the Labour MPs who recommended in a minority report that the Committee should be abolished.

Should the media continue to cooperate with, and indeed to be represented on a Committee which applies formal and informal pressure in favour of censorship? The Committee has become so discredited that no self-respecting editor or media executive should collaborate in its occasional attempts to suppress the truth without legal justification. It still, surprisingly, has some effect: its secretary admitted to having received over a hundred requests for 'guidance' in the course of 1992, and indicated that he had successfully suppressed 'about a dozen' stories. In that year the Government announced yet another 'review' of D Notice procedures. The BBC, obedient as ever, immediately urged that the system should remain in place. The place it remains in is in the Ministry of Defence, where the secretary has his offices and where he functions, in reality, as part of the ministry's public-relations system. There is little informed specialist analysis of defence or intelligence issues in the British media at present, and the D Notice Committee exists in an effort to keep things this way.

MEMORABILIA

Former ministers, retired civil servants, ex-police chiefs and even the public hangman have sought to write accounts of their stewardship in office. Many of these books have been freed from the threat of criminal prosecution by the abolition of Section 2, but may none the less be subject to civil injunctions for breach of confidence. What Whitehall bureaucrats are desperately anxious to suppress are comments or criticisms on their own performance, and premature revelation of differences of opinion in Cabinet discussions. Such differences emerge in unattributed 'leaks' to newspapers by ministers and their advisers at the time, but an insider's account is believed to carry greater credibility and to undermine the constitutional fiction of 'collective responsibility' whereby all members of the Cabinet are assumed fully to support decisions against which they have, in real life, fought tooth and nail. The public interest is alleged to be served by suppressing the truth for many years: ministers will feel inhibited in what they say at Cabinet meetings if they know that one of their Cabinet colleagues might publish a version of the meeting as soon as they return to the opposition benches. These assumptions do not accord with political reality, but none the less form the basis of the legal argument that what happens in Cabinet and at top levels in Whitehall is confidential, and revelations can be stopped by breach-of-confidence actions.

In 1975 these arguments were accepted, up to a point, by the Lord Chief Justice in the breach-of-confidence action brought against the publishers of Richard Crossman's diaries. He ruled that Cabinet discussions were confidential, although the public interest in suppressing first-hand accounts of them lapsed with time, and an eight- to ten-year embargo was the maximum period which the law would uphold in the absence of any danger to national security.[23] He rejected the claim that civil servants should be immune from criticism, and that the Permanent Secretary to the Cabinet has any legal power of censorship over ministerial memoirs. None the less, the case proved a watershed, unleashing a powerful current of civil law which had hitherto been confined mainly to trade secrets. As the criminal sanctions of Section 2 fell into disrepute, injunctions granted by civil courts (backed by criminal sanctions for contempt in the event of disobedience) became a powerful weapon in the hands of the Whitehall mandarins. The 'bottomless purse' of the Treasury Solicitor, who can mount expensive legal actions and carry them through to the House of Lords, is a threat which few publishers can ignore, as memoirs of civil-service life, however interesting for political scientists, are unlikely to sell in sufficient numbers to justify the risk of losing a costly legal action. That is why most publishers of civil-service or ministerial memorabilia do in fact submit their manuscripts for prior censorship to the Cabinet Office, and this may be one reason why such books are so boring. Rare exceptions, such as Hugh Jenkins's *The Culture Gap* and Alan Clark's *Diaries*, were not vetted, and contain vigorous and amusing criticisms of named mandarins and ministers. Neither publisher was subjected to the breach-of-confidence action which had been threatened; both Jenkins and Clark were junior ministers, not members of the Cabinet.

British law is in sharp contrast with American law, as the *Pentagon Papers* case of 1971 shows. *The New York Times* obtained volumes of top-secret documents on the history of the Vietnam War and began publishing. The US Supreme Court refused the Nixon administration an injunction; only if disclosure would surely result in direct, immediate and irreparable damage to the nation would freedom of the press to publish documents from Government sources be interfered with by US courts. It is also significant to contrast the speed of the US decision (so that publication plans were not impeded) with the long period during which the *Sunday Times* had to wait before it could publish the *Crossman Diaries*.

The Government was not satisfied with the amount of secrecy – extensive though it is – which the Crossman decision brought within the law's protection, and it set up a Committee of Privy Councillors on ministerial memoirs. In 1976 that Committee, chaired by Viscount Radcliffe, made proposals which were gratefully and immediately accepted by the Government, which laid them down as new 'conventions' (not laws) which should govern ministerial memoirs.[24] Everything which the Government failed to have decided in its favour in the *Crossman Diaries* case was duly enshrined in the following constitutional conventions:

No minister past or present is to reveal the opinions or attitudes of colleagues as to Government business with which they have been concerned. He is not to reveal advice given to him by civil servants. He is not to make any public comment on the capacity or competence of civil servants who have worked for him. On assuming office he will be told of these conventions and required to sign a declaration that he will follow them. Whenever an ex-minister contemplates making public an account bearing on any aspect of his ministerial life he must show the Secretary of the Cabinet in advance the full text of what he proposes to say. If clearance is refused by the Secretary for reasons of national security or the preservation of international relations, the ex-minister may appeal to the Prime Minister, whose decision is final. If it is refused on the ground of 'confidential relationships' the minister must make his own decision whether to publish in the face of that refusal. An author is free to disregard the above principles relating to 'confidential relationships' fifteen years after the events which they describe, except that in respect of a reference to a civil-service adviser, the embargo period is fifteen years or the remainder of the service life of that adviser, whichever is the longer. There is no fifteen-year limit for questions of national security and international relations. Ministers should leave instructions to their executors in their wills that posthumous publication of their diaries should not take place in breach of these conventions.

These guidelines have clearly been drawn to protect senior civil servants from criticism by the ministers with whom they have dealt, and to remove high-level policy information from public exposure until long after public criticism can have any political impact. They exemplify the secrecy obsession of successive British

Governments, advised by senior civil servants motivated more by protecting their own backs than by any desire to protect the public. They are not laws – neither the Labour Government which accepted them nor its Conservative successors have submitted them to parliamentary debate – but they take the form of a 'gentleman's agreement' which can be relied upon in any future breach of confidence action. It may in fact be doubted whether the courts would today endorse Radcliffe's 'rules of reticence'. Ex-Cabinet ministers are no longer gentlemen, they are greedy players like Nigel Lawson and Kenneth Baker and Norman Tebbit, who cannot wait more than the time it takes to negotiate a large advance before getting their snouts into the lucrative publishing trough. Indeed, in the 1990s it became almost *de rigeur* for discredited Thatcherites to publish memoirs of recent ministerial office, hypocritically claiming that their reminiscences were in the service of 'open government' – a value they had ignored while in office. John Major and his Cabinet Secretary Sir Robin Butler have been prepared to suffer publication earlier than the time lapse recommended by the Chief Justice in the *Crossman Diaries* case, but have required deletions of criticism of individual servants or references to detailed discussions in Cabinet.

Civil servants are subject to the same rules as those concerning ministers and are required to sign a promise to submit any manuscript for approval prior to its publication. When clearance for their books is refused, no reasons will be provided and the author is given no opportunity to argue his case before those who decide – indeed, their identity is concealed from him. This is yet another example of a matter which can affect a person's livelihood being decided by unknown civil servants according to undisclosed rules without the citizen having any opportunity to present argument or test the reasons for refusal. The usual Government apologia – ministerial responsibility for a collective department decision, accountability to Parliament, necessary anonymity of civil servants, decisions of policy, matters of security and so forth – are unconvincing. In 1991 the political motive behind Cabinet Office vetting of civil-service memoirs was hilariously exposed through a mistake by Harper-Collins, publishers of *Kill the Messenger*, the 'authorized' autobiography of Mrs Thatcher's press secretary, Bernard Ingham. They sent to the *Sunday Times* (which had bought serialization rights) a copy of the book proofs *before* it had been submitted for Cabinet Office vetting, and a comparison with the final version allowed the newspaper to deduce which passages had been censored. The Cabinet Secretary, Sir Robin Butler, had not wielded the blue pencil on the basis of national security or justifiable confidentiality, but only to delete or dilute criticisms of still-serving ministers – and particularly of Michael Heseltine – that might be politically embarrassing for the Government.

PUBLIC RECORDS

Most civil-service records are transferred after thirty years to the Public Record Office at Kew, where they can be inspected by historians and journalists. The Government has the power to 'weed out' and withhold records which it thinks should be kept for a longer time, whether fifty or one hundred years, or for ever. The main categories are: distressing or embarrassing personal details about living persons or their immediate descendants, information received by the Government in confidence, some papers on Ireland and 'certain exceptionally sensitive papers which affect the security of the state'.[25] The weeders are super-sensitive to national security and until very recently refused to release any papers which so much as mentioned the existence of MI5 or MI6. The records of these services are not available for inspection, and never will be if civil servants have their way. No public record of any significance is released to the public before thirty years has elapsed, unless a court or Inquiry calls for it, or the Government finds its publication politically advantageous.

By what right does Whitehall withhold the raw material of history for a century or even longer? The Public Records Acts provide that Government papers shall not be available for general inspection until they have been in existence for thirty years 'or such other period as the Lord Chancellor may provide'. In 1967 Lord Gardiner was prevailed upon to grant a 'dispensation' for some forty categories of documents, including all records relating to civil defence, overseas defence planning, atomic energy and the security services. He assumed that documents in these categories would be released as and when they lost any contemporary security significance, but the Cabinet Office tricked him.[26] It interpreted the 'dispensation' as a blanket authorization to withhold all records for as long as it wishes. Hence the documents relating to MI5 activity between the wars and the defections of Burgess and Maclean have never been released. There is no basis for legal challenge: the Lord Chancellor has an unreviewable discretion, and there is no guidance given by the Acts as to what documents should be suppressed.

The British obsession for secrecy is well illustrated by the 4,500 feet (some 5 per cent of the total) of shelf space at Kew containing files which cannot be opened for fifty to one hundred years. Amongst the official memoranda listed as being closed for a century are: prison reform and lengths of sentences (1910–34); forcible feeding in reformatory schools (1910); the sterilization of mental defectives (1911–30); imprisonment and forcible feeding of suffragettes (1913); imprisonment of Emily Pankhurst (1913–17); internment of Sinn Fein leaders (1918); industrial unrest and strikes (1918); experiments on animals with poison gas (1913–16); instructions to police on sedition charges against Socialists (1912–18); Home Office practice in dealings with criminal lunatics (1913); coal-miners' strike (1919); flogging of vagrants (1919); decisions against prosecuting James Joyce's *Ulysses* (1924); Fascist marches (1936); police reports on the activities of the National Council for Civil Liberties (1935–41); opposition to British interests in Palestine (1938); Tibetan relations with China (1938–45); dental service for police in wartime (1939); war crimes – lists of suspects and reports on atrocities (1941–7); interrogations of prisoners of war in London (1942–4); British scorched-earth policy in Malaya (1943); the relief and repatriation of allied internees (1946); and the Albert Speer file (1946).[27] These topics need only be listed to demonstrate how the notion of 'embarrassment to descendants' is being manipulated to cover 'embarrassment to the descendants-in-office of civil servants'. Closure for a century of files relating to official treatment of suffragettes, prisoners and mental patients prior to the First World War cannot conceivably be justified on privacy grounds. Records of field executions in the First World War were withheld for seventy years, ostensibly to avoid embarrassment to relatives of the long-dead soldiers, but when these documents were finally released, it became clear that the secrecy had been used to avoid exposing the arbitrariness and brutality of justice in the trenches.

Quite apart from the absurdity of sealing files about arrangements for police dental treatment during the Second World War, the above examples illustrate how a good deal of information of historical significance in relation to British foreign policy is being deliberately suppressed without any conceivable justification. Historians looking forward to finding out what really happened in 1962 were disappointed, in January 1993, to find that the Public Record Office had decided to withhold most papers on the Cuban missile crisis, together with Macmillan Government documents on British nuclear policy and its policies towards the Middle East. A number of official documents about the royal family's behaviour in 1962 had been ordered to be closed until the year 2062. It was also discovered that files detailing how British troops had used poison gas against Iraqi dissidents (including Kurds) in 1919, which had been released after fifty years in 1969, had been removed from the Public Record Office by Whitehall in the aftermath of the Gulf War. This childish sanitizing of historical embarrassments in hindsight shows why those who control the release of official documents cannot be trusted; least of all William Waldegrave, in charge of John Major's 'open government' initiative, and an architect of the political cover-up over arms sales to Iraq. In 1993 a group of fifty leading British historians declared that despite his posturing about openness, the amount of official documents being withheld from the PRO was actually increasing every year.

In 1992 overwhelming evidence of the corruption of the Public Records Act system came from 'early release' of twenty-seven files on wartime collaboration with Nazis in the Channel Islands, which had been classified as fit for closure for seventy-five and one hundred years. They had been unsealed after fifty years as the result of a long campaign by David Winnick, MP, and they disclosed fascinating and important historical data, including two major investigations by British judges. The prospect of 'embarrassing living persons' was avoided simply by blanking out a few names and identifying details. It became obvious that the real reason for sealing these files for unconscionably long periods was that they contained severe judicial criticism of civil servants, and judicial recommendations to prosecute as war criminals local politicians who were, in fact, subsequently honoured by knighthoods! The disgraceful over-classification of the Channel Islands files to protect the posthumous memory of collaborators and incompetent public servants demonstrates the urgency of the need to reform the Public Records Act, and to provide a legal right to appeal against over-secretive bureaucratic decisions to close files to public inspection for unreasonable periods. (The thirty-year wait for routine historical material is, of course, unreasonable in itself.)

In 1981 a committee of inquiry recommended more liberal access.[28] It criticized the practice whereby the Lord Chancellor can order an entire class of documents to be kept secret for a century, without considering the specific documents which make up that class. It proposed that more files should be released before the thirty-year embargo is up, that 'embarrassment' should no longer be a ground for suppression, that the power to keep files secret for ever should be abolished, and that there should be a right to appeal from secrecy orders. The Government, of course, rejected the report.[29] But what good reason can there be for withholding routine Government records from scholars and historians for longer than the ten years thought appropriate for Cabinet records by the Chief Justice in the *Crossman Diaries* case? The 'thirty-year plus' rule is a typical feature of British public life. A British student of government will often learn more from a short period in Washington about the UK administrative process than he can learn about his own from a lifetime in England, because many of the documents withheld from the public in the UK are sent, under bilateral arrangements, to other countries where they become immediately open to inspection. Modern British historians are becoming more familiar with the US Freedom of Information Act than with our own Public Record Office.

Although historians do sit on the Lord Chancellor's Advisory Council on Public Records, which is chaired by the Master of the Rolls, they complain that because they do not have security clearance they are not allowed to inspect the files about which they are meant to advise. They are particularly critical of decisions to suppress such important documents as those which cover the abdication crisis in 1936, British army action during the Easter uprising in 1916, Nazi subversion in Britain during the war, the attempt on Hitler's life in 1944 and British involvement in the 1953 coup in Iran – all foreclosed to historians for the foreseeable future on bogus 'national-security' grounds. The Government has power to release these immediately, but it is a power that it will only use in response to a specific campaign, or when to do so would suit its political purposes. During the American presidential campaign in 1992, the Home Office was happy to dig for dirt on Bill Clinton in case he had applied for British residence so as to avoid the Vietnam draft. Returning a political favour for George Bush (who had vocally supported John Major during the British elections earlier in the year) was apparently a sufficient reason to breach the 'thirty-year rule'.

PUBLIC INTEREST IMMUNITY

One form of official secrecy which is plainly intolerable in a civilized society is the suppression of evidence which might establish the innocence of a person on trial for a criminal offence. Yet British law provides a procedure whereby the Government may achieve this result, by the device of a minister signing a 'public-interest immunity certificate'. This is a document in which the minister states that he has read the material which is sought to be adduced in evidence, and that it is his opinion that the public interest will not be served by disclosing it. The reasons given normally relate to preserving 'candour' within the public service although in exceptional cases it may be alleged that disclosure would damage national security or interfere with policing operations or expose informers. The judge must accept these arguments, because he cannot challenge Government opinion: what he should then do is look at the documents, and 'balance' the public interest claimed by ministers on the one hand with the important public interest of securing a fair trial on the other. He may then uphold the immunity claim or order some or all of the documents to be disclosed to the defence, with such deletions as he considers will preserve the public interest claimed by the minister. Immunity certificates may be signed because the documents fall within a *class* which the Government does not believe should be made public, or because their *contents* are alleged to damage the public interest. 'Contents' claims carry greater weight, and the weight on the defendant's side of the balance will depend on how relevant the judge considers that the evidence will be to the defence case.

'Public interest immunity' is a euphemism for what was until recently called 'Crown Privilege'. It has for a century been claimed quite often in civil cases, where it has been productive of much injustice. One of the early cases where it was upheld was against *The Times*, which had alleged that a diplomat had sent 'garbled communications' to the colonial office. When the editor was sued for libel, the Government refused to produce the cables, so he had no defence to the action. A similar case occurred in 1991, when John Pilger lost a libel action after the Foreign Office refused to release documents he had subpoenaed to support his defence that the SAS were training Khmer Rouge allies in Cambodia. Alison Halford, the Assistant Chief Constable of Merseyside, was another victim of PII, when the Court of Appeal refused to allow police personnel files to be disclosed to support her action for sex discrimination. It relied upon another Court of Appeal judgement in 1989, when a black woman who had sued the police for racial assault was not permitted to obtain statements made by witnesses in the course of a police complaints investigation. The 'public interest' was deemed to favour the confidentiality of the police complaints procedure rather than the right of the complainant to obtain compensation in the courts.

In civil actions, where plaintiffs are seeking monetary damages, it may sometimes be necessary to override their rights where the public interest is genuinely at stake. It may be doubted whether that interest is really served by protecting police complaints files or other investigations where witnesses cannot reasonably claim confidentiality for imparting what they have seen or heard, but the PII procedure itself is in civil cases unobjectionable. By the time the matter comes to court the issues will have been defined in detailed pleadings, and the judge will be in a position, after reading the documents, at least to appreciate their degree of relevance to the matters in dispute. This is not the position in criminal cases, where the defendant has a 'right of silence' and is entitled to oblige the prosecution to prove its case before entering a defence. The issues are not defined (except in fraud trials) and neither the prosecutor nor the judge will be in a position, merely by reading the documents, to assess their relevance to the defence.

In respect of criminal cases, the proper constitutional practice was announced by Lord Kilmuir in 1956, and approved by the House of Lords in *Conway* v. *Rimmer* in 1968:

If medical documents, or indeed other documents, are relevant to the defence in criminal proceedings, Crown Privilege should not be claimed.[30]

Like so many 'constitutional practices' in Britain, however, this rule did not have the force of law, and in a series of criminal cases beginning about 1990 the Government went back on Lord Kilmuir's promise. It started to issue PII certificates to prevent disclosure of evidence, despite the fact that this evidence was relevant to the case and thus disclosable under the Attorney-General's 'guidelines' for prosecution revelation of documents to the defence. This new approach appeared to have worked at a number of criminal trials, until it was exposed to severe public criticism after the collapse of the *Matrix Churchill* prosecution. In that case no less than four current ministers of the Crown had signed certificates which would have prevented the defence from discovering, and proving, that secret Government policy had been to send defence-related equipment to Iraq prior to its invasion of Kuwait. It was essential to the defence case to establish this fact, which was contrary to the impression given by the evidence of a number of prosecution witnesses, including two former government ministers. Defence lawyers were not able to read the documents, which were said by the prosecution to contain nothing which would assist them, until they disclosed their defence, in order that the judge could appreciate just how relevant the documents were. He rejected the PII certificates based on a 'class' claim but upheld the Government's 'contents' claim, despite the fact that these 'contents' were records of what one defendant had told officers of MI6. The position was reached at the trial where defence counsel had to cross-examine witnesses about documents most of whose 'contents' had been blacked out, but which had been read by the witness, the judge and the prosecutor, although not by anyone on the defence side.[31] This is not a satisfactory state of affairs in a criminal trial.

What was even less satisfactory was the Attorney-General's advice to ministers that they had a *duty* to sign the certificates, irrespective of what the documents revealed. One of the signatories, Michael Heseltine, claimed that he had been unwilling to sign until advised that it was his duty to do so: he was only following orders. Since he claimed to have read and considered the documents, he must have had some knowledge of their import for the trial, and he never managed to explain what he would have done had he succeeded in suppressing them, and had the defendant been convicted. In fact, it is reasonably clear that the Attorney-General's advice was mistaken. Ministers have a *discretion*, not a duty, to claim public interest immunity in relation to documents belonging to their department. Any action designed to withhold relevant evidence from a criminal court calls for the most anxious ministerial judgement. What was so objectionable about the behaviour of Mr Major's ministers in the *Matrix Churchill* case was not that they certified their departmental documents as falling within a class that should ordinarily be protected from disclosure, but the enthusiastic lengths to which they went in their written arguments embodied in the certificate to persuade the judge to uphold the claim, irrespective of the relevance of the documents to the trial. The spectacle of Government ministers enthusiastically urging a judge to uphold their claims to secrecy in a criminal case, where the evidence they sought to suppress could have secured the release of men on charges carrying up to seven years in prison, is not one which should be repeated.

The prospect of a miscarriage of justice in criminal cases cannot be countenanced. On any view of the 'public interest', there can be no weightier value than that of avoiding the conviction of the innocent, or even the conviction of those on whose guilt doubts may be cast by analysis of suppressed evidence. The argument about preserving 'candour' in the public service is debatable in itself, and not of comparable weight even if correct. Other 'public interests' may have more force: the protection of informers from reprisals has always been a concern of the common law, long before PII certificates were invented, but even the names of informers were ordered to be disclosed when there was a real prospect of a malicious accusation. The present vogue for PII certificates should end, and there should be a reversion to the constitutional practice declared by Lord Kilmuir. The danger of disclosure of irrelevant material can be minimized by putting the Attorney-General's guidelines on a statutory footing, so that only the existence of material which throws light upon the circumstances of the case need be revealed. If material can be edited under supervision of the trial judge so as to exclude the identification of informers or undercover agents, the location of police observation posts and the like, and the operational techniques and internal organization of the security services, then there can be no objection to this form of limited disclosure. But if the Attorney-General, as the law officer charged under the Constitution with the responsibility for all criminal prosecutions, cannot countenance the release of relevant evidence to the defence, then he has no reasonable alternative but to exercise his power and his option to withdraw the charges. Under no circumstances should he advise Government ministers to put pressure on judges to permit the Government to withhold evidence the exposure of which may conceivably produce an acquittal.

OTHER POLITICAL OFFENCES

Section 1

Section 1 of the Official Secrets Act makes it an offence punishable by fourteen years' imprisonment to enter top-secret establishments or to collect, publish or communicate any official document or information which might be indirectly useful to a potential enemy, if such acts are done 'for any purpose prejudicial to the safety or the interests of the state'. These are very wide words, and the Act has special provisions designed to reverse the burden of proof if secret information has been found in a defendant's possession, and which enable a jury to draw an inference of intention to prejudice state interests merely from evidence about a defendant's character and associations. Suspects have no 'right to silence' – police have special powers to oblige them to answer questions in the course of a Section 1 investigation, and the trial itself may be held wholly or partly in secret. Section 1 is the most oppressive law on the statute-book, and its provisions which reverse the burden of proof, permit guilt by association and abolish the right of silence are impossible to justify other than in times of war. A particularly unattractive feature of the use of Section 1 has been the savage sentences handed down by the courts: twenty-three years for MI5 officer Michael Bettany, thirty-five years for GCHQ employee Geoffrey Prime, and forty-two years for MI6 traitor George Blake. It was the unconscionable length of the latter sentence which motivated Michael Randle and Pat Pottle to help free him, and sympathy for their motives may have caused a jury to acquit them, twenty-five years later.

Although Section 1 is headed 'penalties for spying', it has on two occasions been used in cases which had nothing to do with espionage. In 1962 a group of anti-nuclear protesters were convicted under Section 1 for immobilizing an airfield used by nuclear bombers: it was state policy to keep the base on constant alert, and the jury was not permitted to hear argument that the immobilization of nuclear weapons might safeguard rather than prejudice the interests of the nation.[32] In 1977 Duncan Campbell was alleged to have breached Section 1 by collecting information for publication in *Time Out* – a purpose claimed to be as prejudicial to the interests of the state as selling the information to the Soviet embassy. This prosecution was a breach of parliamentary assurances in 1920 and 1949 that Section 1 would only be used against spies in the employ of foreign powers, and caused considerable dismay in the publishing world.[33] An A–Z of London, after all, is 'indirectly useful to a potential enemy' – could its publisher be punished for 'prejudicing the interests of the state'? Mr Justice Mars-Jones correctly described Section 1 as 'oppressive', and these charges were in due course abandoned.

It is interesting to note that even with its oppressive features Section 1 charges are still capable of being rejected by a jury. Seven young servicemen were acquitted in 1985 of passing secret information to enemy agents in Cyprus in return for sexual favours, despite their extremely full confessions. A subsequent inquiry found that military police had extracted these confessions by unfair questioning, and recommended that in future servicemen suspected of spying offences should be treated like any other suspect under police interrogation. Michael Bettany was convicted in the same year of attempting to pass information about his work in MI5 to Soviet diplomats. Both the Cyprus and the Bettany trials took place in secret, although the press was allowed to report sections of the prosecution's opening address. While Section 1 cases may sometimes involve evidence which deserves to be kept secret, it is hardly fair to publish the prosecution's allegations of treason without lifting the veil on the answers provided by the defence.

Although the dice are loaded in favour of the prosecution, it is noteworthy that Section 1 was not used against either Blunt or Philby. Both men were offered an immunity from prosecution in return for a confession, the security services apparently believing that the public interest would be better served by hushing up their treachery than by punishing them for it. Blunt was allowed to live in peace for fifteen years until exposed by a journalist (in a book which could not have been published had the 1989 secrecy legislation been in force), while Philby made a brief confession to an MI5 colleague in Beirut and then departed for Moscow. These immunities were later justified on the grounds that Blunt and Philby might volunteer useful information in return for the promise not to prosecute, although the real reason for offering them a secret amnesty was doubtless to avoid public and political embarrassment.

Treason

The crime of treason has played a lurid part in British history ever since the Treason Act of 1351 made it a capital offence for British citizens to give aid and comfort to the King's enemies. This Act remains on the statute-books and the crime still carries the death penalty, although in 1790 Parliament substituted hanging for the traditional punishment of beheading in the Tower. There has not been a treason trial since William Joyce (Lord Haw-Haw) was convicted in 1946 for making Nazi propaganda broadcasts. Those proceedings did little credit to British justice: Joyce was an American who was convicted on the technicality that he had once possessed (but never used) a British passport, and he was executed in defiance of the principle that the death penalty should not be exacted where there is a dissenting appellate judgement.[34] Treason is broadly defined to include 'compassing or imagining' the death of the King or the heir apparent, slaying the Chancellor, the Treasurer, or any judge or magistrate, or having sex with 'the King's companion, or the King's eldest daughter unmarried, or the wife of the King's eldest son and heir'. (Anne Boleyn, it will be recalled, lost her head for being an accomplice in her own treasonable adultery.) In 1848, much disturbed by the republican revolutions in Europe, Parliament passed the Treason Felony Act which makes every person who shall 'compass, imagine, invent, devise or intend to deprive our most gracious Lady the Queen . . . from the style, honour or royal name of the imperial crown of the United Kingdom . . .' liable 'to be imprisoned for the term of his or her natural life'. In theory, the publication of arguments in favour of abolishing the monarchy constitutes an offence under this legislation.

These laws are historical anomalies, and serve no useful purpose other than by exciting the occasional back-bench MP to demand that IRA bombers be hanged for treason rather than sent to prison for life for murder or conspiracy to cause explosions. It is inconceivable that treason would be charged as a means of bringing back the death penalty for politically motivated murder, or that any outspoken republican would face imprisonment 'for the term of his or her natural life'. In 1992 the tabloid press published telephone intercepts and innuendo hinting at Princess Diana's infidelity to the monarch's 'eldest son and heir', but Scotland Yard did not seem interested in sniffing the royal sheets for suspicion of this heinous offence. (If Diana were sentenced to be hanged in the Tower, the European Court of Human Rights would doubtless urge commutation of her sentence.) The heir to the throne was more plainly accused of adultery, but in English law adultery is the prerogative of sovereigns, and not of their consorts. As the Law Commission has commented, with its usual understatement, 'It is our provisional view that there is no need for the retention of any treason-type offence to deal with violation of the royal ladies.'[35] In 1977 it recommended that all treason statutes should be abolished and replaced with a crime of engaging in conduct likely to help an enemy country with which we are at war.

Sedition

Sedition is the political crime *par excellence*, used in the eighteenth and nineteenth centuries in direct attempts to silence critics of Government. The crime is broadly defined as promoting ill-will between different classes of citizens, raising discontent and disaffection among the people, and bringing the Government or the laws into hatred, ridicule or contempt. In 1764 it was used against John Wilkes and the printers of radical papers, who assailed George III with such seditious remarks as 'You have never been acquainted with the language of truth until you heard it in the complaints of your subjects.'[36] The King's judges, and notably Lord Mansfield, were determined to obtain convictions from juries who shared the popular dislike of George III and his ministers, so they themselves ruled that the writings were seditious and instructed their juries that the only issue was whether defendants had published them or not. Juries ignored these directions to convict, and emerged from court to the cheers of crowds who had gathered to celebrate the acquittals. Charles Fox and his Whig supporters finally pushed through Parliament the Libel Act of 1792, which established that it was the province of the jury and not the judge finally to decide whether a particular piece of writing was seditious. The Lord Chancellor and his judges predicted at the time that the Act would lead to 'the confusion and destruction of the law of England' – in fact, it legitimized 'sympathy acquittals' in seditious libel cases and deterred subsequent Governments from using this particular law to muzzle political criticisms of their policies.

Subsequent generations of judges have been less subservient to the Government, and have narrowed the scope of the offence so that it is now virtually useless as a weapon against writers and agitators. In 1886, John Burns and other Socialist speakers were acquitted of sedition at the Old Bailey, after the judge had ruled that the crime required a determined intention on the part of the defendant to incite people to violence – speeches critical of the Government which aroused class hatreds and might lead to violence were not seditious if actuated by 'an honest desire to alleviate the misery of the unemployed' or by a genuine desire to promote lawful reform.[37] In 1990 the Divisional Court rejected a misconceived attempt by Muslims to bring sedition charges against Salman Rushdie and Penguin Books for publishing *The Satanic Verses*. In an important judgement, it limited sedition by stressing that it involved an attack on the state, and thus the prosecution must prove that the speech or writing was both *intended* and *likely to* incite actual violence against democratic institutions.[38]

Sedition now serves no purpose in the criminal law: violent attacks on state institutions may be amply prosecuted and punished by offences in the Public Order Act. The unreformed British law is, however, being used in many Commonwealth countries as a device for jailing dissidents, particularly those who peacefully campaign against corrupt Governments or who urge transition to multi-party democracy. Thus the winner of the 1992 John Kennedy Peace Prize, Chihofwa Chihana, was prosecuted in Malawi by an English QC specially imported for the purpose, for the crime of saying publicly that ninety-three-year-old President Banda was 'too old to run the country' and that most Malawians supported a change in the Government. This is just one example of how oppressive British laws, still on our statute books, are used to diminish human rights in former colonial countries. The failure to abolish them in Britain allows oppressors to justify their use (British lawyers were brought to Malawi, according to its Minister for Justice, 'to show the world that this prosecution is acceptable') and provides the Foreign Office with an excuse to avoid condemning such violations of human rights in 'friendly' countries.

Incitement to disaffection

We have seen in this chapter how the power of the jury to return a verdict of acquittal, irrespective of the evidence, has been a significant deterrent to 'political' uses of official secrets and sedition charges. A further example of the power of a jury to 'unmake' a bad law is provided by the acquittal in 1975 of fourteen pacifists who were charged at the Old Bailey with inciting troops to disaffection by distributing a leaflet explaining how they could conscientiously object to service in Northern Ireland or, as a last resort, desert. The Incitement to Disaffection Act was passed amid great controversy in 1934 – indeed, several of the leading cases on public order examined in Chapter 2 arose from meetings held in protest against this legislation. It punishes those who 'endeavour to seduce' military personnel from their 'duty or allegiance', and aroused understandable fears at the time that it would be used against those who merely distributed pacifist literature or who urged soldiers to disobey orders to fire on striking workers. Those fears have proved unfounded, although the notion of 'duty' is unjustifiably wide, and could theoretically catch both the wife who persuades a husband to stay back from barracks and a protester who urges soldiers to disobey orders on the grounds of conscientious objection to executing them. In neither case would 'allegiance' (in the sense of 'loyalty') be affected, and since the Incitement to Mutiny Act of 1797 punishes any attempt to seduce military personnel from their 'duty *and* allegiance', it is questionable whether the 1934 Act serves any real purpose. It has not been used since the Old Bailey acquittals in 1975, and the then Attorney-General, Sam

Silkin, expressed regret that this much-publicized case was ever brought. The most powerful incitement to disaffection was made during the 1987 election campaign by the Prime Minister, Mrs Thatcher, who announced that service chiefs should consider resigning in protest if the Labour Party were elected and sought to implement its non-nuclear defence policy. It will henceforth be difficult to convince a jury that pacifists should be punished for urging lesser ranks to consider leaving the services in protest against having to implement Government policies on nuclear defence or Northern Ireland.

There are other unjustifiable pieces of legislation which are embarrassing, oppressive and of no contemporary significance. The Aliens (Protection) Amendment Act of 1919 makes it an offence for an alien to attempt any act likely to cause sedition or disaffection or industrial unrest in an industry where he has not been employed for at least two years; and in the same year it was also made an offence to do any act calculated to cause disaffection in the police force or to attempt to induce any policeman to go on strike. Like the laws against sedition and incitement to disaffection, these pieces of legislation have fallen into disuse, and any attempt to revive them would be highly controversial. The Police Federation has certainly not shrunk from inciting disaffection over pay and conditions, and it is difficult to see why aliens should not be permitted to participate in industrial action which is not otherwise unlawful. Attempts to enforce these laws against peaceful protests would probably now be in breach of the European Convention on Human Rights, and the most remarkable thing about them is that the Government has not taken the many opportunities which have been available to have them repealed. Has this been the result of oversight, or of a feeling that they may one day be gainfully deployed?

CHAPTER 5

Censorship

We live in an age where one person's obscenity is another person's bedtime video. The deep division in society over the appropriate limit to sexual permissiveness is mirrored by an inconsistent and largely ineffectual censorship of material which may offend or entertain, corrupt or enlighten, according to the taste and character of individual readers and viewers. The problem of where (if anywhere) you draw the line has been with us since the invention of printing. the exploits of Fanny Hill and Constance Chatterley gained a cinematic dimension with the advent of Linda Lovelace, and now page 3 titillation arrives with the morning milk on millions of breakfast tables. The arguments for and against censorship have worn well throughout the ages: 'Let us renounce the effort to reconcile these two irreconcilable things – art and young girls' exclaimed the Victorian novelist George Moore as his works were personally removed from the bookshelves of Mr W. H. Smith after complaints from elderly ladies in the provinces. The censorhip of art and literature in Britain until the 1960s at least had the one great merit of bringing James Joyce and Henry Miller and D. H. Lawrence to the excited attention of generations of teenagers: the ideologically vapid rubbish which it is now necessary to travel to the Continent in order to procure hardly seems worth investing with the special thrill of the taboo. Britain, until recently, could still boast the best obscenity trials. *Lady Chatterley's Lover* was a tension-packed seminar on English literature, the *Oz* trial produced more letters to *The Times* than the Suez crisis, and during the *Gay News* blasphemy trial readings from the Bible were interrupted by the judge announcing the cricket score while the prosecutrix led prayer meetings in the corridors of the Old Bailey.

The traditional pro-censorship lobby has recently found some strange bedfellows amongst the feminist movement (although, as we shall see, obscenity laws have been much used against outspoken women) while at the same time a new public explicitness about sexual behaviour has been officially sanctioned to help combat the spread of AIDS. The main battleground has shifted to television drama – *EastEnders* and the plays of Dennis Potter and the late-night movies on Channel 4, and the imminent invasion of alien porn from outer space through the satellite dish. The 1990s have so far seen some unsuccessful attempts to press obscenity laws into service against 'rap' music with violent sexist lyrics, but there has been a notable disinclination to mount the extravagant Old Bailey censorship trials of yesteryear. In 1991 the twentieth anniversary of the *Oz* obscenity trial inspired the BBC (whose new Director-General, John Birt, had stood bail for the *Oz* editors) to re-enact the proceedings, to retrospective bewilderment that six weeks of court time and legal talent could have been spent analysing the significance of Rupert Bear having an erection. None the less, persons convicted of selling pornography which is freely available on the Continent were still being sent to prison: Britain and the People's Republic of China are the only significant countries which routinely gaol first offenders for obscenity offences.

For all the absurdity and hypocrisy which has attended the enforcement of obscenity laws, much of the material which could potentially be targeted is obnoxious in the extreme. The fantasies which sell on a blackish market include those depicting the sadistic humiliation of women or children, and freely available 'top-shelf' publications avowedly aim to arouse male lust. Any society genuinely concerned to protect individual rights to adult reading and viewing must balance that value against the danger that what is dilated over in private may encourage antisocial or criminal actions against other, more vulnerable, members of the community. That said, any law enforcement which targets material with literary or artistic pretensions is an objectionable restriction on freedom of expression, and the use of vaguely defined criminal laws against the purveyors of pornography has on any reasonable assessment been unsuccessful. Those who essay the task of making people good by Act of Parliament should eschew criminal law models (except in the specific case of child pornography) and concentrate on workable point-of-sale restrictions. It may be that the national appetite for erotica will reduce once it ceases to be invested with the aura of the taboo; although it is more likely that it will diminish as a result of healthier attitudes towards sexuality promoted through education and community action and the media.

HISTORY OF OBSCENITY

The history of obscenity provides a rich and comic tapestry about the futility of legal attempts to control sexual imagination. The subject-matter of pornography was settled by 1650: writers in subsequent centuries added new words and novel settings, but discovered no fundamental variation on the finite methods of coupling. The central irony of the court-room crusade – what might be termed 'the *Spycatcher* effect' – is always present: seek to suppress a book by legal action because it tends to corrupt, and the publicity attendant upon its trial will spread that assumed corruption far more effectively than its quiet distribution. *Lady Chatterley's Lover* sold three million copies after its prosecution in 1961. The last work of literature to be prosecuted for obscenity in a full-blooded Old Bailey trial was an undistinguished paperback entitled *Inside Linda Lovelace*. It had sold a few thousand copies in the years before the 1976 court case: within three weeks of its acquittal 600,000 copies were purchased by an avid public. That trial seems finally to have convinced the DPP of the unwisdom of using obscenity laws against books with any claim to literary or sociological merit.

The first censorship in Britain was decreed by the Star Chamber, and implemented by the Stationers' Company. Its charter, in 1559, required all serious books to be approved by the Queen, her archbishops, or the Chancellor of Oxford or Cambridge University. The cost of licence fees alone deterred many publishers from submitting their books, and in 1640 the whole system fell with the abolition of the Star Chamber. In 1643, however, it was reintroduced by Cromwell, moving Milton to utter his immortal cry for freedom of the press, the *Areopagitica*:

Promiscuous reading is necessary to the constituting of human nature. The attempt to keep out evil doctrine by licensing is like the exploit of that gallant man who thought to keep out the crows by shutting his park gate

... Lords and Commons of England, consider what nation it is whereof ye are: a nation not slow and dull, but of a quick, ingenious and piercing spirit. It must not be shackled or restricted. Give me the liberty to know, to utter and to argue freely according to conscience, above all liberties.

Milton's plea fell on deaf ears, and the country was saddled with no less than twenty-seven censors, who seem to have been no more effectual than their predecessors. One of their victims was, predictably, Milton himself (his *Defensio* was burned by the public hangman). The Lord Protector's protection was designed to save his subjects from political error rather than lusty thoughts, and Milton's *Paradise Lost* almost fell victim in 1667, but only because it suggested that an eclipse of the sun 'with sudden fear of change perplexes monarchs'. Licensing finally ended in 1695 when Parliament uncovered widespread corruption in its operation. Fraud, extortion, favouritism and intimidation by licensers and their agents had made the whole system a scandal.

During the reign of Charles II, the King's judges wrested control over disorderly conduct from the moribund ecclesiastical courts. To do so they asserted an inherent power, independent of parliamentary or ecclesiastical authorization, of superintending public morality by punishing deviations from what they considered to be desirable standards of conduct. The watershed case, in 1663, involved the poet Sir Charles Sedley, who had been responsible for a breach of the peace one night in Covent Garden. Sedley and his fellow revellers, 'inflamed by strong liquors', had climbed to the balcony of the Cock Tavern, 'and putting down their breeches they excrementiz'd in the street: which being done, Sedley stripped himself naked, and with eloquence preached blasphemy to the people'. A riot almost ensued, and some windows were broken – evidence of a breach of the King's Peace, and therefore appropriately tried by the Court of the King's Bench. But in rejecting Sedley's demands to be dealt with by the more lenient church courts, the Court of the King's Bench announced that it possessed an inherent power to punish moral subversion, whether or not there was a judicial precedent or any law in force against the particular brand of immorality alleged. 'This court is the custodian of the morals of all the King's subjects,' the court ruled, 'and it is high time to punish such profane conduct.'[1] Sedley's case was to become the precedent for the creation by English judges of the offence of obscenity and the crimes of corrupting public morals and outraging public decency. In 1989 the case was used as a precedent for convicting an artist who had exhibited ear-rings made out of human foetuses. The fact that he did so in an art gallery provided no defence (see later, page 247).

The crime of obscenity began in 1727 when the court declared that publication of an erotic book entitled *Venus in the Cloister* was a common-law misdemeanour because it tended to 'weaken the bonds of civil society, virtue and morality'.[2] At first the new crime brought no new prosecutions: it was not activated again until 1763, as part of an attempt to silence the political radical John Wilkes. His popular polemics excoriated George III and his ministers, but he had privately circulated a robust parody of Pope, on the theme that '... life can little more supply / Than just a few good fucks, and then we die'. This *Essay on Woman* was solemnly read to the House of Lords by Lord Sandwich, a target of the publisher's polemics, and when one peer protested the others shouted, 'Go on, go on.' They ultimately resolved that the poem was 'a most scandalous, obscene and impious libel'.

The law of obscene libel created by the judges in 1727 failed to make an impact on the circulation of erotica. By the middle of the eighteenth century the classic of English pornography, *Fanny Hill*, was on sale, with its lurid, if decorous, descriptions of rape, sodomy, flagellation and most other forms of sexual deviation. It was not until 1857 that Britain acquired an Obscene Publications Act, which gave the police powers to take books before local justices to have them 'forfeited' and destroyed for obscenity. The task of defining obscenity was left to the courts, and Chief Justice Cockburn, in the 1868 case of *R. v. Hicklin*, obliged with a formula which has influenced the subject ever since:

I think the test of obscenity is this, whether the tendency of the matter charged as obscenity is to deprave and corrupt those whose minds are open to such immoral influences, and into whose hands a publication of this sort may fall.[3]

Armed at last with a definition of obscenity, Victorian prosecutors proceeded to destroy many examples of fine literature and scientific speculation. James Bradlaugh and Annie Besant were convicted for advocating birth control in *An Essay on the Population Problem*, Havelock Ellis's pioneering classic *Sexual Inversion* was destroyed, and a massive assault was mounted on the works of the 'French pornographers' Zola, Flaubert and de Maupassant. In 1888 Henry Vizetelly, a distinguished bookseller, was brought to the Old Bailey charged with publishing their books. A fortnight before the trial Zola was appointed to the French Legion of Honour for his services to literature and freedom, but this failed to save Vizetelly from a heavy fine. *The Times* gloated that 'In future, anyone who publishes translations of Zola's novels and works of similar character will do so at his peril, and must not expect to escape so easily as Mr Vizetelly.' It was right, of course. Next year Vizetelly, a sick man of seventy, was gaoled for three months for publishing further books by Zola and de Maupassant.

Despite the new law, pornography thrived in the Victorian underworld as never before. This was the time of the great *œuvres* of Victorian prurience: *The New Lady's Tickler* (1860), *Lady Bumtickler's Revels* (1872), *Colonel Spanker's Experimental Lecture* (1879), *The Story of a Dildoe* (1880), *My Secret Life* (1885), not to mention one epic entitled *Raped on the Railway: A True Story of a Lady who was First Ravished and Then Flagellated on the Scotch Express* (1894). Such titles found a new and avid readership as illiteracy declined from 30 per cent in 1861 to an estimated 5 per cent in 1893. These new readers were held to require the protection of the obscenity law. In the first twentieth-century obscenity case, the Common Serjeant of the Old Bailey could confidently assert that a book which sold at 1s. 11d. would 'clearly tend to the corruption of morals ... In the Middle Ages things were discussed which if put forward now for the reading of the general public would never be tolerated.'[4]

Under the old law of obscene libel, almost any work dealing with sexual passion could be successfully prosecuted. The *Hicklin* test focused upon the effect of the book on the most vulnerable members of society, whether or not they were likely to read it. One 'purple passage' could consign a novel to condemnation, and there was no defence of literary merit. D. H. Lawrence's *The Rainbow* was destroyed in 1915, and *The Well of Loneliness* suffered the same fate in 1928 at the hands of a magistrate who felt that a passage which implied that two women had been to bed ('And that night they were not divided') would induce 'thoughts of a most impure character' and 'glorify a horrible tendency'. (In 1974 *The Well of Loneliness* was read as a 'Book at Bedtime' on BBC's Radio 4.) The operation of the obscenity law depended to some extent upon the crusading zeal of current law officers. There was a brief respite in the 1930s, after a banned copy of *Ulysses* was found among the papers of a deceased Lord Chancellor. But in 1953 the authorities solemnly sought to destroy copies of *The Kinsey Report*, and in 1956 a number of respectable publishers – Secker & Warburg, Heinemann and Hutchinson – were all tried at the Old Bailey for 'horrible tendencies' discovered in their current fiction lists. The Society of Authors set up a powerful lobby, which convinced a parliamentary committee that the common law of obscene libel should be replaced by a modern statute which afforded some protection to meritorious literature. The Obscene Publications Act of 1959 was the result.

The 1959 Act emerged from a simplistic notion that sexual material could be divided into two classes, 'literature' and 'pornography', and the function of the new statutory definition of obscenity was to enable juries and magistrates to make the distinction between them. The tendency of a work to deprave or corrupt its readers was henceforth to be judged in the light of its total impact, rather than by the arousing potential of 'purple passages'. The readership to be considered was the actual or, at least, predictable reading public, rather than the precocious fourteen-year-old schoolgirl into whose hands it might perchance fall – unless it were in fact aimed at or distributed to fourteen-year-old schoolgirls, by whose vulnerability to corruption it should then be judged. It was recognized that a work of literature might employ, to advance its serious purpose, a style which resembled, or had the same effect as, the pornographer's: here the jury was to be assisted to draw the line by experts who would offer judgements as to the degree of importance the article represented in its particular discipline. Works of art or literature might be obscene (i.e. depraving or corrupting) but their great significance might outweigh the harm they could do, and take them out of the *prima facie* criminal category established by Section 1 of the Act.

In fact, the 1959 Act has worked to secure a very large measure of freedom in Britain for the written word. It took two decades and a number of celebrated trials for the revolutionary implications of the legislation to be fully appreciated and applied. The credit for securing this freedom belongs to a few courageous publishers who risked gaol by inviting juries to take a stand against censorship, and to the ineptitude and corruption of police 'enforcement' of the law. The first major test case – over D. H. Lawrence's *Lady Chatterley's Lover* – enabled the full force of the reformed law to be exploited on behalf of the recognized literature. In 1968 the appeal proceedings over *Last Exit to Brooklyn* established the right of authors to explore depravity and corruption explicitly described. The trials of the underground press in the early seventies discredited obscenity law in the eyes of a new generation of jurors, and acquittals of hard-core pornography soon followed. These came in the wake of apparently scientific evidence that pornography had a therapeutic rather than a harmful effect. Popular permissiveness was reflected in jury verdicts, and the repeal of obscenity laws in several European countries made it impossible for the authorities to police the incoming tide of eroticism. And if pornography did not corrupt its readers, it certainly corrupted many of those charged with enforcing the law against it. Public cynicism about obscenity control was confirmed when twelve members of Scotland Yard's 'dirty squad' were gaoled after conviction for involvement in what their judge described as 'an evil conspiracy which turned the Obscene Publications Act into a vast protection racket'.[5]

After the acquittal of *Inside Linda Lovelace* in 1976, the authorities largely abandoned the attempt to prosecute books for which any claim of literary merit could be made. The Williams Committee, which reported on the obscenity laws in 1979, recommended that all restraints on the written word should be lifted – a position which they thought had already been achieved *de facto*.[6] Since the Williams Report, the only books which have been prosecuted have either glorified illegal activities, such as the taking of dangerous drugs, or have been hard-core pornography lacking any literary pretension or sociological interest. However, the boast of British literary artistic freedom cannot be made with confidence, given a vague law and a swinging moral pendulum. The forces of feminism have done more than the cohorts of Mrs Whitehouse to challenge public acceptance of erotica: there can be no guarantee that some future legal onslaught against sexually explicit art and literature would not succeed. In 1988, the DPP seriously considered a test-case prosecution against the works of Henry Miller, but in 1991 declined calls to prosecute paperback publishers of the works of De Sade and of Brett Easton Ellis, author of *American Psycho*.

The Obscene Publications Squad did move against the American rap band, Niggaz With Attitude, seizing thirty thousand cassettes and compact discs which it invited a bench of elderly magistrates to destroy on grounds that the lyrics would corrupt teenage listeners. The magistrates declined, having found most of the lyrics impossible to follow while the record was played to their obvious bewilderment over a sound system specially set up in court.

'Censorship' is itself a dirty word for most civil libertarians, and its history in the courts has been comical in retrospect. But there are a number of entirely reasonable claims that can be made in favour of some degree of public reticence about sexual matters. Whatever the claims of 'dirty old men' to dilate over sexual fantasies in private, the colourful display of erotic magazines at local shops and news-stands is offensive to many. Would there be any loss of liberty to require them to be encased in Cellophane, and placed on racks above the reach of children or be confined for sale in licensed sex shops? This is the kind of administrative control that operates in many countries, and avoids the problems of deciding whether particular magazines are likely to deprave and corrupt or be grossly offensive to reasonable people. Although there is no proven link between availability of pornography and sexual crime, many women's groups and senior judges have little doubt that rapes and indecent assaults increasingly involve behaviour that defendants have read about and are in consequence encouraged to try. What is necessary, of course, is to build up societal inhibitions against any form of forcible sex, but although the courts have increased the prison sentences for rape to the point where they approximate to the punishment for armed robbery, this does not seem to deter men whose minds have been warped by something rather more fundamental than the reading of dirty books.

Attitudinal changes are difficult to enforce by criminal laws against publishers who arouse lust in men. The page 3 phenomenon has certainly done more to promote callous salacity than any amount of smuggled Scandinavian pornography, but would a law which banned pictures of nude women in national newspapers be enforceable, or would it merely result in provocative but partly clothed page 3 poses? The lesson to be drawn from the history of obscenity prosecutions is that criminal trials are counter-productive. They polarize opinion and publicize the book or film, and they only succeed in bringing the law into disrepute. They do not always send pornographers to prison, although that is where the Court of Appeal, in a series of sentencing decisions in 1982, insisted they should go, even for first offences. 'When news of this judgement reaches Soho,' the court huffed and puffed and bluffed, 'we think it is likely that there will be a considerable amount of stocktaking within the next seventy-two hours, because if there is not, there is likely to be a depletion of the population of that area in the next few months'.[7] In fact, Soho's pornographers moved most of their wares to licensed sex shops, and increased their prices. Deterrent sentencing in this area does not work in the way that judges imagine, and the jailing of pornographers (who are usually 'front men' for the big importers) merely adds unnecessarily to the prison population and encourages police to spend more public time and money on a social problem which the criminal law is incapable of solving satisfactorily. The availability of pornography on cable television is likely to make the current sentencing tariff all the more difficult to justify: the first 'soft core' channel was approved for late-night viewing in 1992, and in 1993 the Home Office was trying to stop Red Hot Dutch, a hard-core cable channel whose satellite pictures, uplinked from the Netherlands, fell outside the control of the Obscene Publications Act.

THE TEST OF OBSCENITY

The definition of obscenity is contained in Section 1 of the Obscene Publications Act:

For the purposes of this Act an article shall be deemed to be obscene if its effect or (where the article comprises two or more distinct items) the effect of any one of its items is, if taken as a whole, such as to tend to deprave and corrupt persons who are likely, in all the circumstances, to read, see or hear the matter contained or embodied in it.

In any trial, the prosecution must prove beyond reasonable doubt that the material is obscene. It has a number of hurdles to surmount.

The tendency to deprave and corrupt

'Deprave' means 'to make morally bad, to pervert, to debase or corrupt morally' and 'corrupt' means 'to render morally unsound or rotten, or destroy the moral purity or chastity of, to pervert or ruin a good quality, to debase, to defile.[8] The definition implies that the tendency must go much further than merely shocking or disgusting readers.[9] Thus 'obscene', in law, has a very different, and very much stronger, meaning than it possesses in colloquial usage. The convictions of the editors of *Oz* were quashed because their trial judge had suggested that 'obscene' might include what is 'repulsive, filthy, loathsome, indecent or lewd'. To widen its legal meaning in this way was 'a very substantial and serious misdirection'.[10] 'Corrupt' is a strong word, implying a powerful and corrosive effect, which goes further than merely 'leading morally astray', and the courts have recalled the Book of Common Prayer reference to 'where rust and moth doth corrupt'.[11] In one case, however, the Law Lords pointed out that corruption could be all in the mind – it need not take the form of overt sexual misbehaviour. It was a crime to sell pornography to an addict, no matter how far gone in depravity, because dirty old men could be corrupted more than once (a ruling which was no doubt greeted with relief by dirty old men).[12] At the end of the day, the 'deprave and corrupt' test really calls upon the jury to decide whether the material is harmful to likely readers and viewers.

The aversion defence

One important corollary of the decision that obscene material must have more serious effects than arousing feelings of revulsion is the doctrine that material which in fact shocks and disgusts may *not* be obscene, because its effect is to discourage readers from indulgence in the immorality so unseductively portrayed. Readers whose stomachs are turned will not partake of any food for thought. The argument, however paradoxical it sounds, has sometimes found favour as a means of exculpating literature of merit. Thus *Last Exit to Brooklyn* presented horrific pictures of homosexuality and drug-taking in New York. Defence counsel contended that its only effect on any but a minute lunatic fringe of readers would be horror, revulsion and pity. It made the readers share in the horror it described and thereby so disgusted, shocked and outraged them that instead of tending to encourage anyone to homosexuality, drug-taking or brutal violence it would have precisely the reverse effect. The failure of the trial judge to put this defence before the jury in his summing-up was the major ground for upsetting the conviction.[13]

The most valuable aspect of the aversion defence is its emphasis on the context and purpose of publication. Writing which sets out to seduce, to exhort and pressurize the reader to indulge in immorality is to be distinguished from that which presents a balanced picture, and does not overlook the pains which may attend new pleasures. For over a century prosecutors thought it sufficient to point to explicitness in the treatment of sex, on the assumption that exposure to such material would automatically arouse the libidinous desires associated with a state of depravity. Now they must consider the overall impact, and the truthfulness of the total picture. Books which present a fair account of corruption have a defence denied to glossy propaganda.

In 1991 the aversion defence assisted Island Records to argue successfully that a record by rap musicians Niggaz With Attitude was not obscene. Despite the profusion of four-letter words and aggressively unpleasant imagery, it was inconceivable that anyone in their right mind – or even in their wrong mind – would be sexually aroused by songs like 'One Less Bitch' or 'To Kill a Hooker'. These songs were said by the defence to be 'street journalism', reflecting the degradation and depravity of life among the drug gangs in the ghetto suburbs of Los Angeles. The court agreed that the record was more likely to arouse distaste and fear than lust, and directed that the thirty thousand records, cassettes and compact discs seized by Scotland Yard's Obscene Publications Squad should be released.

The target audience

An article is only obscene if it is likely to corrupt 'persons who are likely, having regard to all relevant circumstances, to read, see or hear the matter contained or embodied in it'. Thus the Act adopts a relative definition of obscenity – relative, that is, to the 'likely' rather than the 'conceivably possible' readership. The publication in question is judged by its impact on its primary audience – those people who, the evidence suggests, would be likely to seek it out and to pay the asking-price to read it. The Act rejects the 'most vulnerable person' standard of *Hicklin*, with its preoccupation with those members of society of the lowest level of intellectual or moral discernment, and focuses on 'likely' readers and proven circumstances of publication. A work of literature is to be judged by its effect on serious-minded purchasers, a comic book by its effect on children, a sexually explicit magazine sold in an 'adults only' bookstore by its effect on adult patrons of that particular shop.

The 'significant proportion' test

The 1959 Act requires a tendency to deprave and corrupt 'persons' likely in the circumstances to read or hear the offensive material. But how many persons must have their morals affected before the test is made out? The answer given by the Court of Appeal in the *Last Exit to Brooklyn* case is that the jury must be satisfied that a *significant proportion* of the likely readership would be guided along the path of corruption. The 'significant proportion' test has been applied at obscenity trials ever since. It protects the defendant in that it prevents the jury from speculating on the possible effect of adult literature on a young person who may just happen to see it, although it does not put the prosecution to proof that a majority, or a substantial proportion, of readers would be adversely affected. If the jury feels that a considerable number of children would read or see the article in question, and would be corrupted by the experience, it may decide that this number constitutes a significant proportion of the class which comprises the likely audience.

The dominant effect principle

In obscenity trials before the 1959 legislation it was unnecessary for juries to consider the overall impact of the subject-matter on its likely readers. Prosecuting counsel could secure conviction merely by drawing attention to isolated 'purple passages' taken out of context. The Select Committee on the Obscene Publications Act had stressed the importance of considering the 'dominant effect' of the whole work and this recommendation was duly embodied in the 1959 statute, which provided that 'an article shall be deemed to be obscene if its effect . . . is, if taken as a whole, such as to tend to deprave and corrupt . . .'

The effect of the 'dominant impact' test is to enable the courts to take account of the psychological realities of reading and film viewing, in so far as the audience is affected by theme and style and message, so that isolated incidents of an offensive nature are placed in context. The injunction that an article must be 'taken as a whole' will apply to books and plays and films: in the case of magazines, however, which are made up of separate articles, advertisements and photographs, the 'dominant impact' principle has less force. In such cases the publication is considered on an 'item by item' basis: the prosecution may argue that obscenity attaches only to one article or photograph, and that the other contents are irrelevant.

THE PUBLIC GOOD DEFENCE

Section 4 of the Act provides that the defendant to an obscenity charge 'shall not be convicted' – despite the fact that he has been found to have published an obscene article – if 'publication of the article in question is justified as being for the public good . . .' The ground upon which the defence may be made out is that publication, in the case of books and magazines, is 'in the interests of science, literature, art or learning, or of other objects of general concern'. Section 4(1) looks to the advancement of cultural and intellectual values, and the expert opinion as to the 'merits of an article' must be able to relate to the broader question of 'the interests of' art and science. A publication of obscene primitive art may lack objective merit, but none the less may be defended on the grounds of its contribution to art history. (The DPP once considered a complaint about the ancient drainage ditch at Cerne Abbas, which forms the outline of a giant with a truly giant-size erection. In the interests of history, and the interests of the local tourist trade, he declined requests to allow grass to grow strategically over the offending area.)

In both the *Oz* and *Nasty Tales* cases underground comics were accepted as 'art' for the purpose of a Section 4 defence. Rupert Bear cartoons, it was said by Mr Feliks Topolski, were art of a sort, and when an underground comic superimposed private parts on the much-loved nursery creature, this was satiric art of a high order. In 1975 the New Zealand courts held that drawings of toilet fittings were 'artistic works' – a conclusion which the surrealist school would never have doubted.

In *DPP* v. *Jordan* the House of Lords ruled that the psychiatric health of the community allegedly served by 'therapeutic' pornography was not an 'object of general concern' for the purposes of Section 4, which referred to objects of general concern similar to those aesthetic and intellectual values specifically enumerated in the section. Among the 'objects of general concern' advanced on behalf of *Lady Chatterley's Lover* were its ethical and Christian merits and the Bishop of Woolwich testified to the book's contribution to human relations and to Christian judgements and values. Other witnesses testified to its educational and sociological merits, and the editor of *Harper's Bazaar* was called as an expert on 'popular literature'. In the *Last Exit to Brooklyn* case the Court of Appeal conceded that 'sociological or ethical merit' might be canvassed. Other objects of general concern which have been relied upon at obscenity trials include journalism, humour, politics, philosophy, history, education and entertainment.

These precedents were taken further in the *Niggaz With Attitude* case. Dr Guy Cumberbatch, the Home Office expert on the effects of pornography, had been commissioned by Island Records to carry out field research on the effects of listening to NWA albums, which he did, with the cooperation of large numbers of disc jockeys, school and university students and members of rap clubs. His study was helpful in identifying the age and social profile of likely listeners and in establishing that they understood the lyrics in the context of American black experience, and not as any encouragement to antisocial behaviour. There is no reason in principle why this sort of evidence from social scientists should not be called by parties who are 'showing cause' under Section 3 as to why an article should not be destroyed, and are consequently not bound by the rules of evidence in criminal cases. In any event, evidence of this sort is necessary to acquaint courts with what the case is all about: the Redbridge magistrates in the *NWA* case asked questions such as 'Is rap a cult?' and 'What do people do at rap concerts?' The rules are likely to be more strictly applied at criminal trials for obscenity, where judges are notoriously reluctant to allow defence experts of any sort to sway juries on the central issue of whether material tends to deprave and corrupt.

The last, and undoubtedly the worst, 'serious' book to be prosecuted was *Inside Linda Lovelace* in 1976 – its sociological merits were endorsed by a leading feminist and by the Oxford Professor of Jurisprudence. 'If this isn't obscene, members of the jury, you may think that nothing is obscene,' said the judge. The jury acquitted.

How is a jury to decide whether a work which it has already found to be obscene is none the less justified as being for the public good? It must undertake a 'balancing act' described by the Court of Appeal in the *Last Exit to Brooklyn* case:

The jury must consider on the one hand the number of readers they believe would tend to be depraved and corrupted by the book, the strength of the tendency to deprave and corrupt, and the nature of the depravity and corruption; on the other hand, they should assess the strength of the literary, sociological or ethical merit they believe the book to possess. They should then weigh up all these factors and decide whether on balance the publication is proved to be justified as being for the public good.[14]

Unfortunately, 'corruption' and 'literary, sociological or ethical merit' do not admit of meaningful comparison, and the balancing act is a logical nonsense. 'Depravity and corruption', a predicted change for the worse in the characters of a significant number of readers, cannot be quantified and even if it could, its quantity could not meaningfully be compared with literary ability, or scientific value. No book exists in a vacuum: one of the merits of *Oliver Twist* was to awaken the public conscience, and the value and purpose of Greek tragedy was to purge an audience with pity and terror. Nor is it logically possible to 'weigh' such disparate concepts as 'corruption' and 'literary merit'. Is an ounce of depravity-spreading more or less potent than an ounce of artistic merit? Even if the jury manages to find a common measure, the outcome may well be foreclosed against the defendant by the jury's reluctance to find that it could *ever* be in the public interest to spread depravity. 'The publication of this book is for the public good, although it will deprave and corrupt a significant number of its readers' is a verdict any jury would be reluctant to deliver.

PROSECUTION PRACTICE

The enforcement of obscenity laws is now directed largely at 'hard-core pornography'. This has no legal definition, although juries are often told that 'pornography is like an elephant. You cannot define it, but you know it when you see it.'

Despite the uncertainty of the law, there is some consistency in prosecution targets. Descriptions of sexual deviations are much more likely to be attacked than accounts of 'normal' heterosexual behaviour. In practice prosecuting authorities ignore the message of an article, and concern themselves instead with the physical incidents photographed or described. Stories may degrade women, 'do dirt on sex', by depicting them as objects to be manipulated for fun and profit, but obscenity for most prosecutors hangs on simpler things. DPP and Crown Prosecution Service officials have their lines to draw, and they draw them fairly consistently at the male groin: nudity is now acceptable and even artistic, but to erect a penis is to provoke a prosecution. Bizarre strains of pictorial pornography depicting extreme sexual violence, simulated necrophilia and human excretory functions do exist in Scandinavia and are sometimes imported into Britain, where distributors are almost invariably convicted. Juries which are sometimes inclined to support freedom for voyeurs are less keen to promote freedom for ghouls.

There is no indication in the debates which surrounded the Obscene Publications Act that 'obscenity' pertained to anything but matters of sex, but the courts have interpreted the statutory defini-tion of 'obscene' to encompass encouragements to take dangerous drugs and to engage in violence.[15] In 1984 there was an obscenity blitz on American drug books, and the publishers of *Cooking with Cannabis*, *The Pleasures of Cocaine* and *How to Grow Marihuana Indoors under Lights* were prosecuted in a four-week trial at the Old Bailey. The prosecution failed to convince the jury that drug-taking was necessarily a depraved activity, given the widespread use of cannabis, or that books which provided factual information about both the pains and the pleasures of drugs would necessarily encour-age people to experiment. Some twenty books were acquitted, and only one, a pamphlet which mindlessly promoted the free-basing of cocaine, was found obscene. The Court of Appeal, in an interesting development of the law, approved the calling of expert witnesses to explain the effects of the drugs.[16] Any publication which deals with drug-taking would be well advised to emphasize repeatedly both the physical dangers and the criminal penalties which attach to drug usage.

Any material which combines violence with sexual explicitness is a candidate for prosecution. Yet there are many gradations between a friendly slap and a stake through the heart, and most 'spanking' books and articles escape indictment. 'Video nasties', however, which combine pornography with powerful scenes of rape and terror have been successfully prosecuted. More difficulty is experienced with the depiction of violence in non-sexual contexts. The Divisional Court in one case approved the prosecution of a manufacturer of children's swap cards depicting scenes of battle, on the theory that they were capable of depraving young minds by provoking emulation of the violence portrayed.[17] In 1955 Parliament, in doubt as to whether the obscenity test covered non-sexual violence, passed a special law against 'horror comics' which might deprave and corrupt children. This legislation is rarely invoked, and comics which showed horrific scenes of the 'Green Berets' in action in Vietnam were never taken to court. In 1976, Southampton magistrates acquitted *The Adventures of Conan the Barbarian*, after a child psychiatrist pointed out that the Conan legend would be perceived as moral and even romantic by children inured to the adventures of *Starsky and Hutch*.

The very existence of a law against literature which 'tends to depraved and corrupt' offers a temptation to prosecutors to 'have a go' at publications they – and most of the community – find obnoxious. In 1992 Manchester crown court was invited to uphold the destruction of *Lord Horror* – a science-fiction account of how Hitler and Lord Haw-haw came back from the dead to live in Manchester with their soul-mate, the local chief constable. Although the story was fantastical, it contained offensive accounts of violence against Jews, for which anti-Semitic content it had been condemned by the local stipendiary magistrate. The court heard evidence about the conventions of science-fiction from writer Michael Moorcock (a noted anti-pornography campaigner) and reluctantly lifted the order, although it decreed that a comic on the same theme should be destroyed. Gross anti-Semitic literature may be prosecuted under the Public Order Act if it is likely to incite racial violence (see below, page 95) so there is no reason to press obscenity law into service for this purpose.

The Obscene Publications Act gives a broad discretion to prosecuting authorities to take action against any publication which a jury might consider to 'deprave and corrupt'. In order to achieve some national consistency in prosecution targets, decisions are referred to the DPP, who has been reluctant since the acquittal of *Inside Linda Lovelace* to prosecute the publisher of books and films which have any claim to merit. But the law allows two methods of avoiding a major 'test case' trial. One way is to prosecute the shop-owner who stocks the book or the video, rather than its publisher. The shop-owner will not have the commitment or the resources to mount full-blooded opposition, and will probably rely on a special defence that he had not examined the article and had no reason to believe it obscene. In 1983 the DPP sanctioned a large number of obscenity prosecutions against video shops for stocking so-called 'video nasties' – the results were chaotic, as juries in different parts of the country reached different decisions in respect of the same video title, and major distributors were powerless to intervene to defend their works as they would have wished. In an effort to reduce confusion, the DPP issued an index of some sixty titles which he regarded as candidates for prosecution. Some of these films had claims to merit, but shopkeepers took fright and refused to stock them. The distributors once again were powerless to protest against this back-door state censorship: the DPP was reluctant to prosecute them, but sought to have their films withdrawn from sale by a form of intimidation. The particular problem was resolved by the Video Recordings Act, which requires every sexually explicit or violent video to be submitted to the British Board of Film Classification (BBFC) for classification, and it is to be hoped that law-enforcement authorities never again succumb to the temptation of imposing censorship by threat rather than by prosecution.

The other deficiency in the 1959 legislation is that it permits police to avoid jury trial entirely by seizing books and magazines from local stores and applying for 'forfeiture orders' at the nearest magistrates' courts. This procedure, under Section 3 of the Act, is used in some areas to destroy material which the police are well aware would never be convicted by a jury. Local justices are less broadminded, and can generally be relied upon to make forfeiture orders against 'adult' magazines on national sale.

Section 3 may well have been appropriate to meet the situation where a bookshop or street-stall proprietor stocks only a few obscene books, perhaps inadvertently, and does not deserve to be convicted of a criminal offence. But the forfeiture power has been exploited in a number of cases for the wholly objectionable purpose of depriving publishers of their right to trial by jury. Books – in some cases, many thousands of books – have been seized from publishers who did wish to defend them to the hilt, and condemned by local justices after the most cursory of hearings. The justices of Stony Stratford bankrupted Maurice Girodias and his Olympia Press (which after the war published in Paris the works of Samuel Beckett, Jean Genet, J. P. Donleavy and William Burroughs for the benefit of British tourists who would smuggle them through customs). Thirty-four different novels were condemned, after the justices had retired to read them all in ninety minutes.[18] This was an abuse of the forfeiture power, and was contrary to an undertaking given in Parliament in 1964 that Section 3 would not be used to deprive serious publishers of the right to trial by jury.[19]

To effectuate the 1964 undertaking Section 3 should be amended so that booksellers or publishers who give notice of their wish for a jury trial can be re-charged under Section 2 of the Act, or else the forfeiture proceedings dropped entirely. (As Mr Roy – now Lord – Jenkins put it in 1964, 'I should not have thought that to put upon somebody the right to opt to be prosecuted and to run all the risks, including the risk of prison, was conferring very excessive liberty of choice upon any individual.') This is a difficult choice for publishers to make; nevertheless *they*, and not the state, should be given the right to make it. That, at least, was the conclusion of the Committee on the Distribution of Criminal Business, which reported in 1975 that:

It seems to us especially desirable that a person charged with an offence involving an obscene or indecent publication should have a right to have the matter decided by a jury, which can better reflect contemporary public attitudes towards obscenity and indecency than can a stipendiary magistrate or a bench of lay justices.[20]

Magistrates and justices frequently approach their censorship task under Section 3 in a cavalier fashion, and their decisions are not precedents which carry any weight outside their own locality. A vast amount of police time is currently expended on raiding corner shops, seizing and forfeiting magazines which are on open display in other shops in the same locality. What purpose does this sort of action serve, beyond wasting public time and public money in order to harass publishers of sexually explicit magazines which, however awful, are none the less lawful? The publishers may be unprepossessing people, out to make money by exploiting interest in sex, but there would be a major outcry if such arbitrary destruction of property were visited upon tobacco companies or wine merchants (whose products, by contributing to death rather than to lust, may be the more harmful). If action is to be taken against sexually explicit magazines on open sale, it should be taken nationally (by test-case prosecutions of publishers, or by a classification system which consigns such material to sex shops) and not by having local justices engage in periodic burnings of magazines they do not like.

SHOULD THE LAW BE CHANGED?

The 'deprave and corrupt' test has become a focus for law reform, and the uncertainties in its application remain a matter for concern, both for libertarians who believe that British citizens should have the same right as Europeans and Americans to obtain pornography from discreet suppliers, and for those who believe that the 'soft porn' available from local newsagents is degrading to women and morally dangerous. The problem is to find a better alternative. The best that anti-pornography campaigners could do in 1986 was to draw up a 'laundry list' of activities, the pictorial representation of which would be 'deemed' to deprave and corrupt. Their bill received an enthusiastic second reading in the House of Commons, but the 'laundry list' was withdrawn after sober realization that it would ban the display of Grecian urns, 'safe sex' guidelines, *King Lear*, videos of the Falklands War and David Attenborough's film about the courtship rituals of the praying mantis.

In 1987, Parliament gave a second reading to a bill which would introduce an entirely new concept of obscenity, namely 'whatever a reasonable person would regard as grossly offensive' in dealing with any matters relating to sex or violence or drug-taking. This test would create more problems than it solves. At least the 'deprave and corrupt' formula makes harm the criterion for guilt. The test of 'gross offensiveness' is conceptually very different. It focuses on what might be termed 'gut reaction' – the instant response of shock or disgust to particular written or visual images. The respondent is described as 'a reasonable person', but since magistrates and jurors invariably regard themselves as 'reasonable', they will test the material according to their subjective and immediate response. 'Offensive' merely means that to which offence is taken, whether on grounds of morals or politics or aesthetics; 'gross' would probably be interpreted by the courts as 'obvious' rather than 'extreme'. Thus a reaction of shock and disgust, as distinct from mild disapprobation, would plainly satisfy the new criterion. In this sense, it would cast a very wide net indeed. British criminal law has generally distinguished between actions which harm and actions which err in taste. The former are banned, the latter are contained by nuisance laws which prohibit the public display of indecent pictures or words. The use of such a broad test is justified to protect citizens from gratuitous offence which they do not seek out: the mischief of the 1987 bill was that it sought to apply the 'offensiveness' concept to material which some citizens choose to view, and judge it according to the artificial reactions of others who might never choose to view it.

Thus the test of 'gross offensiveness' is far too vague and subjective to be a fair or proper criterion of guilt for an offence which carries up to three years in prison and which is aimed at regulating artistic freedom. It is a fundamental principle of criminal law that it should be sufficiently certain to enable citizens to regulate their conduct so as to avoid committing crimes. The 'gross offensiveness' test would entirely fail to provide that necessary measure of certainty, and lead to total confusion as to what could be published without shocking the hypothetical 'reasonable person'. In reality reasonable people have very different thresholds of dismay: the new test would enable juries to choose whether to convict material which shocked a person as reasonable as Mrs Mary Whitehouse, or acquit material which failed to shock a person as reasonable as Mr John Mortimer.

Is it possible to produce a different sort of legal definition which will encapsulate what is commonly seen as the real evil of pornography, namely its reduction of women to little more than objects of male lust? A section of the feminist movement in North America has devoted much energy to promoting a law which would punish

the sexually explicit subordination of women, graphically depicted whether in words or in pictures, where

(i) Women are presented dehumanized as sexual objects, things or commodities,

(ii) Women are presented in postures of sexual submission,

(iii) Women's body parts are exhibited, such that women are reduced to those parts,

(iv) Women are presented as whores by nature.

Is this a workable legal definition? If it is illegal to degrade women by treating them as submissive sex objects and to perpetuate notions about women's inferiority and limited role within society, then many newspapers and films become candidates for prosecution. Vast entertainment and advertising industries have been built on these very presumptions. It is difficult to see how pornography infringes women's rights to *equal* treatment, where the actors are as degraded as the actresses and the context is the fantasy enactment of sexual charades. Admittedly, pornography generally attracts a male audience and projects male sexual fantasies, but to justify prohibition the equality argument must go further, and show that women are treated less fairly or favourably in a community which permits men to dilate over pornographic fantasies. This is difficult to maintain, given the fact that many societies which permit pornography are the very societies which also protect women's rights, precisely because they accord a high value to everyone's civil liberties. The notion that obscenity trials should be occasions for judges and juries to scrutinize the texts of novels to decide whether female characters are presented as 'whores by nature' or 'commodities' is asking too much of the criminal law.

The feminist case has been accepted to some extent in Canada, where a recent Royal Commission recommended that material depicting violence against women or female submissiveness should be banned.[21] It argued for a distinction between 'good clean pornography' which would be publicly available as 'erotica', and 'bad dirty pornography' which should be punished by heavy prison sentences. This distinction is being applied, with some difficulty and at enormous expense, by an army of customs censors who carefully scan every word of rubbishy US magazines for innuendoes derogatory to women. It remains to be seen how effectively this well-intentioned censorship works in practice – there is something unedifying and prurient in obliging state officials to decide which sexual fantasies are to be 'authorized' and which are to be turned back at the border. Ultimately, perhaps, it makes the mistake of taking pornography too seriously, dignifying some sexual fantasies with official approval while placing a political ban on certain instincts and imaginings which have always been with us.

The basic problem with any obscenity law which applies a legal test to methods of expression is that it calls for a judgement of *opinion* rather than a finding of fact. Whether the test is 'deprave and corrupt' or 'grossly offensive to reasonable people' or 'derogatory to women', it will inevitably be applied according to the subjective views of the tribunal, which will be unpredictable at the time of publication. Thus obscenity trials reflect the inability of traditional modes of criminal adjudication to comprehend the issues which can arise in the decision to censor. Criminal law has developed as a method for obtaining the truth in a world of fingerprints, alibis, police informers, bloodstains, and the dog that doesn't bark in the night. These are facts able to be tested: the evidence can be weighed; the credibility of witnesses can be shaken by confrontation. The machinery of the criminal law is geared to adjudicate disputes about *facts*. Obscenity cases call for decision, not about truth or falsity, but about which of two plausible opinions is to be preferred. And that is the case, whether they depend upon ambulatory notions of 'community standards' or whether they turn into debates about 'artistic merit'. The only rational solution is to find a system which works by classification rather than censorship, removing public offence by confining clearly defined material to discreet outlets and making the decision for the court a simple question of fact (whether the material has been sold in defiance of a prohibition) rather than an occasion for debating social morality.

In Britain, the case for rational law reform was advanced by the 1979 Report of a Home Office committee chaired by philosopher Bernard Williams. The philosophical axis of the Williams Report is the principle that conduct should not be suppressed by law unless it can be convincingly demonstrated to carry a real prospect of harm to others. An almost clinical fidelity to John Stuart Mill keeps the report on a narrow course. The siren slogan of 'free speech' is set aside: the nasty and dirty pictures which formed the subject-matter of this inquiry were wholly lacking in communicative content. Equally, a deaf ear is turned to rhetorical thunder about 'moral pollution': causation of harm is carefully distinguished from a cultural phenomenon symptomatic of what may (or may not) be an undesirable change in moral standards.

The question is whether the availability of pornography demonstrably contributes to antisocial conduct, and the answer emphatically is 'not according to the evidence'. Pornographic books and magazines, the committee concluded, can be vile and stomach-turning and trashy, but only when their actual production involves the exploitation of persons under sixteen or the infliction of physical harm on participants should they be banned outright. Restriction – to adults who are prepared to search them out in specialist shops – is the only answer consistent with Mill's principle, in that it removes public offence from a trade which cannot otherwise be proved harmful. The committee would sweep soft-core sex magazines from the counters of corner newsagents and place them on sale, together with pornography of much harder core, in soberly fronted 'adults only' sex shops. What the public eye does not see, the public heart will not grieve over.

The present obscenity law assumes that some books and magazines conduce to a particular kind of harm: namely corruption of the mind. The Williams Report found insufficient evidence to support this assumption, and sought to replace it by a law which would punish the sale of pictorial material when production has involved actual harm to young or maltreated models, and a system which restricts to sex shops magazines with pictures prone to give offence to reasonable people if displayed in public. Thus the legal focus would be shifted from speculation about the working of susceptible minds to speculation about reactions in the reasonable mind's eye. The new mischief is aesthetic outrage, not psychological damage: pictures which turn ordinary stomachs must be sought out by those constitutionally capable and desirous of digesting them. The corner newsagent who wishes to continue dispensing sweets and comics must dismantle his shelf of *Mayfair* and *Men Only*. The Williams Committee offered something for everybody: pornography *aficionados* will have access to pictures dirtier than ever before, the clean-up campaigners will have nothing visible to complain about, and the public will have a sensible and workable law commanding general support. These proposals have not, however, been received with gratitude. The consumers of 'men's magazines', who appreciate the delicacy with which local newsagents carefully fold their 'adult' purchases inside a copy of the morning newspaper, do not want the indignity and embarrassment of searching them out in a sex shop. Clean-up campaigners are outraged at the *very idea* that pornography should be lawfully dispensable, even behind drawn shutters.

For those who see censorship as a reflection of society's lack of confidence in itself, the Williams reforms deserve considerable support. Those who fear that tolerance of pornography will demean and diminish the quality of life may not be much impressed by a proposal to legalize the availability of sexually explicit material for consenting adults. But the principle of prohibiting profit-making enterprises from advertising sexual wares in a manner calculated to embarrass citizens going about their ordinary business is unexceptionable, and sexually explicit material on a shelf of a soberly fronted sex shop is hardly an environmental threat. The Williams Committee recognizes that such literature may serve as a boon to the lonely, the ugly, the aged, and those who are forced by circumstances or by personal unattractiveness to live without love and companionship. A system of control which requires responsible management of bookshops presenting a modest front to a public street far from schools, churches and council flats deserves a try, based on a law which echoes the sentiments of Mrs Patrick Campbell: 'It doesn't matter what you do in the bedroom as long as you don't do it in the street and frighten the horses.'

SEX-SHOP CONTROL

Although the Williams Committee Report has not been implemented, its philosophy of 'out of sight, out of mind' is apparent in legislation passed in 1982 giving local councils special powers to license sex shops and sex cinemas in their areas. Sex-shop chains proliferated in Britain in the seventies, to the extent that they threatened to rival Mothercare on local high streets. An Indecent Displays (Control) Act of 1981 cleaned up window displays, obliging them by law to refuse admission to persons under eighteen and to erect a large warning notice in their windows stating that 'persons passing beyond this notice will find material on display which they may consider indecent'. This was hardly an imposition, as it tended to attract rather than repel custom. The Local Government (Miscellaneous Provisions) Act of 1982 was another matter, because it empowered local councils to refuse a licence to shops 'used for a business which consists to a significant degree' of selling books, magazines, films, videos and artefacts which portray, encourage or are otherwise used in connection with sexual activity. A licence may be refused if the applicant is unsuitable, or if the 'character of the locality' makes the presence of a sex shop undesirable. The local council may decide the number of sex shops which are appropriate for the locality, and the legislation specifically provides that 'nil may be an appropriate number'.

The effects of the legislation have varied from council to council: some have decided not to exercise the powers at all, others have used them to ban sex shops altogether, while most have taken the opportunity to extract large licensing fees, limit the number of shops, and lay down rules which exclude them from residential areas or proximity to schools and churches. Sex-shop operators have suffered, but not all that much: licensing has reduced competition rather than demand, and led to some ingenious avoidance devices, such as selling sex articles through 'Tupperware parties' in private homes and reopening sex shops as 'birth-control centres' which solemnly promote 'items which are manufactured as masturbatory aids as an alternative method of birth control'.

The legitimate concern that local-council licensing powers might be used as a form of censorship is somewhat reduced by the fact that 'sex shops' are confidence tricks, selling magazines and videos that may be obtained from local newsagents and video stores, exotic lingerie available at a fraction of the price in Marks & Spencer, and contraceptives and vibrators which are found in most pharmacies. It may be doubted whether these lawful items, when sold under the same roof, really justify the inordinate amount of public time and money which is spent on inspection and application hearings. If (as

Williams recommended) pornography of all kinds was confined to such outlets, then some such system of control would be necessary. The legislation has some unattractive features: it permits no appeal from local-council decisions other than on procedural grounds, and it allows local councils to levy quite extortionate annual licence fees (which range from £10,000 in Westminster to £12.50 in South Kesteven, Lincolnshire). Some over-enthusiastic inspectors have tried to extract licence fees from newsagents and bookshops whose erotic publications form a small part of their trade, but the Divisional Court has now ruled that the 'significant degree of business' test is not satisfied in such cases.[22] The legislation has spawned a great deal of planning litigation, but does not seem to have reduced the national turnover in sexual impedimenta (one million vibrators were reportedly sold each year by one sex-shop chain in the early 1980s). It is interesting that a law which was designed to enable local councils to drive sex shops out of town seems to be working to give them some measure of respectability, as local councillors and council officials up and down the country warm to the task of deciding precisely at what distance from a church one may be permitted to purchase an inflatable rubber doll.

THE THEATRE

Theatre censorship was originally imposed in 1551 to curb opposition to the Reformation, and no play was to be performed without a licence from the Master of the Revels, an officer of the Lord Chamberlain. At first, the royal licence afforded protection from puritan hostility: theatre was an aristocratic entertainment, and so long as no insult was offered to Church or state, dramatic invention was unrestrained. Shakespeare was patronized by the Lord Chamberlain – his sexual candour caused no contemporary offence because his political themes did not overtly challenge the existing social order, and bawdy Restoration drama pandered to the tastes of the King and his court clique. It was Prime Minister Walpole who, goaded beyond endurance by caricatures of himself in the plays of Henry Fielding, first introduced legislation empowering the Lord Chamberlain to close down theatres and imprison actors as 'rogues or vagabonds' for uttering any unlicensed speech or gesture which offended against 'decency and good manners'. The first victim of the Lord Chamberlain was, predictably, Henry Fielding, who stopped writing plays after a series of licence refusals and turned his talents to the novel.

In 1843 a new Theatres Act was passed to consolidate the Lord Chamberlain's power to prohibit the performance of any stage play, or any scene of any stage play, for as long as he thought necessary, 'whenever he shall be of opinion that it is fitting for the preservation of good manners, decorum or of the public peace so to do'. Repressive licensing was in some measure responsible for the sterility of British drama in the nineteenth century. *La Dame aux camélias* and Oscar Wilde's *Salomé* were refused licences, and in 1892 the performance of Ibsen's plays was banned 'in the permanent interests of the stage'. The Lord Chamberlain's Examiner of Plays explained:

I have studied Ibsen's plays pretty carefully, and all the characters ... appear to me to be morally deranged. All the heroines are dissatisfied spinsters who look on marriage as a monopoly, or dissatisfied married women in a chronic state of rebellion against not only the condition which nature has imposed on their sex, but against all the duties and objectives of mothers and wives; and as for the men, they are all rascals or imbeciles.

Many serious writers eschewed the drama, and those few who persisted suffered intolerable restrictions. *Mrs Warren's Profession* was banned from 1894 to 1925, and not even Gilbert and Sullivan were sacred: in 1907 licences for all performances of *The Mikado* were withdrawn for one year to avoid offence to a visiting Japanese prince. The Lord Chamberlain operated a broad definition of 'indecency', and excised all vernacular references to intercourse, gentalia, birth control and venereal disease. Homosexuality could not even be hinted at, and casualties included Lillian Hellman's *The Children's Hour*, Sartre's *Vicious Circle*, Arthur Miller's *A View from the Bridge* and Robert Anderson's *Tea and Sympathy*. Irreverent references to Fascist dictators were suppressed throughout the thirties, and even in 1939 a revue song was banned on account of its opening line: 'Even Hitler had a mother'. This obsessive deference to heads of state extended in the sixties to satires on the Kennedy family, and to aspersions on long-deceased relatives of royalty – as late as 1960 Sadler's Wells Opera were forced to rewrite the libretto of Edward German's *Merrie England* to remove scenes in which

Elizabeth I conspired to poison a rival. Commercial managements accepted political discipline without demur, but state-subsidized companies had no profits at stake, and the Royal Shakespeare Company launched an all-out attack after the Lord Chamberlain objected to the play *US* on the grounds that it was 'beastly, anti-American and left-wing'. In 1966 the Joint Committee on Theatre Censorship commenced its deliberations. Dramatists, state theatre companies and drama critics overwhelmingly demanded abolition of the Lord Chamberlain's powers, and convinced the Joint Committee that pre-censorship provided a service neither to playgoers nor to dramatic art. Its recommendations were embodied in the 1968 Theatres Act. The 1843 Act was repealed, and the test of obscenity installed as the sole basis for theatre censorship.[23]

Section 8 of the Theatres Act duly provides that proceedings shall not be instituted 'except by or with the consent of the Attorney-General'. But when Howard Brenton's play *The Romans in Britain* was first performed at the National Theatre there was considerable critical comment about a scene which called for a simulated homosexual rape, perpetrated by three Roman soldiers upon a young Druid priest. Mrs Mary Whitehouse, the 'clean-up' campaigner, asked the Attorney-General to prosecute under the Theatres Act: the DPP investigated, and reported that no prosecution would be likely to succeed. The Attorney-General refused his consent to allow a private prosecution to go forward, whereupon Mrs Whitehouse sent her solicitor to view the play, and he convinced a magistrate to issue a summons against the director, Michael Bogdanov, under Section 13 of the Sexual Offences Act. This section is directed at male persons who masturbate themselves or others in public toilets and parks, and punishes males who procure the commission of acts of gross indecency in public. The allegation against Bogdanov was that he, being a male, 'procured' a male actor playing the part of a Roman soldier to commit an act of gross indecency with another male, namely the actor playing the young Druid. The artificiality of the proceedings is demonstrated by the fact that had any of the participants been female, Section 13 could not have been applicable.

The prosecutrix had discovered a loophole in the law, applicable in a very limited way to plays directed by males which contain scenes calling for simulation of homosexual activity which a jury might find to be 'grossly indecent'. Although the intention of Parliament was to abolish all residual offences in relation to the staging of plays, the section of the Theatres Act designed to achieve this was not comprehensively drafted. It abolished common-law conspiracy offences, obscene and blasphemous libel and the like, but it overlooked the existence of Section 13. The prosecution evidence was that the act of gross indecency consisted in one male actor holding his penis in an erect position, advancing across the stage and placing the tip of the organ against the buttocks of the other actor. This was the testimony of Mrs Whitehouse's solicitor, who had been seated, appropriately enough, in the gods – some seventy yards from the stage. He admitted, under cross-examination, that he might have mistaken the top of the penis for the actor's thumb, adroitly rising from a fist clenched over his organ. Shortly after this admission the prosecution was withdrawn, relieving the jury from further consideration of a 'thumbs up' defence which might have provided a complete answer to the charge. The jury might also have acquitted on the basis that the actor's performance had not been 'procured' by the director, or that the scene, a necessary part of a highly moral play, was not 'grossly indecent'.

Local councils retain control over front-of-house displays, which they require to remain within the realms of public decency, and they are entitled to withhold licences from theatres which do not comply with fire regulations or other health and safety requirements. They are not, however, permitted to impose any licence conditions relating to the content of plays performed in the theatre. In 1987 Westminster Council contemplated action against the Institute of Contemporary Arts for staging a theatrical performance which featured a 'female Lenny Bruce', but had to accept that it could not use its licensing powers as a back-door method of censorship. The Theatres Act has only been used on one occasion, in 1971, to gaol the promoters of a 'live sex' performance which lacked even the veneer of merit claimed by *O Calcutta*. In 1987, a much more erotic production by the RSC, *Les Liaisons dangereuses*, was performing to packed houses without any public protest, while *No Sex Please, We're British* ended a fifteen-year run which had been justified by little more than its title.

TELEPHONE, POST AND CUSTOMS OFFENCES

It is an offence against Section 11 of the Post Office Act to send 'indecent or obscene' articles through the post. 'Indecency' has a much wider meaning than 'obscenity' (it may include anything that 'offends the modesty of the ordinary person') and there is no public-good defence or right to trial by jury, so it is possible for prosecuting authorities to avoid the safeguards of the Obscene Publications Act in relation to books and magazines supplied by mail order. The 1971 Unsolicited Goods and Services Act specifically proscribes the unsolicited sending of books or leaflets 'which describe or illustrate human sexual techniques' (the word 'human' being added at the insistence of the Ministry of Agriculture to protect its flow of breeding information to farmers). Most people regard the unwelcome arrival of advertisements for pornography as an intrusion on their private life, and the 1971 Act was passed after a public outcry when a leaflet advertising *A Manual of Sexual Technique* was posted indiscriminately to recipients who included schoolchildren and nuns. On the other hand, it is difficult to see why the postal regulations should prevent people from ordering 'indecent' material which, because it is not 'obscene', may lawfully be sold over the counter. This point was made by the Director of Public Prosecutions, and endorsed by the Attorney-General in 1981, to justify their failure to prosecute a distinguished diplomat who had been sending indecent material to his friends. The DPP indicated that henceforth, as a matter of prosecution practice, prosecution under postal indency laws would be confined to cases where indecent material was written on the outside of the envelope or sent to unwilling recipients.

Section 49 of the British Telecommunications Act 1981 makes it an offence to 'send any message by telephone which is grossly offensive or of an indecent obscene or menacing character'. This offence appeared in the earlier Post Office Acts, doubtless to deter unpleasant and unsolicited calls. (Although whether it is apt to catch one breed of telephone nuisance, the 'heavy breather', depends upon whether exhalation of breath amounts to a 'message'.) This section acquired a new importance when the privatization of British Telecom led to the introduction of telephone services which provided allegedly erotic recorded messages at an expensive dialling rate. The exploitation of a former state monopoly to provide crude entertainment was condemned in the press and in Parliament, although providers of this service, carefully supervised by British Telecom, were in fact offering messages so anodyne that to advertise them as 'erotic' was probably a breach of the Trade Descriptions Act. None the less they attracted considerable custom, and became a lucrative service for which telephone subscribers were charged at the same rate as a dialled call to the Republic of Ireland.

In response to public criticism, in 1986 British Telecom required its 'telephone information and entertainment providers' to abide by a special Code of Practice, monitored by an independent committee (ICSTIS) empowered to receive complaints and to discontinue any service which breaches the Code. The Code of Practice excludes 'extreme political or religious messages', establishes careful ground rules for messages designed for persons under sixteen, and provides that in relation to 'adult services', messages should not 'offend against the good taste and decency of reasonable people'.

The 'reasonable people' test would allow some latitude to information services about sexually transmitted diseases, but otherwise the Code is more restrictive than Section 49, confining telephonic jokes to the current level of television situation comedy. In practice, the Code operates to dilute the content of messages designed to titillate, although regrettably it does not stop the misleading advertising of these services. Impersonation of living persons is not permitted if the message is 'grossly offensive to reasonable people'. In 1992 ICSTIS banned the *Sun* from operating a line which enabled callers to listen in to a recording of an intercepted car-phone conversation between Princess Diana ('Squidgy') and a close friend. Thirty thousand callers had dialled the line on its first and only day of operation, many adding £30 to their telephone bill to hear the full tape. Public interest in the state of the royal marriage was insufficient, ICSTIS ruled, to justify profit from the invasion of privacy. While Telecom's concern for royal privacy may be commendable, it has been much criticized for interfering with advertisements for telephone call lines carried in the tabloid press. ICSTIS purports to decide which advertisements are 'unacceptably offensive', by which test it has solemnly ruled that for readers of the *Mirror*, an ad for 'Unzip my Suspenders' is unacceptably offensive, but 'Dial a Bonk' is acceptably offensive. All these restrictions have been justified by reference to the novelty of the British telephone system being used to provide entertainment as well as information, and by the danger of children using their parents' telephones to hear suggestive messages. There is nothing to stop callers in Britain who wish to experience international dirty-talk from dialling ISD to verbally explicit services in the USA or Europe which are available to credit-card holders.

Customs officers have powers to intercept 'obscene or indecent' articles and commercial smugglers of large quantities can be gaoled for up to two years. In 1985 no fewer than thirty-seven customs officers were involved in 'Operation Tiger' directed against Gay's the Word, a small Bloomsbury bookshop which imported a wide range of literature by or about homosexuals. The operation seems to have originated from the actions of zealous customs officers who seized parcels addressed to Gay's the Word for no better reason than that 'Gay' signified to them abnormality, and books by Oscar Wilde, Gore Vidal, Christopher Isherwood and Jean Genet were enthusiastically impounded. Some seventy books, mainly American novels, were selected for prosecution: the bulk of them were alleged to be 'indecent' rather than obscene, and indeed several had for some years been published within the United Kingdom. The proceedings were withdrawn in 1986, shortly before the trial was to commence, as a consequence of the EEC Court of Justice ruling in *Conegate Ltd* v. *Customs and Excise Commissioners* that British customs law could not apply a more stringent test (that of 'indecency') to imported goods the domestically produced equivalent of which were permitted to circulate freely because they were not obscene. The practical consequences of the *Conegate* decision have been to remove the prospect of discriminatory use of customs legislation to prohibit merely 'indecent' material, and to confine its operation to material which would clearly be subject to conviction under the Obscene Publications Act because it depraves and corrupts. Illogically, the Court of Appeal in 1988 refused Gay's the Word permission to call expert evidence to show that 'obscene' books it wished to import could be protected by a public-good defence if printed in England.

Conegate was a sex-shop chain which had imported 'life-size rubber dolls of a sexual nature' from the Continent. A crown court judge had found them to be 'indecent' articles, and thus liable to forfeiture, notwithstanding that they could be marketed within Britain subject only to laws relating to public display and control of sex shops. The EEC Court held that the Treaty of Rome requires 'broadly comparable' moral standards for domestic and imported goods: the UK government could not defend the customs prohibition on 'indecency' when it was not an offence to sell 'indecent' material over the counter.[24] The decision in *Conegate* has had major implications for customs operations. It has been the most important liberalizing development in censorship in recent years, achieved not by Parliament, which has become impervious to any reform smacking of 'permissiveness', but by virtue of our accession to the EEC. In strict law it applies only to importations from Common Market countries, but the Commissioners of Customs and Excise took a policy decision to apply it across the board – it would have been impractical to apply different tests to imports from different countries, and would simply have caused determined American importers to route their goods through Europe. It is likely that a policy will develop of prosecuting importers who smuggle commercial quantities of hard-core pornography, while permitting representations to be made by those who have honestly imported 'borderline' material. Where no agreement can be reached on whether an article is likely to be regarded as 'obscene' if marketed domestically, the question could be tested by allowing the articles entry and leaving it to the DPP to decide whether to bring an obscenity prosecution.

THE COMMON LAW

There are several arcane common-law offences which are occasionally revived 'to guard the moral welfare of the state against attacks which may be more insidious because they are novel and unprepared for'. The case of Sir Charles Sedley (see earlier, page 214) was relied upon by the House of Lords judges in 1961 when they approved the use of a charge of 'conspiracy to corrupt public morals' to convict the publisher of the *Ladies Directory* – a 'Who's Who' of London prostitutes. In ringing tones, the majority affirmed the right of the courts to punish behaviour which was prejudicial to the public welfare, even though Parliament had not legislated against it. ('No one may foresee every way in which the wickeness of man may disrupt the order of society.'[25] This judicial presumptuousness is directly opposed to any democratic theory of government, and has attracted widespread and powerful criticism (as Lord Reid put it in his dissent, 'Where Parliament fears to tread it is not for the courts to rush in'). The Law Lords defended the inherent power of the courts to punish immoral (but otherwise lawful) behaviour on the grounds that guilt would be decided by a jury, although this is clearly contrary to the principle, enshrined in the European Convention of Human Rights, that no penalty should be imposed for actions which are not understood to be illegal at the time they are committed. As Lord Reid pointed out, 'The law will be whatever any jury may happen to think it ought to be, and this branch of the law will have lost all the certainty which we rightly prize in other branches of our law.'

In one remarkable case in 1967, the defendants were found guilty of conspiring to corrupt public morals by 'producing and offering for sale certain whips, leg irons, wrist irons, arm restrictors, belts, straps, chains, gags, hoods, masks, head harnesses, chastity belts, restrictive equipment and other articles, rubber and leather garments . . .' The high-water mark of 'swinging London' was undoubtedly reached when men were convicted at the Old Bailey for conspiring to sell chastity belts.

The law against corrupting public morals is predicated upon the hypothesis that there is one all-embracing moral code to which all classes of the community subscribe – a notion which sociologists have demonstrated to be wishful thinking. Moreover, this assumed moral consensus is further assumed by the conspiracy law to be so vulnerable that a single publication is capable of jeopardizing it. It is not illegal to take advantage of a prostitute's services, but to facilitate this, to help short-cut the sordid and possibly dangerous process of tramping red-light districts by publishing a prostitute's telephone number, may be a serious crime. By allowing juries in effect to make law by deciding what constitutes a corruption of public morality, the criminal law is thrown into an unacceptable state of uncertainty. 'Conspiracy to corrupt public morals' is such a vague and drag-net charge that it is impossible to predict the scope of the law's operation before a jury returns its verdict.

In 1971 the House of Lords reconsidered such drag-net offences as 'conspiracy to corrupt public morals' and 'conspiracy to outrage public decency' and confined them to conduct which was 'reasonably analogous' to conduct which had been punished by prosecution of these offences in the past.[26] The Law Officers have given an undertaking that these conspiracy offences will never be used against any publication which could raise a 'public good' defence if prosecuted under the Obscene Publications Act. None the less, it would be far preferable for Parliament to deal comprehensively with 'contact advertisements' in the course of its reform of the law relating to prostitution rather than by occasional and unpredictable prosecutions against magazine publishers. In 1986, publishers of a contact magazine in Birmingham were convicted of conspiracy to corrupt public morals – the first recorded case for over a decade, and perhaps a harbinger of the revival of common-law charges to punish other 'ways in which the wickedness of man may disrupt the order of society'.

The common-law offence of 'outraging public decency' was revived in 1989 to punish an artist and the proprietor of an art gallery who exhibited a surrealist work featuring earrings which had been fashioned from human foetuses. This prosecution was a breach at least of the spirit of the Law Officers' undertaking, since there were a number of distinguished artists and critics prepared to testify that the work had artistic merit. Defence counsel even discerned a moral message in the work, namely 'a condemnation of a society in which women wear their abortions as lightly as they wear their earrings'. The jury was not permitted to hear anything about art, and the exhibitor's intentions were ruled to be irrelevant. The judge directed the jury to put aside logic and reason and to set standards of public decency by reference to whether the display outraged their emotions. Although the facts of this case were highly exceptional, it showed how the protections for art and literature solemnly enacted by Parliament in 1959 could be circumvented by the device of charging an offence at common law. The Court of Appeal was unconvinced that such a shocking work could possibly have artistic merit, thinking it 'unlikely that a defence of public good could ever arise' in relation to cases properly prosecuted at common law.[27] This approach assumes an ability to discern artistic and literary merit which is no part of the training for membership of the Crown Prosecution Service. The test of 'outrage' is vague and subjective, calling for a value-judgement verdict which will depend not on any provable public standard or any deliberate intention to outrage, but on the 'gut reactions' of the jurors who happen to be empanelled to try the case. The majority-verdict procedure, which allows a conviction despite two dissenters, further undermines the protection for minority tastes and views – it is not surprising that in the 'foetal earrings' case, the *Oz* trial and the *Gay News* blasphemy prosecution, conviction was by a 10–2 majority. If we are to have crimes which pivot upon subjective moral reactions, the least we can ask is that a 'guilty' verdict be unanimous.

BLASPHEMY

The crime of blasphemy was created by the courts in 1677 in order to punish a madman, John Taylor, for denouncing Christ as a whoremaster and orthodox religion as a cheat. In those days, a crime against religion was a crime against the state, and

> ... to say, Religion is a Cheat, is to dissolve all those Obligations whereby the Civil societies are preserved, and that Christianity is a parcel of the Laws of England and therefore to reproach the Christian religion is to speak in subversion of the law.[28]

Taylor was set in the pillory, wearing a placard inscribed: 'For blasphemous words tending to the subversion of all government.'

Until the Darwinian revolution in the latter part of the nineteenth century, the offence was regularly used to punish attacks upon articles of Anglican belief, on the principle that strange gods might subvert familiar government. The evangelical fervour of the Vice Society coincided with fear of French revolutionary atheism to produce a rash of prosecutions against free-thinkers and publishers of the works of Thomas Paine. Blasphemy was irreverence irrespective of motive: in 1840 the Attorney-General secured the conviction of a bookseller named Hetherington for publishing an attack on the violence and obscenity of the Old Testament, 'careless of the effect it might have on the morals of the unthinking working class'.[29] If workers needed protection against the unexpurgated Old Testament, it seemed only fair that literary salons should be protected from the heretical imaginings of great poets, so Hetherington emerged from prison to secure the conviction of a respected bookseller for selling copies of Shelley's *Queen Mab*.[30] The stringency of the blasphemy law became an embarrassment to the government: in 1851 the Law Officers reluctantly advised the Home Office that John Stuart Mill was liable to prosecution for expressing mildly agnostic views in a public lecture, although 'we should in this case consider it highly inexpedient for the Government to institute any such proceedings'.

Judges had made the law, and in the late nineteenth century it was the judges who changed the law to serve different social conditions. They altered the gist of the offence from an attack upon the Christian faith to the mode of expressing that attack. Christianity might be challenged, so long as this was done in moderate and respectful language. There were no blasphemy prosecutions at all between 1922 and 1978, when *Gay News* was charged by Mrs Mary Whitehouse with 'unlawfully and wickedly publishing a blasphemous libel concerning the Christian religion, namely an obscene poem and illustration vilifying Christ in his life and in his crucifixion'.[31]

The Old Bailey had never quite seen the like of *Whitehouse* v. *Lemon and Gay News*, and may not do so again. The prosecutrix led prayer meetings in the corridors; the Bible replaced *Archbold* as the basic forensic reference; the jury (all of whom had taken the Christian oath) were supplied with Test-match scores by the judge – who later wrote a book congratulating himself, the deity and Mrs Whitehouse on the result. He confessed an 'extraordinarily unreal sensation' in writing and delivering his summing-up, which he attributed to his 'being guided by some superhuman inspiration'. One would expect divine inspiration to have produced a summing-up rather fairer to the defence: at any event sales of the newspaper soared after the conviction, and the Law Commission discovered a number of practising Christians who were so disgusted with the prosecution of *Gay News* that 'they ceased to be communicant members of the Church of England'.[32] The Commission, in two comprehensive reports on the blasphemy law, found little to commend the tests which the trial judge had directed the jury to apply in determining whether an offence had been committed:

– Do you think God would like to be recognized in the context of this poem?

– Did it shock you when you first read it?
– Would you be proud or ashamed to have written it?
– Could you read it aloud to an audience of fellow-Christians without blushing?
– Is the poem obscene?
– Could it hurt, shock, offend or appal anyone who read it?

The fundamental defect in the blasphemy law is that it is so uncertain that it is impossible to establish in advance whether a particular publication would constitute an offence. The crime hinges upon the finding by a particular jury that material is unacceptably 'scurrilous', 'abusive' or 'insulting' in relation to the Christian religion, and as the Law Commission points out:

> It is likely to be difficult if not impossible to prophesy in any particular case what the verdict may be ... since the law is so uncertain in ambit, it becomes, to say the least, difficult for any legal advice to be given as to whether or not a jury in whichever part of the country a prosecutor (who may be a private prosecutor) institutes proceedings will find a particular publication blasphemous.

The Law Commission's criticism of the uncertain ambit of the offence was borne out by the experience of the publishers of the film script of *Monty Python's Life of Brian*. Three QCs gave markedly different opinions as to whether it could be published. One said the whole work was blasphemous, and the others advised cuts, some of them substantial. The publishers took the risk of publishing an unexpurgated edition, which was not, in the event, prosecuted.

Another fundamental defect of blasphemy is that, anomalously, it affords protection only to Christianity and the Established Church in a society which is both secular and multi-religious. Lord Scarman has suggested that the way forward for a plural society is to extend the law to cover all religious beliefs – a development which the Law Commission resists on grounds both of principle (religious beliefs are no less firmly held than those which relate to politics or patriotism) and pragmatism (special protection would discredit the law and encourage objectors to seek an easy martyrdom). These objections are surely justified: the identification of Church and state in Iran, for example, would mean that political protest against recent decrees in that country could constitute a blasphemous 'insult' to Islamic beliefs. Moreover, a law criminalizing the wounding of feelings of adherents to any religious group could hardly avoid protecting practices which merit investigation, and possibly condemnation or ridicule. The Law Commission has despaired of any definition which could make workable distinctions between Baptists, Scientologists, Rastafarians, Anglicans and Moonies.

Is it necessary to attempt such a daunting task? Even if it could be accomplished to general satisfaction, a reformed law of blasphemy would serve no purpose necessary to modern society. The claims of public order, morality, and the rights of individuals provide insufficient justification for any offence additional to the existing public-order prohibitions which protect against possible breaches of the peace. This conclusion is reinforced by the absence of prosecutions for blasphemy in England between 1922 and 1977; the withering away of the crime in Scotland (there are no recorded cases since the 1840s, and it is doubtful whether the offence any longer exists); and the demise of prosecutions in Northern Ireland, despite the sectarianism in that society. The scope of the offence in Wales is uncertain, as a consequence of the disestablishment of the Welsh Church in 1920.

The very existence of a blasphemy law is calculated to encourage some Christians to believe they can enforce a conventional presentation of sacred themes in the arts. Martin Scorsese's film *The Last Temptation of Christ* led to demands (most notably from the retired *Gay News* trial judge) that its distributors should be prosecuted. Whilst its presentation of Christ's humanity was challenging and unorthodox, the film lacked any element of vilification or scurrility, and on this basis the BBFC classified it as appropriate for screening to adults and the DPP declined to prosecute. None the less, religious activists prevailed on some local councils to use their powers to prevent it from being screened in some parts of the country, and the distributors had no protection against private prosecutions which could have been brought. If they had been, the defence could not have called evidence as to the film's seriousness of purpose or cinematic merit (there being no 'public good' defence to blasphemy) and the punishment, in the event of a conviction, could have been an unlimited fine or sentence of imprisonment. The episode reinforces the view that a criminal law which holds a publisher strictly liable for an artistic work liable to shock the

Christian on the Clapham omnibus is inappropriate to an age in which the creeds of passengers to Clapham, if they have any, are many and various.

The unfairness of a law which protects only Christian sensibilities was highlighted in 1989 by the outrage felt amongst the Muslim community by the publication of Salman Rushdie's celebrated novel *The Satanic Verses*. This grievance was legitimate only to the extent that Muslims could correctly claim that the blasphemy law in Britain discriminated against their religion. But had it been extended to cover all faiths, Rushdie could have been prosecuted without the right to a literary-merit defence, and without even being given an opportunity to argue that he had no intention to blaspheme. He would have been at risk of conviction merely by proof that the book was likely to outrage and insult believers – which it most certainly did. To punish him in these circumstances would have been offensive to justice, but no more so than the punishment of the editor of *Gay News*. The incident exploded into an international and diplomatic crisis after Rushdie and his publishers were barbarically 'sentenced to death' by Iran: the British government has been unable to take a satisfactory stand on the principle of freedom of speech precisely because it was compromised by a law which had been used in recent years to condemn poetry offensive to Anglicans.

The Divisional Court was squarely confronted with these problems in 1991, when a group of Muslims urged it to reinterpret the law of blasphemy so as to allow a private prosecution of Salman Rushdie and his publishers to go ahead. The judges refused, on the grounds that the crime of blasphemy was confined to attacks upon the Established Church. The court accepted that this was a 'gross anomaly', but the anomaly arose from the 'chains of history', which could be unlocked only by Parliament. Even if the court had power to extend the law to other religions, however, it would refrain from doing so because of the 'insuperable' problems in defining religion, in expecting juries to understand obscure theologies, and because of the danger of divisive and obscurantist prosecutions. The court accepted that 'the existence of an extended law of blasphemy would encourage intolerance, divisiveness and unreasonable interference with freedom of expression', and 'would be likely to do more harm than good'.[33]

That the existing blasphemy law does do more harm than good was emphasized in the same year, when the British Board of Film Classification used it as a basis for banning *Visions of Ecstasy*, a short experimental video about the mystical trances of St Theresa of Avila. The film was not pornographic, although it interpreted these trances (as do most writers on the subject) as sexually inspired. The Board admitted that the contents of the video would have been classified as suitable for purchase and viewing by adults, had it not been for the religious context which might give offence – to persons who would not wish to purchase it in any event. The Board's Appeals Committee admitted to confusion about the law of blasphemy and were unable to agree as to whether any prosecution would be likely to succeed. Three members thought it would and two thought it would not, while a non-sitting member of the Committee, author Fay Weldon, gave evidence on behalf of the makers of the video. The British Government, called upon by the European Commission of Human Rights to defend the ban, conceded that it could not be justified by any public interest in the protection of morals. It was justified, so the Government asserted, because its 'main purpose was to protect the rights of citizens not to be offended in their religious feelings by publications'. The central confusion of principle in this approach is that it seeks to bring within the ambit of 'legitimate' protection persons who may be offended if they are subjected to the video, but who (by the very nature of the limited distribution being sought under an '18' certificate) will never be subjected to it. There was never any reasonable prospect that such persons would purchase and watch the video, unless they did so from a wish to be shocked and offended.

It is a matter of basic principle, emphasized in repeated judgements of the European Court of Human Rights, that freedom of expression is applicable to works of art which 'offend, shock or disturb the state or any section of the population. Such are the demands of that pluralism, tolerance and broadmindedness without which there is no democratic society.' It follows that no aim of a restriction can be legitimate if, without more, it merely protects a section of the population from offence *at the thought* that a work of art might become available to another section of the population. 'Protection of the reputation or the rights of others' in the European Convention exception to freedom of expression refers to citizens who have a 'right' which can be diminished. There may be a 'right' not to have one's religious faith disturbed in a place of worship, or by gratuitous subjection to imaginative video recreation of the passion of a favourite saint, but there is no 'right' to stop others from worshipping in their own way (however much the thought of such worship may offend Christians) or to stop others from viewing, in their own homes, videos which might offend some Christians were they ever to purchase or to screen them. The only 'rights' which can override free speech are real and positive rights, the infringement of which may hurt their victim: they are not rights to avoid disturbance at the prospect that other people may not be shocked by exercising their 'right' to view the video. The purpose of the BBFC ban was to protect a few narrow-minded Christians, not from the video itself, but from self-induced discomfort *at the thought* that some other adult would be able to view it without being shocked. This cannot be a legitimate aim of a restriction on freedom of expression.

CHAPTER 6

Regulation: Film, Video and Broadcasting

Before the children's greedy eyes with heartless indiscrimination are presented, night after night . . . terrific massacres, horrible catastrophes, motor car smashes, public hangings, lynchings. All who care for the moral well-being and education of the child will set their faces like flint against this new form of excitement.

'Cinematography and the Child', *The Times*, 12 April 1913

The recent history of moral and political censorship in Britain has been characterized by a move from criminal law to statutory regulation. The process began, visibly, in 1954, when the inauguration of commercial broadcasting was deemed to require the establishment of a monitoring body, the Independent Broadcasting Authority (IBA), with statutory duties to ensure that political coverage was balanced and that programmes did not contravene the boundaries of good taste. Equivalent obligations were soon voluntarily accepted by the BBC, with the consequence that all radio and television broadcasting is subjected to a regime of institutional censorship, with rules and 'guidelines' which are of powerful effect, although they lack the force of direct law. More recently the Government, distrustful of television executives, has moved to regulate the regulators, superimposing both a Complaints Commission and a Standards Council to exert another level of disciplinary pressure on programme-makers. The film industry had, at an early stage of its development, established a voluntary scheme known as the British Board of Film Censors (BBFC): its certificate carried no legal immunity from prosecution, but in practice deterred police action and smoothed distribution problems with local authorities. In 1984, the BBFC became the official censorship body for video-cassettes, charged by Parliament with the task of cutting out any scenes not suitable for viewing in the home.

There are several reasons for the retreat from law in respect of the new media industries. The criminal law is a blunt instrument, incapable of being framed to take into account the nuances of visual presentation. Moreover, the new media are big business, attracting leading directors and substantial investors who have no desire to see their reputations and their profits at risk in the Old Bailey. For Government, of course, there is the great attraction of avoiding trial by jury: good men and women and true are prone to acquit programmes which can be suppressed, or better still not made at all, by winks and nods from state-appointed licensers. There is, in addition, a deeply felt fear that a free market will lower standards: regulation is necessary to ensure that the public is provided with what it ought to like. These arguments, variously appealing to the industry itself and to politicians from all sides of the spectrum, have produced licensing systems for the new media the like of which have not, since the days of Cromwell, been visited upon books and newspapers. They can cause severe difficulties for makers of films and broadcast programmes, because they set up a form of institutional censorship against which there is little or no appeal. For example, there is nothing that can be done about BBC directives, other than by processes of negotiation within the Corporation. The verdicts of Complaints Commission adjudications are unappealable. Films which are denied certification by the BBFC can be shown if the distributor is prepared to run the risk of an obscenity prosecution, although distribution outlets will be severely limited. Most videos cannot be distributed at all without BBFC approval. The most effective form of appeal will not be to the courts, which have little or no jurisdiction, but to the public through stories leaked to the press. Censorship is news, and some decisions which appear firm when first made within an institution have been rescinded or ameliorated as a result of public criticism. Executives in the higher echelons of broadcasting organizations generally affect liberal sympathies, and dislike the social embarrassment which follows upon publicity about their decisions to censor.

The Thatcher Government made substantial changes in the laws and bodies which regulate radio and television with its Broadcasting

Act, passed in 1990. Although the Act was promoted as a measure to 'deregulate' broadcasting, this was misleading: it provided for a more centralized and sophisticated set of constraints on the media to avoid transmission of discomforting programmes. The IBA was abolished and replaced by the Independent Television Commission (ITC) which inherited the IBA's duties to ensure balance and to eradicate offensive programmes, not by pre-censorship but instead by punishing offenders with a new range of tough sanctions (including financial penalties and the ultimate sanction of licence withdrawal). The ITC is the first level of censorship control for television and cable and for satellite transmissions uplinked from the United Kingdom. A second level of censorship is provided by the Broadcasting Standards Council (BSC), which was placed on a statutory footing and given direct power to monitor sex and violence and to draw up binding programme standards. A third tier of control was achieved by bringing all programmes on all stations within the ambit of the Obscene Publications Act. This three-tier statutory apparatus belies the Government's claim that it wanted to regulate broadcasting with a 'light touch'. Instead, it created three heavy hands: the ITC (with additional powers to punish any lapses in taste or impartiality), the BSC and the police, able to launch obscenity prosecutions against programme-makers if all else fails. The one welcome measure was to abolish the IBA's 'publishing role' of intervening prior to programme transmission; television companies no longer have to submit controversial programmes for 'vetting'. However, it must be doubtful whether relief from this burden will effect liberalization: some controversial programmes will simply not be made for fear that they will incur reprisals in the form of ITC or BSC sanctions, or a possible criminal prosecution. The main reason why programmes of high quality, controversial or otherwise, will diminish, however, is a result of other provisions of the Act, such as the ludicrous 'auctioning' of ITC franchises to the highest bidder. The consequences of what the Government described as 'freedom to match programmes to market conditions' are outside the scope of this book, although it is ironic to note that the advent of 'tabloid television' in 1993 filled the screens with more programmes about sex than ever before, made at an 'acceptable' level of prurience. The ITC's first threatened use of its new punishment powers was against Central Television, for daring to offend religious sensibilities by permitting a puppet of Jesus Christ to appear on *Spitting Image*.

A licensing system is, by definition, a restriction on freedom of expression, although the guarantee of that right in Article 10 of the European Convention is subject to a crucial proviso: '*This article shall not prevent states from requiring the licensing of broadcasting, television and cinema enterprises.*' This exemption permits the establishment of licensing systems, but it does not underwrite specific censorship decisions made by regulatory bodies. Such decisions, if unchallengeable in the English courts, might be taken direct to Strasbourg if they have had the effect of preventing the dissemination of controversial ideas or opinions.

FILM CENSORSHIP

Film censorship today operates on three different levels. The distributors of feature films may be prosecuted under the Obscene Publications Act if the Director of Public Prosecutions deems that audiences are likely to be 'depraved and corrupted' by their offerings. Irrespective of the DPP's decision, district councils may refuse to license controversial films for screening within their jurisdiction. Most councils rely upon the advice of the BBFC, which may insist upon cuts before certifying the film's fitness for the public screen or for certain age groups, or may refuse to issue any certificate at all. Additionally, as a result of new powers granted in 1982, councils may limit the number of 'sex cinemas' in their locality, or prohibit such cinemas altogether. Neither theatre producers nor book publishers suffer institutional restrictions laid down by trade censors or local councillors. Many district councils, prompted by evangelical pressure-groups, have devoted a good deal of public time and money to reviewing films already certified by the Board, so that controversial releases such as *Monty Python's Life of Brian*, *Clockwork Orange* and *The Last Temptation of Christ* have been banned in some districts and licensed in others, sometimes only a short bus-ride away. Local film censorship has been delegated to magistrates or entrusted to standing committees: some district councils rely upon their fire-brigade committees to extinguish any flames of passion which may have escaped the BBFC hose, while one Cornish borough solemnly bans films despite the fact that there are no cinemas within its jurisdiction. Some local councils prohibit 'sex cinemas' entirely, while others allow a reasonable number to operate. The paternalistic axis of the BBFC and the local authorities operates haphazardly, but it does produce a great deal of both national and regional censorship. Chief beneficiaries of this arrangement are the commercial interests involved in film distribution, which are generally happy to obey BBFC directives to expurgate films with the assurance, in practice if not in theory, that certified products will not attract legal action.

The BBFC was established in 1912 in an attempt to protect the new cinema industry from claims that it was destructive of morality. Local councils discovered that they had power to license cinemas in order to protect against fire hazards, and started to use these powers against moral and political hazards as well. The first film to be banned in Britain was an American newsreel of a boxing championship, although the ban had less to do with violence than with the fact that the film showed a Negro defeating a white man. The duty of the British Board of Film Classification (it changed the 'C', somewhat disingenuously, from 'Censors' to 'Classification' in 1984) was to induce confidence in the minds of the licensing authorities, and of those who have in their charge the moral welfare of the community generally. In 1924 the BBFC received its judicial imprimatur when the Divisional Court upheld the validity of a condition that 'No cinematograph film . . . which has not been passed for . . . exhibition by the BBFC shall be exhibited without the express consent of the council.'[1] So long as a council reserved the right to review BBFC decisions, it was entitled to make the grant of a cinema licence contingent upon the screening of certified films.

The cutting-room counsels of the BBFC avowedly err on the side of caution, in an effort to protect the established film industry from criticism as well as from prosecution. Although the BBFC is (save for its role in approving video-cassettes) an unofficial body, unrecognized by statute and financed through fees imposed upon every film submitted for censorship, it exercises a persuasive and in most cases determinative influence over the grant of local-authority licences. 'I freely admit that this is a curious arrangement,' conceded the Home Secretary, Mr Herbert Morrison, in 1942 but the British have a very great habit of making curious arrangements work very well, and this works. Frankly, I do not wish to be the minister who has to answer questions in the House as to whether particular films should or should not be censored.[2]

The present classification, endorsed by all local councils and by the Home Office, is:

U   Universal: Suitable for all.
Uc   Universal: Particularly suitable for children.
PG   Parental guidance: Some scenes may be unsuitable for young children.
15   Passed only for persons of fifteen years and over.
18   Passed only for persons of eighteen years and over.
18R   Passed only for restricted distribution through segregated premises to which no one under eighteen is admitted.

The BBFC has effectively become the authorized censor for feature films in cinemas and on television. Its position derives, not from the law, but from an understanding it has reached with prosecuting authorities, local councils and the Home Office. The basis for this understanding was admitted by the DPP to the Select Committee on Obscenity in 1957:

If I wished to prosecute a film – and it has been suggested on two occasions to me that certain films that had passed the British Board of Film Censors were obscene – my answer would be, as it was in those two cases, I shall have to put the British Board of Film Censors in the dock because they have aided and abetted the commission of that particular offence. So it inhibits me to that extent. As long as I rely on the judgement of the British Board of Film Censors as to the suitability, under the various categories, of films for public showing, which I do, I do not prosecute.[3]

On this basis, the DPP has not prosecuted certified films in connection with cinema screenings, and several private prosecutions have come to grief. A case against *Last Tango in Paris* under the Obscene Publications Act 1959 failed on technical grounds, and a prosecution of the exhibitors of *The Language of Love* for the common-law offence of gross indecency (now abolished in relation to the cinema) was rejected by an Old Bailey jury. Feature films which are certified in the '18' and '18R' categories do not receive the same practical immunity from the obscenity law when marketed on video-cassettes, because there is no control over the age of the audience which may view them in the home. For this reason the DPP has authorized prosecutions against distributors of video-cassette versions of *The Evil Dead* and *The Burning*, certified films which have played without objection to over-eighteen audiences in cinemas.

Films rated '18' are suitable for general release in cinemas which exclude entry to persons under that age. Films rated '18R' are suitable for screening only at film festivals, in private clubs for cinema buffs or in cinemas which are licensed as 'sex cinemas' by local authorities pursuant to the provisions of the Cinemas Act 1985. It is an offence, punishable by the somewhat extravagant maximum fine of £20,000, to use unlicensed premises for film exhibitions. The Cinemas Act allows local councils to restrict, on environmental grounds, the number of cinemas devoted to screening films with explicit sexual content; to ensure that such cinemas are sited well away from schools, churches and private homes; to control public advertising; and generally to impose conditions enforceable by a system of licensing. The '18R' certificate will be granted to films which would not previously have qualified for an 'X' certificate on the grounds of their sexual explicitness, and will generally imply a judgement by the BBFC that the film, although sexually explicit, would survive a prosecution under Section 2 of the Obscene Publications Act. The film will therefore be judged as a whole, in the context of current jury decisions: material which appears to justify or glamorize harmful, illegal or anti-social actions will not receive an '18R' certificate.

It follows that films which encourage the taking of dangerous drugs, or depict extremes of sexual perversion, brutality or sadism, will not be certified. On the other hand, films which show a degree of sexual explicitness within a normal human relationship, whether heterosexual or homosexual, with scenes which are photographed with care and taste, many well receive an '18R' certificate. A more liberal test will be applied to films of recognized social or cinematic merit: by analogy with the 'public good' provisions of the Obscene Publications Act, such merits may redeem an otherwise unacceptable film so that its '18R' certificate will permit it to be shown to members of a cinema club. Pasolini's *Salo* and Oshima's *Empire of the Senses (Ai no Corrida)* are examples of meritorious films which have been made available by this route. However, the lack of '18R' cinemas in most areas means that distributors will rarely be interested in obtaining this classification, but will prefer to cut large chunks of scenes and dialogue in order to obtain an '18' certificate, or even more in order to attract the larger audience able to view a film with a '15' certificate. This means that the British adult public sees less in many major feature films than cinema-goers in other countries.

In its recent reports, the Board has drawn attention to the absurdity of having an '18R' category which, for commercial reasons, distributors will avoid at all costs, insisting that the BBFC wield its scissors as often as necessary to cut their films at least to '18', and preferably to '15'. Yet '18R' is not an 'obscene' category: the Board takes extravagant care to keep this category free from the prospect of obscenity prosecution by regular conferences with the DPP's office. Because there are so few outlets for '18R' films, distributors no longer submit films for that classification. As a result, Board members spend much of their time behaving like over-cautions pornographers, re-editing videos to soften their core to the '18', which will allow a profitable distribution. The consequence is that the Board operates to deny adults access to films and videos which are lawful, in the sense that they would not be subject to an obscenity prosecution. In its 1990 Report, the Board admitted to its behaviour in this respect, and noted that its 'regime is stricter than any of our continental partners in the EC, especially when "18" videos conform to a decency test more stringent than that of most "adult" magazines available in high-street stores'. In other words, the Board is imposing censorship under the guise of classification.

The system of classifying films as not suitable for showing to various age groups is entirely justifiable, but why impose censorship on adult films above and beyond what the law of obscenity demands? The answer, of course, lies in the archaic powers of local authorities to license cinemas, and to object to the content of films. These powers involve not merely a waste of local councillors' time and ratepayers' money, but the constant attention of the BBFC in editing movies so that a BBFC certificate remains acceptable to local councillors. This 'curious arrangement' may protect ministers from being questioned in Parliament about film censorship, although their answer could take the reasonable form of referring the matter to the DPP. The arrangement today is not so much curious as eccentric, and means that the cinema, alone of art forms, is subject to moral judgement by local councillors. Regrettably the 1985 Cinemas Act left local licensing powers in place. It would be sensible to restrict their exercise to health and fire hazards, and to give the BBFC statutory powers to classify films as suitable for screening to particular age groups. It should have no power to ban or to expurgate films for adults: this task should be left to film-makers and distributors, who would at the end of the day be answerable to a jury in the event of an obscenity prosecution.

THE VIDEO RECORDINGS ACT

The home video market in Britain has been a remarkable success: by 1986 there were over 30,000 outlets selling or renting almost 10,000 separate video titles for home viewing. Although video-cassettes were not in existence at the time the obscenity law was passed in 1959, the Court of Appeal soon held that they could be prosecuted in the same way as books and cinema films: the question is whether their contents, taken as a whole, would tend to corrupt people likely to see them.[4] In determining the potential audience, juries could consider the fact that they were designed for screening in the home, and decide whether children were likely to obtain access to them as a result. Pornographic videos presented no additional problems to those posed at trials of sexually explicit books, magazines or 8-mm films. But fears of this novel technology – its fascination for children, the ability to freeze-frame and to replay favourite episodes, and its mushroom growth – were exploited in a manic press campaign against 'video nasties', which led to the Video Recordings Act of 1984.

Only 10 per cent of the feature films available in 1983 on video-cassette had been certified by the BBFC as suitable for universal viewing. Many had been granted an 'X' certificate for cinema screening, and many more had never been certified at all. Amongst these were many run-of-the-mill horror movies, for which there was an early video vogue: to capitalize on it, distributors promoted videos which explicitly depicted violence and brutality. The label 'video nasty' was used indiscriminately, but it reflected the prevailing fear that meretricious movies which dwelt on rape and mayhem would affect the minds of young children permitted to watch them by negligent parents. The Obscene Publications Act was a suitable tool for prosecution of such films, where there was any prospect that a significant number of children might view them, and in 1983 a jury convicted the distributors of *Nightmares in a Damaged Brain* on account of its detailed depictions of sex and violence. But the campaigners – led by the Festival of Light and the *Daily Mail* – saw the opportunity to erect a new censorship apparatus which went far beyond the scope of the Obscene Publications Act. With a remarkable talent for passing off propaganda as scientifically valid research, they convinced politicians and newspapers of the accuracy of such claims as '37 per cent of children under seven have seen a "video nasty"' and that 'the nasty video has replaced the conjuror at children's birthday parties'. 'Scientific' research purportedly showed that very young children in working-class homes up and down the country were watching sadistic sex while their parents were away from home. Sensationalized research claims, timed to coincide with important stages of the Video Recordings bill, created a mild form of hysteria among politicians of all parties and the bill was rushed through with only two Tory MPs and one Labour peer dissenting. Subsequently, the much-publicized 'research' was heavily criticized, but it had served the purpose for which it was apparently designed.[5]

Meanwhile, the climate engendered by the campaign against 'video nasties' affected police forces throughout the country, who were raiding video shops and prosecuting owners for 'X'-certified horror movies perceived as 'nasties'. There was a two-year period of utter confusion, and a few video traders went to prison for stocking films which had been seen by thousands when on previous cinema release. Under heavy pressure from organizations representing the retail trade, the Attorney-General finally issued a 'list' of some sixty film titles which the DPP regarded as obscene because of depictions of violence. Retailers who wished to avoid police seizures could collect a copy of the list from their local police station and remove any offending titles. The 'DPP's list' was the first modern example of an 'Index' in Britain: video traders greeted it with relief, although many of the films on the list had been acquitted by juries while others, such as *The Evil Dead* and Andy

Warhol's *Frankenstein*, had received critical acclaim.[6] The 'list' had no legal force, although fear of prosecution deterred retailers from stocking any film title which appeared on it. The Video Recordings Act has replaced the list by requiring all videos containing sexual or violent scenes to be certified by the BBFC, and imposing heavy penalties on the sale of uncertified videos.

As we have seen, this Act was passed in 1984 with the ostensible object of suppressing trade in about sixty video titles regarded as dangerous if taken into the home by reason of their concentration on sex and violence. But the Act goes much further, and sets up a bureaucratic system of pre-censorship unprecedented since the demise of the Cromwellian 'licensers of the press' in 1695. It establishes by statute an authority (the BBFC) designated by the Home Secretary to classify video-cassettes as 'suitable for viewing in the home', and to censor them if they are not suitable. Fines of £20,000 are visited upon dealers and distributors who make cassettes available to the public without a BBFC classification. The BBFC has been enlarged to cope with its censorship role: it has quadrupled its staff, acquired additional premises, and now has two vice-presidents 'approved' by the Home Secretary – the first direct political link in its eighty-year history.

All video works must be submitted to the Board for censorship, unless they are educational or concerned with sport, religion or music. However, even videos which fall into these categories must also be submitted if '*to any significant extent*' they deal with 'human sexual activity' or 'multilation or torture or other acts of gross violence towards humans or animals'. Thus news and current affairs videos must be submitted if they cover battles or bombings or bullfights, and so must videos which offer counselling in the field of human sexual relations or films which deal with nuclear war or acts of terrorism. Although music is exempted, video-cassettes of operas like *Il Trovatore* and *The Tales of Hoffmann* require certification. A video series of *Great Fights of the Century* would require certification, because it deals to a significant extent with 'acts of gross violence'.

In practice, then, the Act requires the great majority of video titles to be submitted to the BBFC, both for classification as appropriate for sale to particular age groups and for censorship if deemed unsuitable for viewing in the home. The cost of submitting a full-length film on video-cassette is about £500 (the BBFC currently charges £4.60 a minute for its viewing time). The fact that the work has been made by or shown on television is irrelevant: the moralistic minister of state responsible for introducing the Act, Mr David Mellor took pleasure in announcing that BBC programmes like *The History Man, Tinker, Tailor, Soldier, Spy* and *The Borgias* would require classification before they could be sold to the public on video-cassettes.

Section 4 of the Act contains its main censorship implication: the BBFC is to have 'special regard to the likelihood of (certified) video works being viewed in the home'. This test applies to every video submitted for classification, even those which are to be restricted for sale only in licensed sex shops, and is designed to underline the greater potential for harm by the technological capacity to freeze-frame and replay scenes of sex or violence. The Act does not, as some critics mistakenly assume, lay down that videos must be 'suitable for viewing in the home' in the sense of being appropriate for family viewing: that would be to negate the whole system of age-classification and point-of-sale restriction. The video must be 'suitable for classification' in a particular category, having special regard to the impact it will have upon persons in that age group and below through the devices available for home viewing. Thus a video work which is suitable for the classification '18' or '18R', given that it will be viewed by adults at home, should not be refused classification because of the danger that children may obtain access to it when it is left in the home by careless parents. None the less, 'where horror material is concerned, we have exercised a restraining influence on the explicitness of gory imagery because of our awareness that children and younger teenagers may be particularly tempted to watch such material . . .' the BBFC states in its *Guidelines on Violence*. This is a consideration which goes to age-group classification rather than censorship: Section 4 does not justify the deletion of 'gory imagery' from '18' or '18R' films because of the danger that they will be seen by children. Parliament could (as some MP's wished) have insisted that *all* videos be suitable for children: it provided a classification system based on the notion of parental responsibility. This system is logically undermined by the BBFC whenever it makes cuts in '18' videos on the grounds that younger persons may watch.

The Video Recordings Act has necessitated a censorship system which goes far beyond the initial concern about 'video nasties'. It would have been possible to deal with this very limited mischief by legislation which permitted the BBFC, on a complaint by the police or a member of the public, to designate a specific video-cassette as prohibited from public sale. Any subsequent breach of a prohibition order could have constituted a criminal offence, pending a right of appeal by the distributor to a jury. Such a reform, which would effectively have banned the 'video nasty' without exposing much of the industry to a bureaucratic apparatus of censorship, went entirely overlooked. The worst feature of the new system is that it imposes double jeopardy on video distributors because it keeps alive the power of the police, the DPP and private prosecutors to proceed against the suppliers of certified videos for offences against the Obscene Publications Act. Distributors are in breach of one criminal law if they sell uncertified cassettes, and they may still be in breach of another criminal law if they sell certified ones. No censorship system which permits such double jeopardy holds out much hope of rational enforcement.

There have been other unsatisfactory consequences. High classification fees had forced many distributors to delete less profitable videos from their catalogues, thereby reducing viewer choice, especially in relation to vintage movies and minor classics. This is the hidden cultural cost of the Video Recordings Act: its true casualties have not been the trashy films which are banned, but the significant cinematic works which do not have sufficient popular appeal to justify the costs of classification. The Act may have diminished the degree of explicitness of sex and violence, but not the numbers of cassettes dealing with these themes or the prominence given to them. Distributors have discovered the level of 'acceptable' sex and 'acceptable' violence, and their films are full of it. Meanwhile, some films of real worth are not being distributed because the profits from small audiences do not justify the classification fee.

The BBFC at work

The worst result of the Video Recordings Act has been to establish a state censorship apparatus in Britain. The BBFC expanded from a family-size firm of twelve in 1982 to a bureaucratic organization with a staff of fifty (including twenty-two full-time 'film examiners') by 1993. Its members at present are reasonably apolitical, although the powers of 'approval' given to the Home Secretary could at some future date turn into a force for suppressing 'unacceptable' political messages on film or video. As an official censorship body, it believes in its duty to censor, and encounters little opposition from a trade that is more interested in profits than in defending artistic integrity. 'Cuts' are negotiated between the BBFC and the film or video distributors – the voice of the film-maker is never heard, as the system permits no consultation with or complaint from the artist whose vision is being dimmed. For example, distributors who wish to obtain a '15' certificate to maximize audiences will sometimes agree to cuts which seriously undermine or distort the impact of the film.

This is made all the more unsatisfactory because the BBFC purports to adopt artistic judgements. It claims, in relation to violence, to take into account 'the moral position of the film-maker towards his own material' by applying the following tests:

(1) Is the sympathy of the film-maker on the side of the victim or the aggressor?

(2) Is the process of the violence indulged in for its own sake, rather than to tell us anything significant about the motives or state of mind of the persons involved?

(3) Does the camerawork or editing belie the ostensible moral stance of the film by seeking to enlist or encourage our vicarious enjoyment of the atrocities portrayed?[7]

Like Miss Prism's view of fiction, the BBFC's view of feature films is that the good should end happily and the bad unhappily. But these generalized statements are little more than window-dressing, giving some rational justification for cuts which are made because the violence is of a kind which turns the examiner's stomach. Films which glorify wars and mercenary operations have been passed without deletions: those which depict extremes of violence will be censored, however 'moral' the context. 'Moderation is a useful ideal, and the process of violence can often be toned down by judicious cutting' says the BBFC (ever so pleased at being able to improve on the cinematographer's art) in its *Guidelines on Violence*.

Some film-makers, of course, have no wish to have the impact of their images 'moderated' by paternalistic censors. *Christianne F*, a powerfully aversive film about the degradation of heroin-taking, lost some of its impact by four minutes of cuts. Even the comic cocaine-sniffing scene in *Crocodile Dundee* had to be excised before the Board would grant the film a '15' certificate for video release. The BBFC prides itself on being the strictest censorship board in the Western world in cutting scenes of violence (especially sexual violence) against women, 'even where the point of view of the film as a whole is a critical one'.[8] (The Alfred Hitchcock classic *Frenzy* had one of its scenes cut, despite the fact that it had twice been shown unexpurgated on television, while *Death Wish*, which had also been shown on television, was refused a certificate for video release.) Like the Lord Chamberlain's censorship of the theatre, and the prosecutors who applied the 'purple passages' test to books before the Obscene Publications Act of 1959, the BBFC believes itself to be justified in removing images which depict appalling actions, for fear that those actions might be imitated by suggestible viewers. The result is that a great many films and videos have become suggestive rather than explicit, and it may be doubted whether the supposed danger is any the less. Most viewers, of course, receive such scenes as fantasy, and enjoy them as such: the possibility of an appeal to a few unbalanced minds is the basis for curbing the rights of a majority to view as they please. The public, needless to say, are not informed by any message on the video container that the film they are about to buy or hire has been censored.

These platitudes offer ample scope for busy, nit-picking censorship. The fate of *Rambo III* may serve as an example. It was screened uncut to adults (and even teenagers) in America and many European countries. The BBFC, however, insisted on many cuts before it could be screened (for adults only) in the cinema or sold as an '18' video. It was feared that Rambo's weapon-wielding would 'encourage antisocial violence on the streets of Britain', notwithstanding that the film was set in Afghanistan and most of Rambo's military arsenal is unavailable at corner stores. The Board required cuts 'in bloodshed and in glamorization of military weaponry', finding it particularly objectionable that Rambo 'killed, on the battlefield though never at home, with a deadly efficiency which seemed increasingly out of place in a world struggling towards new, more reasonable means of settling international disputes'.

These sentiments are all very fine, but is it any business of the BBFC to promote international harmony? The notion that *Rambo III* would provoke fighting in the streets if shown uncensored to British adults is comical. All that the Board seems to be achieving by its fussy 'topping and tailing' of violent scenes is the sanitization of violence – and sanitized violence is more attractive than the real thing. *Rambo III* is on many counts an objectionable film, but all the BBFC has achieved by cutting it is to make the objectionable 'message' more acceptable.

The BBFC's emasculation of *Rambo* appears absurd beside the scenes of massive violence that were family television viewing during the Gulf War. The Board has always been prone to make political judgements about the kind of violence it cuts, and confessed as much when in 1989 it censored the new James Bond film, *License to Kill*, before it could be certified '15'. Bond films had not previously been expurgated, but the Board admitted that 'the key to this change was the [film maker's] decision to present Bond not as an urbane British intelligence man, but as an embittered vigilante seeking revenge . . .'. It cuts scenes of a woman being whipped and a man being fed to sharks that would, no doubt, have been perfectly acceptable had the urbane 007 loyally taken these actions in the service of British intelligence.

In 1990 the Board refused to reinstate for adult video release cinema cuts it had made in *Lethal Weapon II* because 'the hero indulged his vengeful instincts far beyond the needs of narrative' – a judgement the Board believes itself in a better position to make than the writer or director. More disturbing, however, was the Board's approach to Asian films, a category whose gangster thrillers are traditionally replete with hi-tech but fantasy violence. The Board is appalled that these films have 'no moral dimension in view' (Miss Prism, again) and regards the popularity of their violence as a 'sad comment on the tastes of the occidental audience, or indeed the ethnic communities for whom these untranslated versions are intended'. This approach is both arrogant and ignorant, and appears to reflect Western prejudices.

The Board warms to its task of social engineering by tampering with what it sees as the 'message' of films, and its annual reports read in places like an essay by an enthusiastic first-year sociology student. Thus its 1989 report announced cuts in films that 'by emphasizing the dirt and danger of the drugs scene create an outlaw culture which attracts precisely those to whom the boredom of a safe but sorry existence is no longer enough'. By 1990 the Board had arrogated to itself a parental 'duty of care' in respect of 'older alienated or defeated members of society . . . to such people the risks of drug abuse may offer a kind of challenge, a rite of passage, for which ordeal the easing of pain and the cachet of outlaw status may seem sufficient reward'. The BBFC expresses such opinions throughout its annual reports, often as a justification for censoring scenes that tell it like it is, rather than like the BBFC thinks it should be. Its concern for political correctness extends to the avoidance of 'speciesism': animals too must be protected from psychological stress and alienation. Thus a feature film that depicted a non-life-threatening experiment on a rat by dipping it in liquid oxygen was cut in 1989 on the grounds that 'for the rat, it was a traumatic return to the condition of the womb'. All the rats who viewed the film in British cinemas were doubtless grateful for this concern about their sensitivities.

Some check on the censorious enthusiasms of the BBFC is applied by the Video Appeals Committee, although this body rarely sits because distributors are reluctant to incur further costs in disputing the Board's cuts, and there is no right for directors or film-makers to object to the manner in which expurgation has altered or minimized their message. The Appeals Committee found itself in a hopeless tangle over *Visions of Ecstasy* (see earlier, page 253) although it did intervene in 1991 to lift the ban on *International Guerrillas*, a James-Bond-style epic of the Pakistani cinema which portrayed Salman Rushdie as a mass murderer who tortured victims by forcing them to listen to readings of *The Satanic Verses*. The Board argued, in its usual pseudo-sociological jargon, that the film 'had the emotional weight and symbolic authority that makes the polarization of good and evil a source of moral support and reaffirmation of communal identity'. The Appeals Committee, however, was more inclined to agree with Rushdie himself, who described the film as 'a piece of trash.' It decided the film had as much 'emotional weight and symbolic authority' as an old cowboy-and-Indian movie, and that not even the most gullible viewer of such escapist entertainment would take it seriously. It is noteworthy that the film (pirate video copies of which had been selling for £100 while the ban was in force) was not a commercial success after the appeal, and cinema showings in cities with large Muslim populations were so poorly attended that the legitimate video version was never released.

Film and video censorship has become a comfortable institution in the United Kingdom. The BBFC even offers to advise on film scripts before shooting begins. The film-industry distributors, traditionally motivated by profit rather than principle, have willingly cooperated with the system, recognizing that it helps to protect them from the vagaries of prosecution. They have cooperated to such an extent that many submit videos of films which have been so heavily cut *before* submission that the BBFC has no role other than to approve self-censorship. In 1990 the Board required cuts in forty-two feature films and 278 videos, although its censorship impact is much greater than these figures suggest because the film and video distributors now tend to make their own cuts, following the Board's guidelines, before their films are submitted. Some of the cuts which have been made by the BBFC are quite absurd: five seconds were solemnly chopped from the Douglas Fairbanks classic *The Thief of Baghdad* and six seconds from a trailer for Elia Kazan's *On the Waterfront*, while Walt Disney Productions suffered the loss of seventeen seconds from *The Littlest Outlaw*, sixteen seconds from *Old Yeller* and twenty-four seconds from *Nikki, Wild Dog of the North*. The BBFC justify such cuts on the grounds of 'unsuitability due to the emotional power of the scene, and particularly to its potential for producing nightmares ...' On this basis, should the BBFC allow Bambi's cry of 'Mother' to haunt future video generations?

BROADCASTING

Government control

Television and radio are subject to much more stringent laws and regulatory systems than apply to the press. This discrimination was originally justified on grounds of frequency scarcity, although this could not justify the BBC monopoly, which continued until the introduction of commercial television in 1954 and commercial radio in 1971. It has no logical justification now that the development of fibre-optic cable systems and satellite direct broadcasting provides viewers with a greater multiplicity of channels to choose between than there are newspapers available to purchase. This was pointed out in 1986 by the Peacock Committee, which urged deregulation of the medium.[9] But politicians from all parties were determined to maintain, and even to increase, the regulatory controls on broadcasters, as well as inflicting on them the risk of being prosecuted under the Obscene Publications Act (from which radio and television had hitherto been exempted). There is no acceptance, at any political level, of the simple fact that a viewer may choose a channel as easily as he or she chooses a book or magazine or newspaper. Television is regarded, in the words of Lord Rees Mogg, panjandrum of the Broadcasting Standards Council, as 'a guest in the home', and one which must be carefully groomed and programmed before being allowed to visit. Its political correctness is as important as its politeness of language and its choice of clothes: the most obsessive concern of MPs during the passage of the 1990 Broadcasting Act was that the duty of 'due impartiality' should be rigorously imposed on broadcasters lest their news and current affairs programmes display undue cynicism about Government and politicians. Speech is not free on British television and radio: it is cribbed and confined not merely by the laws which apply to all media, but by a notion of what is 'seemly' for a general audience to hear and view. Lord Reith, founding father of the BBC, insisted that men dress in dinner jackets to read the radio news, and would not allow divorcees on the air waves: his spirit lives on in the innumerable codes of conduct designed and enforced by overlapping bodies of Government regulators appointed to minimize any shock or discomfort caused by the electronic guests in British homes.

Government control over broadcasting is exercised at three levels. It has statutory powers to direct the BBC, and the private companies with licenses from the ITC and the Radio Authority, to transmit (or not to transmit) specific material and programmes. At an indirect level, it has an all-pervasive power to appoint members of the BBC and ITC Boards, and the members of specific regulatory bodies like the Broadcasting Complaints Commission and the Broadcasting Standards Council. Finally, it may put pressure – publicly or privately – on broadcasting executives to discourage them from making or screening particular programmes. In 1985, for example, BBC governors cravenly complied with the Prime Minister's wish to withdraw a programme about an IRA sympathizer in Belfast (*Real Lives*). The Home Secretary thanked the BBC governors for banning it, journalists in both the Corporation and in ITV companies held a one-day strike, and the BBC's reputation throughout the world for independence and impartiality suffered great damage. *Real Lives* was subsequently screened with a few face-saving deletions, but the episode showed that the Board of Governors could not be trusted to uphold freedom of expression when the Government applied pressure, which is always backed by unspoken threats to diminish the BBC's license fee. In 1988, the Independent Broadcasting Authority and Thames Television showed much more resolve in standing up to the Government and refusing to withdraw *Death on the Rock*, a *This Week* investigation critical of the SAS over the killing of three IRA members in Gibraltar. It will be noted that the IBA exists no longer, and that Thames Television lost its license when its replacement body, the Independent Television Commission, awarded new franchises in 1991. There is little doubt that the defiant transmission of *Death on the Rock* influenced the Government when it devised the regulatory framework of the 1990 Broadcasting Act.

The BBC is established under a charter, and is licensed by the Home Secretary to provide radio and television broadcasts. Section 19 of its licensing agreement enables the Home Secretary, when in his opinion there is an emergency and it is 'expedient' so to act, to send troops in to 'take possession of the BBC in the name and on behalf of Her Majesty'. This clause was framed during the General Strike, when Winston Churchill and other members of Government wanted to commandeer the Corporation. It has never been used for that purpose, although Sir Anthony Eden contemplated invoking it for Government propaganda during the Suez crisis, and during the Falklands recapture it provided the legal basis for the Government's use of BBC transmitters on Ascension Island to beam propaganda broadcasts at Argentina.

A more worrying power is contained in Section 13(4) of the Licence Agreement, which gives the Home Secretary the right to prohibit the BBC from transmitting any item or programme, at any time. The power is not limited, like Section 19, to periods of emergency. The only safe-guard against political censorship is that the BBC 'may' (not 'must') tell the public that it has received a Section 13(4) order from the Home Secretary. This safeguard was invoked in 1972 by the Director-General, Lord Hill, when Home Secretary Reginald Maudling threatened a Section 13(4) order to stop transmission of a debate about Government actions in Ulster. Lord Hill called his bluff by threatening to make public the reason why the programme could not be shown. Of course, a less courageous Director-General could simply cancel the programme without revealing the existence of a Government order. For all the public knows, there may be secret Section 13 directives in force at present. In 1981, Parliament unanimously renewed the BBC Licence Agreement until 1996, without debating these powers. Similar powers exist in relation to commercial television in Section 10 of the Broadcasting Act 1990.

The Home Secretary's power to ban broadcasts of specified 'matter or classes of matter' under Clause 13(4) of the Charter and the predecessor of Sector 10 of the Broadcasting Act was invoked in 1988 for the purpose of direct political censorship when the BBC and the IBA were ordered not to transmit any interviews with representatives of Sinn Fein, the Ulster Defence Association, or the IRA, or any statement which incited support for such groups (see earlier, p.101). The broadcasting authorities did not challenge the directive, nor confine it to its narrowest possible interpretation: they made decisions erring on the safe side, and ran to the Home Office for help with its 'interpretation'. The ban is a serious infringement on the right to receive and impart information: it prevents representatives of lawful political parties (Sinn Fein has an MP and sixty local councillors) from stating their case on matters which have no connection with terrorism, and it denies to the public the opportunity to see and hear those who support violent action being questioned and exposed. The Government believes that terrorists survive by 'the oxygen of publicity', but television confrontations generally demonstrate the moral unattractiveness of those who believe that the end justifies the means. The ban prevents the re-screening of such excellent programmes as Robert Kee's *Ireland: a Television History* or Thames Television's *The Troubles*, which contain interviews with IRA veterans. The BBC and IBA meekly complied with the ban, which further underlines the lack of constitutional protection for freedom of speech in British law. In theory, the

Home Secretary's unrestricted powers under Section 10 and Clause 13(4) could permit a directive against transmitting attacks on the Government made by members of the Opposition party.

The broadcasting ban was challenged in the courts, not by the over-deferential BBC, but by the National Union of Journalists. In 1991 the House of Lords in *Brind's Case*[10] upheld it as a reasonable exercise of ministerial powers, although they were much influenced by a method which Channel 4 had employed in 1990 to minimize its effect, namely by dubbing the voices of Irish actors over the voices of Sinn Fein members on the film or tape. The refusal of the BBC and other ITV companies to use this device indicates how, from the beginning, they interpreted the ban far more broadly than was legally necessary. The 'dubbing' option, however, is not appropriate for most of the casualties of the ban, such as confrontational interviews, Irish songs and historical footage. *Brind's Case* was an unsatisfactory decision because the Law Lords refused to apply the freedom of expression standards in Article 10 of the European Convention, ruling that this standard was irrelevant to the application by English courts of domestic statutes, and was not a standard that a British minister could be obliged to take into account when exercising administrative powers to limit media freedom.

The broadcasting ban has had a chilling effect on media coverage of Irish issues which have nothing to do with terrorism. The fault lies primarily with the Government which imposed it, but the degree to which the Government-appointed Boards of the BBC, Radio Authority and IBA/ITC have been complicit in extending it demonstrates the extent to which these bodies have failed to fight for a freedom which should be enjoyed by their viewers. In 1992, for example, the BBC banned a love story accepted and recorded by Radio 4, because it had been written by Sinn Fein publicity director (and novelist) Danny Morrison. The apolitical story was not set in Ireland, and did not even mention the province, yet Morrison was informed by the BBC's director of editorial policy that 'your short story should never have been accepted, and in the existing circumstances you should forget any encouragement from anywhere in the BBC to write a play or other creative work for entertainment purposes'. In the same year, the BBC officiously subtitled the contribution to a debate on violence by Bernadette McAliskey (the former MP Bernadette Devlin) who is not a member of Sinn Fein and who was the only member of the panel who had physically suffered the violence they were talking about.

The BBC

The British Broadcasting Corporation is a body incorporated by Royal Charter. It has nine governors (including the chairman and vice-chairman), who are appointed by the Crown on the advice of the Prime Minister. Three of the governors must be 'national' representatives of Scotland, Wales and Northern Ireland, but otherwise there are no requirements that Board members should be politically balanced or even have broadcasting experience. Appointments are unadventurous and conservative, and guided by the Home Office reluctance to see people of great distinction or originality in any position of power. (The BBC has itself submitted the names of Margaret Drabble, Iris Murdoch, John Mortimer, QC, and Moira Shearer as potential governors: all have been turned down.) In general the Board tries to keep aloof from specific controversies and to allow these to be dealt with by the Director-General and his staff, although in recent years it has proved sadly vulnerable to political pressure. It intervened, as we have seen, to stop the transmission *Real Lives*. The Board was silent when the police raided BBC premises to carry off the *Secret Society* series which included the Zircon film, and in 1987 it notably failed to appoint Jeremy Isaacs, the best-qualified candidate, as Director-General. Both Harold Wilson and Margaret Thatcher have appointed BBC chairmen for personal rather than publicly obvious reasons, and it is difficult to perceive the Corporation as being independent of Government so long as Prime Ministerial patronage is allowed to decide the membership of its governing body.

The BBC's Charter and Licence is silent on the subject of taste and decency, although in 1964 the BBC gave an undertaking, which is now annexed to the Licence, to avoid programmes which would give widespread public offence. The undertaking states:

The Board accept that, so far as possible, the programmes for which they are responsible should not offend against good taste or decency, or be likely to encourage crime or disorder, or be offensive to public feeling. In judging what is suitable for inclusion in programmes they will pay special regard to the need to ensure that broadcasts designed to stimulate thought do not so far depart from their intention as to give general offence.[11]

This undertaking is not legally enforceable, and Mrs Whitehouse and her ilk have spent the last two decades complaining about 'offensive' BBC programmes, from *Steptoe and Son* to *EastEnders*. This has created a climate in which Corporation executives regularly delete expletives and sexual imagery, even in the work of outstanding playwrights like Alan Bleasdale and David Hare, who have had plays performed to acclaim in the theatre either banned or cut by the BBC. BBC censorship operates by a process of 'reference up' the corporation hierarchy. Any producer who foresees possible offence must alert middle management, which may pass borderline cases to departmental heads, who may in turn consult the Managing Director or even the Director-General.[12] Internal directives are issued from time to time about programme content, especially in relation to sex, violence and drugs. The 'middle ground' is occupied by avoiding extreme political views and ensuring that controversial opinions are 'balanced' by dispensation of conventional wisdom either in the same programme, or over a series. 'Gratuitous' bad language or behaviour is 'eliminated' when not essential to plot or purpose, and four-letter words chanted by football crowds are solemnly edited out of *Match of the Day*, but the Corporation promises to strike the balance in favour of creative freedom where it is exercised for genuine or socially redeeming purposes. Such promises are not always honoured: in 1992 it beeped out the word 'fuck' from love poetry being read on a BBC2 arts programme. At the same time, Larkin's famous lines 'They fuck you up, your Mum and Dad', printed on the cover of *Granta*, were on display in bookshop windows.

When Ian McEwan's play *Solid Geometry* was unaccountably banned in 1979 after being rehearsed for some weeks, the Regional Head of Drama explained the decision to David Hare by saying: 'How do you think it would look if in the very week Margaret Thatcher was elected we were stupid enough to record a play which featured a twelve-inch penis in a bottle?' Hare was later reminded that his contract allowed him to be sacked if he leaked the story to the press.[13] This is a good example of the real motivation behind censorship decisions, which frequently belie the seemingly reasonable sound of the Corporation's 'guidelines' and 'policies'. When the BBC banned *The Naked Civil Servant*, the IBA screened it with one alteration: the caption 'Sexual intercourse is a poor substitute for masturbation' was replaced by 'Wasn't it fun in the bath tonight!'

Brimstone and Treacle, a morality play by Dennis Potter, the renowned television dramatist, about the dilemma of reconciling the existence of both God and evil, was vetoed at the highest level although it contained no single scene which was offensive or in poor taste, and it was subsequently made into a successful feature film. It was not blasphemous at common law, because it lacked any element of indecency or scurrility. But its anti-Christian overtones, and particularly its portrayal of the Devil doing good, upset the Director of Programmes, who 'found the play brilliantly written and made' (at a public expenditure of £70,000) 'but nauseating'.[14] The Chairman of the BBC maintained that 'the whole central theme of the play ... would outrage viewers in a way that was unjustifiable'.[15] The play was finally screened in 1987, ten years after it was made, without any public complaint.

In 1978 the BBC banned *Scum*, a violent and disturbing play about conditions in Borstal, based on actual experiences of both inmates and prison officers. This time the BBC deferred to the opinion of Home Office 'experts' invited to view the film prior to transmission. It was conceded that every incident had real-life parallels, but the play distorted reality because they could not all have happened in the one Borstal at the one time.[16]

For twenty years the BBC refused to show *The War Game*, a film about the horrors of nuclear war made for it in 1965, and shown at many public screenings since. Director-General Sir Ian Trethowan said: 'I do not believe that any broadcasting authority could take the responsibility for what the effect might be on elderly people and people of limited mental intelligence, particularly among those three million licence payers whom we know live alone.' The effect might have been to make them enlist in CND – a prospect that many thought was the real reason behind the ban.

BBC censorship is frequently 'political', and its senior executives are vulnerable to pressure from politicians and policemen alike. One play, *Willie, The Legion Hall Bombing* actually had both its opening and closing scenes rewritten by corporation executives to modify criticism of the 'Diplock' non-jury courts in Northern Ireland. The author (Carol Churchill) and director (Roland Joffé) took legal action to have their names removed from the credits, and supplied the original script to the press so that the BBC's action could be publicly criticized. In 1985 the BBC suppressed a *Brass Tacks* film which had been made about a notorious 'supergrass', after 'representations' from Scotland Yard. BBC executives claimed that the film had been canned because of libel difficulties – an excuse which was shown to be threadbare when their researcher took the material to *World in Action*, which remade the film and screened it.

In 1992 the BBC pulled a *Panorama* programme critical of the state of British economy, for no better reason than that an election was imminent. In the same year it succumbed to pressure from the Foreign Office and the British Council to suppress an arts documentary which was hostile to ninety-three-year-old Malawi dictator Dr Hastings Banda, who had recently threatened to feed his dissidents to his crocodiles. The film followed the English Shakespeare Company as it played *Macbeth* to audiences who soon recognized the parallel between Shakespeare's bloody tyrant and their own. This stupid act of censorship was greatly appreciated by Dr Banda, who was beginning to succumb to international pressure over his human-rights record. It was justified on the grounds that although no Malawians had been critical of Banda in the film, he might none the less have taken reprisals against British Council employees who had cooperated with the drama tour. This sent the message to Banda that his threats of brutality would work to suppress informed foreign criticism – which is hardly the message expected of British cultural exchanges, or of BBC arts programmes.

These *causes célèbres* relate only to films which have been made and then withdrawn from screening. The real casualties of political censorship are the subjects which are not tackled in the first place, because of fear of political fall-out. There has been a certain reluctance within the Corporation to devote investigative resources to stories which might directly undermine Government policies, and which are tackled with more enthusiasm by quality newspapers and independent television. The Corporation's independence from Government, which is so vital to the reputation of its external services as the purveyor of unbiased news, suffered a further blow in 1985, at the same time as the *Real Lives* affair, when it was revealed that a

Security Service official, Brigadier Ronnie Stonham, occupied room 105 in Broadcasting House and was employed to 'vet' staff appointments and promotions. Several distinguished journalists had been blacklisted from Corporation jobs as the result of MI5 influence. It also emerged that for many years political journalists and other senior staff had been obliged to sign the Official Secrets Act, and that all staff at Bush House (headquarters of the BBC's overseas broadcasting network) had been routinely required to sign the Act. This obligation, which has in any event no legal force (see earlier, page 165), has never been imposed on journalists working for the press and Independent Television, and seems to have been a grave error of judgement on the part of BBC management. The Corporation promised to end Security Service vetting and to put room 105 to a use more consistent with its proclaimed independence. Ironically, the BBC's tarnished reputation for independence and integrity was partly restored a year later when its offices were raided by the police during the Zircon affair, and the Conservative Party Chairman made a much-publicized accusation of left-wing bias in Kate Adie's coverage of the US bombing of Libya. These accusations were baseless and promptly rebutted by the BBC, but the fact that they were made at least demonstrated to the outside world that the Corporation was not, like many national broadcasters, merely a tool of Government. It deserves to be noticed, however, that when the Gulf War came to be covered in 1991, Ms Adie was dispatched in British battle-dress to play the force's sweetheart in an obscure oasis in the Saudi desert, while her less contentious colleague John Simpson was awarded the prime-time and highly political position of Baghdad.

Independent broadcasting

Commercial radio and television is supervised by a Government-appointed licensing body called the Independent Broadcasting Authority, which has wide powers to interfere with programme content. These powers date from 1954, and reflect the exaggerated fears of that period about untried and untrusted commercial exploitation of the medium. Lord Reith described the introduction of commercial television as 'a betrayal and a surrender ... somebody introduced smallpox, bubonic plague and the Black Death. Somebody is minded now to introduce sponsored broadcasting in this country.[17] One eminent Law Lord confessed to a 'sense of sacrilege' at the very prospect of an advertisement broadcast on the Sabbath. In this atmosphere, it was understandable that commercial television should be placed under the close scrutiny of a licensing body, which is now the Independent Television Commission (ITC). It is obliged by Section 6 of the Broadcasting Act 1990 to do all it can to secure that every service it licenses complies with the following requirements, namely:

(1) that nothing is included in its programmes which offends against good taste or decency or is likely to encourage or incite to crime or to lead to disorder or to be offensive to public feeling;

(2) that any news given (in whatever form) in its programmes is presented with due accuracy and impartiality;

(3) that due impartiality is preserved on the part of the person providing the service as respects matters of political or industrial controversy or relating to current public policy.

The ITC's duties to secure due impartiality go beyond a general supervision of programme output. They are specifically charged to draw up a code 'giving guidance as to the rules to be observed' and must 'do all that they can to secure that the provisions of the code are observed' (Section 6(3)). This duty is somewhat complicated by controversial subsections inserted in Section 6 after pressure from Tory peers who expressed grave dissatisfaction at the way in which they alleged the IBA had watered down the due-impartiality duty under the previous legislation. Clause 6(5) requires that the code shall in particular have rules that reflect the need to preserve due impartiality on 'major matters' of political or industrial controversy or relating to current public policy.

The ITC code on impartiality indicates that 'major matters' relate to political or industrial issues of national importance 'such as a nationwide strike or significant legislation passing through Parliament'. On such questions, licensees must 'ensure that justice is done to the full range of significant views and perspectives', although the rules indicate that 'due impartiality does not require absolute neutrality on every issue or detachment from fundamental democratic principles'. This permits broadcasters to bias their programmes in favour of life, liberty and the pursuit of happiness; even if (say) the resurgence of racism becomes a 'major matter' of political controversy, impartiality will not be 'due' to the racist side of the argument.

In its original formulation Section 6 required only impartiality in respect of matters of 'current' political or industrial controversy, thereby permitting a degree of partisanship in historical programmes. But elderly peers detected an 'insidious' intention behind the amendment to make the Act 'a charter for revisionist historical programmes' about events they could still remember, and the Government quickly backed down, its spokesman expressing the hope that 'long-dead historical political controversies, like the repeal of the Corn Laws' might not, in practice, be subjected to the impartiality rules.

The late amendments to the Act were particularly designed to narrow the exemption from the 'due-impartiality' requirement provided by Section 6(2), namely, that in applying the requirement 'a series of programmes may be considered as a whole'. Section 6 now goes on to require that the ITC shall make specific rules as to what actually constitutes a 'series'; what time-limit shall be imposed before a 'balancing' programme is transmitted; and as to the publicity that should be given to the balancing programme so as to ensure that it reaches a similar audience. These subsections are designed to concentrate the minds of the ITC and its licensees, and to send a clear signal that any current-affairs or feature programme that presents a controversial viewpoint should not be made (or, if made, should not be transmitted) unless or until a balancing programme is well under way. These provisions are most likely to affect current-affairs programmes like *World in Action*, which will need to find space in their schedules for a programme to balance any that is deemed to lapse from the standard of due impartiality. It is nonsensical to expect a current-affairs team that has come to a particular conclusion about a subject of political controversy to make another programme supportive of a conclusion that they do not believe to be justified by the evidence, yet some politicians undoubtedly believe that the 'series' provision should require another *Death on the Rock* supportive of the Government claims about that incident ('Lawful Homicide on the Rock') and another *Who Bombed Birmingham?* (which in 1987 portrayed the Birmingham Six as innocent) portraying the Birmingham Six as guilty. The answer to this dilemma is to confine the 'series' qualification to 'personal view' programmes that have been labelled as such, and to argue that a due degree of impartiality has been provided within the give and take of the current-affairs feature, even if its treatment of the evidence (necessarily, a fair treatment) has favoured a particular side of the controversy. Whether this approach will be sufficient to satisfy the ITC or the courts remains to be seen.

The ITC and the Radio Authority are expected to enforce their statutory duties by monitoring their codes and punishing licensees for any breach of them. Compliance with ITC codes and rulings is made a condition of all radio and television licences: if satisfied that a breach has occurred, the authority may order the licence holder to:

- broadcast a correction or apology;
- refrain from re-broadcasting an offending programme;
- pay a fine up to a maximum calculated by reference to advertising revenue, the ceiling being raised in the case of a second offence;
- accept a reduction of the ten-year licence period by up to two years; or
- rectify a failure within a specified time, or else to suffer revocation of the licence.[18]

The last three penalties are draconian; the maximum level of the financial penalties for most licence holders will be several million pounds, as would the cost of losing one or two years of licensed operation (at least, if the licence were not renewed). The safeguard, in every case, is merely that the licence holder must be given 'a reasonable opportunity to make representations' before receiving punishment. This would be unfair if the licence holder's representations were to be directed to a decision the ITC has already taken, rather than to the question of whether it ought to take such a decision in the first place. It is to be hoped that, in practice, the ITC will operate a system of advance warnings of possible licence breaches, and will give licence holders the opportunity to explain themselves before commencing to decide whether to issue a penalty notice.

The ITC's exercise of its punishment powers will be subject to judicial review on grounds that it has acted irrationally or disproportionately or has not properly appreciated the evidence. However, it is unlikely that the courts will intervene in relation to the merits of an ITC decision: they would only act if there was gross procedural impropriety. In the first case which considered an ITC decision (to award a franchise) the House of Lords was notably reluctant to upset the action of a body of reasonable and experienced people acting on expert advice, although there was evidence that some of the advice was unsound. This was the approach taken by the Court of Appeal in relation to IBA transmission of a documentary about avant-garde artist Andy Warhol: although the judges all thought that the work was indecent and offensive they declined to interfere with the authority's performance of its duty unless its decision could be shown to be manifestly unreasonable.[19]

When Channel 4 first scheduled the film of *Scum*, a powerful drama about violence begetting violence among young offenders in a Borstal, IBA officials refused to approve it. The play on which the film was based had been banned by the BBC (see above, page 279). But they were overruled by the IBA's Director-General, John Whitney, who had been a prison visitor and actually knew something about the subject-matter of the film. His experience enabled him to see its merits, and he ordered it to be screened at 11.30 p.m. Only three viewers complained – two to Channel 4 and one (Mrs Mary Whitehouse) to the courts. In 1985 the Court of Appeal acquitted the Director-General of any error of judgement. The Master of the Rolls, Lord Donaldson, pointed out that the statutory duties of ensuring 'good taste' and 'due impartiality' are imprecise, and require only that Authority members should do their best to establish and supervise a system which provides a reasonable prospect that these values will be preserved by the television companies.[20] The courts should only intervene when convinced that the system adopted by the IBA was so bizarre that no reasonable person could believe it would assist in maintaining programme standards at the general level required by the Act.

The appeal decision in the *Scum* case was useful in the days when the IBA was 'publisher' of all television programmes, and thus expected to preview and pre-censor any which were likely to cause controversy. Many of the IBA's cuts were footling (it insisted that no flowers should be shown on any IRA hunger-striker's grave) but it did stand firm over *Death on the Rock*. It was abolished in 1990 and replaced by the ITC, a licensing rather than a publishing body, which the Government claimed would regulate with 'a

285

lighter touch'. This claim was deceptive, because although it could no longer preview controversial programmes, it was given more draconian penalties to impose if such programmes breached its code. The non-interventionist attitude of the courts now removes much hope of appeal success for companies which are fined or have their licences terminated. The end result has been to make television companies more cautious than ever: they can no longer enlist the support of a previewing authority, but must take their chance of retrospective punishment by the ITC. They are more 'free' than they were before, yet more frightened. They would have much less reason to fear if the ITC were truly 'independent', and if it were not subject to the pressure of rulings from the Broadcasting Standards Council or the Broadcasting Complaints Commission.

The chairperson and members of the ITC and the Radio Authority are appointed by the Home Secretary, sometimes with Prime Ministerial direction, and are as politically vulnerable as appointments to the BBC. There is no requirement for political balance or broadcasting experience, and in 1989 the Thatcher Government was widely criticized for appointing Lord Chalfont, a notorious conspiracy theorist about 'left-wing infiltration of the media' to the position of deputy chairman of the ITC (he later moved to chair the new Radio Authority). Channel 4, which had given Mesdames Thatcher and Whitehouse considerable irritation since its inception as a subsidiary company of the IBA, was made the subject of a particularly petty and unnecessary measure in the 1990 legislation. Its independence and success were partly owed to the fact that its Board was not appointed by the Government, but by the IBA itself. Under the 1990 Act, however, the membership of its Board will be appointed by the ITC subject to Government veto. Since it is inconceivable that the ITC would seek to appoint a professionally unqualified board member, the Government clearly envisages that it may exercise its new right of veto on political grounds.

Broadcasting Standards Council

Both the BBC and the ITC impose censorship through the application of policy guidelines on sex and violence and coverage of terrorism. Bad language, nudity and racism are discouraged, criminal techniques are never demonstrated, and interviews with lawbreakers (whether IRA terrorists or animal-liberation activists) are rarely shown. A 'family viewing policy' operates to increase restrictions until the 'watershed hour' of 9 p.m., when more 'adult' programmes can progressively be screened. There are special provisions for 'news black-outs' on hijackings and kidnaps at the request of the police. The codes on violence are regularly revised and have become increasingly complex, with rules which range from 'dead bodies should not be shown in close-up' to 'film should not dwell on close-up pictures of the grief-stricken in the wake of natural disasters and man-made violence'. Such rules are easy to agree in principle, but frequently ignored in practice. Thus dead bodies *are* shown in close-up, if they are black and lying in some foreign field, and weeping relatives were depicted in television coverage of the 1987 cross-Channel ferry disaster. However, television is notably more restrained in invading personal privacy than the press (it would be inconceivable for any news programme to broadcast a picture of a rape victim on the steps of her church). The balance to be struck, in Hugh Carlton Greene's words, is 'between what is true and what is tolerable'.

Notwithstanding these rigid BBC and ITC and Radio Authority self-censorship codes, which run into many hundreds of pages and are backed by parliamentary undertakings and statutory duties and by the Obscene Publications Act and other criminal and civil laws, the Thatcher Government found it expedient to establish in 1988 a brand new 'watchdog', the Broadcasting Standards Council. It was chaired until 1993 by Lord Rees-Mogg, whose behaviour in stopping the screening of *Real Lives* when deputy chairman of the BBC had been an important qualification for his new role as censor-in-chief.

The Council (now chaired by Elspeth Howe, wife of the former Tory Cabinet Minister Geoffrey Howe) is empowered by the 1990 Broadcasting Act to monitor levels of sex and violence on radio and television, to adjudicate complaints and to draw up more codes of conduct to define standards of taste and decency. It has recruited two thousand 'television monitors' throughout the country who send reports on sex, violence and bad language to its chic headquarters at The Sanctuary, overlooked appropriately by both the Houses of Parliament and by Westminster Abbey.

The BSC is gradually exerting an influence over television

standards. Its codes must be incorporated into the standards issued by broadcasting bodies, and all licence holders must undertake by contract to comply with them. The sanction for disobedience may initially be no more than a 'mogging' (as criticisms issued by Lord Rees-Mogg were called), which will be given some degree of publicity. The BBC will suffer no further adverse action, but companies holding ITC licences may find themselves liable to further punishment as a result of the ITC's powers to fine them, or to reduce or revoke their licences. How many 'moggings' might it take to earn a fine or a revocation?

The BSC issues its adjudications on public complaints in regular monthly bulletins. In a number of respects, these adjudications are displaying both an ignorance of the nature of television and an intention to damage it as a medium for providing education, information and entertainment.

- It condemned as 'unacceptable for showing at any time' scenes from the award-winning and ITC-approved Australian film *Salt Saliva Sperm and Sweat*, shown by Channel 4 between 11.20 p.m and 12.10 a.m. This philistine adjudication, in respect of a brillant and provocative television film, demonstrates how the 'shock of the new' can be too shocking for the old at the BSC, despite overwhelming artistic merit (October 1991).

- Nor will artistic merit save acknowledged writers and directors if they choose to advance their drama with realistic action that the BSC finds violent or erotic, in some cases long after the watershed. The works of Stephen King (*Children of the Corn*), Catherine Cookson, John Irving (*Hotel New Hampshire*) and David Lynch (*Twin Peaks*) were all condemned on this score.

- The BSC has shown no understanding of the importance of live television and radio. It condemned live broadcasts from the 1991 Edinburgh Fringe, and its obsession with 'good manners' caused it to condemn the makers of *After Dark* for not blacking out Oliver Reed's crude and boorish behaviour towards American feminist Kate Millet, when this behaviour was actually proving the point she was making in a discussion of 'men and violence' (as well as amounting to absorbing midnight television, a consideration the BSC never takes in account). In November 1992 it censured Moray Firth Radio over the 'tone' of some of the comments passed on the behaviour of the Duchess of York during a talk-back session from Saturday midnight to 2 a.m. This was an absurd pandering to royalty at the expense of free speech: only Lord Rees-Mogg could be upset at the prospect of unemployed Scots venting what the BSC admitted was 'mild' spleen about Fergie's subsidized summer cavortings, in the early hours of a Sunday morning.

- BSC rulings have constantly interfered with the examination of censorship decisions. When Channel 4 presented a very late night 'banned' season on this subject, the BSC retrospectively declared that three of its offerings should indeed have been banned; scenes in *Sex and the Censors* (a film about the work of the BBFC) were 'wholly unacceptable', while *Damned in the USA* (an account of American responses to the work of gay photographer Robert Mapplethorpe) and the feature film about Wilhelm Reich (*WR – Mysteries of the Organism*) 'went beyond acceptable limits'. Although it may be understandable that censors of the world should unite – they have nothing to lose but their jobs – these adjudications failed to recognize that the programmes had an honest rather than prurient purpose.

Some of the BSC's decisions have been manifestly silly. It solemnly upheld a complaint by the Reptile Protection Trust that Monty Python veteran Michael Palin had been unfair to snakes by selecting a live one to be skinned and eaten in a Canton restaurant while going *Around the World in Eighty Days*. In 1992 it condemned a satirical sketch in *Alas Smith and Jones*, quite missing the point of the satire, and condemned *Baywatch*, a series about life on the beaches of California, because 'there appears to be an emphasis on the presence on the beach of young women rather than young men'. In the same year it displayed homophobic (or celtophobic) tendencies by censuring a programme about a Welsh gay wedding, because it ended with a shot of the bridegroom kissing the bride. More worrying is its evident desire that popular drama and comedy should reflect conventional social and moral attitudes.

In 1992 it condemned *Top of the Pops* for playing a song 'Ebenezer Goode' which some listeners might have interpreted as referring to the drug Ecstasy (many more did, as a result of publicity given to the Commission's adjudication). The fact that (for the initiated) the song contained warnings against drug abuse was considered irrelevant. Older pop fans will simply have to hope that nobody draws the BSC's attention to Bob Dylan's 'Mr Tambourine Man', the Beatles 'Lucy in the Sky with Diamonds', Billy Joel's 'Captain Jack' and other long-time favourites.

The adjudication procedures adopted by the BSC are grossly unfair to the creative artists whose work it criticizes. It usually decides on complaints behind closed doors, without a hearing, so the writers or performers or programme makers are unable to defend their productions. Usually, they will not even be notified of a complaint against them. Only broadcasting bodies are told, and they have no duty to notify, or even to defend, the makers of the work at stake. Yet the adjudication must be published – usually by being broadcast in summary form – and is often the subject of press reports and comment. The BSC watchdogs lead a sheltered life, in more ways than one: those they criticize under legal privilege have no right and often no opportunity to reply. The establishment of the BSC was defended by the government as necessary, in addition to its complaints functions, to engage in research about the effects of sex and violence. This it does at considerable public expense, and is a boon at least to underemployed sociologists and opinion pollsters. In 1990 they discovered that '74 per cent of adults did not subscribe to the view that all television programmes should be suitable for children' and in 1992 a massive study of 'sex and sexuality in broadcasting' revealed that most viewers found it 'awkward' to watch a sex scene in front of their mother or grandmother, but not in front of a father or grandfather. Lord Rees-Mogg claimed that this finding justified its condemnation of the BBC for screening a rape scene in Melvyn Bragg's *A Time to Dance* shortly after 9 p.m., before many grandmothers had been put to bed.

Advertising

Fears of advertising excesses were responsible for the original injunction on bad taste and offensiveness in commercial broadcasting, and the ITC vets both advertising copy and visual material before transmission to remove 'potentially offensive sexual overtones'. Until 1987 the television regulators repeatedly declared that condom advertisements would be offensive to a large section of the British public. This attitude reflected an irresponsible double standard: the media were prepared to promote promiscuity by snigger and insinuation, but refused to help minimize the casualties, and as recently as 1984 the IBA banned advertisements made by LWT for the Family Planning Association. It needs to be stressed that such decisions are entirely ungoverned by rules of law: they reflect the moral prejudices of the regulators as to what constitutes 'good taste'. In 1987, the advent of AIDS made the IBA finally relent in its total ban on condom advertisements, although any trace of humour, or any attempt to put information about condoms across in ways which might actually appeal to a youthful audience, is still rejected as being 'in poor taste.'

The ITC employs forty members of staff on the task of vetting some fifteen thousand scripts and five thousand completed commercials submitted each year, by applying standards that are more restrictive than those applied to programmes. This task is overseen by the BSC, whose remit to monitor 'good taste and decency' applies both to programmes and to advertisements. This duplication causes the advertising industry great concern, given the high costs of advertising campaigns which might have to be aborted if commercials approved by the ITC are declared unsuitable by the BSC.

Section 8(2) of the 1990 Broadcasting Act sets out the three basic rules for advertising on commercial television:

- There must be no advertising by bodies whose objects are 'wholly or mainly of a political nature' or are 'directed towards any political end'.
- There must be no 'unreasonable discrimination' in acceptance of advertisements, either for or against a particular advertiser.
- Programmes must not, without ITC approval, be sponsored by companies whose products or services cannot be advertised under the ITC code.

The prohibition of advertising of a 'political nature' has caused some confusion in the past. The IBA has refused advertisements for left-wing papers like *Tribune* and *New Socialist*, while accepting them for committed Tory newspapers, which make up the majority of the daily press. The ITC claims that the prohibition excludes 'issue campaigning' to influence legislation or Government action. It is doubtful whether its interpretation of the section is correct, or whether it could withstand a challenge under Article 10 of the European Convention. So long as an advertisement is not directed towards an issue of current political or industrial controversy (and is thus in breach of the overriding due-impartiality duty) and is not inserted by or directed towards a party-political end, it is difficult to understand why campaigning organizations should not have the same opportunities on television that they have on public billboards.

The prohibition on 'unreasonable discrimination' is valuable, and should be capable of assertion against ITC attempts to ban advertising by newspapers catering for minorities. The IBA had a deplorable record in this respect, banning Channel 4 advertisements for a homosexual newspaper (on the grounds that it would be 'offensive to public feeling', although the ad was unexceptionally worded and photographed) and for a West Indian newspaper (because of its headlines about a controversial inquest). The ITC must specifically approve any sponsorship of a programme by the manufacturer of products that its code deems unacceptable for direct advertisement; these include all tobacco products, guns and pornography (which the ITC defines as 'including "girlie" magazines and the like', but not, apparently, including the *Sun*). The ITC additionally regards as unacceptable all advertisements for gaming and betting services, private detective agencies and commercial services offering advice on personal or consumer problems (other than firms of solicitors).

Political broadcasts

The BBC accepts a special duty to permit ministerial broadcasts on matters of national importance, which may range from a declaration of war to emergency arrangements for coping with a drought. So long as there is general consensus on the subject-matter of the broadcast, no right of reply will be given to the Opposition. Where there is, however, an element of partisan controversy in a ministerial broadcast, the Opposition must be given equal time to broadcast a reply.[21] When Mr Tony Benn sought to make a ministerial broadcast in 1975 on the Petroleum and Submarine Protection Act, the BBC detected political controversy in his script and informed him that the Opposition would be entitled to put its point of view. He cancelled the broadcast rather than allow his opponents free airtime.

A limited number of party-political broadcasts are allowed each year on all channels, determined by a committee comprising representatives from the BBC and ITC together with the major parties, chaired by the Lord President of the Council. Air-time is parcelled out according to seats held in Parliament and performance at recent polls, although no definitive formula has been adopted. Party propaganda is not welcomed by viewers other than at election time, and after thirty years of complaint the BBC and ITC have finally abolished the rule that party broadcasts should be carried simultaneously on all channels. The SDP/Liberal Alliance felt that it was losing out, not merely in the number of permitted broadcasts but also in news coverage: an analysis of major television news programmes in 1984 showed that 70 per cent of political comment reflected Tory views, 25 per cent Labour and only 5 per cent Alliance. It is natural that Government policy should obtain substantial coverage, but the Alliance complained to the Broadcasting Complaints Commission that it was being denied, as a matter of policy, a coverage in which viewers might perceive it as an alternative Opposition. The courts upheld the Commission's refusal to adjudicate the question, on the ground that it raised issues of policy which were for the broadcasting authorities to determine.[22]

Party-political broadcasts during election periods have become an influential part of the democratic process. In 1987, Hugh (*Chariots of Fire*) Hudson produced a remarkable propaganda film which boosted Neil Kinnock's personal rating by 16 per cent overnight, while the Tories counter-attacked with a theme tune specially composed by Andrew (*Evita*) Lloyd-Webber. One of the main issues in the 1992 election campaign concerned a Labour Party broadcast about the treatment of a young girl by the NHS: Labour was accused of sensationalism, the Tories of breaking medical confidence by feeding details of the girl's treatment to its supporters in the press. These broadcasts, too, are allocated by the Party Political Broadcast Committee: by tradition, the Opposition has the penultimate broadcast and the Government the very last before the election. These arrangements have worked satisfactorily, although a decision in 1974 to give propaganda-time to every party fielding more than fifty candidates led to an inevitably controversial broadcast by the National Front. Much less satisfactory has been the broadcasting authorities' craven acceptance of the right of parties to dictate the choice of spokespeople. Election discussion programmes have become a cosy dialogue between chosen broadcasters and chosen politicians, with none of the fire traditionally associated with the hustings. Questions at carefully arranged press conferences and studio discussions are predictable and deferential – professional broadcasters were put to shame in the 1983 elections, when the only person to subject the Prime Minister to searching questions about the sinking of the *Belgrano*, the Argentinian warship, was a housewife who took part in a phone-in programme. In the 1992 election, the Labour Party was allowed to keep its left-wing candidates well away from the television screen: while much was heard about Ken Livingstone from other parties, he was never permitted to speak for himself to national audiences. Mrs Thatcher and her acolytes were, by the same token, rarely glimpsed in John Major's Conservative cause. The most interesting development in the 1992 campaign was the constant stream of usually unjustified and generally petty complaints from all parties about media distortion: officials were said to have taken a deliberate decision to keep maximum pressure on broadcasters not to rock their boats.

The least justifiable legal infringement on freedom of speech at election time is Section 93 of the Representation of the People Act, which prevents the broadcast of any radio or television programme featuring candidates for a particular constituency unless all of them take part or else consent to the broadcast. This 'candidate's veto' means, in practice, that sitting MPs who decide they have nothing to gain by appearing will often refuse to appear or to consent to the programme going ahead without them. It means, in addition, that a single candidate can veto a programme in order to stop the public from hearing the views of a specific opponent (many Labour candidates for this reason veto programmes which would include a candidate from the National Front). These consequences are wholly unacceptable. The voting public in a democracy should be entitled to see the candidates for local and national elections ranged against each other, and local radio and television stations perform a public service by setting up such debates. The law which permits a single candidate to ban them, from motives of self-interest or political censorship, should be repealed.

British television effectively abdicates any pretence to investigative journalism at election time, and presents the major parties and their leaders as they want to be seen. In other respects, too, it is super-sensitive at this period, postponing any plays or current-affairs programmes which might be thought to carry a political message. In the run-up to the 1987 election (i.e. in 1986) the BBC turned down a play which depicted Mrs Thatcher heroically and compassionately during the Falklands War, and in 1974 it postponed *The Perils of Pendragon* because of its comic portrayal of a Communist. In 1992 it withdrew a long-prepared and objective *Panorama* programme on the state of the economy, featuring interviews with Government ministers, for fear that it might damage the Government's chances if screened a few weeks before the election. In 1964 it agreed to move *Steptoe and Son* from peak time on polling day at the request of Harold Wilson, who feared potential Labour voters would stay at home to watch it. The BBC did, at least, decline Wilson's further suggestion, to 'replace it with Greek drama, preferably in the original'.

The Broadcasting Complaints Commission

The BBC and the independent television companies operate a close control over the ethics of the programme-makers under their supervision, and serious demands for the equivalent of a Press Council for broadcasters did not come until 1971, when the Labour Party took offence at unfair treatment of its leaders in a programme entitled *Yesterday's Men*. The Annan Committee on the Future of Broadcasting, which reported in 1977, recommended the setting-up of a Broadcasting Complaints Commission (BCC) as part and parcel of its proposals for public accountability: it wanted an inquiry board to conduct public hearings which would gauge popular dissatisfaction, and an opportunity for individuals to complain about misrepresentation to a tribunal of persons 'skilled in the assessment of evidence and knowledgeable about broadcasting'.[23] The BCC was finally established in 1981, but in a very much less satisfactory way. It is currently chaired by a cleric who is headmaster of a private boys' school: its members (all of whom are appointed by the Home Secretary) are a retired Foreign Office official, a trade unionist, a social administrator and an ex-newsreader. It has operated not so much to restore reputations unfairly tarnished (victims prefer libel damages) as to give pressure groups and busybodies the opportunity to harass broadcasters who tackle controversial subjects. It does not hold public hearings, it has no investigative resources and it affects to lay down ethical rules which are frequently unrealistic or positively inhibiting for public-interest broadcast journalism. By 1993, it was seen to be attacking good rather than bad programmes, often at the request of con-merchants or propagandists, and finding footling faults with them, which it insisted should be featured on prime-time 'apologies'. The function of the Commission, defined by the statute, is to consider and adjudicate upon complaints of: (a) unjust or unfair treatment in broadcast programmes; (b) unwarranted infringement of privacy in, or in connection with the obtaining of material included in, broadcast programmes.[24]

'Unjust or unfair treatment' is defined to include 'treatment which is unjust or unfair because of the way in which material in the programme has been selected or arranged'. There is a sense in which the broadcast medium must be 'unfair' to those it interviews – in fading light or in harsh studio light, and with the inevitable pressure of editing for a short sharp slot. In its first decision, the BCC accepted that 'fairness' had to be considered in relation to the entire programme rather than its individual elements, and that a short programme could do no more than to highlight a few major issues surrounding a complicated controversy.[25] This is a helpful ruling for programme-makers constrained to edit for brevity. However, by 1985 it was adopting principles more akin to the Queensberry rules than to the expedients to which it is necessary for *Checkpoint* journalists to resort occasionally in order to expose fraudsters and charlatans. For example, it has insisted that people against whom allegations are to be made should be given written details of these allegations well before the interview.[26] Such a rule would mean that fraudsters would simply decline to be interviewed, or would be ready with lawyers and a prepared story. There is, inevitably, a 'catch as catch can' quality about investigative journalism, which would be hopelessly inhibited if this rule were to be stringently applied. (Even the most dedicated libertarians have never suggested that the police should give written notice of questions they propose to ask their suspects.)

The BCC has, in its rulings to date, been over-tender to the wealthy and the powerful: in one palpably foolish adjudication, it upheld a complaint that the Newspaper Society (which represents the most powerful newspaper publishers in the land) had been unfairly treated because it was 'not made sufficiently aware of the distinctive format of *Diverse Reports*'.[27] The notion that a trade association for press barons should be protected from the consequences of its own ignorance of a long-running 'personal view' programme (in order, presumably, so it could decline to participate) demonstrates the extent to which the BCC is capable of twisting the 'fairness' test to protect the powerful from criticism. In another particularly regrettable adjudication it criticized *World in Action* for failing to make clear to the Economic League – an organization notorious for unfairness by supplying 'blacklists' of left-wingers to employers – the extent to which the League's activities would be criticized in the programme.

The BCC has earned the justified contempt of programme-makers by the extent to which it has become a stalking-horse for lobbyists and pressure groups, and for its determination to uphold the most petty complaints. Its 1991 and 1992 reports are full of adjudications that have upbraided, for the most trifling errors, programmes that have been substantially correct and overwhelmingly in the public interest. The two-hundred-word 'broadcast summary' it prepares of its adjudications invariably mentions the most minor errors, and often gives a false impression that the programme has been found 'unfair' when its basic attack on the complainant has been justified.

There is no television current-affairs programme that is 100 per cent factual and fair, so wealthy individuals and corporations can now write to the BCC confident that their complaint will probably be upheld 'in part'. Lately, the BCC has been losing sight of the fundamental public interest in freedom of expression. In 1991 a consumer programme that valuably exposed the low meat content of commercial pasties found itself censured, not for any factual error, but because it had only named one of the corporate culprits. It is, one supposes, unfair to a criminal if he is the only member of the gang who is captured, but it is certainly not unjust on any rational principle.

The BCC shows increasing signs of degenerating into absurdity. Its 1992 report, for example, boasts a number of adjudications which upheld complaints by organizations of dangerous dog lovers. One television station was condemned for allowing a doctor to state 'about a hundred children every year in this country are blinded by toxocariasis' (a disease transmitted by unwormed dogs) because although more recent statistics showed 102 cases of 'significant impairment of vision', not all the children had been rendered 'totally blind'. The Commission found this meant that the programme 'will have given most viewers an inaccurate impression of total blindness'. Children scarred for life by significantly impaired vision may not appreciate the clinical distinction, and certainly would not appreciate the BCC's pettifogging adjudication. Even more ludicrously, it went on to condemn the BBC news for carrying a Home Office description of a dangerous pit bull terrier as 'a cross between a bull terrier and a larger dog'. This description was substantially 'but not entirely' correct, so the Commission solemnly decreed: 'To the extent that the inaccuracy might have damaged the reputation of bull terriers' the description was unfair. It was hardly the hope of the Annan Commission that the BCC would end up functioning as a libel court for dogs.

Yet this is precisely the level to which the BCC has reduced itself: its 1992 report is replete with upheld complaints against the 'rudeness' of talk-back radio hosts; in favour of lobbyists whose tendentious contributions to discussion programmes have been edited out; about the 'unfairness' of accusing BT of running an overpriced telephone service; about one Greenham Common peace camp upset because a BBC programme concentrated on a different Greenham Common peace camp; about the unfairness to the aluminium industry of entitling a *This Week* investigation *Poison in the Water*, when aluminium sulphate had only poisoned the water (at Camelford) on one recent occasion, and not all the time. One egregious American television reporter even had a complaint upheld because his contribution to a BBC2 programme on media coverage of the Gulf War had been confined to one subject (because the rest of his comments were boring). All these complaints involved programme-makers in masses of paperwork and attendance at BCC hearings. The public interest being served – and there is a public interest in rectifying media misrepresentation – is difficult to discern in many upheld complaints.

The BCC could have become a valuable alternative to libel actions by ordering factual mistakes to be speedily corrected. Unfortunately, it is a small and dilatory organization, which takes on average six months before providing an adjudication. This is an unnecessarily long time to correct simple errors of fact, and means that the publication of the decision is of limited use to complainants. Although it does have potentially wide powers to order that its findings be broadcast 'in any manner' it chooses to specify, it generally directs that summaries must be published in small print in the *Radio Times*. As this magazine is now privatized, it charges the BBC and the commercial stations thousands of pounds for this service, which effectively operates as a fine. Since many adjudications actually acquit the broadcasters, yet are still ordered to be published, the BCC ends up imposing a financial penalty on the innocent. Sometimes it directs that an announcement be broadcast to coincide with a subsequent edition of a programme against which it has upheld a complaint. As this will usually be six months after the offending broadcast (in complex cases, adjudication may take a year or so) viewers will be hard put to remember what all the fuss has been about.

The BCC has not functioned, as the Annan Committee recommended, as an effective fact-finding tribunal: it simply does not have the necessary resources for proper investigation, and does not allow procedures that test for truth, such as cross-examination. There is mounting evidence that this tribunal, set up to promote 'fairness' in broadcasting, actually conduces to unfairness to broadcasters. In 1985, for example, it delivered an adjudication, based on 'facts' which were not properly tested, which in effect accused a Thames Television public-affairs programme of putting at risk the lives of dissidents in Czechoslovakia. The programme's editor, presenter and researcher were pilloried in the press, and had to live with this libel for seven years, until the revolution in Czechoslovakia finally produced evidence which exculpated them. In 1992 the BCC formally 'annulled' this unfair finding, although it offered no compensation to the broadcasters whose reputation it had unjustly besmirched.[28] This unhappy episode underlines the consequences of establishing an underpowered tribunal which purports to make 'findings' on wholly insufficient evidence. The BCC made its mistake in this case – and in many others – because it wrongly declines to put any burden of proof on the complainants to justify their allegations. It is a basic principle of all legal proceedings, criminal or civil, that those who bring them must shoulder the burden of proving them, at least on a balance of probabilities. By ignoring this basic principle of procedural fairness, the Commission has, in the words of the distinguished former editor of *World in Action*, Ray Fitzwalter, 'lost the confidence of broadcasters across the spectrum'. There should of course be an independent body which adjudicates disputes fairly and impartially with a keen eye for where the public interest lies: the BCC does not at present serve this purpose.

CHAPTER 7
Freedom of Expression

Free speech does not mean free speech: it means speech hedged in by all the laws against defamation, blasphemy, sedition and so forth. It means freedom governed by law . . .

Privy Council, 1936[1]

British law regards free speech as a very good thing so long as it does not cause trouble, at which point it can become expensive speech, visited with costly court actions, fines and damages, and occasionally imprisonment. It is curious that for all its rhetorical flourish and historic associations – 'freedom of the press' was chanted with 'Wilkes and Liberty' by the mobs celebrating jury acquittals of publishers who attacked George III – the law makes no presumption in favour of freedom of expression when balancing it against rights of property in information. The principle of freedom of expression does find protection in Article 10 of the European Convention on Human Rights, but as this is not directly applicable in English courts it means a long trek to Strasbourg before media organizations can oblige the Government to make any changes in the law.

Journalism is not just a profession. It is the exercise by occupation of the right to free expression available to every citizen. That right, being available to all, cannot in principle be withdrawn from a few by any system of licensing or professional registration, but it can be restricted and confined by rules of law which apply to all who take or are afforded the opportunity to exercise the right by speaking or writing in public. Defamation, breach of confidence and contempt of court are complex laws which can involve heavy damages and legal costs. So newspapers and broadcasting organizations employ teams of lawyers to advise on stories which might otherwise court reprisals. Press lawyers are inevitably more repressive than press laws, because they will generally prefer to err on the safe side, where they cannot be proved wrong. Since most laws pertaining to the media are of vague or elastic definition, the lawyers' caution is understandable if they are instructed by proprietors or insurance companies who want to avoid the high legal costs of defending, even sucessfully, defamation and breach-of-confidence actions brought by the Government or by wealthy private plaintiffs.

One classic example of the way in which the law of defamation, confidence and contempt can be exploited by a wealthy villain to protect ongoing misdeeds from media exposure is provided by the career of Robert Maxwell, a press mogul who litigated obsessively to protect his reputation and his business secrets while he was raiding employees' pension funds. Only six months before his corporate dishonesty could be exposed as a result of his death, he secured a High Court injunction which banned the press from publishing any suggestion that he or his companies had engaged in 'dubious accounting devices' or had 'sought to mislead . . . as to the value of the assets of the company' and the media were even ordered not to report the fact that such an order had been made. Maxwell had already secured the suppression of two books critical of his conduct, by the expedient of threatening libel actions not only against their publishers but against any bookseller who dared to display them. Instead, the public had to be content with a grovelling account of his life by his employed hagiographer, Joe Haines. The suppression of the truth about Maxwell is a sobering example both of the capacity of British law to chill freedom of expression, and the extent to which British publishing declines to wrap itself up more warmly against the cold. It is the threat of costly legal action, and the caution instilled by that threat, which has inhibited many media organizations from standing up for their stories and fighting battles which might secure important liberalizations in the law.

PRIOR RESTRAINT

The Duke of Wellington's taunt 'publish and be damned' reflects an important principle. The media should be free to publish, and to take the risk of being damned in costs and damages afterwards. Journalists cannot claim to be above the law, but they can claim, in any legal system which takes free speech seriously, the right to have their conduct judged after they have chosen to put the information into the public domain. 'Prior restraint' – the use of injunctions obtained secretly to stop information being made public – is obviously an interference with freedom of expression, and it denies the public the right to judge whether the importance of the revelation justified the decision to risk legal reprisals by publishing it. The rule against prior restraint was given definitive shape by the venerated legal writer Blackstone:

The liberty of the press is indeed essential to the nature of a free state; but this consists in laying no *previous* restraints on publications, and not in freedom from censure for criminal matter when published. Every free man has an undoubted right to lay what sentiments he pleases before the public; to forbid this is to destroy the freedom of the press; but if he publishes what is improper, mischievous or illegal, he must take the consequences of his own temerity.[2]

It was this message which went out in the eighteenth century, and became enshrined in the First Amendment to the American Constitution. But in Britain, which lacks a written constitution, the rule against prior restraint has been badly eroded. Almost every week, at secret hearings in the High Court, judges are asked to issue injunctions against the media. An injunction imposes prior restraint, by stopping presses from rolling and film from running. Whether an injunction will be granted often depends on whether the alleged wrong is a libel or a breach of confidence. In libel cases, the rule against prior restraint is still powerful: no injunction will be granted against defendants who swear that they can prove the truth of the defamatory statement or intend to defend it as 'fair comment'. But in confidence cases, injunctions against the media are given on the same basis as in commercial disputes, that is, whenever the 'balance of convenience' warrants it. The judge must balance the commercial interests of the plaintiff against the value of the defendant's right of free speech. For some judges, brought up in a world which accords pre-eminent value to rights of property, this means balancing hard cash against hot air.

One example of 'prior restraint' was the injunction which stopped the scheduled screening of a Thames Television documentary on the pregnancy drug, Primodos. The programme referred to some material which the producer had seen while engaged for a few days as a consultant to the drug manufacturers. Lord Denning thought it should be shown, on the grounds that 'the *public* interest in receiving information about the drug Primodos and its effects far outweighs the *private* interest of the makers in preventing discussion of it'.[3] But he was outvoted by his brethren, who ruled that the producer was bound by an obligation of confidence which should be honoured, at least until the court had decided at a trial, several years into the future, whether the confidence was outweighed by the public interest. The *Primodos* case shows how judges are inclined to give property claims more weight than freedom of expression. The information in that case, as in most cases where breach of confidence is used by wealthy plaintiffs to stop their secrets getting out, was not of itself valuable, like a trade secret which must be kept from competitors. The fact that the producer had once been a consultant to the drug manufacturers was used as a device to stop a television programme which might have proved embarrassing to the manufacturers.

An 'interim injunction' is a device by which the plaintiff obtains an order suppressing publication until trial. In reality, neither side will be concerned about a trial several years in the future, by which time the information will be out of date or published in some other form. The purpose of the 'interim injunction' is usually to stop publication until embarrassing plans can be reconsidered, or become a *fait* sufficiently *accompli* that no public protest can have any effect. In defamation law, as we have seen, the courts will not injunct publication of the alleged libel if the media are prepared to defend the case. The greater willingness of the courts to give prior restraint in cases of confidence and copyright and contempt means that plaintiffs will, wherever possible, rely on these doctrines as a pretext for stopping articles and broadcasts which they fear because of the criticism contained in them, rather than because of secrets divulged as the basis for criticism. It is anomalous that Blackstone's rule against prior restraint, soundly embedded in libel law, should be so precarious when the case is brought within a different legal category.

One deplorable development in use of the 'interim injunction' as a means of political interference with free speech has come about by the Government's exploiting the court's power to order discovery of documents to obtain copies of programmes and articles before they are published. In 1987 BBC Radio 4 made a somewhat academic series about the security services entitled *My Country Right or Wrong*, and advertised it in the *Radio Times*. On the strength of this advertisement, the Government persuaded a High Court judge to grant an 'interim injunction' against the broadcast, because it feared that ex-employees of the security services might have breached confidence in the course of their interviews.[4] It had no evidence of this: the BBC had on principle refused an invitation to submit the programme to the Government for 'vetting' in advance, and its lawyers were satisfied that no breach of confidence had taken place. The interim injunction stopped the broadcast until the matter could be tried, and in due course the court ordered the BBC to 'give discovery' to the plaintiff, i.e. to disclose the tapes of the programmes to the Attorney-General who brought the action on behalf of the Government. After hearing the tapes, and being satisfied that they contained no breach of confidence, the Government discontinued the action and the BBC was finally able to broadcast *My Country Right or Wrong*, six months after it had originally been scheduled, and after being forced in this fashion to submit it for state 'vetting'. The High Court had allowed its interlocutory procedures to be used as devices for enabling the Government to postpone and to preview an entirely innocuous public-interest programme, in the absence of any evidence that the broadcast would contravene the civil or criminal law.

Not only Governments benefit from censorship imposed by breach-of-confidence injunctions. In 1983 a High Court judge granted an injunction against the European edition of the *Wall Street Journal* preventing it from publishing a Lloyds Bank internal memorandum which had been sent to it anonymously. It related to foreign lending policy, a matter of clear public interest, but this, the court held, did not outweigh the claim of confidence.[5] This decision was otiose, given that the *Journal* had published details of the document in its American edition, and disseminated it via its world-wide electronic news services which in turn had been picked up by other British papers. As the *Wall Street Journal* commented after the case:

> The five or six million readers of our American edition and subscribers to our news services throughout the world knew something about the policies of a major international lender that folks in Britain weren't supposed to know. Aside from the more general importance of the news, that is an especially curious result because the Lloyds group itself has shares traded on the London stock exchange. It strikes us as odd that a nation's legal system should try to deny its own investors access to information already available to investors in New York and the rest of the world, unwittingly promoting an Outsiders Trading Law.

This power to restrain publication by an 'interim injunction' is in effect a power to censor – upon hearing claims which may never subsequently be justified. It has been used in recent times to suppress material as diverse as the background to thalidomide manufacture, the financial manipulations of James Slater, the law-breaking of MI5 and the sex life of the Rolling Stones. Since 1986 the Government has abandoned prosecutions under the Official Secrets Act and used civil actions for breach of confidence as a substitute, claiming that any book written by a civil servant without permission could be embargoed. The courts obligingly granted 'interim injunctions', leaving the merits of 'public interest' defences to be decided at trials in years to come. In the case of *Spycatcher* and *One Girl's War*, these books had been published abroad and there was no conceivable public interest in banning them from Britain. This result, which made both the law and the courts which enforced it look asinine, could not have been achieved had the rule against prior restraint, rather than the 'balance of convenience' test, applied to actions for interim injunctions on grounds of breach of confidence. Nor could it have been achieved had the courts adopted the moderate and sensible position of requiring the plaintiff to show, as a condition for any grant of injunction before trial, that there was no significant public interest in the publication. This approach would permit most victims of breaches of privacy by the tabloid press to obtain a worthwhile protection which would be denied to governments and corporations and the likes of Robert Maxwell who seek to suppress information of real public importance.

The US Supreme Court ruled prior restraint impermissible in its historic *Pentagon Papers* decision. The Government got wind of *The New York Times* plan to publish a set of army research papers on the history of US involvement in Vietnam. It sought to injunct the newspaper on the ground that the material contained military and diplomatic secrets, disclosure of which would substantially damage the national interest. The Supreme Court refused to allow any restraint on publication, on the principle that any system of prior restraint on expression comes to the court bearing a heavy presumption against its constitutional validity.

Press

> The only effective restraint upon executive policy and power in the areas of national defence and international affairs may be in an enlightened citizenry – an informed and critical public opinion which alone can here protect the values of democratic government. For this reason, it is perhaps here that a press that is alert, aware and free most vitally serves the basic purpose of the First Amendment. For without an informed and free press there cannot be an enlightened people.[6]

The importance of this principle was emphasized by those justices who accepted that disclosure would substantially harm the national interest, and that publication might even render the newspaper liable to subsequent criminal action under the Espionage Act. None the less, they ruled that only when the Government could prove that disclosure would cause 'grave and irreparable injury to the public interest' (examples given were details of troop deployments in wartime, or information which might trigger a nuclear holocaust) was a court entitled to stop the presses. Because of the *Pentagon Papers* ruling, the British Government was powerless to sue in the USA to stop publication of *Spycatcher*. But when newspapers in Britain published a few extracts, the courts immediately slapped 'interim injunctions' on them.

The European Court of Human Rights in 1991 held that the continuing injunction on publishing *Spycatcher* in Britain long after it had become a bestseller in other countries was an infringement of the Article 10 guarantee of freedom of expression. A narrow majority of the judges was not persuaded, however, that Article 10 prohibited prior restraint in all circumstances, especially when governments were concerned to protect security information that had not yet seen the light of day. The Court did acknowledge that:

> the dangers inherent in prior restraints are such that they call for the most careful scrutiny on the part of the Court. This is especially so as far as the press is concerned, for news is a perishable commodity and to delay its publication, even for a short period, may well deprive it of its value and interest.[7]

It follows that courts in Britain, if they wish henceforth to comply with the Convention, must accept 'newsworthiness' as a public-interest value that weighs heavily against the grant of an interim injunction sought against newspapers and broadcast organizations. This would enable sensible distinctions to be made between 'privacy' cases, where information of prurient rather than public interest is sold to the press by thieves and blackmailers, and cases where the media surreptitiously obtains stories of genuine news value. Since the European Convention is not binding on British courts, it remains to be seen whether this desirable development in the law will take place.

BREACH OF CONFIDENCE

How has this particular doctrine of civil law acquired such an importance as a means of stopping media revelations of misbehaviour in high places? Until recently, nobody would have thought that it could affect information published in books and newspapers, because it had been developed to protect trade secrets and commercial formulae from being pirated by business rivals. It was an action which developed, in effect, to stop unfair competition by exploiting commercial information obtained by industrial espionage. But in 1967 the concept of 'confidential information' was extended by a judge to cover intimate communications made between husband and wife, in a case which injuncted a newspaper from publishing the Duke of Argyll's account of his stormy marriage to the Duchess.[8] Since then, the doctrine has grown like Topsy, and can now be made the basis for stopping any revelation of information which has been imparted under an obligation of confidence. Such an obligation is normally deduced from a contract of employment, a consultancy or merely a 'confidential relationship'. (Thus in the *Crossman Diaries* case, Cabinet discussions were held to be 'confidential', and in 1981 the courts granted an interim injunction to stop alleged tape-recordings of Prince Charles's telephone discussions with his bride-to-be from being published.)[9]

It follows that every business corporation can claim to stop employees from divulging information about what they have seen or heard in the course of their employment. In 1980 British Steel Corporation sued Granada Television for revealing documents, provided by an employee, which demonstrated waste and mismanagement. Although they did not have time to stop the programme, they exploited the discovery process to obtain an order to disclose the name of Granada's source. The House of Lords gave scant consideration to the importance of protecting the free flow of information, especially information about waste in a nationalized industry.[10] BSC had a proprietary right in its own documents, and that was that: the courts were prepared to send journalists to gaol if they did not cooperate to help make good the loss.

After the *Granada* case, Parliament purported to give journalists some protection against being obliged to name their sources, unless this is 'necessary in the interests of justice or national security or for the prevention of disorder or crime' (Contempt of Court Act, Section 10). This protection has proved illusory, and a number of journalists have recently been threatened with imprisonment as a consequence of putting important stories into the public domain. Jeremy Warner, of the *Independent*, was heavily fined for refusing to reveal the source for an article about the use of 'insider information' in share-rigging: his protection was lost because it was 'in the interest of preventing crime' that he should betray his source.[11] It did not seem to occur to the judges that his role in exposing crime would be at an end if he complied, because future sources would dry up. Channel 4 and an independent television company were fined £70,000 in 1992 for refusing to disclose their source for a programme alleging that members of the RUC were assisting loyalist assassination squads in the province: again, the court did not comprehend the importance to the free flow of information of protecting the sources for this kind of information, who, if revealed, are not so much likely to 'dry up' as to crumple up under executioner's bullets.[12] When the *Guardian* avoided a heavy fine by complying with a court order to give the Government the documents which identified its 'mole', Sarah Tisdall, she was jailed for six months and the *Guardian* received no more information from within 'sensitive' ministries in Whitehall.[13]

The demise of any hope that Section 10 would afford real protection to journalists came in 1990 with the case of Bill Goodwin, a young reporter on the *Engineer*, who was tipped off about some refinancing plans being proposed by a well-known private company. When he rang the company for its comments, he received a writ which not only injuncted his story on the grounds of breach of confidence, but threatened him with imprisonment unless he disclosed his source. The Court of Appeal cunningly ordered him to hand over the name inside a brown paper envelope, which would be opened only if the House of Lords ruled against him.[14] By refusing to endanger his source by playing this game of forensic roulette, he put himself in contempt of court. The House of Lords duly held that 'the interests of justice' required disclosure so that the company could identify the 'mole' in its midst, and ordered that he be punished for contempt. (His trial judge sensibly defused a potential clash between media ethics and the courts by imposing a moderate fine of £5,000.) Although there may be rare occasions where the public interest justifies an order for disclosure (e.g. where the name is necessary to establish a defendant's innocence, or when the journalist has been used as the instrument of a serious crime), Bill Goodwin's case arose from a routine situation where a law-abiding journalist received unpaid and unsolicited information of a newsworthy nature, and behaved properly in checking it with the company prior to publication. Yet the private interest of the company, in combating the consequences of its own defects in security, was allowed to outweigh the public interest in encouraging a flow of information to journalists. Until the enactment of a Bill of Rights establishes a presumption in favour of the right to receive and impart information, courts will continue to give more weight to the interests of commerce.

What defences are open to the media against a breach-of-confidence action? The main defences are:

1. *Staleness*. Information ceases to be confidential when it is out of date. Thus the 'Cabinet secrets' of the *Crossman Diaries* could be published because they were ten years old. On the other hand, the

Government claims that security-service secrets remain confidential for ever. *One Girl's War* was injuncted because of its revelations of low-level MI5 operations during the Second World War. As the result of a House of Lords decision permitting the publication of another wartime spy memoir, *Inside Intelligence*, however, the Government will be required to show at least some harm to the national interest before obtaining an injunction.[15]

2. *Public domain.* A confidence is no longer a confidence when it has been published elsewhere. If it has been published at the behest of the person to whom the confidence is owed, then this is a complete defence. However, it is not clear how far the 'public domain' argument will protect those who wish to divulge authoritatively matters which have been placed in the public domain at second hand. Thus an 'insider' may be stopped from confirming what 'outsiders' have long and publicly suspected.

3. *The other side of the story.* Where the owner of the confidence has promoted one version of events or encouraged a favourable image, others are permitted to publish confidential material which shows the proprietor in a true, and less favourable, light. This defence is regularly employed against celebrities who try to stop their ex-employees from telling about the seedier side of their life beneath the glossy PR handouts. Thus when Tom Jones tried to stop his former public-relations consultant from exposing his jumbo-jet orgies, Lord Denning held:

> If the image which they fostered was not a true image, it is in the public interest that it should be corrected ... it is a question of balancing the public interest in maintaining the confidence against the public interest in knowing the truth – the public should not be misled.[16]

4. *Iniquity.* There is no confidence in iniquity, and ex-employees are entitled to reveal evidence of crime or fraud. This defence is absolute where the revelation is made to the police or to other appropriate authorities, but it may be more limited when it is made for profit to a newspaper which will use the revelation as a circulation-building scoop. It may also be unavailable as a defence where the media have obtained the information illegally. Thus the Court of Appeal granted an interim injunction to stop the *Daily Mirror* publishing the transcripts of illegal telephone taps which were alleged to show that a leading jockey might be involved in criminal offences.[17]

5. *The public interest.* The media will not be stopped from publishing confidential material if the court can be convinced that the publication is in the public interest. What is 'in the public interest' for this purpose will depend very much on the outlook of the judge. The courts have unhesitatingly refused to suppress stories about drug-taking and sex orgies involving pop stars and details of courses offered by the 'Church' of Scientology. When the *Daily Express* obtained confidential information about the vagaries of the Intoximeter, an injunction was refused. The Intoximeter case is important because the Court of Appeal conceded that although the information had been obtained in blatant breach of confidence, the possibility that persons were being convicted of drink-driving offences as a result of instrument inaccuracies provided a serious defence of public interest which might be vindicated at an ultimate trial.[18]

The problem with the law of breach of confidence is that it has developed on a case-by-case basis, with interim injunctions being granted on the basis of convenience rather than principle. It is difficult to resist the conclusion that the courts are really deciding the issue on the basis of a subjective appreciation of the merits of the applicant rather than the application, with pop stars and Scientologists being denied the benefits of a legal rule which protects the privacy of royalty, drug manufacturers and nationalized industries. The courts are using the doctrine to provide a form of back-door protection against certain invasions of privacy, but are producing exceptions which justify the revelation of personal sexual peccadilloes while prohibiting serious stories about dubious behaviour in public or corporate office. The result is that 'popular' newspapers devote their energies to 'kiss and tell' stories about people in the public eye without any danger of legal restraint, while serious investigative journalism is hampered by the difficulty in using documentary evidence to expose malfeasance in Government or in powerful corporations. Reform of the law of confidence is long overdue, and should begin by reasserting the rule against prior restraint on publication. Where the media can raise a real defence of public interest, there should be no legal embargo imposed. On the other hand, where the claim of public interest is merely a cloak for public prurience (as it was in the *Sun*'s claim that Myra Hindley's parole application should be published in order to whip up hostility to her before the Parole Board even considered it) there would be a reasonable claim to protect the privacy of the individual.

The Spycatcher verdict

The law against breach of confidence was marginally liberalized for the media by the long-awaited House of Lords decision in the *Spycatcher* case.[19] It will be recalled that Wright, a long-serving MI5 officer now in retirement in Australia, had published in that country and in the USA a book detailing some of his unattractive exploits in the Secret Service (including bugging foreign embassies, trespassing into private homes and plotting against Harold Wilson). The British Government had failed in its action against the book in the Australian courts, on the ground that its claim was of a political nature which domestic courts were unable to adjudicate at the behest of a foreign power, and had been unable to bring any action in the USA because of the 'freedom of expression' guarantee in the First Amendment to the US Constitution. In Britain, however, the Government had taken action against any who published Wright's memoirs: it sued the *Observer* for running a news article about them and the *Sunday Times* for publishing an extract from the book, having paid Wright's publishers for the copyright. In 1987, a 3–2 majority of Law Lords, in this century's most publicly derided legal decision, had upheld an injunction banning any mention in Britain of Wright's allegations (while they were being read throughout the rest of the world) until the proceedings against the *Sunday Times* and the *Guardian* were completed.

It was a differently constituted court which considered the final appeal, and decided that the previous summer's majority decision to prevent publication of *Spycatcher* revelations in the British press had been a mistake – 'a misuse of the injunctive remedy'. The courts, however much they might deplore treachery by people like Wright, cannot put genii back into bottles by stopping British citizens from reading reminiscences already published abroad. Making valuable use of Article 10 of the European Covention, the Law Lords declared that such bootless exercises do not correspond with that 'pressing social need' which alone can justify state censorship in a democracy. Once an MI5 secret is out, albeit in a foreign country, the British

313

public cannot be stopped from reading about it. Short of an international treaty to control the publication of security-service information (an unlikely possibility) there can be no *cordon sanitaire* against the claims of embittered Secret Service men who have emigrated.

However, the Law Lords confirmed that persons who have been employed on secret Government work must, if they wish to be buried in the United Kingdom, take their secrets to the grave. They owe a lifelong duty of confidence to the state, which is defeasible only in three circumstances: where the information they wish to publish is utterly trivial; where it has already come into the public domain (either here or abroad); or where it takes the form of substantial allegations of serious wrongdoing. The overriding principle decided by *Spycatcher*, at the end of the day, is one which should never have been in doubt: a Government which wishes to suppress information by civil action must prove that its censorship is for the public interest. The Government will fail – as it failed, in the end, in its claim against the *Observer* – when the projected publication is manifestly in the public interest and will do little or no damage to national security.

None the less, the Law Lords made it clear that the Government would have succeeded in stopping Wright from publishing *Spycatcher* had he lived in this country. The genuine 'public interest' in his revelations (such as his allegations that those within the Secret Service plotted to have the Wilson Government defeated and, prior to Suez, to assassinate Nasser) extended to only a small proportion of the text. And the Lords applied a qualitative test to decide the point at which editors and publishers are entitled to reveal wrong-doing to the general public rather than to state authorities. There must at least be a prima facie case that the allegations have some substance. It follows that editors will need some corroborative evidence for 'revelations' that may be no more than the product of paranoia or disaffection. Lord Griffiths (who was also head of the Security Commission) thought that editors should loyally report such allegations to the responsible Government minister, and publish them only if 'no effective action had been taken'. But he recognized that this advice was not legally binding, and it is hardly sensible for the courts to encourage editors to inform ministers when the result would be an immediate application for an injunction.

At the end of the day, the Government's extensive and expensive litigation against *Spycatcher* was massively counter-productive, achieving little more than to elevate an otherwise undistinguished book to the top of the bestseller lists throughout the world, and ultimately in Britain as well. The Government took a few crumbs of comfort from a victory over the *Sunday Times*, which was forced to disgorge the money it had paid to Wright's publisher at a time prior to the book's publication in the United States (although in 1991 the European Court of Human Rights obliged it to cancel the account and pay the newspaper's costs). It kept the lid on his allegations being publicly analysed in this country for two years: ironically, when the lid was finally lifted by the House of Lords, some of these allegations were authoritatively refuted and Wright himself was revealed as a conspiracy theorist of McCarthyite proportions. Indeed, the main theme of *Spycatcher* – that Sir Roger Hollis was a Soviet agent – has been discredited by the KGB records and reminiscences which have followed upon glasnost. The revelation of Peter Wright's paranoia, malice and irresponsibility was the real public interest in *Spycatcher* – a public interest which had never been mentioned in any of the court proceedings. How came it that this obsessively right-wing electrician was ever allowed to rise to a position of power and influence in MI5? Although he caught few spies, he and his henchmen destroyed a number of careers; their secret inquisitions drove one Labour MP to suicide and another minister (Niall Macdermott, QC, who might in time have become Lord Chancellor) out of the Wilson Government. The judges contented themselves with reviling Wright for treachery, but the real question was about the control of an organization which allowed his mentality to flourish to the point of damaging both its own reputation and the reputations of innocent citizens. This is the true public interest in *Spycatcher*, which affects the civil liberties of all who may find their liberal instincts anathema to the likes of Wright and perhaps to the likes of his successors in office. The Government took steps in 1989 to ensure that 'public interest' would not be a defence to criminal charges brought under its new Official Secrets Act. Having lost *Spycatcher* in the civil courts, it will in future rely upon the threat of prosecution under a tougher criminal law to deter leaks from the security services.

DEFAMATION

It was originally a crime to speak ill of the living. As early as the eleventh century we find the ecclesiastical courts penalizing slander, on the biblical principle in Leviticus that 'Thou shalt not go up and down as a tale bearer among the people.' But at common law, defamation was only actionable if accompanied by actual injury, such as assault or false imprisonment. However, in 1275 the offence of *scandulum magnatum* was created by statute expressly in order to protect 'the great men of the realm' against discomfiture from stories which might arouse the people against them. Again, it was the threat to civil order which was the gravamen of the criminal offence, hence Lord Coke's famous maxim, 'The greater the truth the greater the libel' – the populace would react more vigorously to real, rather than imagined, grievances. The Star Chamber enforced the libel laws with monumental ferocity – William Prynne had his ears cut off for criticizing the immorality of courtiers; when he repeated his accusations in a polemic entitled *Women Actresses – Notorious Whores* they cut off the stumps of his ears, and branded his forehead with the letters 'SL' for 'seditious libeller'. But this penal jurisdiction was always exercised on the basis of an apprehended threat to the peace.

It was in fact the Star Chamber which paved the way for *civil* libel when it tried to provide an alternative to duelling, which was the traditional method of redressing damage to reputation. The courts became inundated with libel actions and the King's judges tried to discourage them by severely limiting the circumstances in which damages could be recovered. But these early restrictions on defamation were forgotten in the Victorian era, when libel actions became a fashionable and indeed necessary method of answering insults. The idea that large sums of money must be awarded to compensate people for words which 'tend to lower them in the estimation of right-thinking members of society' directly derives from this age, when social and political life was lived in gentlemen's clubs in Pall Mall, an age when escutcheons could be unblotted and society scandals resolved by writs for slander. Libel damages came in this period to call for a metaphysical evaluation of dignity, the notion being that they should show the world a gentleman's real value, rather than be used to punish the publisher for error. Libel was a method for deciding whether the plaintiff really was a gentleman, and leading cases involved allegations of cheating at cards and shooting foxes (it being a dreadful slur on a country gentleman's reputation to suggest he *shot* foxes rather than hunted them down with hounds).

Today, London has become the libel capital of the world. Foreign plaintiffs prefer to sue in this country, because the law favours them more than anywhere else. Tax-free damages awarded in cases which actually come to court are just the tip of a legal iceberg which deep-freezes large chunks of interesting news and comment, especially about wealthy people and companies which have a reputation for issuing writs. There is nothing objectionable in the principle that a person's reputation should be protected from falsehood. The libel law makes an entirely reasonable demand that the media should be restrained from lying or making reckless allegations with impunity. But the strictures of British law sometimes go too far in the opposite direction, restraining investigations into the behaviour of public figures who threaten to sue. The fault lies partly in the complexity of the law, but particularly in certain practices and procedures which work to prevent the exposure of wrongdoing. A rational law would ensure both the speedy correction of false statements and the protection of honest expressions of opinion, but the British libel law secures neither goal adequately. In the United States, the law is much more favourable to the media, which may cast any honest aspersion on a public figure without running the risk of a libel action. In most European countries, a rather better balance between the claims of free speech and personal reputation is achieved by 'right to reply' laws.

So at variance with internationally accepted standards for free speech had British libel law become by 1992 that a US court refused (for the first time since the American Revolution) to enforce English libel judgements. The case involved an attempt to enforce against the magazine *India Today* (headquartered in New York) a judgement for damages of £80,000. The US court was appalled to discover that English law placed the burden of proving truth or fair comment on the media defendant, and imposed strict liability upon it to pay damages even though it had acted in accordance with proper journalistic standards and had honestly believed its statements to be true. Justice Shirley Fingerhood unequivocally held that 'the protection to free speech embodied in the First Amendment [to the American Constitution] would be seriously jeopardized by the entry of libel judgements granted pursuant to standards deemed appropriate in England but considered antithetical to the protection afforded the press by the US Constitution.[20] This decision offers some relief to US publishers with no assets in the UK, but not to their distributors or other publishers with offices in this country. They describe London as 'a town named Sue', as a result of actions brought here by the likes of Armand Hammer, Sylvester Stallone and Bianca Jagger, suing publications which mainly circulate in America, where they would have little prospect of a successful action. When Robert Maxwell wanted to harass the New York magazine *New Republic* over an unflatteringly true profile, he dared not sue in America: he had no difficulty in commencing an action against it in England, where it had only 135 subscribers.

In English law, a libel is simply a statement, either of fact or opinion, which lowers plaintiffs in the estimation of right-thinking people, or exposes them to hatred, ridicule or contempt. Any statement which attributes blameworthy conduct, or any criticism which casts a shadow over a person's fitness for a job or profession is on the face of it defamatory. Judges and juries place themselves (without very much difficulty) in the position of 'right-thinking members of society', and ask themselves whether they think the statement would injure the plaintiff's reputation. The court must bear contemporary social standards in mind in making what will in some cases necessarily be a value judgement. The values of judges in the Deep South in the United States of America, who have held it defamatory to suggest that a white person has 'coloured' blood, would not be shared in England. Not, one hopes, for the reason given in 1848 by the Chief Justice, who argued that being black was 'a great misfortune, but no crime'.[21] Ideas about immorality and what constitutes dishonourable conduct change over time, but the views of judges change more slowly than most. The question, always, is whether the words, in their published context, would be likely to lower the plaintiff in the minds of ordinary, decent readers. That depends, of course, on how the ordinary, decent reader interprets the words, 'reading between the lines in the light of his general knowledge and experience of worldly affairs'.[22]

All that a plaintiff has to prove is that the defendants published a defamatory accusation about him: the burden then shifts to the defence to prove, on the balance of probabilities, that it was true or was published as an honest comment on the basis of true facts, or was 'privileged' in law. The rules relating to these defences are extremely complex, and it is often difficult to disentangle a statement of fact (which must be proved to be accurate) and an expression of opinion (which need only be honest, if there are sufficient facts which can be proved to support it). Privilege may be absolute, as in the case of reporting evidence given in court, or qualified, in cases where the publication is made only to those who have a duty to investigate the allegation, and it is made in good faith. If the defence fails, the jury (or judge, if both sides agree to waive jury trial) may fix damages ranging from one penny to a million pounds to compensate the plaintiff for the slur on his or her reputation. There is no doubt that libel is the chief legal headache for reporters and commentators. In many cases the prospect of heavy damages serves as a spur to accuracy and fairness, in others it prevents or waters down the publication of matters that ought in the public interest to be ventilated. Although British libel law is the most favourable for plaintiffs at the end of the day, it has a number of defects which sometimes prevent them from obtaining corrections for falsehoods published by lazy or incompetent journalists.

One defect in the law is that an action for libel does not rectify all, or even most, false statements. An assertion is not defamatory simply because it is untrue – it must lower its victim in the eyes of right-thinking citizens. To publish falsely, of an Irish priest, that he informed on members of the IRA is not defamatory. It may cause him to be executed by terrorists, but the law offers him no way of securing a correction.[23] In 1981, the Court of Appeal disallowed a libel action by Stephane Grappelli, the renowned jazz musician, who had falsely been described as 'very seriously ill and unlikely to recover', since illness was a misfortune rather than a defect in character.[24]

Another drawback is that defamation is the *only* branch of common law for which legal aid is unavailable. This stark inequity means that wealthy plaintiffs, and those backed by professional associations (like the Police Federation), enjoy privileged access to a powerful weapon of redress. And it means that newspapers may print the most deliberate or reckless lies about poor people, secure in the knowledge that the victim cannot afford the cost of financing preliminary legal skirmishings, let alone the potentially vast fees of a contested trial. An extension of legal aid for libel actions is, in principle, impossible to resist. But this would only mean a more equal application of a bad law. The unreformed law of defamation already restricts far too much public-interest reporting, because massive damages may be awarded for statements on matters of public interest which publishers believe to be true after taking every reasonable step to confirm their accuracy. In 1992 the Court of Appeal mitigated the problems of persons who cannot afford to sue for libel by allowing the very poorest of them, who qualify for legal aid, to bring an action instead for malicious falsehood (a tort which is not, like libel, excluded from the legal aid scheme). The pioneer of this development was Princess Anne's former maid, who had been falsely accused by *Today* newspaper of stealing love letters to the Princess from her future second husband and delivering them to the *Sun*.[25] Her grant of legal aid to sue for malicious falsehood was approved, although plaintiffs in that form of action must prove falsity and journalistic malice, and may only obtain limited damages. This is exactly the sort of law to which the media should answer, not the cornucopia of defamation to which they must answer only if they insult those wealthy enough to take action.

A libel is, in effect, a criticism of a person or corporation. The facts stated may well be true, but the newspaper carries, in law, the burden of proving they are true, by testimony which satisfies strict rules of evidence law. Where the source for a story dies, or is out of the country, or has been promised confidentiality, it will be difficult for the newspaper to satisfy that legal burden. In the United States and in most Western European countries, newspapers are provided with a specific public-interest defence which allows them to escape damages if they show that they had reasonable grounds for believing statements published about important persons and organizations. This defence has no equivalent in British law, and there are a number of recorded cases where damages have been awarded for libellous statements subsequently proved true. John Profumo collected libel damages for the suggestion that he was sharing a prostitute's bed with an officer of the KGB, and Richard Crossman later boasted of how he had perjured himself in the witness-box to obtain damages against the *Spectator* for alleging that he was drunk at a conference in Venice/Liberace, who won large damages against the *Daily Mirror* in 1959 for implying that he was a homosexual – describing him as a 'winking, sniggering, chromium-plated, scent impregnated, luminous, quivering, giggling, fruit-flavoured, mincing, ice-covered heap of Mother Love' – finally died of AIDS in 1987.

In an age of instantaneous communication, satellite television, international magazine distribution and simultaneous book launches, British libel law is not just an eccentric anachronism. US publications are constantly being edited to avoid the possibility that American public figures will descend upon our courts to vindicate reputations they cannot protect at home. There were twenty-two changes made to *Sideshow* – William Shawcross's indictment of US policy in Cambodia – before it was published in the UK. One book about the Sharon Tate murder traced the killer Manson's thinking to the doctrines of an obscure American religious cult. The cult could not sue under US law when the book was widely published in the United States, but it turned up in the High Court to put the British publishers through a long and expensive libel trial. Daniel Moynihan's famous jibe about Kissinger ('Henry doesn't lie because it's in his interests. He lies because it's in his nature') was solemnly edited out of US books about contemporary politics before they were published in this country. In a global village, does it make any sense for public figures to have a different reputation in different parts of town?

British politicians frequently receive tax-free libel awards, which may explain their reluctance to reform the law. John Major promised to remove the unfair liability which attached to magazine printers and distributors, but made lucrative use of this loophole himself in 1993 by obtaining damages from distributors such as Menzies and W. H. Smith for handling an edition of the *New Statesman* which published, in order to deride, widespread rumours that he was having an affair with a Downing Street caterer. The *New Statesman* insisted that its article was not defamatory, and Major declined to face them in a trial he might well have lost. He took the money and ran – leaving the magazine to indemnify distributors who had apologized and paid damages to the Prime Minister in libel actions over an article which might never have been found libellous. 'The curious case of John Major's "mistress"', as the article was titled, turned into a curious case of a libel action which exposed the extent to which defamation has become a game of bluff and counter-bluff, in which the values of freedom of expression find little place. The European Court, to some extent following the US 'public figure' doctrine, has held that politicians are entitled to less protection from media investigation and criticism: if they can't stand the heat, they should get out of the kitchen. Harry F. Truman's robust attitude is not shared by British politicians: those who are most fond of hiding under parliamentary privilege to criticize others are generally the first to sue over criticisms of themselves.

Libel actions launched by wealthy and determined plaintiffs are frighteningly expensive to combat. Even if successful, the defendant is unlikely to recoup all the costs. When the *Daily Mail* was sued by the head of the Unification Church in Britain over allegations that the 'Moonies' brainwashed converts and broke up families, the editor was warned by his lawyers that an adverse verdict might, with legal costs and damages, cost him £1 million. The case lasted one hundred days, required the attendance of many witnesses from abroad, and the defendant's legal costs alone amounted to some £400,000. Libel law has been allowed to become extravagantly complex through special rules for pleading and evidence. In 1989 the Court of Appeal described libel pleadings as an 'archaic saraband' (which the dictionary defines as 'a slow and stately Spanish dance in triple time').

How can a jury assess the 'value' of damage to a reputation? Women who are raped receive about £5,000 compensation, and in recent civil actions for negligence heard by judges plaintiffs have been awarded £50,000 for loss of a leg, £20,000 for loss of an eye and £5,000 for loss of a finger. A worker who contracted asbestosis as a result of his employer's carelessness received £25,000. But when Tory-at-large author Jeffrey Archer was wronged by a newspaper suggesting (albeit on some circumstantial evidence) that he had engaged in sex with a prostitute, he was awarded £500,000 – the price of 100 rapes or as many severed fingers. In 1988 Elton John set a short-lived record with his £1 million libel settlement against the *Sun*, but when the following year Sonia Sutcliffe won £600,000 from *Private Eye* for an article suggesting that she had been prepared to sell her story to newspapers the Court of Appeal reduced her winnings and expressed hope that judges might give some help to juries in future about the real value of money.

In the first case in which such guidance was received, the jury returned with a new British and Commonwealth record of £1.5 million, against an author who had attacked Lord Aldington as a 'war criminal' over his role in the forcible repatriation of Cossacks to their deaths at the end of the Second World War. The judge had warned the jury not to award 'Mickey Mouse money', by which he apparently intended to refer to a sum so large as to be unrealistic (such as £1.5 million). The jury may have understood the phrase to refer to small or trifling amounts, and followed his direction by awarding the sort of sum they imagined in the coffers of Scrooge McDuck. The episode further emphasized the unsatisfactory state of the libel law, and how the prospect of massive awards of damages may serve as a real threat to freedom of expression. In 1992 Jason Donovan won £200,000 against a magazine called *The Face* after his counsel had urged the jury to 'award a large enough sum to ensure that the slur that Mr Donovan was gay was nailed once and for all'. The 'slur' (which was not the attribution of homosexuality as such, but the suggestion that Donovan's denial of it was false) was nailed more effectively than the suggestion that Coronation Street actor Bill Roach was as boring in real life as the character he played, which dreadful supposition was worth only £50,000 (or ten lost fingers).

The prospect of a large libel award has a chilling effect on what is published about powerful people and organizations, especially by small magazines which could be sent into liquidation as a result. Another consequence has been that most publishers are driven to take out expensive libel insurance, which gives their insurance companies the right to insist on copy being 'vetted' by lawyers and the right to settle, often with fulsome or grovelling apologies and secret payments of damages, actions which could possibly (but not certainly) be successfully defended. Awards of libel damages have become so unpredictable and extravagant that it is time to implement the Faulks Committee recommendation that they should be fixed by the trial judge, on a reasoned basis, after the jury has indicated whether they should be substantial, moderate, nominal or contemptuous. When film star Telly Savalas was awarded £34,000 for a gossip columnist's unjustified remark about his drinking habits, the foreman of his jury complained to *The Times*:

> Where a jury has to decide, as men and women of the world, 'how much', the degree of uncertainty is so great that a random answer, consistent only with a total lack of any sort of yardstick, can be expected. Their Lordships would do as well to use an Electronic Random Number Indicating Machine.

The temple of law should not be allowed to become a casino, with entry open only to the wealthy. At the same time, no civilized society can permit a privately owned press to run vendettas against individuals powerless to arrest falsehoods and innuendoes. In the United States, the Supreme Court held in the great case of *The New York Times* v. *Sullivan* that no libel action could succeed if the plaintiff was a public figure and the allegation was honestly and diligently made.[26] This ruling has freed the American media to probe Watergate and Irangate in a depth and a detail which could not be attempted in equivalent circumstances in Britain, where the merest hint of impropriety in public life calls forth a libel writ. But the 'public figure' doctrine denies virtually any protection to persons who are prominent in public affairs, simply because of that fact. True, public figures voluntarily step into a fish-tank which entails close public scrutiny of their every move, and they ordinarily enjoy greater access to channels of communication which provide an opportunity to counter false statements. But that opportunity is circumscribed, none the less, and in a country where for many years Rupert Murdoch, Robert Maxwell and Lord Rothermere, with their powerful and partisan views, controlled 80 per cent of national newspapers, there is an understandable reluctance to give their editors a blank cheque to attack political enemies.

Two essential freedoms – the right to communicate and the right to reputation – must in some way be reconciled by law. British libel law errs by inhibiting free speech and failing to provide a system for correcting factual errors which is speedy and available to all victims of press distortion. US libel law gives no protection at all to the reputation of people in the public eye. Many European countries have opted for a more acceptable solution in the form of 'right to reply' legislation, which allows judges or 'ombudsmen' to direct newspapers to publish corrections and counter-statements from those who claim to have been misrepresented. It is not widely recognized that a legal right of reply has existed, in a limited form, in English law ever since 1881. This has been achieved by granting qualified privilege from libel suit to press reports of defamatory statements made at certain public meetings, company AGMs, and in notices issued by police and Government departments; but this privilege can only be relied upon if the person defamed has been offered the opportunity to provide for publication 'a reasonable letter or statement of explanation or contradiction'.[27]

The first step in defamation law reform would be simply to extend privilege from libel action to newspapers prepared to publish 'a reasonable statement of explanation or contradiction'. In 1991 the Supreme Court Procedure Committee chaired by Lord Justice Neill suggested a much more radical reform, namely that in every case where the libel was not published deliberately or recklessly, the defendant should be permitted to make an 'offer of amends' that would bring the plaintiff's action to a halt. Either the offer would be accepted or the damages in the action would immediately be assessed by a judge and not a jury. This is undoubtedly the most sensible libel reform suggestion to emerge from an official committee, and it deserves speedy implementation. It would confine spiralling jury damages to cases where libels had been published maliciously, and would encourage speedy and effective settlements in other cases. If it were accompanied by a shift in the burden of proof, so that plaintiffs were obliged to satisfy the court that the allegations about them were false in fact or dishonest in comment or lacking in privilege, Britain would have a civil libel law which could stand up in the American courts.

Criminal libel

Criminal libel is an ancient offence which is unlikely to be invoked against the media by prosecuting authorities: the Law Commission has recommended its abolition,[28] and Lord Diplock has pointed out that its provisions conflict with the European Convention on Human Rights.[29] There have only been two modern instances in which it has been invoked by private individuals as part of a vendetta against their journalist-tormentors. In 1977 Sir James Goldsmith was granted leave to prosecute the editor of Private Eye.[30]

The following year a London magistrate, struck by the notion that there should not be one law for the rich unavailable to the poor, permitted a man named Gleaves to bring proceedings against the authors and publishers of a book entitled *Johnny Go Home*, based on a Yorkshire Television documentary which had exposed his insalubrious hospitality to feckless youths. Neither case was an edifying example of law enforcement. Goldsmith was allowed to withdraw his prosecution after a settlement with *Private Eye*, and an Old Bailey jury took little time to acquit the authors of *Johnny Go Home* after a two-week trial. These precedents do not hold out great hope for private prosecutors determined to teach their critics a lesson in the criminal courts.

CONTEMPT OF COURT

The power to punish for contempt is the mechanism by which the judiciary decides where the line is to be drawn between fair trial and free press. Media comment about matters which are subject to litigation may poison the minds of potential jurors or influence or intimidate potential witnesses. It may equally inform public debate and even warn of public danger – for example, when a remand prisoner is armed and on the run. Some publications are blatant contempts, arising from press ignorance or error, and are dealt with by heavy fines after grovelling apologies. (The publication of a defendant's previous convictions before his trial is over is a frequent example.) In most cases there are public-interest arguments on both sides. Anything smacking of 'trial by media' is abhorred by judges, but it is easy to exaggerate the dangers of ephemeral publicity. Prejudicial comment at the time of a suspect's arrest is generally forgotten by the time the case comes to trial, and any residual impact on a jury is attenuated by weeks of live testimony, powerful advocacy and judicial admonition to judge according to the evidence heard in court. We know little about the psychological realities of the jury room, or the extent to which the trial process vacuums the jurors' minds of prejudices they may have picked up from their newspapers, so every contempt case involves guesswork: how great is the risk that the publication will have an impact which cannot be cured by judicial directions to forget about it?

The test to be applied in determining whether a publication amounts to contempt

In deciding whether a publication amounts to a contempt, the court must apply the test of whether it creates a *substantial* risk that justice, either in a particular case or as a continuing process, will be *seriously impeded or prejudiced*. This test was first formulated in the 1981 Contempt of Court Act, which the UK Government was obliged to pass after the European Court of Human Rights held that the old contempt law was so strict that it violated the European Convention guarantee of freedom of expression. The courts had banned the *Sunday Times* from conducting a campaign against Distillers, the manufacturers of the deforming drug thalidomide, and their reluctance properly to compensate victims. There were many legal actions outstanding against Distillers at the time, and the courts took the view that the newspaper campaign would prejudge issues arising in the litigation and put unfair pressure on the drug manufacturers to settle for more than might otherwise be awarded against them. The European Court rejected the British Government's argument that a strict law of contempt was necessary to uphold the authority of the judiciary: the thalidomide disaster was a matter of national concern, and the mere fact that litigation was in progress did not alter the right and indeed the responsibility of the media to impart information and comment about a public tragedy.[31] The old law, by applying the test of *possibility* of prejudice, and by finding that test satisfied whenever media comment prejudged issues under litigation, led to a restraint which went much further than was necessary to protect the authority of the courts in a democratic society. It involved an interference with freedom of speech which was out of proportion to the social need to protect the impartiality of the courts and the rights of litigants.

The 1981 Act, then, originated as a liberalizing measure, and has in some respects had a liberalizing effect. It altered the odds: instead of requiring a *possibility* of some prejudice, it called for a finding of a *substantial risk of serious* prejudice. That the new test is more liberal can be seen from the Court of Appeal's decision in 1986 to refuse to injunct the *News of the World* from publishing allegations about Ian Botham's involvement with drug-taking during a cricket tour of New Zealand. These allegations were already the subject of a libel action brought by Botham against another newspaper which had published them some time before, and the case would be tried by a jury some ten months after the date of the proposed republication in the *News of the World*. The Court of Appeal accepted that there was a possibility that fresh publication in a national newspaper would influence a jury at a later date, but in view of the ten-month delay such a risk could not be assessed as 'substantial'.

This occasion marks an important judicial recognition of the psychological phenomenon that involvement in the immediate drama of a trial will help to eradicate dim memories of media comment. As Lord Donaldson put it,

This trial will not take place for at least ten months, by which time many wickets will have fallen, not to mention much water having flowed under many bridges, all of which would blunt any impact of the publication ... the fact is that for one reason or another a trial, by its very nature, seems to cause all concerned to become progressively more inward-looking, studying the evidence given and submissions made to the exclusion of other sources of enlightenment.[32]

This phenomenon is amply evidenced by the jury which awarded Jeffrey Archer £500,000 for an allegation which had been the talk of every pub and party in the country after the press exposure of his dealings with a prostitute, and the jury acquittal of Jeremy Thorpe after years of press speculation about his involvement in a conspiracy to murder Norman Scott. But there are limits to the extent to which the media may be permitted to vilify individuals facing trial, either by publishing prejudicial facts which would be inadmissible as evidence against them or by whipping up hatred against them generally. The *Sun* newspaper clearly exceeded those limits when it publicly accused a doctor of sexually assaulting a small child, and then (after the DPP had refused to prosecute, on the basis of insufficient evidence) itself funded a private prosecution. The court held that the newspaper had published the attack with the specific intention of prejudicing the proceedings which it had already determined to bring: the day before it began its character assassination of the doctor ('a beast and a swine') it had secretly signed up the child's mother, in whose name the prosecution would be brought, to provide the *Sun* exclusively with interviews and pictures.[33] This is a particularly odious form of 'trial by newspaper', and the newspaper was fortunate to escape with a fine of £75,000. When the *Daily Mirror* published sensationalized suggestions that a man arrested for one particularly foul murder was not only guilty, but guilty of other murders as well, its editor was gaoled for three months.[34]

Notwithstanding the frequent condemnation of 'trial by news-paper', there have been only two occasions on which the courts have actually quashed a conviction because of the danger that the verdict was influenced by prejudicial publicity. In the first case, three young Irish defendants – the Winchester Three – were facing charges of conspiracy to murder Northern Ireland Secretary Tom King.[35] On the day after they had claimed their 'rights of silence' and declined to give evidence, King announced that he was going to abolish the right of silence because it was being claimed by Irish defendants who were guilty of terrorist offences. The timing of King's announcement was extraordinary, and the prejudice was heightened by the instant appearance on television and radio of former judges like Lord Denning (much respected in the Winchester area) to opine that Irish defendants who claimed the right of silence were probably guilty. The Court of Appeal had no doubt that this publicity, a few days before the jury retired to consider its verdict, was devastating to the prospects of a fair result. It did not criticize the media for its coverage of an important political development which had coincidentally been timed so as to make one particular trial impossible of fair resolution. In other cases – especially notorious murder trials – the tabloid press may not be exculpated so readily, if sensational and slanted coverage while the trial is underway is designed to reverse the presumption of innocence. That was what the Court of Appeal in 1993 found had happened during the murder trial of the Taylor sisters, when press coverage which headlined prosecution allegations as fact and featured private photographs doctored so as to prejudice their defence created a public expectation that they would be found guilty. The Court quashed their convictions on the basis that they had not received a fair trial, both because police had withheld evidence which favoured them and because the media had sensationally distorted the highly circumstantial evidence against them.

A society's respect for the values of fair trial is judged by the protection it affords to those charged with the ugliest of crimes, and the liberalizing intentions of the 1981 Act were in some respects restrained by the unedifying media circus which accompanied the arrest of Peter Sutcliffe, the 'Yorkshire Ripper', while the law was passing through its parliamentary stages. The series of gruesome murders of young women for which Sutcliffe ultimately accepted

329

responsibility had fanned fear and terror in northern cities, but relief at the arrest did not justify the police holding triumphant press conferences or the media publishing every kind of prejudicial detail which its reporters, with blank cheque-books, could purchase from potential witnesses. Had Sutcliffe denied the charges, it would have been difficult to empanel a jury unaffected by the publicity given to his arrest, and his trial in any event badly miscarried when his plea of guilty of manslaughter on grounds of diminished responsibility was rejected by a majority verdict despite unanimous medical evidence that he was suffering from paranoid schizophrenia. (Subsequently his illness became so pronounced that he had to be removed from prison to a secure mental hospital.) Although no prosecutions were brought as a result of this episode – the Attorney-General lamely explained that he would have to put all of Fleet Street in the dock – it influenced Parliament to set a strict timetable within which 'strict liability contempt' may be committed

'Intentional contempt', i.e. when a newspaper deliberately sets out to influence a trial (as in the case mentioned above of the *Sun* criticizing and privately prosecuting a doctor) is rare, but may be committed at any time, arguably even before charges are brought (see later, page 333). 'Strict liability contempt' – the normal case of publishing prejudicial material negligently or in ignorance of a forthcoming trial – can be committed only during the period when proceedings are deemed to be 'active'. In criminal cases, this is as soon as the first formal step in launching a prosecution is taken, either by arrest or the issue of a warrant for arrest or a summons to appear in court. Civil cases become 'active' as soon as the case is listed as being ready for trial. Publication of prejudicial material outside these time-frames will not be capable of amounting to contempt unless intended to prejudice some further trial, while publication within the 'active' period will be contemptuous if it constitutes a substantial risk of serious prejudice. A case ceases to be 'active' when it has concluded, although it 'reactivates' when an appeal is lodged. The reactivation period causes the media little concern, as appellate judges are reluctant to concede that they are influenced by anything they might read in newspapers. They are, however, only human, and advocates who strive to appeal deterrent sentences which have been stridently endorsed by popular newspaper can feel they have an uphill task.

The media won an important victory in the House of Lords in 1990, when the *Observer* was acquitted of contempt for publishing the very document the disclosure of which it was seeking in legal proceedings which had reached the House of Lords. The editor of the *Observer* had received the document (a DTI investigation of the takeover of Harrods, accomplished by the Al Fayed brothers to the fury of 'Tiny' Rowland, proprietor of the *Observer*) from an anonymous source, and deemed it of such overwhelming public importance that he published it as a 'special edition' of the Sunday *Observer*, on a Thursday. He also sent free copies to all the important people in Britain, including the five Law Lords due to hear the appeal. Although the *Observer* editor had acted as judge in his proprietor's cause, the Law Lords acquitted all concerned of contempt, noting with a disdain amply justified by the newspaper's extraordinary behaviour that 'it is difficult to visualize circumstances in which any court in the UK exercising appellate jurisdiction would be in the least likely to be influenced by public discussion of the merits of a decision appealed against or of the parties' conduct in the proceedings'.[36] The Law Lords also emphasized that the Contempt of Court Act should be construed, as far as possible, to conform with Article 10 of the European Convention, with its requirement that suppression of information by law must be justified by 'a pressing social need'.

Another liberalizing aspect of the 1981 Act was its introduction of a 'public interest' defence which ensures that public debate on matters of current controversy can continue even if it reflects upon issues before the courts. Section 5 exonerates publications which discuss in good faith matters of general public interest 'if the risk of impediment or prejudice is merely incidental to the discussion'. The first beneficiary of this defence was Malcolm Muggeridge, who had written critically of the 'common practice' of doctors who allowed deformed babies to die, in a newspaper article which appeared during the trial of a doctor who was alleged to have committed manslaughter in these very circumstances. Incidental prejudice to the trial was insufficient, the House of Lords held, to curtail robust criticism of medical euthanasia.[37] Sir John Junor, however, was heavily fined for a snide and misleading personal attack on the doctor while his trial was in progress, made without any attempt to discuss the wider issues. Section 5 will not protect publications which directly relate to imminent or ongoing jury trials and which criticize witnesses or vilify defendants or set out inadmissible evidence or encourage a particular outcome.

Contempt creates a difficult problem for individuals who are not witnesses, but who receive adverse publicity as a result of attacks at the trial. Can they rebut false allegations while the trial is in motion? Not, it seems, when the result would be to suggest that a party to it or a witness in it is a liar.

When Greville Janner, MP, was falsely and irrelevantly accused of buggery by a witness at the trial of Frank Beck in 1991, he maintained a stoic silence 'on legal advice' until the jury convicted, and then launched a parliamentary campaign to remove the absolute privilege attached to press reports of court proceedings where allegations are made against third parties. (Janner and his supporters showed no enthusiasm for removing the absolute privilege attaching to reports of MPs' speeches in Parliament, a source of much greater unfairness to third parties.) When a victim of outrageous allegations, made under privilege in a court in which he is neither a party nor a witness, puts on public record immediately a short and emphatic denial, he should not be regarded as having committed a contempt of court. When Lord Goodman was mentioned in an unattractive light by a witness in the Thorpe committal hearings, he went to the Attorney-General to demand redress, only to be advised that the best thing he could do was to stand on a soapbox in Trafalgar Square and proclaim his innocence.

The basic thrust of the 1981 Act, with its test of substantial risk of serious prejudice and its public-interest defence, reasonably balances the conflicting values of fair trial and free press. It allows courts to impose a stricter test where trial is by jury rather than by magistrate or judge, and the 'cut-off-point' at the moment of arrest allows the media latitude to expose wrongdoing which may otherwise go unprosecuted. It does make it more difficult than in America or Europe to criticize the conduct of particular prosecutions or the behaviour of those engaged in court cases while they are 'active', but it serves to dampen the sensationalistic hue and cry against unpopular defendants which disfigures justice in other countries. Contempt prosecutions may only be brought by the Attorney-General, whose control prevents trivial prosecutions but has also served to immunize the police force, whose press statements and public conferences and inspired 'leaks' are directly responsible for much avoidable prejudice. On occasions politicians − including Government ministers − have been unable to resist grabbing headlines by denouncing prospective defendants or announcing police breakthroughs in proving their guilt: the Attorney-General has taken no action.

There are several respects in which the law of contempt still overvalues the claim of due administration of justice. First, the absolute prohibition of any kind of post-trial interview with jurors precludes sensible and serious analysis of how that system works (see later, page 361). Second, the powers given to judges and magistrates to postpone reports of proceedings or to ban the mention of names or other items of evidence are apt to be used in contravention of the open-justice principle (see later, page 341). The third unsatisfactory feature of contempt is the 1981 Act's failure to reform the law of 'intentional contempt', which survives with all its common-law features intact. It applies outside the statutory periods imposed on 'strict liability' contempt, and requires only a potential risk − not a substantial risk − of prejudice to litigation. The 'public interest' defence given by Section 5 of the Contempt Act does not apply.

Although there was good reason to condemn the *Sun* for intentionally prejudicing the trial of a doctor whom the newspaper itself had decided to prosecute privately, it is questionable whether the Divisional Court was correct in deciding that at common law contempt can be committed before any kind of proceedings have been commenced. As a High Court judge pointed out in a subsequent case, in which he refused to follow the Divisional Court ruling in this respect, it is very much in the public interest that the media should be free to expose wrongdoers and demand that they be brought to trial.[38] To render them liable to a contempt prosecution for doing so is to deter them from performing this public service. Hard cases make bad law, and it is to be hoped that courts in future do not treat the *Sun* case as authority for prosecuting newspapers for exposing suspects whose prosecution may be seen as 'imminent', in retrospect, but may not have been instigated without the publicity. The *Sun* decision should be confined to its own unpleasant facts, and in particular to the fact that the prosecution had effectively begun the day before the attacks on the doctor were published, when the child's mother signed the 'world exclusive' agreement with the newspaper to prosecute for its benefit.

[handwritten margin note: Example of the use of intentional contempt to restrict free speech]

The Attorney-General's deployment of the device of 'intentional contempt' to punish newspapers which published revelations by Peter Wright was also controversial. These complicated contempt proceedings were commenced in 1987 against the *Independent* and two evening newspapers which reported detailed extracts from Wright's book just before it was published in America. The previous year, the Government had obtained injunctions against the *Guardian* and the *Observer* over brief reports of Wright's main allegations, on the ground that these amounted to breaches of a duty of confidentiality owed to it. The *Independent* was not a party to these proceedings, had not had the opportunity to contest the injunction and could not in natural justice be said to be bound by it. Its decision to publish Wright's allegations on the eve of their publication in America was, if anything, a further breach of confidence. Yet the House of Lords upheld the Attorney-General's contention that the *Independent*'s publication could amount to 'intentional contempt' because it 'destroyed the subject-matter' of the Government's action against the *Guardian* and the *Observer*. (It would not amount to 'strict liability' contempt, because that earlier action had not yet been set down for trial.)

This case – *Attorney-General v. Newspaper Publishing plc* – shows just how far the law of contempt can be stretched when combined with another exceedingly supple common-law doctrine, namely breach of confidence.[39] The 'subject-matter' of the initial confidence action against the *Observer* was a report of Wright's allegations. This subject-matter was likened to an ice-cube: it would 'evaporate' if exposed to the light of day by the *Independent*. There would be no point in the Attorney-General continuing his action against the *Observer* if Wright's revelations were published elsewhere. Since contempt is a power deployed by the courts to prevent interference with the due administration of justice, the courts were entitled to punish the editor of the *Independent* by way of a criminal action for contempt of court on the grounds that by publishing Wright's allegations he had destroyed the confidential nature of information that another court had injuncted the *Observer* from publishing pending the trial of the Government's claim to exclusive possession of this information. It was, said the Court of Appeal, as if the Government and the *Observer* had commenced a legal action over the ownership of a racehorse, and the court had ordered the horse to be kept alive until the dispute over its possession could be resolved after a full trial. The editor of the *Independent* had shot the horse prior to that full trial, and thereby rendered the proceedings pointless. The Attorney-General, in his role as guardian of the administration of justice, was entitled to seek to commit the *Independent* editor to prison for intentionally aborting legal proceedings in which, quite coincidentally, the Attorney-General happened to be a party.

There can be no objection to the principle that courts should have power to protect judicial proceedings from third parties who deliberately set out to prejudice or subvert them. Where the argument in the *Newspaper Publishing plc* case becomes metaphysical is in assimilating Wright's allegations (that MI5 plotted to assassinate Nasser, bug foreign embassies and destabilize the Wilson Government) to items of physical property like ice-cubes and racehorses. Information of this kind is not 'subject-matter' which can be possessed exclusively by a department of state, any more than a conspiracy to murder is the exclusive property of the conspirators. The 'subject-matter' of an action for breach of confidence is not the information itself, but the confidential relationship in the course of which it was acquired. In fact, the *Independent*'s publication did not abort the proceedings in the case against the *Observer*: they continued to trial and appeal, irrespective of the fact that over a million copies of *Spycatcher* had been published throughout the world and many copies had been imported into Britain. The ice-cube had by this stage been transformed into a flood of dirty water, but what was at stake in the litigation was the question of whether the *Observer* had become party to Wright's breach of his duty owed to the Crown by publishing his allegations. The *Independent* did not frustrate the administration of justice in that case by further publishing Wright's allegations, although by so doing it may well have become a party to his breach of confidence. The *Independent* should have been sued for breach of confidence, and not prosecuted for the crime of contempt.

None the less, *Attorney-General* v. *Newspaper Publishing plc* stands for the proposition that it can be a crime for one newspaper to breach the spirit of an injunction imposed upon another, despite the fact that it has had no opportunity to present a case against the imposition of any restraint. It must go cap in hand to the court and

335

ask for permission to publish. This was the course taken by Derbyshire County Council to request permission for its local library to stock a copy of *Spycatcher*. Although numerous copies of the book had by this time been imported into the country, and were being sold by enthusiastic entrepreneurs at inflated prices, the High Court followed the *Newspaper Publishing plc* case and held that the book's availability in a public library would 'constitute an interference with the due administration of justice' in the ongoing cases against the *Guardian* and the *Observer*.[40] This decision shows just how far the contempt/confidentiality doctrine has moved in the direction of prior restraint: had the Council simply ordered a copy of the book pursuant to its duty to provide a comprehensive and efficient library service, it is doubtful whether it would have been charged with intentional contempt. This crime is only committed by those who specifically intend to impede or prejudice the administration of justice, and even recklessness as to whether such prejudice may be caused is insufficient to ground a conviction. For this reason, individuals and bookshops who sold a handful of imported copies of *Spycatcher* were not prosecuted for contempt.

It must be remembered that the *Newspaper Publishing plc* case was a decision on a theoretical point of law – and not an actual finding of guilt against the *Independent*. Its editor hoped to exculpate himself from contempt charges by claiming that his intention was not to prejudice existing legal actions against others but rather to fulfil a public duty by placing important facts in the public domain. There is, however, no public-interest defence against 'intentional contempt', and all the prosecution has to prove is foresight of some risk, not of 'substantial risk of serious prejudice'. The editor is not permitted trial by jury, and if convicted is liable to up to two years' imprisonment and unlimited fines. So, when the *Independent* editor returned from losing his legal argument in the House of Lords, the trial judge had no difficulty in finding that he 'intended' to interfere with the administration of justice, although he did not desire to do so. The newspaper was fined £50,000 for its contempt, and other newspapers which had jumped on the *Independent*'s banned wagon were fined similar amounts. (The Government's rejoicing at recouping a fraction of the taxpayers' money it had squandered on *Spycatcher*-related actions was short-lived: the Court of Appeal quashed the fine, but not the conviction, on the grounds that the law had been hopelessly unclear at the time the *Independent* decided to publish.) Should a similar situation recur, many newspapers will choose, like Derbyshire County Council, to apply to the court for guidance as to whether they can properly publish material which has been made the subject of an injunction in some other action – a procedure calculated to give High Court judges a good deal of experience in editing newspapers.

MURMURING JUDGES

One form of contempt which should have been abolished by the 1981 reforms is the arcane crime of 'scandalizing the court' by criticizing the judiciary (in Scotland, the offence goes by the delightful name of 'murmuring judges'). It was deployed in the eighteenth century against radicals like John Wilkes, and was revived in 1900 to punish the editor of the *Birmingham Daily Argus* for describing Mr Justice Darling, not inaccurately, as 'an impudent little man in horse-hair' who was 'a microcosm of conceit and empty-headedness'.[41] In 1930 the *Daily Worker* was fined for describing a conservative judge as 'a bewigged puppet exhibiting a strong class bias', but there have been no successful prosecutions in Britain since then. Some of the credit for this restraint must be accorded to Quintin Hogg, MP (later Lord Chancellor Hailsham), who was privately prosecuted for contempt in 1968 over an article he had written in *Punch* which was severely and inaccurately critical of the Court of Appeal. That Court declined to regard itself as scandalized, ruling that no criticism of a judgement, however vigorous, could amount to contempt if it was made in good faith and with reasonable courtesy.[42]

The bounds of reasonable courtesy may well have been exceeded by the *Daily Mirror* in 1987, when it published upside-down photographs of the Law Lords who had injuncted *Spycatcher* under the banner headline 'YOU FOOLS!' No prosecution was forthcoming. The danger, however, of leaving such a crime on the books is well illustrated by recent contempt prosecutions in other countries which have inherited the common law, where robust condemnation of court decisions (Trinidad), suggestion that a decision was influenced by trade-union demonstrations (Australia) and justifiable

The danger of [st]/having a crime of 'scandalizing the court'

337

criticism of the conduct of proceedings against an opposition MP (Singapore) have all been treated as contempt. This crime has been declared unconstitutional in the United States, and is difficult to reconcile with Article 10 of the European Convention. The most detailed and recent analysis of the English law has been in the courts of Canada, where the crime of 'scandalization' has been ruled incompatible with the 'freedom of expression' guarantee in that country's Charter of Rights and Freedoms.[43] It may be that the British press has itself to blame for Parliament's refusal to abolish this head of contempt. During the 1981 reforms, an amendment to this effect was rejected, after Lord Hailsham recalled a recent incident which had arisen after the Court of Appeal denied a divorce to a woman who claimed that her husband was unreasonable in having sex with her only once a week. A journalist from the Fleet Street gutter telephoned the wives of the three appellate judges to ask how often a week they regarded as reasonable. The offence of scandalizing the court, said the Lord Chancellor, was still required to deal with such conduct.

The British press was responsible for Parliament's refusal to abolish the crime of scandalizing the court

CHAPTER 8

Fair Trial

Trial by jury is revered by radicals and reactionaries alike. It is seen as the bastion of liberty, 'the lamp which shows that freedom lives'.[1] Freedom, of course, is alive and well in most European countries, which have long abandoned the jury in favour of trial by professional judges, often sitting with lay or expert assessors. Yet for Britain and its traditional cultural allies – the USA, Canada, Australia and the West Indies – it remains the basic institution upon which we pin our faith for fairness of trial. Ironically, the jury has won its laurels in the rhetoric of liberty because of its ability to acquit the guilty – to nullify laws which are unpopular or prosecutions which are perceived as oppressive. The jury, it is said on high authority, may 'do justice', whereas a judge, obliged to follow the letter of the law, has no such discretion. In this chapter, the jury's constitutional role as a check on executive power to prosecute will be considered, together with some of the more recent Government efforts to avoid legal confrontations with the 'gang of twelve'.

The central irony in our reverence for jury trial is that it is the lynch-pin of an adversarial system of criminal justice which has palpably failed to do justice in a number of very serious cases exposed in the early 1990s. The Birmingham Six, the Guildford Four, the Maguire Seven and Judith Ward suffered many years of imprisonment for crimes they did not commit, as have less-well-known defendants wrongfully convicted of murders, robberies and sexual offences. These scandals were with hindsight variously blamed on perjurious policemen, deceitful scientists, unfair prosecutors and biased judges, but whatever their immediate causes the fact remains that the adversarial system failed to compensate for them: far from being foolproof, the jurors at these trials allowed themselves to be fooled. There is no reason to believe that an inquisitorial system

339

would have achieved better results: such systems tend to give even more credence to the conclusions of policemen, scientists, lawyers and judges. The adversarial process, which permits ordinary members of the public to judge whether a defendant, provided through legal aid with the skills of a solicitor and a barrister, has raised a reasonable doubt about the police conclusion as to guilt, simply failed to detect doubts which were verified years later through advanced scientific analysis of police notebooks and revelations from documents undisclosed at the original trial. The jury system is precious, but it never will be perfect: there is an urgent need to establish a 'court of last resort' with the resources to investigate and rectify miscarriages of justice long before the unconscionable seventeen years spent in prison by Judith Ward and the Birmingham Six. Failure to make these urgent reforms will not only mean a continuing risk of wrongful convictions, but a new danger of wrongful acquittals. It is important to realize that the state of public confidence towards 'the case for the prosecution' is reflected in the attitudes of members of the public called for jury service: a profound scepticism towards prosecutions will be reflected in verdicts which find 'reasonable doubts' in cases which are truly watertight. This is the real damage that miscarriages of justice do, by diminishing the public confidence which is essential if the system is to perform its fundamental task of convicting those proven to be guilty.

The Royal Commission on Criminal Justice, chaired by Lord Runciman, emphasized the need to restore public confidence when it finally reported in 1993. It made wise recommendations for improving the rights of suspects and minimizing the danger of false confessions (see Chapter 1), but its suggestions for changes in trial practice were less astute. Some of them would actually increase the risk of convicting the innocent – by, for example, abolishing committal proceedings (where weak prosecutions can be identified and aborted); encouraging 'plea bargaining'; cutting back the duties of disclosure on the Crown (notwithstanding that inadequate disclosure has proved to be a prime cause of error); and removing many cases from trial by jury to trial in magistrates courts, where they will receive cheaper but less careful scrutiny and a higher conviction rate. These unattractive features of the Runciman Report may be the result of a familiar tendency of the Royal Commissions to come up with a 'package deal' with concessions to all interested parties:

the danger of this approach is that most parties will be unhappy with the compromise. Criticism of the proposal to limit the right to jury trial overshadowed analysis of the Report when it was published, and detracted from the urgency of adopting its main recommendation for the establishment of a Criminal Cases Review Authority, independent of both the courts of the Home Office, empowered to investigate controversial convictions and to refer them back to the Court of Appeal as soon as real doubt has been established. This reform is essential if we are to provide a remedy, albeit belated, for innocent victims of our adversarial system of justice, although it will not help to minimize their numbers. It is a modest advance to provide a remedy for miscarriages after they have taken place, preferably before the victim has completed the prison sentence: it is more important to advance further, by adopting a set of rules which reduce the risk of justice miscarrying in the first place.

THE OPEN JUSTICE PRINCIPLE

The most fundamental principle of justice is that it must be seen to be done. Lord Halsbury, in the great constitutional case of *Scott* v. *Scott*, proclaimed that 'Every court in the land is open to every subject of the King.'[2] The rule became established almost by historical accident from the fact that courts in the Middle Ages were badly conducted public meetings in which neighbours gathered to pass judgement on their district's notorious felons. The Star Chamber followed the practice and heard all its cases in public, in order that its vicious punishments would have a general deterrent effect. In time, jurists like Blackstone and Bentham elevated the practice into a fundamental precondition of justice. They acclaimed it on a number of grounds, principally as a safeguard against judicial error or misbehaviour. In Bentham's words, 'Publicity is the very soul of justice. It is the keenest spur to exertion and the surest of all guards against improbity. It keeps the judge himself, while trying, under trial.' Moreover publicity deters perjury, in that witnesses are likely to come forward to confound lies when they learn that they are being told. Press reporting of court cases enhances public knowledge and appreciation of the workings of the law, it assists the deterrent function of criminal trials and it permits the revelation of matters of genuine public interest. Indeed, the very first newspapers were 'chapbooks' consisting entirely of reports of Old Bailey trials, hawked in the streets of seventeenth-century London for a penny a piece. The advantage of the open-justice principle to the press, of course, is that contemporaneous reports of what is said in court are absolutely privileged from any action for defamation – the court-room is the only place outside Parliament where an Englishman may cry '*J'accuse*' and be utterly safe from a libel action.

The open-justice principle is now found in many constitutions and Bills of Rights, including the European Convention. In Britain, its somewhat insecure legal basis is the 1913 House of Lords decision in *Scott* v. *Scott*, which confirmed the general rule that courts must be open to press and public unless statute specially provided that they must or might be closed. To this 'general rule', alas, several of the Law Lords grafted an exception: the court could sit in secret if justice could not be done at all if it were done openly. They had in mind cases involving young children and litigation about secret processes, but like most exceptions to legal rules there has been much ingenuity expended upon extending them. Parties and wit-nesses – especially in criminal cases – will frequently be embarrassed by press reports of their misconduct, and their lawyers sometimes convince judges (and, more often, lay-justices) that justice cannot be done unless names or addresses are withheld or portions of evidence suppressed. Thus reporting restrictions have been imposed to protect police informers from reprisals, to encourage witnesses to testify, to avoid publication of extravagant allegations, and even on occasions where a court has thought that publicity would be too harsh a penalty for a minor offence. These claims are usually spurious – all the Law Lords in *Scott* v. *Scott* made it clear that considerations of humiliation or embarrassment should never be a ground for suppress-ing reports or closing the court.

The Divisional Court has disapproved of some attempts at secrecy, ranging from withholding the name of a witness from a celebrated family lest publicity interfere with her treatment for drug addiction,[3] to suppressing the address of a former Tory MP who feared that his ex-wife would read it and harass him.[4] Section 11 of the Contempt of Court Act allows courts to order that names or other matter may not be mentioned in open court or published in the press, but only when such orders are justified by statute (such as the law which prevents the naming of rape victims) or by the *Scott* v. *Scott* exception for circumstances where justice could not otherwise be done. This exception has been too widely interpreted: it relates to the doing of justice in the case itself, rather than any unfortunate consequences which might attend publication of the details of the court action. In 1991 the High Court rightly quashed a secrecy order imposed by magistrates because a restaurant owner feared that publicity given to allegations that he had violated health standards would reduce custom, yet the Court of Appeal allowed some of the proceedings against the Polly Peck company to be heard in private, because investor confidence in a financial institution might be damaged by unproven allegations. The civil and the criminal legal process invariably involves the making of accusations which damage reputations and trade: the answer is not to hear them in private, but to hear them with sufficient speed and efficiency to expose those which are false, and thus minimize the damage. Until 1988 no remedy existed against gag orders imposed by crown court judges. In 1987 the European Commission of Human Rights ruled, after applications from Channel 4 Television and Old Bailey reporter Tim Crook, that this absence of legal remedy against court-ordered interference with freedom of expression was a breach of the Convention.[5] The United Kingdom Government settled these cases by legislating to allow the media to challenge crown court secrecy orders by making a special and urgent application to the Court of Appeal.

Temptations to secrecy are difficult for courts to resist at a time when the popular press is distrusted and the open-justice principle is not embedded in a written constitution. In the 1980s this gap emboldened a number of magistrates' courts to adopt a policy of anonymity, refusing to divulge to reporters the identity of JPs sitting on any particular case. The *Observer* newspaper and its chief reporter, David Leigh, successfully challenged this policy in the Divisional Court, which condemned it as inimical to the administration of justice and an unlawful obstruction to the right to know who sits in judgement.[6] This was a significant case because Britain has no constitutional provision requiring open justice, and the magistrates argued that there was no law which required their clerks to cooperate with the media. The Divisional Court was prepared to acknowledge 'open justice' as a basic principle of the unwritten constitution, and to recognize that it implied a right to know the identity of all who sit in judgement, and to make an order which would prevent that right from being circumvented by procedural arrangements. Those who distrust judges to apply the provisions of a Bill of Rights should study *Leigh* v. *Felixstowe Justices* as an example of how judges can develop a constitutional principle to protect the public against officious and unjustifiable encroachments. 'There is no such person known to the law as the anonymous JP' the Court concluded. Court reporters were the 'watchdogs of justice', and were entitled to know the identity of those over whom they watched.

There are, however, a number of areas where secrecy is quite sensibly imposed by law in order to avoid prejudice to the outcome of a trial. Details of committal proceedings, for example, cannot normally be reported until the case is over, lest publicity be given to evidence which is subsequently ruled inadmissible. Nor can legal arguments heard in the absence of the jury, which frequently involve discussion of evidence which is deemed too irrelevant or prejudicial for them to hear in court, let alone read about in the press. Parliament has decided that the peculiar problems of rape cases justify anonymity for victims, in order to mitigate their humiliation and encourage other victims to come forward, and the same consideration is frequently extended to victims of blackmail. Trials under the Official Secrets Act may also be partly heard in camera. There are special statutory protections for juveniles charged with crime: the press may attend their trials and report the evidence, but without identifying the children involved. The sordid details of divorce proceedings, once the stock-in-trade of popular newspapers, are now published only rarely: undefended divorces, and maintenance and custody proceedings, are heard 'in chambers' – in a judge's room to which reporters are not permitted entry.

These exceptions may be reasonable, but there are many aspects of British justice which are unnecessarily hidden from public scrutiny by the 'in chambers' proceedings which form a large part of the work of the High Court. In 1987, two senior Family Division judges severely criticized the automatic exclusion of the press from chambers hearings involving important issues of sorting out property and income in divorce proceedings. The absence of press and law reporters was said to have led to 'lax and sloppy advocacy' and poor conduct of cases: Mrs Justice Booth admitted that 'Everything is in danger of becoming too cosy and too informal and we are forgetting that we are lawyers. We do not have the press or the public or even members of our own profession there to keep us up to the mark'[7] – an echo of Bentham's point that publicity 'keeps the judge himself, while trying, under trial'. A more extraordinary anomaly is provided by the routine practice of the Queen's Bench Division of the High Court to hear applications for injunctions or eviction orders in chambers, whilst its Chancery Division hears such applications in open court. Since there is a good deal of overlap in jurisdiction, plaintiffs may opt for secrecy by bringing their actions in one Division rather than the other. In 1987, when the Government embarked upon its court-room crusade to stop the media from publishing interviews with former security-service personnel, its first actions against the press were commenced in the Chancery Division and were fully reported. By the end of the year, when it sought an injunction against the BBC in relation to the programme *My Country Right or Wrong* it chose the Queen's Bench Division, where its arguments were heard in secret.

There is no sensible basis for this distinction, and no reason why the open-justice principle should not apply to applications, which may be of great public interest, made to Queen's Bench judges. (The anomaly is made more glaring by the fact that any appeal against a decision in chambers is heard in open court.) Nor is there any justification for recent regulations which require bail applications and similar matters at crown courts (but not in magistrates' courts) to be heard in chambers. If there is any danger that the press will publish prejudicial matter, the court can invoke Section 4(2) of the Contempt of Court Act, which requires such reports to be postponed until after the conclusion of the trial.

In short, Britain does not live up to the open-justice principle which has been its most enduring contribution to the law of other nations. Secrecy in some divisions of the High Court, and in pre-trial proceedings in crown courts, has become routine. In criminal trials, advocates are allowed to make secrecy applications in secret, and so the public may never know whether bogus reasons are being advanced or, more importantly, whether bogus reasons are being accepted in order to close the court doors. Orders 'postponing' reporting of parts of criminal trials are granted far too readily:

while it is right that matters which are likely to prejudice a jury should not be reported until the trial has ended, many legal arguments (which are routinely 'postponed') are not likely to have this effect and can be of considerable public interest. The practical effect of a 'postponement' order is to empty the press benches, because the news will be stale by the time it becomes reportable. At the Matrix Churchill trial in 1992, all reporting relating to the Public Interest Immunity certificates was postponed, and the public was not permitted to know anything about the attempts by ministers to withhold evidence of Government policy towards arms sales to Iraq until after the trial collapsed. The press had not bothered to attend the legal arguments, and could not inform the public debate which followed until transcripts were obtained some months later.

Press reporting can, at times, be shallow, sensational or just plain incompetent. Courts have some corrective powers and can usually protect parties from any prejudice. A more persuasive objection to entrenching the right to report is the desire to protect witnesses against loss of face or loss of job, or even, where police informers are concerned, against possible loss of life. Does it really matter if a few cases go unreported so that prosecution witnesses are relieved from the anxiety of reading their names in newspapers? It does, for the reasons given by Blackstone and Bentham. Trials derive their legitimacy from being conducted in public; the judge presides as a surrogate for the people who are entitled to see and approve the power exercised on their behalf. Those who assist the prosecution can and should be protected by other means. No matter how fair, justice must still be seen before it can be said to have been done.

But how far should the open-justice principle stretch? If every court in the land is open to every subject of the King, does it not logically follow that subjects should be entitled, quite literally, to see justice done through the medium of television? That conclusion has been reached in many American states, which permit radio and television broadcasts from their court-rooms. Bar associations, initially hostile, report some good results: the lawyers are better prepared, the judges better behaved, and the public better informed. In Britain, the Criminal Bar Association is in favour of some television coverage. The communications revolution can bring benefits to justice, and we are beginning to accept the advantages of videotaped testimony of child witnesses and the possibility of cross-examining overseas witnesses via satellite link-up. Appeal courts would be better able to evaluate the testimony of trial witnesses if they could see and hear it being delivered, and most barristers have had occasions to regret that they could not include in grounds of appeal against judges' summings-up some reference to prejudicial tones of voice or body language which are not apparent from a typed transcript.

If the public is entitled to see justice done, it is entitled to see it done on television, the main and the most accurate medium for the communication of news and information about public events. Court cases at all levels are of genuine public interest, yet their evidence and their atmosphere is not accurately or adequately conveyed in newsprint, nor by the present television expedient of breathless reporters pictured outside the court quoting snatches of evidence, followed by a distorted 'artist's impression' of the scene inside the court. Experiments suggest that proceedings are not disrupted by a discreetly placed television camera, and nor are witnesses disquietened, deterred or flustered. Television coverage discourages time wasting and irrelevance, and enables the public to make up its own mind about the testimony.[8] The arguments against televising the courts are similar to those deployed until very recently against televising Parliament: nobody now suggests they had any substance in the latter case. They can have no substance at all in relation to televising or permitting radio coverage of the legal arguments heard in appeal courts, or the proceedings of public tribunals. There is some concern that coverage of 'the day's play' in sensational Old Bailey trials will feature heavily edited 'highlights' chosen for entertainment value rather than as fair and accurate reporting, but this can be dealt with by carefully drawn rules and by proper supervision. No coverage, for example, could be permitted which might identify jurors, or witnesses who are protected by existing anonymity rules (such as children and alleged victims of rape and blackmail). Television coverage of the courts requires careful and gradual introduction, but introduction none the less if England is to take its 'open justice' principle seriously. Scotland does: television was permitted in some courts for the first time in 1993.

For the present, we must be content with 'dramatic re-enactments'. Channel 4 has pioneered this device, albeit with some difficulty. In 1985 it launched a late-night 'court report' in which actors were to re-create the day's proceedings in the official secrets trial of Clive Ponting. The trial judge insisted that they should be replaced by newsreaders, which may have made the programme more boring, but it was none the less watched by half a million people at 11.30 p.m. each evening. In 1987 the Court of Appeal ordered a ninety-minute reconstruction of the first Birmingham Six reference-back appeal to be postponed until after the Court's decision: it did not view the programme, but feared that it might 'undermine public confidence in the Court's judgement' if it fostered expectations that the judgement did not fulfil. (What did undermine public confidence in the Court's judgement was the fact that it resoundingly rejected the appeal of men the wrongfulness of whose convictions was finally established three years later.) What the Court overlooked was the simple fact that citizens who watched a careful ninety-minute reconstruction of the evidence would be better informed about the serious issues involved in the appeal than by reading the desultory and disjointed newspaper reports which had trickled out during the six-week hearing. In 1991 the BBC finally plucked up the courage to produce a dramatized re-enactment of the *Oz* trial, on the twentieth anniversary of that extraordinary event. They had rejected the idea in 1971, when the case was attracting more letters to *The Times* than had the Suez crisis, and would have produced many more had the public been allowed to see what had really gone on.

Justice is not, as a great judge once remarked, a cloistered virtue. It must suffer the scrutiny of an informed public, because it is on the goodwill of that public that it depends for respect and support. The serious miscarriages of justice which were exposed in the 1990s damaged that respect, which can only be retrieved by proof that those charged with operating the system are in fact operating it fairly and responsibly. Nobody involved in the justice system in 1993 could doubt that serious attempts were being made to address past failings, but the capacity to restore public confidence in the system will depend in part on whether the public is permitted to see the results.

TRIAL BY JURY

If Britain had a written constitution, its most predictable clause would provide that no citizen should be liable to lose his or her liberty for longer than a year without at least the opportunity of submitting to trial by jury. With the exception of the crime of contempt (which has a two-year maximum sentence, and is triable by judges alone) this reflects the actual position today. The jury system is too deeply entrenched to be directly supplanted, however much senior police officers may despair of its propensity for acquitting one in four defendants who contest their charges in crown courts. Undermining the defendant's right to trial by jury can take more subtle forms than outright abolition, however: there has been a steady increase in offences which are triable only by magistrates; 'jury vetting' has been instituted for official secrets and terrorist cases; civil injunctions, backed by contempt powers, are preferred to politically controversial jury trials; and in 1989 the defendant's right to challenge up to three members of the jury panel was abolished. The Runciman Report leaves little doubt that further restrictions on the right to jury trial will be attempted in years to come, in order to reduce the public expense of criminal justice and in an attempt to boost conviction rates. The only satisfactory way to boost conviction rates, of course, is to bring fewer flawed prosecutions and to take steps to avoid those scandalous miscarriages of justice which are prone to make juries think twice about convicting anyone on apparently unassailable police evidence.

Jury trial is a unique British institution. It was hit upon by happy accident over seven hundred years ago, to replace trials by the ordeal of fire or water, in which guilt or innocence was decided by ritual tests overseen by parish priests. Divine providence was getting a bad name from priests who accepted bribes to rig the trials – by choosing shallow ponds, or making sure that water did not boil – so in 1215 the Pope refused to allow them to participate, and the system collapsed. It was replaced by the procedure which Henry II had instituted to resolve land disputes: a group of worthy citizens from the district, summoned by a judge to decide between rival claimants on the basis of their knowledge of local history and customs. In criminal cases their verdict, delivered after solemn conclave, was endowed with some of the ritual and sanctity which had attended 'the ordeal' before it fell into disrepute. Some centuries passed before juries won the right to stand out against the prejudices and partiality of the King's judges – they could be starved into submission by being locked up without food or fire until they returned a 'guilty' verdict, and the Star Chamber went so far as to punish jurymen who refused judicial invitations to convict by seizing their lands and goods. The turning-point came in 1670, when twelve courageous jurors at the Old Bailey refused to convict two Quakers, William Penn and William Mead, of holding a seditious assembly. They were locked up for two nights without food or water or even a chamber-pot. When they nevertheless insisted upon a verdict 'according to conscience' of 'not guilty', the Recorder of London sentenced them to prison. Four of them, led by Edward Bushell, challenged the legality of their punishment by a writ of *habeas corpus*. The Lord Chief Justice, Sir Robert Vaughan, decided that a jury was entitled to act according to its own conscience and appreciation of the evidence, irrespective of judicial direction or expectation.[9] *Bushell's Case* is the foundation of the constitutional independence of the jury: it can do justice, whatever the law may be.

Since jurors all swear solemn oaths to 'give true verdict according to the evidence', how can an acquittal in the face of overwhelming evidence of guilt be morally or logically justified? The answer was given, most reluctantly, by Lord Mansfield at the sedition trial of the Dean of St Asaph in 1784, 'the most important case in English law not to be discussed in the textbooks'.[10] The jury, he said, has in its verdict the duty of 'blending law and fact', a process in which they might follow 'the prejudices of their affections or passions'. The judge could tell them how to do right, but they had it in their power to do wrong, 'which is a matter entirely between God and their own consciences'. Although crown court judges today invariably direct their juries that they must accept the law as they declare it ('there is a Court of Appeal which can put me right'), this direction is not constitutionally correct: juries have never been required to swear to follow the law as laid down by the judge. On this difficult, but precious, distinction rests the power of an English jury to take the law into its own hands.

This independence remains the most remarkable feature of the modern jury, and an important safeguard against oppressive prosecutions. It means that an ordinary, everyday sense of mercy is built into our criminal-justice arrangements, in a way which defies strict logic but has won popular acceptance. Throughout the brutal period of the late eighteenth and early nineteenth century, when the death penalty was visited on all who stole goods valued at more than forty shillings, juries consistently undervalued property so as to enable petty thieves to escape the gallows. Recent studies estimate that some 14 per cent of acquittals are 'sympathy verdicts', where the jury strives to find a reasonable doubt because it believes, with good cause, that the defendant has been the victim of oppressive police behaviour or has in any event suffered enough.[11] The rule in *Bushell's Case*, by enabling the jury to temper the legal wind to the shorn lamb, has had important implications in politically motivated prosecutions brought under vague or unpopular laws. The jury most noticeably lit 'the lamp which shows that freedom lives' by ignoring judicial directions to convict radicals charged with publishing seditious attacks on George III and his ministers. In 1985, the Old Bailey jury which refused to convict Clive Ponting, a civil servant who had clearly breached Section 2 of the Official Secrets Act by supplying classified information to an MP, was duly celebrated in many quarters for upholding the traditions of the 'gang of twelve'. So was the jury which in 1991 acquitted the pacifists Michael Randle and Patrick Pottle of freeing the traitor George Blake in 1966 – despite the fact that they had written a book entitled *How We Freed George Blake – and Why*. The jury were evidently impressed by their reasons (moral outrage at the unconscionable length of Blake's forty-two-year sentence) and unimpressed by a prosecution, brought after the baying of back-bench MPs, which sought to put them in prison for a crime committed a quarter of a century previously. In America, Penn and Mead had their counterpart in Peter Zenger, a New York printer whose colonial jury refused to convict him for publishing anti-British sedition just before the Revolution. In some states in the USA, judges even remind jurors of their constitutional right to nullify unpopular laws by acquitting defendants.[12] In Britain, this right is celebrated in theory but regarded as subversive in practice: it is not allowed to be mentioned in court. This secrecy may explain why some unpopular prosecutions do succeed, such as that in 1992 of the distinguished hospital consultant Dr Cox who shortened the life of a terminally ill and pain-racked patient at her own and her family's request. The Winchester jurors were in tears when they returned a verdict which would probably not have been reached at the Old Bailey, where a gold plaque recounting the story of the jury which refused to convict Penn and Mead tends to inspire modern jurors with the spirit of the men who went to prison to establish their right to bring humanity and compassion to the harsh letter of the law.

The other feature which contributes to the esteem in which the modern jury is held is that it is drawn at random from a representative cross-section of society. This is not a historical survival, but a very recent adaptation of the system to satisfy democratic ideals. Before 1972, juries were mainly 'male, middle-aged, middle-minded and middle class' – because only those who owned property could serve upon them. But in that year Parliament accepted the recommendation of the Morris Committee that almost all who were entitled to vote should be eligible for jury service.[13] Then the modern jury – the very modern jury – became, in Lord Simon's words, 'a microcosm of democratic society'. It was an important change of principle, from the idea that only sound citizens with a proprietary stake in society were fit and proper persons to pass upon questions of guilt or innocence, to the principle that every class – the dispossessed, young people, members of minority groups – should be available for selection. Since 1972 the jury has become, truly, the people's court.

The right to jury trial

There has been some erosion of the right to jury trial in recent years, by the simple expedient of making certain criminal offences triable only by magistrates. The state forgoes the prospect of a heavy prison sentence in return for a cheap and speedy trial and a better chance of conviction. The most commonly deployed public-order offences, such as obstruction of the highway and the use of threatening or abusive or insulting language and the new crimes of disorderly conduct and disobedience to police bans or restrictions on demonstrations, do not carry the right to jury trial. It is ironical that were the Quakers Penn and Mead to return today to hold their meeting in Gracechurch Street in the City of London, they would be brought before a stipendiary at Tower Bridge Magistrates' Court rather than Edward Bushell's 'gang of twelve' at the Old Bailey. Cases of assaulting police carry no right of jury trial, although conviction is a serious matter which often occasions a prison sentence. Crimes which can severely affect personal reputation, such as kerb-crawling and homosexual soliciting, have carefully been made triable only by magistrates, and forfeiture proceedings against books and magazines and videos are regularly used to destroy 'obscene' material which might well be acquitted by juries. The notable thing about many of these offences is that they generally involve contests between the evidence of the police and the evidence of the defendant – contests which cry out for jury adjudication. Often, too, they raise questions of civil liberty or morality which are better decided by a tribunal which is in touch with ordinary and contemporary standards than by lay justices drawn from an unrepresentative class base.

Another method of evading the right to jury trial is to give prosecuting authorities the discretion to decide whether to proceed against defendants in a way which permits them to elect trial before a jury in the crown court. In the case of an allegation of criminal damage, for example, this right of election is reserved to defendants charged with damage exceeding £2,000. Police now have High Court approval to select from amongst damaged property only items which total less than £2,000, and so remove the defendant's right to elect.[14] In public-order cases, they may pick and choose those charges which are triable only by magistrates – a common tactic at Greenham Common and in the wake of the miners' strike (when magistrates generally convicted, while juries usually rejected more serious allegations of riot and unlawful assembly). It would, in principle, be preferable that all cases carrying a substantial risk of imprisonment or involving a value-judgement about community standards should be capable of trial by jury, but the pressures of cost and convenience are hostile to such a reform. It is difficult enough to hold the line against powerful lobbies in favour of abolishing jury trial for simple theft charges where the goods are valued at less than £50 – a reform which a Labour Government attempted to institute in 1979. It would have covered precisely those shoplifting cases which have the capacity for destroying hitherto unblemished reputations. We are in grave danger of reserving the 'palladium of liberty' for occasions involving the liberty of persons charged with bank robberies and burglaries, rather than the occasions which are most likely to threaten the character and careers of ordinary citizens.

This danger became acute with the Runciman Report recommendation that the right to claim trial by jury should be withdrawn from 35,000 of the 100,000 defendants who currently exercise it each year when asked by magistrates whether they elect to have their cases tried by them, or by a jury at the crown court.[15] Although serious crimes must be tried by a jury, and most minor offences must be tried by magistrates, many offences of moderate seriousness which may destroy a defendant's career if convicted (such as theft, obtaining by deception and handling stolen goods) fall within the category of offences which may be tried by either system. Instead of allowing the defendant to choose, Runciman would require the magistrates to decide: an invidious question, on which they would obviously be biased, since what they would be asked to decide is whether they (or their magisterial ilk) can do justice as effectively as a judge and jury. They certainly do it more cheaply, and more prosecution-mindedly (Runciman's statistics show that magistrates convict in almost twice as many of these 'either-way' cases as do juries). What is so objectionable about this Runciman recommendation is that no sensible reason (other than savings in cost) is offered for destruction of this valued right. The Commission falls back on a complacent act of faith – 'magistrates should be trusted to try cases fairly' – without any appreciation of the drawbacks of lay justice (see later, page 362). It notes the phenomenon of the 'cracked trial', whereby most of those who elect for jury trial in fact plead guilty before a jury is ever empanelled to try them, but fails to draw the obvious conclusion that this is because the justice system works more effectively at the crown court level than in the 'police court' atmosphere which still prevails in many magistrates' courts. It is in the interests of the public, and of most defendants charged with 'either-way' offences, that they should be dealt with speedily and sensibly by magistrates: the way forward is not to abolish their right to obtain what is at present a better class of justice, but rather to improve the standards in magistrates courts so that they can begin to compete with crown courts in the eyes of defendants and in the experience of the lawyers who advise them.

Jury challenges

A more direct attack on a traditional right associated with jury trial was made in 1989, when the defence right to challenge was abolished. It had been reduced from twenty (in serious cases of murder or treason) to seven in 1948, and further reduced to three per defendant in 1977. It was the only mechanism available to assist the defence in obtaining a representative jury: the first twelve 'called to the book to be sworn' may be wholly unbalanced in terms of sex or age or class or race, and the availability of challenges offered some prospect of readjustment. In the great majority of cases, no challenge was offered to the panel. But where a black defendant was arraigned before twelve white jurors, or a young woman before twelve middle-aged men, the exercise of the challenge could secure a 'peer' or two amongst the decision-takers.

There is, of course, no art to find the mind's construction in the face, but there are a number of cases where brief visual inspection will indicate a juror's unsuitability to participate in a particular trial. A juror who evinces fear or hatred of the defendant before taking the oath, who appears disruptive or uncomfortable, or mentally unbalanced or half-drunk, or who smiles encouragingly at the police or who seems to be wearing a badge or carrying a publication which indicates possible partisanship in relation to the facts of the case, or gives every indication of being likely to react over-emotionally to the nature of the evidence – all give grounds for genuine apprehension about ability to judge calmly and dispassionately. Such apprehensions on the part of defendants and their counsel may well be misplaced, but a system which boasts that justice must be seen to be done was right to provide some mechanism for dispelling them. At the very least, it could be said that no defendant was obliged to be tried by someone whose face he did not like.

The impetus for abolition came in a particularly unattractive way, from back-bench Tory MPs enraged at the acquittal of a number of young servicemen who had been accused of leaking secrets about a GCHQ base in Cyprus to enemy agents. A number of the original panel had been challenged and replaced by younger jurors, and the Government yielded to demands that the 'retirement age' for jury service be increased from sixty-five to seventy and that the defence right to challenge without cause be entirely abolished. This was an irrational response to the Cyprus case, in which any jury would have been influenced by the brutal methods of interrogation used by RAF police which were subsequently condemned by an official inquiry. The notion that a jury panel which has been subject to defence challenges is more likely to acquit had been exploded in 1986 by a study conducted by the Crown Prosecution Service, which demonstrated that conviction rates in court cases where jurors had been challenged were identical to those in trials where they had not. But Government MPs were not interested in facts, and the myth that the right to challenge was being 'abused' to obtain dim-witted jurors likely to be hoodwinked by clever advocacy carried the day. As it happens, jury studies show that intelligent jurors are much more likely to find 'reasonable doubts' about the logic of the prosecution case, and there is some reason to believe that older jurors are more resistant to judicial direction than persons under thirty.

It was otiose to make the right of challenge the scapegoat for inconvenient acquittals, which on closer examination will generally be shown to be justified by some reasonable doubt arising from the evidence or from some justifiable doubts about the conduct of officials. At the Old Bailey in the first month after abolition of the right to challenge, defence counsel unavailingly protested that a black youth was to be judged by a panel of twelve white jurors and that the question of whether the display of earrings made from foetuses was 'an outrage to public decency' was to be decided by a panel ten of whose members were women. In 1989 the Court of Appeal ruled that judges are powerless to order a fresh and more balanced jury panel, no matter how important it is to achieve a racial or sexual balance in order that justice may be seen to be done.[16] One reform which is plainly necessary is to give judges by statute this very power, which some had been prepared to exercise in the interests of justice until the Court of Appeal unhelpfully decided they did not have it at common law. The Runciman Commission recommended this, although only in cases which have a sensitive 'racial dimension', where black defendants might apply to have up to three jurors from ethnic-minority communities.[17] There is no reason why the defence should be confined to a few sensitive cases involving black defendants: such a power should be available whenever the interests of justice demand its exercise. It is manifestly unfair that the prosecution retains its right to challenge, and although this is used only exceptionally, it is these exceptional cases – where information is obtained by secret 'vetting' of the panel – that cause most concern.

Jury vetting

The practice of 'vetting' goes back to the time of the French Revolution when Pitt, concerned to crush republican stirrings, introduced 'special juries' of loyalists to try cases of sedition. They were 'guinea men', paid a guinea a day and made well aware that continued lucrative employment by the Crown was contingent upon their ability to reach verdicts congenial to the Crown. It was, said one defendant, 'like offering a man a basket of rotten oranges from which he was at liberty to take his choice', and it was a tribute both to the advocacy of Thomas Erskine and to the unpopularity of George III and his ministers that on some occasions even 'special juries' acquitted. The best that can be said for the system is that it brought to prominence Jeremy Bentham, whose first book was entitled *Elements in the Art of Jury Packing*. He condemned a system of vetting 'which is become regular, quietly established and quietly suffered. Not only is the yoke already about our necks, but our neck is already fashioned for it.' In due course special juries were abolished, and replaced by juries comprising men (and a few women) of property.

In 1972, as a result of the report of the Morris Committee, the property qualification was abolished and all persons on the electoral role were made liable to jury service, subject to appropriate exclusions for lawyers, policemen, court staff, MPs, clergymen, and the mentally ill. All persons who have in the past ten years received any prison or suspended prison sentence or a community service order, or have been put on probation at any time in the previous five years, are disqualified. The Morris Committee made no reference to 'vetting' other than by court inquiries to check that disqualified persons did not serve. Both prosecution and defence were to be entitled to a list of the names and addresses and occupations of persons on the jury panel, although in 1973 the right to know a juror's occupation was abolished by Lord Chancellor Hailsham as a result of allegations that defence counsel at trials arising from industrial picketing were using the information to deduce whether a juror might be a member of a trade union. Like so many Government tamperings with the justice system, this was a petulant and politically motivated change brought about by reaction to an exceptional case. The result has been that occasionally juries do contain persons who are likely to be prejudiced against the accused, whose defending lawyers are not allowed to know the factual basis which would found a challenge for cause. Regrettably the courts are reluctant to act, even when such a fact subsequently emerges. Thus in 1985, they refused to quash the conviction of a striking miner for picketing offences, after it was discovered that one of the jurors had in fact been a strike-breaking miner. In the heightened atmosphere of the miners' strike, it was plainly unfair that the defendant should have been tried by a foe.[18] This kind of problem will recur, unless and until the defence has restored to it the right to know the occupations of the jury panel – a right which (because it was not laid down by law) could be abolished by the unilateral executive action of one Government minister.

The 'jury vetting' controversy exploded in 1978, after it was revealed that the prosecution at Duncan Campbell's trial (the *ABC official secrets* case) had secretly obtained access to the jury panel six weeks before the trial started in order to run Special Branch checks on potential jurors. The Attorney-General, Sam Silkin, was forced to admit that he had personally sanctioned such vetting in twenty-six cases over the previous four years. In 1979 the press got hold of a police vetting report about a jury empanelled to try a group of Anarchists: it revealed long-spent convictions, and the fact that one juror lived at an address 'believed to be a squat' and another had made a complaint against the police.[19] In that trial the defence had convinced a judge to extend £5,000 of legal aid to enable it to conduct its own 'vetting' of the panel by employing private detectives. The following year the issue of jury vetting split the Court of Appeal – or rather, two differently constituted Courts of Appeal reached diametrically opposed conclusions about the legitimacy of the practice. One set of judges thought that the practice was reasonable and even desirable when conducted to supply information about previous convictions,[20] while another thought the whole business was unconstitutional.[21] In 1990 the Court of Appeal declined to criticize the challenging of a juror empanelled to try the Winchester Three after a vetting operation produced information about him which had not been shared with the defence.[22] The prosecution had obtained the details of jurors (including their addresses and occupations) from court staff, who had refused to give this information to the defence. If this situation recurs, it may well be challengeable under Article 6 of the European Convention, which requires an 'equality of arms' between prosecution and defence as the foundation of a fair trial.

These great issues of principle have, in familiar British fashion, been ducked and defused by the issue of 'guidelines', both by the Attorney-General and the Association of Chief Police Officers (ACPO). 'Guidelines' as we have seen so often are not law, and there is neither any sanction against their breach nor any likelihood, given the secrecy in which vetting is conducted, that any breach will be made public.

The Attorney-General's guidelines approve Special Branch vetting of jurors in official-secrets and terrorist cases to ascertain whether any hold extreme political views which might colour their appreciation of the facts or, in security cases, lead them to divulge in-camera material to others. Presumably any potential juror discovered with Communist or Anarchist or Sinn Fein connections would be challenged, although it is unclear whether Militant Tendency or National Front views would be regarded as extreme, or whether journalists would be regarded as a risk in official-secrets cases. The guidelines permit vetting to uncover whether any juror on the panel belongs to a 'pressure group' with views which might affect the 'fair assessment' of a case. Does this mean that jurors in official-secrets trials will be vetted to ensure that they are not supporters of the Freedom of Information Campaign?

The ACPO guidelines permit police officers to undertake 'vetting' exercises whenever a juror is suspected of being disqualified or there is reason to suspect that 'jury nobbling' will be attempted – both perfectly reasonable grounds for checking on criminal records. But vetting is also approved 'in any other case in which in the opinion of the DPP or the chief constable it is particularly important to ensure that no disqualified person serves on the jury'. As to what cases these might be, the guidelines give no guidance. They permit a general trawl through police records (which may contain much information other than a record of previous convictions); they permit the use of information by the prosecution in order to challenge jurors (whether disqualified by law or not); and they do not require the fact that the vetting exercise has been undertaken, or the information it has disclosed, to be shared with defending counsel. These guidelines legitimize jury vetting without providing any equality to the defendant or any protection for the vetted jurors. It came as little surprise that in 1987 one police district admitted to making regular Criminal Records Office checks on all persons summonsed for jury service.

The principal objections to 'jury vetting' are that it is conducted in secret according to deliberately vague guidelines, that it has become the prerogative of the police and the prosecution, that it goes far beyond what is required to ensure that persons disqualified by law do not sit as jurors, and that it involves an invasion of the privacy of those summonsed to do a public service. Where checks are desirable, they should be made not by police officers involved in a particular case but by senior court staff, who could be given access to police computer records for the strictly limited purpose of ensuring that persons who attend in response to a jury summons do not have a conviction which disqualifies them. In a particular case where 'jury nobbling' is suspected, police checks may be legitimate as part of a general investigation. In view of the majority-verdict provisions, which permit one or two dissenters to be overriden, it should not (even in 'terrorist' cases) be necessary to check on the 'loyalty' or politics of potential jurors. As there is little prospect of this view being accepted by the present Government, the procedure for vetting should at least involve an application to the trial judge, after notice to the defence, so that the court can control both the obtaining of information and the use which is made of it.

The dangers of jury vetting are easy to exaggerate: there is no evidence that police or prosecutors regard membership of a left-wing branch of the Labour Party as indicative of political views so extreme as to disentitle a person to sit on a case involving security issues. However, so long as the situation remains unregulated other than by vague and unenforceable 'guidelines', that possibility can never be excluded. If it should ever happen, it is highly unlikely that it would come to be exposed.

The future of the jury system

There is no aspect of the criminal law so bedevilled by myth and anecdote than the system of jury trial. Until 1981 it was possible to interview jurors and for them to write about their experiences: on the whole the results were reassuring, and confirmed the general experience of legal practitioners that juries approached their task in a serious and intelligent way and produced common-sense results. A careful monitoring of jury verdicts in contested cases undertaken by the Oxford Penal Research Unit concluded that the great majority of acquittals were justified by the evidence, or the lack of it. After the much-publicized acquittal of Jeremy Thorpe on charges of conspiracy to murder, one juror gave an interview to the *New Statesman* explaining the decision, and the High Court refused to find that the journal had committed a contempt of court.[23] A new clause was speedily inserted in the Contempt of Court Act prohibiting any disclosure of jury deliberations, for whatever purpose. While some restriction was necessary to prevent newspapers purchasing juror memoirs, the clause is couched in blanket terms to ban even anonymous accounts of deliberations in unnamed trials. It effectively prohibits serious research into the ways in which juries arrive at their verdicts. It has not worked as its advocates predicted to protect the jury system from attack: on the contrary, it has imposed yet another layer of secrecy which handicaps those who would wish to defend the system with more than anecdotal evidence.

The law which makes it a crime (punishable by up to two years' imprisonment) for researchers to ask, or for jurors to answer, any questions about their deliberations once the trial is over, is not only an unjustified infringement of freedom of expression, but a formidable obstacle to any rational understanding of the cornerstone of the criminal justice system. It frustrated both the Roskill Committee on Fraud Trials and the Runciman Royal Commission, the latter being moved to recommend that the Contempt Act be amended 'so that informed debate can take place rather than argument based only on surmise and anecdote'.[24] It may well be that such informed debate would have saved Runciman from its mistake of recommending cut-backs in the right to elect for jury trial, especially if comparative research were also permitted into the social assumptions and deliberating procedures of lay justices.

Recent attention to the composition of jury panels – the abolition of the right of defence challenge at the same time as the legitimization of methods of police vetting – may foreshadow further changes. In the United States, the search for unbiased jurors is taken so seriously that many weeks can be expended in questioning the panel so as to winnow out any hint of prejudice from beliefs or back-ground or even 'body language' assessed by psychiatrists sitting in solemn attendance on trial counsel. This does not always assist the defence – it can enable the prosecution to exclude jurors who manifest that same independence of spirit which led to the acquittals of William Penn and Peter Zenger. We need to work towards a system which preserves the randomness of jury service, with built-in safeguards against jury panels that are unrepresentative in particular cases or that contain individuals whose occupations or commitments provide a clear reason to apprehend bias. To this end, the right to know occupations should be restored, any information available to the prosecution should be shared with the defence, and judges should be prepared to question jurors in general terms about any associations they might have which would make it difficult for them to keep an open mind. Trial judges must be given the power to order a fresh panel when the jurors initially summoned contain no members of the defendant's peer group: in cases where black youths alone are accused of riot or affray, for example, it is unseemly to have them tried by twelve white jurors. What must be preserved is the public acceptability of the jury verdict: justice must be seen to be done by representative and unbiased groups of citizens, and not by panels which are secretly manipulated behind the scenes or which appear to be wholly ignorant of the pressures and predicaments of the defendant's social environment. The jury system will never be fully appreciated until the secrecy provisions of the Contempt of Court Act are relaxed to allow jurors to speak more freely, at least to *bona fide* researchers.

TRIAL BY MAGISTRATES

The alternative to trial by jury is trial by stipendiary magistrate or lay justices. Magistrates' courts dispose of over 93 per cent of criminal charges brought in England and Wales, and function additionally to decide whether there is sufficient evidence to commit cases for jury trial. Justices have important powers to decide whether to issue search and arrest warrants, make care orders in respect of children, and supervise payments of maintenance in family split-ups. These courts deal with half a million citizens each year, dispatching some 25,000 of them to prison and imposing fines in relation to upwards of two million offences. There are seventy full-time stipendiary magistrates – experienced lawyers who sit alone – and 24,000 unpaid JPs who generally sit on twenty-six days a year in benches of two or three, advised by a legally qualified clerk. The lay justice system goes back to the fourteenth century, when men were selected 'from amongst the most worthy of the locality' to punish blemishes of the parochial peace. Its reputation for common sense and guardianship of liberty is poor beside that of the jury, but it has weathered the ridicule of Shakespeare and Dickens, the fury of radicals and the contempt of historians to play what is currently an important part in the administration of justice. It holds a monopoly over trials of routine public-order offences, and many cases of an intermediate category such as theft and possession of drugs may be tried by magistrates if the accused so elects. Lay justice has the undoubted virtues of cheapness and speed: its critics claim that it often lacks consistency and fairness.

Politically, the lay bench is heavily weighted with Tory supporters. This emerged from figures released in 1992 by the Lord Chancellor's Department, which asks all candidates for the magistracy about their voting habits. In Southampton, where each of the main parties received 43 per cent of the vote, 71 per cent of the justices supported the Conservative Party and only 17 per cent voted Labour. In St Helens, where Labour won 60 per cent of the vote in the last general election, it was supported by only 16 per cent of lay justices: most of the magistracy voted Conservative. Those figures were repeated over eighteen randomly selected constituencies, demonstrating a serious imbalance in political affiliations. Part of the blame rests with local Labour Parties, which have done little to find or promote candidates, and part with Lord Chancellor Hailsham, who deterred many applicants by dismissing justices who had taken part in CND demonstrations and by insisting that all JPs should be prepared, if necessary, to cross picket lines in order to undertake court duties. It may be that any system which requires volunteers to make considerable sacrifices of time and money in order to judge and punish others is bound to attract a greater proportion of authoritarian personalities who think and vote Conservative: while better political balance would give greater appearance of fairness, the real issue is whether justice would be better served by trained professional magistrates than by unpaid amateurs with time on their hands.

Lay justices certainly do not represent the class, race or age of those (other than motoring offenders) who beg for their mercy. They are overwhelmingly culled from the middle and upper classes – the most comprehensive study suggests that only 8 per cent can be described as 'working class'.[25] In 1984 a survey of the 150 Stockport justices revealed an average age of fifty-three (the youngest was thirty-seven) dealing with offenders over half of whom were under twenty-one.[26] The reason for the imbalance lies partly in the voluntary nature of the service, which can attract Ladies Bountiful and deter workers whose employers are reluctant to give them time off for magisterial duties. Selection procedures have also been to blame. The names of members of local advisory committees are kept secret in order to protect them from lobbying, which simply means they are lobbied by those 'in the know'. (There are several examples of undue influence by organizations like the Freemasons or Rotary.) Too much attention is paid to recruitment from local political parties, business organizations and charities, and too little to the claims of welfare and minority groups. There is a gross under-representation of the black community: in 1988 it had 455 representatives (1.9 per cent) out of a total of 23,730 active justices. Outside large cities, the local bench 'must be seen as part of a series of overlapping networks of doing, belonging, leading people – who in any community must form a small though egregious minority'.[27]

But if the lay magistracy is unrepresentative, does this affect the quality of justice on offer in their courts? Not according to Sir Thomas Skyrme, former president of the Magistrates' Association:

If one may take account of comments made to me by wage earners who have become involved in court cases, it would seem that they prefer to be tried by someone who is not a member of their own class. The right of every Englishman to be tried by his peers is not of overriding importance on these occasions.[28]

The idea that the poor really prefer to be tried by posher people is novel, but is hardly borne out by the fact that they and their lawyers generally opt for trial by jury when the alternative is available, and the case involves a conflict between their evidence and that of police officers. After all, the essential legal task of fact-finding in such cases is to judge whether the defendant's story *might* be credible, and thereby raise a reasonable doubt. Correct assessment of that credibility depends upon some ability to stand in the defendant's shoes, to test the account as a matter of common sense, compassion and street wisdom. Twelve randomly selected jurors offer a better chance of correct judgement – or, at least, a lesser likelihood of wrongful conviction – than three local worthies. Advocates often notice that in cases where there exists, objectively, a reasonable doubt about guilt, lay justices will convict (thereby 'supporting' the police) but reflect that doubt in handing down a lighter sentence than the tariff for the offence really requires.

The Lord Chancellor's Department has recognized that the social imbalance is serious enough to justify advertising in popular newspapers for 'ordinary people' to come forward as candidates. This is a welcome departure from the old-boy network, but the root problem remains of attracting wage-earners who fear that magisterial commitments will jeopardize their chances of promotion or of obtaining new jobs. Employers are bound by statute to give trade-union officials paid time off for union duties, but are under no similar obligation towards those of their workers who are JPs. They may take such time off as is 'reasonable in the circumstances' and are paid a small allowance for loss of earnings, but career and remuneration disincentives still make service on the Bench primarily a charitable service. Less secrecy about the selection process, a more active search for candidates from minority groups, proper remuneration and statutory protection from discrimination in employment will all be necessary before the lay Bench is perceived as presiding over a people's court rather than a police court.

One factor which has led to concern over the even-handedness of lay justice is the emergence of disparate sentencing patterns in different parts of the country. A comprehensive survey published by *Liberty* in 1991 revealed that lay justices in some police areas were two or three times more likely to impose jail sentences than justices in other divisions in relation to similar offences. In 1987 the BBC's *Panorama* programme contrasted the penal policies of Benches in two neighbouring towns, where similar crimes were punished in the one place by invariable imprisonment and in the other by community service. The disparity reflected the attitude of the local court clerks – officers whose responsibility for selection and training of justices and advising them on the law gives them an overweening influence on their local Bench. The influence of the court clerk is also seen in legal-aid refusal rates, which vary greatly from court to court, even within the same locality. Clerks are legally trained, and are called in to advise justices on points of law when they retire to consider verdict or sentence – an unhappy practice which can give the impression that the clerk is playing a determinative part in the outcome. If justices wish for legal advice, there is no reason why they should not return to court and obtain it in the presence of prosecution and defence lawyers.

Amateur justice has drawbacks other than the difficulty in obtaining representative Benches, the inevitable dominance of the clerk and the expenses of training. As criminal law becomes more complex, and as 'duty solicitor' schemes ensure that more defendants are represented, most contested cases generate legal arguments which lay justices cannot be expected to resolve. Hearings are protracted, and rulings are increasingly appealed to the Divisional Court. Hence the preference, in major city areas, for stipendiary magistrates appointed from the ranks of experienced criminal practitioners. Their courts function more efficiently, and their rulings are less prone to error. The 'stipe' or 'beak' has had his detractors since the days of Dickens's Mr Fang (within whose court 'enough fantastic tricks are daily played to make the angels blind with weeping') but recent appointments have been of higher quality and hold out hope that the stipendiary magistracy will become a greater bulwark of the liberty of the subject than it has appeared in the past, especially if the problem of the 'case-hardened' stipendiary is alleviated by treating the job as a stepping-stone to the circuit Bench. Stipendiaries who have had experience of both prosecuting and defending criminal cases are on the whole more likely to detect disingenuousness and dishonesty in police evidence than local worthies summoned from desirable residences to judge those who live on the wrong side of the tracks.

THE JUDICIARY

Judges cannot convict anyone of crime, although they frequently direct acquittals when the evidence is weak. The verdict is often decisively affected by the trial judge's rulings, made in the absence of the jury, to admit or reject prosecution evidence. Appellate judges, by declaring a new rule for trial judges to apply, will affect the outcome of future trials, while decisions made by High Court judges in reviewing executive conduct can settle the ambit of police and CPS powers in subsequent prosecutions. In making such decisions, judges will be guided to some extent by the letter of the law, and by past cases. But there is usually some element of subjective appreciation: the art of judging is the art of juggling, of shading and eliding, and ultimately the art of choosing. The English language is rich with ambiguity, and English jurisprudence is teeming with case law: at the point where legislative words have more than one meaning, at the moment when accumulated cases offer different solutions, there comes the necessity for choice. A judgement is not a computer printout from fed-in facts, but a decision between competing tenable arguments. Most law is settled, but many issues are not, which is precisely why they come to court. Most of these issues are unsettled because they are new, thrown up by the advance of technology, the sophistication of police and criminals and the aspirations of groups or individuals who want to live better or more convenient lives. The *choice* which the judges make will affect these lives, and it lies in their discretion alone. It is a decision which involves what judges call 'policy', and what others loosely call 'politics'. The age, the class, the received social and political opinions of the judge will play an influential and in some cases a determinative role. Nobody really believes the hoary myth that Parliament makes laws and judges, mere technicians, simply apply them. (Lord Radcliffe thought that the mark of a great judge was to make law while pretending not to.) The important question is the nature of the men who, in the process of 'interpreting', 'developing' and 'elaborating' increasingly complex, ambiguous or non-existent law, in reality are shaping and creating it.

Judges are generally men appointed from the practising bar in their late forties or early fifties. Their responsibility for ensuring justice in criminal proceedings operates at three levels:

- Crown court judges supervise the fairness of jury trials, refereeing disputes over the admission of evidence, directing the jury as to the law, summarizing the factual issues and imposing punishment;

- Court of Appeal judges scrutinize the record of trials which have resulted in 'guilty' verdicts, and are empowered to quash convictions if there have been errors of law or mistakes in procedure, or if 'fresh evidence' or any other consideration suggests there has been a miscarriage of justice. The Court of Appeal also reviews the level of sentence;
- The House of Lords judges sit as a final appellate court, interpreting legislation and pronouncing the basic principles of criminal law and procedure.

The performance of the English judiciary at each of these levels has been mixed. On the credit side is a unique record for personal integrity and incorruptibility, and a high level of legal science and learning and technical competence. On the other hand, it is plain that justice in many important criminal trials has miscarried, and has not been corrected on appeal. There have been much-publicized occasions on which individual judges have displayed smugness, arrogance, racism, sexism and lack of understanding of contemporary social and moral attitudes. Where basic human rights are concerned, the House of Lords does not have the benefit of a Bill of Rights, and hence its jurisprudence is less impressive than that of the US and Canadian Supreme Courts. Chris Mullin, MP, whose work was important in exposing the wrongful convictions for the Birmingham pub bombings, claimed in 1992 that 'the truth is that the judges, both at trial and on appeal played a large part in the most recent miscarriages of justice and there is nothing to be gained from suggesting otherwise'. What is to be gained is a sense of proportion, because those judges were not responsible for the perjury of police officers, the unfair withholding of evidence by prosecutors and the dishonesty of Home Office forensic scientists, or indeed the anti-Irish prejudice after murderous IRA bombing campaigns, which all played a more significant part than judicial bias in securing those wrongful convictions. None the less, judicial intransigence there was, epitomized by Lord Denning's comment (after they had served five of their eventual seventeen years of wrongful imprisonment) that any further proceedings which might uncover police perjury must be stopped because this would open up 'an appalling vista'.

How can judicial performance be improved? Most reform agendas focus upon the selection of candidates, made at present by the Lord Chancellor after 'soundings' taken in secret from senior judges. This procedure guarantees integrity and legal ability, but tends to judicial cloning, advancing successful appellate advocates who have conformed with the dominant culture of the robing room and the Inns of Court and circuit dinners. Qualities of managing and chairing and umpiring (important for trial judging), of inquisitiveness, street wisdom and cynicism (vital to the evaluation of police evidence) and of wide-ranging scholarship, social concern and literary craft (essential for appellate jurists) tend to be overlooked. The system has been operated as an old-boy network, which has never admitted a woman to the highest court, and by 1993 could produce only one female amongst twenty-seven members of the Court of Appeal, three out of eighty-three High Court judges, and only twenty-two out of 467 on the circuit Bench. While three members of the Court of Appeal were South African (all, it should be said, of outstanding judicial calibre), only three black judges had ever been appointed, and merely to the circuit Bench. Solicitors were still few on the ground, and notable academics were noticeable by their total absence. Although sexual, racial and social balance in the judiciary is less important than in juries, in the sense that professionalism should itself serve to minimize prejudice, a worrying study published in 1992 by the Commission for Racial Equality demonstrated a sentencing bias against blacks by some crown court judges,[29] and in the same year Helena Kennedy, QC, collected convincing evidence of judicial prejudice and ignorance towards female defendants and witnesses who did not live up (or down) to traditional male expectations.[30] The failure of the judicial establishment to be other than well-off white men all older than the President of the United States is beginning to irk a public whose confidence in the judiciary has been shaken by too many wrongful convictions.

Reform within institutions, as distinct from reform of institutions, can only be effective up to a point. The Lord Chancellor's Department, under Lord Mackay, has responded much more genuinely to these concerns than it did under Lord Hailsham, by attempting to broaden the appointment base, but it is reluctant even to set goals for the appropriate number of women and minority judges, let alone to achieve them. A new Chief Justice (Lord Taylor) has shown much more enthusiasm than his predecessors for reversing dubious convictions and exhorting prosecutors to fairer play, but he is handicapped by the statutory rules and lack of resources which prevent the Court of Appeal from turning itself into an effective body for remedying most miscarriages of justice. (This problem requires special legislation of the sort recommended by the Runciman Commission.) The secrecy and clubbability of the appointments system is no longer acceptable: it is now widely recognized that the patronage of the Lord Chancellor should be replaced by a lay-dominated Judicial Appointments Commission, using acceptable criteria and accessible methods to select candidates with the range of qualities and skills appropriate to the modern, professional judge.[31] Black and female candidates must be advanced, not by 'positive discrimination' but by simple recognition of the character qualities they have had to possess in order to combat the negative discrimination operating against them in the legal profession. The claims of solicitors, employed lawyers and academics must be considered as well as practising barristers, at the highest as well as the lowest judicial level. Some of the greatest common-law judges (Oliver Wendell Holmes, Felix Frankfurter, Bora Laskin, William Douglas, Jerome Frank) were university law professors: it is chastening to think that one of England's finest common lawyers, the late Rupert Cross, was doubly disqualified from appointment to the House of Lords, because he was both a solicitor and an academic.

No reform, however, can be permitted to infringe the fundamental principles of the independence of the judiciary, which is a precondition of any political system which aims to protect citizens against abuses of state power. It is one of the few rights ever won in Britain by a revolution – the Glorious Revolution of 1688–9 – which put an end to the pretensions of James II to dispense with the law when it suited his government. The principle was entrenched in the Act of Settlement of 1701, and is reflected in the judicial oath to 'do right to all manner of people after the laws and usages of this realm, without fear or favour, affection or ill-will'. It means, in modern terms, that judges after their appointment should be immune from the influence of the Government of the day, whether from fear of dismissal or hope of advancement or, less directly, by formal involvement with the executive whose powers they may be called upon to curb. In the words of Article 6 of the European

Convention, they must constitute 'an independent and impartial tribunal established by law'. A High Court judge can only be removed for misbehaviour after a vote by both Houses of Parliament; crown and county court judges may be dismissed by the Lord Chancellor for 'incapacity or misbehaviour'. This power was used in 1983 to sack an Old Bailey judge caught smuggling whisky, although it has never been used against judges who drink and then drive, or who make racist or sexist remarks or who frequently get the law or their sentencing wrong. Judicial independence is certainly not inconsistent with the overdue establishment of a procedure to investigate citizen complaints against the judiciary, or with a rule that any judge who commits an imprisonable offence automatically loses office, or with the monitoring of performance and standards by a judicial commission. Nor is it incompatible with a provision for regular medical and psychiatric examinations, which would avoid the unedifying situation which occurred some time ago when the Lord Chief Justice began to lapse into senility. Nothing was done about this until one public-spirited Queen's Counsel made some veiled references to the problem in an anonymous article in the *New Statesman*.

The most serious incursions into the principle of judicial independence from the executive has been made by recent Governments which have sought to exploit the confidence reposed by the public in judges by using them to inquire into political scandals, to chair tribunals with unfair procedures and to supervise the behaviour of the security services. The Thatcher Government, in particular, chose to resist demands for proper legal controls of telephone tapping and MI5 entries on to private property by legislation appointing 'judicial monitors' to check the warrants signed by the Home Secretary and to reassure the public by issuing annual reports. The monitoring process involves judges being initiated, behind the scenes, into Whitehall's secret world, hugger-mugger with the buggers, the very officials they may be asked in court to call to account. A similar objection applies to the use of senior judges to preside over the deportation tribunals set up during the Gulf War, which sat secretly to consider MI5 information without affording a fair hearing to prospective deportees (see later, page 404). Judges have cooperated, from the best of motives, with these and other 'inquiries', for which their public stature has been a political benefit for an embarrassed Government, but as Professor A.W.B. Simpson warns,

such work involves joining the executive, becoming *pro tempore* incorporated into the civil service . . . the very nature of these activities stands in direct opposition to the ideal of the rule of law. Judges should have absolutely nothing to do with secret hearings where there is no legal representation, no confrontation of witnesses, no giving of judgement in open court after a hearing in open court. Their involvement in such goings-on may in the short term confer a spurious legitimacy on what is done, but they should remember that what is involved here is the debilitation of the judicial function and ultimately the degradation of the judicial office.[32]

Lord Denning's secret inquiry into the Profumo affair, wholly lacking in forensic procedures for testing truth, now appears incredibly naïve in its conclusions, which were unfair to Stephen Ward and over-kind to ministers and MI5; in 1993 the Prime Minister accepted that Lord Widgery's inquiry into 'Bloody Sunday' twenty years before had wrongfully put the blame on the innocent victims, thereby beginning a long process of disenchantment with 'British justice'. The most serious criticism to be made of modern British jurisprudence is that it has been over-impressed by executive claims of 'national security' and has consistently failed to permit legal challenge to unfair actions which ministers have unconvincingly but successfully justified by this magic formula. By allowing themselves to be drawn into this secret world, judges offer even less hope that they will demonstrate their true independence from the state by breaking its last taboo, the legal invincibility of actions taken 'in the interests of national security'.

The quality and independence of the judiciary has a particular relevance to demands for a written constitution and a Bill of Rights. In recent years judges have displayed a commendable determination to protect citizens' rights by overturning unfair executive decisions (other than in the 'no-go' area of national security): would a Supreme Court of British judges be capable of acceptably applying fundamental human-rights standards to strike down or read down infringing parliamentary legislation? This issue is considered in greater detail in Chapter 12, where it will be seen that Law Lords in their Privy Council capacity are making valuable contributions to human rights abroad through their interpretation of Commonwealth constitutions, and that many senior judges are beginning to adopt approaches to statutory interpretation and common-law development which are influenced by the European Convention of Human Rights. Their learning curve would be accelerated if the British Government were prepared to appoint members of its own judiciary to the European Court and Commission: because it fears their independence, it usually makes such appointments from the ranks of its own tame legal advisers.

MISCARRIAGES OF JUSTICE

No system of justice is infallible. No matter how careful the investigation, how capable the lawyers and how conscientious the jury, mistakes will sometimes be made. Errors by magistrates, confirmed on appeal by circuit judges, may rankle and dog defendants, who will at least be at liberty to complain to the Home Office, which may grant a 'royal pardon' if they can furnish absolute proof of innocence. But for the long-term prisoner whose appeal on points of law has failed, the jury verdict is almost impossible to dislodge unless a book or television programme or a retired Law Lord takes up the case and persuades the Home Secretary to make a 'reference back' to the Court of Appeal, in which event the court may decide, on hearing fresh evidence, that the conviction should be quashed. There were very few references by the Home Secretary until 1990, when Lord Denning's 'appalling vista' of English injustice was made plain to all the world: first the Guildford Four, then the Maguire Seven, the Birmingham Six and Judith Ward: accused by perjurious policemen and inadequate forensic scientists, wrongly convicted by juries, mistakenly turned down by appeal judges (twice, in the case of the Birmingham Six, whose 'reference back' had been confidently rejected in 1987), and wrongfully imprisoned for bombings and murders in the mid-seventies. Revelation of this shameful record at last brought a respite from serious calls for the reintroduction of the death penalty (which would have been inflicted on most of these defendants) and produced some important exhortations about the need for full prosecution disclosure of evidence from chastened Courts of Appeal, and then a devastating critique of the integrity and competence of Government forensic scientists from an inquiry chaired by Sir John May.[33] What, unconscionably, it did not bring was any Government action to establish an independent review tribunal to investigate dubious convictions. Instead, the Prime Minister opted for the traditional stalling device of a Royal Commission, which predictably reported in 1993 in favour of reforms which have been obviously necessary for many years, notably widening the powers of the Court of Appeal to quash convictions about which it entertains serious doubts, and establishing a Criminal Cases Review Authority, independent of the Home Office, to investigate allegations that justice has miscarried in trials of serious crime.

There are no authoritative statistics as to how many wrongful convictions occur: Justice, the organization with most experience in unravelling them, has estimated that as many as two hundred defendants are sentenced to terms of imprisonment each year for crimes they did not commit. The most comprehensive study, which analysed three hundred contested crown court trials in London and Birmingham concluded that sixteen of the convictions – 5 per cent of the sample – were 'doubtful', in the sense that the trial judge, the prosecution solicitor and the police officers involved in the case thought that a 'reasonable doubt' had emerged by the end of the evidence.[34] Most of these defendants were sentenced to prison, and only two of them appealed, both unsuccessfully. This same study uncovered a serious under-representation of black jurors in the Birmingham courts, and noted that half of those who had been 'doubtfully convicted' were black. In 1992 the Court of Appeal quashed the convictions of 299 appellants. This is a fraction of the 14,661 persons convicted by juries in crown courts in the same year, but the real concern is that some of the 1,500 or so who are refused leave to appeal because they cannot show grounds convincing enough to justify a full appellate hearing might in fact have their claims to innocence substantiated by further and fuller investigation.

Inevitably, police officers charged with solving serious crimes will become psychologically committed to the guilt of their chosen suspect: it is the function of the adversary system to test those suspicions according to the very high standard of 'proof beyond reasonable doubt', which is designed to protect the innocent by protecting those who are probably (but not certainly) guilty as well. This device (the 'golden thread of the criminal law') is a necessary, but plainly not sufficient, safeguard against wrongful convictions. Attention must additionally be turned to developing effective procedural safeguards against certain types of evidence, and certain kinds of prosecution behaviour, which have a proven tendency to cause wrongful convictions. These safeguards are especially necessary in an adversarial system, which only works if there is equality between prosecution and defence and a judicial referee who enforces rules designed to keep irrational prejudice out of the courtroom. A consideration of trials which have resulted in miscarriages of justice indicates that our criminal procedure offers insufficient safeguards against the most common causes of wrongful convictions, namely:

1. *Confessions.* Many innocent persons are convicted on the strength of apparently reliable confessions to police. Occasionally, these can be proved, by ESDA testing of police notebooks, to be fabricated. More often, they are volunteered by persons in custody through fear or mental breakdown or in a desire to curry favour with police custodians. Although requirements for tape-recording and video-taping of interviews reduce the danger, they do not remove it, for some people (like Judith Ward) can be subject to mental pressures which cause them freely to confess to crimes they did not commit.[35] The only satisfactory safeguard is a new evidential rule that no conviction can be registered wholly on the strength of a confession; there must be some independent evidence confirmatory of guilt. The Runciman Commission was not prepared to go this far, although it conceded that such a rule would apply in only a small number of cases and would encourage police to look for corroborative evidence so as to put the matter beyond doubt. It recommended lesser safeguards, namely that trial judges should be more willing to withdraw cases which hinge on questionable confessions and should warn juries about the dangers of convicting defendants upon their confessions alone. There is a certain illogic in saying 'this evidence is dangerous, but convict upon it if you can', although it is an illogic that is found throughout the English law of criminal evidence, which avoids principles whenever possible so as to preserve the discretion of judges to act as the 'feel' of the

case seems to require. Their intuitions have not always proved correct.

2. *Circumstantial evidence*. Those familiar with Ripley's *Believe It or Not* will understand how the most convincing circumstantial evidence can convict an innocent person. Thus Sir Henry Fisher, the former High Court judge who held an inquiry into the Confait killing, concluded that the circumstances proved the guilt of two of the young defendants. A few weeks after his report was published, the real murderer was identified and both boys were cleared. There should be a strict rule that circumstantial evidence must point to only one possible conclusion before a finding of guilt based entirely upon it is upheld.

3. *Identification*. Many of the worst miscarriages have been inflicted on defendants 'identified' by prosecution witnesses. This evidence is notoriously unreliable because it cannot be tested by cross-examination: witnesses instinctively and honestly believe that the defendant is the person they saw at the scene of the crime, unaware of how memory plays tricks with visual impressions. The courts require warnings to be given to juries about the dangers of convicting on identification evidence, but as with confessions a 'warning' may prove insufficient: there is a need to go further and to require independent evidence which corroborates guilt.

4. *Unsound science*. The evidence of prosecution scientific experts – especially those attached to Government forensic science laboratories – can be invested with a credibility which subsequent discoveries demonstrate to be misplaced. The trial process is much at risk from overconfident prosecution experts, whose evidence may be reckless (Sir Bernard Spilsbury, the 'father' of forensic science, can with hindsight be condemned for contributing to many wrongful convictions) or grossly incompetent (a finding made against Home Office scientist Dr Alan Clift in 1977, when a number of convictions obtained on his evidence had to be quashed). The Birmingham Six trial miscarried partly as a result of the unreliable tests used by Dr Frank Scuse; the Maguire Seven were convicted after scientists from the Royal Armament Research Development Establishment (RARDE) had not only used unreliable tests but had improperly withheld evidence of their unreliability from the court.[36] The problem of partisanship by Government-employed scientists needs to be addressed through professional discipline, by ensuring that

laboratories are independent of the police and by providing defence access to a pool of scientific experts with equivalent experience to those in Government service. The lesson from the Maguire Seven case is that there must be complete disclosure by prosecution experts as well as by the police. Finally, there should be a statutory duty to retain prosecution exhibits in all cases which have involved substantial sentences of imprisonment: it is remarkable how many disputes over convictions could now be resolved by recently developed ESDA and DNA testing, if only police notebooks, human samples and other trial exhibits had been retained.

5. *Guilt by association.* This remains a danger for innocent defendants jointly tried with those who are palpably guilty. Judges may order separate trials, but are reluctant to do so in conspiracy cases, where the gravest dangers arise. It is not easy for jurors to understand why evidence against one defendant should not be considered as evidence against others (if it seems to implicate them) and mud thrown against a guilty party will inevitably stick against an associate by application of the adage that 'birds of a feather flock together'.[37] The problem calls for particular judicial vigilance, not merely at appeal level (the victim may by then have suffered a period of wrongful imprisonment) but at the 'half-time' stage of a trial, when judges should dismiss charges which rest on evidence which carries more prejudice than proof.

6. *Non-disclosure.* One factor common to most miscarriage cases is the failure by the prosecution to disclose evidence which it regards as irrelevant, but which turns out, on subsequent analysis, to point towards innocence. Such conduct is usually the result, not of dishonesty or malice, but of ignorance. Policemen, Crown solicitors and prosecuting counsel all become to some extent 'committed' to their case: they know little of the defence case, and cannot begin to appreciate its requirements. They should never take upon themselves the decision as to what evidence is 'relevant' and what is not: all their evidential material should be available for the defence to inspect. This simple rule should be given statutory force, with rare exceptions (such as revelation of the identity of informers) to be decided by the judge. Non-enforceable 'guidelines' from the Attorney-General are not enough, now that we know how vital psychiatric reports on Judith Ward were never revealed at her trial, and how evidence of Gerald Conlon's alibi lay unappreciated

amongst 'non-material' prosecution papers throughout the fifteen years he wrongfully served in prison, and how material discrediting the most important witness against the Taylor sisters at their trial for murder was withheld by police, even from the prosecution lawyers. The Runciman Commission made wholly unsatisfactory recommendations on this subject, perhaps as a sop to the police: it would allow them to withhold evidence they deem 'irrelevant', or 'relevant but sensitive', and leave these categories to be sought in pre-trial proceedings by defence lawyers who would not be entitled to know what was available to be sought for. Non-disclosure by the prosecution is the most infuriating of all causes of miscarriage of justice: Runciman failed to recognize that it is also the most easily avoided, if only everyone involved in the prosecution process can be forced to recognize that their conduct must in principle be open to examination on behalf of those whose liberty it may jeopardize.

7. *Previous convictions.* Defendants who attack – sometimes truthfully – the credibility of police or other prosecution witnesses face the prospect of their own past criminal record (which would normally be excluded from evidence) being put before the jury if they step into the witness-box. This tit-for-tat rule of evidence means that defendants with previous convictions for similar offences – which may well have aroused police suspicions against them in the first place – cannot fully develop their defence for fear of the prejudice they will suffer in reprisal. This is one of the commonest causes of wrongful conviction of previous offenders, faced with the Catch 22 that they cannot accuse police of lying without being placed at an unfair disadvantage. It intrudes an element of gamesmanship into trials in which results may hinge on tactics rather than truth. The tit-for-tat rule should be abolished, as the Runciman Committee has now recommended, in cases where the attack on the credibility of the police or other prosecution witnesses is a central plank of the defence.[38]

8. *Defence inadequacy.* Some defences are not properly prepared by solicitors, who may be negligent or incompetent or so strait-jacketed by legal-aid limitations that they lack the resources to do the necessary detective work on behalf of clients who are themselves locked up in prison prior to trial. A defence barrister's performance may be affected by lack of experience or competence, by late delivery of the brief or simply by making a tactical mistake or

failing to appreciate a potentially important aspect of the case. Appeal courts have been reluctant to upset convictions on this ground, requiring evidence of 'flagrantly incompetent advocacy', rather than of the inadequacy which occasionally affects advocacy in courts where the majority of legally aided defendants meet their barrister for the first time on the morning of the trial. Runciman valuably recommends that the stringent test of 'flagrancy' should be jettisoned, and that appeal courts should be more prepared to consider whether errors of legal judgement, and inadequacy in lawyers' performance, may have led to a wrongful conviction.[39] Regrettably, the Report is sprinkled with exhortations to trial judges to 'punish' barristers who appear to them to waste court time, by recommending that their fees be reduced or by ordering that they personally pay prosecution costs. The danger is that these powers will be used to inhibit defence counsel from pressing their client's cause against the wishes of a hostile judge, undermining that independence of the bar which remains a defendant's most important safeguard against wrongful conviction. Another Runciman recommendation – to undermine the accused's 'right of silence' by requiring solicitors to disclose the defence case long before trial – is a recipe for more wrongful convictions, as ill-considered and incomplete defence statements, made at a stage before legal aid permits the involvement and advice of counsel, will assume disproportionate evidential significance at the eventual trial.

9. *Informers.* This class of evidence is notoriously unreliable, tainted as it usually is by motives of malice, greed or self-exculpation. Judges are required to tell juries to find corroborative evidence before convicting defendants on the testimony of accomplices who have participated in the crime, but this rule does not apply in respect of other informers, or even to *agents provocateurs*. A disturbing number of dubious convictions have been secured by evidence from 'prison grasses' likely to be rewarded in the disposal of their own cases by inventing evidence against others.[40] Any prosecution which depends on such obviously tainted sources should be viewed with suspicion, yet our rules give this evidence more credence than the testimony of a rape victim (which must be independently corroborated before a conviction can ensue).

10. *Delay.* Although Magna Carta promises that 'to no man will we deny, to no man will we defer, justice or right', it is only very

recently that English courts have permitted defendants to argue that their trials should not go ahead after unconscionable delays, during which evidence becomes stale and witnesses (or their memories) fade. The circumstances in which a trial can be stopped on the grounds that it would be an 'abuse of process' to continue depend on the subjective evaluation of the judge, and it may be better to adopt statutory limitaion periods as well. There is little likelihood that this would appeal to Members of Parliament, who support the inevitably unfair prosecution of alleged war criminals, on identification evidence, after a delay of fifty years.

11. *Plea bargaining*. The practice of plea bargaining sometimes induces innocent defendants to plead guilty in order to obtain a lesser sentence than they have been led to expect in the event of a conviction. There can be no objection to judges who indicate openly the kind of 'tariff' sentence which an offence, if proven, is likely to receive: the problem (as with so much in English law) is caused by secrecy: the private negotiations between prosecutors and defence counsel, sometimes in the judge's chamber, result in 'nods and winks' which can convey insidious pressures to frightened defendants. People with previous convictions can be particularly susceptible to such pressures, which are increasingly being justified in the interests of saving time and money. With proper safeguards, the acceptance of a genuine plea after public discussion of an appropriate sentence can serve everyone's interests, but at present the safeguards are neither agreed upon nor in place. The Runciman Report, which advocated increasing resort to the judge's chambers for secret plea-bargaining (euphemistically labelled 'sentence-canvassing') in the absence of the defendant, ignored the danger of improper pressure on the innocent, as well as the tendency of such a system to produce 'instant reaction' sentencing which fails to take into account subsequent recommendations of the probation service or indeed the public interest in the careful disposal or treatment of dangerous or mentally disordered offenders.

12. *Sensational security*. An intractable problem in 'terrorist' trials is their very description, and the atmosphere it engenders inside and outside the courtroom. It is impossible to expect juries to be unaffected by distressing prosecution pictures of bomb victims, or by security arrangements made on the assumption of guilt, namely that a 'terrorist trial' is the trial of a terrorist. There are always body

searches of counsel, judges and jurors; armed guards (sometimes allocated to jurors), sharpshooters on the court roof, police dogs patrolling the court yard, police helicopters hovering overhead – all these security measures being emphasized daily in sensational television coverage and breathless press accounts. From the outset of the trial, jurors are made to fear the defendants and the hypothetical IRA hit squads against whose attacks all these precautions are being taken. It takes an exceptionally courageous and unprejudiced jury to acquit defendants whom the state so obviously believes are dangerous, and this was undoubtedly the most important (but least recognized) factor in the wrongful convictions of innocent Irishmen after the mainland bombing campaigns in the seventies.

Given that the adversarial system of trial produces, each year, a significant number of wrongful convictions, it might be expected that the criminal justice system would provide some form of longstop – an agency empowered to investigate all the evidence in doubtful cases and to recommend release when those doubts magnify alarmingly. The Court of Appeal, however, cannot act in this capacity. It has no investigative staff, and its function is limited to assessing the reliability of the trial record. Most appeals succeed, not on merit, but because the trial judge has misstated the law or permitted a technical irregularity. Jury verdicts are notoriously difficult to dislodge: rarely do appeals succeed on the ground that the verdict is against the weight of the evidence. The court is reluctant to assess 'fresh evidence' not placed before the court of trial, unless it is clearly material which could not have been discovered at the time by diligent defence solicitors. In such cases, the defendant will be penalized for the inadequacies of his lawyers (or, more often, the inadequacies of the legal-aid system which may not have covered the cost of adducing the evidence at the trial). There are good reasons for limiting the Court of Appeal to a review of the written record, but these very reasons make it imperative that some other agency should exist to go behind the transcripts and to examine the whole case afresh, when serious doubts have been raised.

The only recourse after appeal for an innocent prisoner is to petition the Home Office, which Runciman found to demonstrate a 'reluctance to inquire deeply enough into the cases put to it'. It has no trained investigators, does not even interview the prisoner, and turns down the vast majority of petitions without giving reasons. It adopts a narrow, legalistic test for deciding whether to refer a case back to the Court of Appeal: the prisoner must advance 'convincing grounds for thinking he is innocent'. On this test, it has turned down the petitions of a number of prisoners who were subsequently proved to be innocent by the BBC's *Rough Justice* team.[41] Even when a reference back is made – generally on powerful evidence and after political pressure – the Court of Appeal must in the end ask itself a subjective question, 'whether we are content to let the matter stand as it is, or whether there is not some lurking doubt in our mind which makes us wonder whether an injustice has been done'.[42] In the words of Viscount Dilhorne in *Stafford* v. *DPP*, 'this is a reaction which may not be based strictly on the evidence as such; it is a reaction which can be produced by the general feel of the case as the court experiences it'.[43] It is the 'general feel' of three appellate judges as to whether the original jury might have been content to convict had it known the full story, which will decide the fate of cases referred back by the Home Secretary. This approach undermines the principle of trial by jury. Whenever a conviction is reopened, the test must be related to the effect of fresh evidence on the minds of a jury, and not to some 'general feel' about the case entertained by appellate judges.[44] Rather than reject a 'reference back' which has been made on the basis of fresh evidence, the Court of Appeal should be more willing to order a retrial, so that the new evidence can be assessed by a jury. This may be impractical where many years have elapsed since the conviction, but it does preserve the constitutional principle that the jury should be the final arbiter of guilt or innocence.

The problem with the 'reference-back' procedure is that it raises expectations that it cannot fulfil. The judges decline, reasonably enough, to turn themselves into a public inquiry: they have no investigatory powers. The evidence put before them is still confined by rules of admissibility, rather than the need to get at the truth. They are naturally predisposed towards believing that the system has worked: to shake their faith in a conviction requires some convincing proof. By adopting the test of whether fresh evidence and analysis shakes their faith, rather than the test of whether it might well have induced a reasonable doubt in the minds of a trial jury, they are led to uphold a number of convictions in relation to which reasonable doubts abound in the minds of intelligent observers. Such was the public disquiet over the failure of two references back to the Court of Appeal in the Luton Post Office murder case that the Home Secretary eventually took it upon himself to release two men, Cooper and McMahon, from the life sentences they were serving. Public clamour, of course, is confined to sensational cases, generally of murder, which are taken up by MPs or investigative journalists: it took representations from the Irish Government to obtain a 'reference back' for the men convicted of planting the Birmingham bombs. Obscure defendants who may have been wrongly convicted have little chance of being afforded even the opportunity to have their protests judicially considered.

So what should be done to provide the safety net that is so clearly needed to identify, investigate and rectify miscarriages of justice? There is no doubt that the situation will remain unsatisfactory until responsibility is taken away from both the Home Office and from the Court of Appeal. A new institution – a 'court of last resort' – must be established. The Devlin Committee proposed an Independent Review Tribunal, unfettered by the evidential rules restricting the Court of Appeal. In 1986 Parliament's Home Affairs Committee endorsed the proposal, but the Government initially responded with a glib White Paper which rejected any need for an independent safety-net.[45] The Home Office intransigence weakened after its own inadequacies as a 'referral-back' agency were exposed first by Lord Justice May's inquiry into the Maguire Seven case and then by the Royal Commission into Criminal Justice. The Report of the latter concluded with a chapter recommending the establishment of a Criminal Cases Review Authority, empowered to investigate allegations of wrongful convictions and to refer appropriate cases back to a Court of Appeal with sufficiently flexible rules to enable it to consider such evidence as the Authority had turned up in favour of quashing the conviction. The advantage of this approach is that it removes entirely from the Home Office, which is responsible for policing, the incompatible function of exposing police mistakes, while maintaining the independence of the Court of Appeal as the only body which can ultimately decide to reverse the verdict of a trial jury. If this recommendation is accepted (and the Royal Commission will have been a waste of time if it is not), much will hinge upon whether the Government devotes sufficient resources to enable it to fulfill its investigative role, and is prepared to appoint persons of requisite experience and calibre (who should not invariably be lawyers) to direct its work.

The only substantial reforms to criminal procedure made by Parliament in recent years have been in the specialized area of serious fraud, where the safeguards of committal proceedings and the right to silence have virtually been abolished, and defendants have been required to disclose their defences in advance. The results have not been encouraging: all convictions in the Blue Arrow trial were quashed because prosecution overloading of the indictment produced complexity and confusion, and the second Guinness trial proved too onerous even to begin. A number of recent fraud trials have lasted over a year, placing intolerable strains on jurors, who may well think that they have to bring in some guilty verdicts in order to justify the massive public expense. Any trial which lasts more than four months carries inherent dangers of unfairness. While there is no alternative to prosecuting the prime mover of any major fraud on the public for offences carrying lengthy terms of imprisonment, there is no reason why lesser figures whose involvement delays and lengthens the trial could not be dealt with by charging summary offences. A better alternative to a lengthy, expensive and unfair trial in cases of very complex fraud would be a public inquiry, which would have the inestimable advantage of ending with a reasoned statement of what really happened. What the public would lose is the prospect that a few major players would go to prison: what it would gain is a reasoned account of what happened, and reform proposals to prevent it happening again. Public inquiries could punish persons involved in major frauds by convincingly condemning them for posterity, disqualifying them from directorships, ordering them to pay costs, producing evidence for civil actions against them or (in the case of unethical solicitors or accountants, who generally escape prosecution in any event) for professional disbarment proceedings, and by recommending perjury prosecutions (which carry prison sentences) against those it caught out in lies. The experience of other common-law jurisdictions is that fraud and corruption are more effectively investigated and deterred by immediate public inquiries than by drawn-out criminal proceedings. The trial of the sons of Robert Maxwell (a case of playing Hamlet without the ghost) may satisfy desires for revenge, but will take place long after a public inquiry might have uncovered the truth, allocated blame and provided compensation to all those who had been wronged.

CHAPTER 9

Freedom of Movement

As I went aboard the steamer I asked myself with anxiety under which flag would she sail – Norwegian, German, English? And then I saw floating above the stern the Union Jack, the flag under which so many refugees, Italian, French, Hungarian and of all nations have found an asylum. I greeted that flag as from the depths of my heart.

Prince Kropotkin (1899)[1]

Although British citizens have no legally enforceable right to move freely about the United Kingdom or to travel abroad, Government interference with their freedom to do so has been minimal. The Prevention of Terrorism Act is responsible for turning back or removing to Northern Ireland hundreds each year who are 'suspected' (without hard proof) of being sympathetic to terrorism and are somewhat irrationally viewed as being of greater danger on the mainland than at home in the province. Police peace-keeping powers may be used to stop people travelling to demonstrations (see earlier, page 79) and there have been occasions when the Foreign Office has declined to issue passports to citizens wishing to travel abroad for politically unattractive purposes. But it is the freedom to enter Britain for settlement which has been massively restricted in recent years, as the result of a wider political debate which has been racist in both rhetoric and result. The two principal statutes, the Immigration Act of 1971 and the British Nationality Act of 1981, together with the all-important Immigration Rules, effectively throw a *cordon sanitaire* around the country, which may be breached permanently only by those who prove close family affinity with British citizens or who can satisfy increasingly difficult tests for political asylum or refugee status, or whose wealth or special skills give a privileged route to settlement. The weapons of deportation and removal are widely used to extirpate those who 'overstay' or have entered unlawfully, and sometimes to rid the country of aliens whose political activities are regarded by the Government as non-conducive to the public good. The power of extradition is also available, with dwindling legal safeguards, to remove persons resident in Britain for trial in foreign states on charges of serious crime. Although 'political' offences were long regarded as non-extraditable, the rise of international terrorism has led to domestic laws, implementing international conventions, which severely restrict this historic exemption.

Every nation has the right to limit entry and to decide, subject to international conventions, to whom it shall afford shelter or the protection of citizenship. Historically, the United Kingdom has a more liberal record than most: the blue plaques around London bear testimony to the home it once was to Marx, Mazzini, Garibaldi, Lenin, Engels, Kropotkin, Kossuth and Sun Yat-sen. Some of their modern counterparts would today be deported as undesirable aliens, and the liberal tradition survives only in respect of those refugees who can persuade an increasingly unsympathetic Home Office that their fear of persecution is well founded. It survives as a political rather than a legal judgement: the courts are unable to interfere with the Home Secretary's decision unless it is manifestly irrational. The twin features of modern immigration control are administrative discretion and administrative secrecy: the broadest of legal powers are bestowed upon officials, who exercise them according to secret guidelines approving procedures (such as the X-raying of children and 'virginity tests') which cannot be justified once they see the light of day. Officially approved immigration after the war brought the challenges and the benefits of a multiracial country: lack of compassion (especially towards the reuniting of families) in administering immigration rules has proved a potent factor in exacerbating racial tensions. Both Labour and Conservative Governments are responsible for the present set of controls, which allegedly provide a 'fair but firm' basis for administration. Of the firmness there can be no doubt: this chapter will consider the claim of 'fairness', and the limited extent to which the law is available to promote it.

Freedom of movement is increasingly affected by Britain's membership of the European Community. It has been massively extended in respect of nationals of EC countries and to their dependents, who are entitled to enter and work and remain with minimum restrictions. This development has been counterbalanced by a tightening of immigration controls on prospective entrants from outside Europe, especially refugees whose chances of successfully exerting their claims are diminished by the Asylum and Immigration Appeal Act of 1993. Although European law is generally helpful to human rights in Britain, and the EC Court has struck down some discriminatory aspects of immigration control, it has ignored or cut back the rights of non-EC nationals, including the ten million settled for many years in Europe (one million of them in Britain) who remain nationals of countries outside the EC. At a time of increasing racism and Fascism in Europe, there are concerns that all governments will agree to adopt a 'lowest common denominator' approach to the refugee crisis, refusing by agreement between themselves to lower the drawbridge of 'Frontier Europe' to accommodate many fugitives in genuine fear of persecution. As internal travel has been made easier, so has extradition: there is little role now left for courts to scrutinize demands made by member states. The borders within Europe have been broken down: the borders of Europe are being made much more difficult to cross.[2]

THE HISTORY OF IMMIGRATION CONTROL

The main shifts in immigration control in this century have come about as the result of war, entry into the European Community and the end of the British Empire. Nineteenth-century Britain was a confident country which exuded sympathy for those struggling against despised European monarchs, but this long tradition of tolerance ended in 1905, as a result of Jewish migration after the pogroms in Russia and Eastern Europe. The Aliens Act of that year was passed by a Conservative Government which found political mileage in anti-Semitism and workers' fears about competition for jobs. Henceforth, alien immigrants 'likely to become a charge on the rates' could be excluded, although refugees were excepted and immigration officers were required to set out full reasons in writing for refusing leave to land and there was a right of appeal to a tribunal. Forty per cent of appeals were successful, but this brief experiment in fairness was ended by the Aliens Restriction Act of

1914, an oppressive piece of war hysteria rushed through all stages in Parliament in one day. It gave the Home Secretary untrammelled power to exclude and expel aliens, without any rights of appeal or even the right to make representations, and without any protection for refugees. Although described as a 'temporary measure', it was re-enacted after the war and then extended each year until 1969, and deployed as the spirit of the time (and the need for skilled workers) appeared to the Home Secretary.

Commonwealth citizens, meanwhile, enjoyed at common law a virtually automatic right of entry. There was a shortage of labour after the Second World War, and immigrants from the Caribbean and Asian colonies were encouraged to do the 'dirty jobs' of the 1950s, and in due course became scapegoats for fears about jobs and housing. In 1962, the Government introduced the Commonwealth Immigrants Act, a measure to deal with the 'troublesome phenomenon' of recent racial disturbances (by whites) in Notting Hill and elsewhere. It instituted a system of work vouchers, but it did not affect those who carried British passports – a precaution taken out by many Asians in East Africa as their countries prepared for independence. In the following years, as their fears of victimization became well founded, they applied to enter Britain. Some 200,000 Kenyan Asians were principally involved, and the prospect of their arrival unleashed the racist passions and predictions of Enoch Powell's 'rivers of blood' speech. Secret reports in 1967 predicted further large-scale expulsions of Asians from East Africa, and caused the Government to make what Richard Crossman was subsequently to describe as 'plans for legislation which we realized would have been declared unconstitutional in any country with a written constitution and a supreme court'.[3]

This legislation took the form of the Commonwealth Immigrants Act of 1968, which was passed through both Houses of Parliament in thirty-six hours. It was a dishonest, unjust and racist measure, later condemned as degrading and discriminating by the European Commission of Human Rights. It was designed to dishonour promises of citizenship previously made to East African Asians, but in doing so it adopted a formula which is now applied across-the-board to would-be immigrants from outside the EEC. The formula is that of ancestral connection (termed 'patriality') made by reference to parental or grandparental birth or naturalization in the United

Kingdom. For the purposes of 1968, this had the advantage of discriminating against Kenyan Asians in favour of white settlers, without actually using discriminatory language. The European Commission, in its *East African Asians* decision of 1973, found that the Kenyan and Ugandan Asians holding British passports who were refused entry under the Act had been the victims of degrading treatment by virtue of legislation which intentionally discriminated by dispossessing them of a right to enter which they had been led reasonably to expect.[4] By that time, however, the patriality formula had become the basis of the main immigration measure, the 1971 Immigration Act. The mentality which could deceive the Kenyan Asians in 1968 is reflected, a quarter of a century later, in the UK Government's stubborn refusal to ratify the fourth protocol to the European Convention on Human Rights, viz. 'no one shall be deprived of the right to enter the territory of the state of which he is a national'. What sort of Government would refuse its nationals the right to re-enter their own nation?

The 1971 Act (together with the Immigration Rules and the 1981 British Nationality Act) is inordinately complicated, and its detailed provisions are outside the scope of this book.[5] In general terms, it places Commonwealth citizens on the same footing as other foreigners, save for citizens of EEC countries who have special rights of entry under the Treaty of Rome. Ironically, given the extent to which the fear of immigrants taking jobs was exploited in order to close the door on Asians, accession to the Common Market with its philosophy of freedom of movement has meant that business people, workers and self-employed may enter from EEC countries without let or hindrance, with their families, and remain even after their work has ceased. Immigrants from the Commonwealth, and from countries outside the EEC, are subject to stringent immigration control unless they are British citizens either through birth in the UK or through having a UK-born parent (in some cases, grandparent) or through naturalization or through having been settled in the UK for substantial periods prior to the 1971 Act. This effectively removes the 'right of abode' in Britain from most Commonwealth citizens: it bears disproportionately on blacks, although it also affects the migration of many whites from the 'old' Commonwealth. The citizenship arrangements made by the 1981 British Nationality Act were designed with the hand-over of Hong Kong to the Chinese very much in mind: citizenship of 'British Depe~~ carries no right of abode in the United Kingdom ~ at least grandparental connections. This measure many Falklanders from settling in Britain, and w 'signals' that made Argentinian generals think that h not resist their invasion of the islands the following y~ the Government found that the logic of its 1981 Act wa~ impaled on the Prime Minister's rhetoric that the islanders were British to their bootstraps: the British Nationality (Falkland Islands) Act of that year specially extended full-blooded British citizenship to all of them. There has been no such indulgence to the citizens of Hong Kong, although to discourage the most influential from emigrating before the lease is surrendered in 1997, the UK Government has guaranteed several thousand of them entry rights to Britain should Chinese rule be unpalatable. (This preferential treatment for a tiny caste of business and political élite is typical of the way considerations of class – usually less obtrusively – permeate discretionary entry decisions.) The most drastic change made by the 1981 Act was removal of the centuries-old principle that birth in Britain was sufficient for citizenship. This simple and symbolic test has been replaced with a patriality requirement.

Those of 'good character' who do not qualify for citizenship may of course obtain it by naturalization (usually by marriage or by a period of at least five years' lawful residence) or in certain circumstances by registration – a slow process without the fair political wind which set an immigration record for South African sprinter Zola Budd in 1984, whose registration was arranged after a conversation between the Home Secretary and Budd's sponsor, the editor of the *Daily Mail*. Would-be immigrants are at the mercy of the rules and the administrative 'guidelines' which implement them. A voucher system is operated to allow a very limited immigration (to a maximum of 5,000 heads of households a year) by those holding UK passports, many of whom live in the Indian subcontinent. Most have been forced out of East Africa, and must queue for many years before their turn to enter comes. Their treatment contrasts remarkably with the one remaining permissive immigration rule, which permits residence to 'persons of independent means' who have amassed (however dishonourably) capital of at least £200,000 which they bring into the country. In this respect, at least, the

of an immigrant's money has replaced the colour of his skin
the test for welcome: crooked South American generals, Australian media moguls, Arab princes and Asian millionaires may purchase
with little difficulty the right to settle in the UK.

FAMILY LIFE AND PRIVACY

Immigration policy must primarily be determined by political
considerations, but its implementation should respect the fundamental rights of those who live or are permitted to settle in Britain. The
worst features of the implementation of the Immigration Rules have
stemmed from failures to respect the rights to family life and to
privacy. On an administrative level, examples are provided by long
delays in processing applications and the rigorous and intrusive
questioning which often accompanied them. X-rays have been done
on the bone structure of children to determine age, and 'virginity
tests' carried out on the assumption that Asian women who failed the
test were likely to be married already. Both practices were authorized
by secret guidelines, and were discontinued after public outcry after
they had been 'leaked'. (It is typical of British administration to
publish generalized 'rules' which are interpreted by officials according
to unpublished 'instructions' and 'guidelines'; much confusion and
unfairness would be avoided if these secret 'instructions' were
supplied to applicants and their advisers.) One particularly insensitive
provision in the Immigration Rules precludes entry to men who
intend to marry women already settled here unless the entry clearance
officer 'is satisfied that the parties to the proposed marriage have met'
– an attitude to arranged marriages which, in Lord Scarman's words,
implies 'an attack on the social habits and custom of people who have
come to this country and who are living according to the customs in
which they were brought up'.[6] A requirement which subverts
European notions of family life is the rule which allows the exclusion
of dependent relations if they would require some maintenance from
public funds, e.g. by claiming supplementary benefits or housing
benefits. In the absence of a written constitution or a Bill of Rights
which entrenches entitlement to family life, British courts are
powerless to strike down decisions by immigration officers which
have the result of keeping families apart.

The rule which has caused most anguish is the 'primary purpose' test for the entry of a spouse. There is nothing wrong in principle with the requirement that the parties should intend to live together as man and wife, but the Rules now additionally place the burden on the applicant to prove 'that the marriage was not entered into primarily to obtain admission to the UK'. The 'primary purpose' rule and the burden of proving it allow several thousand spouses and fiancées to be turned back each year on mere suspicion – 71 per cent of those who applied for entry visas from Pakistan in 1989, for example. Inevitably, it is a racist rule with a racist application, rarely considered in the case of applications by Australian or American couples. Many mistakes are made (as the statistics of successful appeals demonstrate) by immigration officials who have no cultural background or training to assess marital purpose amongst different communities. Ludicrously, a marriage which fails the test to begin with 'will still retain its non-qualifying character whatever happened afterwards and even if the husband applied for entry on their Golden Wedding day'.[7] It has been used to justify the most intimate and intrusive questioning of applicants, by customs officers who sometimes seem to hold a Mills & Boon view of personal relationships. One applicant was turned down because his letters were not 'sufficiently affectionate', while those who honestly hesitate over the sixty-four-dollar question, 'If your fiancée did not live in England, would you still go to her home to live?', are turned away.

The 'primary purpose' test was originally applied only to men who wished to marry women settled in Britain, but in 1985 the European Court ruled that this amounted to sex discrimination.[8] The Government responded by applying the test to women seeking entry as well. Where entry is permitted the marriage is subject to a 'probation period' of twelve months, with deportation for those who do not display sufficient commitment by the end of that period. This limited respect for family life is extended only in the context of marriage: the Immigration Rules recognize no other relationships, however successful or permanent (although there is discretion to admit a woman whose unmarried permanent relationship with a man is established 'by a local custom or tradition'). Local British custom and tradition was vindicated by the 1988 Immigration Act which precluded a wife of a polygamous marriage from exercising her right of abode if another wife preceded her into the United Kingdom. Needless to say the Rules are entirely silent about the plight of homosexual couples: British citizens have no entitlement to be joined by foreign lovers of the same sex.

Rules relating to the entry of 'dependants' are even more strict. Children may not join their parents if they are aged over eighteen. Elderly parents and other close relatives are not permitted entry to settle with their children unless they have become 'wholly or mainly dependent' on these children, are over sixty-five and have no other relations to turn to in their present place of residence. 'Dependence' means financial dependence, and not 'the normal love and affection of a united family', although officials have been urged by the courts to interpret this rule with a 'broad humanity' which recognizes the need for children settled here to care for chronically ill or isolated parents.[9] Even temporary reunion of families for weddings or funerals may be prevented where immigration officers have any suspicion that a visitor may 'overstay'. The introduction of visa requirements for visitors from the Indian subcontinent and from Ghana and Nigeria in 1986 led to 11,575 visa refusals in the first six months of the system's operation. By subjecting black Commonwealth citizens, rather than white, to the need for visas (as well as other entry documents), the Government sent a clear signal to black communities in Britain that its immigration policy was driven by considerations of colour.

A particularly agonizing problem arises when husbands settled in this country die or decide to leave it or to end their marriage before members of their families have been granted permanent-residence status. In these circumstances, the wife and children will generally have to leave, especially if they cannot maintain themselves without 'recourse to public funds'. In 1984 the European Parliament condemned as callous the decision to deport a wife and family whose husband was killed in a fire. The assumption in many of these 'family deportation' cases is that the wife is a mere appendage, and the links that she and her children forge with a local community count for little once their 'bread-winner' has been removed.[10] In 1992 the EC Court of Justice struck an important blow against the racist and sexist assumptions of UK immigration practice in this respect by ruling that the legal rights of movement and residence within the community granted to nationals of an EC country could be enjoyed by their non-EC-national spouses. It followed that an

Indian who married an English woman and worked in Britain and Germany had acquired a community right to reside and work, and could not be deported from Britain after the marriage had ended in divorce.[11] European law will be of little use to non-Europeans when the discriminatory practice they complain about is one which favours Europeans – as it does in respect of *au pairs*, who are permitted to enter and work with English families only if they are from Western Europe (Mexican and Filipino maids are not even permitted work permits). The rules rigidly define an *au pair* as 'an unmarried girl aged 11–27', and in 1992 immigration officials were made to look ridiculous when they detained a nineteen-year-old male *au pair* from Sweden, arranged by a family 'as a way of showing their children that child care is the responsibility of both sexes'. The Home Secretary personally intervened to reverse the decision – which he would not have done had an *au pair* of either sex arrived from Africa or Asia. British middle-class traditions may learn to cope with equality of the sexes, but not of races.

Literal compliance with these Immigration Rules can appear heartless to severed families, and although discretion to decide compassionately exists at every level there is little doubt that indulgence is more readily extended to white immigrants than to blacks and Asians. This is a major cause of the bitterness and anger which exists within ethnic communities in Britain, and the limitations of the appeal system have done little to defuse it. The appeal system is in two stages: first to an adjudicator, and then to the Immigration Appeals Tribunal. The major deficiency is that most people refused entry clearance, either in their place of residence or by being turned away on arrival, will not be in Britain to prepare or present their appeal. Unless the claim is for patriality or the applicant has already obtained a work permit or entry clearance, the appeal will have to be mounted from abroad.[12] Communication with lawyers will be difficult, and as Lord Bridge recently noted 'the person removed, being unable to attend the hearing of his appeal, has no realistic prospect of presenting it with success'.[13]

The 1993 Asylum and Immigration Appeals Act abolished the right of would-be visitors and short-term students to lodge an appeal against the refusal of an entry clearance. This backwards step means that immigration officials will make decisions about visitors to Britain without any form of accountability to the courts. It will mean more arbitrary and racist decisions, as many blacks and Africans seeking entry for family reunions, weddings and the like will find themselves refused entry, without reason and without appeal. The abolition of these appeal rights, which visitors and students had enjoyed since 1971, came after 1,500 out of 9,000 appeals in this category had proved successful in 1992. This indicates the extent to which decisions have been cavalier and ill-informed, and will be all the more so without the discipline of an appeals system. Despite strong objections from a number of law lords, the Government cynically insisted on ending the embarrassingly high number of successful appeals by ending appeals altogether.

To help immigration officials decide whether and on what terms entry will be granted, they possess wide powers to detain and examine passengers, take copies of their correspondence, and order airlines and shipping companies to remove immediately those they reject. Regrettably, there is no 'duty solicitor' scheme for those detained at British ports: the only protection is an ancient, traditional right of Members of Parliament to intervene and request a 'stop' on a removal until the MP has time to make representations to the Home Secretary. This power was valuable, in that it enabled detainees to obtain legal advice and allowed information to be produced which sometimes led to an official rethink, but in 1988 this privilege (which rested only on convention) was severely restricted. MPs' intercessions are now limited to requesting a review (if they are quick enough) of decisions to send visitors back on the next plane. Such decisions will only be reversed in 'compelling circumstances'.

DEPORTATION

The extirpation from a country of persons settled within its borders is the most direct infringement of freedom of movement: it requires the clearest justification and unobstructed rights of appeal. In the United Kingdom expulsion may be accomplished:

(1) by administrative directions to expel illegal immigrants;

(2) by deportation of those who 'overstay' or fail to observe other conditions of entry;

(3) by deportation on the recommendation of a court after conviction for a criminal offence;

(4) by deportation deemed 'conducive to the public good' by the Home Secretary;

(5) by extradition at the request of foreign countries to stand trial for alleged crimes abroad.

Removal of allegedly illegal immigrants by administrative direction is drastic, in that rights of appeal cannot be exercised except after removal, when they are virtually valueless. An 'illegal immigrant' is one who has secretly entered the country without passing through immigration control, or has presented false documents or otherwise secured entry by fraud. In 1980 the House of Lords extended this category alarmingly by ruling that it included persons who had not made full disclosure of every relevant fact to immigration officers, but this decision (which meant that jet-lagged applicants had a legal duty to answer questions they were never asked) met with an avalanche of criticism and was reversed three years later by *Khawaja*.[14] In that case the Law Lords opted for 'a robust exercise of the judicial function in safeguarding citizens' rights' against detention and removal without proper rights of appeal. The Government has not shown similar robustness in extending a right of appeal to persons detained on the allegation of being an illegal entrant.

Another unattractive incident of the power is the way it is sometimes exercised by 'rounding up' members of ethnic communities in raids on homes, factories and supermarkets, and detaining them in custody until the legality of their status has been established. Detention often lasts for several months before removal: supervision is privately contracted to Securicor, whose employees are not subject to police-discipline codes. It amounts to imprisonment without trial and without a right of appeal, and in 1991 was inflicted on 4,500 people.

The Home Secretary will normally order deportation of those who 'overstay' in breach of entry conditions, unless they have put down roots in circumstances which warrant compassion or recognition of good character and input into their local community. The Home Secretary's decisions, usually delegated to middle-ranking civil servants, could be reviewed on their merits by adjudicators and then by the Immigration Appeals Tribunal (IAT) until 1988, when the Immigration Act of that year excluded appeals in all cases where the 'overstay' has been less than seven years. This unjustified destruction of appeal rights means that most deportees can only resist an order if it is susceptible to judicial review – i.e. has been made irrationally, or as the result of an error of law. Humanity is henceforth the unappealable prerogative of the Home Office.

A deportation order made by a court as part of the sentence for a criminal offence may be reviewed by the Court of Appeal, and is in any event no more than a recommendation upon which the Home Secretary is not obliged to act – he is enjoined by the Rules to take 'all relevant circumstances' into account, including representations, before giving effect to it. Deportation recommendations, the Court of Appeal has recently stressed, are serious matters, requiring 'full and proper inquiry' to produce evidence that the offender's continuing presence would be a potential detriment to the country. Where EEC nationals stand convicted, a deportation order must not be made unless they constitute a real threat to public order and security,[15] and in the case of other aliens minor offences do not justify a recommendation unless there is a gang element or a likelihood of more serious repetition.[16] In 1992 the Court of Human Rights further insisted that deportations should not violate the respect for family life guaranteed by Article 8 of the European Convention: the French Government was not permitted to expel an Algerian national who had committed several serious offences, because he had lived in France for many years, his wife was French and deportation 'might imperil the unity or very existence of the marriage'.[17]

Despite these self-denying ordinances, there have been occasions when magistrates' courts have succumbed to the temptation to rid the country of foreign students convicted of minor offences in the course of demonstrating support for unpopular causes. Particularly bad examples were set by London magistrates who made mass deportation recommendations against Iranian and Libyan students, many of whom had been convicted of no more than minor obstruction offences outside the United States Embassy. Immigrants should not have their right to protest chilled by the possibility of expulsion for an offence of highway obstruction committed by most trade-union picketers, and in these instances the magistrates were made to look foolish when the deportees delightedly accepted free trips back to Tehran and Tripoli to receive acclamation on their arrival. Most offenders, of course, will not relish their homecoming and may in some cases be subjected to persecution on political grounds. The Court of Appeal has stubbornly insisted that such considerations are irrelevant to the judicial decision to recommend deportation: they are 'political' matters of which the Home Secretary must alone be judge. This is one of many points in immigration law where the courts shrink from impinging upon the Government's exclusive prerogative to decide 'political' questions, although it might be thought that a judge is a better tribunal to decide, on evidence, whether an individual is likely to be persecuted on return to a particular country than the Home Secretary, who is likely to be swayed by considerations of diplomacy rather than justice.

POLITICAL EXPULSIONS

The Home Secretary's power to expel aliens where he deems this 'conducive to the public good' was used during the cold war years to deport American Communists, and in 1965 the Labour Government deported an American pacifist who was a member of the 'Committee of 100'. There was no right of appeal, and the court's attitude to natural justice in security matters was exemplified in 1962 in the case of Dr Soblen, who had been convicted of espionage in the USA after a trial much criticized for its unfairness. Soblen fled to Israel prior to sentence, where pressure from the US Government soon had him put back on a plane bound for New York. Over British air space he slashed his wrists, and he was landed and hospitalized in London. Under extradition law Soblen was safe – he was a political offender. But Washington's wish for his return was the British Home Secretary's command, and a deportation order was made on the ground that his presence – thus far confined to a prison hospital – was 'not conducive to the public good'. His application for *habeas corpus* was rejected by the Court of Appeal, on the basis that deportation was purely an administrative action and he had no right to make representations or to any other of the other protections normally afforded by the rules of natural justice.[18]

The order could only be challenged if it was made in bad faith, i.e. as a device to achieve an illegitimate extradition requested by the United States Government. US Embassy officials had admitted as much to *The Times*, but its articles were not evidence. The crucial documents were the exchange of correspondence between the two Governments, and this the court refused to order to be disclosed, on the grounds of national interest. Soblen committed suicide on the morning he was due to be escorted to the airport by a US police officer.

The denial of natural justice to Soblen was a factor in the Wilson Committee recommendation, a few years later, that 'security' cases should not be exempt from the fundamental principle that 'any administrative decision should be subject to scrutiny and appeal before execution'. It accepted that the Appeal Tribunal might have to hear evidence in camera, 'but there would be no question of withholding from the appellant particulars of what is alleged against him'.[19] But when the Labour Government came to implement the Wilson Report by setting up an immigration appeals machinery, it provided that appeals in security cases were to be heard by a specially vetted panel whose judgement would not be binding on the Home Secretary.

This short-lived attempt to do a little justice in national security cases was soon tested when the incoming Conservative Home Secretary, Reginald Maudling, desired to rid the country of Rudi Dutschke. Once a radical student leader in Germany, Dutschke had been allowed entry to convalesce from an assassination attempt, and had been offered a research post at Cambridge. At his appeal, it was alleged he had engaged in political activities in this country, and some of the evidence against him was inspected by the tribunal in secret. None the less he was given a 2,500-word statement of the case against him, which he was able to challenge with a large measure of success. Indeed, the tribunal found that he had the qualities to make a 'significant contribution to historical research' and that 'up to the present time his presence in this country has not constituted an appreciable danger to national security'. But then, blandly and illogically, it ventured the view that 'there must be a risk in his continued presence', and Maudling confirmed the deportation order expressing the fear that Dutschke might become 'a focal point for student and political unrest'. The obvious unfairness of this decision caused justified outrage and demands for changes in the composition of the tribunal, which had included two retired diplomats and a Deputy Chief of the Defence Staff.

But this was not the lesson taken to heart by the Home Secretary. Acting on the principle that the less that is known the less there will be to complain about, he abolished the right of appeal altogether in security cases. The 1971 Immigration Rules now permit only 'representations' to a civil service panel of 'three wise men' which proffers 'advice' to the Home Secretary in secret. The Government had been criticized for not allowing Dutschke to see *all* the evidence against him, so its solution was to allow others no right to see *any* of the evidence. Maudling claimed that the 'three wise men' system had worked well in civil-service 'purge' cases, which it had not (see earlier, page 150) and that the convention of the Home Secretary's responsibility to Parliament would be a safeguard against abuse of power – which it is not, for the simple reason that there is another convention which entitles Ministers to refuse to answer questions about decisions taken on security grounds.

The Labour Party, to its discredit, supported the abolition of appeal rights, and made first use of the new system to deport Philip Agee and Mark Hosenball. Agee was an ex-CIA officer living in Cambridge and writing books exposing his former employers, whilst Hosenball was an experienced journalist working for the *Evening Standard*. Agee had no secrets relating to British intelligence, and was not infringing US law: the damage he was doing to a friendly intelligence agency was presumably thought sufficient to justify his expulsion. Hosenball was given no information at all as to the reason his presence was not conducive to the public good. Both men attended at secret hearings of the 'three advisers' to recite their life stories: they were given no opportunity to cross-examine witnesses or to learn, let alone to test, the evidence against them. The 'three wise men' comprised a solicitor who had served in the security service, a retired civil servant who had formerly been Permanent Secretary to the Admiralty, and a retired Post Office official. It is not known how they 'advised' the Home Secretary, but both deportation orders were confirmed.

Hosenball appealed on the grounds that he had been denied natural justice by the Home Secretary's refusal to give him any details of the case against him. The Court of Appeal conceded readily enough that he had been the victim of an unjust proceeding, but the rules of 'natural justice' were not to be applied to deportation decisions taken by the Home Secretary on 'national security' grounds. Lord Denning was prepared to sacrifice legality, fairness and equality in favour of blind obedience to Government claims of 'national security' ('The rules of natural justice have to be modified in regard to foreigners who prove themselves unwelcome and ought to be deported').[20] His words are enthusiastically quoted by counsel for repressive regimes throughout the common-law world which deport their critics or detain them without trial. Hosenball has for the past fifteen years been working as a Washington correspondent for the *Sunday Times*: he is still not permitted to re-enter the United Kingdom.

Central to Hosenball's case is the proposition that British courts cannot and will not examine the justification for executive actions which are alleged to be 'in the interests of national security'. This excuse has been used by the British Government to ban publications like *Spycatcher*, to prevent disclosure of documents relevant to court proceedings and to outlaw trade unions at GCHQ. These are all infringements of civil liberties, but they are not as devastating for their victims as a decision to detain without trial and to deport a person who has long been settled in this country. In this context in particular, 'the rule of law' is a fairy-tale if the legal process is precluded from examining the validity of the executive's action. Yet the British judiciary has consistently held that 'national security is the exclusive responsibility of the executive': as Lord Diplock explained in the GCHQ case, 'it is *par excellence* a non-justiciable question'. Why? The question of whether national security grounds really exist is no more or less 'justiciable' than whether other grounds, of the sort that courts examine every day, exist as the basis for disputed action. The question of whether procedures in national-security cases are 'fair' is never difficult to decide. It may be that sources of information need to be withheld (as often happens in criminal trials) or that certain information should be heard in closed court or that security-service witnesses should testify anonymously. It may be that judges should accept 'hearsay' evidence, and be content with deciding whether it is *reasonably believed* that national security is at stake, rather than deciding whether it really is. The burden of proving that it is not at stake might be put upon the applicant. But surely it is false to assert that these questions are 'non-justiciable'. They *can* be decided: British judges simply do not *want* to decide them. In relation to this issue, and to this issue alone, they have adopted this inflexible formula in relation to 'national security' claims: 'The Government knows best.'

There was hope, after the bogus claims of national security had been exposed during the *Spycatcher* saga, that judges would take the next available opportunity to change their approach. The powers available to the court to examine the legitimacy of detention under the writ of *habeas corpus* would permit scrutiny of 'national security' claims, and the onset of the Gulf War provided the opportunity to reconsider Hosenball's case when the UK (unlike any other allied power) detained for deportation 160 Iraqi and Palestinian residents whose presence was no longer deemed 'conducive to the public good'. The round-up was badly mismanaged, being based on outdated and often incorrect MI5 files, and the detainees included some who had actually come to the UK as refugees fleeing from Saddam Hussein. One of his most prominent opponents was Abbas Cheblak, a distinguished author and teacher who had publicly protested against the invasion of Kuwait. He had been settled in England with his wife and family for sixteen years. On the day after Operation Desert Storm begun in January 1991, he was arrested and imprisoned to await deportation. At first the Home Secretary declined to give any reasons at all for this action: under pressure as a result of Cheblak's *habeas corpus* proceedings, he would say merely that the applicant had 'known links' with an organization (which he refused to specify) which could take terrorist action in support of the Iraqi Government. The Court of Appeal refused to examine this allegation, or the grounds for it, or to order the Government to give further reasons. The Home Secretary had said that provision of further details 'would prove an unacceptable risk to national security' and the oracle had spoken – the Court would not examine the logic or the reasonableness of his belief. In the light of Cheblak's 'known links' with anti-Saddam organizations and his pacifist commitments, the Home Secretary's decision was surprising, but the Master of the Rolls hastened to add darkly 'Those who are able most effectively to undermine national security are those who least appear to constitute any risk to it.'[21]

This is Alice-in-Wonderland language, out of place in a court of law. While the other judges approached the case more narrowly, blaming Parliament for conferring a draconian power on the Home Secretary to 'deem' a deportation conducive to the public good, Lord Donaldson went out of his way to defend the Government, and even to praise its 'three wise men' procedure, which he described (with some difficulty) as 'independent quasi-judicial scrutiny'. He proclaimed:

The Home Secretary is fully accountable to Parliament for his decisions whether or not to deport and, as part of that accountability, for any failure to heed the advice of the statutory panel.

This is a statement neither of law nor fact. The Home Secretary's accountability is meaningless under a convention which permits him to refuse to answer parliamentary questions which touch upon 'national security'. The advice of the statutory panel is a state secret, as is the fact of whether the Home Secretary has chosen to heed it, so there can be no question of any accountability on that score. It is true that the Government appointed a senior judge to head the advisory panel for these Iraqi cases, in order to give it some public credibility. Lord Donaldson equated this advisory panel with the City takeover panel, but the comparison is bizarre: one regulates private corporate behaviour, the other replaces the courts as the only 'safeguard' against Government destruction of a subject's liberty and perhaps life. The 'three wise men' may be turned into three blind mice: they have no statutory powers or proper procedures, they refuse legal representation, they are told only what the security services decide to tell them about the case, they cannot inform detainees of what is alleged against them, they cannot insist on receiving evidence from the Home Secretary and the security services (let alone on testing it) and their secret 'advice' is not binding in any event. Abbas Cheblak later related how the panel merely listened to him and his witnesses, asked very few questions and said they would read the papers. 'They smiled a great deal and stressed that they only had power to advise the Home Office. After that I went back to my cell.' The 'three wise men' procedure is so conspicuously lacking in fairness that it cannot be regarded as a satisfactory safeguard against the abuse of executive power over the liberty of the subject.

By the time the Gulf War had ended, nineteen of the thirty-three detainees to appear before the panel (including Cheblak) had been released – an indication of the obvious unreliability of the security 'evidence' on which they had been detained. The episode had damaged race relations, by associating residents from the Middle East with unproven 'terrorist' propensities. What was most noticeable was the total failure of Labour and Liberal politicians to criticize the Government action while the war was continuing. This is a familiar phenomenon: MPs criticize abuses of power when it is safe to do so, and are silent when popular passions are raging against the victims of such abuses. This is why victims must in such a climate be able to turn to the courts for a protection which they will certainly not receive from Members of Parliament. There is no reason, as the Wilson Committee explained, why they should not have an appeal to the courts, and the reasons advanced in the cases of Hosenball and Cheblak are spurious. Both Mark Hosenball and Abbas Cheblak were innocent of any danger to national security and the courts should have said so, adopting the approach of Lord Atkin during the Second World War to the case of *Liversidge* v. *Anderson*:

It has always been one of the pillars of freedom, one of the principles of liberty for which on recent authority we are now fighting, that the judges are no respectors of persons and stand between the subject and any attempted encroachments on his liberty by the executive, alert to see that any coercive action is justified in law.

That was a courageous dissenting speech, for which Atkin suffered social ostracism: his brethren childishly refused to eat with him in the House of Lords. Only ministers and their civil servants would find these words indigestible today, when the public increasingly expects judges to live up to them. The real damage which cases like *Hosenball* and *Cheblak* have done as authorities for the principle that 'national security' is non-justiciable is not in Britain so much as to human rights throughout the British Commonwealth, in countries where political dissidents are actively detained without trial under security legislation modelled on British examples (usually including an 'advisory panel' chaired by a judge). The courts in these countries still follow English legal decisions, and counsel for repressive regimes invariably cite *Hosenball* (and now *Cheblak*) to convince the judges that they have no powers to interfere with any tyrannical action which is justified by the magic words 'in the interests of national security'. Thus can British common law, composed in comfort by luminously learned Law Lords, contribute to the failure to remedy human rights outrages in some of the world's worst political prisons.

The Home Secretary has an unappealable power to direct that foreigners should not be allowed to enter the UK on the grounds that their presence would not be conducive to the public good. In the late sixties and early seventies this power was used to stop North Vietnamese politicians, European student leaders, Marxist professors and American radicals from entering the country to speak at political gatherings, and until 1980 it was regularly invoked against Scientologists. In the case of EEC nationals the power must not be used unless the person poses a clear danger to public health or order, but otherwise the Home Secretary has an absolute discretion to exclude any individual whose life-style or beliefs might outrage the British public. The most ridiculous exercise of the power was to stop an Oxford University debate in 1986 between Professor Timothy Leary, jaded apostle of sixties radicalism, and Gordon Liddy, defender of executive secrecy who organized the 'Watergate' break-in. These two had performed double-act debates across American campuses, but the Home Office had no doubt about which side was most conductive to British public good: Liddy was allowed to enter and Leary was turned away.

POLITICAL ASYLUM

The United Kingdom is a signatory to the 1951 UN Convention and Protocol relating to the status of refugees, which is incorporated into domestic law by Section 1 of the 1993 Asylum and Immigration Appeals Act and provides that applications for asylum may be made by any person

on the ground that, if he were required to leave, he would have to go to a country to which he is unwilling to go owing to a well-founded fear of being persecuted for reasons of race, religion, nationality, membership of a particular social group or political opinion.

Applications for asylum and for refugee status are decided by the

Home Office, subject to rights of appeal to the adjudicator and in certain cases to the IAT. The question for the Home Office is whether the applicant would suffer persecution, and if this is determined in his favour, he is entitled to remain. The courts will not second-guess the Home Secretary, but exercise a supervisory jurisdiction to ensure that his decisions are made rationally, with procedural fairness, and take cognizance of all relevant factors. In this respect, it must be said the judges have displayed a commendably tough attitude towards Home Office callousness and incompetence, and have devised procedural methods to ensure that asylum seekers are protected until their claims can be properly considered.

The lengths to which they have been prepared to go were demonstrated in 1991, when Home Secretary Kenneth Baker was held in contempt of court for disdaining a court order aimed at saving the life of a refugee from torture in Zaïre, who had been put on a plane back to that country by immigration officials.[22] Baker did not resign (so much for 'ministerial accountability') but the account of high-handedness, legal ineptitude and official arrogance set out in the Court of Appeal's judgement illustrates the lack of concern for human rights which is all too often displayed behind closed doors in Whitehall. It took this first-ever contempt conviction of a Cabinet Minister before the Government was prepared to establish in British law (Section 6 of the 1993 Act) the international law principle that refugee claimants have a right to remain in the country until their claim is decided. (Even so, Section 6 does not go far enough to incorporate this principle, because it does not permit them to remain in order to appeal an adverse decision.)

In 1993 the House of Lords, in a decision of resounding constitutional importance, ruled in the *Kenneth Baker* case appeal that courts had power to grant injunctions against ministers of the crown and their officials, and to hold them in contempt of court if they disobeyed. Where that disobedience was the fault of his departmental officers rather than of a minister himself, the contempt finding would be against the minister 'in his official capacity', but it could be made against him personally if the contempt related to his own default. Although the court exonerated Baker of personal liability, the prospect of a criminal conviction will henceforth concentrate the minds of ministers who may be tempted to ignore inconvenient court orders made to protect asylum-seekers. It is a measure of how degraded Government thinking has become towards refugee claims that this was the first time that the courts had squarely to respond to executive defiance of their orders. The robustness of that response was a welcome sign of a willingness to protect both their own authority against the state, and the people on whose behalf that authority is exercised. The Government's argument that since its ministers and officials were obliged to obey the law there was no power in the courts to enforce it against them by injunctions or contempt proceedings was met with incredulity. The notion that the executive obeyed the law as a matter of grace and not of necessity was, Lord Templeman riposted, 'a proposition that would reverse the result of the Civil War'.[23] The refugee to whom Britain owes the affirmation of this fundamental constitutional principle has not been heard of since the plane on which he had unlawfully been placed landed in Zaïre, the country where he feared torture and death.

One disgraceful example of political expediency overriding international obligations was the case of *Amekrane*, a Moroccan air-force officer who in 1972 fled to Gibraltar and requested political asylum after a plot to overthrow King Hassan's Government collapsed. The request was immediately refused and although no extradition treaty existed with Morocco, Amekrane was immediately handed over to its Government for execution. An application to the European Commission on behalf of his wife and children, alleging that he had been subjected to inhumane treatment by the UK Government in returning him to certain death for a political offence, was declared admissible: the Government bought off an adverse verdict by an *ex gratia* payment of £37,500.[24] As in the case of Dr Soblen, the Home Secretary had used his discretionary powers under the immigration laws to effect an 'extradition' which would not otherwise have been lawful: the lack of any substantive right to appeal the refusal of political asylum sealed the applicant's fate.

In *Bugdaycay* v. *Secretary of State*, Lord Bridge endorsed the crucially important principle that the

most fundamental of all human rights is the individual's right to life and, when an administrative decision under challenge is said to be one which may put the applicant's life at risk, the basis of the decision must call for the most anxious scrutiny.[25]

In that case the applicant was a Ugandan refugee whose father and cousins had been killed by the secret police, and who had reason to believe that the same fate would befall him should he return. He had lived for some years in Kenya, to which country the Home Secretary had decided to deport him, ignoring a good deal of evidence that Kenya had (in contravention of its own obligation under the UN Convention) returned such refugees to Uganda in similar circumstances. The House of Lords held that the Immigration Rules must not be interpreted so as to conflict with the Convention on the Status of Refugees, Article 33 of which requires that:

No state shall expel or return a refugee in any manner whatsoever to the frontiers of territories where his life or freedom would be threatened on account of his race, religion, nationality, membership of a particular social group or political opinion.

Although Kenya was not a territory where the applicant would be directly threatened, the risk that it would return him to Uganda made his removal to Kenya a contravention of the convention.

This aspect of *Bugdaycay* is a welcome 1987 decision which shows what courts can do when they try, even under the severe limitations of judicial review which confines them to inspection of procedures rather than consideration of merits. It is impossible to read the facts, as set out in the speech of Lord Bridge, without despairing at the Home Office's consistent failure to inform itself of the political realities in East Africa. Its conduct at various stages was described as 'strange' and 'even stranger', and 'doing little to inspire confidence in its procedure'; its affidavits were 'at worst self-contradictory, at best ambiguous'. How many of the 3,882 applications for political asylum in that year (only 450 of which were granted) were dealt with in such slipshod ways, by incompetent or ignorant officials whose decisions cannot be reviewed on their merits? The importance of *Bugdaycay* is that the court used its powers under *habeas corpus* writs to get to grips with the real merits of the life-or-death nature of a decision to grant or withhold asylum. Faced with this determination on the part of the judiciary, the Government conceded in the 1993 Act that asylum seekers could at least remain in the UK for long enough to pursue initial appeals to special adjudicators. Further appeals on the merits to the IAT will not be allowed, however, if the Home Secretary certifies they are 'without foundation' and the adjudicator agrees; a mean-minded limitation, given that most asylum claims upheld subsequently by the courts are initially refused by the Home Office as 'without foundation'. Moreover, many asylum seekers will be forced under the fast-track procedures of the 1993 Act to submit their appeal against rejection of refugee status within forty-eight hours, and it will be decided within seven days – a procedure which manifestly sacrifices justice to expedition. (The European Committee of Ministers, which is hardly generous to asylum rights, recommended a month as the minimum time which fairness requires for claim submission and assessment.) The fairness and humanity of the new system will depend heavily on the independence and awareness of the 'special adjudicators' to be appointed by the Lord Chancellor; regrettably the Act does not require them to have any special knowledge of the refugee situation.

Although asylum applicants are described as 'refugees', the concept does not extend to those who flee from their birthplace because of famine or poverty or earthquake. Nor does it include those who are innocently caught up in riots or revolutionary strife between contending parties, no matter how painful or distressing the experience awaiting them on their return. Refugees must not only fear personal persecution, but their fear must be objectively well founded, in the sense that they must be able to demonstrate a reasonable degree of likelihood that they will be persecuted in their own country for one of the reasons listed in the International Convention. This ruling by the House of Lords in another 1987 case disposed of applications by six Tamils who genuinely feared they would suffer violence if they were returned to Sri Lanka, where civil war between Government forces and guerrillas had brought suffering to most Tamil families. The court held that it was not sufficient for the fears to be genuine or even understandable if on an objective basis there was no reasonable likelihood of them being realized.[26] Four of the six were actually imprisoned and tortured after their enforced return to Sri Lanka, and were finally allowed back to Britain as refugees in 1989.

What amounts to 'persecution'? It does not mean prosecution for an ordinary criminal offence, unless the defendant has been made a scapegoat as a result of his political opinions or race. All that the refugee should have to show is that, given the opinions which he holds, his fear of future persecution is well founded. In some cases, however, the IAT has quibbled with distinctions (when does 'harassment' amount to 'persecution'?) and has displayed a certain naïvety about the behaviour of the police and military forces of 'friendly' governments. Home Office decisions defer excessively to the United Kingdom's current political alliances, because the Government is afraid to cause diplomatic pique by suggesting that allies persecute their citizens. Thus it is reluctant to give asylum to fugitives from Commonwealth countries, although some have appalling records of jailing and torturing dissidents. Before the collapse of Communism, defectors from behind the Iron Curtain could much more readily establish a 'well-founded' fear of persecution than people like Amekrane, who had plotted against a Government whose support Britain needed at a time of its dispute with Spain over Gibraltar. All sorts of spurious reasons have been given by British ministers for denying asylum to dissident Americans, however well-founded their fears were of being persecuted for the political opinions which led them to dodge the Vietnam draft or to escape the McCarthyite purges. Just how far Home Secretaries are prepared to go by way of condoning the malpractices of allies is demonstrated by the strange case of Dr Joseph Cort, a brilliant US pharmacist lecturing at Birmingham University when the McCarthy hearings began. He suffered from polio and myopia, and his US military service had been indefinitely deferred, but when his name was mentioned by the Committee for Un-American Activities as a 'Communist sympathizer' he was promptly recalled for active service. He was ordered to leave Britain after his application for asylum was refused, on the grounds that 'The Government of the supplicant's country does not employ methods of political persecution.' Cort was accepted by the Czech Academy of Science, where he developed drugs now in worldwide use for diabetes and kidney disease, and in 1977 he was welcomed back to New York as a professor at Mount Sinai Hospital and a vice-president of a major drug company.[27]

Britain's current record in granting claims to refugee status is one of the worst in Western Europe. It accepts less than one thousand asylum seekers each year, despite the fact that it has comparatively few applicants (about twenty thousand, compared with two hundred thousand who seek entry into West Germany). The UK limits claimants by applying a 'first safe country' rule, namely that a refugee whose plane has touched down in another country *en route* to Britain will be sent back to that country to seek his asylum there. This is not a rule of international law, however convenient for a country which is the last stop on airline flight paths. (It is likely, however, to become a rule of European law, as EC governments agree to allow applicants only one chance to find a safe haven within the Community).[28] The most effective method of limiting asylum applications, however, has been the heavy fines imposed on airlines and shipping companies which carry fugitives whose entry documents are not correct – and the papers of genuine refugees rarely are, because people fleeing for their lives do not have time to wait around for a visa. (Political refugees may have escaped from prison, or would be denied exit visas by their governments, or fear surveillance by attending the local UK embassy.) The Government has in effect 'contracted out' immigration control of refugees to the airlines, which have avoided financial penalties by refusing to fly refugees and in several cases by removing them from passenger planes by tricks or force. What makes this treatment so unconscionable is that refugee status is a legal right, which all civilized nations have a duty to recognize. Instead, the United Kingdom forces international carriers to treat them as if they were illegal immigrants. The position is made the more untenable by the fact that claims on our compassion are so minimal compared with the burden shouldered by other and poorer nations: Pakistan is home to 3 million refugees, Jordan has 800,000, and Somalia and Malawi give sanctuary to 600,000.

EXTRADITION

There is no branch of civil-liberties law which has undergone such a sea-change in public attitudes as extradition, the process by which the courts and the Home Secretary decide whether to surrender a resident (frequently, a British citizen) for trial in a foreign country. In 1988, the Criminal Justice Act removed the traditional safeguard of the *prima facie* case, extended the definition of extradition crimes, and made it much easier for foreign Governments to obtain the return of those they claim to be fugitives from their country's justice. These changes made it possible for Britain to implement the

European Convention on Extradition, which came into force in 1991 to smooth the surrender process between the nineteen signatory countries.

Extradition is based on reciprocal treaties between states: the UK Government undertakes to hand over persons within its power accused of crime in another country in return for that country promising to return persons within its borders who are wanted in Britain. Unlike domestic laws relating to criminal offences, extradition treaties are given the broadest possible interpretation to effect their purpose of bringing to justice those who are guilty of grave crimes.[29] The procedure, broadly speaking, is that a foreign state requests the extradition of a fugitive and the Home Secretary decides whether to accede to the request: if yes, a warrant is issued empowering arrest, and the evidence is forwarded to a stipendiary magistrate who must decide (subject to appeal) whether the extradition conditions have been met. The magistrate could only commit for extradition if satisfied that the evidence was sufficient to justify sending a defendant for trial – i.e. that there was credible evidence upon which a reasonable jury, properly directed, could convict. This test remains for extradition to Commonwealth countries, which is governed by the Fugitive Offenders Act of 1967. However, it had long proved irksome to European nations, whose inquisitorial system requires the attendance of an accused during the course of investigation by a magistrate. The 1988 Criminal Justice Act permits the Government to sidestep the *prima facie* case requirement by entering into arrangements with foreign states (e.g. by the European Extradition Convention) which preclude its application: in such cases the magistrate need only be satisfied that the offence is an 'extradition crime' – i.e. that it relates to conduct punishable in Britain by a prison sentence of twelve months or more. The fugitive, if committed, may apply for *habeas corpus*, and the High Court is given a discretion to order his discharge if satisfied that extradition would be 'unjust or oppressive' because of the triviality or staleness of the offence or because the accusation 'is not made in good faith in the interests of justice'. Governments are still bound to honour the 'rule of speciality', by which the extraditee may only be prosecuted for the crimes for which extradition has been granted. There was an outcry in 1991 when Dessie Ellis, the first Irishman to be extradited to Britain from the Republic, was committed for trial on different charges because the magistrate ruled that English courts had no jurisdiction to try the actual charges on which he had been extradited. The Government was obliged to honour the speciality rule, drop the new charges and restore the original ones, upon which Ellis was acquitted.

The 1988 reforms, by permitting 'extradition on demand', abolish an important civil liberty hitherto guaranteed to citizen and foreigner alike. Once an appropriate treaty is in place, the magistrate becomes merely a rubber stamp, making no examination of the evidence other than to ensure that the crime alleged has an equivalent in British law carrying a sentence of twelve months or more. There will be no presentation of the facts of the case, and no prospect of challenge or review of the evidential sufficiency of the request. The High Court's power to discharge a fugitive if the extradition would be 'unjust and oppressive' is limited to three circumstances (triviality, delay or bad faith) and the broadest – that the accusation has been made in bad faith – will be virtually impossible to prove, as Dr Soblen's lawyers discovered. Moreover, the 1988 Act permits 'special arrangements' to be made for particular cases with states with which Britain has no extradition treaty, suggesting that retrospective political bargains may be struck over the return of individual suspects. The Government resisted amendments which would have prevented extradition to countries which impose the death penalty. At present, some extradition treaties (e.g. with the USA) provide that the Home Secretary *may* ask for an assurance that the death penalty will not be carried out, but in 1987 the Divisional Court refused to require him to seek such an assurance before a mentally abnormal suspect was returned to a US state which was likely to execute him for murder.[30] It took the European Court of Human Rights to intervene on behalf of decency and humanity by finding that the decision would breach the Article 3 prohibition against infliction of 'inhuman or degrading treatment or punishment'. *Soering* v. *UK* imposes a most important limitation on extradition power; although the Court did not find capital punishment impermissible *per se*, it located ill treatment in the mental anguish that the applicant would suffer while waiting on death row for the five or so years it would take before US appeal rights were exhausted and the execution carried out.[31]

As Dr Soblen's fate indicates, the UK has long been prepared to overlook barbarities in American law or procedure, and *Soering* required it to pay them some attention. In 1992 the Divisional Court emphasized the point when it took the extraordinary step of declaring that the Home Secretary acted irrationally in acceding to a US request to extradite a minor offender named Sinclair, ten years after his conviction. Sinclair had actually sought to return to the US in order to serve his sentence shortly after it had been imposed, but had been denied an entry visa on the grounds that he was a convicted criminal! Over the following decade he had established a settled family life in Britain, and the Court pointed out that the Home Secretary's agreement to his belated extradition would destroy the rights to respect for family life guaranteed to him under Article 8 of the European Convention. It severely criticized the Home Secretary for failing to give any reason for a decision for which no reason was obvious (other than a desire to truckle to the US) and quashed his extradition warrant.[32] The case is procedurally important, because Sinclair had already taken it to the House of Lords, which had ruled that the magistrate had no power to take these considerations into account in deciding whether or not to commit. This means that despite a proper committal for extradition, the warrant itself may be challenged in separate judicial review proceedings on the grounds that its issue was manifestly unreasonable.

British courts have been less prepared to stand up against oppressive behaviour where the victims have been drug dealers and money launderers. It is difficult to object if US undercover agents lure greedy suspects into the jurisdiction by offers of money,[33] or have subjected them to illegal telephone taps in other countries,[34] but would the English courts refuse to order their release if they had been brought here drugged and kidnapped? The question arose in Barbados, when some mercenaries landed with their prize, kidnapped Argentinean citizen and Great Train Robber Ronnie Biggs. The local court refused to order his extradition to Britain to complete his twenty-five-year sentence, on the grounds that the courts should not allow their procedures to be used in a way which would reward or otherwise encourage unlawful behaviour. The United States Supreme Court, its judgement perverted by partisanship in the 'war on drugs' and an arrogant assumption that American might makes right, took a different position in 1992 by permitting the trial of a Mexican national who had been forcibly abducted from that country by the CIA to face charges of murdering an undercover agent of the Drugs Enforcement Administration. The Supreme Court majority conceded that the kidnap was 'shocking' but irrelevant to the power of an American court to put him on trial. Justice Stevens concluded his dissent with the prediction that 'most courts throughout the civilized world will be deeply disturbed by the monstrous decision the court announces today. For every nation that has an interest in preserving the Rule of Law is affected, directly or indirectly, by a decision of this character.'[35]

In 1993 the House of Lords fulfilled Justice Stevens's prediction in *Bennett* v. *Horseferry Road Magistrates Court*, when it upheld the rule of law by deciding that English courts should investigate the circumstances by which a defendant had been brought into the country and should release him if these had been tainted by illegality or breaches of international law or deliberate defiance of proper extradition procedures. Bennett was wanted in England for prosecution on theft charges: he had been arrested in South Africa, and claimed that English and South African police had colluded to have him brought back to the jurisdiction against his will and without an extradition hearing. The High Court had ruled that it could not investigate his allegations, but the Law Lords decided that if substantiated they would amount to an abuse of the courts' process and entitle him to freedom. Although there was no doubt that Bennett would have received a fair trial, the courts have a responsibility 'to oversee executive action and to refuse to countenance behaviour that threatens either basic human rights or the rule of law'.[36] The decision in *Bennett* stands in stark contrast to that of the US Supreme Court in the Mexican kidnap case, and demonstrates that notwithstanding the public interest in prosecution and punishment of crime, the courts will refuse to allow their legal processes to be used in a way which countenances abuse of power by the executive. The cases of *Bennett* and *Sinclair* offer some hope that the wretched decision against Dr Soblen may one day be buried in a jurisprudential cemetery reserved for victims of cold war case law.

There remains the safeguard that no person who is accused (or has been convicted) of an offence of a political character shall be sent to a foreign country for trial. The 1988 Act brings extradition law into line with political asylum by further providing that there shall be no surrender if the request is in reality made for the purpose of punishment on account of race, religion, nationality or political opinions. The courts have been reluctant to define the concept of a 'political offence' with any precision, other than by requiring the fugitive to be at odds with the state applying for extradition over an issue relating to political control or government.[37] In 1954, when seamen on a Polish trawler mutinied, wounded their captain and sailed into Whitby, there was a *prima facie* case of piracy and unlawful wounding, but the Polish Government's request for extradition was rejected because the mutineers' purpose was to escape from political tyranny.[38] Today, however, the scope of the 'political offence' exemption has been severely restricted by international conventions on terrorism. Thus the Suppression of Terrorism Act (1978) lists a wide range of offences – murder, wounding, hostage-taking, possession of firearms and explosives, etc. – which are not to be regarded as being of a 'political character' when application for extradition is made by most European countries and the United States. The exception for fugitives who are in danger of political persecution did not originally apply to those sought by Common-wealth countries, but it was added to the Fugitive Offenders Act in 1967 after the Home Secretary had ordered the return of suspects to Nigeria and Cyprus to face blatantly political proceedings.[39] The provisions are reciprocal: had the British Government applied to extradite *Spycatcher* Peter Wright to face charges under the Official Secrets Act, the Australian courts would have had no hesitation in refusing the request on the grounds that such proceedings would be blatantly political.

FREEDOM OF TRAVEL

Magna Carta asserts the right of every free man to leave the realm at his pleasure in time of peace. In the eighteenth century, Blackstone held that this right was part of the common law, subject to the prerogative of the Crown to restrain departure by the writ of *ne exeat regno* in cases where the traveller is required for military service or court appearances.[40] This writ has been superseded by the advent of the passport, surrender of which to the police is a common condition of bail. The passport has become a form of international currency, serving as an identity card at frontiers, a symbol of nationality and a certificate of immigration status. It is not a legal document, merely *prima facie* evidence of nationality and identification, yet its convenience has made it indispensable for the modern traveller. Despite a common belief to the contrary, immigration officials have no power to stop citizens from leaving the country without a passport. They may request evidence to establish identity and nationality, but cannot detain or turn back persons who cannot produce such evidence in the form of a passport. Citizens re-entering Britain will be required to prove their right of abode, and production of a valid passport is the simplest and speediest means of so doing.

Although UK citizens are free in law to enter and leave Britain without a passport, they will encounter innumerable difficulties in practice if they try to do so. Airlines and shipping companies may be contractually entitled to insist on production of a passport prior to boarding. At the journey's end, foreign immigration control may well refuse to admit passengers without a passport, at least if they cannot produce a separate visa. Many countries have reciprocal treaties with the UK whereby they undertake to admit British citizens without visas but on condition that they produce a passport as proof of nationality. So for all practical purposes, a passport is crucial for overseas travel, and it is all the more remarkable that British citizens do not have an enforceable right to obtain one.

Passports are issued by the Foreign Office under the royal prerogative – the most discretionary form of power, and hence the most difficult to review in the courts. The Foreign Secretary may refuse to issue or review a passport, or may cancel it or even insist on it being handed back – the passport itself is so worded that it remains at all times the property of the Crown. A number of passports are withheld each year, in four classes of case:

(1) where it is suspected that the intention is to take children out of the jurisdiction illegally;

(2) where stranded tourists have been brought back to the UK at Government expense, and have not yet paid their fare;

(3) when the applicant is a person suspected of leaving the country to avoid imminent arrest; and

(4) in the case of persons whose activities 'are so notoriously

undesirable or dangerous that Parliament would be expected to support the action of the Foreign Secretary in refusing them a passport'.[41]

It is the last category which gives rise to most concern. In the absence of any legal right, the Foreign Secretary can stop British citizens from travelling abroad for purposes which, although legal, are popularly or politically deplored. During the cold war, British scientists who wished to attend conferences in Moscow were refused passports, and the same treatment was meted out to several British supporters of the Smith regime in Rhodesia. These actions of withholding passports on political grounds are outside the review powers of the Ombudsman, because they are said to relate to matters affecting relations between Governments. The situation is typical of the British attitude towards 'rights': what ought to be a constitutional entitlement is entrusted to Government, and decided in secret. The position is defended by recourse to the fiction of ministerial responsibility to Parliament, which means, as one participant in a debate over passport withdrawal in 1968 pointed out, 'The only action open to one aggrieved would be in fact to defeat the Government.'

The royal prerogative was regarded by lawyers as untouchable until the GCHQ case in 1984, where the House of Lords held that in certain instances the exercise of a prerogative power (in that case, the banning of trade unions) was subject to the limited discipline of judicial review.[42] In 1988, the Court of Appeal applied this ruling to permit review of the Foreign Secretary's refusal to issue a new passport to a British citizen living in Spain.[43] Although the Foreign Secretary was entitled to refuse to issue a new passport to fugitives from justice, the decision in each case had to be a carefully considered one. Since the denial of a passport is an administrative act affecting the citizen's freedom to travel, the Court of Appeal was prepared to review it on the same principles as it reviews official decisions in immigration cases. This case at least opens up the prospect of overturning refusals and withdrawals of passports if they are made irrationally or unfairly. Prerogative powers only survive to the extent that Parliament has not intervened to place them on a proper statutory footing: the practical importance of passports to freedom of movement demands such legislation, in which the grounds for refusal should be both narrowly defined and appealable.[44]

The most controversial exercise of the freedom to travel is by British mercenary soldiers, who have played a wretched part in civil wars, especially in Africa. They are recruited, generally from the ranks of ex-servicemen, through newspaper and magazine advertisements in Britain, and have notoriously figured in 'war crime' trials when captured. Several hundred left for Angola in 1976, when they killed innocent civilians and in some cases murdered each other. The Foreign Enlistment Act of 1870 makes it an offence to recruit for or enlist in the military service of a foreign state at war with any country which is 'at peace' with Britain. The Government declined to take action against the Angolan mercenaries or their recruiters because of legal doubts about whether the Act could apply to enlistment for another country's civil war, and a committee chaired by Lord Diplock recommended additional legislation to provide the Government with power to ban recruitment in respect of particular conflicts in which it was not in the public interest for British citizens to participate.[45] This begs difficult questions, and no Government has yet attempted the task of distinguishing the right to leave the country to risk one's life for a cause from 'the right to be a hired killer in a foreign war'.[46] The time for making this distinction should have come with exposure in 1990 of the role played by British mercenaries in training and equipping the murderous forces of the Colombian drug cartels. A few of the old Angola hands, and some new recruits (most of them dishonourably discharged from the SAS) were lavishly paid to travel to secret camps in Colombia, where they were engaged to 'turn untrained killers into trained killers'.[47] There is a fundamental difference between allowing mercenaries to travel abroad to fight for one side – even a despised side – in a civil war or insurgency, and allowing them to travel to help a gang of criminals attack officers of state in order to protect a drugs operation. There comes a point when the right to travel gives way to the need to protect the human right to life, and the US senate was severely critical of a UK Government which claimed (falsely) to be powerless to act against those of its nationals who assisted the Medallin drugs cartel to murder over sixty Colombian judges, journalists and politicians.

The Prevention of Terrorism Act

Special Branch Officers may examine at random travellers departing to or arriving from Northern Ireland (or the Republic of Ireland) for up to twelve hours to determine whether they may be involved in terrorist activity. They may detain them for a further thirty-six hours if reasonable suspicion of such involvement arises, and for a further five days if a minister certifies approval. The power to examine is reasonable enough, given the problems of terrorism in relation to Ireland, although permitting interrogation to last for twelve hours in the absence of any reason for suspecting terrorist involvement exposes innocent travellers to unnecessarily lengthy ordeals (one hour should be sufficient to gauge whether there is any basis for suspicion). Detention for up to seven days on ministerial order, either at entry points or at any police station, is permitted by the Prevention of Terrorism Act in relation to persons who are suspected of involvement in international (not specifically Irish) terrorism. The length of this imprisonment without charge is contrary to the European Convention on Human Rights, but the UK Government has made a special derogation from the Convention in the hope that guilty suspects may 'crack' towards the end of the period (see earlier, page 23). Innocent suspects, and those against whom insufficient evidence has been obtained, may be made the subject of an 'exclusion order' to ban them from re-entering Great Britain, if they have resided here for less than three years and are suspected of harbouring terrorist sympathies.

Exclusion orders are a dramatic interference with the right to enter Britain, imposed for the most part on British citizens from Northern Ireland, who often have close family ties with the mainland. An exclusion order is virtually unchallengeable in the courts because of the judicial mind-block on requiring (let alone examining) reasons for decisions taken by the Home Secretary on grounds of 'national security'. An excluded person's only 'right' is to an interview with an 'adviser' appointed by the Home Secretary, who does not have to follow his advice. This 'one wise man' procedure is as unsatisfactory as the panel of 'three wise men' for national-security deportations: the excludee tells his life story, and then is ushered out of the room. He is not told, even in general terms, of the basis for suspicions against him and so has no opportunity to refute them by producing facts or logical argument.

A review of the Prevention of Terrorism Act by Lord Colville in 1987 concluded that the ends did not justify the means, and recommended that the powers to make exclusion orders should be repealed 'both in terms of civil rights in the United Kingdom and this country's reputation in that respect among the international community'.[48] The Government refused, and every Irish person who is acquitted on terrorist charges by a jury is immediately re-arrested and 'excluded' from Britain as a terrorist because the Home Secretary refuses to accept the jury's verdict. Most exclusions are to Northern Ireland, but how does it help to diminish terrorism to oblige a suspect to live in one part of the United Kingdom rather than another? A number of Irishmen active in Sinn Fein have been banished from England and obliged to live in Northern Ireland, in circumstances which suggest that their political activities in Irish communities on the mainland is the danger that is really feared. Terrorists are intolerable wherever they reside: does the notion that a suspect is less of a problem in Belfast than in London imply that English lives are more valuable than Northern Irish lives?

CHAPTER 10

Freedom from Undue Control

This chapter is about various forms of state paternalism. The traditional justification for the exercise of power over individuals – to prevent them from harming themselves or harming others – justifies the withdrawal from prisoners and mental patients of certain rights enjoyed by free citizens. It does not, however, justify the infringements of basic rights which have gone on within British penal and mental institutions, such as denial of access to the courts and unfair trial of disciplinary offences. It is here that the European Convention has made its most marked contribution to the enhancement of civil liberties in Britain, in providing an external and objective standard by which to judge the fairness of prison rules and mental-health regulations. Improvements in the past five years have been dramatic, and have owed nothing to parliamentary democracy ('there are no votes in prisons', Home Secretary Kenneth Clarke pointed out in 1992). They have been required by Strasbourg rulings against secrecy, arbitrariness and political (rather than judicial) exercises of power; by British judges beginning to adopt European human-rights standards to test for 'unfairness' in judicial review proceedings, and by the prison riots which gave impetus to the recommendations of two reforming judges, Harry Woolf and Stephen Tumin. There is much more to be done, but those who argue that Bills of Rights change nothing are refuted by the remarkable changes achieved in the past few years by prisoners and mental patients who have taken the back-door Bill of Rights route to Strasbourg.

There has been much controversy over the rights of children to make decisions about their own future without parental veto when they come of an age to appreciate the consequences. The House of Lords decision in *Gillick* makes clear that parent power begins to evaporate long before the age of eighteen, inversely to the growth of intelligence and understanding. It is also subject to the power of the state to intervene, through local authorities and social-work agencies, to rescue children from abuse. That this necessary control requires a greater measure of legal scrutiny was demonstrated by the Cleveland and Orkney inquiries, which exposed how magistrates were permitting paediatricians and social workers to separate children from their parents on inadequate evidence and with insufficient accountability. When errors of judgement are made by social workers the consequences can be catastrophic, but public outrage at the deaths of children like Kimberley Carlile and Jasmine Beckford needs to be tempered by an appreciation that 'erring on the safe side' would deprive many children of a tolerable family environment, and deprive some innocent parents of their children. Further changes in the law are required to give parents greater legal rights to challenge the diktat of doctors and social workers, and to avoid the danger that child welfare powers will be used oppressively against parents who are poor rather rather perverse.

State paternalism is manifesting itself in attempts to control citizen access to advances in birth technology. The right to bear children, denied to many by physical impediment, can now be overcome by *in vitro* fertilization (IVF) and surrogacy techniques. The latter have to some extent been prohibited by criminal law, and access to IVF treatment is limited by resources, doctors' discretions and debatable ethical judgements. This field promises a great deal of legislation and litigation, in which the right to family life on terms convenient to individual couples will be balanced against moral standards assumed, perhaps optimistically, to reflect community values. Finally, this chapter looks at the prohibitions upon euthanasia. The law no longer embodies the Gilbertian paradox of suicide as a crime punishable by death, but it severely punishes those who help others to die with some measure of dignity.

PRISONERS' RIGHTS

The principle that 'people come to prison as a punishment, not for punishment' is difficult to credit at a time when 48,000 prisoners are crammed into accommodation originally built for 5,000. The prison inspectorate concedes that in many closed prisons one-person cells that now carry two or three prisoners are 'spartan, gloomy and stagnant', without access to sanitation; prisoners are locked up, sometimes for twenty-three hours a day; they are allowed to write one censored letter a week and receive two visits a month; and must defecate in each other's company at night and 'slop out' the next morning. In 1991 a Council of Europe delegation, having inspected a number of British prisons, concluded that 'the pernicious combination of overcrowding, inadequate leisure activities, the lack of integral sanitation and poor hygiene . . . amounted to inhuman and degrading treatment', a judgement confirmed by a Helsinki Watch report the following year. After the prison riots of 1990, the Woolf Report recommended revolutionary changes in the management of prisons and the treatment of prisoners, which the Government has promised to implement. The problem, of course, is that no Government bound by its own law-and-order rhetoric can tackle the root problem, which is that too many people are unnecessarily sent to prison for too long. It takes 32,000 prison staff, backed by 2,000 Home Office overseers, to manage the present prison population, at a public cost of £300 per prisoner per week. Statistics show that blacks, unemployed and homeless are grossly over-represented in the prison population; that some magistrates courts remand excessively instead of granting bail, and that the obsession with 'tariff' sentencing has served to increase the length of all sentences on deterrent principles rather than to allow mercy and mitigation to reduce these appropriately in individual cases. The Government strategy of building more prisons and privatizing others may in the short term mean less overcrowding and more variety: unless sentencing policies are changed, these new jails will simply overcrowd and produce more riots and more jail suicides. Britain may have abolished capital punishment, but fifty prisoners commit suicide each year, mostly as a result of staff negligence or failure to stop bullying or to do anything about the conditions that induce despair.

The closest Britain comes to having a written constitution is the Bill of Rights of 1688, which prohibits the infliction of 'cruell and unusuall punishment'. The degradation caused by overcrowding comes in some prisons well within that description. Reliance on the 1688 Act in court was once regarded as the last resort of a desperate advocate, but in the 1987 case of *Ex parte Herbage* (*No. 2*) the Court of Appeal was prepared to make it the basis for a judicial review of a prison governor's decision to keep a sane prisoner in a psychiatric wing because of accommodation problems.

If it were to be established that the applicant as a sane person was, for purely administrative purposes, being subjected in the psychiatric wing to the stress of being exposed to the disturbance caused by the behaviour of mentally ill and disturbed prisoners, this might well be considered as a 'cruell and unusuall punishment' and one which was not deserved.[1]

The decision is a welcome reminder of an often forgotten power in the courts to protect all those in detention against inhumane treatment, although in 1981 the High Court limited the effect of the Bill of Rights by requiring that the punishment (solitary confinement in a 'control unit') be 'unusual' as well as 'cruel'. The phrase is better understood as a compendious expression of a minimum standard of decency, directed against excessively harsh and unjustified regimes, rather than as a sanction for outrageous treatment which happens to be common within the prison system. At least it was acknowledged that the moral standard to be applied is contemporary, and not that which prevailed in 1688, so the Bill of Rights would certainly provide a basis for challenging, for example, the use of tranquillizers to control behaviour rather than to restore health or the deployment of brain-washing techniques to break the spirit of 'trouble-makers'.[2] In the 1991 case of *Ex parte Haque* the House of Lords confirmed as a general principle that prisoners had remedies against being subjected to 'intolerable conditions': they could have them terminated by order of the court in judicial review proceedings, and could win damages for assault or negligence if they had been subjected to threats or injuries to their health.[3] The difficulty will be to convince British courts to adopt the same definition of 'intolerable' as the Council of Europe and Helsinki Watch.

The Prison Rules, made under the Prisons Act of 1952, have been the subject of many actions taken to Strasbourg in an effort to secure acceptable standards of treatment for prisoners. Until these European Court cases, the Rules imposed a blanket of censorship over prisoners' contact with the outside world, even in relation to correspondence seeking legal advice. The turning-point came with the 1975 decision in *Golder* that the rule which forbade a prisoner from seeking advice from a solicitor in relation to his rights against a prison officer was a breach both of his right to freedom of access to the court (Article 6) and of his right to respect for his correspondence under the privacy guarantee of Article 8.[4] The Rules were slowly liberalized, under the pressure of further European Court rulings against the United Kingdom and decisions by domestic courts prepared to scrutinize the Prison Rules for compliance with natural justice. In *Raymond* v. *Honey* in 1983 the House of Lords went so far as to hold a prison governor in contempt of court for refusing to forward to the High Court a prisoner's application for leave to apply for judicial review. The Prisons Act of 1952, it held, did not empower the making of any rule which would interfere with a prisoner's right of unimpeded access to the courts: 'Under English law, a convicted prisoner, in spite of his imprisonment, retains all civil rights which are not taken away expressly or by necessary implication.'[5] Attempts by the Home Office to make the right to legal advice about complaints against prison authorities subject to conditions – e.g. that the complaint should first have been taken up with prison authorities – have also been held to be impediments on access to the courts.[6] In these recent cases, English courts have been adopting and applying broad human rights principles to strike down petty prison rules, such as that which empowered officials to stop letters to solicitors for 'prolixity' and 'objectionability'. In 1993 the court held this rule *ultra vires*, on the ground that it unnecessarily infringed the rights to confidentiality of correspondence and unimpeded access to legal advice.[7]

The Home Office owes a duty of care to all prisoners, to protect them from any harm which may befall them as a result of following orders or being required to work under dangerous conditions or being assaulted by other prisoners or by prison officers. It also has a duty to provide an appropriate standard of medical and psychiatric treatment to those in need, although in 1990 the High Court held that the standard of such care required in prisons was less than in 'outside' institutions. The action was brought by the family of a young schizophrenic who had, in the past, as officials well knew, attempted to jump out of a window, stab himself in the eye, cut his face with a razor blade and hang himself from the bars of his cell. Incredibly, authorities at Brixton only bothered to observe him once every quarter of an hour, which gave him ample time to try once again to hang himself from the bars of his cell, and to succeed. If this is not negligent supervision it is difficult to know what is, yet

Mr Justice Pill held that it did not involve any breach of the 'lower standard of care' appropriate to prisoners.[8] This objectionable and discriminatory decision requires reversal, in the interests of reducing the unacceptable number of prison suicides.

Prisoners still suffer some deprivations of civil rights which are not justified by the need to maintain discipline or security. They are deprived for no logical reason of the right to vote in both national and local elections, and they only acquired in 1983 the right to marry while in prison, as the result of another application to Strasbourg. The Rules permit only two personal visits a month (within the sight and often hearing of prison officers) and it is asking too much of British politicians, the Prison Officer's Association or the tabloid press to acknowledge any human need for conjugal visits. Under the pressure of the Woolf Report, however, much of the routine and petty censorship of correspondence has been relaxed, and cardphones have been installed in all prisons to enable greater family contact. The Home Office remains neurotic about publicity, and generally refuses 'professional visits by journalists and writers', although the European Court forced it to make some concessions by condemning its infringement of Jimmy Boyle's freedom of expression by stopping his letters because they were addressed to a 'media personality'.[9] In 1993 the Court of Appeal gave short shrift to the Home Office's arguments for stopping a television documentary about serial killers because it featured a short interview with mass-murderer Denis Nielsen: the risk of distressing relatives, the court pointed out, could be eliminated by the relatives declining to watch the programme.[10] While the Government is justified in maintaining rules to ensure that serving prisoners do not profit from or promote their criminality, there have been petty examples of refusing to allow prisoners to have books published or plays performed on the grounds that this would amount to a 'business activity'. This approach is almost certainly a breach of Article 10 of the European Convention, and it is difficult in any event to understand why some interest in legitimate business by prisoners in their spare time should not be encouraged rather than banned. Another particular concern is the treatment of unconvicted prisoners who have been refused bail. Although presumed innocent, they can be made to suffer the same indignities as convicts. In 1988 the Home Office took the mean-minded and unnecessary step of abolishing their traditional 'right' to receive food parcels from friends and family.

Another battlefield in the struggle for prisoners' rights has been over fairness in disciplinary proceedings. Over eighty thousand charges are laid by warders against prisoners each year; the vast majority are dealt with by the governor (who may order temporary loss of privileges, or loss of up to twenty-eight days of their entitlement to early release) but the more serious offences were tried by a panel selected from the Board of Visitors – Justices of the Peace and other local citizens who meet each month to make recommendations about the state of the prison and the welfare of its inmates. After the Hull Prison riot in 1976, some long-term prisoners were punished by losing 720 'remission days' – the equivalent of an additional three-year sentence – imposed in secret, non-jury proceedings. At first, attempts to secure basic rights failed in the courts, where judges could see no difference between prison discipline and army discipline: speed was of the essence, and legal representations would produce delay. There was, however, a duty on the Board to act fairly, and some of the heavy punishments handed down to the Hull rioters were quashed because they had been given no opportunity to cross-examine the evidence against them.' [11] It took the European Court, in *Campbell & Fell* v. *UK*, to give full effect to the principle that 'justice cannot stop at the prison gates': there had been a breach of the Article 6 right to a fair hearing by denial of legal advice and representation at a trial which imposed a 'sentence' of loss of fifteen months' remission. [12]

Campbell & Fell was a watershed decision in the struggle for prisoners' rights. The European Court accepted that there was a distinction between criminal law proceedings (which required full due-process safeguards) and disciplinary proceedings, but it depended on the seriousness of the charge and its consequences. Prisoners have a legitimate expectation of early release, and allegations which may lead to them serving rather longer than they might otherwise expect require to be adjudicated fairly. Many more cases followed, alleging various forms of unfairness by Prison Visitors, who were not in any event suited to a punitive role, because it compromised their independence from the prison establishment and detracted from their real purpose of assessing prison conditions. In 1992, at Lord Woolf's instigation, the jurisdiction of Prison Visitors to punish prisoners was finally abolished; in future, all disciplinary offences are to be dealt with by the governor, unless they are sufficiently serious to be sent to the Crown Prosecution Service for proceedings in criminal courts, where full safeguards will apply. Another welcome reform, instituted in 1993 again as a result of the Woolf Report, is a 'prison ombudsman' to deal with complaints from individual prisoners which cannot be resolved within the existing prison complaints systems.

The 1991 Criminal Justice Act abolishes 'remission' altogether, and replaces it with 'early release'. Prisoners sentenced to four years or less will automatically be released after serving half their sentence, and longer-term prisoners will be eligible for parole between the half-way and two-thirds stage of their sentence, with automatic release (albeit on licence) after the latter stage is reached. The governor may award up to twenty-eight 'additional days awards' as punishment for breaches of prison discipline. In a most significant decision in 1988, *Leech* v. *Governor of Parkhurst Prison*, the House of Lords ruled that even with their limited power to punish, prison governors were none the less subject to judicial review.[13] They quashed a disciplinary finding against a prisoner who had not been permitted to cross-examine the accusing warder or to make a proper defence to the charge. Lord Bridge rejected the analogies with discipline imposed by military commanders and schoolmasters, which had previously dogged so many prisoners' rights cases in the courts (judges being able to recall their days at school and in the army rather more realistically than any time they had passed in prison), and refused to be cowed by arguments about cost and inconvenience and encouraging 'trouble-makers'. He pointed out that 'nothing is so likely to generate unrest among ordinary prisoners as a sense that they have been treated unfairly and have no effective means of redress'. This approach warrants revision of the disciplinary offences, several of which allow for too much discretion to prison officers to persecute prisoners for complaining. Over half the charges brought before prison governors are of 'offending against good order and discipline' and 'being disrespectful to a prison officer'. (In women's prisons, punishments are regularly meted out under these heads for swearing, talking-back and other such 'unladylike' behaviour.)

The latest stage in securing prisoners' rights to due process concerns those serving life sentences, whose release after the 'tariff period' set by judges as being appropriate to punish them for their actual offence has hitherto been at the discretion of the Home Secretary, and has often been affected by political considerations. Life sentences fall into two categories: they are mandatory for those convicted of murder, but may also be imposed at the trial judges' discretion for lesser offences where the offender is judged to be a danger to the public for the indeterminable future. The point at which this danger dissipated sufficiently to justify release was decided by the Home Secretary after secret reports from the Parole Board – a body which allowed the prisoner no legal representation or sight of the evidence against him or reasons for whatever recommendations it made. This arbitrary and unfair procedure was ended only after the European Court ruled that it violated Article 5(4) of the European Convention on Human Rights, namely that 'Everyone who is deprived of his liberty by arrest or detention shall be entitled to take proceedings by which the lawfulness of his detention shall be decided speedily by a court and his release ordered if the detention is not lawful.'

In the landmark case of *Thynne Wilson & Gunnell* v. *UK*, the European Court decided that once a prisoner had served a period fixed by reference to deterrence and rehabilitation for his actual offence – his punishment period, or 'tariff' – and his liberty thereafter depended on his future dangerousness (a quality which could change over time) then he was entitled to the protection of Article 5(4).[14] That meant he should have the right to have his position reviewed at reasonable intervals of time by a judicial body acting fairly towards him, empowered to order his release once satisfied that he no longer constituted a risk to the public. This ruling, once again, forced the Government to make radical changes (which it did in the 1991 Criminal Justice Act) to provide 'discretionary lifers' with rights of legal representation before Parole Board panels chaired by a judge and newly empowered to direct their release without the Home Secretary being able to veto their decision. In the spirit of this European Court decision, in 1992 the Court of Appeal ordered that a seventy-six-year-old prisoner, given a life sentence for a sexual assault twenty years before, should be entitled to see and to challenge all the secret reports which might influence his Parole Board to rule that he still remained a danger to the public.[15]

These victories for 'discretionary lifers' leave only those convicted of murder ('mandatory lifers') whose liberty remains at the unappealable and highly political mercy of the Home Secretary, rather than at the procedurally fair determination of an independent judicial body. This anomaly arises from the mandatory life sentence for murder, first adopted by Parliament as a quid pro quo for the abolition of the death penalty in 1965, and which must be passed on murders of such varying gravity as mercy killings and *crimes passionelles* on the one level and criminal gang assassinations on the other. For most murderers 'life does not mean life', but how much it means should depend firstly on an assessment of a sentence length which fits the circumstances of the actual crime (an assessment made by the trial judge) and thereafter by a decision on future dangerousness decided by a panel independent of the Government. It is likely that the European Court will in due course come to this conclusion, and in 1993 the House of Lords moved the law in this direction by ruling that a life prisoner was entitled to know both the period of years which his trial judge recommends to the Home Secretary that he should serve to satisfy the requirements of retribution and deterrence, and the reasons for any decision by the Home Secretary to increase the length of this period. This important case – *Doody* v. *Home Secretary* – marks a watershed in prisoners' rights by overruling earlier judgements which had left prisoners sentenced to life at the uncontrolled mercy of Government ministers as to when they would first be considered eligible for release. Evidence in the case demonstrated how cavalierly the Government had handled this responsibility, delegating it to junior ministers who, frequently and secretly, increased the 'tariff' period recommended by judges. *Doody* brings to an end this preposterous practice whereby a politician could on a whim 're-sentence' an offender without giving reasons, and the leading speech of Lord Mustill emphasizes that the courts will be concerned to ensure that all prisoners are treated with basic fairness and rationality in administrative decisions made within the Home Office which affect their futures.[16]

It is unacceptable that a Government minister should decide whether and when persons who have served the tariff for their murders (which usually confines them to prison for ten to twenty years) should be set at liberty, because on such subjects Home Secretaries are particularly prone to political pressures from their party and from the media. Myra Hindley, for example, has been in prison since 1965 and it cannot now be contended that she poses any danger to the public, yet in prison she will remain for ever if MPs and the popular press have their way. However heinous the original offence, there comes a point at which incarceration without hope of release is, in the absence of public risk, no more than a form of pure revenge, psychologically cruel and morally inhuman. The 'mandatory life sentence' is an idea whose time has passed, and which operates now only to distort the sentencing and parole process and to inflict cruel and unnecessary punishment on those who have done more than enough time for their crime. There is no reform more universally favoured by judges, prison governors and psychologists than the abolition of the mandatory life sentence for murder, yet as recently as 1991 the Government threw out a bill to this effect which had passed the House of Lords.

MENTAL PATIENTS

It is wrong to punish the 'unblameworthy' – those who cannot be held morally responsible for actions arising from a disorder of the mind. They are 'not guilty', but having committed antisocial actions there is every justification for a court to order an appropriate treatment, which may include confinement in a secure mental hospital until, if at all, they are cured. The principle that it is wrong to punish mentally disordered persons was recognized far back in our legal history, by judges who, although they had no compunction in burning witches, drew the line at hanging village idiots. As one Chief Justice, Edward Coke, explained four centuries ago:

The execution of an offender is for example, but so it is not when a madman is executed; that should be a miserable spectacle, both against law, and of extreme inhumanity and cruelty, and can be no example to others.

At first, the law demanded that the madness should be obvious and overwhelming: it had to be proved that the defendant 'doth not know what he is doing, any more than a brute or a wild beast'. This test remained until 1800, when Lord Erskine, the greatest advocate of that or perhaps any other age, was called upon to defend James Hadfield, a schizophrenic who had attempted to assassinate George

III. Erskine opened the door to forensic psychiatry when he spoke to the jury of 'an insanity where imagination still holds the most uncontrollable domination over reality and fact; and there are cases which frequently mock the wisdom of the wisest in judicial trials; because such persons often reason with subtlety . . .'[17] Erskine established the broad principle that those who commit crimes under the influence of delusions are not responsible in law. Hadfield was acquitted, to the bewilderment of the Government. He was held in custody until a Criminal Lunatics Act could be rushed through Parliament, providing indefinite hospitalization for those found 'not guilty on grounds of insanity'. They were, in time, committed to the care of doctors in Bedlam (the Royal Bethlehem Hospital) rather than to the hangman.

This humane development of the law met with a serious reversal in 1843, when the judiciary succumbed to political pressures whipped up as a result of the acquittal, on grounds of insanity, of Daniel M'Naghten. He was a young Scot who killed Sir Robert Peel's private secretary (mistaking him for Peel) under the influence of schizophrenic delusions. The press vilified the 'mad-doctors' who had given evidence for the defence, and some editorials, noting M'Naghten's Chartist sympathies, wondered whether socialism was a disease of the mind which might save other assassins from the gallows. The politicians were furious, and Queen Victoria was outraged. M'Naghten was 'not in the least mad', she declared. Twelve senior judges were ordered by Parliament, 'in consequence of the M'Naghten verdict', to restate the law of insanity, and they produced the 'M'Naghten rules' – a test of insanity which remains the law in Britain today. They abandoned Erskine's principle that a defendant is not criminally responsible for an act committed under the influence of delusions stemming from a disease of the mind. They decided that he was guilty, unless the disease was so severe that 'he did not know the nature and quality of the act he was doing, or if he did know it, that he did not know he was doing what was wrong'.[18]

Seen in historical context, the M'Naghten rules were in fact designed to hang future M'Naghtens. The assassin's ability to make careful preparations and penetrate the security around public figures requires an intelligence which, however disordered, must apprehend the illegality of the action. Judged in the light of our contemporary knowledge, the rules are based on the erroneous belief that if an ability to reason exists, it can control behaviour. The paranoid schizophrenic may retain an ability to reason within certain limits of his general alienation, without being able to exercise cerebral control. He cannot help his actions, even though he realizes they are against the law. An irresistible inner order, coupled with a delusion that it is morally right, provides no insanity defence. For lawyers, the definition of a madman is a person who cannot understand the law.

In 1953, the Royal Commission on Capital Punishment condemned the M'Naghten rules, and Parliament provided a special defence of 'diminished responsibility' to defendants charged with murder. It operates to reduce that crime, with its mandatory sentence of life imprisonment, to manslaughter (where the sentence is entirely at the option of the judge). To return a verdict of 'diminished responsibility' the jury should be satisfied that the mental disorder was a substantial causative factor in the killing. But how debilitating must a mental disease be before 'impairment of responsibility' is deemed 'substantial'? The test of causation is difficult for experts and juries to apply in the context of serious mental disorder. In cases of schizophrenia, where diagnosis must largely depend on what the defendant says about himself, there is no sure way of deciding whether he is ill, or feigning illness. One well-read but perfectly normal defendant recently managed to convince seven psychiatrists that he was suffering from schizophrenia (he was subsequently convicted of perverting the course of justice), while the most deadly of paranoid schizophrenics – Peter Sutcliffe (the 'Yorkshire Ripper') had his 'diminished responsibility' defence rejected by a jury which thought he was feigning (after his illness became apparent in prison, he was transferred to Broadmoor). In many cases where the mandatory life sentence would operate harshly – in respect, for example, of women who have killed brutal partners – 'diminished responsibility' is the only way to avoid harshness and courts are minded to accept the plea on evidence of post-traumatic stress, depression and similar disorders which are not serious or long-lasting mental illnesses. These confusions and fudges would not be necessary if the mandatory life sentence for murder (and the distinction with manslaughter) were abolished, and courts were simply left to decide the appropriate punishment warranted by a particular act of 'unlawful killing'.

Defendants whose actions are caused by mental illness may not be morally guilty, but most of them plead guilty. The 'not guilty by reason of insanity' plea is rarely heard because the M'Naghten rules are so restrictive, and because acceptance of the plea means an indeterminate confinement in a mental hospital for as long as authorities believe the defendant remains a danger to the public. There is, moreover, a social and legal stigma in being labelled 'insane' and 'lunatic'. But if the mentally ill offender pleads 'guilty' to any offence other than murder, the court has a whole range of humane treatments at its disposal, from which it can select the most appropriate. Thus schizophrenics who commit offences under the influence of delusions, which are then brought under control by treatment before trial, plead 'guilty' in order to receive a probation order, perhaps with a requirement that they continue out-patient treatment. Because of their illness, they were not responsible for their crime, but the M'Naghten rules afford them no defence. Even if the mental illness was severe enough to satisfy the M'Naghten test, what candidate for probation would plead 'not guilty' when the result would have to be indefinite confinement?

There is always a danger that mentally disturbed defendants will plead 'guilty' to offences they have not committed in order to obtain psychiatric treatment by court order which they need in any event, while avoiding the stigma of being labelled 'insane'. Where the disorder is so debilitating that they cannot give rational instructions to their lawyers, they can be found 'unfit to plead' and the charges remain on file against them while they are hospitalized. Some protection against assumption of guilt in these circumstances was provided by the Criminal Procedure (Insanity and Unfitness to Plead) Act 1991, which requires a jury to hear evidence about the facts of the offence and to make a 'finding' that the defendant committed the criminal act only if satisfied beyond reasonable doubt. This 'finding' is not a verdict of guilty, because the defendant's mental state cannot be put in issue, but if the jury is unable to find that the defendant did the act, this counts as an acquittal. The importance of clarifying the status of mentally disabled suspects is demonstrated by the curious case of David Mackenzie, the 'serial killer' who turned out to be a serial confessor. He was found 'unfit to plead' to charges of murdering a number of elderly women, to which he had confessed in extensive but unconvincing detail (including the murder of anti-nuclear campaigner Hilda Murrell). A few years later, his mental condition was thought to allow him sufficient insight to plead to the charges, and he was convicted of two of the murders. The Court of Appeal quashed his convictions, establishing an important rule that uncorroborated and inconclusive confessions by mentally disordered persons cannot henceforth be the basis for a 'guilty' verdict.[19]

The Committee on Mentally Abnormal Offenders, chaired by the late Lord Butler, reported in 1975.[20] It recommended abolition of the M'Naghten rules and the installation of a new verdict: 'not guilty on evidence of mental disorder'. This verdict would be brought in if the jury were satisfied that at the time of the act charged as a crime, the defendant was suffering from severe mental illness or severe subnormality. Psychiatrists could testify to the question of fact – is he, the defendant, severely ill or is he not? The question of causality, so tortuous and speculative in relation to most forms of schizophrenia, would not need to be answered. After an acquittal 'on evidence of mental illness', the court would be empowered to make the most appropriate order, ranging from an absolute discharge for those demonstrably cured and harmless to indefinite detention in Broadmoor if there were any danger that violent episodes would be repeated. Now that the gallows no longer casts its shadow over the design of the criminal law it is time to adopt Butler's recommendation, which gives proper effect to the principle that persons in the grip of mental illness should not be branded as criminally responsible for their actions.

In other respects, British law relating to mentally disordered offenders has developed more rationally. Judges may make 'restriction orders' confining them in mental hospitals rather than prison, for fixed or unlimited periods, where the evidence shows that their disorder would make them a danger to the public if set free immediately. Mental Health Review Tribunals, comprising a lawyer, a psychiatrist and a lay person, advise the Home Secretary as to when an offender subject to an unlimited 'restriction order' can safely be released. Until 1983 release was always 'on licence', and the offender could be recalled at any time at the Home Secretary's discretion. The drawback in this system was that release and recall were decided entirely by the Home Secretary – a politician easily deterred by fear of adverse publicity. It took the European

Court of Human Rights to produce a change in the law which has helped to make the restoration of liberty a matter of independent judgement rather than political discretion.

X v. *United Kingdom* involved a man who had been sent to Broadmoor for assaulting a workmate. After several years he was released into the community, to live for three years without problem until he was suddenly 'recalled' by the Home Secretary for reasons, it subsequently emerged, of unsubstantiated gossip by his wife during their divorce. The European Court held that the Home Secretary had been in breach of Article 5(4) of the Convention, which requires that all who are deprived of their liberty by detention should be entitled to have the lawfulness of their confinement decided speedily by a court. Although the Mental Health Review Tribunal was capable of being a 'court', it failed the test because it had no power to 'decide', but merely to make recommendations to the Home Secretary.[21] As a consequence of this ruling, the 1983 Mental Health Act abrogates the Home Secretary's discretionary power and leaves him to make representations to the Tribunal, which now has the final duty to decide questions of release, although the Home Secretary retains the power to recall an offender who has been conditionally released.

Tribunals have a delicate and sometimes agonizing task in predicting how offenders and patients will behave when set at large; on the occasions when mental illness reasserts itself and results in another act of violence or sexual assault, angry and sensational allegations of incompetence will follow in the press. It is necessary for tribunals to have the strength of mind to act on the evidence placed before them in cases of individuals who have recovered from a mental illness that caused them to commit serious offences, and failure to give cogent reasons for refusing a discharge in such cases will be reviewable in the High Court.[22] Judges in several recent cases of this sort have been prepared to quash tribunal decisions where inadequate or irrational reasons have been given, and where the suspicion must be that the decision has been dictated by prejudice about the original offence rather than a fair appreciation of the offender's current mental state.[23] A 'restriction order', after all, may be imposed for a minor offence, and may last for life: it must not be viewed as 'punishment' for a 'crime' (for which it would be grossly disproportionate) but as confinement in order to treat a mental state – a confinement which must end as soon as that state is manageable enough for release. This point ought to be reached when detention in hospital is no longer necessary for the patient's own health. However, the courts have fudged this issue in the difficult case of offenders released by tribunals because there is no evidence that they are suffering from mental disease, but who are later 'recalled' to secure hospitals by the Home Secretary because they have committed an offence. Logically, a person cured of mental illness who re-offends while on licensed release should be sentenced to serve a finite term of imprisonment rather than be recalled to a hospital which can do nothing for him other than to deprive him of liberty for an indeterminate period.[24] But courts, like mental-health review tribunals and Home Secretaries, find it difficult to apply logic to a dangerous person who was once mentally sick.

The 1983 Mental Health Act now sets out comprehensively the law relating to state power over those suffering from mental disorder. Compulsory admission to hospital must be upon the application of a relative or a social worker, supported by the recommendation of one doctor in any emergency (where the patient may be detained for up to three days – a 'Section 4' order) or by two doctors in cases requiring up to twenty-eight days' detention for assessment (a 'Section 2' order). There must be evidence of 'mental disorder', which is widely defined to encompass 'mental illness, arrested or incomplete development of the mind, psychopathic disorder and any other disorder or disability of the mind', although drug or alcohol dependence and promiscuity are excluded as sole grounds for admissions. Admissions for emergency treatment are lawful if doctors think it necessary or appropriate for the health of the patient: when longer-term detention is sought for assessment (Section 2) or for up to six months of hospital treatment (Section 3) the test of danger to self or others becomes the governing standard, and confinements must be reviewed by the Mental Health Review Tribunal after six months at the patient's request, and a review must take place after a year if consecutive Section 3 orders have been made. The other method of compulsory admission to hospital is by order of a court, on the evidence of two doctors that an offender is suffering from a form of mental disorder specified in the Act which can be ameliorated by hospital treatment. A court can make the more severe 'restriction order' only in cases where it is of the opinion that this 'is necessary for the protection of the public from serious harm'. Voluntary admission, of course, may be sought at any time, but patients in this category who seek to discharge themselves may be detained by a doctor under 'emergency treatment' powers.

These provisions are designed to balance the rights of mentally disordered individuals with the powers of professionals to put them out of circulation for a short period of examination or a longer period if they are assessed as dangerous to themselves or others. Ultimately, there is judicial control through *habeas corpus* applications and the supervisory role of the Mental Health Review Tribunal, but in the short term there is still considerable potential for abuse.[25] A single, inexperienced GP may react to a patient in emotional crisis by making an emergency order; some doctors are tempted to let 'assessment' run the full twenty-eight days. The catch-all phrase 'any other disorder or disability of the mind' is extraordinarily wide (one youth who laughed at police officers ended up in hospital allegedly suffering from 'euphoria').

Mental Health Review Tribunals are the only protection for 'restricted' patients who have committed such serious offences that politicians – represented by the Home Secretary – are reluctant ever to release them. It frequently happens that killings are committed under the influence of mental disorders that are either ended or brought under control by medication after a stay in a secure mental hospital. The offender, who is no longer a danger to himself or to members of the public, is entitled to be released under Section 72 of the Mental Health Act, after a tribunal hearing at which the Home Secretary will be represented or to which he will make written submissions. In 1991 the Court of Appeal held that the tribunal is a 'court' for the purposes of the law of contempt, with the result that the press is limited in its power to agitate sensationally against the release of the unpopular patients.[26] Although the prospect of the release of any person who has many years before committed serious offences is a matter of public interest upon which reasonable comment is permitted, before the 1991 ruling the absence of legal restraint had encouraged hysterical press campaigns of vilification against some 'restricted' patients and their expert witnesses in the weeks before the tribunal sat. Tribunal proceedings are precisely the kind of hearings which most need to be insulated from this type of passion and prejudice.

Some mental patients are unable to understand, let alone to give consent to, medical treatment which their own best interests may warrant. Routine operations occasion no difficulty, as doctors and relatives are entitled to make reasonable decisions as to what the health of the patient requires, just as they would in treating a young child. In the case of operations which raise serious ethical questions, such as sterilization or kidney donation, the approval of the High Court should be sought, although this is not necessary for abortions if the necessary medical approvals have been obtained.[27] In 1989 the courts ruled in *Re F* that approval will normally be given if the operation is regarded by the general body of medical opinion as best calculated to promote the patient's true welfare and interests.[28] The court's decision that 'the right to reproduce is of value only if accompanied by the ability to make a choice' may be doubted as a general principle, although on the facts of the particular case the decision to approve sterilization was humane (a thirty-five-year-old woman with a mental age of five for whom pregnancy would be 'a disaster' was having a sexual relationship but could not be protected by normal methods of contraception). The ruling indicates both that the courts are prepared to oversee drastic medical decisions which affect the fundamental rights of mental patients, but that they will not override 'the general body of medical opinion'. Where there is a substantial conflict in that opinion, the judges will decide according to their perception of the public interest. It is of some comfort that such ethical conundrums will at least be resolved openly and by an independent body, rather than be left to the discretion of individual practitioners and health authorities.

The European Convention influenced a number of reforms in the 1983 Act, such as giving mental patients the right to vote and removing certain restrictions on their correspondence. But there are still gaps in the protection which the Act affords to society's most vulnerable members. Although patients cannot resist routine treatment while they are detained, psycho-surgery must not be undertaken without consent or, where the patient is incapable of giving consent, without independent confirmation of that incapacity and approval of the treatment proposed. Treatment in the category of 'medication', however, which includes the controversial electro-convulsive therapy (ECT), may be given without consent where an 'independent doctor' has certified its benefits. This is a wholly inadequate protection against a form of treatment which some psychiatrists recommend but which has been shown to have dubious benefits and a potential for abuse.

Psychiatrists are permitted to breach their ethical duties of confidentiality towards their patients by notifying authorities of any 'dangerousness' which they apprehend in the course of consultation. This serious inroad into professional confidentiality is necessary in the public interest in cases where a life is under direct threat (e.g. if a patient makes a credible threat to kill another person) but it is hardly justified when a psychiatrist merely suspects that his patient has not been cured. None the less, the case of *W* v. *Egdell* shows that mental patients cannot stop their own psychiatrists from sending, without their consent, confidential and damaging opinions about them to the Home Secretary and to their review tribunal. This ruling is not calculated to give mental patients the confidence to speak freely to psychiatrists, or to retain 'experts' who claim the right to make any adverse subjective impressions they form about their client available to the other side.[29]

Mental patients are particularly vulnerable to abuse, from both doctors and staff, yet they suffer discrimination in not being allowed to take legal proceedings unless the claim is based on allegations of negligence or bad faith, and even in such cases they must first obtain leave of the High Court, which is withheld unless there is 'substantial ground' for the allegation. High-security 'special hospitals' can easily become places of illegal brutality and malpractice, as a series of scandals recently uncovered by inquiries and inquests relating to Rampton, Broadmoor and Ashworth have shown. No amount of high-minded legal principles can protect against a culture of brutality of the sort revealed in 1992 by the Blom-Cooper inquiry into the sadistic physical and psychological abuse of patients by their 'nurses' at Ashworth Special Hospital – connived at by some doctors and covered up by the Prison Officers Association (which acts for special hospital nurses). The role of law is limited to retrospective exposure and punishment; mental patients will continue to be treated as a subhuman species until new management practices, ethical standards and codes for caring rather than demeaning come to counteract the prison culture which pervades special hospitals.

CHILDREN AND PARENTS

The legal right of parenthood is, at common law, 'a dwindling right ... It starts with a right of control and ends with little more than advice.' Statute law provides certain rights on the basis of age gradations; at birth, still reflecting Victorian values, it permits inheritance and the possession of bank accounts and Premium Bonds; at ten it allows criminal conviction if the prosecution can prove knowledge of wrong-doing (full criminal responsibility comes at fourteen, together with the right to own a shot-gun and to enter pubs); at sixteen come the rights to buy lottery tickets and liqueur chocolates and cigarettes, pose naked for page 3 of the *Sun*, consent to medical treatment, leave school and work full time and have sex and join the army, while eighteen is the age for full civil rights except those of standing for Parliament or adopting a child or having male homosexual relationships, which are not bestowed until the twenty-first birthday.

These age limits are inevitably arbitrary and those relating to sexual conduct in particular call for careful discretion in enforcement. Outside the framework of statutory rights, there lies a fertile area for conflict between the interests of parents, their children, and the state. The present Government has devised social legislation (the Child Support Act 1991 and the Maintenance Enforcement Act 1991) which threatens bad parents with fines and imprisonment, at a time of increasing divorce and dislocation and evidence of widespread child abuse. Somehow, the child-welfare system must be geared to social intervention at a point which will protect children from the possibility of abuse while at the same time preserving the rights of parents to have their child-raising capabilities judged carefully and fairly. The errors of assessment which led to the deaths of Maria Colwell and Jasmine Beckford and Kimberley Carlile received condemnation from a public which expects social workers to take children to places of safety whenever danger signals appear, but zeal for playing the Pied Piper without proper heed for parents' rights produced the crises in Cleveland and Orkney.

The general rights of a child vis-à-vis its parent were considered by the House of Lords in 1987 in a case brought by a moral crusader, Mrs Victoria Gillick, against her Area Health Authority because it refused to assure her that its doctors would never prescribe contraception to her daughters under sixteen without her consent. The decision – that parental consent was not required in cases where a doctor formed an honest view that contraception was necessary to the welfare of a girl who insisted upon confidentiality – was reached by reference to the capacity of individual children, below any arbitrarily set age, to make decisions for themselves. Parental rights to control a child exist for the benefit of the child and not of the parent, and they are justified only to the extent that is necessary to enable the parents to fulfil their duties of care and support. 'That parental right yields to the child's right to make his own decisions when he reaches a sufficient understanding and intelligence to be capable of making up his own mind on the matter requiring decision.'[30]

The effect of Gillick is to remove any right of parental veto over medical treatment, including abortion, which doctors believe to be necessary and which their patients are of sufficient mental development to comprehend and approve. Henceforth, the courts should be reluctant to exercise a paternal power over minors who are sufficiently intelligent to decide their own best interests, at least where the conduct concerned is lawful. When the young Jessica Mitford was made a ward of court by her family in an attempt to stop her marrying Churchill's nephew and fighting against Franco, the Government diverted a destroyer to collect the runaway from Spain. The decision in Gillick should signal the end of the use of wardship powers to impose such restraints upon headstrong youth.

None the less, recent decisions of the Court of Appeal demonstrate a reluctance to follow the logic of Gillick if to do so would allow competent adolescents to harm themselves in ways open to competent adults. In Re R (1991) the Court had no hesitation in overriding the refusal of a 'Gillick competent' fifteen-year-old to undergo a treatment course involving the administration of anti-psychotic drugs, which offered the only protection against onset of a mental illness marked by tendencies to violence and suicide.[31] Although the teenager had considered the treatment and declined it rationally, the Court doubted her overall competence and in any event decreed that it could substitute its own (and her doctor's) view of what was in her best interests. A more difficult decision was Re W (1992) in which the wishes of a 'Gillick-competent' sixteen-year-old girl suffering from anorexia nervosa were overridden.[32] The girl had lived a wretched life, and was rationally determined to cure herself, if at all, in her own time and way and without additional clinical treatment. The Court directed her to undergo the treatment, forcibly if necessary, on hearing that she was in danger of suffering permanent damage. It questioned her 'competence' in view of the evidence that a feature of the addictive illness was a wish not to be cured. Although it paid lip-service to *Gillick* by acknowledging a presumption in favour of granting intelligent and informed adolescent wishes, it nevertheless emphasized the unlimited power of the Court to override them by exercising its inherent jurisdiction to protect minors from permanent injury.

These cases demonstrate that decisions to accept or refuse medical treatment by competent persons under eighteen must be respected by doctors unless a court can be persuaded that they are not in the best interests of the patient – and if medical experts apprehend serious consequences for the patients' health, that will be persuasion enough. Good judging, like good parenting, will consist (in Lord Donaldson's homely aphorism) of 'giving minors as much rope as they can handle without an unacceptable risk that they will hang themselves'. The judges in *Re W* saw little realistic danger of courts intervening to force abortions on unwilling sixteen- or seventeen-year-olds so as to comply with their parent's wishes, but the 'best interests of the child' formula will continue to superimpose adult value-judgements on youthful freedom of choice. In other respects, however, reverberations from the *Gillick* decision have echoed more loudly in the law relating to teenagers; this good woman's legal crusade to control children has ironically associated her name with a landmark in their liberty. This 'dwindling rights' doctrine permits doctors to prescribe contraception to stable and intelligent fifteen-year-olds without their parents' consent or even their knowledge. *Gillick* has encouraged courts to give more weight to the views of intelligent children as to their own best interests. For example, in 1992 the Court of Appeal quashed a decision that a fourteen-year-old child of divorced parents should go away to board (as his mother desired) because the boy, sensibly enough, preferred to attend a good local day school.[33] In the same year the Court refused to allow 'intelligent and articulate' children to leave the country with their mother against their wishes,[34] and a High

Court judge went so far as to permit a fourteen-year-old girl to remain with her father who had unlawfully abducted her, such was the strength of her feeling in favour of remaining with him.[35] Parents can no longer be said to have a legal entitlement to custody of their children until the age of sixteen: many thousands of youngsters run away from home each year, and *Gillick* lends support to the hostels which hide these refugees from angry parents until family problems can be resolved.

The most dramatic result of the 'dwindling rights' doctrine, allied to the central presumption outlined in the 1989 Children Act that a child's welfare must be the paramount concern of the court, first emerged in 1992, when the media claimed that children were beginning to 'divorce' their parents. Here were cases where children of sufficient understanding to instruct solicitors had brought proceedings to obtain orders that they should live with grandparents (in one case with a boyfriend's parents) rather than with negligent or inconvenient natural parents. Such cases emphasize how 'parental responsibility' has replaced 'parents' rights': the court must decide custody issues under the 1989 Act by considering who will best undertake the responsibility of looking after the welfare of the child, applying a presumption in favour of natural parents which can be rebutted by other evidence including the child's own assessment of his or her welfare.[36]

The power to make a child a ward of court is sometimes used as a device for testing the legitimacy of actions which are open to question on grounds of morality. The yardstick applied by the court is not, however, moralistic: it decides strictly according to what it conceives to be the best interests of the child. In 1987, judges were criticized for permitting the sterilization of a mentally handicapped girl of seventeen who was made a ward of court by the local authority in order to obtain court approval for the operation, which had been unanimously recommended by doctors and was supported by the girl's mother.[37] Although the irreversible nature of such an operation should make it a last resort, the evidence established that the girl, who had a mental age of six and would not develop further, could not cope either with pregnancy (which would be an 'unmitigated disaster' for her) or with any other form of contraception. The courts – all the way up to the House of Lords – were called upon to sanction the decision which, while obviously humane in the particular circumstances, raised moral issues that made experts nervous. The case shows that doctors who fear accusations of 'playing God' can, at least where children are concerned, always obtain the approval of a higher authority.

Parents are entitled to object to others inflicting corporal punishment on their children. In *Tyrer*'s case, the European Court held that the birching of juvenile offenders, even those convicted of acts of violence, amounted to 'degrading punishment' contrary to Article 3 of the Convention. It was a form of 'institutionalized violence', constituting an assault on the individual's dignity and physical integrity. Although the British judge dissented (pointing out that he had come to no harm from being beaten at school), the UK Government was obliged to stop corporal punishment in the Isle of Man, and in 1982 the court once again indicated that Britain was in breach of the Convention by allowing children to suffer canings in schools contrary to their parents' wishes and beliefs about how they should be educated. In 1986 Parliament formally passed – by one vote – a law prohibiting corporal punishment in state schools. Parents who want their children beaten must pay to send them to independent schools which remain, anomalously, free to administer corporal punishment, although the Government would be held responsible under the European Convention if it permitted them to inflict the floggings familiar to Nicholas Nickleby.[38]

Undoubtedly the most common, and the most brutal, way in which teenagers have their rights infringed is by being subjected to severe corporal punishment within their homes. English law traditionally protects the authoritarian parent or guardian who 'reasonably chastises' children with cane or belt or gym-shoe. This is an urgent area for a reform in the law: now that canes are banned in schools, it is anomalous that they should be wielded in the privacy of the home. Some European countries forbid parents to beat teenage children and the Scottish Law Commission has recently recommended that hitting a child with any implement, or else with the intention to cause more than transitory pain, should be a criminal offence. It must be hoped that *Gillick* will herald the demise of 'reasonable chastisement' as a common-law defence to assault charges brought against parents: their 'right' to bruise their children should be the first to dwindle.

The abuse of young children by their custodians is such an

appalling fact of life that inroads must be made on the right to have family life respected by agencies of the state. The law until 1989 allowed magistrates to grant 'Place of Safety Orders' if social workers had 'reasonable cause to believe' that a child was at risk of ill-treatment or neglect. These orders removed children for up to twenty-eight days, and were unchallengeable if the correct procedures were followed. In 1989 the Government replaced these orders, which had proved so destructive of family relationships during the Cleveland crisis, with a new 'Emergency Protection Order' which lasts only for eight days and is challengeable by parents after seventy-two hours have elapsed. This reform, contained in the Children Act, was long overdue. It permits a court to remove a child from home if satisfied that social workers' belief 'that the child is likely to suffer significant harm' is reasonable. The court may further order that the child be examined by doctors or psychiatrists and that it should not have contact with any person who might harm it, although subject to such orders reasonable access must be permitted to parents or those who have been exercising parental authority. The 'Emergency Protection Order' is intended to encourage social services to act immediately on strong suspicions that children are in danger (they were previously reluctant to take the serious step of removing a child for a whole month without having clear medical evidence) but at the same time it improves the opportunities for parents to assert their own rights in court. Regrettably, their rights are generally asserted before lay justices: the difficulty of assessing evidence about suspected child abuse makes these cases more apt to be decided by county or crown court judges. The 1989 Children Act additionally strengthens the powers of police officers to act in an emergency by taking children into protection for up to three days if it is believed they would otherwise be likely to suffer significant harm. This temporary power can be used to safeguard children in the period before a court can be convened to hear an application for an 'Emergency Protection Order', although whether parents will be allowed access will depend on police judgements as to whether this is in the child's best interests.

Local authorities have a duty to protect children within their area. Social services departments may apply to the court for 'care orders' (which can last until the age of eighteen) if the child is otherwise likely to suffer significant harm (whether by ill-treatment or by impairment of health or development), or is simply 'beyond parental control'. There are about 80,000 children 'in care' in Britain, yet the House of Lords has held that the courts have no power to review on their merits decisions which local authorities take in respect of these children.[39] Such decisions frequently deny or restrict parental access, and five parents who were thus deprived complained to the European Court. In 1987, the court ruled that local-authority procedures had failed to respect the right to family life (Article 8) and had violated the guarantee of fair trial (Article 6), because social workers had not consulted parents about decisions to deny them access to their children, and these decisions were not appealable other than by way of judicial review. A judicial review did not amount to a 'fair trial' because the High Court could only examine the legitimacy of the procedures employed, and could not reassess the merits of the decision.[40] In an attempt to bring British law into conformity within the Convention, the Government legislated to provide a right of appeal for parents who are totally denied access to their children. The 1989 Children Act goes further by creating a presumption that a child taken into care should have reasonable contact with its parents, and by providing that a care order may be challenged by 'any person who has parental responsibility for the child' and by the child itself. The Act permits children with sufficient understanding to instruct solicitors and to be represented, when appropriate, before courts which make or reconsider care orders. The Act strives to keep state intervention to a minimum, however, by adopting as an overriding principle that a court should only make an order if it would positively improve a child's welfare, and not merely because the statutory criteria are made out.

Any system must strike a balance between the rights of parents to respect for family life and the right of the state to break up a family if there is evidence of children being ill-treated. The 1989 legislation had the welcome purpose of making allegations of child abuse both easier to investigate and easier to challenge. It drew upon the lessons of the Cleveland inquiry, and previous inquiries conducted by Louis Blom-Cooper, QC, into the deaths of two children – Jasmine Beckford[41] and Kimberley Carlile[42] – who were murdered despite being under the 'care' of social services departments. The Blom-Cooper reports argued strongly for a 'child assessment order' which would require parents to take children to a clinic for examination when child abuse was suspected – a much simpler and less coercive procedure than police protection followed by an eight-day 'Emergency Protection Order'. The most important result of the 1989 reforms has been to effect a shift of power from local authorities (which are no longer able to take control of children by committee resolution) to the courts. Although the courts concerned will initially be magistrates' courts, they will be able to transfer more complex care proceedings to the county court or to the High Court. Regrettably, the 1989 reforms did not create a structure for a Family Court, which alone could bring order and expertise to all disputes over the best interests of children.

Child sexual abuse poses intractable problems for the courts, especially in their preventive jurisdiction. Medical tests are rarely conclusive (in the absence of pregnancy or venereal disease or gross injury) and children abused by fathers or stepfathers have generally been emotionally blackmailed into secrecy. Obtaining disclosure from very young children by use of 'anatomically correct dolls' (one of the great euphemisms of our time) and other methods of interpreting children's play is open to ambiguity and allegations of 'coaching'. At what point does mere suspicion that a child is being sexually abused justify removing it from the family? This is one of the most agonizing dilemmas for a court, yet it is often entrusted to lay justices, who have shown themselves incapable of resolving it fairly and responsibly. It was the incompetence of lay justices, more than the doctrinaire beliefs of paediatricians and social workers, which produced the crisis in Cleveland in 1987, when so many children were suddenly removed from their families on inadequate and untested evidence. These removals were not ordered by the doctors (whom the media chose to blame) nor by the social-services department: neither had any power to make a 'Place of Safety Order'. These orders were made, often recklessly and without proper documentation, by lay justices. The majority lasted for the full twenty-eight days and were made by a single justice, at home rather than in court, and often at times when a full juvenile bench was sitting at Cleveland. As Louis Blom-Cooper, QC, concluded, reviewing the Cleveland inquiry report, 'The magistrates acted as rubber stamps to applications to remove and detain children on the say-so of social workers . . . (their) rush to *ex parte* judgement was inexcusable.'

The Cleveland crisis provides case-study support for the argument made in Chapter 8 that the lay justice system is a major weakness in the protection of civil liberties. It is particularly susceptible to panic when confronted by naïve but authoritarian social workers peddling horrific tales about ritualistic or 'satanic' abuse, as they subsequently did in Rochdale and Orkney – after the Cleveland inquiry but before the 1989 Act had come into affect. The Orkney affair was carefully planned: teams of police and social workers flew from the mainland for a dawn raid, abducting terrified children and holding them for weeks without contact with their families or even each other in order (as the senior social worker admitted) 'to disorient and deprive the children of all sense of security'. This inhuman treatment of 'displacement, disorientation, isolation and disempowerment' was justified on the same grounds as 'in-depth interrogation' in Northern Ireland – as a means of extracting the truth. What it extracted – by children frightened and abused by dogmatic social workers – was not the truth, but what police and social workers wanted to hear in order to justify their own behaviour. Subsequent inquiries have found no evidence of ritualistic abuse, although the children suffered trauma at the hands of those empowered to detain them in a misnamed 'place of safety' and to expose them to so-called 'disclosure therapy'. At no stage of these proceedings did anyone heed the wishes of the children, who all wanted to remain with, and then be reunited with, their families. The most sinister aspect of the operation was the use of disorientation and isolation techniques to strip children of their own identity (in which they allegedly cooperated with or accommodated to sexual abuse) prior to constructing a new identity for them. The scandal of Orkney was to put this Orwellian strategy into effect before any court had decided whether 'satanic abuse' had occurred at all. As at Cleveland, the most painful aspect of the Orkney affair was the plight of parents who were powerless even to put the case for reclaiming their children until the system permitted it, and it was this frustration which did some of the permanent damage to family relationships. Doctors, social workers, police and council officials shared the public blame, but the real failure lay in a justice system which gave their victims – both parents and children – no choice and no voice.

In 1991 the British Government ratified the UN Convention on the Rights of the Child, which emphasizes the fundamental principle of the Children Act that the best interests of the minor must be the primary consideration in all action towards it undertaken by public or private agencies, and underlines the importance of the child's freedom to express views and to have these views taken in account according to its age and maturity. In the same year as the Convention was adopted, an inquiry into children's homes in Staffordshire revealed that senior social workers had enthusiastically experimented with an unethical and brutal 'pin-down' regime which had caused lasting damage to 150 teenagers in residential care. In the same year, a court case revealed a long history of appalling sexual crimes inflicted on children under the residential 'care' of Frank Beck and his associates in Leicestershire. These Dickensian outrages cannot be stopped by an international Convention, but only by the creation of a rigorous and human-rights-orientated national inspectorate, to act as a 'children's ombudsman'. Meanwhile the Convention, which states that children are entitled to state benefits, has already been breached by the Government's decision to withdraw such benefits from children aged between sixteen and eighteen.

BIRTHRIGHTS

The right to become a parent has been put in issue as a result of the development of *in vitro* fertilization (IVF) techniques. Science has relieved much of the anguish and frustration of human infertility, which dogs an estimated 10 per cent of relationships in Britain. The first 'test-tube baby' was born in 1979, and many hundreds have followed. The creation in a test-tube of an embryo formed from a husband's sperm and a wife's egg, and its subsequent implantation so as to bypass an obstruction in the womb, is now scarcely controversial. But those who fear that licensed laboratories will lead to the hatcheries of *Brave New World* point to the way in which early human embryos are used for research and experimentation, and then tipped down a sink. They can be frozen, for implantation years or even centuries later, and they may soon be able to grow to babyhood in artificial wombs, or even in the male abdominal cavity. A committee chaired by Dame Mary Warnock comprehensively surveyed the ethical issues in human reproductive technology which had emerged by 1984, and many of its recommendations were implemented by the Human Fertilization and Embryology Act 1990. This legislation prohibits the creation, keeping and use of embryos outside the human body, except with a licence for their treatment, storage or research issued to clinics by a new statutory body, the Human Fertilization and Embryology Authority. This Authority takes over the supervision of IVF treatment conducted previously by a voluntary body, and its duties include the provision of advice and information about new developments to Parliament and to the public. Parliament has so far narrowly resisted back-bench MPs' attempts to outlaw research on human embryos, which is conducted for the purpose of finding cures for infertility and unlocking the causes of genetic disease. The Warnock Report recommendation, which would permit experimentation with em-bryos for up to fourteen days after fertilization, at present has the support of the Authority.

The difficulty of making people good by Act of Parliament is compounded where the objective deemed to be 'bad' is the creation of a child. Now that IVF techniques are available to married couples, what right has the state, or its hospital doctors, to withhold the benefits of treatment from unmarried couples, or from lesbian couples or single women? Article 12 of the European Convention guarantees to all citizens 'the right to found a family', and it is likely to be asserted against doctors who make value-judgements about applicants deemed 'unsuitable' for the opportunity of motherhood. The first such case was brought unsuccessfully by a prostitute who had been denied the opportunity of infertility treatment. The Hospi-tal Ethics Committee's decision to turn her away was wrong in principle, although justified in terms of the practical need to give priority to married couples while waiting-lists are long. (The court at least conceded that judicial review would lie against a hospital whose unethical 'ethics committee' refused to treat 'anyone who was a Jew or coloured'.)[43] As *in vitro* treatment becomes widely available, it will be wrong in principle to deny certain women access to it on moralistic grounds, or because they happen to be unwed. However, during the passage of the 1990 Act, the paternalis-tic voices of hereditary peers and back-bench MPs brayed about the 'danger' of extending IVF birthrights to single women (who might even, they feared, be lesbians) and the Government compromised by adding Section 13(5) of the Act which requires that:

a woman shall not be provided with treatment services unless account has been taken of the welfare of any child who may be born as a result of the treatment (including the need of that child for a father) . . .

The words in brackets were designed by Virginia Bottomley, then the Cabinet's sole woman, to discriminate against single women. If hospital ethics committees wish to avoid such discrimination, they might consider the hypothetical views of a child born to a single applicant as to its own best interests: would it prefer to be born and brought up by a single mother or lesbian couple, or would it prefer not to be born at all?

One matter which vexed the British Parliament at an early stage was surrogate motherhood. The whole idea of surrogacy is abhorrent to many, although from the perspective of individual rights this total hostility is difficult to understand. For women who cannot or should not bear children as a result of a medical condition (such as heart disease or a defective womb or a propensity to miscarry) the artificial insemination of a willing surrogate may produce a wanted child 'fathered' by the husband of the marriage. A woman with functioning ovaries but a damaged womb can achieve children who are genetically hers as well as her husband's by a combination of laparoscopy for ovum recovery and *in vitro* fertilization, followed by embryo transfer to a surrogate. Such cases may be rare, but they argue against the total legal prohibition on surrogacy recommended by Warnock. In the United States, surrogacy services operated by doctors and lawyers fulfil a powerful need, notwithstanding the legal problems which occasionally ensue when surrogates decide to renege on their contract and to keep the child. The rights of infertile couples to enter into surrogacy arrangements, with professional advice and subject to safeguards such as medical supervision, genetic screening of the surrogate and adequate counselling, would seem to follow from the right to found a family.

It was precisely this right which was ignored by Parliament in 1985 when it rushed through the Surrogacy Arrangements Act, which has the familiar defects associated with legislation inspired by moral panic. The much publicized saga of 'Baby Cotton', the offspring of a proselytizing US surrogacy agency, outraged MPs and convinced them that 'something ought to be done'. The Act imposes a fine or short prison sentence on any person who receives a fee for advising or assisting a surrogacy arrangement. It does not prohibit surrogacy as such, but by punishing professionals who would otherwise be involved, it forces the infertile couples and the surrogate to make amateurish 'do it yourself' contracts and to proceed without the benefit of medical, legal and other counselling services. It is a squalid piece of legislation, which places the burden of proof on defendants and denies them the right to jury trial, as well as effectively denying citizens who wish to make lawful arrangements their basic entitlement to legal advice and professional help.

There can be no objection to the state regulating surrogacy services or restricting the opportunities for profiteering from them. There is an obvious danger of exploitation, which calls for carefully drafted contracts which make provision for the surrogate to receive adequate counselling prior to signing, adequate remuneration and an effective right to change her mind and keep the child, at least if it is genetically hers. In 1986 one meddling Social Services Department seized a surrogate's baby after its birth and had it made a ward of court: the judge, sensibly, decided that since there was no dispute between the parties the child's best interests obviously lay with the infertile couple who had commissioned it. By the time of the 1990 Act, Parliament's panic over surrogacy had receded sufficiently for it to provide a statutory basis for couples to obtain a court order that the child borne by their surrogate should be treated in law as their own; this avoids the absurdity of couples having to adopt a child which is genetically theirs, before it can be theirs in law. Although many find surrogacy arrangements unpalatable, they are a measure of the desperation of otherwise childless couples who are asserting their freedom as individuals to make private arrangements with another individual to bear their wanted child. Instead of providing a compassionate and supportive framework in which this aspiration may be realized, British law isolates them from professional help. Wealthy couples, of course, may (and do) find the liberty they seek in the United States.

THE RIGHT TO DIE

The bodies of suicides were once buried by night at crossroads, with a stake through their hearts and a stone on their heads. Until 1961, self-murder was a crime, and would-be suicides could be prosecuted for botching their own demise. The law took its cue from Blackstone, who condemned the suicide for the spiritual presumption of 'invading the prerogative of the Almighty, and rushing into His immediate presence uncalled for'. The Suicide Act of 1961 abolished the old crime, but perpetuated punishment for any person 'who aids, abets, counsels or procures the suicide of another or an attempt by another to commit suicide'. The compassionate doctor who, by request, shortens the life of a dying patient remains technically guilty of murder, while anyone else who dares to help or advise a sufferer commits an offence of 'aiding and abetting suicide', punishable by up to fourteen years' imprisonment.

The harshness of the law can be mitigated in practice by a certain turning of blind eyes by coroners and prosecuting authorities when terminally ill patients are put out of their misery by close family members unmotivated by greed for inheritance, and genuine 'mercy killers' who are prosecuted for aiding and abetting generally receive suspended sentences. Where the evidence is clear that life was taken with an intention to kill, however, there is no defence to a prosecution for murder no matter how compassionate the circumstances. Moreover, the penalty for murder is fixed at life imprisonment. At Manchester Crown Court in 1988, a man who admitted to smothering his crippled and dying wife with a pillow after she had repeatedly begged him to cut short her sufferings in precisely that way was ruled to have no defence to a murder charge. When he changed his plea to guilty and was sentenced to life imprisonment, his jury published a joint statement of outrage at the result. It was a barbaric outcome, but one dictated by the inflexibility of the law, providing yet another reason why the mandatory life sentence for murder should be repealed.

The case for a more fundamental change was made in 1992 by the conviction for attempted murder of hospital consultant Nigel Cox, who had injected a pain-racked and terminally ill seventy-year-old patient, for whom he had cared for many years, at her (and her family's) desperate request with a lethal dose of potassium chloride. The evidence demonstrated that the decision was taken courageously and compassionately, to relieve her from unbearable torment (she had built up a resistance to painkillers) and in the only way which would allow her to die while holding the hand of her son. The doctor's act was reported by a devoutly Catholic nurse, and neither the Crown Prosecution Service nor the jury had the humanity to stay the hand of the criminal law. The judge, while imposing a suspended sentence, fulminated that 'what you did was not only criminal, it was a total betrayal of your unequivocal duty as a physician', but the General Medical Council disagreed, and to widespread public approval refused to withdraw the consultant's license to practice. The case demonstrated that a bad law cannot be tolerated on the basis that it will be sensibly administered. Doctors may continue to administer heroin in potentially lethal doses to dying patients, protected by the fiction that their prime object is to kill pain rather than to cause death (whereas in fact it is to cause death in order to kill pain), but the boon of oblivion will be denied to those who most need it, whose pain is terminal, unrelievable and unbearable. In these circumstances, British law is irrevocably committed to the distinction expressed in Arthur Hugh Clough's 'The Latest Decalogue', 'Thou shall not kill, but need'st not strive officiously to keep alive.'

The embodiment of officiousness in the legal system is the Official Solicitor, charged with the worthy task of representing those who cannot represent themselves. His office has in recent years caused large amounts of court time and money to be expended in attempting to stop doctors from allowing their patients to die with as much dignity as is possible in their circumstances. The courts can never, as the law stands, approve of positive actions to hasten death, but they have declined to order doctors to undertake major or invasive surgery to keep alive patients so damaged that any life which might be prolonged would be so cruel as to be intolerable for the patient.[44] Nor will judges encroach upon a doctor's professional duty to his patient by dictating some possibly life-saving treatment which is contrary to the hospital medical team's honest clinical judgement as to the treatment which is required.[45]

In 1993 the courts decided the landmark case of *Airedale National*

Health Trust v. *Bland*, which concerned a twenty-one-year-old boy who had suffered irreversible brain damage in the Hillsborough disaster, and had lain in a 'persistent vegetative state', from which he could never recover, ever since. Could the hospital, with the approval of his doctors, parents and friends, allow artificial feeding and antibiotic drugs to be withdrawn so that he could die in a gentle and controlled way, rather than 'live' a non-existent life? This is, of course, an ethical and not a legal question, although only Lord Justice Hoffman (in the Court of Appeal) treated it as such, in an eloquent essay on moral philosophy which acknowledged his 'discussions' with Professors Bernard Williams and Ronald Dworkin. (If the Official Solicitor persists in bringing moral conundrums to court, there seems no reason why they should not be settled by cross-examination of doctors of philosophy rather than of medicine.) Conveniently, the philosophical and legal conclusions coincided; the right to individual autonomy, or self-determination, like the legal approach of hypothesizing the opinion of the patient as to his own best interests, envisaged Tony Bland as a boy who would wish to end the ordeal of his family and who would wish to be remembered as a 'cheerful carefree gregarious teenager' rather than observed as a grotesque 'living' carcase. The solution imaginatively arrived at – ('we should try our honest best to do what we think he would have chosen') marks a valuable development in the law. It does have three consequences, however, that the Court of Appeal failed to explore. First, if Tony Bland had been a devout Catholic, or a selfish youth who enjoyed causing parental pain, the decision would have to be to keep him 'alive' as long as possible. Secondly, if Tony Bland had been a logical and practical youth, he would have preferred to be given a lethal injection to bring about his death directly (a device the court eschewed with horror) rather than to be denied food, which is a slower and more distressing form of death, however 'natural' to our curious way of thinking. And, thirdly, if the test were applied to Dr Cox's patient (and to most 'victims' of euthanasia) she would devoutly have wished the lethal injection.

The House of Lords decided that Tony Bland should be left to die simply because death, objectively speaking, was in his best interests. The medical treatment which was keeping him alive (tubal feeding and antibiotics) was futile, since there was no earthly prospect of any improvement in his condition, and doctors were not legally or ethically obliged to continue futile treatment.[46] They accepted that had Tony positively expressed a wish not to be subjected to medical treatment then doctors would be obliged to respect it, but they discouraged the Court of Appeal's hypothetical approach of asking what he might have wished had he ever been asked to imagine the circumstances his body was in. The Law Lords were at pains to explain the importance of distinction between 'letting die' (an *omission*) and euthanasia, which involved a positive *act* of causing death to relieve suffering, such as a lethal injection. This distinction is disingenuous, when the so-called 'omission' involved acts of withdrawing food and antibiotics over several weeks, administering sedatives and obtaining a declaration from the courts. The case of *Airedale NHS Trust* v. *Bland* at least shows how judges are coming to occupy the place for them imagined in More's *Utopia* (see later, page 461), in which they may absolve doctors from criminal prosecution (and perhaps from some moral anguish) by declaring proposed conduct to be lawful. To the extent that they are slowly finding ways to give legal effect to the wish to die with dignity, the judge may become a welcome visitor to those dying patients who choose last rights instead of last rites.

The judgements in *Bland* mark an important recognition of rights to die and of 'a principle of kindness which is the badge of our humanity'. They endorsed, too, a presumption in favour of self-determination which affords some protection against the moral absolutism of others. It is a presumption, however, which must be applied to all decisions by competent adults about their medical treatment, however irrational or superstitious they may appear. As a Canadian court pointed out, in stopping a hospital from transfusing blood to save the life of a card-carrying Jehovah's Witness:

At issue here is the freedom of the patient as an individual to exercise her right to refuse treatment and accept the consequences of her own decision. Competent adults are generally at liberty to refuse medical treatment even at the risk of death. The right to determine what shall be done with one's own body is a fundamental right in our society.[47]

This statement was approved by the Court of Appeal in *Re T*, which involved a tug-of-war around the hospital bed of a woman who had been brought up as a Jehovah's Witness, and who needed a blood transfusion to survive after an operation. In a drugged state, and after talking to her mother (a fanatical Jehovah's Witness), she indicated she did not want a transfusion and lapsed into unconsciousness. Her father and boyfriend, who were not members of the faith, urged a High Court judge at 11 p.m. at night to save her life by ordering medical staff (who were twiddling their thumbs) to give her a transfusion. The Court of Appeal approved the order, because of doubt about T's real wishes (her mother had exerted undue influence) but confirmed the right of patients to decide their own treatment if they were capable of doing so by ratiocination, even if their conclusion was irrational. The respect for the sanctity of life will obviously incline English courts to err on the safe side if there is any doubt at all about a patient's competence, or if the decision will affect the life of another. Thus the President of the Family Division of the High Court had no hesitation, after a ten-minute hearing, in ordering an emergency Caesarean to be performed, against both the patient's and her husband's wishes, because this operation was the only way to save the life of the patient's unborn child as well as of the patient.[48] Hard cases make bad law, and there must be limits to using the coercive power of the state over women who choose to act in ways which may impede the health of their foetus. Protection against the crazed beliefs of its parents (the couple were members of a 'born-again Christian' sect) should only begin when a baby is capable of being delivered alive: the courts have yet to injunct women from drinking and smoking and drug-taking in the course of pregnancy.

What alternatives are open to those who urge legal recognition for the right to decide the time and place of one's own death? Two enthusiastic euthanasiasts who offered to dispatch elderly members of 'Exit' with plastic bags and sleeping pills were convicted and gaoled for aiding and abetting suicide, but the High Court refused to injunct *The Guide to Self-Deliverance*, a 'do-it-yourself' instruction manual for members of the organization which set out the arguments against committing suicide before proceeding to explain how it could be accomplished effectively, without resort to desperate and unreliable measures such as wrist-slitting and drug-overdosing.[49] The Voluntary Euthanasia Society has many supporters who believe that terminally ill and bedridden individuals have a right to choose death with dignity, and to receive the assistance of doctors and relatives in effectuating that choice. Several European countries have legislated to permit doctors to ease the passing of dying patients, but attempts to modify the law in Britain have been unsuccessful.

The subject of euthanasia calls for careful distinctions which the present law does not draw, and which are left, unsatisfactorily, to police and prosecuting authorities. There are cases (which are increasing with the ability of medical science to prolong the pain-racked life of the terminally ill) where assistance to a free and rational decision to end life requires neither condemnation nor punishment. In Sir Thomas More's *Utopia*, priests and magistrates were obliged to counsel the incurably ill towards an 'honourable death'. After proper inquiry, a citizen was entitled to 'either dispatch himself out of that painful life, as out of a prison or a rack of torment, or else suffer himself willingly to be rid out of it by others'. The danger is that total repeal of the 'aiding and abetting' offence in the Suicide Act would leave the elderly open to artful persuasion by greedy relatives, and even permit the kind of manipulated hysteria which produced the mass suicides at Jones Town. *The Guide to Self-Deliverance* might be acceptable in the hands of adult members of a euthanasia society, but should it be on open paperback sale to any temporarily depressed teenager? Applications to the courts for the right to have an 'assisted death' would be prone to difficulty and delay, and would in any event be doomed to failure in Britain so long as Section 2 of the Suicide Act is unamended. The choice for reformers is between a new law carefully enumerating the circumstances in which assistance may be given, or an amendment providing a defence if assistance is given with legitimate reason. Those who choose to attempt suicide by drug overdose sometimes leave notes withdrawing their consent to any treatment designed to revive them, and such an instruction would protect a doctor from prosecution for manslaughter if he obeyed it, although the courts would draw the line at awarding damages for assault if he disobeyed it and was sued by the patient whose unbearable life had been saved.

CHAPTER 11

Freedom from Discrimination

'We hold these truths to be self-evident, that all men are created equal . . .' begins the Declaration of Independence. Of course, all men and women are not created equal in physical or intellectual attributes, and their entitlement to equality is really a right to have the same respect accorded to them as is shown to others who share their characteristics as human beings. Discrimination on grounds of race or sex involves the application of criteria which are irrelevant to the intrinsic human quality of an individual. It is behaviour we have come to regard as immoral and to recognize as socially divisive. Law does not and cannot change the way people think about each other, but it can deter the translation of prejudice into actions which disadvantage and harm fellow citizens. In performing this deterrent function, it may further promote equality by educating others to recognize and despise racist and sexist actions, and encourage reconsideration of socially ingrained customs and prejudices which have hitherto justified discriminating behaviour. It may also – much more controversially – have a remedial role to play, by subordinating other freedoms to an overriding social objective of eliminating the root causes of inequality. British law has yet to endorse 'positive discrimination' – the policy of specially favouring minorities in order to redress existing imbalances – although this may offer the only prospect of tackling the pattern of distributional inequality which remains endemic in British society, as women and blacks fare disproportionately worse in terms of employment and income, as well as in representation in professional and public life.

The common law failed abjectly to counter inequality. Freedom of contract prevailed, and the providers of goods and services could discriminate against women and blacks to their heart's content. But in the USA, beginning with the great case of *Brown* v. *Board of*

Education in 1954,[1] the Supreme Court was able to use constitutional guarantees of equality to strike down discriminatory rules, and in 1964 Congress passed the momentous Civil Rights Act. Under the influence of this American example, and shaken by the racial disturbances in Notting Hill and the racist hysteria whipped up during the Smethwick by-election, the British Parliament passed its first Race Relations Act in 1965. This was a modest measure, improved in 1968 and extended in 1976. In 1975, and also associated with the commitment of Roy Jenkins as Home Secretary, came the Sex Discrimination Act and the implementation of the Equal Pay Act. This web of legislation gave victims of discrimination the right to sue for damages, and established commissions with the powers to receive complaints and assist in bringing them before the courts. Judicial reception of the legislation was at first hostile to the exercise of these new powers and courts took refuge in technicalities to deny necessary relief and to circumscribe the investigative functions of the Commission for Racial Equality (CRE) and the Equal Opportunities Commission (EOC). Shamed (and overruled) by the much more robust decisions of the European Court of Justice, and buffeted by binding EC directives, British courts and tribunals are gradually accepting the objectives of anti-discrimination legislation and rejecting beguiling excuses for noncompliance. Seemingly inconsequential sexist or racist practices cannot be overlooked on the principle that *de minimis non curat lex* (the law does not concern itself with trifles). Petty apartheid is not petty at all to those who suffer it all the time.

Freedom of religion is a fundamental human right, and its inclusion in a chapter on discrimination does not imply otherwise. The untrammelled freedom of worship in Britain should not obscure the more subtle ways in which minority faiths face prejudice in schools and workplaces and professions, or the increasingly absurd and anachronistic consequences of the 'establishment' of the Church of England. There is growing recognition of how rights are denied to disabled people, as often by architecture as by choice, and of how the law should make better provision for their special needs. What has emerged as the most virulent and obnoxious form of contemporary intolerance is denigration and discrimination aimed at homosexuals. There are probably more homosexuals than there are black people in Britain, yet the law affords no special protection against discrimination on the basis of sexual orientation. Indeed the law itself still positively discriminates against homosexuality in a number of respects. Its total prohibition of homosexual acts between consenting adult men was repealed as recently as 1967, and it will take many more years for society to come to terms with the rights of gay people to be treated with the respect due to them as law-abiding human beings. It is ironic that for all the progress made over the past decade in improving the legal lot of women and ethnic groups, prejudice against homosexuals has been allowed free reign, fanned by the advent of Aids. In 1988 MPs gave further expression to that prejudice by passing a special law – Section 28 of the Local Government Act – designed to prevent local authorities from taking positive action to counter hostility to homosexuality. Trans-sexuals, too, suffer special legal disabilities. There is no more urgent change required in the law securing civil liberties than the inclusion of 'sexual orientation' as a ground of wrongful discrimination.

At the outset, and as a measure of the failure of anti-discrimination law to secure much more than procedural justice, it must be recognized that all these forms of discrimination are endemic at every level of the legal profession and in the institutions of law. There has never been a woman appointed to the highest court (nor, for that matter, has there been a Lady Chancellor, or a Madame Attorney- or even Solicitor-General) and appointments of women and black judges have been merely token (see earlier, page 369). In 1992 only thirty-one of about two thousand lay members of industrial tribunals (which hear complaints of racial discrimination in employment) were themselves from racial minorities. There are few Afro-Caribbean or Asian lecturers in law, and black students have three times the failure rate at the Council of Legal Education (due in part to the notorious 'practical exercises' where individual performance in advocacy and conferencing is assessed by practising barristers, who tend to be more impressed by the performers who most resemble themselves). The problem of 'clonesmanship' exists at most levels, as prospective partners for solicitors' firms and applicants for chambers membership are judged by standards of congeniality and like-mindedness which tend to exclude 'outsiders' and minorities. Rejection of women and black and gay candidates is often justified on the basis that they 'are not quite as good' as the successful white heterosexual male: rarely is it remembered that their ability to overcome discrimination so as to reach serious candidature is a quality which, if properly assessed, probably makes them 'that much better'. Many courts and most chambers and solicitors' offices are not wheelchair-accessible, which makes life difficult both for disabled lawyers and for disabled clients. The Bar and the Law Society have promoted equal opportunities policies (although as late as 1991 there was still a sufficient number of homophobes on the Law Society Council to veto protection for gay solicitors), but there is a marked reluctance to give these rules any teeth. A large number of senior lawyers have a profound psychological attachment to 'men only' clubs. (This was seen at its most comical in the recent attempts to admit women to the Garrick made by 'liberal' lawyers, who neglected to resign when they failed, or to explain why they chose to join such a sexist institution in the first place.) The law exists primarily to serve the social values of fairness and equality: by failing to reflect these values in its human composition, it undermines the respect which is necessary before its anti-discrimination work can begin to succeed.

RACIAL DISCRIMINATION

Britain has no laws which expressly impose disabilities on persons according to their race or colour. Subject to satisfying rules about nationality and residence, members of all races may vote or travel on public transport or apply for the benefits of education and social services. The Race Relations Act is necessary, however, to protect those who are liable to be treated less favourably, in a whole range of situations, simply because of their colour or race or ethnic or national origin. That is the basic test for unlawful discrimination, applied by the 1976 Race Relations Act. It protects 'racial groups', defined not by strict reference to biology but to cultural traditions and community perceptions. If a group of people regard themselves, or have long been regarded by the community, as a distinct racial group, as a result of common history or social actions or language or religion, their members will be able to invoke the Act to combat discrimination which is based on their membership of the group.

This broad interpretation of the Act was laid down by the House of Lords in *Mandla* v. *Dowell Lee*, where a private school was held to have discriminated on racial grounds by refusing to admit an orthodox Sikh because he would have been obliged to wear a turban in contravention of its rules about school uniform.[2] The Law Lords decided that Sikhs, although biologically no different from other Punjabis, were a 'racial group' as a result of their distinctive history, language and religious beliefs. The discrimination in this case would not be 'justified' under the Act because the rules had no purpose other than to prohibit a display of ethnic origin. (A rule discriminating against Sikhs on public-health grounds – e.g. preventing beards being worn in a chocolate factory lest hairs fall into the vats – has been held to be justifiable.) When the landlord of the Cat and Mutton pub in the East End displayed a sign saying 'Sorry, No Travellers' he was held to be indirectly discriminating against gypsies, who form a racial group on the test established in *Mandla*'s case.[3] A Rastafarian, however, could not claim discrimination when ordered by the Department of the Environment to cut his dreadlocks before he could work as a van driver: the Court of Appeal ruled in 1993 that for all their religious and cultural tradition, Rastas lacked a 'long shared history' which was a prerequisite for a racial group.[4] Sixty years of reggae music was not enough to distinguish them from other Afro-Caribbean people, although it was enough for a Government department to act in a petty and stupid fashion (the dreadlocks, concealed beneath a multicoloured hat, were not a hazard to his work as a driver). This case shows how acts of discrimination which are 'racist' in a broad sense may fall outside the Act. It would be unlawful in Northern Ireland, where religion is included as a ground of discrimination.

The Act entitles members of racial groups to bring proceedings if subjected to less favourable treatment than members of other racial groups in a wide range of situations where discrimination has proved a serious social problem. The first area specified is in the provision of any goods, facilities or services. These wide expressions cover places of public entertainment or refreshment like dance halls, public houses, theatres, cinemas, cafés and public libraries. The Act covers hotels, boarding houses, trains, buses and air services. Businesses and professions which provide services are included (doctors and estate agents, for instance) and so are public bodies which provide services. There must be no discrimination in educational facilities or in banking or insurance facilities. In decided cases, it has been held that a car-hire firm could not refuse a car to a Trinidadian on the ground that its insurance cover did not extend to those born outside the UK. Lloyd's had to rewrite its car insurance policies to replace the 'born abroad' test with merely a residence requirement and proof of driving experience. A life-assurance company was required to desist from asking applicants whether they were 'Caucasian, Negroid or Asian'. Mecca could not refuse black youths admission to its Locarno Ballroom, Streatham, merely on the ground that to admit any black person might result in disturbances, or because youths of the same race had caused trouble in the past. A Lancashire estate agent who offered mortgage facilities to house buyers could not refuse to put up to the building society for whom he acted as agent an application by a Pakistani. The motive or reason for an act of direct discrimination may be good, bad or indifferent; the result is what counts. The question is simply 'Would the complainant have received the same treatment from the defendant but for his or her race?' or, in most cases 'Would the same treatment have been received had the complainant been white?'

The Act prohibits an employer from discrimination in recruiting schemes or by refusing a black applicant employment, or by giving him or her different terms of employment or opportunities for training or promotion. Segregation will, almost inevitably, mean discrimination – separate toilets for white and Asian employees have been held to infringe the Act. Bodies like the Law Society and Bar Council which license people to practise in particular professions are not supposed to discriminate in conferring authorization or qualification. It is unlawful for trade unions or employers' organizations to discriminate by denying membership or refusing benefits. The 1976 Act specifically makes it unlawful for clubs with twenty-five or more members to discriminate on racial grounds in the admission of or treatment accorded to members. There is a special exception for clubs whose main object is to promote the interests of a particular racial group, so long as colour is not a factor in membership rulings. The Australian Association would be entitled to exclude Frenchmen and Filipinos, but not Australian Aborigines.

The Act applies to discrimination in housing, either by refusing to dispose of a home to the applicant (whether by sale or lease) or by treating him differently when he is in the accommodation. There is an exception where the landlord lives there, shares accommodation with others and has accommodation for fewer than seven persons other than those in his or her household. Municipal housing is covered, so that local authorities cannot have rules for allocating council houses which discriminate against blacks or coloured people or foreigners. A property owner could not refuse accommodation to a Kenyan on the ground that he did not mix white and coloured tenants; an Indian doctor was discriminated against when he was told on the telephone that a house on a new estate was available but when he promptly called at the agent's office in person was informed that all the houses were sold. In housing, employment and elsewhere discriminatory advertisements are also prohibited. The obsessive racist Robert Relf was eventually gaoled for refusing to take down the sign outside his house which read 'For sale to an English family'. Most racist advertisements are less obtrusive, and classifieds seeking New Zealand nannies or Jewish flat-mates may well be over-looked by the CRE, which has the sole responsibility for enforcing this section of the Act, in order to avoid vexatious prosecutions. None the less, as the Government White Paper on the Act points out, 'the public display of racial prejudices and preferences is inherently offensive and likely to encourage the spread of the discriminatory attitudes and practices'.[5]

The most important innovation in the 1976 Act was to outlaw 'indirect discrimination', which occurs where a condition applies in theory to persons of all racial groups, but is in practice such that a considerably smaller proportion from one racial group can comply with it than the proportion from other groups. The concept was imported from American law, where it is founded on the US Supreme Court ruling in *Griggs* v. *Duke Power Co.* that a condition requiring applicants for manual work at a power station to have graduated from high school or to have passed an IQ test discriminated in practice against Negroes and could not be justified as a necessary qualification for the job.[6]

British law permits the indirect discriminator to prove that the policy is 'justifiable' on non-racial grounds – a test that has caused a good deal of confusion in the courts. Some judges have mistakenly permitted indirect discrimination to continue where the condition in question is justified merely in terms of sound and acceptable business practice, while others have required proof that the condition is necessary to the economic viability of the business. An example of how the House of Lords approaches the question of indirect discrimination and whether it can be justified on non-racial grounds is provided by *Orphanos* v. *Queen Mary College*.[7] The college had sought to implement government cost-cutting by charging overseas students at an increased rate, unless they could show that they had been ordinarily resident in Britain or the EEC for the preceding three years. It was held that this rule indirectly discriminated against students of non-British or non-EEC nationality who wished to be admitted to the college, a considerably smaller proportion of whom could comply with the residence condition than the proportion of British or EEC nationals who could take advantage of it. Moreover, the discriminatory condition itself was not capable of being justified without regard to race. Although the motive for introducing it was to cut expenditure in the interests of economy (a reasonable and non-racist consideration), none the less the method chosen for cost-cutting was directed against foreign students. An across-the-board fee increase, or restrictions by reference to academic qualifications, would have been acceptable: but the college could not implement its chosen policy without having regard to the nationality of the applicants at whose expense the policy was carried into effect. This approach is welcome in that it requires the justification for indirect discrimination to be scrupulously devoid of racial considerations and to be related to reasons for imposing the actual condition and not to background motives.

A policy which discriminates is not 'justifiable' merely because non-racist reasons can be given for imposing it; there must be a real need for that particular policy, and a lack of realistic alternatives. Thus a Department of Education policy to accept only teachers who had trained for the length of time required in Britain, and a Council of Legal Education policy requiring non-law graduates of foreign universities to take longer courses than non-law graduates of British universities, indirectly discriminated against qualified persons of other races and were not justified by the non-racist need for sufficient accreditation, because this could be accomplished in other ways (e.g. by individual assessment) which did not bear disfavourably on applicants from races other than British.[8] The Department of Education, in the teacher-training case, relied also on the statutory defence that it was acting in pursuance of a law, but the House of Lords pointed out that this could not avail a defendant if the discriminatory policy or action it chose was merely sufficient, and not necessary, to comply with a statutory duty. It is lawful to discriminate in favour of employing members of a particular racial group to look after the welfare of members of that group if this is the best way to promote their welfare: thus it is not discriminatory to appoint an Afro-Caribbean rather than a white to a nursery job which entailed reading books to children in West Indian patois.[9] (If the white applicant spoke the patois fluently, the discrimination would be insupportable, at least on any basis envisaged by the Act.)

Members of the armed forces are denied the right to complain to courts about racial discrimination – the complaint is considered by their commanding officer and on appeal by a military board (two senior officers). The unwillingness of the army to do justice to black soldiers has recently been condemned by the Divisional Court; it imposed some procedural safeguards, but it is quite plain from this case that racist behaviour in the services will continue until victims are given the right to appeal to a tribunal independent of the military establishment.[10]

True to British tradition, acts 'done for the purpose of safeguarding national security' are entirely exempt. This means that MI5 and MI6 may be as racist as they wish in their employment policies. Spying on particular nationalities may best be done by members of that nationality, but there is no reason why desk jobs in the secret services should be reserved for white, as distinct from black, Britons.

The prime responsibility for making the Race Relations Act work belongs to the Commission for Racial Equality. It has a chairman and not more than fourteen members appointed by the Home Secretary; the various racial minorities are substantially represented in its composition. It is the aggrieved individual, not the Commission, who instigates a complaint of discrimination. The Commission will, on application, be able to give assistance to a claimant or potential claimant where the case raises an issue of principle or where it is unreasonable, for instance by reason of the case's complexity or the respective positions of the parties to the dispute, to expect claimants to proceed on their own behalf. 'Assistance' includes advice, conciliation, arranging for legal advice and assistance, and representation.

If the alleged discrimination is in the field of employment, the individual complains to an industrial tribunal, which may award compensation up to £10,000, or recommend that the employer take action to obviate or reduce the adverse effect on the complainant of the act of discrimination. All other complaints are made to the county court, where complainants have the burden of proving discrimination. If they succeed the court has power to award damages (including damages for injured feelings) and to grant an injunction restraining the defendant from discriminating unlawfully against the plaintiff. For many years judges failed to appreciate the impact of racism, and awarded merely nominal damages for 'hurt feelings'. Some improvement came in 1987, when the Court of Appeal decided that £3,000 was an appropriate sum to compensate a Sri Lanken scientist for the degrading experience of being refused employment by a local health authority because of her colour, and that £500 rather than £50 should be awarded to a black prisoner who had been treated unfairly by prison authorities.[11] In 1991 the Court again increased compensation to a teacher who had been turned down on racial grounds for the headship of a college department, and authorized the awarding of additional punitive damages in exceptional cases where the discriminatory treatment was insulting or high-handed.[12] Although these levels are still derisory compared with awards for libels of more fleeting impact than a racist rejection, they indicate a dawning judicial willingness to take race discrimination seriously. In the same spirit, the Court of Appeal has reduced the burden on complainants by encouraging tribunals to draw an inference of real discrimination where an employer's explanation for apparent discrimination is inadequate or unsatisfactory. There is no 'right to silence' in civil proceedings; the Great Britain–China Association had refused to explain why it had failed even to shortlist an outstanding Chinese applicant for its deputy-directorship, and there was evidence that it had never employed an ethnic Chinese. In these circumstances, although the burden of proving discrimination was on the complainant, the court could infer from the proven facts that the Great Britain–China Association was disinclined to associate with employees born in China.[13]

One of the Commission's main purposes is to conduct investigations into discriminatory practices. It has powers to require the furnishing of information and the production of documents and to issue 'non-discrimination notices' which last for five years. The

CRE's power to conduct formal investigations has been the subject of much litigation and a good deal of judicial hostility. In 1984 the House of Lords confirmed that the Commission's procedures could be challenged by judicial review (which is reasonable enough) but that it could only conduct a 'named-person investigation' (which carries the power to subpoena evidence) where it already has concrete reason to suspect that the targeted individual or organization is guilty of unlawful discrimination.[14] This ruling has severely restricted the work of the Commission, by depriving it of the power to investigate thoroughly organizations or industries in which blacks are severely under-represented, although there is no evidence pointing towards any specific unlawful act of discrimination. The subpoena powers attaching to named-person investigations are frequently the only way that such evidence can be produced. The dangers inherent in 'fishing expeditions' by state agencies with powers of compulsion must be balanced against the social evil they combat, and such powers have greater justification when the fruits of their use are confined to civil action rather than criminal prosecutions. A drafting error in the Act required the CRE to grant hearing rights at the preliminary stage of its investigations, as well as at later stages, and this process is so frustrating and time-consuming for an under-funded and understaffed Commission that very little of its potential as an investigative body has been achieved.

Under Section 71 of the Race Relations Act local authorities have a duty to carry out their functions with due regard to the need to eliminate discrimination and to promote good race relations. The courts, however, have been reluctant to allow councils free reign to use this power other than against organizations involved in acts of unlawful discrimination. Labour-controlled Leicester City Council took the view that it was entitled, given its 25 per cent population of blacks and Asians, to refuse its sporting facilities to the local football club, because the club refused to criticize those of its members who had played in a politically controversial tour of South Africa. The House of Lords held that although a council is entitled to exercise its discretions in a way which conduces to good race relations, it was an 'abuse of power' to punish a club which had 'done no wrong'.[15] It is difficult to see how local authorities can give much meaning to Section 71 if their policy decisions may only disadvantage 'wrongdoers': good race relations are frequently jeopardized by actions which are entirely lawful. What was unfair and objectionable on free-speech grounds was the council's heavy-handed insistence that the club should make a public statement condemning the tour, irrespective of the real beliefs of its members.

The law cannot produce racial harmony, but it can remove some causes of tension and grievance. In 1988, the Home Secretary announced that the Government was satisfied that the Act had worked to make private acts of discrimination much less virulent. While it is true that such acts have become decreasingly overt, recent studies suggest that the real level of racial discrimination in employment has remained constant since 1975, with over one third of private employers favouring white applicants over blacks with equivalent qualifications. (Discrimination can rarely be proved in court against companies which secretly instruct employment agencies and consultants to exclude members of certain races before the final job interview.) Over the same period, only a small proportion of cases brought under the Act in county courts and industrial tribunals were successful, despite CRE backing. In 1989 only fifty-four cases succeeded in tribunals, and in 1990 the figure was sixty-one – approximately 5 per cent of those which had been brought (although 20 per cent were settled by ACAS conciliation).

The Race Relations Act has done little to address the yawning disparities between blacks and whites in employment rates, income, housing quality, representation in professions and public offices, imprisonment rates and the like. Expecting it to do so is to ask too much of a process geared to promote individual betterment through an adversarial system focusing on proof of unlawful 'acts' rather than controlling patterns of conventional behaviour which happen to promote or prolong racial imbalances. The Act has broken down barriers for individuals fortunate or courageous enough to use it, whose cases have set standards which have unobtrusively assisted many other individuals to receive their due. It has served a valuable educative purpose in stigmatizing racism and in slowly gaining acceptance for the proposition that it is the discriminatory *result* rather than the non-discriminatory or even benign *intention* of policies, conditions and criteria for judging people, which really matter. If the law is expected to do more to combat the manifest imbalance between black and white, it must add to the 'individual rights' guaranteed by the present Race Relations Act the possibility of asserting group rights to equal treatment, through procedures which can identify the behaviour which entrenches discrimination and can authorize affirmative action to overcome its consequences, and overcome them sooner rather than in the fullness of a very long time. But British law rarely allows 'class actions', and court-imposed restrictions have hamstrung the C R E in its attempts to gather evidence of discriminatory behaviour patterns through formal investigations.

More frustratingly the Act itself makes affirmative action unlawful (because 'positive discrimination' in favour of blacks will disadvantage whites) except in relation to education and training schemes in a few areas where it can be shown that blacks have 'special needs'. Lord Scarman concluded his report into the Brixton disorders with a finding that 'it is clear from the evidence of ethnic minority deprivation I have received that if the balance of racial disadvantage is to be redressed, as it must be, positive action is required'. Ironically, as the Race Relations Act now stands, the most effective 'positive action' programmes would amount to unlawful discrimination. It is difficult to see how the representation of blacks (or women, for that matter) will improve in industries and professions where recruitment and promotion is carried on through sponsorship, informal 'words of mouth', 'old white-boys' networks', interviews which test skills at communicating to the interviewers or at speaking B B C English, and so on, without programmes which encourage affirmative action. Such programmes are necessary – if only to recognize the real qualities of minority candidates normally passed over – and must be backed by targets and realistic timetables for achieving fairer represen-tation. Such programmes seem to have worked for corporate manage-ment in America (so much so that business strongly resisted President Reagan's ideologically motivated attempt to dismantle them)[16] and are permissable under Northern Ireland's 1989 Fair Employment Act. But at present, the British Race Relations Act outlaws the one kind of initiative which might help to enhance racial equality in Britain.

DISCRIMINATION AGAINST WOMEN

Nineteenth-century judges stood firmly against the advancement of women, relegating them to the same legal status as dogs and lunatics when excluding them from statutes which entitled 'persons' to be admitted to universities and professions. It was not until 1928 that women were given equal voting rights with men. The courts could have brought about this result as early as 1868, by applying to the Representation of the People Act of that year a statute which required that legislative words importing the masculine gender should be interpreted to include the female gender. The Court of Common Pleas, however, rejected the suit, reasoning that the denial to women of the right to vote

is referable to the fact that in this country, in modern times, chiefly out of respect to women, and a sense of decorum, and not from their want of intellect, or their being for any other reason unfit, they have been excused from taking any share in this department of public affairs.[17]

More than a century later, when the Sex Discrimination Act of 1975 came into force, the same male paternalism was immediately evident. 'I must say it would be very wrong to my mind,' said Lord Denning in an early test case, 'if this statute were thought . . . to do away with the chivalry and courtesy which we expect mankind to give womankind.'[18] For eight years the notorious El Vino's Wine Bar in Fleet Street survived legal challenges to its obviously discriminatory practice of refusing to serve women journalists and lawyers who stood in un-ladylike fashion with male colleagues at its bar, rather than sitting demurely to be waited on at a table. In the view of a succession of male judges, this was a long-standing traditional practice born of courtesy and chivalry which reasonable people would not find objectionable. In 1983, at last, the Court of Appeal applied the simple terms of the Act to hold that El Vino's had plainly discriminated against women by denying them goods and services on the sole basis of their sex.[19] Considerations of 'chivalry' and 'courtesy' can no longer excuse differential treatment in employment or education, or in the provision of goods, services, facilities or premises.

The 1975 Sex Discrimination Act contains most of the provisions of the Race Relations Act that have already been discussed, including the prohibitions upon unjustifiable indirect discrimination. It applies to all aspects of employment recruiting policy (for example, advertising only for male school leavers), arrangements for interviewing, training methods, selection for promotion or transfer, lay-offs, redundancy or dismissal. Trade unions and employment agencies are also within the net of the 1975 Act. A printing union operating where there is a closed shop cannot maintain a male preserve by barring women from the union. Complaints about discrimination in employment and training are made to an industrial tribunal which may award compensation up to a present maximum of £10,000.

The Act defines discrimination under four heads: treating a woman less favourably than a man on account of sex; conversely treating a man less favourably than a woman; treating a married person less favourably, on grounds of marriage, than a single person; and fourthly, victimization against a complainant who has invoked the Act. Indirect discrimination is also outlawed when tests are applied which appear neutral but which in practice place one sex (or married people) at a disadvantage – for example, a rule that all clerks must be at least 6 ft tall. The leading case, *James* v. *Eastleigh Borough Council*, decided by the House of Lords in 1990, establishes that criteria for making decisions which are gender-based infringe the Act, irrespective of the benign or non-discriminatory motive of the decision-maker.[20] The Council's humanitarian intentions to help pensioners by allowing them free access to its swimming-pools did not protect it from a finding of unlawful discrimination at a time when the pensionable age was sixty for women and sixty-five for men. When Mr and Mrs James, both aged sixty-one, turned up to do their laps at their local pool, Mr James suffered discrimination on the grounds of sex when he was charged 75p while his wife was admitted free on producing her pension book.

The Council had the best of motives for its policy, and was not to blame for the statutory discrimination in pension ages (which has since been repealed) but the result of its policy discriminated between sexes. The test for direct discrimination is to ask whether the plaintiff would have received the same (and more favourable) treatment as others *but for* his or her sex, irrespective of the motive for the difference in treatment. This decision makes it easier to prove direct sex (or race) discrimination by looking objectively at results rather than subjectively at the reasons. One of the first casualties of this approach was the *Lady* magazine, which had adopted a policy of refusing 'position vacant' advertisements from single gentlemen living abroad, for fear that young 'ladies' who applied would be more likely to be sexually molested by single men than by single women. This motive, which would undoubtedly have been held to justify the discrimination in the days of Lord Denning, could not save the magazine from a breach of the Act.

The 1975 Act also affects education. It is unlawful for those responsible for an educational establishment (including school governors and university governing bodies) to discriminate on grounds of sex in admissions policy. No institute can lawfully operate a quota system for females, or require higher A-levels from them, or discriminate in the benefits and facilities offered. A local education authority may not provide worse science laboratories in its girls' schools than its boys' schools and nor may it, by supporting a greater number of grammar schools that are only for boys, produce a situation in which girls require a higher examination mark than boys in order to obtain a grammar-school place.[21] Other areas where sex discrimination is outlawed include: the provision to the public of goods, facilities or services, including facilities offered by building societies, insurance companies, banks, credit institutions and HP companies; restaurants, public houses and places of entertainment; and local authorities and transport authorities. These changes in the law banned many common business practices, such as making a husband sign an HP contract when his wife, who had a good job of her own, was buying the goods, and the building-society practice of looking askance at spinster borrowers. In 1980 a furniture store was held by the Court of Appeal to have acted illegally when it required a woman buying a suite on credit to have her husband enter into a guarantee.[22]

In all these cases, the female complainant must prove that she was less favourably treated than a man, in the same circumstances, would have been, and that the predominant reason for this unfavourable treatment pertained to her being a woman. The principal target of the Act has been stereotyped assumptions of the sort: 'I like women but I will not employ them because they are unreliable.' The indirect discrimination provisions bring more subtle, and sometimes unconscious, forms of prejudice within the net. Thus a civil-service rule that all applicants for executive-officer position must be under twenty-eight years of age was struck down because in practice a much lower proportion of women than men could comply with it, given the propensity of women to have children during their twenties and return to employment later in life.[23] (The age limit was subsequently amended to forty-five.)

One particularly difficult problem has been how the Sex Discrimination Act affects women who are treated less favourably not on account of their sex as such, but as a result of the prospect of pregnancy, which is an additional characteristic of their sex. The English courts failed to develop a coherent and intellectually satisfactory approach to such 'sex plus' discrimination, which does not admit of comparison because men are incapable (subject, perhaps, to IVF developments) of bearing children. They compared pregnant women to men who suddenly contract hepatitis thereby managing both to degrade childbirth and to misunderstand the prejudice behind, say, a decision not to promote a woman because she is likely to have children. It took the European Court of Justice, in its historic *Dekker* decision in 1990, to make British courts accept the truism that pregnancy is unique to women. To take maternity – or the possibility of maternity – into account when refusing employment to a woman is discrimination based automatically on her sex.[24] The Court emphasized that a refusal to employ a woman because of the potential cost of her maternity leave cannot justify the discrimination. This ruling, delivered in a case from Germany but by way of interpretation of an EC 'Equal Treatment Directive' which is binding on Britain, has changed the approach of English law to pregnancy. The House of Lords now accepts that dismissals by reason of pregnancy are *per se* unlawful discrimination, without any need for comparisons with sick men.[25] The 1993 Trade Union Reform and Employments Rights Bill, which incorporates the EC directive on pregnancy and comes into force in 1994, will make it automatically unfair to dismiss a woman for any reason 'connected with' her pregnancy. (The Employment Protection (Consolidation) Act of 1978 already guarantees pregnant women the right to return to work, together with maternity pay and time off for antenatal care and treatment.)

Notwithstanding the progress made under pressure from Europe, some forms of British hypocrisy seem ineradicable. An example is provided by the case of Ms Berrisford, matron of a Church of England boarding school, who was congratulated on her pregnancy by the headmaster until she told him she had no immediate intention to marry, whereupon she was sacked. Incredibly, this unchristian behaviour was approved by the Employment Appeals Tribunal, on the basis that matron had been expelled not because of her pregnancy, but because her pregnancy would remind pupils of the possibilities of extramarital and non-marital sex.[26] This reason is wrong both in law (see *James* v. *Eastleigh* above) and in common sense, at a time when the most sheltered of teenagers are well aware of the extramarital activities of pop stars, politicians and princes.

There are some exceptions to the law, and these are set out in Section 7 of the 1975 Act. It is permissible to discriminate by imposing height or weight requirements for policemen and prison officers, and to discriminate in the employment of ministers by those religions which believe that the Deity declines to communicate through female intermediaries. The overriding test is whether 'being a man is a genuine occupational qualification for the job' in a set of carefully defined situations which are for the most part sensible (e.g. in dramatic roles, or attendance in male lavatories). One curious exemption, inserted after frantic lobbying from the CBI, permits sex discrimination in employment or promotion to jobs involving work in countries whose customs are such that the duties could not effectively be performed by a woman. The assumption that Arabs will not do business with British women other than Mrs Thatcher is highly dubious, but is unlikely to be invalidated so long as British firms appoint only salesmen. In any event, why should Britain kowtow to the sexist prejudices of foreign businessmen? This loophole, quite indefensible in terms of the Act's own logic, applies to work in any overseas country, so that firms might justify a 'men only' policy on the basis of male mateship rituals in Australia or the amount of business transacted in West German brothels.

The Act establishes an Equal Opportunities Commission, with similar (although not quite so extensive) powers as the CRE to monitor compliance with the legislation. It may conduct formal investigations, compel evidence and the production of documents, serve non-discrimination notices, seek injunctions against discriminatory practices and support action in the courts by aggrieved individuals. But most of these powers have proved ineffective, as a result of the complexity of the law and court rulings which have complicated and cut down the investigatory powers. In consequence, relatively few formal investigations have been completed, and any which are can be challenged by way of a complete rehearing in the courts. A serious slap in the face was delivered to the EOC in 1992 by a Court of Appeal ruling which denied it the standing to bring a judicial review action against the Government in an attempt to improve the rights of part-time workers (80 per cent of whom are women) to receive redundancy payments.[27] This case demonstrates the deficiency of English law in its refusal to permit 'class actions': if judicial review is not available to allow the EOC to challenge discriminatory Government policy in respect of groups of women, then these individual cases may only be taken to industrial tribunals, which have no power to order changes in policy.

Moreover, the women who bring cases can easily be 'bought off' by out-of-court settlements which do not result in any alteration of the discriminatory practice. Thus Alison Halford, the doughty assistant chief constable of Merseyside, whom the EOC backed when she took to an industrial tribunal her claim to have been passed over for promotion, was forced to settle in mid-action by an offer of £10,000 (the statutory maximum) and £5,500 (the maximum additional award to cover a claimant's expenses). The police and the Home Office thereby avoided having to justify under cross-examination the sexist practices that make the upper echelons of British policing a man's world. In 1990, only eighty-six women succeeded in proving discrimination at tribunal hearings, twenty of them in cases where they alleged sexual harassment (which constitutes discrimination where it involves, as it generally does, men treating women less favourably on the grounds of their sex). The awards in these harassment cases averaged a mere £2,000 – hardly a fair recompense either for the ordeal of enduring sexist humiliation or the ordeal of proving in public that it took place.

In 1993, the European Court of Justice delivered a landmark ruling in *Marshall* v. *Southampton Health Authority* to the effect that the statutory limit on compensation which tribunals could award to victims of sex discrimination was contary to EC law; the object of securing real equality of opportunity in employement could only be achieved by providing full and effective compensation to victims of discrimination.

'Equal pay for equal work' has long been recognized by the European Court of Justice as a fundamental human right, and Article 119 of the EEC Treaty requires all member countries to secure not only equal pay for the same work, but equal pay for work to which 'equal value' can be attributed. The Treaty applies directly to the United Kingdom, and it was in preparation for membership of the EEC that the first Equal Pay Act was passed in 1970, although it did not come into operation until 1975. It writes an equality clause into every woman's employment contract. The Act applies not only to basic pay, but to other matters in the contract of employment. It may require equality in provisions for overtime pay, bonus payments, sick-pay schemes, health insurance, holiday pay and length of holidays, luncheon vouchers, and other fringe benefits.

A woman who proves that she is not getting equal pay for work similar to a male colleague's will succeed unless the employer can show that there is a 'material factor' in their situations which constitutes a genuine reason for the pay differential. However, a 'material factor' is not confined to a difference in personal qualities, such as skills, experience and training. In 1987 the House of Lords opened the door to pay discrimination where a 'material circumstance' could be found in economic factors affecting the efficient running of the employer's business. It is difficult to understand why external business considerations, rather than the personal qualities of employees, should justify a deviation from the rule of 'equal pay for equal work'. Economic history shows that market forces, when left to their own devices, exploit women's weaker bargaining position in the labour exchange to push them down into segregated, part-time and low-paid work, the very kind of discrimination which the EPA should protect them against.[28] Whether the 'market-forces' defence developed by British courts is consonant with Article 119 of the EEC Treaty will in due course be decided by the European Court in the case of Mrs Enderby, an NHS speech therapist paid 60 per cent less than male pharmacists and psychologists employed by a local health authority on work of equal value. The EAT upheld the authority's 'market-forces' defence, on the basis that the differential had arisen over many years of collective bargaining by professional associations of disparate power. The European Court is likely to take the view that this is exactly the kind of process which has produced much of the workplace discrimination that Article 119 is designed to eradicate.

The Equal Pay Act has not, as its detractors predicted, led to any significant shrinkage in the jobs offered to women. Its initial weakness stemmed from the high degree of job segregation between men and women, so that it was in many cases difficult for complainants to find male employees in order to make comparisons. Job-evaluation schemes, intended to provide for such contingencies, were blocked by many organizations. In 1982 the European Court of Justice held that in consequence Britain was in breach of its EEC duties, and the Equal Pay (Amendment) Regulations of 1983 were necessary to allow a woman to claim equal pay not only where there is 'like work' or 'work rated as equivalent' being done by men, but also where she is employed on work where the demands made upon her (e.g. in terms of effort, skill or decision-taking) are of equal value to those of a man in the same employment. It took further pressure from Europe to impose equality in retirement age, which was not implemented until 1987. The House of Lords has recently shown a more robust determination to construe British law according to the 'equal pay for work of equal value' philosophy of the Treaty of Rome. It has insisted that basic-pay terms in employment contracts should reflect that equivalence, thus preventing employers from arguing that non-wage benefits enjoyed by women could compensate for discriminatory pay terms.[29] It has also foreclosed the 'token male' defence, whereby employers could point to a few men who were treated just as badly as the women complainants. When a woman claims equal pay for work of equal value, she need only specify a man doing equivalent work who is paid at a significantly higher rate, irrespective of whether there also happens to be a male who is earning her lower salary.[30] In reaching these and other recent decisions the British courts have been concerned to follow the approach of the European Court of Justice, and to interpret UK Acts of Parliament in line with our EC Treaty obligations and with European directives. Such achievements as there have been in combating discrimination against women could not have been won – either at the time or at all – without the impact of EEC membership.

Almost two decades after the Sex Discrimination Act, women workers remain concentrated in low-paid unskilled jobs, are excluded from many skilled manual jobs and suffer disadvantages in training and discouragement to break through the 'glass ceiling' and occupy positions of influence and responsibility in professional and public life. The Act has deterred overt discrimination, has assisted some individual aspirations and has marginally compensated others for hopes which have been dashed, but it actually deters most 'affirmative action' programmes which might be devised to redress the worst imbalances, because these would temporarily discriminate against men. As a result of the Equal Pay Act and the European Court, women's pay is rising faster than men's, and the gap between them is slowly narrowing – although by 1992 the differential was still seventy-nine female pence to the male pound. The rights of part-time workers have not been secured, there is still inadequate deterrence of sexual discrimination and harassment, and employers are allowed too many 'material factors' as justification for less favourable treatment. The ease with which the law may be side-stepped by employment consultants whose instructions to discriminate can rarely be proved has become notorious, and provides a strong argument for giving the EOC wider power to conduct formal investigations. The most glaring defect of all is the non-availability of legal aid to bring sex-discrimination cases before industrial tribunals: the costs (especially if the case goes to appeal) preclude most women from complaining unless they receive financial backing from a trade union or the EOC. This is a breach of the spirit of our obligation, under EEC law, to provide a procedure whereby all employees with an 'equal pay for work of equal value' complaint can ventilate it in court. There is particular need for reform so that 'equal value' claims may be brought by groups and classes of persons, as well as by individuals.

SEXUAL ORIENTATION

Discrimination on grounds of sexual orientation is not outlawed by any of the legislation discussed in this chapter, although it is rife both in the law and in the community. Male homosexuality was not 'legalized' in 1967: it was merely permitted in private between two consenting males aged over twenty-one. It remains a criminal offence if it involves more than two persons, or a consenting male under twenty-one. It is a crime, without heterosexual equivalent, for a man to procure an act of gross indecency with another man, or for male homosexual acts to take place between adults in the locked cubicle of a public lavatory. Homosexual contact advertisements, facilitating meetings between men for sexual purposes, have been held by the House of Lords to amount to the common-law offence of 'outraging public decency' in circumstances where similar heterosexual advertisements would not offend.[31] This residual impact of the criminal law on homosexual men (lesbians, for arcane historical reasons, labour under no such restraints) provides an excuse for much discriminatory and degrading police action in and around public toilets, as members of 'importuning squads' arrest men for the offence 'importuning for an immoral purpose' under Section 32 of the Sexual Offences Act 1956. This crime can only be committed by a male, and the courts have consistently assumed that to ask consent to gay sex – even if it is to take place in private – is an invitation to immorality.[32] In consequence, several thousand men are prosecuted each year, often for responding to sexually provocative policemen in public lavatories. This discriminatory law – the source of so much unnecessary public humiliation and police malpractice – should be repealed, or at the very least made subject to a defence of entrapment (see earlier, page 61) and a requirement that no prosecution should be brought without at least one civilian witness.

Homosexuals suffer additional prejudice in criminal-law enforcement, fanned by the advent of AIDS. Men are sometimes arrested under local by-laws for displaying affection in public: massive raids are occasionally mounted on 'gay' parties in private homes; police are often issued with plastic gloves in order to raid the houses of homosexuals. Customs officers, too, can display an obsessive homophobia: thirty-six of them were involved in a long operation to intercept books imported by Gay's the Word, at a time when the influx of cocaine and heroin might have seemed a higher priority in the allocation of resources. This ludicrous exercise (code name 'Operation Tiger') was in vain (see earlier, page 244) but it was followed by the Obscene Publications Squad's 'Operation Spanner', a much more successful attempt to criminalize consensual homosexual conduct. The target was a group of middle-aged sado-masochistic men, who had for ten years obtained sexual satisfaction in private by giving each other bizarre and painful beatings, brandings and penile rough handlings which left no permanent injury. They were jailed for assault, and the House of Lords subsquently confirmed that consent was no defence to the infliction of harm in the course of a sado-masochistic encounter. Although assaults in the course of 'manly sport', chastisement or 'rough but innocent horseplay' are always justifiable on grounds of 'good reason', most of the judges could not bring themselves to find that the achievement of sexual pleasure was a reason which could be other than 'bad'. Lord Chief Justice Lane seemed to think that 'the function of the court is to mark its disapproval of these activities' by approving 'substantial' prison sentences. Others might think that the court's function is to punish those who harm others and not themselves, and that sentencing men to years in prison for private sexual fetishes is a more significant act of brutality than those acts to which they consented.

The House of Lords in 1993 divided three to two over 'Operation Spanner', opting narrowly but emphatically for prejudice and paternalism instead of individual liberty.[33] There was no trace of the philosophical or social (let alone street) wisdom displayed in the *Bland* decision the previous year: the majority judgements are informed only by an ignorance about, and revulsion towards, sado-masochistic sexuality. 'Sex is no excuse for violence'; 'pleasure derived from the infliction of pain is an evil thing'; 'sado-masochistic homosexual activity cannot be regarded as conducive to the enhancement or enjoyment of family life or conducive to the welfare of society'; its exponents 'wish to satisfy a perverted and depraved sexual desire' were some of the pejorative slogans by which private and consensual sexual rituals were declared to be serious offences against the person, assisted by graphic descriptions of harm (such as the transmission of AIDS) which might – but, over ten years, never did – affect the willing participants. Quite absurdly, sado-masochistic sexuality was equated with duelling and street-brawling, as an evil to which consent could provide no defence (other than in 'trifling and transient' cases). The result of the judgement was to jail men for playing private games which hurt no one but themselves, producing minor injuries which would have been acceptable had they occurred in the course of manly sports rather than homosexual sports.

The 'Operation Spanner' decision is not only objectionable on classic liberal principles: it encourages police to expend public time and resources investigating private sexual behaviour, examining willingly spanked adult bottoms (male or female) to decide whether the sting lasts long enough to amount to an offence against Section 47 of the Offences against the Person Act 1861. The decision also opens up a lucrative area for blackmail, and provides the tabloid press with a splendid excuse for buying up 'smack and tell' memoirs and for investigating 'evil interests in consensual S & M'. The decision cannot be faulted for its rhetoric condemning cruelty, but for identifying cruelty in rituals designed to enhance erotic pleasure through the giving and receiving of pain. The law relating to sexual offences already criminalizes behaviour which is organized and touted to this end (thereby amounting to the crime of keeping a disorderly house), and consent cannot avail a participant who causes serious ('grievous') bodily harm to another. It is right that the courts should offer protection to unwilling participants, and negative any 'consent' which has been obtained by oppression or drugs or undue influence. But sado-masochists, however repulsive their sex-play, should in principle be entitled to the same level of tolerance as the criminal law extends to other fetishists, namely to go to hell in their own way, so long as they do not drag others with them or travel by public paths.

It must be said that international human-rights law has been unconscionably slow to protect the human rights of homosexuals. Egalitarian principles fashioned to combat race and sex discrimination have not taken the next logical step, as a result both of religious taboos and secular prejudices (Catholic and Communist dogma on the subject has at times been equally cruel). However, a number of European countries have either abolished the age of consent or lowered it to sixteen or eighteen in the case of homosexuals, and in 1988 the European Court of Human Rights ruled that some particularly harsh laws against homosexuals in the Irish Republic violated their right to privacy. The Court has insisted upon uniformity within each nation, and in 1982 the United Kingdom was obliged to lift the total prohibition on homosexuality in Northern Ireland and to incorporate the 1967 reforms, notwithstanding the efforts of the Reverend Ian Paisley and his cohorts to 'save our sons from sodomy'.[34] By 1993, the UK was one of only four remaining EC countries which offer no legal protection in cases of discrimination against homosexuals.

Discrimination against homosexuals takes place in some areas of the civil law. In family disputes, the courts have been reluctant to award custody to a parent who has entered a homosexual relationship, and the notion that it may not be 'in the best interests of the child' to be exposed to a homosexual environment can sometimes affect adoption and fostering decisions as well. The law, and the officials who apply it, are still unwilling to equate a permanent homosexual relationship with either marriage or a permanent hetero-sexual relationship. In consequence, homosexual couples are discrimi-nated against in housing, and in the operation of taxation and immigration rules. The Sex Discrimination Act is of no assistance, other than in the rare case where a male homosexual can prove that he has been treated less favourably than a lesbian in the same circumstances (or vice versa).

The worst examples of legally sanctioned discrimination have occurred in the context of employment, where some tribunals have pronounced it 'fair' to dismiss workers for no reason other than a sudden discovery of their homosexuality. Although it has been held in several cases that an entirely irrational prejudice on the part of fellow workers does not justify dismissal, the courts have allowed 'strong feelings amongst the general public' to justify the sacking of law-abiding homosexuals from jobs entailing supervision of young persons. (In other words, blameless citizens are punished because of an assumed public ignorance of the distinction between homosexual-ity and paedophilia.) In the context of national security the Divi-sional Court has refused to find unreasonable a decision by GCHQ to sack a homosexual employee (see earlier, page 149). There is a disinclination in Britain to follow the refreshingly value-free logic of the Supreme Court of California:

[A] particular sexual orientation might be dangerous in one profession and irrelevant to another. Necrophilism and necrosadism migh. be objectionable in a funeral director or embalmer, urolagnia in a laboratory technician, zooerastism in a veterinarian or trainer of guide-dogs, prolagnia in a fireman, undinism in a sailor, or dendrophilia in an arborist, yet none of these unusual tastes would seem to warrant disciplinary action against a geologist or shorthand reporter.[35]

Combating any form of discrimination requires, in the first place, a firm resolve by Government. The laws relating to sex and race discrimination were introduced by a committed Home Secretary who had a considerable measure of cross-party support. John Major has been prepared to meet for a 'photo opportunity' with Sir Ian McKellen, and has announced that there should be no discrimination against homosexuals in the civil service, but has otherwise done little to reverse the prejudices which were promoted by his predecessor. In 1988 the Thatcher Government responded irresponsibly to the AIDS virus: instead of setting up a national commission to provide advice, research and information on the subject, like most other Western countries, it promulgated new regulations enabling the detention of HIV sufferers under the Public Health (Control of Disease) Act 1984. It then singled out gay and lesbian lifestyles for legal disapproval by passing Section 28 of the Local Government Act 1988, which purports to prohibit the promotion of homosexuality or 'the teaching in any maintained school of the acceptability of homosexuality as a pretended family relationship'. For all its malign purpose, Section 28 has little direct effect: it applies only to local authorities, i.e. bodies which have no direct responsibility for, or control over, what is taught in schools. As a result of the 1986 Education Act, the conduct of maintained schools is under the direction of the governing body and it is the ultimate responsibility of the head teacher to determine and organize the secular curriculum. Thus Section 28 does not permit teachers to be dismissed for discussing homosexuality sensibly and truthfully. Even where local authorities have an advisory role, Section 28 must be read subject to the Education Act, whereby the need 'to encourage pupils to have due regard to moral considerations' permits the teaching of tolerance in order to counter pupils' ignorance or hatred of homosexuals.

A local authority does not infringe Section 28 unless, at the time it decides to grant funds to a homosexual group, it either desires or is well aware of the fact that its action will 'promote homosexuality', i.e. result in an increase in the number of homosexuals. It follows that there is nothing to stop a local authority from funding gay youth groups or counselling services where the intention is not to 'promote' homosexuality but rather to assist homosexuals to cope with an existing sexual orientation. There is a crucial distinction between promoting homosexuality and promoting tolerance towards homosexuals. None the less, Section 28 has had a chilling effect on some local authorities, who have used it as an excuse for withdrawing from homosexuals services similar to those provided for other disadvantaged groups. A council which is panicked into misusing Section 28 as an excuse for prejudice and discrimination in the provision of services will be open to challenge in the courts.

What the advent of Section 28 does show, quite dramatically, is the depth of the prejudice which will have to be overcome before discrimination on the grounds of sexual orientation is made unlawful.

The British Government's mean-minded and discriminatory attitude towards its homosexual population contrasts with the US administration under President Clinton, who vowed immediately after his inauguration to appoint several homosexuals to important executive positions and to end the ban on their admission to the armed forces. Between 1989 and 1991, 272 men and women were 'dishonourably discharged' from British military service on suspicion of being homosexual, and a further thirty-four were court-martialled and jailed for up to two years for the crime of consensual homosexual conduct in barracks. The Government has announced that criminal proceedings will no longer be taken, but has ruled out any acceptance of gay or lesbian soldiers on the grounds that their presence would be 'incompatible with good order and discipline' and create difficulties in 'cramped barrack conditions'. This is nonsense, of course: entry to the forces of most of our NATO allies are now open to gays and lesbians, and US Defense Department studies demonstrate that sexuality is unrelated to work performance and that homosexuals display military suitability 'that is as good or better than the average heterosexual'.

Transsexuals, whose psychological commitment to a gender at odds with their biology is reinforced by hormone implants and surgical acquisition of artificial vaginas and even serviceable penises (phalloplasty), invite reinterpretation of the words 'male' and 'female' in the statutes which determine sexual status. In *Corbett* v. *Corbett*, a 1971 case which decided that seaman-turned-model April Ashley had no right to marry a man, the High Court settled on a strict biological determination.[36] This rule – simple to apply at the end of the day, but productive of much misery for those who have to all intents and purposes shed their biological sex – has been vigorously applied, and transsexuals are denied any remedy against instant dismissal by employers who discover their former identities. The right to have a change in sexual status officially acknowledged was in 1992 recognized by the European Court of Human Rights, which has required national laws concerning homosexuals to be kept under review in the light of 'scientific and societal developments'. Although it has (narrowly) declined to require the UK Government to alter the entries registering sex on birth certificates,[37] since these documents are intended as accurate historical records rather than to serve purposes of identification, it has obliged the French Government to permit transsexuals to use their acquired gender on identity cards, passports and all other documents the production of which may be routinely required by police and other authorities.[38]

Laws which publicly confine transsexuals to their biological gender fail to show the respect for their private life which is guaranteed by Article 8 of the European Convention, and the Court was dismissive of the French Government's suggestion that they could avoid humiliation and embarrassment by adopting ambivalent forenames like 'Claude' or 'Camille'. In due course it may be that the European Court will require a reversal of the decision in *Corbett*, to give transsexuals the right to marry – not a person of their own sex, but a person whose gender they have, for all relevant purposes, discarded.

FREEDOM OF RELIGION

The last British heretic to be burnt at the stake by order of a Church court suffered his punishment in 1612. In the nineteenth century, Unitarians, Roman Catholics and Jews were relieved from legal disabilities, and Charles Bradlaugh won emancipation for atheists – the Oaths Act of 1888 permitted them for the first time to take seats in Parliament and to give evidence in court by way of a solemn affirmation. The major religious disability which remains today is the requirement that the Sovereign must be a member of the Church of England, and that his or her spouse must on no account be or become a Roman Catholic. The Acts of Settlement which define the monarchy are in blatant breach of the European Convention guarantees of religious freedom, and enshrine religious and sexual discrimination at the very bedrock of the British Constitution. It is difficult to understand why Prince Charles would be unfit to mount the throne were he to become a Methodist, or had his wife taken communion with priests rather than with tabloid journalists. Should his children convert to Catholicism, the sexist rules of royal primogeniture would require Andrew, or even Edward, to succeed to the throne ahead of their elder and more popular sister Anne, the Sex Discrimination Act notwithstanding. Like a number of ancient laws applicable to the Crown – the Treason Act 1361 still punishes with death any adulterous Royal Consort – these obnoxious rules seem to have acquired a historic immunity to rational reform.

The Church of England retains a few unfair advantages as the 'established' religion – notably seats for twenty-four bishops in the House of Lords and a theoretical protection for its doctrines by the law of blasphemy (see page 248). The price it pays for these favours is to crown the monarch as head of Church as well as state, to have its doctrinal changes approved by Parliament and to give the Prime Minister final say in the appointment of its bishops (a power last used by Mrs Thatcher in 1981 to promote a 'conservative' over the Church's choice for the Bishopric of London). These arcane constitutional arrangements came under criticism in 1993 as a result of the impending royal divorce and the prospect of an adulterer as Defender of the Faith: a better ground for objection to them is that they allow Anglican leaders a significant role in Government which is denied to all other religions, and provide a discriminatory legal protection for Anglican doctrines. The Church of England clings to its privileges for reasons of power rather than of logic: a faith which rests upon the support of the present British Government and monarchy is hardly built upon a rock.

The United Kingdom tolerates all religions and permits freedom of worship, and in this respect mainstream religions compete on even terms: 'collective worship' in state schools must not favour any particular Christian religious denomination. There is a tradition of moderation in religious education, avoiding the contradictory US extremes of outlawing all prayer in school yet permitting education authorities to sanction the teaching of 'creationism'. The head of religious education in a Hertfordshire comprehensive lost his claim before an industrial tribunal for unfair dismissal when he refused to comply with the agreed county syllabus by insisting on teaching the biblical account of creation as historical fact. In 1988 Parliament insisted that 'collective worship' should 'reflect the broad traditions of Christian belief', although schools with a significant number of children from other faiths may make adjustments which are appropriate to the 'family background' of these pupils or obtain an exemption which permits them to provide for the worship of non-Christian faiths. The Secretary of State for Education has not yet approved an application for voluntary aided status by a Muslim school, although the ready bestowal of such status on Jewish, Catholic and Methodist schools would make any refusal on non-educational grounds difficult to justify under the provisions of Article 2 of the first protocol to the European Convention on Human Rights, which requires the state to respect the religious convictions of parents in the provision of education. The United Kingdom has accepted this protocol 'only so far as it is compatible with the provision of efficient instruction and training and the avoidance of unreasonable public expenditure', but this reservation is curiously limited to the 'efficiency' of the teaching rather than to the content of what is taught.

The Sunday Observance Act of 1780 is one of the few operational relics of ecclesiastical influence: the Lord's Day Observance Society and a few killjoy local councils still prosecute an occasional shopkeeper or entertainer for livening up the 'British Sunday'. It was trade-union opposition, however, that was primarily responsible for the Government's defeat in 1986 over its attempts to reform the Shops Act to allow more extensive Sunday trading. Fresh foodstuffs (but not canned food), alcohol (but not powdered milk), motoring accessories (but not Bibles) may be sold on the Sabbath, and in recent years exemptions have been made for cinemas, theatres, galleries and museums. Many general retailers, both large and small, determinedly flout the law in response to consumer demand, secure in the knowledge that most local councils will turn a blind eye and that any fines incurred will be insignificant by comparison with the profits of Sunday trading. The European Court of Justice has declined to intervene, on the basis that restrictions on trading hours are entitled to reflect local socio-cultural eccentricities. The resultant shambles serves only to bring the law into disrepute, as a prohibition imposed by a self-righteous moral minority and an intransigent trade union vainly strives to deny both consumers and business a harmless but valued freedom.

Although the law no longer imposes special disabilities on adherents to particular religions, to what extent should it require special allowance to be made for those whom conscience impels to behave in unusual ways? This question has assumed some importance in the quest for a multi-racial and multi-cultural society, where respect should be accorded to firmly based religious beliefs so far as is consonant with the public interest. Spiritual obligations cannot be prayed in aid by way of defence to criminal charges – Jehovah's Witnesses who physically prevented a doctor from giving their child a blood transfusion would be guilty of manslaughter if the child died as a result, and Rastafarians can claim no special religious defence when charged with possession of cannabis. Sikhs were routinely convicted of driving motor-cycles without crash helmets until Parliament amended the law to allow them to wear turbans – a religious duty to which it should have been sensitive when the law was first introduced. In civil law there is obviously scope for greater flexibility, although employers have been held to have acted fairly by dismissing workers whose religious devotions prove unreasonably disruptive and put them in breach of their contract of employment.[39] Anomalously, discrimination on religious grounds is specifically prohibited in Northern Ireland, but not in England, Scotland or Wales, where discriminatory actions are lawful unless race has also been a factor. Employment tribunals have on these grounds refused relief to Sikh and Muslim nurses denied their religion-dictated wish to wear trousers under their uniforms, and have been reluctant to find against employers who insist that orthodox Jews keep 9–5 hours on winter Fridays. Public opinion is ahead of the law in condemning such ignorant inflexibility: in 1992 the Metropolitan Police was forced to change its rostering policy so as to accommodate religious observance after widespread criticism of its orders to Jewish police constables to work on their Sabbath. There is no reason why discrimination on religious grounds should not be unlawful, at least in circumstances where it is perfectly practicable for employers to make reasonable accommodation for conscientious belief.

In 1978 employers in 'closed shop' industries were forbidden to dismiss workers for refusing to join the trade union where such refusal is based on 'conscience or other deeply held conviction', although regrettably the burden of proof is placed upon the employee and several industrial tribunals have failed to understand the religious requirements of certain Hindu sects. There is a special advisory committee which considers claims by members of the armed forces for discharge on grounds of conscientious objection, which may arise from religious convictions acquired in the course of service. In these instances, of course, the 'conscience' need not be affected by religious beliefs – a rationally developed, unshakeable conviction against trade-union membership or service in Northern Ireland would also be entitled to respect. Conscientious objections to jury service should be respected by judges, at least where genuine religious beliefs would make it difficult for that service to be performed rationally.[40]

Article 9 of the European Convention guarantees freedom of 'thought, conscience and religion' and the right to manifest religion in worship, teaching, practice and observance, subject to considerations of public health and safety and the need to protect the rights and freedoms of others. Toleration of religion is most severely tested in relation to cults and cranks whose activities, while profitable spiritually to their adherents and financially to their leaders, are both socially offensive and objectively nonsensical. In the absence of incorporation of the European Convention into British law, and of any protection against religious discrimination, cults are especially vulnerable to local hostility, often reflected in planning decisions which deny them places of worship. Judicial review is an insufficient remedy for decisions like the one ordering closure of the Hindu Krishna Consciousness temple at Letchmore Heath in Hertfordshire, because it cannot investigate the extent to which the opposition of local residents is really based on prejudice against the nature of the worship rather than on the noise or inconvenience it is alleged to cause. Scientologists have been the most notable victims of unfair treatment. Until 1980 foreign members of this church were denied entry to Britain, and the courts have refused to concede that it is a 'religion' for the purpose of rates and tax relief. These decisions conflict with a recent Australian High Court ruling that Scientology fulfils the only general criteria for religion: 'First, belief in a supernatural Being, Thing or Principle and second, acceptance of canons of conduct in order to give effect to that belief.'[41]

The real question is not whether 'E meters' and 'dianetics' have the same validity as the communion and the catechism, or whether brain-washing Moonies, sexually promiscuous Children of God, callous Exclusive Brethren and the zombie followers of fashionable Bhagwans are as socially acceptable as those who heed the words of the Pope or Jimmy Swaggert or the Reverend Ian Paisley. The issue should be whether *any* religion is entitled to special benefits which are withheld from other idealistic endeavours with equal or greater claim to social utility. Positive discrimination in favour of religion is most objectionable in charity law, which in large measure exempts trusts for the advancement of religion from the obligation of paying tax. This benefit it does not extend to ethical or humanist societies, nor to such worthwhile secular enterprises as Amnesty International. The antisocial activities of registered charities like the Moonies and the Children of God simply emphasize the irrationality of a law which exempts an organization from a civic duty for no better reason than its commitment to spreading belief in a super-natural Being. In 1981 the libel jury which sat for six months to hear evidence of how the Unification Church of Sun Myung Moon brainwashed young followers and destroyed families, added a rider to its verdict recommending that charitable status should be withdrawn. The Attorney-General promised to investigate, but his successor announced in 1988 that the Moonies were, so far as the law was concerned, unassailably engaged in tax-free charitable pursuits.

DISABLEMENT

Disabled citizens are accorded no special protection from discrimination which has been based, not on their actual capacities, but on their lack of access to workplaces or the disinclination to make reasonable changes to accommodate them. The Disabled Persons (Employment) Act is outmoded: it was passed in 1944, to assist men wounded in war by requiring medium- and large-scale employers to accept a 'registered disabled quota' comprising 3 per cent of their workforce. This rule is rarely observed and hardly ever enforced; there have only been ten recorded prosecutions, the last (in 1975) resulted in a £60 fine. In 1991 the Government admitted that only one of its departments reached this target, and the Home Office could only muster 0.32 per cent. In the light of this and other overwhelming evidence of unfair discrimination, it is understandable that organizations representing the disabled should abandon any faith in 'codes of practice' promoted by the Government and employer organizations over the past decade, and demand legal protection against unreasonable discrimination. Recent legislative initiatives in Canada, Australia and the US have demonstrated the value of this approach, especially in placing a positive duty on businesses and organizations to make their premises wheelchair-accessible, and in combating ignorant prejudices which disadvantage sufferers from conditions such as controlled epilepsy or the AIDS virus.

The bestowal of 'rights' on disabled citizens would be a new departure in British law, which has always viewed them as dependent and pitiful, requiring services rather than capable of providing services (other than stereotypically as lift or car-park attendants). There is no difficulty in devising legislation: the Americans with Disabilities Act of 1990, for example, prohibits employers from discriminating against 'a qualified individual with a disability', and 'qualified' simply means having a capacity to perform the essential functions of the job. Employers are required to make 'reasonable accommodation' to physical and mental limitations of qualified individuals, unless they can prove that to do so would impose 'undue hardship' on their business operations. The Canadian Human Rights Act guarantees freedom from discrimination on grounds of physical handicap, and investigations by its Human Rights Commission have led to damages awards for many unfair actions against citizens whose form of disablement does not rationally disqualify them from jobs or services. The British Government has approved some recent regulations to encourage disabled access to transport and new public buildings, but its obsessive preference for 'voluntary' solutions and 'codes of practice' is in stark contrast to most European countries (French law punishes discrimination on grounds of 'health or handicap' as a crime), and is demonstrably inadequate to ensure equality of opportunity. A human-rights approach would be consistent with developments in other Western countries and could be readily integrated into existing anti-discrimination laws and procedures involving commission investigation and tribunal enforcement. Perhaps most importantly of all, it would serve to promote confidence and self-esteem amongst citizens who have hitherto been required to look to the state for charity, rather than for freedom.[42]

CHAPTER 12

A Bill of Rights for Britain?

It can confidently be asserted that such improvements in civil liberties as have been achieved in the past decade have come about more as a result of Britain's obligations under the European Convention of Human Rights and the Treaty of Rome than from initiatives by its own Government or by its elected Members of Parliament. That this should be so is an emphatic refutation of the traditional theory elaborated by Dicey that liberty is best left to unwritten constitutional conventions, statutes passed by a sovereign Parliament and a common law developed by judges. Something is missing in our complacent constitutional arrangements if the only remedy for so many abuses of state power is an appeal to a European Court which may, years after the injustice has occurred, oblige the United Kingdom to legislate so as to ensure it does not happen again. What is missing is a set of fundamental principles, contained in a statute which would provide the courts of this country with a power to strike down official decisions that infringe the liberty of the subject unless those decisions are directly sanctioned by laws approved in Parliament. Most of the objectionable decisions and practices described in this book have never received the stamp of parliamentary approval, but have been based upon ministerial or bureaucratic discretions, Home Office circulars, exercises of the royal prerogative, 'guidelines' issued by Attorneys-General and police chiefs, or codes of practice and 'standards' issued by bodies of Government appointees and never debated in Parliament. They are largely outside the control of the courts other than by way of 'judicial review', which cannot consider their merits but only check that the decisions have been procedurally fair and have not been made irrationally. Why not short-cut the long trek to Strasbourg by bringing the European Convention back home, making it a part of British law, to be interpreted and applied by British judges in deciding cases which raise issues of fundamental freedoms?

The present Government opposes this reform on the ground that a Bill of Rights would undermine the principle of parliamentary sovereignty, by which ministers are accountable to Parliament rather than to the courts for the unfair actions of their officials. But this theory has little relevance to the real world of modern party politics, where ministers preside over vast bureaucracies run by anonymous public servants for whose mistakes they are in no meaningful sense responsible. True accountability, in any event, presupposes the availability of information about the workings of Whitehall – which will not be forthcoming without a Freedom of Information Act. MPs may ask questions or refer individual cases of maladministration to the Ombudsman or investigate departmental functioning through select committees of the House: their powers in each case are limited and capable of deflection by a defensive civil service or a determined Government. Occasional back-bench revolts in the governing party may block a controversial clause in a particular bill, but most MPs will cower under the three-line whip. As the Commons debates over Maastricht in the summer of 1993 showed, back-benchers utterly opposed to their Government's policy will rally to that Government if the alternative is its loss of office. Politicians, moreover, cannot be trusted to champion the liberties of all who elect them. Some of our most oppressive legislation – the original Official Secrets Act, the Commonwealth Immigration Act of 1968, the Prevention of Terrorism Act and Section 28 of the Local Government Act of 1988 – have had all-party support at the time they were passed. Many attacks on specific freedoms, such as the right to challenge jurors or to give professional advice on surrogacy arrangements, have been initiated by back-bench MPs.

In no advanced democratic country – other than in Britain – does 'democracy' mean unbridled rule by the elected Government. There are invariably checks and balances, provided by Constitutions and Bills of Rights, by state or provincial legislators, by Upper Houses or by heads of state. These institutions work, in different ways, to filter and to fetter the exercise of power by central government. They are not thereby 'undemocratic', even if comprised of persons who are unelected, or elected to represent sectional interests rather than to govern the nation-state. Nobody could suggest that America is less of a democracy because its executive president is frequently checked by Congress, or by the Supreme Court, or by state rights. British Government has no such balance: the House of Lords may delay but not override, the monarch is a cipher, there is no devolution and no written constitution to set clear and objectively enforceable limits to the exercise of power. The 'separation of powers' between the executive, the legislature and the judiciary is not a true or equal separation: executive government by definition commands the vote in the legislature, and appoints the judges who have no authority to strike down laws and have limited procedural means to correct decisions which infringe liberty. Majority rule resulting from free and fair elections does make most of us safe most of the time, and there is little likelihood that any Government would risk electoral reprisals by passing laws which deprive the majority of any right which they value. But it is minorities who are at risk – immigrants, homosexuals, persons suspected of crime, demonstrators, parents of children taken into care, mental patients and other classes of persons insufficently numerous to wield electoral power but large enough to attract obloquy or resentment. Their only remedy, once Parliament has legislated, is to appeal to the European Court in Strasbourg on the grounds that the legislation is contrary to the British Government's undertaking to abide by the European Convention on Human Rights.

The Convention was drawn up in 1951. Politically, it was the product of a desire for Western European unity: its ideals were shaped by the need to have some legal bulwark against a resurgence of Fascism, and by a wish to articulate those civil rights which seemed threatened by Communist regimes in Eastern Europe. Ironically, it was drafted by the senior legal adviser at the Home Office, and supported by the Attlee Government despite the dire predictions of the Lord Chancellor that it would 'jeopardize our whole system of law, which we have laboriously built up over centuries, in favour of some half-baked scheme to be administered by some unknown court'. Britain ratified the Convention in 1951, but did not accept the right of individual citizens to petition until 1966, when a less complacent Labour Chancellor, Lord Gardiner, came to office. Its impact on English law did not begin until the next decade, when the European Court at Strasbourg began to hand down decisions holding the United Kingdom in breach of the Convention for failures to guarantee certain basic rights to its citizens. Any person who believes that his or her rights under the Convention have been infringed by a court ruling or an administrative act, and who has exhausted all the possibilities of redress in the British courts, may complain to Strasbourg. If the complaint is upheld, the British Government is required by the Convention to change the law which permitted the original infringement.

In recent years, 'going to Strasbourg' has become an increasingly important journey for those denied any remedy by domestic law in Britain. The path was blazed by Stanley Golder, a prisoner denied by prison rules the right to consult a lawyer. In 1975 his complaint was upheld and the Government was obliged to alter the rules so as to allow all prisoners access to legal advice. Subsequently, European Court rulings were responsible for: putting an end to 'in depth' interrogation of suspects in Northern Ireland, birching of juveniles in the Isle of Man, and caning in state schools; liberalizing the test for contempt of court, permitting journalists to see 'discovered' documents read in open court, and allowing the media a right of appeal against suppression orders; providing some safeguards against lawless telephone tapping; ending the prohibition on homosexuality in Northern Ireland; removing certain discriminatory clauses in the immigration rules; securing some citizenship rights for British passport holders in East Africa; requiring changes in the law to enlarge the rights of prisoners, parents of children in care, and mental patients; ensuring that parents have access to information on which local authorities have decided to take their children into care or send them to foster homes, and even (in an important case in 1990) upholding the right of poor persons accused of serious crime to have legal aid extended for their trials and appeals.

Every chapter in this book records cases where the European Court has forced alterations in British laws which have proved deficient in protecting fundamental freedoms. At the last count over one hundred separate changes since 1975 — to laws or to regulations or to administrative practices — have been attributed to actions brought against the British Government under the European Convention. Other milestones in civil liberties, such as the Data Protection Act, the Equal Pay Act and the abandonment of customs powers to intercept 'indecent' books and films, have come about only because of the United Kingdom's obligations under the EEC Treaty, which is being interpreted by reference to the principles in the European Convention of Human Rights.[1] These decisions, made by the European Court of Justice in cases relating to commerce and employment, are directly binding on British courts through our accession to the Treaty of Rome and the Single European Act of 1986. It is paradoxical, to say the least, that Parliament has required our judges to apply directly European Community law (which may embody human-rights principles) in cases relating to business but refuses to allow them to apply those fundamental principles in cases where they matter most.

This paradox has serious practical consequences. It means that British citizens cannot obtain speedy and effective relief in the courts of their own country when they are the victims of obvious violations. It means that Britain is denied the opportunity of contributing to the development of human-rights law – here, in Europe, and abroad – through the distinctive perspective and experience of our own judges. And it means that Britain has the worst human rights record amongst Council of Europe members, whose locally enforceable Bills of Rights allow them to provide remedies which are not available in Britain. Moreover, Strasbourg decisions are always cautious and conservative: the Convention embodies basic rather than progressive standards, which are interpreted so that they may be applied in practice to countries far less economically and socially advanced than the UK. For this reason, the European Court gives the UK Government the benefit of doubts and latitudes which it would not always receive from an astute judiciary in Britain.

It has to be said, too, that the Strasboug route to human-rights protection is one which will become of diminishing importance for this country, because of new pressures on the Commission and the Court. By 1993, twenty-six of the member states of Europe had accepted the right of individual petition (including Bulgaria and Hungary, with Romania, Albania, the Ukraine and the Russian Federation in the queue to join).[2] With complaints running at 5,500 a year, the average waiting time for a final judgement has lengthened to five years. Even assuming procedural reform and additional funding, it is inevitable that the Court will turn its attention towards the protection of freedom in the new democracies. This may mean a dilution in the most basic standards of treatment it is prepared to prescribe across the new Europe: it will certainly mean even longer delays. It cannot be said that the right of individual petition to Strasbourg is a satisfactory protection which itself obviates the need for any British Bill of Rights.

Why have so many British laws and procedures and administrative decisions fallen foul of the bedrock standards embodied in international treaties? The absence of any written constitutional guarantees of liberty which would empower our courts to correct abuses of power by state agencies, an over-reliance on doctrines about the sovereignty of Parliament and the accountability of ministers, and the reluctance to guarantee to citizens enforceable legal rights have produced a society in which civil liberties are regarded as privileges granted at the discretion of the powerful rather than as rights capable of direct assertion by members of the public. There are gaps in the pieces of common and statute law, precisely because the politicians and judges responsible for producing the jigsaw have no clear idea of the ultimate picture. Amongst the main characteristics of the 'rule of law' in Britain can be included the following:

Discretionary justice. We repose wide discretions in police and other officials in the hope that they will act fairly. These discretions are not controlled by the law, or by the courts, although they may be informed by 'guidelines' issued by the Home Office or the Attorney-General. 'Guidelines' cover such important matters as the use of informers and secret surveillance devices, the criteria for collection of information on law-abiding citizens, the operation of the security service, the handling of pickets and demonstrators, the censorship of films, the vetting of jurors, the use of CS gas and rubber bullets, and the treatment of immigrants. They do not have the force of law, and there is no sanction for disobedience. As one senior police officer said, when taxed with mounting secret operations in contravention of a Home Office circular, 'there is no reason to respect an obscure piece of paper'. There is no right of peaceful assembly guaranteed by British law – instead, we have a polite letter from the Home Office to chief constables, reminding them to bear such a 'right' in mind when exercising their powers under the 1986 Public Order Act to control meetings and processions. Even the Association of Chief Police Officers has taken to issuing its own secret guidelines, one of which advocates the striking of demonstrators 'in a controlled manner with batons about the arms and legs and torsos' in certain crowd–control situations. In this way, the rule of law is replaced by the rule of thumb, and occasionally the rule of fist.

Nominal ministerial control. Many basic decisions about civil liberties are made the responsibility of the Home Secretary rather than the courts. These include such important matters as the power to: issue warrants to tap telephones and burgle homes; detain suspects for up to seven days under the Prevention of Terrorism Act; refer doubtful convictions back to the Court of Appeal; exclude aliens on the ground that their presence is contrary to the national interest; decide how long 'life-sentence' prisoners will serve; grant asylum and carry out deportations. The notion that the Home Secretary makes all these decisions himself, with the care expected of a judge, after weighing the evidence, is the sheerest nonsense. For the most part, he has little time to do more than rubber-stamp the decisions advised by his officials. His 'accountability' to Parliament can be avoided by invoking the rule that no explanation is required where issues of national security are concerned, or because the case is *sub judice*: his decisions about individuals are rarely the subject of full parliamentary debate.

Pervasive secrecy. Most decisions and many policies which affect civil liberties are made and even implemented in secret. The Official Secrets Act supplemented by the extended common law of confidentiality casts a blanket of secrecy over the operations of the public service. The Public Records Act ensures that work within Whitehall will not see the light of day for at least thirty years, and for much longer if there is any prospect of embarrassing civil servants who are still alive, or casting any light at all on security operations. Unjust practices develop for years unchecked by public outcry; jury vetting had been institutionalized for five years before it was accidentally uncovered, and 'virginity testing' of immigrant wives and X-raying of their children's bone structures went on for some time before these practices were publicized and prohibited. Even when questions were asked in Parliament – as they were about the trade in arms to Iraq – responses were carefully drafted so as to disguise the true picture. The Security Service Act shrouds every activity – lawful or otherwise – of the intelligence services. Freedom of information, now a routine characteristic of most comparable democracies, is firmly resisted. *SCOTT REPORT*

Variable local practices. The extent to which you are allowed to enjoy a particular freedom may depend upon the part of the country in which you happen to reside. Police discretion means that the forty-three different chief constables have different policies on such basic matters as the use of summonses instead of warrants for arrest and imposition of blanket bans on marches under the Public Order Act. While John Alderson, as chief constable of Devon and Cornwall, shredded Special Branch intelligence on CND activists, Phillip Knights, Chief Constable of Birmingham, defended surreptitious surveillance of those who write letters in their local newspaper critical of nuclear weapons. The powers given to local councils over cinemas have led to marked inconsistencies, as controversial films are banned in some localities but not in others. Rates of conviction and sentencing patterns and legal-aid grants differ markedly from one magistrates' court to the next. There are remarkable variations in implementing duties to provide caravan sites for gypsies and facilities for the disabled; some local authorities purport to apply Section 28 by discriminating against homosexuals, while others ignore it. *MORE DETAIL*

Limited powers of judicial review. The courts have a narrow role in examining the exercise of discretion by agents of the state. They will seldom upset a decision unless it can be shown to be so irrational that no reasonable official or tribunal could come to the same conclusion, or unless it has been made in 'bad faith' (i.e. corruptly or from some ulterior motive). Courts hardly ever find a police chief's operational decisions to be unreasonable, and are usually reluctant to question the logic of ministerial decisions in immigration cases. They can intervene if the minister has applied the wrong legal test, or acted unfairly by refusing to receive representations, but their 'supervisory role' is limited to ensuring that due process is observed. And when proprieties are not observed, the victim of abuse of power has no claim for compensation or damages. The courts are not permitted to apply directly the principles of the European Convention on Human Rights, or to require ministers to take them into account when making decisions which affect the liberty of the subject.

Sham protections. Reliance is placed on certain institutions to protect citizens' rights or to check the oppressive use of power. Some of these are little more than confidence tricks. The Press Complaints Commission, for example, merely pretends to combat invasions of privacy by the press: its decisions are neither respected nor obeyed. The Police Complaints Authority has serious defects. Lay justices are meant to scrutinize police applications for search warrants, but rarely do more than rubber-stamp applications, and the Cleveland affair exposed them as unwilling to protect the rights of parents accused of abusing their children. Coroners' courts are expected to resolve the most serious disputes over deaths caused or contributed to by police action: their personnel and procedures are inadequate for uncovering truth or placing blame. The Commission for Racial Equality and the Equal Opportunities Commission lack the powers necessary to uncover and eradicate pervasive but hidden forms of discrimination. The independence of the BBC can be undermined by the Government's power of patronage, as it appoints its supporters both to the boards and to watchdog bodies like the BSC and BCC. The commissioners and tribunals appointed to monitor telephone tapping and MI5 lack the power to make proper investigations and to provide effective remedies.

Parliamentary sloth. The theory of parliamentary sovereignty assumes that Governments and MPs will act to remedy defects in the laws affecting human rights. The Law Commission drafted a bill in 1979 to reform the law of breach of confidence: had it been enacted, much of the *Spycatcher* confusion would not have occurred. The Law Commission's reports on the need to reform the laws of treason, sedition, blasphemy and criminal libel have similarly been consigned either to the 'too hard' basket or to the waste basket. No action has been taken to implement the Younger Report on privacy, the Faulks Committee or the Neill committee recommendations for reforming the law of libel, the Wilson Committee Report on the Public Records Act, the Williams Committee Report on altering the law of obscenity or the Butler Committee's report urging changes in the law relating to mentally disordered offenders. Parliament has failed to establish, either as an independent body or as a committee of the House, any Human Rights Committee to warn of deficiencies in draft legislation or of laws which are in urgent need of reform. When its existing committees do venture into areas which relate to civil liberties, their performance is unimpressive: they lack investigative resources and skilled counsel, and tend to accept ministerial assurances. Thus the 'Supergun' committee, which held hearings on arms-related trade to Iraq in 1990, was unable to extract even a smattering of the true story which emerged at the Matrix Churchill trial and the ensuing Scott Inquiry.

Vulnerability to emergency legislation. Parliament's failure to implement carefully considered recommendations for improving the standards of civil liberties contrasts starkly with its capacity to rush into action to cut down freedoms when Government convenience dictates or where public emotions have been whipped up on the strength of an isolated case. Emergency legislation is generally bad legislation, which has a habit of remaining on the statute books long after the so-called emergency has passed. The Official Secrets Act, the Prevention of Terrorism Act, the Commonwealth Immigration Act and the ban on Sinn Fein broadcasts are leading examples. Back-bench MPs obsessed with getting their names in newspapers in response to moral panics are a particular nuisance for civil liberties. In recent years they have erected a massive censorship apparatus to deal with a handful of 'video nasties', abolished the right to challenge jurors, passed the 'Surrogacy Arrangements Act' and inflicted 'Section 28' after one local council was alleged to have stocked a Danish sex-education book in one of its libraries. In these repressive exercises they have been incited and supported by the popular press, which frequently uses its own freedom to agitate against that of others, especially against the rights of prisoners and mental patients and unpopular minorities (such as blacks, immigrants and homosexuals) as well as against the freedom of speech of its competitors in television. The 1992 War Crimes Act, twice rejected by the House of Lords because of the necessarily unfair trials it envisages, is another example of how heightened emotions can produce laws which lead to injustice.

Lack of awareness of rights. There is a remarkable reluctance on the part of officialdom to acknowledge the existence of such rights as can be extracted from statutes and case law. This was epitomized in the parliamentary debates over whether a person 'invited' to a police-station interview should be told of his clear statutory entitlement to leave at will unless or until he is arrested. The Government resisted, on the ground that explaining this fundamental liberty to suspects 'would impose an enormous administrative burden on the police'. The same reluctance was apparent throughout the debates on PACE. 'Rights' are too much trouble, and there is always the danger that, if they are publicized, they might be exercised. (For this reason, juries are never told of their 'right' to bring back a verdict according to their consciences.) This is an attitude frequently displayed by officials towards complainants, who are perceived as 'trouble-markers' rather than citizens to be assisted in obtaining their due. It is partly explained, of course, by the lack of any formal constitutional guarantee of basic freedoms. It is difficult to be aware, let alone be proud, of 'rights' which derive from obscure sources – convoluted legal cases and complicated statutes – and which require the assistance of lawyers to extract and to explain. It is, conversely, easy to dress up in the rhetoric of 'rights' initiatives like the 'Citizen's Charter', which encourage public servants to wear name badges and to answer telephones more promptly, but provide no enforceable guarantees whatever that the answers provided by named bureaucrats will be consistent with fairness and justice.

Vulnerability to cost-cutting. One consequence of the lack of public appreciation of civil liberties is that politicians are unable to detect many votes in enhancing them at times of financial stringency. Cutbacks in the health service arouse a public outcry far more vehement than the drastic 1993 cut-backs in legal aid. Lay justices are cheaper than juries, so new penal statutes wherever possible exclude the right to elect for jury trial. Prisoners are treated inhumanely as a result of overcrowded prisons: the solution is to house them in squalid police cells (rather than to devote resources to bail hostels) and to experiment with privatization of prison and custodial services. The opposition to enacting freedom-of-information legislation is based on the expense of answering requests for information. Laws requiring caravan sites for gypsies and provision for the disabled are not enforced because of the expense that compliance would cause.

The Asylum Act and Home Office directives are designed to cut costs by reducing the number of fugitives who may fairly claim asylum, irrespective of the strength of their case. The Home Office has for many years resisted demands for an independent tribunal to review doubtful convictions on the grounds that this would be too costly. The *value* of rights is rarely brought into account.

There is no single panacea which will cure all, or even most, of these unattractive features of British law relating to the liberty of the subject. Specific legislative reforms are required in almost every topic treated in this book, and may sooner or later receive piecemeal parliamentary attention. Changes in substantive law (such as the introduction of a Freedom of Information Act) are necessary, but not sufficient: attention must be paid to the procedures and remedies available to correct abuses of power. There is scope for considerable extension of administrative law, by providing the High Court with power to award compensation to victims of maladministration, to require that reasons be given for every decision – whether made by a minister or by a civil-service mandarin – which infringes the liberty of the subject, and in some cases to scrutinize those reasons for justice as well as for due process. But the deepest defects lie in systems and in attitudes, with their pervasive secrecy and their preference for pragmatism over principle. The Government's refusal to make the European Convention of Human Rights part of British law represents both a symptom of the disease and a rejection of the best hope for a cure.

There is a hypocritical aspect to the British Government's refusal to enact a Bill of Rights, namely that we are not prepared to adopt the standards we urge on others. In the days following the Tiananmen Square massacre in 1989, MPs at Westminster insisted that a Bill of Rights should immediately be introduced in Hong Kong, so that its courts could develop a 'human-rights culture' in the colony before its hand-over to the Chinese. As a result, Hong Kong judges (most of them British lawyers) have been developing human-rights law with the help of English Law Lords in the Privy Council, the colony's final court of appeal. The Chinese point out, accurately, that the United Kingdom by this arrangement seeks to impose upon them obligations to respect civil liberties more onerous than obtain in England. The double standard is flagrant, because Britain has bequeathed Bills of Rights to most of those former colonies which retain appeals to the Privy Council, where English Law Lords protect liberties with more force than is allowed them in England. In 1990, for example, the Privy Council struck down a criminal libel law passed by the Antiguan Government and used to prosecute a newspaper editor who exposed that Government's corruption.[3] The Law Lords said that criminal libel was contrary to the guarantee of freedom of expression in the Antiguan Constitution – a decision they could not, sitting as English Law Lords, reach in respect of criminal libel law in England, because we have no similar constitutional guarantee.

It frequently happens that judges in British courts who are constrained by existing law to turn down applications for relief against executive action remark that the action does, or may, conflict with the European Convention. This anomalous position is reached because the Convention, for all its influence, forms no part of British law. It cannot be applied by the High Court or used as a basis for suing the Home Office or raised by way of a defence against oppressive criminal prosecutions. There is no obligation on the Home Secretary or any of his officials to take it into account when exercising their discretion in deciding, for example, whether to allow an immigrant family to stay in the UK. It is only relevant in British court-rooms in two respects. Where a statute is ambiguous, the judge should not choose the interpretation which would breach the Convention (on the principle of construction that Parliament does not intend legislation to conflict with international treaties unless it uses the clearest language) and its terms may be taken into account when courts are considering questions of public policy. In these limited respects, the Convention has been useful. Indeed, it has encouraged judges to interpret legislation so as to give effect to the purpose for which it was passed by Parliament, and to take account of progressive thinking. But it does not permit them to judge executive infringements of liberty according to the approach required by the Convention, by deciding (for example) whether they are necessary in a democratic society, or justified by a pressing social need, or are proportionate to a legitimate aim. These legal techniques, applied by courts in Europe and at Strasbourg to keep government infringements of individual liberty to a minimum, find no place in British law.

Parl. is sovereign.

'Going to Strasbourg', through all the procedures of the Commission and then of the Court, is a very slow process. So why not short-circuit the procedure, by making the Convention directly enforceable in British courts? If an administrative practice is in stark conflict with a Convention guarantee, why permit it to continue for many years when it might be struck down in a matter of months by the High Court? Why the humiliation of Britain being condemned once again at the international bar by foreign judges, for abuses which British judges could have stopped years before, if only they had possessed the power?

The short answer is that the Government has blocked legislation, passed on several occasions in the Lords, which would incorporate the European Convention into British law. The most recent bill, drafted by Lord Scarman, simply provides that no minister, bureaucrat or public body shall do any act which infringes the fundamental rights and freedoms set forth in the Convention. Any victim of such infringement may sue in a British court – for an injunction to stop the practice, and for damages to compensate for any loss it has caused. The bill would not alter the balance of power between Parliament and the courts: it provides that legislation should not be interpreted as permitting any action which infringes fundamental rights, unless Parliament has specifically indicated in the legislation that human-rights considerations should not apply. In other words, Parliament remains sovereign, and may override the Bill of Rights (as far as UK courts are concerned) simply by indicating its intention so to do. It hardly seems an unreasonable imposition for a Government bent on infringing a basic freedom to declare its intentions openly. There are different views on the most appropriate method of incorporation, and many supporters of the measure would prefer to see a Bill of Rights 'entrenched' in the Constitution, so that Parliament could not pass any law which countermanded its provisions. This may be too radical a solution for a country without a written constitution of any sort, and which is committed to the principle that an elected Parliament can do anything. Lord Scarman's approach, which does not stand in the way of an elected Government hell-bent on infringing liberty, is likely to be the most practical way of introducing the Convention in domestic courts.

The enactment of the European Convention as part of English

Lord Scarmans way most practical. Halfway house

law would measurably improve the protection for individual freedom. It would enable full-blooded challenges to be made to the way discretionary power is exercised by ministers and officials, not merely by way of procedural review but from the first principles set forth in a Bill of Rights. There would, in addition, be the prospect of compensation for victims of abuses of power which is not available to them at present. There would be added protection against hasty legislation which impinges upon individual freedom, if only because its promoters would have the burden of justifying the clause which excluded the operation of the Convention. It would improve the quality and comprehensibility of judicial decision-making, since arguments from first principles are apt to be more logical, realistic and understandable than those artificially constructed from the rag-bag of case-law precedents. New generations of law students would be required to study human rights as a central part of constitutional law, and not merely as a diverting option or summer-term seminar. In criminal cases, it would provide a defence which could be raised against drag-net laws: juries could be reminded of their duty to uphold the rights of freedom of expression and peaceful assembly when considering their verdicts in cases brought under the Official Secrets Act or the Public Order Act.

Enactment of the European Convention would conduce to greater respect for the rights of minorities and provide the basis for challenging untrammelled discretions in Whitehall. It would not, however, provide a remedy for all, or even most, of the ills identified in this book, which require careful parliamentary amendment to specific pieces of legislation. In fact, its most beneficial force would be educative, as Harold Laski perceived in his pertinent comment on Bills of Rights:

Granted that the people are educated to the appreciation of their purpose, they serve to draw attention . . . to the fact that vigilance is essential in the realm of what Cromwell called fundamentals. Bills of Rights are, quite undoubtedly, a check upon possible excess in the Government of the day. They warn us that certain popular powers have had to be fought for, and may have to be fought for again. The solemnity they embody serves to set the people on their guard. It acts as a rallying point in the state for all who care deeply for the ideals of freedom.

It is not surprising that Governments and their servants should oppose a reform which would limit their opportunities to be judges in their own cause. Incorporation would bring administrative acts squarely within the supervision of the High Court – a prospect seen at best as inconvenient and at worst as meddlesome. The Government claims that a directly enforceable Convention would undermine the traditions of parliamentary sovereignty and ministerial accountability – traditions which notably serve to hide civil servants behind ministers with parliamentary majorities. These traditions do not in real life accord with their descriptions: Parliament is controlled by the Government of the day, and ministers disclaim responsibility for the mistakes of their departments. It is inconceivable that a minister would resign if caught approving an infringement of human rights: Home Secretary Kenneth Baker, condemned in 1991 for contempt of court for putting a refugee's life at risk by deporting him in defiance of a judge's order, did not consider this course for a moment. The obligation to answer MPs' questions, as anyone who has watched Question Time in the House of Commons will appreciate, is no substitute for a citizen's entitlement to make ministers answer a claim in court. The argument – used by the present Government – that a Bill of Rights would be alien to British jurisprudence is refuted by the valuable work being done with Bills of Rights by British judges in the Privy Council. Its hollowness can also be perceived by reference to the recent experience of Canada, which engrafted a 'Charter of Rights and Freedoms' on to its common and statute law in 1982. After some initial judicial hiccoughs, it is now accepted as a dynamic and valuable legal presumption in favour of individual freedom: its popularity is such that politicians want it strengthened rather than revoked.

The Conservative Party, in office since 1979, has shown no disposition to promote a Convention which has been responsible for checking some of the worst abuses of Government power, let alone to entrust its principles to British judges who have, through their development of public law in recent years, provided a more effective bulwark for the liberty of the subject than the parliamentary Opposition or the press. The Labour Party made a 'deathbed conversion' to the Bill of Rights in an attempt to woo social democrats just before the 1992 elections, and in 1993 its new leadership announced a commitment to incorporation of the European Convention. Pockets of opposition on the left remain from some power-thirsty politicians, no doubt nostalgic for the days when the last Labour Government persecuted pacifists for conspiracy, deported Philip Agee and Mark Hosenball, secretly approved jury-vetting, tried to suppress the Crossman diaries and made a very serious attempt to put Duncan Campbell behind bars on spying charges carrying up to thirty years' imprisonment (charges thrown out by a High Court judge on the grounds that they were 'unfair' and 'oppressive'). That era is conveniently captured in the story of James Malone, the antiques dealer who sued in the High Court when he discovered his telephone was tapped. The Labour Government sent its Solicitor-General hot-foot to the High Court to defend the lawless and unaccountable basis of state surveillance. The judge was unimpressed: he condemned the system as a blatant breach of the right to privacy guaranteed by the European Convention, but regretted that British law afforded no remedy. Malone took his case to Strasbourg: the Home Office spun it out for six years before their inevitable defeat. The moral, of course, is that all Governments, irrespective of their political philosophy, will put individual liberty at risk in the course of their exercise of the power of the state.

Opposition to enactment of a Bill of Rights from a few academics and commentators on the left appears to stem from a knee-jerk antipathy to giving lawyers an opportunity to make money (an objection which can be made to any law) and from a concern about the 'conservatism' of the judges who will be called upon to apply it. To this last objection there are a number of answers, the best provided by the recent record of the judges themselves, who have shown little compunction (outside the 'no-go' area of national security) in striking down unfair decisions made by Tory ministers and their departmental officials. Indeed the Cabinet Office has become so concerned about judicial scrutiny of executive decisions that it has published several editions of a booklet – *The Judge over Your Shoulder* – instructing bureaucrats on how to make their actions less prone to challenge in the courts. Judicial activism in the interests of fair play has been heavily influenced by the indirect effects of the European Convention: its incorporation would boost the power to do justice (to which the left should not be averse) and would assist in the process of predisposing the judiciary in favour of the liberties it guarantees.

The law, after all, is a discipline which trains and controls those who apply it. Should fundamental principles of liberty become part of that law, they will be reflected in the attitudes of the law's disciples. The great majority of judges may at present be white males from upper-middle-class backgrounds, but this will change as new generations with a more acceptable social, sexual and racial mix are appointed. In any event, the fear that incorporation of the European Convention would enable the courts to prohibit the policies of a future Labour Government is entirely misplaced: the rights set forth in the European Convention are not so much fundamental as elemental, and are no threat to socialist proposals for nationalization or redistribution of income.

Incorporation of the European Convention does not foreshadow government by judges. It would simply mean equipping the most appropriate institution – the courts – with better principles and procedures for identifying and remedying abuses of power perpetrated against citizens by Government departments. What the judiciary can never possess is any power to strike down the sovereign Acts of an elected parliament, but what it needs to have – because no other person or institution independent of Government has it – is authority to ensure that decisions which affect the lives of people, taken by officials in purported compliance with such Acts, are made and executed fairly, and as consistently as the law permits with the fundamental principles of human rights. This does not involve judges in deciding Government policy, although it may involve them in ensuring that as regards individuals, the policy is implemented justly and humanely. This does not infringe any sensible concept of 'parliamentary sovereignty' or 'ministerial accountability', although what it may infringe is the sovereignty and lack of accountability of departmental officials and police and prison officers and secret servicemen and other agents of the state. The evidence given to the Scott Inquiry which followed the Matrix Churchill case in 1993 emphatically revealed how significant decision-making within Whitehall is hidden from Parliament, even from the ministers allegedly accountable for the consequences. It is a remarkable irony that a nation whose style of government has accurately been held up to the popular ridicule of *Yes Minister* has done so little to clothe its courts with power to remedy its deficiencies, when they cause injustices which are no laughing matter.

Objections to a Bill of Rights made by self-styled civil libertarians are disingenuous. Roy Hattersley was fond of alleging that incorporation of the European Convention would mainly assist the 'articulate and middle classes' – notwithstanding the fact that the majority of citizens who have obtained remedies from Strasbourg have been impoverished prisoners, mental patients and immigrants (often represented free of charge by lawyers who have cared about their plight). Now that it is difficult to imagine a future Labour Government adopting any programme of nationalization, scaremongering opponents of a Bill of Rights have racked their imaginations for examples of something of value which might be struck down by reactionary judges. Their current suggestion is the law permitting abortion. What they fail to recognize is that the whole point of bringing the Bill of Rights back home is to enable its guarantees to be interpreted in accordance with British social needs, history and culture. It is inconceivable that British judges would strike down the law permitting abortion, which has been accepted as according with pressing social need in this country for a quarter of a century. (The Canadian Supreme Court used the privacy provisions of its charter to make it easier for women to obtain abortions.) Conservative interpretations of the Convention may disappoint, but will not damage existing rights. The likelihood is that after an initial period of uncertainty, decisions will emerge which enrich the understanding of Convention guarantees by reflecting that spirit of liberty which appears so abundantly in British history, literature and political rhetoric, yet so circumspectly, at present, in British law. The beneficiaries of such a development would not only be citizens of this country, but those seeking their rights in Commonwealth courts which are still persuasively influenced by English legal precedents.[4]

The objection to judges having the necessary power to protect the liberty of the subject fails, at the end of the day, for want of any sensible alternative. The courts remain the only place where oppressive Government action against individuals may be checked. The parliamentary Opposition does not, by definition, have the numbers to intervene, short of a revolt by Government back-benchers. MPs may harass and embarrass ministers over individual cases: they may call for explanations, but have no power to interfere further. The notion of Parliament as the sole guardian of liberty is risible: 3,000 pages of statutes and 2,000 separate statutory instruments receive

Westminster's imprimatur each year, many of them without proper scrutiny or debate, their contents understood only by a handful of administrators and draftsmen. The media may take up particular cases of injustice, subject to their ability to obtain sufficient information and to the political allegiances of editors and proprietors. But trial by media – partial, simplistic and usually sensational – is no substitute for trials by judges, decided by application of fundamental principles of law.

A Bill of Rights is only a danger if it induces complacency about the state of civil liberties. Although the culture and history of England have produced a powerful public commitment to 'fair play', decisions taken by Orwell's 'striped trousered ones who rule' behind closed doors in Whitehall will always be liable to lack fairness, scruple or consistency. While Strasbourg is necessary as a court of last resort, it remains a serious reproach to British law that it lacks the internal dynamics to provide speedy and effective redress for many breaches of fundamental freedoms. The generalized promises of a Bill of Rights are no substitute for statutes which limit, precisely and clearly, the powers of officialdom, but they do provide a bedrock upon which such statutes may be built. A return to the first principles of a Bill of Rights would mark the recognition of the simple and demonstrable fact that individual freedom needs greater protection than Governments and their legislation, Parliaments and their elected representatives, or civil servants with their 'Home Office circulars' and *Yes Minister* styles are capable of providing.

Recognition of the need for some checks on executive power has prompted many thousands of people to sign Charter 88 – a demand for a new constitutional settlement which would enshrine in English law the fundamental freedoms guaranteed by the European Convention, provide effective domestic remedies for abuses of power, establish freedom of information and subject all executive prerogatives to the rule of law. The Charter was launched to mark the tricentenary of the 'glorious revolution' of 1688, which produced a Bill of Rights designed not to safeguard individual liberty but to effectuate a shift of power from the monarch to what was, by modern standards, an undemocratic Parliament. Today, the supremacy of Parliament means in practice the supremacy of the leaders of the party with a majority in the House of Commons, who are subject to few of the checks and balances which work to ensure the fair and effective distribution of power in other advanced democracies. This book argues the case for law reform and incorporation of the European Convention as a moderate means of securing respect for basic civil liberties, but beyond the Bill of Rights lies a further debate about the nature and form of a new and written British constitution, of which it should form a fundamental part. The present Government has responded to that debate by pilfering from the rhetoric of freedom the phrase 'citizens' charter' to dress up a puny public-relations exercise: the only charter that can have any meaning for citizens is one that lives up to its name by bestowing upon them rights against the state which are enforceable in law.

Notes

Introduction

1. *Human Rights* (Central Office of Information, 1992), p.11.
2. *The Citizens Charter*, First Report, (HMSO, November 1992, Cm 2101).
3. Roger Bowles, *Law and the Economy* (Macmillan, 1982), pp. 90–91.

CHAPTER ONE: Personal Liberty and Police Powers

1. Report of an Inquiry by Sir Henry Fisher (HMSO, 1977).
2. *The Brixton Disorders* (HMSO, 1981, Cmnd 8427).
3. *Royal Commission on the Police* (HMSO, 1962, Cmnd 1728), para. 30, approving the comment by the *Royal Commission on Police Powers and Procedure* (HMSO, 1929, Cmnd 3297).
4. *Rice* v. *Connolly* (1966), 2 QB 414.
5. *R.* v. *Lemsatef* (1977), 1 WLR 812; *R.* v. *Houghton and Franciosy* (1979), *Crim. LR* 383.
6. Police and Criminal Evidence Act 1984, s. 29.
7. *Miranda* v. *Arizona* (1966), 384 US 752.
8. *R.* v. *Metropolitan Police Commissioner, ex parte Blackburn (No. 3)* (1973), QB 241 at p. 136.
9. ibid.
10. *R.* v. *Dytham* (1979), QB 722.
11. See *ex parte Blackburn* (1973), QB 241; *The Times*, 1 December 1979 and 7 March 1980.
12. *Arrowsmith* v. *Jenkins* (1963), 2 QB 561.
13. See McConville, Sanders and Lang, *The Case for the Prosecution* (Routledge, 1992); Report of the Royal Commission on Criminal Justice (HMSO, Cmnd 2263), chapter 5.

14. Police Act 1964, s. 4(1). And see generally, Laurence Lustgarten, *The Governance of Police* (Sweet & Maxwell, 1986).

15. PACE, s. 24.

16. (1914), 1 KB 595.

17. *R.* v. *Self* (1992), 95 Cr App R 42.

18. PACE, s. 25(5).

19. *Shaaban Bin Hussein* v. *Chong Fook Kam* (1970), AC 942.

20. *Casterina* v. *Chief Constable of Surrey, The Times,* 15 June 1988, per Woolf, LJ. See Archbold, *Criminal Pleading, Evidence and Practice* (Sweet & Maxwell, 1993), vol. 1, paras. 15–44.

21. *Chapman* v. *DPP,* 89 Cr App R 190; and see *Edwards* v. *DPP,* 23 March 1993 (Divisional Court).

22. *Plange* v. *Chief Constable of South Humberside,* The Times, 23 March 1992.

23. *R.* v. *Gardner* (1979), 71 Cr App R 13, and see also *Chapman* v. *DPP, The Times,* 30 June 1988. But 'reasonable cause to believe' is decided objectively: the honesty of the appellant's belief is irrelevant (*Casterina* v. *Chief Constable of Surrey,* note 20 above.

24. *Christie* v. Leachinsky (1947), AC 573.

25. *R.* v. *Taylor* (1895), 59 JP 393; *R.* v. *Vratsides* 1988, *Crim. LR* 251.

26. See Criminal Law Act 1967, s. 3, PACE, s. 117, and *Swales* v. *Cox* (1981), QB 849; *Abbassy* v. *The Metropolitan Police Commissioner* (1990), 1 All ER 193.

27. See P. A. J. Waddington, *The Strong Arm of the Law* (Oxford, 1991), chapter 3.

28. *Royal Commission on Criminal Procedure* (HMSO, 1981, Cmnd 8092), paras. 3.69–3.70.

29. Barry Irving, interviewed for *Tree of Liberty* (Granada Television, 1982, programme 3: *Arrest*).

30. *Sunday Times,* 18 March 1973; and see John Walkley, 'Police Interrogation: a Handbook for Investigators', *Police Review,* 1990.

31. *R.* v. *Hudson* (1980), 72 Cr App R 163.

32. *Report of the Royal Commission on Criminal Justice* (HMSO, 1993, Cm 2263), chapter 3, para. 37.

33. See McConville, Sanders and Lang, 'Has PACE changed the rules?', *Legal Action,* October 1991, p. 9.

34. *Re Maychell,* Divisional Court, 3 February 1993.

Cash Scorer and Pat Hewitt, *The Prevention of Terrorism Act: The Case for Repeal* (NCCL, 1981).

36. See Lord Shackleton's *Review of the Act* (HMSO, 1978, Cmnd 73) and Lord Jellicoe's *Review* (HMSO, 1983, Cmnd 8803).

37. *Miranda* v. *Arizona*, 384 US 436 (1966).

38. Annex B, 'Delay in Notifying Arrest or Allowing Access to Legal Advice'.

39. Sanders and Bridges, 'Access to legal advice and police malpractice', 1990, *Crim. LR* 494.

40. See, for example, *R.* v. *Silcott, Braithwaite and Raghip*, *The Times*, 9 December 1991; *R.* v. *Samuel* (1988), 87 Cr App R 232; *R.* v. *McGovern* (1992), 92 Cr App R 228, and *R.* v. *Dunford* (1991), 91 Cr App R 150.

41. Jacqueline Hodgson, 'Tipping the scales of justice: the suspect's right to legal advice', 1992, *Crim. LR* 854; John Baldwin, 'Legal Advice in the Police Station', *New Law Journal*, 18 December 1992, p. 1762.

42. *R.* v. *Yvonne Jones* (1978), 3 All ER 1098.

43. See *Lindley* v. *Rutter* (1981), QB 128, and *R.* v. *Naylor* (1979), *Crim. LR* 532.

44. *Holt* v. *United States* (1910), 218 US 245 at 252.

45. Roger Leng, *The Right to Silence in Police Interrogation* (HMSO, 1993).

46. *Bishopsgate Investment Ltd* v. *Maxwell* (1992), 2 WLR 991.

47. *R.* v. *Maguire* (1990), 90 Cr App R 115, and *R.* v. *Matthews* (1990), 91 Cr App R 43.

48. See Mike McConville, 'Video interrogations: police behaviour on and off camera', *Crim. LR* 532.

49. See the Compton Report on *In Depth Interrogation* (HMSO, Cmnd 4823), and the Parker Committee on *Interrogation Procedures* (HMSO, Cmnd 4907).

50. *R.* v. *Fulling* (1987), QB 426.

51. *R.* v. *Mason* (1987), 3 All ER 481.

52. *R.* v. *Keenan* (1990), 90 Cr App R 1; *R.* v. *Barry* (1992), 95 Cr App R 384.

53. *R.* v. *Silcott, Braithwaite and Raghip*, *The Times*, 9 December 1991.

54. *R.* v. *Mackenzie* (1992), 96 Cr App R 98.

55. See *R.* v. *Isquilla* (1975), 1 WLR 716.

56. *R. v. Nottingham Justices, ex parte Davies* (1980), 2 All ER 775. See s. 154 of the Criminal Justice Act 1988, and *R. v. Dover JJ, The Times*, 22 August 1991.

57. *Sommersett's Case* (1772), 20 State Tr. 1.

58. *R. v. Governor of Wormwood Scrubs Prison, ex parte Boydell* (1948), 2 KB 193.

59. *R. v. Governor of Brixton Prison, ex parte Kolczynski* (1955), 1 QB 540.

60. *R. v. Board of Control, ex parte Rutty* (1956), 2 QB 109.

61. *Ex parte Daisy Hopkins* (1891), 61 LJQB 240.

62. *Phillip and Others* v. *DPP of Trinidad* (1992), 1 All ER 665.

63. Compare *R. v. Norwich Crown Court, ex parte Stiller* (1992), *Crim. LR* 501, with *R. v. Norwich Crown Court, ex parte Parker* (1992), *Crim. LR* 500.

64. *Hill* v. *Chief Constable of West Yorkshire* (1988), 2 All ER 238.

65. *R. v. Dytham* (1979), 3 All ER 641.

66. *White* v. *Metropolitan Police Commissioner, The Times*, 24 April 1984.

67. *Taylor* v. *Metropolitan Police Commissioner, The Independent*, 6 December 1989.

68. *Daly* v. *Metropolitan Police Commissioner, The Times*, 18 and 23 July 1980.

69. *Sturley* v. *Metropolitan Police Commissioner, The Times*, 27 June 1984.

70. See Harrison and Clegg, *Police Misconduct: Legal Remedies*, 2nd edn (Legal Action Group, 1991), chapters 1 and 3.

71. *The Broadwater Farm Inquiry* (Karia Press, 1986), pp. 81–7.

72. *Fraser* v. *Mirza*, House of Lords, 25 February 1993.

73. *Lester Cooper* v. *Chief Constable of Merseyside, The Times*, 9 July 1985.

74. See HC Written Answers, col. 725, 15 October 1990.

75. *R. v. Bow Street Magistrates, ex parte Cherry* (1990), 91 Cr App R 283.

76. 'Police pay £87,000 for Wapping assaults – six Met officers will keep jobs', *Guardian*, 15 June 1993.

77. Administration of Justice Act 1982, s. 62.

78. *R. v. Hammersmith Coroner, ex parte Peach* (1980), 2 All ER 7.

79. Paul Foot, *The Helen Smith Story* (Fontana, 1983), pp. 389–96.

80. HMSO, 1971, Cmnd 481.

81. Coroners' Rules 1953 (SI 1953, No. 205), p. 27 as amended by Coroners' (Amendment) Rules 1980 (SI 1980, No. 557), p. 8.

82. *Matto* v. *Wolverhampton Crown Court*, 1987 *Crim. LR* 641. See also *Fox* v. *Chief Constable of Gwent* (1985), 3 All ER 392, decided prior to PACE coming into force.

83. *R.* v. *Bailey and Smith* (1993), 3 All ER 513.

84. See Lord Devlin in *Connelly* v. *DPP* (1964), 2 All ER 401.

85. *R.* v. *Dean* (1993), *NLJ* Reports, p. 508.

86. See Martin Short, *Lundy: the Destruction of Scotland Yard's Finest Detective* (Grafton Books, 1991).

87. See G. Robertson, *Reluctant Judas* (Temple-Smith, 1976).

88. Report to the Home Secretary on the Actions of Police Officers Concerned with the Case of Kenneth Joseph Lennon (the Starritt Report), HC Paper 351.

89. See Maguire and Norris, *The Conduct and Supervision of Criminal Investigators* (HMSO, 1992).

90. *R.* v. *Macro* (1969), *Crim. LR* 205.

91. *Sorrells* v. *United States* (1932), 287 US 435; and *Shurman* v. *United States* (1958), 356 US 369; and see *Bunning* v. *Gross* (1978), 19 ALR 641; *R.* v. *Ireland* (1970), 44 ALJR 263.

92. *R.* v. *Ameer* (1977), *Crim. LR* 104.

93. *R.* v. *Christou* (1992), 4 All ER 559.

94. *Williams* v. *DPP* (1993), 3 All ER 365; and see *DPP* v. *Marshall* (1988), 3 All ER 683.

CHAPTER TWO: Public Protest

1. *Hubbard* v. *Pitt* (1976), 1 QB 142.

2. *Hickman* v. *Maisey* (1900), 1 QB 142.

3. *Harrison* v. *Duke of Rutland* (1893), 1 QB 142.

4. *Thomas* v. *National Union of Mineworkers* (1985), 2 All ER 1.

5. *News Group Newspapers* v. *SOGAT* (1987), ICR 181.

6. *Arrowsmith* v. *Jenkins* (1963), 2 QB 561.

7. *Hague* v. *Committee for Industrial Organizations*, 307 US 496 (Justice Roberts).

8. *Duncan* v. *Jones* (1936), 1 KB 249.

9. *Bailey* v. *Williamson* (1873), LR 8 QB 118, and see *Brighton Corporation* v. *Packham* (1908), 72 JP 318.

10. See 'Replies of Governments to the Secretary-General's Inquiry

Relating to the Implementation of Articles 8–11 of the European Convention on Human Right': Council of Europe, October 1976.

11. A local authority which cancels a firm booking of its hall by the National Front is liable for breach of contract: *Webster* v. *Newham Borough Council* (1980), *The Times*, 22 November.

12. *R.* v. *Liverpool University, ex parte Caesar-Gordon* (1990), 2 All ER 821.

13. *R.* v. *Clarke* (No. 2) (1964), 2 QB 315.

14. Public Order Act 1986, s. 11.

15. See note 6 above.

16. Public Order Act 1986, s. 12.

17. ibid., s. 13.

18. See *Kent* v. *Metropolitan Police Commissioner, The Times*, 15 May 1981, and Application No. 8440/78, *Christians against Racism and Fascism* v. *UK* (1981, European Commission of Human Rights).

19. *News Group Newspapers Ltd* v. *Society of Graphical and Allied Trades, The Times*, 1 August 1986.

20. See, for example, *Kent* v. *Metropolitan Police Commissioner, The Times*, 15 May 1981; *R.* v. *Secretary of State for the Home Department, ex parte Northumbria Police Authority* (1987), 2 All ER 282.

21. *R.* v. *Howell* (1982), QB 416.

22. Templeman, LJ, in *R.* v. *Chief Constable of Devon and Cornwall, ex parte Central Electricity Generating Board* (1982), QB 458. This is a confused case, in which Lord Denning seemed to say that anyone who physically obstructs a worker would be guilty of breach of the peace. However, Lawton, LJ, makes clear that passive resistance cannot amount to a breach of the peace, and his view is consistent with *R.* v. *Howell* and later cases.

23. *Thomas* v. *Sawkins* (1935), 2 KB 249.

24. *Lavin* v. *Albert* (1982), AC 546.

25. *Parkin* v. *Norman* (1983), QB 92.

26. *Moss* v. *McLachlan* (1984), *The Times*, 29 November.

27. See *R.* v. *Mansfield JJ ex parte Sharkey* (1985), 1 All ER 193.

28. See 'The hounding of Valerie Waters', *Sunday Times*, 21 August 1977, and 'The justice of Mrs Mercy', *Daily Mirror*, 20 March 1980.

29. *Lanham* v. *Bernard and Teye, The Times*, 23 June 1986.

30. *R.* v. *South Molton Justices, ex parte Ankerson* (1989), 90 Cr App R 158.

31. *Nagy* v. *Weston* (1965), 1 All ER 78.

32. *Hirst* v. *Chief Constable of West Yorkshire, The Times,* 19 November 1986.

33. Once a section of the public is deprived of its *legal* right to use a road for travel, it ceases to be a 'highway' for the purpose of the Act. A physical obstruction does not affect a legal right, but exercise by police of these statutory powers to withdraw a lawful right (e.g. of vehicular access) by certain classes of persons may make a highway lose its character of a 'highway' in law: see *Bailey* v. *Jamieson,* 1978, 1 CPD 329; *Metcalf* v. *Australian Racing Club,* 78 WN (NSW) 1158.

34. *Hunt* v. *Broome* (1974), AC 587; *Kavanagh* v. *Hiscock* (1974), QB 600.

35. See Peter Thornton, *Public Order Law* (Financial Training, 1987), pp. 99–100, 119–20.

36. See *News Group* case, note 19 above.

37. *Platform 'Arzte für das Leben'* v. *Austria,* European Court of Human Rights, 21 June 1988.

38. *Beatty* v. *Gillbanks* (1882), 2 QBD 308.

39. *Wise* v. *Dunning* (1902), 1 KB 167.

40. *Duncan* v. *Jones* (1936), 1 KB 218.

41. *Forbutt* v. *Blake* (1980), 51 FLR 465.

42. *Jordan* v. *Burgoyne* (1963), 2 QB 744.

43. *Brutus* v. *Cozens* (1973), AC 854.

44. *Masterman* v. *Holden* (1986), 3 All ER 39.

45. *Parkin* v. *Norman* (1983), QB 92.

46. *R.* v. *Horseferry Road Magistrate, ex parte Siadatan* (1991), 1 All ER 324.

47. *DPP* v. *Oram* (1988), 3 All ER 449.

48. *DPP* v. *Clarke; DPP* v. *Fidler, The Times,* 27 August 1991.

49. See P.A.J. Waddington, *The Strong Arm of the Law* (Clarendon Press, 1991), p. 178.

50. *R.* v. *Secretary of State for the Home Department, ex parte Northumbria Police Authority* (1989), QB 26.

51. 1975, Cmnd 6234.

52. *R.* v. *Malik* (1968), 1 All ER 582

53. *Wiggins* v. *Field* (1968), 112 *Sol. J* 656; (1968), *Crim. LR* 503.

54. *Lees* v. *Parr* (1967), 3 All ER 181.

55. *Abrahams* v. *Cavey* (1967), 3 All ER 179.

56. See the Law Commission, *Offences against Religion and Public Worship,* Working Paper No. 79 (1981).

CHAPTER THREE: Privacy

1. *Gordon Kaye* v. *Andrew Robertson & Sport Newspapers* (1991), FSR 62.

2. *Baron Bernstein of Leigh* v. *Skyways* (1978), QB 479.

3. *Report of the Committee on Privacy* (HMSO, 1972, Cmnd 5012).

4. *Breach of Confidence*, Law Commission Report No. 110 (HMSO, 1981, Cmnd 8388).

5. *Report of the Committee on Privacy* (HMSO, 1990, Cm 1102); *Review of Press Self-regulation*, (HMSO, 1993, Cm 2135).

6. *Duke of Argyll* v. *Duchess of Argyll* (1967), Ch 302.

7. *Lennon* v. *News Group* (1978), FSR 573.

8. *Woodward* v. *Hutchins* (1977), 1 WLR 760.

9. *Kashoggi* v. *Smith* (1980), 130 NLJ 168.

10. Sir Robert Megarry, VC, in *Malone* v. *Metropolitan Police Commissioner* (1979), 2 WLR 700.

11. *Francome* v. *Mirror Group Newspapers* (1984), 2 All ER 408.

12. See *Janvier* v. *Sweeney* (1919), 2 KB 316.

13. *Sheen* v. *Clegg*, *Daily Telegraph*, 22 June 1961, and see *Daily Mail*, 15 May 1982, 'Love bug planted by the man next door'.

14. *Press Conduct in the Sutcliffe Case* (Press Council, 1983), chapter 18, paras. 22 and 29.

15. See G. Robertson, *People against the Press* (Quartet, 1983).

16. 'Press Council: Ealing Vicarage rape case', *UK Press Gazette*, 9 March 1987.

17. See *Report of the Data Protection Committee* (the Lindop Committee) (HMSO, 1978, Cmnd 7341).

18. *Oxford* v. *Moss* (1978), 68 Cr App R 183; *DPP* v. *Withers* (1975), AC 852.

19. House of Commons Home Affairs Committee, *Criminal Records Session 1989–90, 3rd Report* (HMSO, 1990), p. ix.

20. See Michael Spencer, *1992 and All That* (Civil Liberties Trust, 1990), p. 63.

21. Consumer Credit Act 1974, s. 158.

22. *Eighth Report of the Data Protection Registrar* (HMSO, June 1992).

23. Richard Norton Taylor, *In Defence of the Realm* (Civil Liberties Trust, 1990).

24. *Semayne's Case* (1604), Eliz 908.

25. *Entick* v. *Carrington*, 19 State J 1029 at 1066, per Lord Camden, CJ.

26. *Wilkes* v. *Lord Halifax* (1763), 19 State Tr. 981.

27. *Robson* v. *Hallett* (1967) 2 QB 939; *Davis* v. *Lisle* (1936) 2 QB 434.

28. *McArdle* v. *Wallace* (1964) 108 Sol. J 483.

29. See *Snook* v. *Mannion* (1982) RTR 321; *Gilham* v. *Breidenbach* (1982), RTR 328.

30. *R.* v. *Reading Justices, Chief Constable of Avon & Somerset and Intervention Board for Agriculture and Produce, ex parte South West Meat Ltd* (1992), *Crim. LR* 672.

31. K.W. Lidstone, 'Magistrates, the police and search warrants' (1984), *Crim. LR* 449, and, post-PACE, see Lidstone (1989), 40 *NILQ* 333.

32. David Feldman, *The Law Relating to Entry, Search and Seizure* (Butterworth, 1987), p. 75.

33. *Barclays Bank* v. *Taylor* (1989), 3 All ER 563.

34. *R.* v. *Bristol Crown Court, ex parte Bristol Press and Picture Agency Ltd* (1987), 85 Cr App R 190. For the position of untransmitted television film on subpoena, see *Senior* v. *Holdsworth, ex parte ITN*, 1976, 1 QB 23.

35. *The Brixton Disorders* (Lord Scarman) (HMSO, 1981, Cmnd 8427).

36. Code of Practice on Power of Stop and Search, Annex B: 'Reasonable Grounds for Suspicion'.

37. PACE (1984), s. 2(9)(a).

38. *R.* v. *IRC, ex parte Rossminster Ltd* (1980), AC 952.

39. *Boyd* v. *United States*, 116 US 616 at 625. And see Polyvios G. Polyviou, *Search and Seizure* (Duckworth, 1982); pp. 10–11.

40. *Columbia Picture Industries and Others* v. *Christopher Robinson and Others*, 19 December 1985, transcript p. 111.

41. *Report of the Commissioner, Interception of Communications Act 1985* (HMSO, May 1992, Cm 1942), chapter 56, p. 1.

42. See Richard Norton Taylor, *In Defence of the Realm* (Civil Liberties Trust, 1990), p. 79.

43. *Report of the Committee of Privy Counsellors Appointed to Inquire into the Interception of Communications* (Chairman, Lord Birkett), (HMSO, Cmnd 283).

44. *Malone* v. *Metropolitan Police Commissioner* (No. 2) (1979), 2 All ER 620.

45. *Malone* v. *UK* (1985), 7 EHRR 14.

46. *Klass* v. *Federal Republic of Germany* (1978) 2 EHRR 214.

47. Royal Commission on Criminal Procedure (HMSO, 1981, Cmnd 8092), chapter 3, paras. 53–60.

48. *R.* v. *Effick* (1992) 95 Cr App R 427.

49. *R.* v. *Preston* (1992) 95 Cr App R 355.

50. Viscount Whitelaw, Interception of Communications Bill, House of Lords, 6 June 1985, col. 919.

51. See 75 H Official Reports, pp. 159–60, 12 March 1985.

52. Interception of Communications Act 1985, s. 10.

53. See 75 H Official Reports, pp. 159–60, 12 March 1985.

54. *R.* v. *Secretary of State for the Home Department, ex parte Ruddock* (1987), 2 All ER 518. See also Ian Leigh, 'The security service, the press and the courts', *Public Law*, Spring 1987, p. 15.

55. See C. Walker, 'Police surveillance by technical devices', 1980, *Public Law*, 1980, 184.

56. Such is the obsession with secrecy that these 'Guidelines on the Use of Equipment in Police Surveillance Operations' have not been formally published. They can be found in the House of Commons Library, attached to a written answer on the subject given by the Home Secretary on 19 December 1984, and marked 'Not to be removed'.

57. *United States* v. *United States District Court*, 407 US 297, Mr Justice Powell.

58. See statement by the Prime Minister, vol. 177 HC Deb, cols. 159–61, written answer 24 July 1990.

59. *R.* v. *Director of GCHQ, ex parte Hodges, The Times*, 26 July 1988.

60. *Statement on the Findings of the Conference of Privy Counsellors on Security* (HMSO, 1956, Cmnd 9715).

61. *Security Procedures in the Public Service* (HMSO, 1962, Cmnd 1681).

62. Vol. 197 H L Deb, col. 1275, 21 June 1956.

63. *R.* v. *Home Secretary, ex parte Hosenball* (1977), 1 WLR 766; *R.* v. *Home Secretary, ex parte Cheblak* (1991), 2 All ER 319.

64. *Council of Civil Service Unions* v. *Minister for the Civil Service* (1985) AC 374.

CHAPTER FOUR: Official Secrecy

1. James Madison, cited by Mr Justice Michael Kirby, *The Right to Know* (Granada, 1984), p. 49.

2. See David Leigh, *Betrayed: The Real Story of the Matrix Churchill Trial* (Bloomsbury, 1993).

3. Official Secrets Act (1989), Section 1(1).

4. See David Hooper, *Official Secrets – The Use and Abuse of the Act* (Secker & Warburg, 1987), chapter 3.

5. *Report of the Select Committee on the Official Secrets Act* (HMSO, 1938).

6. See 22 November 1976, Hansard, H C Deb, vol. 919, col. 1878 ff, and *Reform of Section 2 of the Official Secrets Act* (HMSO, 1978).

7. See Andrew Nicol, 'Official secrets and jury vetting', *Crim. LR* 284, 1979, and Crispin Aubrey, *Who's Watching You?* (Penguin Books, 1981).

8. See *Chandler* v. *DPP* (1964), AC 763, where four House of Lords judges considered the phrase 'interests of the state'. Lords Reid and Hodson said that 'state' meant the organized community, and implied that the phrase meant something akin to 'in the national interest'. Lords Devlin and Pearce adopted a narrower interpretation, indicating that the interests of the state were to be decided by having regard to the policies of the government of today.

9. Geoffrey Cannon, *The Politics of Food* (Century, 1987), p. 32.

10. See Peter Thornton, *The Civil Liberties of the Zircon Affair* (NCCL, 1987).

11. See Police and Criminal Evidence Act, Schedule 1, paras. 12 (a)(11) and 14(c).

12. Hooper, op. cit., p. 201.

13. Departmental Committee on Section 2 of the Official Secrets Act 1911 (HMSO, 1972, Cmnd 5104), vol. 1.

14. *R.* v. *Boyer* (1949), 94 Can. Crim. Cases 195.

15. *The New York Times* v. *United States*, 403 US 713 (1971) at 729.

16. *Attorney-General* v. *Jonathan Cape Ltd* (1975), 3 All ER 484.

17. The *Spycatcher* saga is reported as *Attorney-General* v. *Guardian Newspapers (No. 1)* (1987), 3 All ER 316, and *(No. 2)* (1988), 3 All ER 545.

18. *Attorney-General* v. *Brandon Book Publishers Ltd*, judgement of

Ms Justice Carroll, 2 December 1986. The book was finally published in the UK in 1992.

19. Lord Denning's *Report on the Profumo Affair* (HMSO, 1963, Cmnd 2152).

20. *Report of the Security Service Commissioner (Stuart-Smith, LJ) for 1991*, (HMSO, Cm 1946), para. 23.

21. *R. v. Central Criminal Court, ex parte Randle and Pottle* (1991), 1 WLR 1087.

22. Third Report from the Defence Committee 1979–80 HC 773 'The D Notice system'. See also *The D Notice System: Observations Presented by the Secretary of State for Defence* (HMSO, 1981, Cmnd 8129).

23. *Attorney-General* v. *Jonathan Cape* (see note 16 above).

24. *Committee of Privy Counsellors on Ministerial Memoirs* (Chairman Lord Radcliffe) (HMSO, 1976, Cmnd 6386).

25. See Lord Chancellor (Gardiner's) Parliamentary Statement: Hansard (1967), vol. 282, 5th series, col. 1657–8.

26. Lord Gardiner, interview with author, 1986.

27. See David Rose, 'The secret world', *Guardian*, 7 January 1989.

28. *Modern Public Records* (HMSO, 1981, Cmnd 8024).

29. *Modern Public Records – White Paper Response* (HMSO, 1982, Cmnd 8531).

30. Lord Kilmuir, 197 HL Official Report, 5th series, col. 745, approved by Lord Reid in *Conway* v. *Rimmer* (1968), AC 910 at 942.

31. See David Leigh, *Betrayed* (note 2 above).

32. *Chandler* v. *DPP* (1964), AC 763.

33. See G. Robertson and A. Nicol, *Media Law*, 3rd edn (Penguin, 1992), p. 429.

34. *R.* v. *Joyce* (1946), AC 347.

35. Law Commission, *Treason, Sedition and Allied Offences*, Working Paper No. 72 (1977), pp. 31–2.

36. See *R.* v. *Miller* (1770), 20 State Tr. 870.

37. *R.* v. *Burns* (1886), 16 Cox's Crim. Cases 355.

38. *R.* v. *Bow Street Magistrates Court, ex parte Choudhury* (1991), 1 All ER 306.

CHAPTER FIVE: Censorship

1. *R.* v. *Sedley* (1663), 1 Sid. 168.

2. *R.* v. *Curl* (1727), 2 Stra. 788; 93 ER 849.

3. *R.* v. *Hicklin* (1868), LR 3 QB 360 at p. 371.

4. *R.* v. *Thompson* (1900), 64 JP 456.

5. See Barry Cox, John Shirley and Martin Short, *The Fall of Scotland Yard* (Penguin Books, 1977), p. 160.

6. *Committee on Obscenity and Film Censorship* (*The Williams Committee*) (HMSO, 1979, Cmnd 7772), chapter 4, para. 2.

7. *R.* v. *Holloway* (1982), 4 Cr App R (S) 128.

8. See C. H. Rolph, *The Trial of Lady Chatterley* (Penguin Books, 1961), pp. 228–9.

9. *R.* v. *Martin Secker & Warburg* (1954), 2 All ER 683.

10. *R.* v. *Anderson* (1971), 3 All ER 1152 at p. 1160.

11. *Knuller* v. *DPP* (1973), AC 435 at 491.

12. *DPP* v. *Whyte* (1972), 3 All ER 12.

13. *R.* v. *Calder & Boyars Ltd* (1969), 1 QB 151 at p. 168.

14. ibid., p. 171.

15. *Calder* v. *Powell* (1965), 1 QB 509.

16. *R.* v. *Skirving* (1985), 2 All ER 705.

17. *DPP* v. *A & BC Chewing Gum* (1968), 1 QB 159.

18. *Olympia Press* v. *Hollis and Others* (1974), 1 All ER 108.

19. See Hansard, 7 July 1964, cols. 296, 302 and 358. The undertaking was reaffirmed in 1975 (letter from Solicitor-General, Mr Peter Archer, to Sir Geoffrey Howe, 22 May 1975).

20. *Committee on Distribution of Criminal Business between Crown Courts and Magistrates' Courts* (HMSO, 1975, Cmnd 6323), p. 73.

21. *Pornography and Prostitution in Canada* (Canadian Government Publishing Centre), 1985.

22. *Lambeth Borough Council* v. *Grewel, The Times*, 26 November 1985.

23. *Report of Joint Committee on Censorship of the Theatre* (HMSO, 1967), HC 255 and 503.

24. *Conegate Ltd* v. *Customs and Excise Commissioners* (1986), 2 All ER 688.

25. *Shaw* v. *DPP* (1962), AC 220 at p. 268.

26. *Knuller* v. *DPP* (1973), AC 435.

27. *R.* v. *Gibson* (1991), 1 All ER 439.

28. *R.* v. *Taylor* (1677), 1 Ventris 293.

29. *R.* v. *Hetherington* (1840), 4 State Tr. (NS) 563.

30. *R.* v. *Moxon* (1841), 4 State Tr. (NS) 693.

31. *R.* v. *Lemon and Gay News Ltd* (1978), 68 Cr App R 381.

32. Law Commission, *Offences Against Religion and Public Worship*, Working Paper No. 79 (1981).

33. *R. v. Bow Street Magistrates Court, ex parte Choudhury* (1991), 1 All ER 306.

CHAPTER SIX: Regulation: Film, Video and Broadcasting

1. *Mills* v. *London County Council* (1927), 1 KB 213.

2. (1942), 385 HC Deb 504.

3. See John Trevelyan, *What the Censor Saw* (Michael Joseph, 1973), p. 141.

4. Attorney-General's Reference, No. 5 of 1980 (1980), 3 All ER 816.

5. See Martin Barker (ed.), *The Video Nasties* (Pluto Press, 1984), and Michael Tracey, 'Casting cold water on the ketchup', *The Times*, 25 February 1984.

6. See Statement of Attorney-General, House of Commons, 23 June 1984.

7. British Board of Film Classification, *Annual Report* (1986).

8. ibid.

9. *Report of the Committee on Financing the BBC* (chaired by Professor Alan Peacock) (HMSO, 1986, Cmnd 9824).

10. *R. v. Secretary of State, ex parte Brind* (1990), 1 All ER 469.

11. Letter from Lord Normanbrook (Chairman, BBC) to Postmaster-General, 19 June 1964. The contents of this letter are noted in the prescribing memorandum under Clause 13(4) of the BBC Licence.

12. *Report of Joint Committee on Censorship of the Theatre*, Appendix 3, 'Control over the Subject Matter of Programmes in BBC Television', p. 113.

13. David Hare, 'Ah mischief: the role of public broadcasting', *Guardian*, 15 August 1981.

14. Letter from Alastair Milne (Director of Programmes, BBC) to Dennis Potter, 19 March 1976.

15. Letter from Sir Michael Swann (Chairman, BBC) to Ben Whittaker (Chairman, Defence of Literature and the Arts Society), 25 March 1976.

16. Peter Fiddick, 'Brutal truth barred from the screens', *Guardian*, 23 January 1978, p. 8.

17. Hansard, House of Lords, 22 May 1952, col. 1297.

18. Broadcasting Act 1990, ss. 40–42.

19. *Attorney-General ex rel. McWhirter* v. *IBA* (1973), 1 QB 629 per Lord Denning at p. 652.

20. *R.* v. *IBA, ex parte Whitehouse* (1985), Court of Appeal, 3 April 1985.

21. See 'Aide-Mémoire' of 3 April (1969) (between the BBC and the Conservative and Labour Parties).

22. *R.* v. *Broadcasting Complaints Commissions, ex parte Owen* (1985), 2 All ER 522.

23. *Report of the Committee on the Future of Broadcasting* (see note 19 above), chapter 6, para. 11.

24. Broadcasting Act (1981), s. 54(1).

25. *National Anti-Fluoridation Campaign* v. *Medical Express, Report of BCC* (1982), p. 7.

26. *Report of the Broadcasting Complaints Commission*, 1985, para. 2.

27. *Newspaper Society* v. *'Diverse Reports', Report of BCC* (1985), p. 22.

28. *Report of the Broadcasting Complaints Commission* (HMSO, 1992).

CHAPTER SEVEN: Freedom of Expression

1. *James* v. *Commonwealth of Australia* (1936), AC 578.

2. William Blackstone, *Commentaries* (1765), Book IV, pp. 151–2.

3. *Schering Chemicals* v. *Falkman Ltd* (1981), 2 All ER 321 at p. 334.

4. *Attorney-General* v. *BBC, The Times*, 5 and 18 December 1987.

5. *Lloyds Bank International* v. *Dow Jones (Publishing) Europe Ltd* (1983), 27 May, unreported.

6. *The New York Times* v. *United States*, 403 US 713.

7. *Observer and Guardian* v. *UK*, ECHR, Strasbourg, 26 November 1991, para. 60.

8. *Duke of Argyll* v. *Duchess of Argyll* (1967), Ch. 302.

9. *Attorney-General* v. *Jonathan Cape Ltd* (1975), 3 All ER 484.

10. *BSC* v. *Granada Television Ltd* (1981), 1 All ER 484.

11. *In Re an Inquiry under the Company Securities (Insider Dealing) Act 1985* (1988), 1 All ER 203.

12. *DPP* v. *Channel 4 and Box Productions, The Times*, 1 September 1992.

13. *Secretary of State for Defence* v. *Guardian Newspapers Ltd* (1985), AC 339.

14. X v. *Morgan Grampian Publishers Ltd and others* (1990), 2 All ER 1.

15. *Lord Advocate* v. *Scotsman Publications Ltd* (1989), 2 All ER 852.

16. *Woodward* v. *Hutchins* (1977), 2 All ER 751.

17. *Francome* v. *Mirror Group Newspapers* (1984), 2 All ER 408.

18. *Lion Laboratories Ltd* v. *Evans and Express Newspapers* (1984), 2 All ER 417.

19. *Attorney-General* v. *Guardian Newspaper Ltd* (*No. 2*) (1988), 3 All ER 545.

20. 'Bachnan v. *India Abroad*: Non-recognition of British libel judgements: the American Revolution revisited', Laura Handman and Robert Balin, *Communications Lawyer*, vol. 10, no. 3, Fall 1992.

21. *Hoare* v. *Silverlock* (1848), 12 QB 630.

22. *Lewis* v. *Daily Telegraph* (1964), AC 234 at p. 258, per Lord Reid.

23. *Mawe* v. *Pigott* (1869), IR 4 CL 54.

24. *Grappelli* v. *Derek Block* (1981), 2 All ER 272.

25. *Joyce* v. *Sengupta* (1993), 1 ALL ER 897.

26. *The New York Times Co.* v. *Sullivan*, 401 US 265.

27. See Section 7 of the Defamation Act, Part II.

28. The Law Commission, Working Paper No. 84 (HMSO, 1982).

29. *Gleaves* v. *Deakin* (1980), AC 477 at p. 483, per Lord Diplock.

30. *Goldsmith* v. *Pressman Ltd* (1976), 3 WLR 191.

31. *Sunday Times* v. *United Kingdom* (1979), 2 EHRR 245.

32. *Attorney-General* v. *News Group Newspapers* (1986), 2 All ER 833 at p. 842.

33. *Attorney-General* v. *News Group Ltd* (1988), 2 All ER 906.

34. *R.* v. *Bolam, ex parte Haig* (1949), 93 SJ 220.

35. *R.* v. *Cullen, McCann and Shanahan* (1990), 92 Cr App R 239.

36. Re *Lonrho plc and Observer Ltd* (1989), 2 All ER 1100.

37. *Attorney-General* v. *English* (1982), 2 All ER 903.

38. *Attorney-General* v. *Sports Newspapers* (1992), 1 All ER 503.

39. *Attorney-General* v. *Newspaper Publishing plc* (1987), 3 All ER 276 (Court of Appeal); *Attorney-General* v. *Times Newspapers* (1991), 2 All ER 398 (House of Lords).

40. *Attorney-General* v. *Observer and Others, in re Application by Derbyshire County Council* (1988), 1 All ER 385.

41. *R.* v. *Grey* (1900), 2 QB 36.

42. *R.* v. *Metropolitan Police Commissioner, ex parte Blackburn* (No.2) (1968), 2 QB 150.

43. *R.* v. *Kopyto* (1987), 47 DLR 213; and see *Bridges* v. *California*, 314 US 252 (1941).

CHAPTER EIGHT: Fair Trial

1. Lord Devlin, *Trial by Jury* (Stevens, 1956), chapter 6.

2. *Scott* v. *Scott* (1913), AC 417.

3. *R.* v. *Central Criminal Court, ex parte Crook* (1984), *The Times*, 8 November (Divisional Court).

4. *R.* v. *Evesham JJ, ex parte McDonagh* (1988), 1 All ER 371.

5. *Godfrey Hodgson, Dennis Woolf and Channel 4 Television* v. *United Kingdom* (1987), 10 EHRR 503.

6. *R.* v. *Felixstowe JJ, ex parte Leigh* (1987), 1 All ER 551.

7. Speech at Annual Conference, Family Law Bar Association, 1987.

8. The positive results of televising tribunals are described in the Report of the Antiguan Royal Commission into the trafficking of weapons to the Colombian drug cartels. See Louis Blom-Cooper, QC, *Guns for Antigua* (Duckworth, 1990), pp. 44–6.

9. *Bushell's Case* (1670), 6 State Tr. 999; Vaughan 135.

10. Lord Devlin, 'The conscience of the jury', *Law Quarterly Review*, July 1991, p. 401, discussing *R.* v. *Dean of St Asaph* (1784), 4 Dougl 73.

11. See *The Shadow Jury at Work* (Oxford University Penal Research Unit, 1974).

12. See *United States* v. *Dougherty*, 473 Fed. Rep. (2nd series), p. 1113.

13. Morris Report (HMSO, Cmnd 2627).

14. *R.* v. *Canterbury Justices, ex parte Klisiak* (1981), 2 All ER 129.

15. Report, Royal Commission on Criminal Justice (HMSO, 1993, Cm 2263), chapter 6.

16. *R.* v. *Ford (Royston)* (1989), 3 WLR 762.

17. Royal Commission on Criminal Justice (HMSO, 1993, Cm 2263), chapter 8, para. 63.

18. *R.* v. *Pennington* (1985), *Crim. LR* 394.

19. See David Leigh, *The Frontiers of Secrecy* (Booklist, 1980), p. 168ff.

20. *R.* v. *Mason* (1980), 71 Cr App R 157.

21. *R.* v. *Sheffield Crown Court, ex parte Brownlow* (1980), 2 All ER 444.

22. *R.* v. *McCann and others*, 92 Cr App R 239.

23. *Attorney-General* v. *New Statesman and Nation Publishing Co. Ltd* (1981), QB 1; and see *Attorney-General* v. *Associated Newspapers* (1992), *NLJ* Reports, 1647.

24. Royal Commission on Criminal Justice (HMSO, 1993, Cm 2263), chapter 1, para. 8.

25. See M. King and C. May, *Black Magistrates* (London Trust, 1985).

26. *Brass Tacks* (BBC Manchester), April 1984.

27. Elizabeth Burney, *Justices of the Peace: Magistrate, Court and Community* (Hutchinson, 1979).

28. Sir Thomas Skyrme, *The Changing Image of the Magistracy* (Macmillan, 1979).

29. Roger Hood, *A Question of Judgement* (CRE, 1992).

30. Helena Kennedy, *Eve was Framed* (Chatto, 1992).

31. See the recommendations of Justice, *The Judiciary* (1992), the report of a committee chaired by Robert Stevens.

32. A. W. B. Simpson, 'The judges and the vigilante state', Child & Co. lecture 1989, p. 22.

33. *Reports on the Maguire Case* by Sir John May (interim report, 9 July 1990; final report, 3 December 1992) (HMSO).

34. Baldwin and McConville, *Jury Trials* (Clarendon Press, 1979).

35. e.g. the defendant in *R.* v. *Mackenzie* (1992), 96 Cr App R 98; and see Dr Gisli Gudjonson, 'The psychology of false confessions', *New Law Journal*, 18 September 1992, p. 1277.

36. *R.* v. *McIlkenny and others* (1992), 2 All ER 417 (Birmingham Six) and *R.* v. *Maguire* (1992), All ER 433.

37. See G. Robertson, *Whose Conspiracy?* (NCCL, 1974).

38. Report of the Royal Commission on Criminal Justice (HMSO, 1993, Cm 2263), chapter 8, para. 33.

39. ibid., chapter 10, para. 59.

40. Bob Woffinden, *Miscarriages of Justice* (Coronet, 1989), p. 487.

41. See Martin Young and Peter Hill, *Rough Justice* (April 1983).

42. Lord Widgery, CJ, *R. v. Murphy* (1975), 61 Cr App R 215.
43. *Stafford* v. *DPP* (1974), AC 878.
44. Patrick Devlin, *The Judge* (Oxford, 1979), chapter 5.
45. HMSO, Cmnd 8856.

CHAPTER NINE: Freedom of Movement

1. Peter Kropotkin, *Memoirs of a Revolutionist* (London, 1899), p. 377.
2. See Michael Spencer, *1992 and All That* (Civil Liberties Trust, 1990).
3. Richard Crossman, *The Times*, 6 October 1972, quoted in Vaughan Bevan, *The Development of British Immigration Law* (Croom Helm, 1986), p. 81.
4. *The East African Asians* v. *UK (No. 2)* (1981), 3 EHRR 76.
5. The most detailed account is Macdonald and Blake, *Immigration Law and Practice*, 3rd edn (Butterworth, 1990).
6. Home Affairs Committee on the Immigration Rules and the European Convention, Evidence, para. 110 HC 434.
7. *R. v. Immigration Appeal Tribunal, ex parte Arun Kumar* (1986), IAR 446.
8. *Abdulazis, Cabales and Balkandali*, case no. 15/1983/71.
9. *R. v. Immigration Appeal Tribunal, ex parte Singh* (1987), 3 All ER 690.
10. See *Worlds Apart: Women under Immigration and Nationality Law* (Pluto Press, 1985).
11. *R. v. Immigration Appeal Tribunal, ex parte Secretary of State for the Home Department* (1992), 3 All ER 798.
12. *Swati* v. *Secretary of State* (1986), IAR 88.
13. *R. v. Secretary of State, ex parte Khawaja*, 1984 AC 74.
14. *R. v. Secretary of State, ex parte Khera, ex parte Khawaja* (1984), AC 74, reversing *Zamir's Case* (1980), AC 930.
15. *R. v. Bouchereau* (1977), ECR 1999.
16. *Beljoudi* v. *France* (ECHR), 26 March 1992, Strasbourg.
17. *R. v. Nazari* (1980), 3 All ER 880.
18. *Ex parte Soblen* (1963), 2 QB 243.
19. Report of the Committee on Immigration Appeals (HMSO, 1967, Cmnd 3387), para. 144.
20. *Ex parte Hosenball* (1977), 3 All ER 452.
21. *R. v. Secretary of State, ex parte Cheblak* (1991), 2 All ER 319.

22. *M* v. *Home Office* (1992), 4 All ER 97 (Court of Appeal); (1993), 3 All ER 537 (House of Lords).

23. *M* v. *Home Office and Kenneth Baker* (1993), *The Times*, 28 July.

24. *Amekrane Case*, 16 Year Book ECHR 356 (1973).

25. *Bugdaycay* v. *Secretary of State* (1987), 1 All ER 940.

26. *Ex parte Sivakumaran* (1988), IAR 147.

27. Compare Sir David Maxwell-Fife, Written Parliamentary Answer, 24 June 1954 (529 HC Deb 50) with 'Noted scientist ends his exile after 25 years', *The New York Times*, 1 April 1977.

28. See the Dublin Convention (1990), discussed in MacDonald and Blake, *Immigration Law and Practice*, 3rd edn (Butterworth, 1990), pp. 308–10.

29. *Government of Belgium* v. *Postlethwaite* (1987), 2 All ER 985.

30. *R.* v. *Governor of Brixton Prison, ex parte Soering* (Divisional Court, 11 December 1987).

31. *Soering* v. *United Kingdom* (1989), 11 EIIRR 439.

32. *R.* v. *Secretary of State for Home Department, ex parte Sinclair, The Times*, 5 February 1992.

33. *Liangsipiprasert* v. *UK Government* (1990), 2 All ER 866.

34. *R.* v. *Governor of Pentonville Prison, ex parte Chinoy* (1992), 1 All ER 317. Compare *R.* v. *Bow Street Magistrates, ex parte Makeson* (1981), 75 Cr App R 24.

35. *US* v. *Alvarez-Marchain* (1992), 112 S Ct 2188.

36. *Bennett* v. *Horseferry Road Magistrates Court* (1993), 3 All ER 138.

37. See *Cheng* v. *Governor of Pentonville Prison* (1973), AC 931; *Schtraks* v. *Government of Israel* (1964), AC 556.

38. *R.* v. *Governor of Brixton Prison, ex parte Kolczynski* (1955), 1 QB 540.

39. *R.* v. *Governor of Brixton Prison, ex parte Enaharo* (1963), 2 QB 455; *Zacharias* v. *Cyprus* (1963), AC 634.

40. The writ of *ne exeat regno* was revived in an unsuccessful attempt to stop a New Zealand rugby team from travelling to South Africa: *Parsons* v. *Burk* (1971), NZLR 244.

41. 209 HL Deb 860 (16 June 1958) and see HC Deb. 265 (Written Answers), 15 November 1974.

42. *Council of Civil Service Unions* v. *Minister for the Civil Service* (1985), AC 374.

43. *R.* v. *Secretary of State for Foreign and Commonwealth Affairs ex parte Everett, The Times*, 1 November 1978.

44. There is an arguable right to a passport under EEC law. See directive 68/360, art. 2.

45. *Report of the Committee of Privy Councillors Appointed to Inquire into the Recruitment of Mercenaries* (HMSO, 1976, Cmnd 6569).

46. See Wilfred Burchett and Derek Roebuck, *The Whores of War – Mercenaries Today* (Penguin Books, 1977).

47. Report of the Royal Commission on Arms Trafficking to Colombia – Louis Blom-Cooper, QC, *Guns for Antigua* (Duckworth, 1990).

48. *Lord Colville's Review of the Prevention of Terrorism (Temporary Provision) Act* (HMSO, 1987), p. 40.

CHAPTER TEN: Freedom from Undue Control

1. *R. v. Secretary of State for the Home Department, ex parte Herbage (No. 2)* (1987), 1 All ER 324.

2. *Williams v. Home Office (No. 2)* (1981), 1 All ER 1211.

3. *R. v. Deputy Governor of Parkhurst Prison, ex parte Haque (1991)*, 3 WLR 340.

4. *Golder v. UK*, ECHR series A, vol. 18 (1975).

5. *Raymond v. Honey* (1983), AC 1.

6. *Ex parte Anderson* (1984), 2 WLR 725.

7. *R. v. Secretary of State for the Home Department, ex parte Leech (No. 2)*, The Times, 20 May 1993.

8. *Knight v. Home Office* (1990), 3 All ER 237, and contrast *Kirkham v. Chief Constable of Manchester* (1990), 3 All ER 246, in which police were liable in negligence to a suicide's family for failing to tell prison officers of his suicidal tendencies.

9. *Boyle & Rice v. UK*, ECHR, Series A, vol. 131, 27 August 1988.

10. *Home Office v. Central Television*, The Times, 28 January 1993.

11. *R. v. Hull Prison Board of Visitors, ex parte St Germain (No. 2)* (1979), 2 WLR 47.

12. *Campbell & Fell v. UK* (1983), 5 EHRR 207, (1984) 7 EHRR 165, and see now *ex parte McCartan* (1988), 2 WLR 177.

13. *Leech v. Deputy Governor of Parkhurst Prison* (1988), AC 533.

14. *Thynne Wilson & Gunnell v. UK* (1990), 13 EHRR 666.

15. *R.v. Parole Board, ex parte Wilson* (1992), 2 All ER 576.

16. *Doody v. Secretary of State for the Home Department* (1993), 3 All ER 92.

17. See Richard Moran, *Knowing Right from Wrong* (Macmillan, 1981).

18. ibid.

19. *R.* v. *Mackenzie* (1992), 96 Cr App R 98.

20. *Report of the Committee on Mentally Abnormal Offenders* (HMSO, 1975, Cmnd 6244).

21. *X* v. *United Kingdom* (1981), 4 EHRR 188.

22. *Home Secretary* v. *Oxford Regional Mental Health Review Tribunal* (1987), 3 All ER 8.

23. e.g. *ex parte Pickering* (1986), 1 All ER 99; *ex parte Clatworthy* (1985), 3 All ER 699.

24. See *R.* v. *Merseyside Mental Health Review Tribunal, ex parte K* (1990), 1 All ER 562.

25. See, for example, *R.* v. *Hallstrom* (no. 2) (1986), 2 All ER 306.

26. *Pickering* v. *Liverpool Daily Post and Echo* (1990), 1 All ER 335; (1991), 2 WLR 513 (House of Lords).

27. *Re G, The Times,* 31 January 1991.

28. *F* v. *West Berkshire Health Authority* (1990), 2 AC 1; *J* v. *C* (1990), 3 All ER 735.

29. *W* v. *Egdell* (1990), 2 WLR 471.

30. *Gillick* v. *West Norfolk and Wisbech Area Health Authority* (1985), 3 All ER 402.

31. *Re R* (1991), 3 WLR 592.

32. *Re W* (1992), 4 All ER 627.

33. *Re P* (1992), 1 FLR 316.

34. *M* v. *M, The Times,* 1 August 1992.

35. *Re R* (1992), 1 FLR 105 (Bracewell, J).

36. See, for example, *Re H* (1991), 2 FLR 109.

37. *R.* v. *B* (1987), 2 All ER 206.

38. See *Costello-Roberts* v. *UK, The Times,* 26 March 1993, where the European Court held that a 'moderate slippering' in a private school did not infringe the severity threshold of the Article 3 prohibition on 'inhuman or degrading punishment'.

39. *A.* v. *Liverpool City Council* (1981), 2 All ER 385; *in re M and H (Minors),* The Times, 29 July 1988.

40. *O* v. *United Kingdom,* European Court, 8 July 1987.

41. *A Child in Trust – Report of Inquiry into the Death of Jasmine Beckford* (London Borough of Brent, 1985).

42. *A Child in Mind – Report of Inquiry into the Death of Kimberley Carlile* (London Borough of Greenwich, 1987).

43. *R.* v. *Ethical Committee of St Mary's Hospital (Manchester)*, *ex parte H* (1988), 1 FLR 512.

44. *Re J* (1990), 3 All ER 930.

45. *Re J* (1992), 4 All ER 614.

46. *Airedale NHS Trust* v. *Bland* (1993), 1 All ER 821.

47. *Re T* (1992), 4 All ER 649.

48. *Re S* (1992), 4 All ER 671.

49. *Attorney-General* v. *Able* (1983), 3 WLR 845.

CHAPTER ELEVEN: Freedom from Discrimination

1. *Brown* v. *Board of Education* (1954), 347 US 483.

2. *Mandla* v. *Dowell Lee* (1983), 2 AC 548.

3. *CRE* v. *Dutton* (1989), 1 All ER 306.

4. *Dawkins* v. *Department of the Environment* (1993), 29 January (Court of Appeal).

5. Cmnd 6234, p. 19.

6. *Griggs* v. *Duke Power Co.*, 401 US 424 (1971).

7. *Orphanos* v. *Queen Mary College* (1985), 2 All ER 233.

8. *Hampson* v. *Department of Education and Science* (1991), AC 171 (teacher training); *Bohon-Mitchell* v. *Common Professional Examination Board* (1978), IRLR 525 (Bar qualification).

9. *Tottenham Green Under-fives' Centre* v. *Marshall No. 2* (1991), IRLR 162.

10. *R.* v. *Army Board of the Defence Council, ex parte Anderson* (1991), 3 All ER 375.

11. *Noone* v. *North West Thames Regional Health Authority* (1988), IRLR 968.

12. *Bradford City Council* v. *Aurora* (1991), 2 WLR 1377.

13. *King* v. *The Great Britain–China Association* (1991), 11 October, Court of Appeal.

14. *Commission for Racial Equality* v. *Prestige Group plc* (1984), 1 WLR 335.

15. *Wheeler* v. *Leicester City Council* (1985), AC 1054.

16. See Lawrence Lustgarten, 'Racial Inequality, Public Policy and The Law' in Hepple and Szyszczak, *Discrimination: The Limits of the Law*, Mansell, 1992.

17. Willes J in *Chorlton* v. *Lings*, LR 4 CP 374 (1868).

18. *Peake* v. *Automotive Products* (1977), 1 CR 968.

19. *Gill* v. *El Vino Co. Ltd* (1983), QB 425.

20. *James* v. *Eastleigh Borough Council* (1990), 2 All ER 607.

21. *EOC* v. *Birmingham City Council* (1989), AC 1155.

22. *Quinn* v. *William Furniture Ltd* (1980), *The Times*, 18 November

23. *Price* v. *Civil Service Commission* (1978), 1 CR 27.

24. *Dekker* v. *VJV*, *The Times*, 20 December 1990; (1992), ICR 325.

25. *Webb* v. *Euro Air Cargo* (House of Lords, 26 November 1992).

26. *Berrisford* v. *Woodard Schools (Midland Division)*, 6 March 1991. See *Equal Opportunities Review*, No. 38, July/August 1991.

27. *R.* v. *Secretary of State for Employment, ex parte Equal Opportunities Commission* (1992), *The Times*, 12 November.

28. See Camilla Palmer, *Discrimination at Work*, 2nd edn (LAG, 1992), chapter 10.

29. *Hayward* v. *Cammell Laird* (1988), 2 All ER 257.

30. *Pickstone and others* v. *Freemans plc* (1988), IRLR 337.

31. *Knuller* v. *DPP* (1973), AC 435.

32. See *R.* v. *Kirkup*, and Helen Power, 'Entrapment and gay rights', *New Law Journal*, 15 January 1993, p. 47.

33. *R.* v. *Brown* (1993), 2 All ER 75.

34. *Dudgeon* v. *United Kingdom* (1981), 4 EHRR 188, and see *Norris* v. *Ireland*, 26 October 1988, Series A, No. 142.

35. *Morrison* v. *State Board of Education*, 461 2d 375.

36. *Corbett* v. *Corbett*, (1971), p. 83.

37. *Cossey* v. *UK* (1990), 13 EHRR 622.

38. *B* v. *France*, 25 March 1992.

39. See *Ahmad* v. *Inner London Education Authority* (1978), QB 36; *Essen* v. *United Transport Executive* (1975), 1 RLR 48.

40. *R.* v. *Guildford Crown Court, ex parte Siderfin* (1989), 3 All ER 7.

41. *Church of the New Faith* v. *Commissioner for Payroll Tax* (1983), 57 ALJR 785.

42. See Bynoe, Oliver and Barnes, *Equal Rights for Disabled People* (Institute for Public Policy Research, 1991).

CHAPTER TWELVE: A Bill of Rights for Britain?

1. See *Johnston* v. *Chief Constable of the Royal Ulster Constabulary* (1987), 1 CR 83.

2. Andrew Drzemczewski, 'The need for a radical overhaul', *New Law Journal*, 29 January 1993.

3. *Hector* v. *Attorney-General of Antigua and Bermuda* (1990), 2 All ER 103.

4. See Ronald Dworkin, *A Bill of Rights for Britain* (Chatto, 1990), pp. 45–51.

Table of Statutes

CANADIAN LEGISLATION

EUROPEAN LEGISLATION

UN LEGISLATION

US LEGISLATION

Table of Cases

Index

READ MORE IN PENGUIN

In every corner of the world, on every subject under the sun, Penguin represents quality and variety – the very best in publishing today.

For complete information about books available from Penguin – including Puffins, Penguin Classics and Arkana – and how to order them, write to us at the appropriate address below. Please note that for copyright reasons the selection of books varies from country to country.

In the United Kingdom: Please write to *Dept. JC, Penguin Books Ltd, FREEPOST, West Drayton, Middlesex UB7 OBR*

If you have any difficulty in obtaining a title, please send your order with the correct money, plus ten per cent for postage and packaging, to *PO Box No. 11, West Drayton, Middlesex UB7 OBR*

In the United States: Please write to *Penguin USA Inc., 375 Hudson Street, New York, NY 10014*

In Canada: Please write to *Penguin Books Canada Ltd, 10 Alcorn Avenue, Suite 300, Toronto, Ontario M4V 3B2*

In Australia: Please write to *Penguin Books Australia Ltd, 487 Maroondah Highway, Ringwood, Victoria 3134*

In New Zealand: Please write to *Penguin Books (NZ) Ltd, 182–190 Wairau Road, Private Bag, Takapuna, Auckland 9*

In India: Please write to *Penguin Books India Pvt Ltd, 706 Eros Apartments, 56 Nehru Place, New Delhi 110 019*

In the Netherlands: Please write to *Penguin Books Netherlands B.V., Keizersgracht 231 NL–1016 DV Amsterdam*

In Germany: Please write to *Penguin Books Deutschland GmbH, Friedrichstrasse 10–12, W–6000 Frankfurt/Main 1*

In Spain: Please write to *Penguin Books S. A., C. San Bernardo 117–6° E–28015 Madrid*

In Italy: Please write to *Penguin Italia s.r.l., Via Felice Casati 20, I–20124 Milano*

In France: Please write to *Penguin France S. A., 17 rue Lejeune, F–31000 Toulouse*

In Japan: Please write to *Penguin Books Japan, Ishikiribashi Building, 2–5–4, Suido, Tokyo 112*

In Greece: Please write to *Penguin Hellas Ltd, Dimocritou 3, GR–106 71 Athens*

In South Africa: Please write to *Longman Penguin Southern Africa (Pty) Ltd, Private Bag X08, Bertsham 2013*